pgs 122-127

pgs 309-317

Mark H. McCormack's

EBEL

World of Professional Golf 1988

Dedication

GEORGE BLUMBERG

(1912-1987)

Golf has lost a great friend, a man whose true contributions and love for the game will never be truly or fully appreciated. Nowhere has the sport been more genuinely and selflessly supported throughout the world by one individual during the past four decades.

Mark H. McCormack's
EBEL
World of Professional
Golf 1988

Photographs by Lawrence Levy

William Morrow and Company, Inc.
New York   1988

Library of Congress ISSN: 0891-9909
ISBN: 0—688—07029—9

Printed in the United States of America

First U.S. Edition

1 2 3 4 5 6 7 8 9 10

Contents

1. The Year In Retrospect

The United States loses the Ryder Cup?

To those cozy isolationists of the U.S. PGA Tour, that prospect was unimaginable. It would not happen, not again, not on captain Jack Nicklaus' own Muirfield Village course.

You would see Deane Beman approve the paying of appearance money before that would happen.

You would also see...another major championship wrenched from Greg Norman's hands...the four major titles held by Larry Mize, Scott Simpson, Nick Faldo and Larry Nelson...the measurement of iron grooves as golf's most hotly-debated topic...Ian Woosnam of Wales winning eight tournaments and over $1.8 million, and Mark McNulty of Zimbabwe winning seven tournaments...an American, David Ishii, leading the Japanese circuit with six victories.

You would even see Tom Watson win again.

It was an unusual year, 1987.

The Ryder Cup was the most meaningful golf tournament in two decades because America's weaknesses were blatantly exposed. The Europeans had the better team, led by two of the world's three current superstars, Seve Ballesteros and Bernhard Langer. The U.S. was held back by an unrealistic selection system, and by an all-exempt tour with purses that were too evenly distributed, producing complacency among the players.

The frequent lament from the American tour had been, "What have they (Europeans) done over here lately?" Often, the speaker had won perhaps three tournaments in his career, but enough to be rated among the current top five on the U.S. tour.

In September at Muirfield Village, near Columbus, Ohio, that question was forcefully answered, as the Europeans won for the second time in succession, for the first time ever in this country and while, also for the first time, the American public was taking notice.

It's beyond me how you could play the Ryder Cup without Nicklaus, Watson or Raymond Floyd, to name but three proven winners excluded by a points system that afforded the captain no role in the selections.

"We had some matches we could have won, but the European players are tougher," Nicklaus said. "Because of the all-exempt tour now, our guys don't find themselves in position to win very often. Two or three times a year at most. They don't get the taste of winning. Some of them have forgotten what it's like. These Europeans have won a lot, even if it is the Hong Kong Four-Ball. Winning breeds winning."

While the European margin was merely 15-13, that could be attributed perhaps to an overly-cautious attitude after they entered the final day with a 10½-5½ lead. The Europeans were strongest when they had to be, over the closing holes. Even the sole European player who didn't contribute a point, Ken Brown, went on the following week to win the Southern Open.

After the Ryder Cup, it was suggested that the U.S. tour must now open its doors to overseas players. Nicklaus said, "If the Ryder Cup loss does one thing, it will be to wake up our tour to the archaic rules that bar foreign players. I can't understand why Seve and other players who have proved themselves should not play our tour."

The present rules dictate a minimum of 15 tournaments for members, or a maximum of eight for non-members. Commissioner Beman has said he favors allowing "more flexability" in player movement, but "to allow them to cherry-pick our tour and the world would not be fair and it would not be right."

The restrictive policies are a result of the U.S. tour being run by the players and controlled by the 150 or so who are beneath the top echelon, which I have criticized previously. The tour is insular and isolationist by definition. Through its one-man one-vote system, the group controls the tour with considerable self-interest.

If I were a young golfer, my response might be: Why bother playing in America? Twenty years ago a European had no choice but to go to the United States to prove himself as a world-class player. Now that is not necessary. He can go, or he can stay in Europe. It makes no difference. Conversely, young Americans might now be well advised to develop their games in Europe.

The talent is not limited to those two tours. One could pick a team from the Sony Ranking that would be a match for either Ryder Cup side. It's a shame that first-rate international competition occurs so infrequently, that we have made so little progress toward anything resembling a world tour, and that the U.S. tour continues to try to strangle the growth of the game around the world. Golf will not accept that status quo very much longer.

Meanwhile, the U.S. tour has only become more insular, in part because of RJR Nabisco's insistence on more value for its multi-million dollar investment. The sponsor was even allowed to pay appearance money to players entering the $2 million Nabisco Championship. Supposedly, this was a $1 million bonus pool to reward year-long performances (and also to encourage the leading golfers to play more on the domestic circuit), with the top 30 qualifying for the big late-season event in San Antonio, Texas. The problem was that the first year, 1986, not all went to San Antonio to receive their bonuses. In other words, put the check in the mail, please.

The renegotiated terms were that the players had to compete in the Nabisco Championship to receive bonuses; further, depending on the amount received, they had to perform services such as to have Nabisco identification on their golf bags or shirts, and to play in corporate outings. It was also agreed that the bonuses would be official earnings. (In this annual, the bonuses have been excluded from the World Money List.)

I applaud Nabisco's negotiations. It's the U.S. tour's attitude that bothers me. Appearance money has always been a factor on the tour, despite the denials. If a golfer has an endorsement deal with a company, and that company (its subsidiary or its customer) sponsors a tournament, it's logical that the golfer would play in the tournament. At least part of his compensation then is appearance money.

That issue is a mere dog-fight in comparison to the legal battle pending between the United States Golf Association and Karsten Manufacturing

Corporation over "square-grooved" irons. The USGA declared that Karsten's Ping Eye 2 clubs cannot be used in competition (most notably the U.S. Open) after 1989, and that the clubs will be illegal on January 1, 1996.

We all know by now that the Ping Eye 2 clubs enable a golfer to generate spin on the ball out of the rough that is far greater than is possible with traditional irons. The technical aspects are too complex to be discussed here without diagrams, and have been amply covered since the clubs were introduced in 1985 — notably by Frank Hannigan in the USGA's *Golf Journal,* Jaime Diaz in *Sports Illustrated* and Lew Fishman and Dwayne Netland in *Golf Digest,* which were among my own research sources.

Battle lines have been drawn. Karsten responded to the USGA's announcement by ceasing to manufacture any clubs except Ping Eye 2, and the debate over square grooves and the recent improvements in golf balls — which probably have a greater impact — has created a rift on the tour. Nicklaus, Watson and Norman are among those who believe the innovations have benefited the weaker players. "Mis-hit shots don't curve the ball into trouble so much anymore." Watson said. "We all complained about the narrow fairways at the 1986 British Open at Turnberry. And I was the most outspoken of all. But maybe that's not right. Maybe we should play 15- to 17-yard fairways now that the balls go so straight."

Average players do seem to be making the biggest gains. The 36-hole cut scores are declining. Comparing the 1966 and 1987 U.S. Opens at San Francisco's Olympic Club, the average score dropped 2.5 strokes, but the winning total fell only one stroke.

Nicklaus has suggested that one ball be used, an official ball for the tour. "It's just ridiculous," he said. "I'd get rid of square grooves and go back to playing golf with talent rather than equipment. Then we'd have one ball out here for the tour. It would be made to go only so far."

David Graham, noted as a clubmaker, has said, "Of course the new equipment has made the game easier. It's so much more available to everyone. In the 1960's a player had to scrape around to find the right clubs, and there wasn't much of a choice. Now there is a large variety, honed to suit each player. But how do you prevent progress? If the automobile business had stopped innovating, we'd still be driving Model-T Fords."

The alleged decline in shotmaking, according to two other veterans, Curtis Strange and Peter Jacobsen, may also be attributed to improved course conditioning and to the architects, building longer courses. Strange said, "You don't have to finesse the ball anymore; you just need one shot, long and high." And Jacobsen noted, "The ball sits up in the fairway and you can spin it right at the flag."

Often singled out among the "high-tech pros" is Mark Calcavecchia, who won the 1987 Honda Classic and $522,398 officially on the U.S. tour. "They think the only reason I'm winning is that I'm playing Pings," Calcavecchia said. "That's their problem. Equipment might help a very small amount, but 98 percent of it is that the young guys out here are just better. If everybody used the same clubs and the same ball, you'd still have the same result — the young guys winning."

There's no doubt in my mind who *should* prevail between the USGA and Karsten Manufacturing. However good his intentions, however good his arguments, Karsten Solheim, the 75-year-old founder, is wrong to undermine the USGA's authority over rules and equipment, which it shares worldwide with the Royal and Ancient Golf Club of St. Andrews.

It should be left to the USGA, sensibly, for the good of the game. Just listen to the USGA's Hannigan: "The players are saying that the world is coming to an end, as they tend to do periodically. I don't think golf can stand another quantum jump in equipment like the one it made from hickory shafts to steel, because we would simply run out of real estate. But nothing is telling me anything like that is happening. And I think the safeguards are in place to prevent it."

Incidentally, Hannigan laughs at suggestions of a decline in shotmaking ability: "That's what all the guys over 30 say. The fact is, these kids are just terrific players. Calcavecchia, for one, putts like God."

Enough of that. Let's now consider the year in professional golf, 1987. An appropriate comment was made by Gary Adams of the Taylor Made golf club company, "Equipment is never going to replace talent. The only real equipment that gets a golfer to the top is his heart." Which leads us to the best golfers in the world, according to the Sony Ranking:

SONY RANKING LEADERS
(As of January 1, 1988)

1.	Greg Norman, Australia	1231
2.	Seve Ballesteros, Spain	1169
3.	Bernhard Langer, W. Germany	1112
4.	Sandy Lyle, Scotland	879
5.	Curtis Strange, U.S.	873
6.	Ian Woosnam, Wales	830
7.	Payne Stewart, U.S.	717
8.	Lanny Wadkins, U.S.	697
9.	Mark McNulty, Zimbabwe	673
10.	Ben Crenshaw, U.S.	668
11.	Paul Azinger, U.S.	649
12.	Larry Mize, U.S.	645
13.	Rodger Davis, Australia	626
14.	Nick Faldo, England	623
15.	Tsuneyuki Nakajima, Japan	617
16.	Tom Watson, U.S.	616
17.	Scott Simpson, U.S.	592
18.	Masashi Ozaki, Japan	591
19.	Isao Aoki, Japan	580
20.	Hal Sutton, U.S.	579

(The complete Sony Ranking may be found in the appendixes of this annual.)

There are nine Americans among the top 20 golfers in the world. Last year there were 13, so the rankings reflect the continued downward spiral which many, myself included, have attributed to the socialistic and all-exempt U.S. tour. "Mediocrity excels," Nicklaus said. "I'd like to see American guys who want to win...I know those guys from 30th to 200th on the money list will say, 'There goes Nicklaus again,' but I'm going to keep preaching. Without stars you don't have a tour. The tour is based on stars."

One of the tour's real battlers for all his career, Hale Irwin, agrees. "I never finished No. 1 on the money list, but I would have given anything if I could. It doesn't seem to make much difference to these guys one way or the other. The foreign players have the discipline ours don't."

Even Beman, in an interview with *Golf* magazine, said: "I don't subscribe to the notion that you have to be the best player or one of the 10 best players in the world or you had better get another job. But I do believe in survival of the fittest and I do believe — and this is probably more surprising to me than anything else I've encountered — that a number of golfers hang on too long without accomplishing anything. They may be making money, but they might also be better off directing their lives somewhere else where they could be more productive...I played for the competition. So, yes, I'm disappointed when I see some players use their winnings as a cushion for leisure rather than as a springboard for more achievement. But some people are here to tread water and some are here to sprint. That's a personal choice. I don't think our system should decree their decisions."

Fortunately, golf has always had some real competitors, regardless of nationality, and throughout this century they've seemed to march three abreast: there were Harry Vardon, James Braid and J.H. Taylor; then Bobby Jones, Walter Hagen and Gene Sarazen; then Ben Hogan, Byron Nelson and Sam Snead; then Nicklaus, Arnold Palmer and Gary Player; as Nicklaus outlasted the others, Lee Trevino, Johnny Miller then Watson took up the challenge.

The New Triumvirate is Norman, Ballesteros and Langer. Who's No. 1 is open for debate; there's no question they're the three best golfers in the world and have been for three years. They are not immune to outside threats, particularly if certain golfers were to win in the majors, such as Curtis Strange, Sandy Lyle, or one of the two players who won the most tournaments in 1987, Woosnam and McNulty. But for now, Norman, age 32, and Ballesteros and Langer, both 30, are in a class by themselves.

Ballesteros moved back into first place in the Sony Ranking briefly in November, ahead of Norman, who took that position after winning the Panasonic European Open in September, 1986, in the midst of his 10-victory year. But Norman responded immediately with only his second victory of 1987, a 10-stroke triumph in the National Panasonic Australian Open, and reclaimed the No. 1 position. Surprisingly, Ballesteros won only one tournament, the Suze Open in France, But he was second twice, third three times and a top-10 finisher in 10 of his 13 European Tour events. He played just eight times in America, but won $305,058 with three seconds (including the Masters playoff), a third in the U.S. Open and 10th in the PGA Championship.

Norman's other win came at the Australian Masters. The playoff that Norman and Ballesteros lost to Mize at the Masters — with Seve failing on a putt on the first extra hole, then Mize making that incredible 140-foot chip shot on the second — probably took something out of both. Norman's year was also typical of the nature of the game (a reason why the Sony Ranking is based on a three-year rolling total, not just one year). Even a golfer as great as Player, for example, never had two consecutive superb seasons. Norman's explanation was, "Basically I was trying too hard to top last year."

The third member of the Triumvirate, Langer, had a very good, if not a spectacular year, winning in great style at the Whyte & Mackay PGA Championship and Carrolls Irish Open on the European circuit, and was runner-up in the German Masters which he co-promoted with our company, International Management Group. His U.S. record included seven top-10 finishes, a tie for fourth in the U.S. Open and seventh in the Masters. The biggest disappointment for Bernhard probably was the British Open, which he had been on the verge of winning three times previously. He was two strokes behind after 36 holes, then faded to a tie for 17th place.

None of the three led the World Money List for 1987. That honor was destined for Woosnam, who earned $1,793,268 including $1 million for winning the Sun City Million Dollar Challenge in Bophuthatswana, southern Africa. Woosnam became the second golfer to earn more than $1 million in prize money in one year, surpassing Norman's $1,146,584 in 1986. He also earned $66,667 at Sun City in bonuses for the low daily rounds, pushing his total past $1.8 million.

WORLD MONEY LIST LEADERS

1.	Ian Woosnam, Wales	$1,793,268
2.	Curtis Strange, U.S.	911,671
3.	Paul Azinger, U.S.	844,506
4.	Sandy Lyle, Scotland	767,891
5.	Greg Norman, Australia	715,838
6.	Scott Simpson, U.S.	713,067
7.	Miller Barber, U.S.	709,571
8.	Payne Stewart, U.S.	704,426
9.	Tom Watson, U.S.	694,587
10.	Ben Crenshaw, U.S.	671,844
11.	Bernhard Langer, West Germany	667,797
12.	Severiano Ballesteros, Spain	655,256
13.	Bruce Crampton, Australia	645,621
14.	Lanny Wadkins, U.S.	643,571
15.	David Ishii, U.S.	643,030
16.	Chi Chi Rodriguez, U.S.	623,395
17.	Masashi Ozaki, Japan	613,867
18.	Mark Calcavecchia, U.S.	602,350
19.	Larry Mize, U.S.	574,027
20.	Tom Kite, U.S.	571,791

(The complete World Money List may be found in the appendixes of this annual.)

If years in professional golf are usually remembered for the major champions, 1987 was not very memorable except from a British perspective, with Faldo's victory in the Open at Muirfield. Mize, Simpson and Nelson are not regarded as great or exciting players — never mind what they might have done, respectively, to win the Masters, U.S. Open and PGA Championship. We were close to having these names on the championship rolls: Norman or Ballesteros (Masters); Watson (U.S. Open); Floyd (British Open); Ballesteros, Floyd or Lanny Wadkins (PGA Championship).

This could have been the year that Ben Crenshaw won the Grand Slam. He tied for fourth in the first three, and tied for seventh in the PGA. Evidence of Crenshaw's near brilliance was also reflected in his 15 top-10 finishes to lead the tour. He won only the USF&G (New Orleans) Classic, but was third on the U.S. money list with $638,194.

In fairness, the major championship winners had more than one good week. Simpson and Nelson were among the U.S. tour's six multiple winners and Mize had 10 top-10 finishes. Simpson, who scored three birdies in the last five holes to hold off Watson in the U.S. Open, also won the Greater Greensboro Open and was fourth with $621,032. Nelson, who had done little before defeating Wadkins in a playoff at the PGA Championship, later also won the Walt Disney World/Oldsmobile Classic and closed over the $500,000 mark.

The highlight of the U.S. tour was Watson's win in the Nabisco Championship, his first since 1984. It would be a tremendous boost for American golf if Watson, age 38, winner of 32 tour events and eight major titles, were to continue the resurgence that enabled him to earn $616,351 this year, his best-ever U.S. total and fifth-best on the current tour. "If I come out next year and win five or six times, then I will be all the way back," Watson said. "People who say that's impossible to do now don't know what they're talking about."

Coming closest to Watson's former dominance in recent years has been Strange, age 32, with 11 U.S. victories in the 1980's, second to Watson's 16. Curtis won three times, starting in late June — Canadian Open, Federal Express St. Jude (Memphis) Classic and NEC World Series of Golf. For the second time in three years, Strange set a money-winnings record with $925,941 (including a first-place Nabisco bonus of $175,000). He was chosen Player of the Year by several magazines and the Golf Writers Association of America.

The PGA Player of the Year was Paul Azinger, who was second on the U.S. list with $822,481 and also won three tournaments — Phoenix Open, Panasonic Las Vegas Invitational and Canon Sammy Davis, Jr., Greater Hartford Open. Azinger missed a great opportunity when he stumbled at the finish to lose the British Open. He impressed the British nevertheless, with his game and his manner. Age 27, Paul had not won since joining the tour in 1981, but indications are he could be quite a player.

That's a risky assumption, based on recent history.

It might have been expected that a previously undistinguished golfer such as Azinger would rise, and that the sensation of 1986, Bob Tway, would fall. Like Azinger, Tway had not won before he posted four victories last year, including the PGA Championship. He did not win in 1987, except in the Chrysler Team Championship with Mike Hulbert. Also without a victory (but three second places) was the man once proclaimed as "the next Nicklaus" — Hal Sutton, the 1983 PGA Champion and No. 1 money-winner in his second year on the tour. And Scott Verplank, winner of the 1985 Western Open as an amateur, played so poorly he was sent to the qualifying school to keep his card.

Corey Pavin started as if the year would be his, winning the Bob Hope Chrysler Classic and Hawaiian Open, then disappeared from the leader boards. That pre-Masters portion of the year was the most interesting. Beman's former nemesis, Mac O'Grady, won the season-opening MONY Tournament of Champions. Johnny Miller won for the first time since 1983, and at a favorite venue, in the AT&T Pebble Beach Pro-Am. Chen Tze Chung became Taiwan's first U.S. winner, defeating Crenshaw in a playoff for the Los Angeles Open title. Payne Stewart finally got above second place in the Hertz Bay Hill Classic. Sandy Lyle won the prestigious Tournament Players Championship to signal a great year for the Europeans.

Steady Tom Kite won the Kemper Open to register a tournament victory for the seventh consecutive year. South African David Frost was another frequent contender, although he did not win until returning home for the Safmarine Masters. Frost was second to Crenshaw with 13 top-10 finishes, and was runner-up in three tournaments.

Mike Reid, the first golfer to earn more than $1 million without winning a tournament, got his first victory in the Seiko Tucson Open. Chip Beck, who won $523,003 in 1987, now tops that list with over $1.2 million without a victory.

Three players won in their first year. Keith Clearwater was the most successful rookie, winning $320,007 and two tournaments — Colonial National Invitational and Centel Classic. Sam Randolph won the Bank of Boston Classic and John Inman, the Provident Classic.

Among the older players, in addition to Miller at Pebble Beach, the winners included Irwin in the unofficial early-season Fila Invitational, and J.C. Snead in the Manufacturers Hanover Westchester Classic, where he won a playoff against Ballesteros.

Without victories in the U.S. were the world's three best golfers — Norman, Ballesteros and Langer. Others who did not win included Nicklaus, Floyd, Fuzzy Zoeller and Craig Stadler. Hindered by injury, Andy Bean did not have an official win, but started playing well late in the year and took the ABC Cup individual title then the Isuzu Kapalua International.

The most unusual occurance was Stadler's rules infraction in San Diego, which was only detected a day later by television viewers during a replay. Stadler had knelt on a towel to protect his trousers, while hitting from his knees on a trouble shot in the third round, and thus violated a rule for having built a stance. When this came to light, Stadler was disqualified for signing an incorrect scorecard, without the penalty stroke. It cost him a tie for second place.

(Stadler also inadvertently broke a rule at the British Open, but was saved from disqualification by alert officials, although for a time it seemed the penalty stroke might cost Stadler the championship.)

There were two notable holes-in-one. Don Pooley had a million-dollar shot at Bay Hill — worth $500,000 each to Pooley and the tournament charity, the Arnold Palmer Children's Hospital. Trevino scored an ace worth $175,000 en route to winning $310,000 in the Skins Game at PGA West. Trevino had not anticipated such a boost until he became eligible for the Senior PGA Tour in 1990.

The over-50 circuit continued to provide bonanzas for newcomers while, for the first time, Arnold Palmer, age 58, did not win. Chi Chi Rodriguez, the personable Puerto Rican who won eight times in his career on the regular tour, had seven senior victories in 1987 alone, and 10 for his two years on the circuit. Australian Bruce Crampton also won seven times, four in unofficial events, bringing his two-year total to 15 wins, the same number he won on the regular tour. They were one-two on the official money list, with Rodriguez earning $509,145 and Crampton, $437,904. Including $250,000 from the Mazda Champions, Miller Barber was the overall money leader with $709,571.

Rodriguez won the General Foods PGA Senior Championship in February, then went on a roll in May, winning four in succession — Vantage at the Dominion (San Antonio), United Hospitals Seniors Championship (Philadelphia), Silver Pages Classic (Oklahoma City) and Senior Players Reunion Pro-Am (Dallas). In August, Rodriguez won two more, Digital Seniors Classic (Boston) and GTE Northwest Classic (Seattle).

Rodriguez' highlights included his final-round 63 in the United Hospitals Seniors, when he missed five birdie putts inside the 10-foot range and had his sights on a below-60 score ("If I didn't do it today, I don't know if I ever will.") and his 65 to overtake Crampton in the Senior Players Reunion.

Crampton's three unofficial wins were the Australian World Seniors Match Play Championship, Doug Sanders Kingwood Celebrity Classic and Legends of Golf (with Orville Moody). His first official victory was the Denver Champions of Golf, when Rodriguez was taking a week off between his third and fourth consecutive wins, then Bruce later won the Greenbrier American Express Championship, MONY Syracuse Classic and Bank One Classic (Lexington, Kentucky).

Player won four tournaments, three significant titles — Senior Tournament Players Championship, USGA Senior Open and PaineWebber World Seniors Invitational — and the unofficial Northville Invitational. Bob Charles also won four times, while Moody, Gene Littler and newcomer Al Geiberger each scored three victories.

Geiberger's arrival was perhaps a signal to Rodriguez and Crampton that their time at the top might be short-lived. He became eligible for the tour in September and one month later won the $1 million Vantage Championship. He soon added the Hilton Head International and Las Vegas Classic titles. But even Geiberger had cause to look over his shoulder: former U.S. Open champion Lou Graham would join the circuit in January, 1988, and within two years, Trevino and Nicklaus would be eligible.

The U.S. LPGA Tour was dominated by three players — Ayako Okamoto, Betsy King and Jane Geddes. They won 13 tournaments (Geddes five, and Okamoto and King, four each) and were one-two-three in nearly every statistical category. Okamoto, who is incredibly popular in her native Japan, became the first non-American to win the money title with $466,034 in official earnings.

Okamoto's victories included the Nestle World Championship, with its LPGA-high $81,500 first prize, and King was just behind her on the money list with $460,385, including her Nabisco Dinah Shore victory. Geddes, winner of the Mazda LPGA Championship, earned $396,818 for third place on the money list. The winners of the other LPGA major events were Britain's Laura Davies in the U.S. Women's Open and Jody Rosenthal in the du Maurier Classic.

Pat Bradley, the tour's leading player of 1986, won just one tournament and fell to 15th on the money list. Jan Stephenson came closest to challenging the leading three, having three victories and $227,303 for fourth place on the money list. Ever-popular Nancy Lopez also won three, including the rich Mazda Champions with Barber, and Rosenthal and Cindy Rarick each had two wins.

IAN WOOSNAM'S 1987 PERFORMANCE

TOURNAMENT	POS.	SCORES				TOTAL	MONEY
Hong Kong Open	1	70	71	65	69	275	$25,000
Australian Masters	10	75	68	72	72	287	A$7,080
Victorian Open	8	76	68	71	71	286	A$3,278
Moroccan Open	T5	72	71	73	74	290	£5,950
Jersey Open	1	68	67	72	72	279	£16,160
Suze Open	2	73	64	68	70	275	£16,993
Madrid Open	1	67	67	69	66	269	£27,500
Epson Match Play	T17	Lost second round					£3,000
Spanish Open	T14	71	74	75	77	297	£2,512
British PGA	T15	69	78	70	68	285	£3,030
Memorial	T39	71	69	73	73	286	$3,980
Dunhill Masters	2	67	68	72	68	275	£21,117
French Open	T15	73	66	67	69	275	£3,468
Belgian Open	T2	66	66	69		201	£11,183
Irish Open	T3	72	74	69	67	282	£12,099
Scottish Open	1	65	65	66	68	264	£33,330
British Open	T8	71	69	72	72	284	£18,667
Dutch Open	MC	70	77			147	
Scandinavian Open	T7	66	74	70	71	281	£5,314
PGA Championship	MC	86	75			161	
Benson & Hedges	T14	71	71	68	71	281	£2,820
Batley International	T18	70	70	70	70	280	£1,704
European Masters	MC	73	69			142	
European Open	5	73	71	74	65	283	£9,320
Lancome Trophy	1	65	64	69	66	264	£50,000
German Masters	T5	79	68	69	66	282	£9,550
World Match Play	1	Won final					£75,000
Kirin Cup	2	71	68	67		206	$35,000
Kapalua International	5	68	70	70	68	276	$30,000
World Cup	1	67	70	65	72	274	$150,000
Million Dollar Challenge	1	67	71	68	68	274	$1,000,000

A leading player on the European Tour for six years, Ian Woosnam gained worldwide attention in 1987 with his eight victories and over $1.8 million earnings. The victories doubled his career total since starting out in 1978. The richest, of course, was the Million Dollar Challenge, but the most important was the Suntory World Match Play Championship, where "Woosie" defeated Faldo, Ballesteros and Lyle in succession to become the first Briton to win that prestigious event at the Wentworth Club, near London.

Woosnam, 29 years old and from Wales, was a great favorite of the American crowds at the Ryder Cup because of his small stature (five feet, four and a half inches) and his tremendous power (I reckon he is Britain's best long-iron player). It was fabulous publicity, especially for someone who was snubbed by the Masters earlier in the year, but ignored the fact that Woosnam is merely four inches below the ideal height for a golfer, and that he is very muscular for his size and weighs 147 pounds.

His first triumph was the United Airlines Hong Kong Open, followed by four European Tour victories as he led the money list with £253,717 — Jersey Open, Cepsa Madrid Open, Bell's Scottish Open and Lancome Trophy. Then came the World Match Play, World Cup individual and team (with David Llewellyn) titles and Million Dollar Challenge. In 31 worldwide appearances, Woosnam was a top-five finisher 17 times.

Not far behind Woosnam was another international star that the Masters overlooked, Mark McNulty. Continuing his domination of the South African circuit, McNulty (or McMagic, as the press labeled him) won four times including the Southern Sun South Africa Open. In Europe, McNulty won three — London Standard Four Stars Pro-Celebrity, Dunhill British Masters and German Open — and ranked second to Woosnam on the money list with £189,303. Four others — Langer, Faldo, Howard Clark and Gordon Brand, Jr. — won twice each on the European circuit. Most surprising among the non-winners were 1986 rookie sensation Jose-Maria Olazabal and Australia's Rodger Davis, another who deserved a Masters invitation off his 1986 performance, but was overlooked. And Paul Way, mired in a two-year slump, produced a gratifying victory in the Panasonic European Open.

In almost any other year, Faldo would have been the toast of Britain and Europe. The 30-year-old Englishman had not won since 1984, and had undergone a controversial swing change. He gave notice of his return to Europe's top echelon by winning the Peugeot Spanish Open, then scored a determined triumph at the British Open, recording 18 consecutive pars on the final day. Faldo also was on England's winning Dunhill Cup team, with Clark and Gordon J. Brand.

Although not gaining a place on the Ryder Cup team, the Swedes continued to show promise of a great future. Mats Lanner won the Epson Grand Prix, succeeding Ove Sellberg, Anders Forsbrand won the Ebel European Masters-Swiss Open and Magnus Persson was runner-up in a playoff at the Scandinavian Enterprise Open.

There were further signs of a golf awakening on the continent: 18-year-old Oliver Eckstein tied for sixth in the German Open, three places ahead of Langer, once Germany's "only" golfer.

In Africa, there were three tournaments leading into the European Tour, won by Gordon J. Brand, Carl Mason and Paul Carrigill, plus a full slate of Sunshine Circuit events in South Africa. Behind McNulty on that tour were Tony Johnstone with three victories and Fulton Allem with two, plus a playoff loss to McNulty in the South African Open. Allem also played several U.S. events, and was runner-up in the NEC World Series of Golf.

A big winner in Australasia was Peter Senior, who took three titles on that circuit plus one in Europe. In addition to Norman, two-event winners were Roger Mackay (including the Australian PGA title) and Northern Ireland's Ronan Rafferty, who had not won since the 1982 Venezuelan Open in his first year. David Graham returned home for his only 1987 victory in the Konica Queensland Open and fellow Aussie traveler, Ian Baker-Finch, won the Australian Match Play. Another champion of note was Gerry Taylor, a surprise challenger in the British Open, who recorded his first important title at the National Panasonic Western Australia Open.

The Asia/Japan Tour produced perhaps the year's most far-fetched scenario: an American led the circuit, the first time a foreigner had ever done so.

That was Ishii, who won six times including a first-place tie with Isao Aoki when the year-end Japan Series was cancelled by snow after 36 holes. Ishii, age 32, is of Japanese extraction, from Hawaii, and once starred on the golf team at the University of Houston. His success was not totally out of the blue; he had won in Japan once in 1985 and twice in 1986. Tops among Ishii's victories were the Japan PGA Championship and Casio World Open.

In contrast to Ishii's campaign was a one-victory year by Tsuneyuki (Tommy) Nakajima, who had won 28 tournaments over the past five years and risen to fourth on the Sony Ranking. Winning only the Tokai Classic, Nakajima remained the leading Japanese player in the Ranking, but fell to 15th place overall, just ahead of Masashi (Jumbo) Ozaki and Aoki, who were also among the world's top 20. Ozaki was Ishii's main challenger for the money title and had three victories — Chunichi Crowns, Fuji Sankei and Jun Classic. Aoki had four triumphs, including the Japan Open.

Other Asia/Japan results of particular note included Brian Tennyson's two wins on the Asian circuit, and Chen Tze Ming's three, one in Japan and two in Asia. Australians Baker-Finch, Brian Jones and Graham Marsh also scored victories in Japan, as did America's Stadler. Marsh, the most successful foreign contestant in Japanese golf history, won the Taiheiyo Club Masters, followed a week later by Stadler's win in another important autumn event, the Dunlop Phoenix.

And, yes, Team USA won. After losing the Ryder Cup, Dunhill Cup, World Cup and ABC Cup, the Americans came away with a win in the Kirin Cup. "There isn't a damn thing wrong with our golf," said Strange.

Maybe, but at least this was a positive conclusion to the first 100 years of American golf. The second century would begin with the New Year, or more precisely, February 22, the date on which in 1888, a group of men from New York gathered in a cow pasture in Yonkers, north of the city, and laid out three golf holes, becoming the "Apple Tree Gang" — the first golf club in the country.

Before turning to the 1987 season in detail, we recall the passing of. . . George Blumberg, 75, a pioneer of golf in South Africa, and great friend of golf and golfers worldwide. . . Arthur D'Arcy (Bobby) Locke, 69, also of South Africa, winner of the British Open four times and South African Open eight times, among more than 60 pro titles. . . Henry Cotton, 80, winner of the British Open three times, among more than 30 pro titles. . . Ralph Guldahl, 75, whose 11 PGA Tour victories included two U.S. Opens and one Masters. . . Dan Sikes, 58, winner of six PGA Tour and three Senior PGA Tour events. . . Laurie Auchterlonie, 83, honorary professional to the Royal and Ancient Golf Club of St. Andrews for 24 years, and a clubmaker of note. . . Tom Scott, 80, and Geoffrey Cousins, 86, respected British golf writers.

2. The Masters Tournament

Larry Mize stood on the 10th tee in the dying light of a spring afternoon on the most hallowed grounds in American golf, but nobody saw him. A playoff for the 1987 Masters Tournament was about to begin, and all the world would see were the other two golfers on the tee: Greg Norman of Australia and Seve Ballesteros of Spain.

The debate over who ruled the world of golf would be settled at the Augusta National Golf Club. The dark-haired, dashing Spaniard, a winner of four major championships but none since 1984, had in the week of his 30th birthday sported a maturity heretofore unseen. Ballesteros would duel the white-haired, dashing Aussie who had captured the hearts of golf fans worldwide when his magnificent 1986 season collapsed in the sandstorm of Bob Tway's PGA Championship victory.

Mize, the third man who completed 72 holes at three-under-par 285 (the highest winning score since Jack Nicklaus' 286 in 1972) had spent his childhood right here in Augusta, Georgia. As a teen, Mize had played golf next door, at the Augusta Country Club which nestles up to Amen Corner. Mize had never played Augusta National until 1984, when he competed in the Masters. Though he had worked on the scoreboard next to third green in his youth, he refused to play on Bobby Jones' course until he had earned it.

Now, he had earned a place in this playoff, earned it with a birdie on the 72nd hole, but no recognition came forth. Mize may have won the 1983 tour stop in Memphis, but he was most known for his collapses. In the glow of Nicklaus's final-round 66 to win the 1986 Masters, no one but Bonnie Mize remembered her husband had shot the low round of the day (65).

But everyone recalled that Mize had lost a four-stroke lead on the final nine of the 1986 Tournament Players Championship. He had lost the 1986 par-three tournament at Augusta in a playoff to Gary Koch. He had lost a six-hole sudden-death playoff in the 1986 Kemper Open — to Norman.

Mize saved his response for the 11th green, on the second hole of the playoff. What more competitive answer to Norman, the victim of a sand-wedge shot at the PGA, than to hole an even more difficult shot to snatch the Masters away from him.

Ben Hogan used to play the 455-yard downhill par-four 11th by bailing out to the right so as to avoid the pond which guards the left side of the green. In the dark of twilight, Larry Hogan (for his grandmother, not the Wee Icemon) Mize blocked his approach too far to the right. He had 140 feet to negotiate, 140 feet to come up and over a crest, yet stop the ball on a slick green all too willing to allow it to continue into the pond.

Mize stroked his pitch, and as it neared the hole, the patrons lined all the way up the hill of the 11th fairway began a roar that would be the equal of any heard in the cathedral of pines. As the ball rolled into the cup, Mize leapt into the air with both fists raised, a photograph that would appear around the world.

At the outset, the worry of the 1987 Masters centered on the problem of providing an encore. Nicklaus' sixth victory in Augusta left the golf world agape. As always, the wonders of Augusta National quickly erased all worry. Simply arrive, celebrate the coming of spring, appreciate the beauty on which so many depend for a boost out of the late-winter blahs.

Still, few wished to admit that it was time to let go of the Nicklaus miracle. When asked about an encore, tournament chairman Hord Hardin replied, "I don't worry about that because I don't think it's possible."

Nicklaus also sounded a note of, if not resignation, for no one believed the Golden Bear had packed it in, then satisfaction. He sounded as if he would take the time this year to smell the azaleas. "If I do well this week, that's great," Nicklaus said. "If I don't do well this week, obviously I'll be disappointed, but it's not the end of the world. Last year sort of put a lot to rest, and I had a very enjoyable year because of it. Last year, when I came in here, I was a bit frustrated with myself because I hadn't been able to put much together or make much happen. This year I'm very relaxed. I'm not worried about my play."

The record which Nicklaus, 47, brought to Augusta showed he had played sparingly and poorly in 1987. He had entered four tournaments, missed one cut, and finished no better than 15th. Nicklaus had won $18,678, 109th on the money list.

But he appeared upbeat at the beginning of the week. A tip received before the TPC from his old friend Phil Rodgers had restored power that had been missing for a few months. Rodgers, through the magic of videotape, showed Nicklaus that he hadn't been lowering his right hip.

"It puts me in the position of being able to coil and to be able to uncoil from that position with some power," Nicklaus said. "I put on considerable distance and found that the center of the golf club gets used occasionally again."

After the final round of the 1986 Masters, no one would dare write Nicklaus off. However, the mantle of favorite cloaked the broad shoulders of Norman. In the previous autumn, Norman had doused the disappointment of the PGA by winning everything that wasn't nailed down.

Norman won seven tournaments, six in succession, and 10 for the year. Prior to the Masters, he won the Australian Masters but had played only five stops on the American tour: the Tournament of Champions on the second weekend of the year, the AT&T Pebble Beach Pro-Am and three events in his adopted home of Florida. Though he had played well enough, gaining three top-five finishes, Norman had dominated the Wednesday pro-ams, winning two team events and one individual.

Perhaps, to his chagrin, this boded well for Norman's chances in the par-three tournament. History has told us — quite loudly, in fact — that no winner of the par-three tournament has gone on to win the Masters. However, this would be a different par-three tournament.

The Augusta National Golf Club for years has been able to withstand the clamor for tickets — "badges", in the local parlance — to the Masters. The course can hold only so many people, they say, if not with some measure of glee. Even Hardin has only eight tickets at his discretion.

In order to assuage the public, tickets to the practice rounds on Monday and Tuesday and to the Wednesday afternoon nine-hole tournament, on the par-three course east of the practice area, were placed on sale on the day of the event. This worked well for some time, until recent years, when the demand for par-three tournament tickets became such that one had to line up at dawn to be assured of a purchase. I know that in 1986 one friend who got in line — located at the front of the patrons' parking at Gate 4, on Washington Road — before 9 a.m. and had made little progress toward the ticket window when the "sold out" announcement was made.

As it turned out, 1986 would be the last exclusive par-three tournament. Showing a sensitivity toward the non-badge-holding public not seen often in these parts, the Masters redesigned the short course to allow for more spectators (one suspects the lure of several thousand more patrons paying $20 a head carried some weight).

The redesign of the course included Ike's Pond, behind and below President and Mrs. Eisenhower's cottage next to the 10th tee. Trees were cleared out to make room for two holes, of 120 and 135 yards respectively, one going over the pond and the other one coming back toward the cottage. They were designated the final two holes of the par-three course. The old Nos. 1 and 2 were used for gallery space, and the course began on what had been No. 3.

Not only did the change make more room for spectators, but it opened all eyes to how picturesque Ike's Pond was. The natural amphitheatre provided by the slopes toward the water allowed more people to experience the fellowship of the par-three yet without losing its coziness.

After all, there aren't many tournaments where kids can walk the course while Dad plays. Old friends Scott Simpson and Craig Stadler were joined by four-year-old Brea Simpson and seven-year-old Kevin Stadler. Some of the officials didn't cotton to the kids — Brea and Scott performed a high-five on one green — but the children are an example of the charm of the Masters par-three. It is the loud paisley tie against Augusta National's Brooks Brothers image.

Take Tournament of Champions winner Mac O'Grady. Mac the Life of the Party played the course in two-over 29. Not bad for a right-handed player going southpaw. O'Grady always has putted left-handed. As he showed here, he is a talented golfer from either side of the ball.

O'Grady had tongue-in-cheekily announced in 1986 that he planned to petition the USGA to allow him to compete in the U.S. Open as a left-handed amateur. Based upon his play, it's safe to say he wouldn't embarrass anybody on the course. Then again, O'Grady usually waits to get off the course before he becomes, shall we say, colorful.

Bernhard Langer, the 1985 Masters champion, provided something to cheer about with an ace at No. 7, only the fourth in the last nine par-three tournaments. Tom Kite finished early in the par-three and put up a four-under 23 that stood for most of the afternoon. Late in the day, however, he would be overtaken by Ben Crenshaw, his boyhood friend and rival.

Do you think Kite, an even-keeled sort, ever looks up and asks, "Why me?" Here is one of the most talented golfers of the last decade — Kite is the only player to win a tournament in each of the last seven years — and yet the 37-year-old has been unable to take that biggest step and win a major championship.

His most agonizing loss came in the 1986 Masters. Kite turned in consecutive rounds of 68 on Saturday and Sunday, only to finish one stroke short of Nicklaus' winning score of nine-under 279. That one stroke will be remembered for many years. Kite's 12-foot birdie putt on the 72nd hole seared the edge of the cup before staying out. "I still don't see how the putt missed," Kite said a year later.

Kite currently carries the title of best player to never win a major. It has been his since Crenshaw, his teammate at the University of Texas, relinquished it by knocking him out on Amen Corner in the fourth round of the 1984 Masters. Kite's challenge on that day fell short when his tee shot at the par-three 12th hole plopped into Rae's Creek.

"There's a big difference between 'can't' and 'haven't,'" Kite said. "It depends on your perspective. I prefer to say 'I haven't.' I'll let the negative guys say 'I can't.'"

Crenshaw was stuck with a similar dilemma as he walked to the ninth and final tee of the par-three tournamentt. His father, Charlie, told him, "Son, you know if you win this thing, you're not going to win the big tournament." As he prepared to hit his shot, Charlie spoke again.

"On the tee," he said, " 'put this thing in the water'," Ben would say at the awards presentation. "I told him I was going to try to win the big one too. I know what's happened to the winner of the par-three tournament every year. But my wife, Julie, has informed me that this is a new par-three course so we're gonna have to break that old tradition."

Crenshaw, in fact, had to be a favorite in 1987's field of 86 golfers. He had finished in the top 15 in all but one of his starts in 1987, and had won at New Orleans. He arrived in Augusta fourth on the money list, with $254,956.

The others attracting the most attention were Norman and Ballesteros. "I feel I have a good chance to win the tournament, the best I've had," Norman said early in the week. "I was very keen to get back here just to play in it. I have no reservations, no doubts in any part of my game."

Mize drew attention from the local paper during the tournament, but only because he is a local boy. Actually, Larry and Bonnie Mize, and their infant child David live in Columbus, Georgia, but the *Augusta Chronicle* and *Herald* ignore that, as do Mize's parents and all his friends who come out in force every year to root for him.

"I feel good about my game," said Mize. "I've been playing well. I've got confidence going into this week."

Both the field and the course would be fine-tuned in the days leading up to Thursday's morning start. On the Sunday prior to the tournament, Augusta National would have to inscribe another invitation. Scott Simpson won the Greater Greensboro Open and snuck under the wire into the Masters field. A bit of a mudder — despite being from southern California, Simpson plays well when conditions are less than ideal — Simpson would not threaten here, and finished tied for 27th.

Weather was poor in Greensboro and along the south Atlantic coast on that weekend, but Augusta welcomed its players with sunny weather once the week began. Sunny, brisk, blustery weather, actually. The wind blew constantly, keeping the greens hard and fast. Now, we all know that there's never been an Augusta green too fast for the men in the green jackets or too slow for the players. By Wednesday, however, Hardin and his greenskeeping staff allowed as how maybe they could ease up on the mowers a tad.

Nicklaus, for his part, wondered if maybe the trees on the course were due for a trim, too. He pointed out several holes on the course which had changed because of the growth of the treeline. "At No. 3, you used to be able to set it up at the left of the fairway and cut into it," the defending champion said. "Now you really have to hit the ball straight. You can't bring it in right to left.

"You used to be able to draw the ball over the bunker at No. 5, but you've got to play it up the fairway now. No. 7 has gone from a wide hole to a very narrow hole, and you have a similar situation at No. 9. On No. 13, it's harder to get it around the corner. The trees on the left side of No. 14 force you to hook the ball. At No. 15, the trees have grown so far out on the right that you almost have to start the ball left, and the hole isn't set up for that."

This may not have been the course Nicklaus has been so used to for three decades, but nine players were seeing it for the first time: David Frost, Paul Azinger, Ernie Gonzalez (the first lefthander since Japan's Yutaka Hagawa in 1982), Georgians Fred Wadsworth and Gene Sauers, Mike Hulbert, and amateurs Brian Montgomery, Chris Kite (no relation to Tom), Billy Andrade and Louisiana State University golf coach Buddy Alexander, the 1986 U.S. Amateur champion. Alexander's father, Stewart, Sr., had played in a half-dozen Masters in his prime, finishing as high as 14th.

As long as the invitation list had become — 88 golfers, for the second consecutive year — the international list again looked thin. The questions concerned Rodger Davis of Australia, Ian Woosnam of Wales and Mark McNulty of Zimbabwe, all ignored by the Masters.

As usual, the oldest participants would start it all at 8:30 a.m. Thursday morning. There is no other sporting event, much less a major one, which honors its own as does the Masters. Sam Snead, Byron Nelson and Gene Sarazen teed off shortly before their scheduled starting time. Their annual nine-hole round has developed about it the sense of ritual. In the sense that the rounds blend from year to year, I suppose it has become that. The memories become indelible.

No matter what the weather (and this year it was magnificent, if windy), it's always cool enough to see your breath. Those hardy souls who appear in the gallery huddle around the first tee, waiting for the threesome to hit their drives. Then the patrons fan out to the sunnier areas of the course, some to wait for several hours on the back nine, others to watch a favorite among the early golfers, others still to the nearest cup of coffee.

Among the 85 starters (former champions Bob Goalby and George Archer each withdrew because of illness or injury in the days leading up to the first round, and back pains caused Peter Jacobsen to withdraw Thursday morning) were, at 12:29 p.m., the defending champion, Nicklaus, and the current U.S. Amateur victor, Alexander; U.S. Open winner Raymond Floyd with British Amateur champ David Curry at 1:04 p.m.; the golden-boy duo of Crenshaw and Norman at 1:32 p.m.; and the similar set of Payne Stewart and Hal Sutton at 2 p.m.

The star of the first round wouldn't come from that group. In fact, the star wasn't a golfer, but the greens. The windy conditions endured all week had so glazed the putting surfaces that the greenskeeping crew attempted to slow them down a notch on Wednesday. Nonetheless, Norman, who shot a one-over 73, would describe the greens as "the fastest I've ever had."

"In one word — brutal," Norman said. "The back nine was extremely brutal on your concentration. The greens were extremely quick and there were some places out there where you just couldn't put the ball. If the pin placements were a little more liberal in the right places, the greens wouldn't have seemed that fast... They are going to have to water the greens or they will lose a couple."

"This is the best the greens have been by a long shot," said Tom Watson, who birdied No. 16 to come home in 71, two shots out of the lead. "They're firm and require excellent shotmaking. They've gotten very, very hard around the hole. They'll be very, very treacherous with any wind at all."

Under those conditions, those who have early tee times tend to fare best. Such was the case with veteran Calvin Peete, who played in the third pairing of the day with 1959 champion Art Wall, Jr. Going off at one minute before 9 a.m., Peete, who played the last two rounds of 1983 in 87-80 and the first two in 1984 in 79-66, took the early lead with a one-under 71. After saving one-putt pars at the first two holes, Peete holed birdie putts at Nos. 3, 5 and 8. A bogey at the par-three fourth meant he went out in 34. "Then," said Peete, "the wind came up."

Peete also bogeyed both par-threes on the back side, Nos. 12 and 16, before birdieing the 17th to finish under par.

"I'm basically trying to be more patient," Peete said. "I feel good about my chances."

He should have, thanks to the gusts that shook the pines. Mac O'Grady (10:51 a.m.), three-under after 10 holes, finished even; Craig Stadler (12:15 p.m.), two-under through 12, turned in a 74; the defending champion, one-under through 11, was two-over after 13 holes and completed a round of 74.

The leaders at the quarter-pole watched each other's every shot. They were the 9:48 a.m. twosome of John Cook, with a three-under 69, and one stroke behind him, Larry Mize. Before they stand accused of benefitting from a defanged course, it must be pointed out that Cook birdied Nos. 16 and 17, while Mize reached two-under by making birdies on the final two holes. They didn't play those holes until mid-afternoon.

Cook holed a 12-foot putt at the par-three 16th, "one of the scariest" of his career, he said. "If the ball had missed the hole, it would have rolled to the front of the green." To his credit, Mize came out of the back bunker to make a six-foot par putt.

Both made threes at the 400-yard uphill No. 17, Mize by sinking an eight-footer, Cook, a three-footer. Then, Mize pulled within a shot by jamming home a 35-foot uphill putt at the home hole. His charge came so late that he didn't make the leader board per se. Off to the side, under "Messages", read the legend "Mize 2 18". The "2" was in red.

As we shall see, it wouldn't be the last time he was shunted to the side. But even Mize wasn't all that impressed. "It was a kind of a so-so round, then boom, it turned into a 70," Mize said. "I'm happy, but there's a long way to go."

Cook, the 29-year-old 1978 U.S. Amateur champion, won two tournaments in his first four years on tour, yet had been winless since 1983. Wrist and elbow ailments had held him back until the 1986 tour, when he rebounded to win more than a quarter-million dollars. He is a soft-spoken, personable father of three. The key to Cook's round had been his 24 putts. The key to his putting had been the retention of the Bullseye he had used at Ohio State. Cook didn't return to the Bullseye of his own volition. He had been forced to do so. When he arrived in New Orleans for the USF&G tournament in March, Cook discovered that his clubs had not followed him. He was still looking for them.

"If you see any clubs in an old black bag with my name on it anywhere," Cook said, "you can have that putter. Maybe it was a blessing in disguise that I sent home for my old Bullseye. I used it last week (sixth at Greensboro) and it's as comfortable as I've ever felt with a putter."

Peete and Watson would be joined by four others at 71. Bernhard Langer, Curtis Strange, Payne Stewart and Corey Pavin each had felt the heat of the final nine holes of Augusta National on previous Sundays. Here it was Thursday and they stumbled.

Langer and Strange had joined O'Grady in reaching three-under. Langer, in his best opening round in his five Masters, birdied three of the opening four holes — the only par had been a three-putt at No. 2. But Langer didn't finish minus-one until he made a three at No. 17. Stewart's iron play lifted him among the leaders. The four birdie putts he made were all inside 10 feet.

Strange made the turn at 33, but finished at 71 by making bogey at the final hole. Pavin, who already had two victories before getting to Augusta, played textbook conservative golf. Standing on the 12th tee two-over, he didn't miss a green coming home and made birdie attempts of seven and six feet at Nos. 12 and 14 before draining a monster 30-footer at the 170-yard 16th.

"Monster" is the right description, for No. 16 was the demon in Pavin's golfing life. He played the hole six-over par in 1986. He finished six strokes behind Nicklaus. The birdie there signified that he had exorcised all memories of that collapse.

A recap of the first round wouldn't be complete without mentioning Pavin's partner, Scott Verplank. The one-time amateur wunderkind had fallen on hard times. He had been playing poorly for the better part of a season, listening for advice to every Tom, Dick or caddie who walked past him on the range. But maybe this Masters would be different. Verplank eagled the first hole — yes, the 400-yard par-four — out of the fairway bunker, 189 yards away.

"I hit a three iron out of the bunker and somehow it went into the hole," Verplank said. "It hit on the front of the green and started rolling up by the pin. I just figured it would stop on the back fringe and be pretty close. You know when the ball goes in from the crowd reaction."

Just as he started his career with a boom — winning the 1985 Western Open as an amateur — before going astray, Verplank frittered the eagle away. He bogeyed the final three holes to finish four-over.

Perhaps the most refreshing result of the first round was the caliber of players atop the leaderboard. When asked if the exacting conditions of the course favored the better players, Nicklaus said, "Absolutely. We don't see these conditions on tour." Nicklaus and Norman both referred to the greens as turning "blue". When greens are their slickest, and driest, they do take on a purplish tint. Some say it's because they're choking for water.

Strange has been accused of turning blue in his day, one day in particular two years ago. His bold, losing gamble on the par-fives of the back nine in the 1985 Masters placed upon him a bittersweet legacy. Just as it still is difficult to look at Ed Sneed without wincing over his collapse in the 1979 Masters, a dark cloud will follow Strange about the grounds until he wins a green jacket.

To his credit, Strange didn't allow the 1985 Masters to destroy him. He would prove that throughout 1987, when he won his second Arnold Palmer Award as the leading money-winner, but his second round at Augusta National also would be a strong indication. The 32-year-old Virginian, just as he had in the second round of the 1985 Masters, fired a slew of birdies on Friday. Two years ago, he had six birdies and an eagle en route to a 65. This time, Strange made five birdies and an eagle. Unfortunately, they came accompanied by five bogeys. Still, the 70-141 total left Strange in first all by his lonesome.

The leaderboard looked like this:

Curtis Strange	71-70—141
John Cook	69-73—142
Corey Pavin	71-71—142
Larry Mize	70-72—142
Roger Maltbie	76-66—142
Tom Watson	71-72—143
Bernhard Langer	71-72—143
T.C. Chen	74-69—143

"Obviously, I have thought about it," Strange said of atoning for 1985. "Obviously, this is one I'd like to win. It's a most important tournament for me now, the biggest tournament for me to win some day."

Strange's surge wouldn't come until late in the day. Again, there would be a big move made among the morning players. One of the manners in which the Masters displays its specialness is the repairing of players according to their scores after the first round. Most tournaments wait until the 36-hole cut to change. The meaning of this is that any move made by an early player will bring him only back to the pack, not send him in front. Such was the case with veteran Roger Maltbie.

The 35-year-old had qualified for the 1987 Masters by finishing tied for 23rd in 1986. Maltbie's undistinguished first round of 76 had left him and Jim Thorpe the relatively early tee time of 10:15 a.m. Maltbie jumped on the unsuspecting front side with birdies at the second, third and fifth holes. After six consecutive two-putt pars, he made his only bogey at the 12th when he bunkered his tee shot.

After that pause, Maltbie took off again. He pitched to one foot at the par-five 13th and tapped in a birdie. Then, as the USA cable network began its coverage, Maltbie closed by making birdies on the final three holes. He hit a five iron to five feet at the par-three 16th, then made putts of 10 and 28 feet on Nos. 17 and 18.

The 66-142 total not only brought Maltbie back to the pack, it left him only one shot out of the lead. "I went into today wanting to shoot under par because you have to look at the cut after shooting 76," Maltbie said.

As it turned out, he would look at much more. "I wanted to get back in the tournament, so if I play well on the weekend...I hopefully will take one day at a time, one shot at a time. The tournament is won on the final nine."

Quite a metamorphosis in thinking for one who began the day thinking about surviving the cut. Maltbie's Good Time Charlie attitude has changed just as completely. The one-time party boy still likes his cocktails — he plays out of a Michelob bag — but his recent entrance into fatherhood had calmed him down. Spencer Davis Maltbie came to Augusta five weeks old. Roger and Donna Maltbie had been so intent on bringing him that Donna wrote "Baby Maltbie" on the form for family badges. The Maltbie baby operation worked out of a friend's motor home in the Augusta National parking lot.

Maltbie gave acknowledgement to the early start. "It's certainly nicer to be off at 10:15 than at 1:53," Maltbie said. "The wind wasn't much of a factor, but it did get stronger. The greens held shots much better today. They were softer," no doubt because of his early play. Dave Barr, whose opening 79 forced him off the first tee at 9:12 a.m., turned in a nifty 68. Other than those rounds, however, the conditions remained stringent. Both Pavin and Strange would reach five-under, only to fall back.

The first-round leader would feel their bite early. Cook fell apart on the front nine. He stood on the sixth tee four-under for the tournament, alone in the lead. A poor tee ball at the par-three sixth left him 40 feet away, and he three-putted. At No. 7, he left his third shot in the back bunker and had to get up-and-down for another bogey. Another three-putt at No. 8 dropped him to one-over, and a poor drive off the ninth tee provided his fourth consecutive bogey.

"At No. 9," Cook said when the day was done, "I wanted to walk in the clubhouse and say good-bye to everyone."

A four-foot par putt at the 10th steadied his nerves, and Cook tightened his wheels down the back nine. Then, after he had drifted out of everyone's attention span, Cook pounded home an 18-foot birdie at No. 17. A seven iron to three feet gave him a birdie on the home hole (only the seventh of the day at No. 18) and brought him back to a 73—142, within a shot of the lead.

While Cook stepped out of the spotlight, Pavin took over. He burst out of the chute with birdies on the first two holes. He holed a 20-foot putt on No. 1, then chipped six feet away and holed it on the 555-yard downhill second hole. Birdie putts of 12 feet at No. 7 and 15 feet at No. 9 dropped him to five-under, two shots ahead of Strange and Mize.

"It was almost two rounds," Pavin would say when it was done, "the front nine and the back nine. I had a chance to be in the lead but I just didn't get the job done on the back nine."

Pavin missed the green at the 12th, 14th and 15th holes, and failed to get up-and-down at any of them. The round of 32-39 left him tied with Maltbie and the final twosome of Cook and Mize at 142. Pavin's year peaked on the ninth green during the second round. After stumbling home on the back nine, Pavin followed with a third-round 81 and finished back in the pack at seven-over 295. He would continue to slump throughout the season, a mystery to those who had seen him dominate the early season with victories at the Bob Hope and the Hawaiian Open.

Mize played most of the day at three-under. A bogey at No. 2 dropped him to one-under, but consecutive birdies at Nos. 8 and 9 — while his playing partner, Cook, was making bogeys — gave him a front-side 35. He made eight straight pars on the back side, then dumped his second shot at No. 18 into a bunker. His sand shot failed to stay on the top tier, and rolled back to the front fringe, from where he got up-and-down for bogey.

Sensing the missed opportunity, Mize proclaimed himself "not very happy with the way I played today. I'm pleased with the score. The course is playing tough and if you don't hit the ball very good, it will wear you out."

Strange hit it good, bad and indifferent. He only made one par in the first eight holes, which he played in two-under. To wit: bogey-birdie-bogey-par-eagle-bogey-birdie-birdie. As he had during his 65 in the second round of the 1985 Masters, Strange made a two on a par-four. Then it had occurred at No. 3. This time, he holed a six iron from 185 yards out at No. 5.

Strange blitzed Amen Corner, making birdies at Nos. 12 (20 feet) and 13 (two-putt from 40 feet) to reach five-under. A poor pitch at No. 14 resulted in a bogey. Strange sandwiched missed birdie attempts at Nos. 16 and 18 around a three-putt bogey at No. 17. He spent 45 minutes on the putting green before coming to the interview room.

"It's not a round I'm very proud of," Strange said, "but I made five birdies and an eagle. I should dwell on that, and not on the five bogeys."

Strange's last bogey allowed nine golfers to sneak in under the 36-hole cut. The Masters makes its cut at 44 players and ties, but includes everyone within 10 strokes of the leader. Those at 151 included Mac O'Grady, who tacked a 79 onto his opening 72, and Hubert Green, who, after a first-round 80, turned in a 71, despite an 8 at No. 15. "The golf course played a lot fairer today," Green said. "Yesterday, they made a mockery of the game of golf. The pins and the greens yesterday were not fair for a round where you had early and late tee times. (They) would have been fair today, for all the leaders went out roughly at the same time."

Same old shy Hubert.

Shot of the round goes to Tommy Aaron, the 50-year-old 1973 Masters champion. Aaron's tee shot at No. 17 never came down. It lodged itself in Ike's Tree, the pine named after President Eisenhower after he requested that it be taken down. He salvaged a bogey, despite the lost ball, and his 72-76—148 comfortably made the cut.

The stars lurked just behind the scenes. Langer and Watson were only two shots out. Ballesteros shot a 71 to pull to even-par 144. Norman added a 74 to his opening 73. It would be Saturday before he made his charge. What a charge it was.

The Sunday *Atlanta Journal-Constitution* would headline its story "The stars come out in Masters". Twenty-three players began the third round within five strokes of the lead. Two of the early contenders, Pavin and Cook, took themselves out of contention early: Pavin, en route to his 81, and Cook, who bogeyed the first two holes. He would finish only two-over for the day, but never challenged.

Actually, the biggest splash was made by the Great White Shark lurking six strokes out. Norman beat par by the same amount. They don't call him Shark for nothing. The nickname would take on added importance on Saturday, thanks to Norman's longtime caddy, Pete Bender. But first, the round itself. Not only did Norman birdie four of the first seven holes. He birdied the difficult ones — the par-three fourth, the second toughest hole on the course, and the long par-four fifth — as well as Nos. 2 and 7. He re-appeared on the leaderboard shortly after 1 p.m., after the birdie at No. 5. Norman would be there for the rest of the tournament.

The last pairing, Strange and Maltbie, went off the first tee shortly before 2 p.m. Maltie immediately grabbed a share of the lead with a birdie on the first hole. They would remain tied at three-under for several holes, one stroke ahead of Cook, who again started wildly, with a bogey at No. 2 and a birdie at No. 3, and Ballesteros, who made birdie at the second and seventh holes to go to two-under.

Norman would soon join them, to the delight of his mushrooming gallery. At the dogleg par-five 13th hole, the Shark knocked his drive through the bend into the crowd at the rise of the sloping fairway. He still had a clear shot to the green however, and knocked it on the green 25 feet away. Two putts gave Norman his fifth birdie and moved him to two-under. A similar two-putt birdie at No. 15 put Norman at three-under and gave him, ever so briefly, a share of the lead.

At 3:40 p.m., the leader board read:

Strange	three-under through 7
Maltbie	three-under through 7
Norman	three-under through 16
Ballesteros	one-under through 10
Mize	one-under through 7
McCumber	one-under through 13

The last name, that of veteran Mark McCumber, appeared when the Floridian, who began the day two-over, eagled No. 8 and birdied No. 13. This would be the apex of his charge.

Norman routinely parred the final two holes to complete a round of 32-34-66—213, and left his red "3" on the board for everyone to joust.

The difference in the Norman of Saturday and of Friday could be seen best on those back-nine par-fives. On Friday, he had knocked the ball into the water on each hole and made bogey.

"I putted more aggressively today," Norman said. "Maybe the first two rounds were a blessing in disguise for me. I played them like I was afraid of the course. I tried so hard, but fell so far back. Today I went out more relaxed. I decided, 'You love this place, so just have fun.' I did what I had to do. The third round is a crucial one. If you play well, you get your name back up with the leaders. It gives you a lot of confidence."

Laura Norman said her husband's relaxed demeanor came about because of a gathering of his mates Friday night. The organizers of the Australian Masters tournament, Frank Williams and David Inglis, visiting Augusta from Down Under, annually put on an "Aussie Barbeque" at their rented home, complete with lamb and dozens of cases of Swan lager flown in just for the occasion.

"We just had a great time. He needed to relax," Laura said. "I told him he was going to shoot a 65."

Bender, Norman's caddy, also created something of a stir himself by wearing a patch which featured a shark. Bender had shoved it in his bag over the winter and forgotten about it. He discovered the patch Friday night. A quick perusal of the Masters caddy guide showed no rule against wearing the patch, so Bender sewed it onto the back of his caddy coveralls. He received a lot of comments, nice comments, during the round. Afterward, however, Bender barely had left the 18th green when Augusta National officials indicated the patch would have to go.

"I guess you could say he was a little rude about it," Bender said. "He said, 'I don't want you to wear that again.'"

Oddly enough, the back nine that had knocked down so many pretenders in the opening two rounds would prove to be paved with gold on Saturday. Only Strange stumbled. Both he and Maltbie moved out of the tie with Norman and stood in the lead at four-under. Those on their heels, however, increased in number and stature, and through Amen Corner, no less.

- Lanny Wadkins, who began the day one-over, birdied Nos. 11, 13 and 14 to go two-under.
- Crenshaw, the 1984 champion, would string up four straight birdies beginning at No. 12 and go to three-under.
- Ballesteros sandwiched birdies at Nos. 12 and 14 around a bogey at No. 13 and stopped, at the moment at two-under.

Strange conquered No. 13, his old nemesis, for a birdie and took sole possession of the lead at five-under. With the crowd swelling and cheering, Strange once again gave the lead away. A poor approach at the par-four 14th left him an impossible third shot from the bottom of the two-tiered green, and he could get within only 20 feet. He missed that long par and dropped to four-under and into a tie with his partner, Maltbie, and yes, Crenshaw. A birdie on the closing hole gave the Texan a 31 on the back nine and a 67 for the day.

"That was something I needed," Crenshaw said of the round. "I gave myself a chance to score on the back side. I told my caddy that if we could be patient, something good would happen, and I'll be darned if it didn't. I hit a lot of nice shots."

Crenshaw pointed out two keys to his play. The first was an eight-foot par putt at the 10th hole. "That gave me the spur of confidence I needed" for the birdie streak, he said. The second was his refurbished home life. Crenshaw had a new wife, Julie, and they would have a daughter late in the summer.

"I've never been a happier person," Crenshaw said. "I know that." The pre-eminent historian among the golfing pros (he mused aloud about naming his newborn Merion, after the course, only to be nixed by Julie), Crenshaw always beams when at Augusta. "It's safe to say I'm a sentimental sort," he said.

"I can't help it but I feel privileged to play at a tournament such as this. I'm happy as heck I've won it once before. There are too many elements that make it so special to me. This is a beautiful place, but it goes beyond that. It's a matter of taste and people's feeling. Bobby Jones, in a large part, is here. It's his expression of the game and, as I've said before, he's the one I look up to more than anybody.

Sorry to interrupt the elegy, but on the course, Strange's game suddenly needed a eulogy. The most glaring error of 1985, hitting into the water at No. 15, re-appeared and cost him another bogey, leaving Maltbie and Crenshaw in the lead at four-under. Then, at No. 16, Strange simply didn't think. He put his tee shot 12 feet above the pin, and boldly charged with his birdie putt. The ball hardly slowed at the cup and stopped 40 feet below the hole. It would be his last bogey, but by that time, he was two-under.

"Sometimes this golf course can really humble or embarrass you," Strange said. "You feel pretty silly when you have it 12 feet for birdie and 40 feet for par. Don't ask me what I did on the first putt. I still don't know. It exploded. I didn't think it was going to run all the way down the hill."

While Strange plummeted at the 16th, his partner crested. Maltbie ran home a 12-foot birdie, holding his putter aloft as the ball dropped. He held sole possession of the lead at five-under, but only for one hole. Maltbie left his approach at No. 17 in the front bunker, and blasted within only 20 feet. The two-putt bogey moved him back to four-under, where he ended the day. His score of 70 left him tied with Crenshaw for the lead.

The leader board:

Ben Crenshaw	75-70-67—212
Roger Maltbie	76-66-70—212
Greg Norman	73-74-66—213
Bernhard Langer	71-72-70—213
Seve Ballesteros	73-71-70—214
T.C. Chen	74-69-71—214
Larry Mize	70-72-72—214
Curtis Strange	71-70-73—214

With Strange mishandling the pressure of Augusta, and Crenshaw waxing poetic about it, Maltbie seemed the perfect antidote for the end of the round. Bob Verdi of the *Chicago Tribune* asked him, "What if you win?"

Maltibie smiled. "We'll have a helluva party somewhere. I'm noted for that aren't I?"

He pooh-poohed the idea that Everyman, in the form of himself, couldn't win. "I don't think my golf clubs know who's leading the tournament," said the 1985 World Series of Golf winner. "If it came down to No. 15, who knows what I'll do? I'll take a chance to be the Masters champion. Hopefully, I'll perform like Roger Maltbie. I'm pleased and surprised with my play, but you don't just walk on Firestone and someone gives you a trophy."

Someone asked Maltbie about the importance of this tournament. "Obviously, it will be very special if I can win," he said. "For the rest of your life, they say, 'There goes a former Masters champion.' But let's play. I play with these guys every week, so I know what they can do. It's not like I just see them here."

Finally, Saturday's shot of the day, would be a 12-foot par putt. The approach shot at No. 14 had stopped eight feet above the hole, and the delicately struck birdie attempt had still rolled well below the hole. But Larry Mize rolled the par in, and began the final round only two shots out of the lead.

In few places does one feel the sense of anticipation one feels on Sunday morning at Augusta National. The grounds fairly crackle. One follows the morning golfers with one eye cocked downward, at the wristwatch. It's imperative that one is stationed along the first two or three holes in early afternoon, ready for the leaders to begin their long march toward immortality.

The first twosome of the day, Bob Lewis, the only one of the six amateurs to make the cut, and O'Grady, went off the first tee at 10:47 a.m. The final pair, Crenshaw and Maltbie, would go off at 2:15 p.m. In the interim, the fireworks would be provided by Jodie Mudd. Short of Mize himself, Mudd presented the most heartwarming story of the 1987 Masters.

The Louisville native first played in the Masters in 1982, when as a 22-year-old amateur he shocked the crowd by shooting a 67 in the third round to leap into contention. The score is still tied for the best performance by a first-year player. Mudd played collegiately at Georgia Southern in Statesboro, well south of Augusta but close enough that the gallery took a liking to him. A 76 in the final round left Mudd with a 72-hole total of 294, 10 shots out of the lead but good for a tie for 20th and an invitation back the following year.

His return engagement in 1983 was, for three rounds, stunning. Mudd's scores of 72-68-72 left him tied for third with Watson, two shots behind Craig Stadler and Floyd and one behind Ballesteros. Collapse, however, would be inadequate to describe his final round. The 86 sent Mudd into a slump that would last for two years. He regained his confidence in 1985 and has become a solid, if winless, veteran of the tour.

A tie for 15th in the 1986 U.S. Open allowed him access to the Masters to attempt to atone for his wretched performance. He began the final round five strokes out of the lead, at one-over 217 following scores of 74-72-71.

On the first hole, a fine pitch to eight feet enabled him to birdie and reach even par. At No. 2, he nearly holed out his second shot, and left himself an eagle putt "in the leather". The roar that went up, which dissolved into extended applause, telegraphed instantly what had happened. When Mudd and his partner, Chip Beck, walked up the third fairway, the scoreboard confirmed the message with a red "2" next to Mudd's name.

Mudd followed the eagle by ramming home a 12-foot birdie putt at No. 3. He wore a big grin as he walked to the adjacent fourth tee. When he dumped his tee shot into the front left trap, it appeared that the glory ride had ended. But Mudd pitched to six feet and holed the putt. He had played the first four holes 3-3-3-3. The string would end at No. 5, when he again missed the green, yet saved par.

Having watched Mudd cool off, it was time to turn attention to the other leaders. Norman came out attacking and birdied the first hole to draw into a tie with Crenshaw and Maltbie at four-under before they even had a chance to record a score. Mize birdied the second hole, which would turn out to be the easiest hole on the course (average score 4.77) and moved into a tie at three-under with Mudd and Langer. Already six players were within one shot of the lead. It would be that kind of final round, a lifeboat which tossed about, shifting every time one of its occupants so much as hiccupped.

When Mize bogeyed both the third and fourth holes, it was thought that he had done more than hiccupped. It appeared that the minute he had thrust himself into contention, he had choked. When Crenshaw picked up a birdie at No. 2 to go into the lead at five-under, well, Mize already was four strokes out of the lead. It appeared that no one would wait for Mize.

Then, however, the wind or the nerves or whatever it is that grabs hold of Augusta National on Sunday took effect. Norman, as tough a golfer mentally as there is, fought the course and himself from the start. He could only par the second hole, then he bogeyed No. 3. But he birdied the fifth hole to get back to four-under, one stroke behind Crenshaw.

At this point Mize showed he could swat down the beast in his throat. He birdied the sixth and seventh holes to move back to three-under. As he moved up, those in front of him came back. Norman, two groups behind Mize, bogeyed those same holes. Crenshaw, a group behind Mize, bogeyed Nos. 6 and 7, too.

Maltbie broke the tie at No. 8 when he placed his second shot on the 535-yard uphill par-five only 20 feet away. The two-putt birdie moved him to four-under. Up ahead, on the ninth hole, Langer drained a seven-foot birdie putt to go three-under. Norman, less than two feet from the hole, missed his birdie and made the turn at two-under. Maltbie and Crenshaw followed them to No. 9, and each placed his approach shot 20 feet above the hole on the sharply sloping green.

Crenshaw putted first. Few golfers have been as demonstrably emotional as Crenshaw. Not in a McEnroesque way; when a putt doesn't go in, Crenshaw looks at it as if it's his best friend who just turned him down for a favor. This birdie putt rolled downhill and stopped six agonizing inches short. Crenshaw put his hands on his hips in disbelief.

Maltbie reacted characteristically as well. After "going to school" on Crenshaw's putt, he left his birdie in the exact same spot. Then he turned to Crenshaw and convulsed into laughter.

With the leaders on the 10th tee, it was the traditional time for the tournament to begin. Let's look at the leaderboard:

Maltbie	four-under through 9
Crenshaw	three-under through 9
Langer	three-under through 9
Mudd	two-under through 12
Norman	two-under through 9
Ballesteros	two-under through 10
Chen	two-under through 10
Mize	two-under through 10

As Crenshaw and Maltbie putted out at the ninth hole, an enormous roar wafted up from the 15th green below. Seconds later (and they always put his scores up fast), the leaderboard near the 18th green showed Nicklaus plus-one through 15. The Golden Bear, wearing the same yellow shirt, plaid slacks ensemble he had worn on his victorious Sunday a year before, had eagled the par-five 13th from 15 feet, but could do no more. "That was the only putt I made this week," he said afterward. Still, Nicklaus would finish with a 70—289, good for a tie for seventh.

After it was all done, Norman would say, "You had no time to notice what anyone was doing. That was a lot of golf course today. It demanded your total attention. Those final nine holes were as intense as I've ever played."

Maltbie and Norman would falter immediately. Norman missed the green at No. 10 and failed to get up-and-down. Then he three-putted at No. 11 from 20 feet. Suddenly the Shark was even par, but only three shots out. Maltbie also missed the 10th green, and missed a par putt of eight feet.

Few noticed that Mize, after bogeying the 10th hole, made a 20-foot par putt at the 11th from the back right side of the green. He followed with birdies at Nos. 12 and 13 to climb to four-under and take sole possession of the lead.

The field began to thin out. Strange played the first three holes of the back nine in four-over and disappeared again in the heartbreak of a final-round failure. One would have to think that he will win here someday. Langer bogeyed four of the first six holes on the back nine and came home in 40. Chen double-bogeyed No. 11 and also shot 40 on the final nine.

All of which left Mize, Crenshaw, Maltbie, Mudd, Norman and Ballesteros, lurking at one-under through 12. Mudd, the picture of steadiness after his blazing start, made 13 pars over the final 14 holes. The bogey came at No. 12. However, there wasn't one of the golfers on the course who wouldn't have taken a two-under score in the clubhouse and been happy with it.

Crenshaw saved par with a 10-foot putt at No. 12, which also gave him a share of the lead. Mize had missed the green at the 14th, and a poor chip left him no realistic par-saving putt. Norman followed a birdie at No. 12 with another, two-putting from 40 feet at No. 13, to go back to two under. Mize splashed a four iron into the pond at No. 15, and again everyone reached for their throats. He had bogeyed two holes in a row down the stretch.

The bogey dropped him to two-under, and left Crenshaw in the lead, one shot ahead of Mize, Norman, Mudd, and Ballesteros. A year ago, the Spaniard had collapsed at No. 15, hitting a four iron into the pond. This time around, he succeeded with a two-putt birdie.

Norman then made his third birdie in four holes. As he stood over the short putt, the sun broke through the clouds to shine for the first time in several hours. Then Norman backed off after some applause from No. 16 broke his concentration. He settled down again and calmly stroked the birdie in to get back to three-under and a share of the lead.

Just as swiftly he fell back into second, missing a 12-foot par putt. But Crenshaw wouldn't hold the lead by himself. Ballesteros stroked a 12-foot birdie attempt in at No. 17 to move to three-under.

As Ballesteros walked to the 18th tee, Mize approached the 18th green. He was two-under, one stroke out of the lead. Mize had hit a three wood and a nine iron only eight feet away. With no hesitation, he sent the ball right into the heart of the cup. He had tied Ballesteros and Crenshaw for the lead.

"I knew I had to make it to have a chance," Mize said. "It wasn't a winning putt. It almost fell into the hole."

The roar which began on the veranda would echo down at No. 16, where Crenshaw was making his eighth consecutive par. The hometown boy had made good. Mudd, watching his outside chance for victory dissipate, said with a smile, "Right now, I just don't have any idea what the hell's going on."

Ballesteros joined Mize at three-under with a routine par at the final hole. Both would go to the practice green to putt and watch for Norman, Crenshaw or Maltbie to follow them into a playoff, or move past them to four-under.

Norman rebounded from his bogey at No. 16 to birdie No. 17. Bender, his caddy, said Norman approached the 25-footer and said, "I'll make this one for sure." Now there was a foursome at three-under.

In 1986, Norman had launched his second shot at No. 18 into the gallery right of the green and bogeyed, thus missing the opportunity for a playoff with Nicklaus. He would find more success, but not quite enough. His approach shot stopped 22 feet to the right and slightly above the hole.

He hit the putt, and as it rolled toward the hole, Norman raised his putter in his left hand and clenched his right fist. Four times he began to jump, but only stayed down. The putt burned the low edge of the hole and, to Norman's disbelief, stayed out.

"I still don't know how it stayed out," he said afterward. "I thought it was in. I couldn't believe it missed. I could feel the ball going into the hole."

Which left only Crenshaw and Maltbie, on the 17th green. Or rather, near it. A critical mistake would cost Crenshaw his share of the lead. Caddy Carl Jackson had suggested a pitching wedge from the fairway, but Crenshaw insisted upon a nine iron, which he hit "a teaspoon too hard." "It was just a feeling," Crenshaw said. "I hit the littlest nine iron I know how, but it was probably five yards off line."

Crenshaw didn't get his chip close to the hole, and two-putted to fall to two-under. Maltbie sent home a birdie putt and, after playing the first six holes of the back nine in three-over, Maltbie had climbed back into the fray.

But neither could get close enough to the 72nd hole to have a genuine chance at birdie. Maltbie missed from 35 feet; Crenshaw, from 20 feet. Both were philosophical in defeat. "I can't say it was fun today," Crenshaw said. "It was work all day. It seemed like, on my iron shots, all day I was guessing clubs. I never felt comfortable and it played tough out there today. You needed to play very precise iron shots to give yourself a chance to win the tournament and we did not do that.

"I had my chances like everybody else, but I couldn't make a birdie when I needed to," Crenshaw said. "I knew that the worst I could do was be in a playoff if I parred in. As it turned out, that's the way it was. Just too many bogeys."

Maltbie just gave a shrug and a smile. As he grabbed a post-round beer, he said, "This is the second best thing to happen to me today. The first was playing the last hole of the Masters with a chance to win. What more can you ask? Not many people have that opportunity. Sure it hurts a little. If it didn't I wouldn't be human. But this was one of the most exciting experiences of my life.

"You know, it didn't come out the way I'd have liked, but regardless of that, this will go in the memory bank. I can always say I was right there. That's worth something in itself."

Only three people had the opportunity to win. Norman walked out of the cabin adjacent to the 10th tee, where the playoff would begin, and Mize and Ballesteros followed him seconds later. This would be the third playoff since the sudden-death format was adopted in the late 1970s. In 1979, Zoeller had birdied the 11th hole to defeat Sneed and Watson. In 1982, Stadler beat Dan Pohl with a par on the 10th hole.

Mize walked over and kissed his wife Bonnie, who was holding their infant son, David. She seemed to be the only one paying attention to her husband.

"Maybe that's the best time to win," Bonnie Mize said. "When they're looking at everybody else and not you."

"When we went to sudden death," Larry said, "I was pretty nervous standing there with those two boys. But I wasn't intimidated by them."

All three hit adrenalin-charged drives far down the sloping 10th fairway. Mize, the smallest of the three, hit the longest drive, far down the right side.

The gallery stretched several-deep all the way up to the tee, excluding those that had moved ahead to Amen Corner to watch the expected action at the 11th and 12th holes. It was well after 6 p.m., and the early spring light had begun to fade, making it difficult for most of the gallery to see.

All three hit the green in two. Ballesteros, 20 feet away, putted first. As he always has done, Ballesteros charged right at the hole. He sent it five feet past, but no one believed for a minute he had been too strong. Norman, about 15 feet away, never gave his putt a chance to go in. He would tap in for par. That left Mize, with a 10-foot uphill putt to win, and all the world watching.

"I had the putt in the best possible place to be in," Mize said. "I just missed it." The ball approached the hole and broke left.

Attention shifted to Ballesteros, except for those who broke in a sprint for the 11th fairway. Somehow, Ballesteros missed the putt. He had three-putted his way out of a chance for his third Masters title. As Norman and Mize walked to the 11th tee, a teary-eyed Ballesteros walked up the 10th hole, figuratively and literally in the wrong direction. He was too devastated to meet with the press.

Norman unleased another 300-yard-plus drive on No. 11. Mize nailed his drive, too, hitting down the right side but about 25 yards short of Norman. But then, again, as everyone expected, Mize hit an awful shot, blocking a five iron that stopped some 40 yards right of the hole. "The second shot was just poor," Mize said. "I didn't mean to put it there. But I thought about the water on the left. It's such a treacherous hole."

Norman seemed to follow Hogan's philosophy when his second shot stopped on the right fringe, 40 feet away. "When I saw Larry's ball go to the right, I knew where my ball was going to go — to the right of the flag," Norman said. "I told my caddy Pete I knew I could get down in two." Mize, however, was much further away. How far? "I'm not sure," Norman said, "because I've never been as far right as Larry was."

The gallery watched knowingly as Mize played out the string. All day long, he had been expected to choke. He had done so three times: consecutive bogeys at the third and fourth holes, and again at Nos. 14 and 15. But twice he had come back.

"I was on the same line as the 20-footer I'd made for par earlier in the day," Mize said. "I walked up on the green and it was firm and baked, like they've been all week. I knew I couldn't land it on the green, so I took my sand wedge and bumped it a yard or two in front of the green. I had to pitch it low. I had to get it on the green and give it a chance. I tried to hit a firm, aggressive chip."

The roar began to build as the ball approached the hole. The explosion came as the ball went in. Mize threw his club and jumped up and down, both fits raised. "I probably could have dunked a basketball," said the six-foot Mize.

Norman gamely attempted to equal Mize's feat. His putt broke away from the hole, and Bender never took the flagstick out of the hole. Norman turned and shook hands with Mize. He and Bender got into a golf cart and were driven back to the clubhouse. Halfway up the 11th fairway, they stopped, and Laura Norman walked out into the fairway to console, and be consoled by, her husband. She rode back in his lap.

Instead of winning his third consecutive major, Norman had been floored by a lightning bolt for the second straight time. He had won the British Open in July. In August, Tway had holed a bunker shot to steal the PGA Championship from Norman. But even there, Norman was in the thick fringe on the front of the green. He would likely make par, as would Tway. You have to expect a tour pro will make a par out of the bunker.

But here, with Mize where no man had gone before, well...

"I couldn't believe my eyes," Norman said. "I just couldn't believe it was going in. Larry's shot was 30 percent harder than Bob's, because Bob was in a bunker. You can control the ball a little better there. If Larry misses, the ball goes five feet past. I just couldn't believe it was going in.

"All I can say," said Norman, masking his severe disappointment with as game an attitude as any athlete has ever taken, "is that at least I was there for both of them."

"I've been trying to think of what to say," Mize said. "You have big dreams as a child, and mine came true today. Growing up here, those who live here know what this means."

The boy who wouldn't play Augusta National until he had earned his way on became the man who conquered it. In doing so, he conquered his past failure to maintain his cool under pressure.

"A lot of it I expected," Mize said of the flak he drew, "but sometimes I think some of the people went overboard. There is no doubt when the pressure was on I played some bad golf in some tournaments. I had some bad breaks but I do say I played some bad golf at times. I got tired of it at times. I expected some of it. I deserved some of it."

Mize mentioned the thrill of having Nicklaus, in his role as defending champion, present him with his green jacket. "Jack was telling me out there that this would open a lot of doors for me, be very special and be with me for the rest of my life. I think he knows what he's talking about, doesn't he?"

No question as to the shot of the day or of the year. For that matter, Mize made this a shot that would be remembered for all the days of his life. Every time he appears at Augusta, from now until his death, people will point at Larry Mize and say, "Remember when..."

3. The U.S. Open

Thoughts about the great occasions in golf inevitably lead to memories of the great champions — the Joneses, the Sarazens, the Hagens, the Hogans, the Nelsons, Palmers, and Nicklauses. We forget at times that the big championships are won more often by the lesser golfers, who rise to the occasion, then settle back into shadows. For every Open won by Jones, another was won by a Willie Macfarlane; for every PGA won by Hagen, another was won by a Tom Creavy; for every Masters won by Palmer, another was won by a Charles Coody; for every Open won by Hogan, another was won by a Jack Fleck; and for every Open won by Nicklaus, another was won by a Hubert Green.

His superb finish notwithstanding, Scott Simpson falls into the category of the unexpected winners. In his 10 years on the PGA Tour he had never indicated he had the all-around game to stand up to either the shot-making demands of a course so strong as the Olympic Club in San Francisco, or the emotional tension of the U.S. Open.

Thirty-one years old, Simpson grew up playing in junior golf programs around San Diego, went on to play for the University of Southern California, and won the NCAA Championship in 1976 and 1977. Since becoming a professional the following year, Simpson had become known as a reliable player, but something less than one of the great men of the age. He had won only three tournaments, taking the 1980 Western Open, 1984 Westchester Classic, and earlier in 1987, the Greater Greensboro Open. Although he had not been a major winner, he was making a comfortable living, only once since 1980 earning less than $140,000 a year, and twice topping $200,000.

Nor did Simpson's record in previous U.S. Opens indicate he might be ready to win. Indeed, it showed quite the opposite: a tendency to wilt once he climbed within range of the lead. He had played in seven previous Opens without finishing higher than 13th. He clearly was expected to become little more than one of the supporting cast. However, with Tom Watson, who seemed moribund the previous few years, threatening to win his second Open, Simpson birdied three of the last six holes and won by one stroke.

Thus, this Open was similar to the two previous championships held at Olympic. Hogan seemed to have won a fifth title in 1955, but Fleck, an obscure player from Davenport, Iowa, with an indifferent record and a new set of Hogan clubs, birdied two of the last four holes to tie Hogan, then beat him in a playoff the next day. Eleven years later, in 1966, Palmer led Billy Casper by seven strokes with nine holes to play, and had Hogan's 72-hole record in sight, but Arnold shot 39 on the home nine, Casper tied him with 32, then beat him in a playoff.

No one knew what to expect when the 1987 field gathered on Olympic's Lakeside Course. On the one hand, American dominance of the major events was in decline; all the star players were foreign, but Greg Norman, who for a time had seemed the brightest of them all, had done nothing since losing the Masters in a playoff, Seve Ballesteros, the most exciting player of his time, had had a spotty record in the Open, threatening only once, and Bernhard Langer, the German, had done nothing in his two previous Opens.

Among the Americans there was no clear indication of who might rise to the occasion. Raymond Floyd, who had won the Open at Shinnecock Hills a year earlier, had been having a bad year. Leading the list of money-winners was Paul Azinger, a tall, lean 27-year-old Floridian. He had won the Phoenix and Las Vegas events, finished third in Hawaii, sixth in the TPC, and had won $450,000 by mid-year. Payne Stewart was next. A fine ball-striker but unreliable putter, Stewart had won at Bay Hill and had finished among the leading five scorers in four of the 16 others he'd played. Nevertheless, he had shown a knack of playing well on the big occasions, finishing one stroke behind Sandy Lyle in the 1985 British Open, and two strokes behind Floyd in the 1986 U.S. Open. He was followed on the money list by Larry Mize, who had holed his pitch-and-run and defeated Norman in the Masters playoff, Mark Calcavecchia, and Ben Crenshaw.

From the moment Olympic and the U.S. Golf Association had signed their agreement, it had been obvious the championship would be financially successful. Evidently eager to see the Open, San Franciscans snapped up tickets at such a pace, the club had sold out by August of 1986, 10 months before the first ball was struck. After that, tickets could be had only by buying program advertising. Hospitality tents grew all over those portions of the Ocean Course adjacent to the Lakeside, the program sold over $1.6 million in advertising and Olympic generated revenues of $11 million.

Olympic was as difficult to play as any Open course since Oakmont had been in 1983. Although it measured only 6,709 yards, one to two hundred yards shorter than most, with a balanced par of 35-35 — 70, it seemed longer because of the lengthy carries into the greens. The greens themselves were not only small, they grew progressively more firm throughout the week, until at the end they were extremely difficult to hold with even a precisely struck shot.

Perhaps more than anything, Olympic was a difficult driving course. Its fairways wove among stands of tall Monterey pines and cypress, several clusters of eucalyptus, and some California redwood. Most had been narrowed to 30 yards although the seventh, a short par four of only 288 yards, had been cut down to 26 yards, and the extremely difficult 17, a par four of 428 yards, was allowed to play at 34 yards.

Widths can be misleading, though; on many holes the actual targets were much smaller, sometimes only about 10 yards. Because the teeing ground of the fifth, for example, was set so that a shot came in on a right-to-left angle, the drive had to be held along the right side; balls that didn't either kicked left into the rough, or found themselves blocked by an overhanging cypress intruding into the fairway. The drive to the fourth had to be played into a level spot on the right or risk kicking off a hill on the left and running across the fairway into the right rough.

As exacting as the fourth and fifth might have been, and even though the 17th was the more notorious, the ninth fairway turned out to be the most difficult to hit and hold. The line of play bent slightly from left to right, but a slight bulge of rough coming in from the right channeled the drive to the left, where it might kick off the slightly tilted ground into the belt of two-inch rough bordering the fairway.

The 17th deserves special attention. A 517-yard par five for members, it was set up shorter for a special reason. Olympic normally finishes with two par fives (the 16th and 17th), and a short par four of 343 yards. Had those three been played as the members play them, the Open would have finished with three wedge shots. To avoid what was clearly an undesirable condition, the markers were moved ahead by 89 yards, shortening its length to 428 yards, bringing the green within range of a medium to long iron second.

By doing this, however, the drive now landed on a portion of the fairway that had a pronounced right-to-left tilt. This wouldn't have mattered under ordinary conditions, but since the fairway mowers were set at a quarter of an inch, which gave a cut of three eights of an inch, the grass was so short it wouldn't hold the ball. Drives that hit dead center, or even on the left half of the fairway, most often rolled down the hill and into the light rough, and many of those that hit to the right of center rolled into the heavy primary rough two yards beyond the light cut. Built to accept a pitch, and crowded by steep-faced bunkers, its small green was hard enough to reach from the fairway, but when the approach was played from the rough, making a par was reason to celebrate.

While the rough was not as unyielding as it had been at Oakmont four years earlier, it was particularly intimidating on those holes where the drive had to be played so precisely.

The greens themselves were fast as well as hard. They were of a perennial annual bluegrass, a term that seems contradictory, but because the climate of San Francisco is so ideal for grass, without the hot, humid summers of the East, the *poa annua* survives the year around. Different varieties of *poa* caused the greens to have a mottled look, but they were cut so close (an eighth of an inch), the different varieties had no effect on a putted ball. (The fairways, too, were of *poa*, and the rough had some coarse-bladed ryegrass.) On some steeply graded greens, a ball might gather speed as it approached the hole and glide yards past the cup. This was especially true on the 18th where a putt from above the hole was the most dangerous on the course. Playing together in practice rounds, both Tom Watson and Jack Nicklaus found that from above the hole at some of the more severe locations, a good putt might roll six feet past, and a bad one might go 35 feet past.

While golf took hold in this country only in the early 1890s, Olympic originated in the middle 1850s, in the back yard of Charles and Arthur Nahl, where a group of young San Franciscans passed their time exercising and developing their bodies. From boyhood, the Nahls had spent hours performing difficult gymnastic maneuvers. As they grew older they accumulated an inventory of equipment, developed into accomplished gymnasts, and invited more and more young men of the neighborhood to join them in their afternoon sessions. The recruits included Reuben H. Lloyd, an able organizer who became an eminent lawyer later on. Looking around at all the young men taking advantage of the Nahls' facilities, Lloyd suggested they organize an athletic club. On May 6, 1860, 23 young athletes met at the Lafayette Hook & Ladder Company fire house and founded The Olympic Club.

After several moves, the club found quarters in an old warehouse and settled down to steady expansion. It's growth seemed slow at first, with its programs centering principally around gymnastics, but the newer recruits brought wider interests with them, and the club's activities grew. Eventually

Olympic had everything — individual sports like track and field, boxing, wrestling, fencing, gymnastics, rifle shooting, cycling, handball, billiards, bowling, crew, squash racquets, and swimming (water from the Pacific was piped about four miles into the club's pool) and team games like baseball, football, basketball, cricket, ice hockey, rugby, soccer, volleyball, water polo, and even polo.

As it grew, the club moved its quarters to newer buildings, until finally, in 1912, it found a permanent site on Post Street, a few blocks west of Union Square, in a new multi-storied building with a sandstone face based on Greek architecture on its lower floors, and red brick on the upper floors.

With professional sports small time, athletes fresh from college had no outlets other than the athletic clubs, like Olympic, and the Los Angeles and New York Athletic Clubs. Under first-class coaching, they continued to develop, competed in AAU competitions, and some of them went to the Olympics.

Olympic's roster of prize athletes was remarkable: Gentleman Jim Corbett, a former Wells Fargo clerk who knocked out John L. Sullivan, the great bare-knuckle champion, for the world's heavyweight championship; Hank Luisetti, who as an all-America basketball player at Stanford made the one-hand shot popular; Cornelius Warmerdam, the first man to pole vault over 15 feet, in 1942; Parry O'Brien, who put the shot 60 feet 8½ inches in 1955; Lon Spurrier, who set the 880-yard record at 1:47.5, also in 1955; Fortune Gordien, who set the discus record at 186 feet 3/5 of an inch; and Grover Klemmer, who set the 400-meter record at 46 seconds in 1941. All of them represented Olympic in amateur competition, and its track and field teams were so strong, they won seven Amateur Athletic Union championships between 1915 and 1950.

Its football teams were among the best in California. Olympic played an intercollegiate schedule against powerhouse schools like Stanford, coached then by Glenn (Pop) Warner; the University of California, in the era of its Wonder Teams, under Andy Smith; and Santa Clara, coached by Slip Madigan. Olympic also played St. Mary's, St. Ignatius, the West Coast Marines, and other athletic clubs. Olympians considered their 1929 team their best, even though it won only four games and lost three: those losses were to Stanford, by 6-0, to California, by 21-19, and its only decisive loss, to St. Mary's by 17-0. Two years later, Olympic shut out St. Mary's, 10-0, the school's first loss in two years.

With the rise of professional sports late in the century, the college-trained athlete had other outlets, and the glories of the athletic clubs faded. Rather than for its track and field program, or its basketball and baseball teams, Olympic's name grew more closely associated with golf, one of the later additions to its diversified roster of activities. The downtown facility remained, with all its capacities for gymnastics, and swimming, and fencing, and boxing, and all those other games, but the club's reputation shifted to the golf club.

Golf came to Olympic at about the time the United States entered the First World War. The Lakeside Country Club, located west of the city a few hundred yards from the cliffs overhanging the Pacific Ocean, fell into such desperate financial condition, club officials invited Olympic members to use the course and all the facilities, and gave the club an option to buy its 365 acres at a favorable price. In return, Olympic would assume Lakeside's operating costs. Since Olympic's membership had been agitating for golf for some time, the club accepted the offer, and shortly afterward, took over Lakeside completely.

The course was not the same then as the one that became so familiar after Olympic reached its full glory. Anyone familiar with the Olympic of the late 20th century would be surprised at pictures of the original site. Known as a heavily forested course, covered with dense stands of eucalyptus, Monterey pine, and redwood, it was barren and treeless then, a not particularly testing course designed early in the century by three immigrant Scottish professionals: Wilfrid Reid, a protege of Harry Vardon, who was among the leading golfers of his day (he was among the 36-hole leaders in the 1913 Open), Walter Fovargue, and James Donaldson.

Shortly after Olympic took over Lakeside, the club called in Willie Watson, another Scottish emigre, who had designed the Minikahda Club, in Minneapolis, to lay out an additional 18 holes closer to the ocean and redesign the Lakeside Course. With help from Sam Whiting, who had been brought in recently as the club's professional and greenskeeper, Watson created two new courses. Built between 1922 and 1924, they lasted only two years. A few holes of the Ocean Course had been terraced to run along the shoreline, but savage storms during the winter of 1926 washed away some of the spectacular holes along the sea, and it was time to rebuild again.

Whiting handled the job himself, creating two new courses, and altering the landscape permanently by planting 43,000 trees, 30,000 of them on the Lakeside Course, the rest on the less ambitions Ocean Course, transforming the bleak, windswept landscape permanently. As they aged, the trees grew to immense heights, perhaps 60 to 80 feet. They bordered every fairway, turning them into narrow avenues from 75 to 80 yards wide.

Except for modifications over the years, the Lakeside course remained essentially faithful to Whiting's design, but more storms during 1985 and 1986 undermined more holes on the Ocean Course, and once again it had to be redesigned.

While those holes along the sea were the more scenic, with their panoramic views of the Pacific and the craggy bluffs of the California coastline, the Lakeside Course was the club's pride. It was there that three Opens and two Amateurs had been played.

Those championships didn't come to Olympic without further changes, though. While Olympic's governing authorities felt Whiting's design was perfectly suitable for the membership, they also believed it had to be strengthened before it was exposed to players of Open quality. To bring it up to strength before the first Olympic Open, they brought in Robert Trent Jones, the golf course architect. Jones effected extensive changes, adding about 30 yards to nearly every hole (50 to the 16th, creating a crescent-shaped par five of 609 yards, among the longest holes in championship golf) adding or modifying greenside bunkers, creating tighter approaches, re-shaping fairway paths of some others, and bringing in the rough lines. In his most dramatic change, Jones practically re-created the seventh, a 266-yard par four whose green was so open and vulnerable it could be driven. He drew a bunker across the front of the green and eliminated nearly all the fairway, leaving only what he termed a dewdrop landing zone, 27 yards long and 26 yards wide.

It was evident from the Monday morning of Open week that the fans of San Francisco were eager for the championship. Crowds roamed over the hills and glades as the practice rounds began, and swarmed over the steep hillside rising from the 18th fairway to the Spanish-style clubhouse above.

The galleries were even heavier as the Open began early on Thursday morning, under overcast skies and in cool temperatures, following several days of bright, sunny weather. The conditions seemed ideal for scoring, because in the moist climate around San Francisco bay, fairways are usually lush, and greens seldom become dry and crusty, but as the scores began coming in, it was clear Olympic would yield only to the very best golf, and that its strength lay in its first six holes. The players would have to struggle through them, and hope to make their birdies from the seven hole on.

Among those who began early on the first day, Jay Don Blake, a former NCAA champion, and Lennie Clements matched the par of 70. With better luck, Blake should have been at least one stroke better, if not two. He lost those strokes on the eighth, where he four-putted from 30 feet, trying with every stroke, and taking no careless, half-hearted jabs at the ball. After making his double-bogey five, Blake had a stretch of four consecutive threes on the home nine, beginning with the 12th, and finishing with 34. Clements made threes on four holes of a five-hole stretch, again on the second nine, and actually had a chance to finish under 70, but he lost a stroke at the devilish 17th, and came in with 34.

With three holes to go, Bobby Wadkins seemed a cinch to break par. Out in 36, he had birdied the 12th and 13th and stood one under par on the tee of the 16th, the long par five. Par fives are normally birdie holes, but Wadkins made six there, losing one stroke, parred the 17th, which was pretty good, but then bogeyed the 18th. A 71.

Crenshaw was the first to break Olympic's par. Beginning just after nine o'clock, paired with Mize and Bob Tway, the tall, sandy-haired 1986 PGA champion, Crenshaw reversed what by then had become the established pattern. Smiling at the crowds lining the fairways, and occasionally waving to familiar faces in the gallery, Ben birdied the very difficult third hole, a par three of 233 yards played from an elevated tee, by dropping a four iron within four feet, then, driving with a three wood to control his ball, he played his approach to the fourth with a five iron, and holed from six feet for another birdie. Two under par then, he was out in 33, picked up two more birdies on the early holes of the home nine in typical Crenshaw style, holing an uphill putt from 60 feet on the 11th and another from 35 on the 12th. With six holes to go, he stood at four under par, threatening the course record of 64, set by Rives McBee during the second round of the 1966 Open.

Thoughts of a record score disappeared on the 14th, and his round seemed to be falling apart. An inconsistent driver throughout his career, Ben pushed his ball into the right rough, dropped a seven iron into a greenside bunker, and in his first attempt, failed to recover from the fluffy sand. A six; two strokes gone. Two holes later he seemed to be in deeper trouble. Leaving his second shot in the heavy rough bordering the left of the 16th fairway, and realizing he had no real chance to reach the green with his third, Ben laid up about 80 yards short of the green, and played a marvelous wedge within six feet of the cup. He holed the putt, saved his five, and clung to his two-stroke edge over par.

After a par four on the 17th, Ben played a two iron from the 18th tee, then a pitching wedge that carried over the flag and drew back within three feet of the cup. A closing birdie and a round of 67, three under par. Once again, as it had so often in the past, his 20-year-old putter had been his salvation, for Ben had one-putted eight greens.

Crenshaw had come quite a distance from 1985. He had fallen from 16th on the money-winning list during the 1984 season, the year he won the Masters, to 149th in 1985, Winning only a little more than $25,000. For more than a year he had been suffering from a hyperactive thyroid that had gone undiagnosed until December of 1985. The condition had left him weak, sluggish, and often ill. He lost 20 pounds, dropped several sizes, and his clothes drooped from him as if they belonged to a bigger man.

A man who lives in hope that someday he'll win all the game's major championships, Crenshaw had done badly in the last few Opens, opening with rounds of 80, 78, then 76 in the previous three, missing the cut in 1984 and 1985, but finishing with three consecutive rounds of 69 in 1986, placing sixth.

"I should have gone to a doctor right away," he admitted at day's end. "It's my own fault for not getting a checkup. I feel fine now."

His condition relieved, Crenshaw was going through a revival. Earlier in the year, he had won at New Orleans, finished second in the Los Angeles Open, and fourth in the Masters. Now he was threatening in the Open.

Still, this was only the first round, and he had some of the game's leading players close behind him. Ballesteros stood at 68, tied with Floyd and Tommy Nakajima, with Denis Watson, Nick Price, and Langer another stroke behind, at 69.

Ballesteros's round, the best start he'd ever had in the Open, was without question the most adventurous of all the leaders'. Olympic begins with a mild par five of 533 yards that runs downhill. It could be reached with a long, well-played drive and a big second shot, perhaps with the longest irons, or more likely a wood. Ballesteros of course drives long enough, although he can be erratic, and he is perhaps the game's finest long iron player. He began by driving into the heavy stand of trees that borders the fairway. Finding his ball, he punched it back to the fairway, played a four iron into a bunker about 60 feet short of the green, recovered to about 10 feet, and holed the putt. Par five. After that he had to scramble — three wood pulled into the rough on the second, five iron pulled left of the third green, two more three woods into the rough on the fourth and fifth. He hit the sixth fairway, drove behind a tree on the seventh, and with a restricted swing, punched his ball over a bunker and onto the green, parred the eighth, a par three, and missed the ninth fairway as well, and yet shot 35 going out. In spite of his labyrinthine route, his score might have been better. His putt on the seventh barely slipped past the edge of the cup, and he missed makeable birdie putts on the eighth and ninth.

Coming back he holed a 20-footer on the 10th, nearly holed a wedge after missing the 11th green, and holed an eight-footer on the 12th. Two under then, he pulled his five iron to the left of the 13th, but pitched into the hole. Three under. Another chip stopped inches from falling on the 14th, and when his tee shot to the 15th hit a tree and dropped into a bunker, he came out within six feet and holed it. Ballesteros lost one stroke when he played down the left rough on the 16th and bogeyed, but he finished with two pars.

His was one of the more entertaining rounds of the first day. Even though he had hit only eight fairways, he had bogeyed only once, birdied three holes, just missed five more, and had saved six pars through his genius around the greens, one-putting eight of them.

Floyd, on the other hand, had played according to the instruction manual. Driving with precision and playing his irons so superbly, he hit 16 greens. On the few holes where he missed the fairways, his ball stopped in the first cut of two-inch rough; it grew to five inches farther out. This was Floyd's best golf since the last round of the 1986 Open (he never figured again, finishing at 290, 13 strokes behind Simpson).

Meantime, Jack Nicklaus had brought the first day alive with a round of 70. He began by birdieing the first hole, and he was still one under par after 17, but he three-putted the severely sloping 18th, dropping back to even par.

Among the other leading players, Norman birdied the second, but then bogeyed the 13th, 14th, and 15th and shot 72, Mize shot 71, losing a stroke on the 17th, and Johnny Miller matched him, even though he had six birdies. At the end of the day, 17 players had either matched or broken par, and 16 others had slipped one stroke over.

The first-round leaders:

Ben Crenshaw	67
Seve Ballesteros	68
Tommy Nakajima	68
Raymond Floyd	68
Nick Price	69
Denis Watson	69
Bernhard Langer	69

Other scores of interest:

Jack Nicklaus	70
Larry Mize	71
Mac O'Grady	71
Scott Simpson	71
Tom Watson	72
Greg Norman	72
Lee Trevino	73

Some disappointments:

Payne Stewart	74
T.C. Chen	75
Rodger Davis	75
Mark O'Meara	76
Paul Azinger	76
Fuzzy Zoeller	78

A light drizzle fell early the next morning, the skies remained overcast throughout the day, and the temperatures never once climbed into the 60s. The rain softened the greens somewhat, improving the chances for low scoring, and the field took advantage of it. At the end of the day 24 men had broken par, matching the Open record, and 11 more had shot 70. In one of the more stirring rounds, Nicklaus played as if he had forgotten he was 47 years old. Followed by an enthusiastic gallery, perhaps the largest of the day, that raced along the fairway ropes and cheered his every shot, Nicklaus scrambled as he had seldom done in his career, missing six greens between the fourth and 15th holes, and yet saving his pars on each of them. He had done what all the great players have been able to do: made his figures even though his game was not at its best, shooting a three-birdie 68, and thrusting himself into the thick of the fight.

No one could remember having seen Nicklaus play this kind of golf. Throughout his career he had usually hit more greens than anybody (61 of the 72 during the 1967 Open, for example), and yet on this day nothing seemed to go where he aimed. He made his most spectacular par on the 11th, a good par four of 430 yards, pushing his drive behind a tree on the right, playing his second shot across the fairway into the left rough, then nearly holing his pitch, and leaving himself a six-inch putt for the par. Two holes later he pitched from the rough within three feet and saved par, and saved still another par from a bunker by the 15th green. Putting aside his oversized putter, Jack had gone back to his old blade and holed two birdie putts of 20 feet and another of 30.

Nicklaus stood at 138, but he was one stroke behind, for up ahead Watson had been driving as superbly as he had five years earlier, when he had won the Open at Pebble Beach, and he was tearing Olympic apart. After his dull 72 in the first round, he had begun holing some outlandish putts, rolling in a 50-footer on the third that slammed into the back of the cup and somehow dropped, and a 30-footer on the ninth. Out in 33, he picked up two more birdies, one after a monstrous drive on the 14th that must have gone 300 yards. The ground of this hole, a 417-yard par four, runs level for the first 270 yards, then plunges down a steep incline to a deep depression before it rises again to the green, which sits on the same level as the tee. Watson's drive split the fairway and rolled to the bottom of the depression. His sand wedge settled within eight feet of the pin, and he holed the putt. He seemed to have another birdie in hand after an eight iron left him within 10 feet on the 15th but he missed the putt.

Another birdie on the 16th and he was five under par for the day, and once again the record was in reach, with only the 17th and 18th to play. The 17th fairway was becoming impossible to hold. With the grass shaved so close, even shots played well to the left were kicking off the hill and rolling into the right rough. Only a few drives had held this fairway, and some players, like Andy North, had tried so hard to draw the ball against the tilt of the ground, they had driven out of bounds. Watson's ball hit the fairway, but it rolled into the light rough, and he bunkered his approach. A day earlier he had birdied the 17th by holing from one of those steep-faced bunkers, but here he played his recovery about eight feet from the pin and struggled to get down in two. A bogey: four under. Now for the little 18th, a par four of 338 yards played from a high tee into a valley, leaving a pitch to the high green. Driving with a two iron, Watson had only a little more than 100 yards to the green, and played a soft pitching wedge that hit beyond the cup, bit, and stopped three feet away. It was a terrific shot, but putts of this length were missable on this treacherous green, and Watson was not the putter he had been. Using his freshly adjusted stroke (he was using his arms and shoulder more than he had been), he tapped the ball lightly and held his breath while it crept toward the hole, and tumbled into the cup. A 65 and 137.

"This was one of the top 10 rounds of my life," Wason said when it ended.

Between them Nicklaus and Watson had aroused old memories by rising racing to the front, and as they had done so many times in the past, threatening to turn the Open into another *a deux* occasion.

This time, however, they were not alone. Mark Wiebe, a husky 6-foot-2, 210-pounder from Oregon, shot an adventurous 67, hitting only 10 greens and making just two pars on the first nine, and matched Watson's 137. Birdies on the first and third were canceled by bogeys on the fourth through sixth, but he took two of those strokes back with birdies on the eighth and ninth, and then made the shot of the day, holing a full wedge for an eagle-two on the 12th.

Crenshaw, meanwhile, was having an indifferent day on the greens and shooting 72, dropping a stroke behind Watson and Weibe, and Ballesteros, still having trouble hitting Olympic's narrow fairways, shot 75 without making a bogey, dropping six strokes behind the leaders, with 143.

At the end of the day, five men lurked a stroke behind Watson and Weibe — Nicklaus, Nakajima, Langer, John Cook, and Jim Thorpe. Both Cook and Thorpe had matched Nicklaus's 68, Langer had shot a second 69, and Nakajima a 70.

The 36-hole cut fell at 147, three under par. Seventy-seven men qualified for the last two rounds, the most ever, causing the USGA to change its policy for the third round. Ordinarily the last two rounds are played in pairs, but because of the field's size, three men would play together in the third round.

The second-round leaders:

Tom Watson	72-65—	137
Mark Weibe	70-67—	137
Jack Nicklaus	70-68—	138
Tommy Nakajima	68-70—	138
Bernhard Langer	69-69—	138
John Cook	70-68—	138
Jim Thorpe	70-68—	138

Other scores of interest:

Ben Crenshaw	67-72—	139
Larry Mize	71-68—	139
Scott Simpson	71-68—	139
Mac O'Grady	71-69—	140
Raymond Floyd	68-73—	141
Greg Norman	72-69—	141
Seve Ballesteros	68-75—	143

Missed the cut:

Paul Azinger	76-27—148
Johnny Miller	71-77—148
Payne Stewart	74-74—148
Larry Nelson	76-75—151
Lee Trevino	73-78—151
Fuzzy Zoeller	78-74—152

Olympic would never play easier than it had on Friday. While the city was covered by low-hanging clouds early Saturday morning, the sun broke through the overcast toward mid-day and combined with a gentle breeze to dry out the course. The greens became harder and faster, and the scores shot upward. Where 24 men had broken par on Friday, only 10 shot under 70 on Saturday. Even though he shot 71, a stroke over par, Watson held onto his lead, with 208, for Wiebe backed off, shooting 77, and was never a contender again, Thorpe and Langer shot 73s, Nakajima 74, Cook had 76, and most disappointing of all, Nicklaus also shot 76. He was never a factor again, shooting 77 in the fourth round.

Finally, though, someone matched the course record. Keith Clearwater, a raw-boned tour rookie who had won the Colonial National Invitational with two closing rounds of 64 on the same day, shot another here, passed 54 men, and leaped into second place, a stroke behind Watson. Lennie Clements shot his third consecutive 70, leaving him at 210, Crenshaw shot another 72 and yet lost only one stroke, leaving him at 211, three behind Watson, Ballesteros shot back into the fight with 68, matching Crenshaw, and most significant of all, although no one realized it at the time, Scott Simpson, who had followed his opening 71 with 68 on Friday, shot 70, and climbed to within one stroke of Watson.

The scramble had been intense throughout the day as first one man, then another fought to the top, then fell back. At one stage, six men shared first place.

Five over par for the first 36 holes, and eight strokes behind Watson and Weibe, Clearwater left the first tee at 8:20, three and half hours ahead of the last group. He had picked up only one stroke through the first seven holes, holing a good six-footer on the fourth, and making solid pars on the other six, and he seemed headed nowhere. Just then, though, he began playing outstanding irons, hitting a seven iron within 10 feet on the eighth, and another seven iron to six inches on the ninth. Three under par now, and out in 32.

An eight iron to the 10th and two putts from 25 feet, then a 20-footer fell on the 11th after a four-iron approach. Some shaky play, missing the next three greens but saving pars by holing five-footers on each of them, then he closed out the round by holing a good 12-footer on the 16th, and best of all, playing a drive and three iron to eight feet on the 17th and dropping the putt. Back in 33.

A 27-year-old Californian who had played golf for Brigham Young University, Clearwater wouldn't have been in the field had it not been for his wife. He had joined the tour the previous fall and had to go through both local and sectional qualifying to win a place in the starting field. The local round was set for the day after the Colonial, in late May, but after winning, he had celebrated well into the night, and hadn't gone to bed until 2:30 the next morning. When the alarm sounded at 5, he groaned there would be other Opens, and he'd just as soon stay in bed today.

Planting her feet in the small of his back, Sue Clearwater gave him a push, told him that if he wasn't at Olympic he'd be watching on television and wishing he were, and to get up and get going. He did, qualified handily, made it through the sectional trials as well, and now, with his 209, he was in with the best 54-hole score so far, and he had made up a vast amount of ground.

Watson, meantime, had begun as if he would fall out of the race. He bogeyed three of the first four holes, three-putting both the first and third, then overshot the fourth with a six-iron approach, and missed from 12 feet. Just then some putts began to fall — a 10-footer for a birdie-three on the seventh, and an eight-footer for a saving par on the ninth. Out in 36, a stroke over par, he began the home nine with five steady pars, then birdied the 15th, holing a good 15-footer. By then he had made up two of the three strokes he had lost on the early holes.

Once again, though, the 17th, which had been so kind to him on the first day, cost him a stroke. His drive drifted into the light rough, his six iron rolled to the back edge of the green, and he three-putted, missing a difficult six-footer.

Clearwater had finished by then, and when Watson bogeyed, he had fallen back into a tie for the lead. He had to birdie the home hole to move ahead once more. Setting himself on the tee, he played his two iron once again and left himself with a nine-iron pitch. His ball cleared the front bunkers, soared to the back of the green, and settled about 15 feet to the right of the flagstick. He had as difficult a putt as he had faced in some time, with a slick green tilting from back to front. Watson had practiced that putt early in the week, and he knew he would have to borrow about 10 feet. He also knew that if his ball missed the hole, he could have trouble two-putting.

Watson studied the line for a long time, finally stepped up to the ball, set himself with his back partially toward the hole, and in that quick, no-nonsense style, rapped the ball up the hill toward the back of the green. He held his breath while the ball took the break and began gliding slowly downhill, picking up speed as it approached the hole. It dropped; he had his birdie and had fought back into the lead.

While a big crowd had rushed out to see Clearwater as word of his hot round raced through the gallery, and another huge throng had followed Watson, hardly anyone was watching Simpson. As his round began to unfold, he was giving precious little reason why anyone should bother. After having bogeyed three holes in the first round and only one in the second, Scott had begun the third round like Watson, missing the greens of three of the first six holes and dropping a stroke on each of them. The strokes were piling up, but just as it looked as if his game had collapsed, Scott turned it around. A six iron to eight feet won back one stroke on the ninth, he picked up another with an eight-footer on the 15th, then pulled back to even with an eight iron to 10 feet on the 18th. He had caught Clearwater, and he stood within one stroke of Watson.

A final scene. Tommy Nakajima had carried the stigma of making very big numbers on key holes in the major competitions. He had hit an approach into the Road Bunker at St. Andrews during the 1978 British Open and made nine; had hit several balls into the water in front of the 12th green at Augusta and made 13 in the Masters, and standing among the leaders going into the last round at Turnberry in the 1986 British Open, had hit into another bunker and had begun his round with a six. At Olympic he had come to the 18th needing a par four for 72 and a 54-hole score of 210, which would have left him only two strokes behind Watson. He pushed his drive a bit to the right leaving a tall Monterey pine between his ball and the hole. To reach the green he would have to play a high pitch almost directly over the tallest branch of the tree. His pitch soared true enough, but not high enough. It rattled around in the upper branches, but as far as anyone could tell, it never fell to earth. A teenaged spectator shinnied about 40 feet up into the branches, but he couldn't find it. Nakajima, therefore, had to declare the ball lost and play another. He made six, shot 74, and dropped to 213. He was never within reach of the lead again. The leaders, with 18 holes to play:

Tom Watson	72-65-71	—208
Scott Simpson	71-68-70	—209
Keith Clearwater	74-71-64	—209
Lennie Clements	70-70-70	—210
Jim Thorpe	70-68-73	—211
Seve Ballesteros	68-75-68	—211
Ben Crenshaw	67-72-72	—211
John Mahaffey	72-72-67	—211
Larry Mize	71-68-72	—211
Bernhard Langer	69-69-73	—211

Early on the morning of the last day, a thick fog lay over San Francisco, covering the city from downtown to Olympic. Driving along the Great Highway, which skirts the beach to the west, the sea was hidden in the mist. The fog was so heavy at Olympic, it sounded like rain as it settled against the huge tent housing the press facility.

By 10 o'clock, though, the fog had burned away, and the sky shone clear and blue; in the distance, San Francisco Bay shimmered under the warming sun, and the mountains above Cavallo Point, on the far side of the Golden Gate, lay under a blue haze. The crowds began to arrive early, avoiding the heavy traffic to come, and many of them found strategic points on the hillside above the 18th green, where they would sit all day watching the field finish. Those who chose to follow early players went out with Nicklaus or Norman while they waited for the leaders, who were to begin after noon. Among the 10 leaders within three strokes of Watson, Thorpe and Langer were first off, beginning at 10:24, followed nine minutes later by Crenshaw and Mize, then Ballesteros and Mahaffey, followed by Clements and Simpson, and finally Watson and Clearwater.

The tension began to show from the start. While both Ballesteros and Simpson began with birdies on the first hole, almost every one of the leaders stumbled through the early holes. Ballesteros quickly bogeyed three holes in succession, after holing a 10-footer to save his par on the second; Simpson bogeyed three of the next four; and Watson bogeyed three of the first five. Obviously nervous, Clearwater went out in 39, and played no part in the outcome.

Throughout most of the day the situation changed by the hole as first one man, then another looked as it he would race ahead, but then stumbled and dropped back. After Watson and Simpson had played through the sixth and stood at one over par for 60 holes, they were tied with Mize, Langer, and Mac O'Grady, who was on the 12th hole by then, one under for the round, and with Crenshaw, Ballesteros, Nakajima, and suddenly Curtis Strange just a stroke behind — nine men within a stroke of one another well along in the final round. A playoff seemed likely, particularly since no one seemed to be making a move; the leaders were falling back to the field. For example, Strange had come into contention by simply playing the first 12 holes in even par.

Watson had been playing some terrible stuff. After three-putting the first hole from nowhere, certainly not more than 15 feet, he drove into the left rough on the second and bounced an eight iron over the green for another bogey, and then, after routine pars on the third and fourth, he three-putted the fifth. From two under par he had fallen to one over.

With the toughest part of the course behind him, his game suddenly came together. A putt fell for a birdie-two on the eighth after a nine-iron tee shot had fallen inside 15 feet, and then, after another big drive and a pitching wedge inside 20 feet, another dropped on the ninth. Two consecutive birdies, and he was under par once again.

Meantime, one-by-one the others continued to fall back. Ballesteros had made two birdies through the 15th but squandered them with two bogeys; after pulling back to even par by birdieing the 10th and climbing into a tie for the lead, Crenshaw bogeyed four holes coming in; O'Grady had worked himself into position, but then he bogeyed three of the last four holes; Mize grabbed a share of the lead with a birdie at the 10th, but bogeyed the 12th, 13th, and 14th; and Langer made only one birdie after the first hole and was left behind.

By the time Watson had played through 12 holes, the mood of the crowd had changed. Sensing his three years of frustration might be over, they abandoned the players up ahead and dropped back to follow him in, cheering every shot, and groaning when a putt slipped past the cup. The Open was his, they felt, for no one else was playing well enough to stop him. Only Simpson was still within range and they felt Scott was lucky to be so close; they ignored him, expecting him to collapse, like the others.

They had good reason to feel this way, because Scott had been playing some unsteady stuff since he had birdied the seventh, missing three of the next four greens but saving his pars on each of them, the most spectacular on the 11th, where his poor recovery from a bunker caught in the folds of the flag and dropped within two feet of the cup; if it hadn't it might have gone off the green. Now, though, like Watson, he began playing superbly through those final six holes, the key holes of the championship.

Both men made their pars on the 13th, a strong par three of 186 yards to a green set behind a high-walled bunker. Playing first, Simpson hit a five iron 50 or 60 feet past the hole and lagged it up close. Moments later Watson used one club less, and although he cleared the steep face of the bunker, which rises abruptly from the flattish ground, his ball didn't quite reach the putting surface, settling in the rough about 30 feet short of the flagstick. He played a lovely soft lob that ran to within two or three feet of the cup, then holed it for the par. Watson still ahead by one.

By then Simpson had driven into the fairway of the 14th, and from 160 yards had lofted a seven iron within five feet of the cup. It was his best iron of the day, and it came at just the right time. Except for a sand wedge to 10 feet on the eighth, it was his first approach inside 20 feet. He holed the putt, and had his third birdie of the day. One under par for 68 holes, and even with Watson. On to the 15th, the last of the par threes, 149 yards with its green hiding behind another of those high-walled bunkers that block a clear view of the cup, and occasionally confuse the players' judgment of distance. In his long, unhurried, even-paced stride, Simpson strolled onto the tee, and with the hole set to the back of the green, left his eight iron 30 feet short of the cup.

Although Watson had begun the fourth round immediately behind Simpson and Clements, he and Clearwater had lagged a clear hole behind, and they were only now driving on the 14th. To stay short of the depression, Watson drove with a three wood, expecting to give himself a view of the hole as he played his approach. Tom turned a little on the downswing and pulled the shot into the left rough. Controlling a ball from that thick and tangled grass is as difficult as any shot the players face, and here Watson played it superbly. Using his pitching wedge, he dug the ball out of the grass and flew it to the back of the green 20 or 25 feet past the cup.

As Watson crouched to study his line, Simpson stroked his putt on the 15th. Scott's ball eased to the hole slightly off center, caught the right lip of the cup, and curled in. A second consecutive birdie; now he was one under par, and had moved a stroke ahead of Watson.

The gallery around the 15th roared as Simpson's ball fell into the hole, and hearing the cheers, Watson realized he would have to hole his 20-footer to remain level. Stepping up to his ball, he rapped it firmly and stared, willing it to dive into the cup. It did. Even once again, one under par for the day, two under for 68 holes.

Through frequent glances at the scoreboards, Watson had kept himself apprised of the fluid situation, and as he stood on the 15th tee, he knew he and Simpson were both two under par. Drawing out his nine iron, Watson seemed to move into the shot nicely enough, but when it settled at least 30 feet short of the cup, it was evident he had either miscalculated the distance, or had not hit the shot as solidly as he would have liked. He needed birdies now, and he couldn't make them if he continually left himself putts of this length. Here he didn't; his first putt was both short and off line to the right, and his second caught the lip of the cup and spun nearly all the way around before it dropped. A close call, but still level with Simpson, three strokes clear of the field. Ballesteros was closest to them, but just then he was about to bogey the 17th and drop four strokes behind, and Crenshaw and Mize were already five behind through the 17th and out of the fight.

Simpson, meanwhile had driven from the 16th tee, and had pushed his drive into the right rough. Although he was in the primary rough, he was in no danger; his ball was lying cleanly enough for him to play a two iron to center fairway and leave himself a shot of about 130 yards to the center of the green. From there Scott played just the kind of shot he needed — a nine iron about 15 feet to the right of the hole.

By then the field had bunched up, and Watson had played two wonderful shots straight down the center to within 100 yards of the green. As Simpson stood crouched over his ball preparing to putt, Watson stood watching him, with his feet spread, his hands clasped behind his back, and wearing an expression of grim, tight-lipped concentration.

Simpson rapped his ball right into the hole. As it dropped, he smiled in a quiet, understated way, but as he walked toward the cup, the grin spread wider, and after he picked his ball from the hole, he raised an arm and waved to the crowd. He was three under par for 70 holes now, and a stroke ahead of Watson. Still, he had two holes to play, and Watson was in good position to catch up once again.

Watson next. Knowing he needed a birdie, Tom attacked the hole, playing the kind of shot that has made him so dangerous under pressure, a crisp sand wedge straight at the flag that cleared the frontal bunker, and dropped onto that hard surface with so much backspin it bit and braked about 12 or 15 feet past the cup. Now it looked as if he would catch up once again. Again he took his time studying the line, and again tapped the ball carefully. He had misjudged; the ball rolled just a hair off line, and barely missed the left edge of the hole. A stroke behind now, with two holes to play.

Just then, up ahead on the 17th, Simpson's drive had trickled off the tilted fairway and settled against the edge of the light rough. He was in trouble, in a difficult lie, with his feet above the ball, a stance that without compensations would ordinarily cause a slice. In making his adjustment, Scott evidently overcompensated; his ball shot off to the left and settled in the left greenside bunker, perhaps 70 feet or so from the pin. It seemed to be a bad break for Simpson, but it should give Watson the opening he needed, because with the ground tilting not only from back to front, but also slightly away from where Simpson's ball lay, it seemed like a certain bogey. Surely Watson would catch up once again.

Here Simpson surprised everyone, playing the shot of the championship. With Watson walking up the 17th fairway toward his ball, Scott dug in his feet and played a marvelous recovery. The ball popped out of the sand, landed well short of the pin, rolled dead at the hole, and somehow stopped only about six feet past. He holed it. It was the most important par he had ever made, and it kept Watson under extreme pressure, for once again Tom had seen it all. Now he knew he would have to birdie either the 17th or the 18th, perhaps both, to force a playoff.

Watson had played a solid drive that had stopped on the right side of the fairway, and then a forcing four iron that carried onto the green, hit hole high, but had come in on such a low trajectory it rolled about 30 feet past, leaving him a nasty downhill putt. Again taking his time, he sized up the putt, tapped it gently, and frowned as the ball ghosted down the slope. He had judged the speed just right, but he had misread the slope. Expecting the ball to break much more than it did, he had borrowed too much and left himself a tricky six-footer. Under intense pressure now, he holed it.

He was still two under, and still a stroke behind, for up ahead Simpson had played the 18th perfectly — a two iron from the tee, an eight iron to 20 feet, and two putts for the four. He was in with 68, and 277 for the championship, three under par, 10 strokes better than Hogan and Fleck 33 years earlier, and one stroke better than Casper and Palmer in 1966. Now let Tom catch him if he could.

No man walks with more determination than Watson. After holing that wicked putt on the 17th, he stalked to the 18th tee, and with his lips set in a tight, thin line, looked out at the huge gallery crowding from the amphitheater-like hillsides rising from the green, and into the deep valley below. Drawing out his two iron, he took very little time over the ball, then played it perfectly, into the fairway 112 yards short of the flagstick. Sizing up his approach, he decided the shot was either a pitching wedge or a nine iron. He chose to play the wedge. He hit the ball crisply and watched as it soared almost directly at the pin. If he had chosen the proper club, he could be within holing distance, and he might still force a playoff.

He saw the ball carry over the bunkers, but because the fairway lies so far below the level of the green, he couldn't see exactly where it had stopped. Those who could see watched the ball carry onto the green short of the flagstick with so much spin it drew back onto the collar, and stop resting against the higher cut of grass at least 45 feet below the hole. Perhaps his nine iron would have been the better choice.

Facing a putt of that distance up an incline, and knowing he would not only have to hit it hard to drive it up the slope, but also borrow enough for a slight right-to-left break, Tom gave the ball a firm rap. It raced up the slope, took the break, and for one heart-stopping moment seemed certain to drop. The crowd, which had been watching nervously, screamed as the ball approached the hole on line, but he hadn't borrowed enough. His ball nearly grazed the lip of the cup, and the crowd moaned as it stopped inches away. It was as courageous a putt as he had ever played, but it wasn't quite good enough. A par; 69 for the round, and 278 for the 72 holes. Simpson was the champion.

Folding himself into a chair sometime later, Simpson marveled at the sensation of having won the Open.

"I feel overwhelmed that I could win a tournament like this," he said. "Winning the Open is special enough, but to beat Watson makes it more so. It's incredible."

It was indeed more incredible than he realized at the time. Although his closing 68 will never rank among the great rounds, it was considerably better than it seemed at the time. It's last 12 holes were remarkably good, and its last six were the best in relation to par since 1967. Furthermore, even though his 277 was five strokes above the record 272, set by Jack Nicklaus in 1980, his 206 for the final 54 holes (68-70-68) was only two strokes off the record Nicklaus had set in 1967.

From the seventh hole, where he and Watson had been tied, through the end of the round, Simpson had played a very hard course with seven fours, four threes, and one two — six under fours, and four under par — while Watson was playing those same holes in five under fours and three under par. In playing such first-class golf and applying such pressure to the rest of the field, Simpson and Watson had shaken off many of the best players in the game. Ballesteros finished third, but he was five strokes behind Simpson and four behind Watson. Langer, Crenshaw, Mize, Strange, and Bobby Wadkins finished a further stroke behind.

What was more impressive, with the Open there to be won, and with the tension growing with every stroke, Simpson played the last six holes with three birdies and three pars. No one had played the last six holes so well since Nicklaus had birdied three of the last six as he finished with 65 in the last round at Baltusrol, in 1967, when he won the second of his four Open championships. But there was a big difference: By the time he had reached the 13th tee at Baltusrol, Nicklaus was already four strokes ahead of Palmer, his closest challenger, and he was, therefore, playing under less pressure than Simpson.

By playing the last nine holes in 32, and more especially by running in three successive birdies while all around him men of greater reputation were losing their games, Simpson had one of the strongest finishes anyone had ever had in the Open, from the standpoint of both skill and emotional control, because he knew he was in position to win, and he knew he had to make birdies, because Watson was there behind him.

It is unfortunate in a way that great rounds of the past are remembered more because of who shot them than because of their quality, and it is possible that because Simpson's was not among the more famous names in golf, memories of what he did at Olympic will be forgotten too soon. That would be unfortunate, for this was truly among the more stirring of all Open finishes, bringing out as it did not only all of his skill, but revealing his strength of character as well, for golf of this kind, under these conditions, over a course as severe as Olympic, demanded a vast amount of both.

Open lore is filled with inspiring stretches of great golf played when it mattered most, several during the 1980s. Only a year earlier Raymond Floyd had ripped through the home nine at Shinnecock Hills in 32 when he too birdied three holes on the second nine, although not three of the final six, when he knew he needed the strokes. In 1981 David Graham shot 32 on the second nine at Merion with George Burns, his closest rival, playing alongside him. In remembering the 1982 Open, at Pebble Beach, everyone was too dazzled by Watson's pitch into the cup of the 17th to remember he also birdied the 18th and two other holes on that demanding home nine (of course he also bogeyed two holes).

There was no question, however, Nicklaus's final nine holes at Baltusrol, in 1980, when he staged a magnificent finish of two closing birdies to hold off Isao Aoki, was the most inspiring of the decade. Nicklaus and Aoki had come to the 17th with Nicklaus leading by two strokes but expecting Aoki to birdie both the closing holes. Nicklaus then rolled in a 22-footer on the 17th before Aoki holed from five feet, and dropped another putt at the 18th. This was a case of Nicklaus's not only knowing what he must do, but also wanting desperately to win that fourth Open, all the while realizing he was 40 years old, and this could be his last chance.

Even though Simpson's round did the job, however, it wasn't one of the classic rounds of our time. It wasn't nearly on the same plane as Graham's surgically precise 67 at Merion, which will remain a standard of excellence until someone does better than hit 18 greens and 13 of the 14 fairways on driving holes.

Simpson had, however, held his game together over some rough spots, and played the shots he had to play when he had to play them. No one could ask for more.

4. The British Open

Few sporting events put as much pressure on an individual as does the British Open on the home favorites. The weight of empire, some call it. Or carrying the flag. Nick Faldo had carried the flag for years, without success. Faldo had a strong Open record, however. In 11 previous Opens, he had never missed the 36-hole cut, he had five top-10 finishes and two other finishes in the top 15. Only Tom Watson, who won five times, had a better average finish than Faldo in that span.

Two years before Faldo won at Muirfield, Scotland, producing 18 consecutive pars over the final round, he underwent a tortuous swing change. The effort had begun to pay off earlier in the spring. He won the Peugeot Spanish Open for his first victory since 1984, and his 15th triumph in 12 years as a professional. He also had four other top-five finishes in 10 European events. But Faldo was not satisfied. His teacher, David Leadbetter, flew over from Florida for a last-minute session.

In most minds at the time, Faldo's swing change had been a mad decision — suicidal. But not in Faldo's mind. His swing, always graceful and fluid, had been too upright, and it tended to break down under pressure. So much so that some had taken to calling him *"El Foldo."* Leadbetter advised a more compact swing. "Athletic" is the way he put it. That sounds simple enough. Faldo had a different view of it.

"It's very difficult to change something you've been doing for 13 years," Faldo said. "If you've been walking backward, it's very difficult to walk forward. I had to go through — well, it's almost a pain barrier. I find it amazing to read that Ben Hogan would work on a swing change for two weeks and go off and win a tournament."

Leadbetter had him stand more erect and keep his right elbow close to his body, thus flattening the swing plane. So much for the technical. What about the man behind the club, the man who invested so much effort and hope, and who struggled with doubt?

"This morning, I said to myself, 'This is a chance you may never get again,'" Faldo said after the victory. "I just wanted to try. In 20 years it would have been sad to hang up your hat and say. 'I was so close once, but I missed.'"

And in so saying, he fulfilled the belief that got him to Muirfield. "I knew I'd do it — I knew I'd do it this week," he said. "And I knew I had to do it."

It wasn't news anymore that the American grip on world golf had been broken. What was new was that most of the world's big guns had lost their grip. Greg Norman was the quietest of all. His 1986 record was staggering: Two victories and four seconds in the U.S. for a record $653,296; the British Open, the European Open, the Suntory World Match Play, the three consecutive events back home in Australia. All told, some $1.3 million in winnings. So far in 1987, he had won only the Australian Masters, and second in the U.S. Masters, where he lost to Larry Mize's chip-in on the second playoff hole. "To put it simply," he said, "I've basically been trying too hard to make 1987 a better year than 1986 instead of just letting it happen."

There was Seve Ballesteros. He was the odd man out in that Masters playoff, three-putting at the first playoff hole. He came back to Europe and won the Suze Open the next week, and that was it. Watson was in the deepest slump of all. He had not won since the 1984 Australian Open. "My kids used to come up to me and say, 'Daddy, did you win?' " Watson said. "Now they say 'Daddy, did you make the cut?' " Bernhard Langer, however, was holding steady. He tied for fourth in the U.S. Open, and he had done everything but win the last three British Opens — tied for second in 1984 followed by two ties for third. Coming into this one, he was fresh from a tremendous victory in the Carrolls Irish Open two weeks earlier, a 19-under-par performance and a 10-stroke victory.

Scott Simpson had won the U.S. Open just a month earlier, and Paul Azinger had won three tournaments on the American tour and arrived at Muirfield as the leading money-winner. Those are no little accomplishments. One might expect that such players would practically lust for the British Open crown. Actually, neither man had particularly wanted to enter.

"My No. 1 goal," Simpson had said, on winning the U.S. Open when Watson missed a long tying putt on the final hole, "is to make as much money as possible for my family. Golf is a job. It's as simple as that." So at the moment, the U.S. Open was a nothing but a big payday. Simpson had entered the press tent carrying a plastic envelope through which could be seen the title "116th Open Golf Championship." Someone had handed it to him just moments before. Which means the British Open had just entered his picture. He admitted as much a month later at Muirfield. "I would not have been here," he said, "if Watson hadn't missed that putt."

Azinger had shown plenty of fire. He had struggled mightily for years just to win and keep his playing card on the U.S. tour. Suddenly, he broke through in 1987, not only scoring his first victory, but winning three times before mid-season — the Phoenix Open, the Hawaiian Open, and the Hartford Open. Despite his $586,962 in winnings, he wasn't interested in the British Open until he got a scolding from Bert Yancey, an American tour player from an earlier day. "He told me the majors are the only tournaments which matter," Azinger said. "A lot of guys my age don't appreciate their importance. We're not obsessed with them the way Nicklaus, Lee Trevino, Tony Jacklin and the rest were. There's just so much money out there."

There was no lack of men to watch. There was Larry Mize. He had a history of tailing off when victory threatened, but he certainly didn't tail off in the Masters against Norman and Ballesteros. There was Corey Pavin, who mysteriously went cold after winning twice early in the season. Raymond Floyd was hungry. He needed only the British Open to join four others who had won all four of golf's majors. But Floyd hadn't played well since winning the 1986 U.S. Open. Nor had Bob Tway, after his skyrocket year in 1986, which he capped by holing a bunker shot on the final hole to blast Norman out of the U.S. PGA Championship. Then there was "Little Woosie" — Ian Woosnam, the five-foot, four-inch-tall Welsh Terrier — the terror of the European Tour at the time. He had won the Jersey Open and the Cepsa Madrid Open early in the season, then picked up his third victory, a 20-under-par, seven-stroke runaway in Bell's Scottish Open just the week before the British Open.

Who could win the Open? Time was when the figure was modest — 15, maybe 20 people. That number had grown over the years. Even so, few were ready for Langer's answer. "Fifty to 70," he said. "But give us a wind, and that figure might come down to 15." Could wind make that much difference? Jack Nicklaus thought so. "British Open courses aren't difficult unless there's wind," he said. Watson put it more picturesquely. Muirfield without wind, he said, "is like a woman without any clothes on — there's no challenge." Wind had become the big topic because there wasn't any. During practice days, Muirfield lay quiet in very rare calm.

Wind has a way of thinning out the field. Some welcome the mere thought. "The worse the weather is, the harder the course is, the better chance I feel I have," said Tom Kite, often described as the best current golfer never to have won a major. "In America, we hit the ball through the air to there, then hit it through the air onto the green, and take one or two putts. But you have to learn a course like Muirfield. You could play it 40 or 50 times and think you knew something about it, and then the wind would blow slightly differently and everything's shot to hell. I love the British Open."

This was the 13th Open at Muirfield, the home since 1891 of the Honourable Company of Edinburgh Golfers, dating to 1744 and acknowledged as the world's first golf club. A total of 1,407 golfers, second highest in the Open's 116 playings, had entered. Eighty-seven were exempt, leaving 66 players to come in through the qualifiers, which did not lack for drama. Among those who didn't qualify was one Jack Nicklaus, only this one carried the numeral II after his name. His caddy had the same name. "I had no yardages — nothing," said Jack Nicklaus, the caddy-father. "If I worked for me I'd be fired."

Playoffs were needed at three of the four qualifiers. At Longniddry, three players dueled for two spots, and at North Berwick, nine battled for three spots. These paled in comparison to the action at Luffness, where one spot was left for eight players. Among the casualties at the first hole was Deane Beman, commissioner of the U.S. PGA Tour. Beman qualified at Turnberry the year before, but got turned away this time. Five survivors proceeded to the second playoff hole. It was just after 8 p.m., and it took three more holes before Wayne Westner, a South African pro on the European Tour, claimed that precious berth. It was off to Muirfield, then.

Muirfield had been the scene of some great Opens. Among the more recent was Lee Trevino's victory in 1972, when he chipped in four times from off the green to beat out Nicklaus and Tony Jacklin. It was more than just his second consecutive British Open title. It was the death of Nicklaus's chance at the Grand Slam. Nicklaus had come over carrying both the Masters and U.S. Open titles that year.

When it comes to memorable British Opens, the 1980 edition will do for Ben Crenshaw, that most congenial of golfers. When he arrived at Muirfield for this Open, it was as though he had stepped back in time seven years. There was that man again, that stocky, powerful-looking older man, the broad face and the stern look behind the eyeglasses. The last time Crenshaw met this man, the conditions were less than reassuring. It was that Sunday evening in 1980, not long after Tom Watson had won his third Open. That's when that Crenshaw met Captain Paddy Hanmer, then secretary of The Honourable Company, the hard way. Hanmer was famed for guarding Muirfield the way the Tower of London guards the crown jewels. It's a celebrated tale now: Crenshaw and Watson, in the company of Tony Jacklin and a few others, had gone out to play a few holes with old clubs and a gutta percha ball. Just for old times' sake. They were at the 18th green, just a short distance from the window of Hanmer's office. He came rushing up in a paternal fury. The conversation (reconstructed) went about like this:

Hanmer, furious: "What are you doing on my golf course!"

Crenshaw, et al.: "Uh, Captain Hanmer..."

"And as for you, Ben Crenshaw, your shadow will never again darken our door!"

Hanmer's iron rule at Muirfield has been written about at length, but perhaps no one captured him with such waspish humor and economy as Peterborough, a columnist who used that pen name in *The Daily Telegraph*. In 1983, after Hanmer announced that he would retire as secretary, Peterborough created this imaginary dialogue between Hanmer and another club official discussing an outsider who asked to play Muirfield:

"School?"

"Eton."

"College?"

"Trinity."

"Service?"

"Coldstream Guards."

"Decorations?"

"M.C., V.C."

"Handicap?"

"Scratch."

"Give him nine holes."

Wrote Peterborough in conclusion: "Such is the man who, when grudgingly giving me a press pass, said I had a face like a pork pie."

So Crenshaw faced Hanmer again, on the Monday of the 1987 British Open. The meeting took Crenshaw back to 1980. "At the time, I was scared to death." Crenshaw said, recounting that first episode. "But after 10 minutes, he cooled down. He said, 'Ben, you know better. You know to come to me before you go on the golf course.' Then he said 'Let's go have a drink.' " Their reunion this time was equally warm. Some say Hanmer never smiled. They should have seen him smiling when he shook Crenshaw's hand.

"Quite a guy," Crenshaw said.

The Open had returned to Muirfield, rekindling almost a century of history and creating yet another chapter.

Bob Tway, the surprise of 1986 and now the disappointment of 1987, was what you might call the lead-off prophet for this Open. He was inspired by his own accomplishment. Tway started early, when the weather was agreeable and the winds calm, and took the first-round lead on a four-under-par 67, a record for the altered Muirfield (the ninth and 15th holes had been changed). "The key to the round was that I hit the ball very well," Tway said. "I missed only two greens, and only a few fairways." One of the missed greens cost him his only bogey, a four at No. 7. The Bob Tway of 1986 had returned, it would seem. Who could forget that season — four victories, including the PGA Championship, when he holed from a bunker beside the 72nd green to beat Greg Norman. He also won $625,780, just $516 behind Norman's American tour record. But now, about halfway through the 1987 season, Tway was winless. "I don't think I have played up to my capabilities," he said. The 67 was one of his outstanding performances of the year. But he didn't think it would hold up for long. "Someone could shoot a 64 today," he said.

There was a parallel between the young careers of Tway and Paul Azinger. Like Tway, Azinger had trouble even qualifying for the American tour. Then he came from nowhere to dominate it. He spent four years winless (Tway spent one), but when he finally broke through this year, he broke through big. It took him no time at all to stake his claim to the old cup. Playing in the morning just behind Tway, Azinger returned a 68 that was marred by only one bogey, a four at No. 16, where he missed the green. He birdied twice going out, a 10-footer at No. 3 and a 14-footer at No. 4, and he closed with two straight birdies on some spectacular play.

First came No. 17, a sweeping dogleg-left par five of 550 yards. It can be a pivotal hole, depending on the wind, and helped settle the 1972 Open dramatically. That's where Lee Trevino chipped in to save his five, and Tony Jacklin three-putted. Azinger conquered No. 17 by no known chart. He hit his driver and ended up on a cart track. He hit a one-iron over the bunkers and ended up in a sandy divot. Wearying of this adventure, he hit a pitching wedge 105 yards to within 18 inches of the cup and holed for the birdie four. At No. 18, he hit a four-iron approach 200 yards through a cross-wind to within 25 feet of the pin, and got a gift. "I was looking for two putts, with a break of about three feet on the first one," Azinger said. "And it went in. Now, that was an unexpected pleasure."

Azinger had mixed feelings about his round. "By No. 13 and No. 14, I thought — I'm not getting much out of a good ball-striking round," he said. "I made a few good putts, but I let a lot of good chances get away. But I like my score a lot." Like Tway the year before, he was playing his first British Open. He was pleased with his debut. "Conditions helped my appearance," he said. "I didn't have the jitters on the first tee as I thought I would. I'm really surprised that the weather is like this, and I didn't expect it. It's a good break for me." Then it was Azinger's turn to play prophet. "I'm surprised that someone isn't six or seven under already," he said. In fact, Tway held the record and the lead for about one hour, that's all.

Leave it to me, said Rodger Davis, the mustachioed, fashion-plate Aussie in his plus-twos, and he put a 64 on the board. It looked easy. "It was one of my best rounds ever," he said. "I only made one mistake." At the 10th, a 475-yard par four, the bunkers on the right pinch the fairway in toward the left rough, leaving the golfer with chancy tee shot. Davis deliberated: The one iron, as he had in practice, or the driver? He chose the driver. "And I paid the penalty and finished in a fairway trap," Davis said. "If you hit a fairway trap, there's no way to get it on the green. The lip is too high." A procession of sad souls would learn that lesson as the week wore on. That was Davis' only bogey of the day. He had seven one-putt greens, five in an outward 31 for birdies ranging from two to 20 feet. He finished birdie-birdie, with two putts from 35 feet at No. 17 and one from 12 feet at No. 18. It was scary to think that he had come within about six inches of shooting 60. Three birdie putts stopped short by two inches or less at No. 8, from 12 feet; No. 14, from 50, and No. 15, from 20. And at No. 17, his birdie tap-in was what was left of an eagle try from 35 feet.

On the leader board, it looked like the good old days for the Americans, who held nine of the first 18 places by day's end. Tied for second with Tway were Ken Green, playing in his first British Open, and the ubiquitous Lee Trevino. Trevino opened with a bogey, then ran off four consecutive birdies on putts of 12, 15, 20 and 10 feet. "I told those guys yesterday," he said, "that maybe I'n not hitting it so hot, but this flat stick is working awfully good." It was the old putter he cut down and gave to his mother-in-law. It didn't work for her, and she was delighted to give it back. So he put a nine-iron shaft in it, and off he went. "The feel was unbelieveable," he said.

Some other marquee names were taking a beating. Defending champion Greg Norman, an afternoon starter, ran into the face of a rising wind. At the 559-yard fifth, he hit a driver and a one iron and was 100 yards short of the green. He scratched out his par. Despite a variety of problems, he had suffered only one bogey, and was in good position coming to No. 18. Then up jumped trouble. He hit a one iron off the tee and a two iron into the left greenside bunker, and then needed two to get out. The double-bogey six left him at par-71. "We may have had the toughest conditions this afternoon," Norman said. "Anyway, it's a four-round tournament, and it needs patience." Seve Ballesteros, two groups behind Norman, ground out 17 straight pars, then also double-bogeyed No. 18 from the same bunker. He shot 73. Jack Nicklaus bumped around to a 74. Some semblance of order was kept by Bernhard Langer, whose 69 missed being a stroke lower by inches when his pitch at No. 12 stopped just short of becoming an eagle-two. Tom Watson, who narrowly missed a hole-in-one at No. 3, also posted a 69. "Any time you start two under, you are still in the thick of it," said Watson, brightening under one of his better performances of the year and hoping for a sixth Open title.

There would have been a four-way tie at 67, except for Craig Stadler, prime target for the prankish gods of golf this year. Back at the San Diego Open early in the year, Stadler knelt on a towel to hit his ball from under a low-limbed tree in the third round. He was merely trying to keep his trousers clean. Television viewers called in, and the next day, when he finished the final round, he was informed that kneeling on a towel violated the rule against building a stance. That cost him a two-stroke penalty. Since he signed that third-round card without the penalty, he was disqualified for having signed an incorrect scorecard.

His fortune was better this time — but only just. At Muirfield's fifth hole, his tee shot was embedded in the rough. Accustomed to a local rule on the U.S. tour, and with the assurance of his playing partner, Ian Woosnam, Stadler lifted the ball in the belief that he was entitled to a free drop. He went on to birdie the hole with a 40-foot putt. What a waste. Some spectators passed word of the drop to the R&A committee, who informed Stadler after the round — but before he signed the card — that the drop was illegal. Result: Two-stroke penalty.

"You learn something every day," Stadler said later in the press tent, mustache twitching from a wry grin. "One of these days, I'm gonna take a month off and read the rules and the decisions. And it'll probably take that long." The penalty cancelled out the eagle-three he had scored with a 12-foot putt at No. 9, and left him with a 69. Stadler said he was happy that the R&A informed him of the penalty before he could sign the scorecard. This, of course, saved him from disqualification. "A 69 is better than going home tomorrow," he said.

With European Tour leader Ian Woosnam mustering only a serviceable par 71, the task of carrying the British flag remained with Nick Faldo, who shot 68. It was a calm and collected 68, considering that he faced a crisis of sorts halfway through the round. Falso opened the day with the best start of the 153-man field — three consecutive birdies on putts of 12, five, and 12 feet. "A start like that sets you up," he said. "It gives you something in store and something to play at." A bogey at No. 6 still left him in good shape, and he was at two under par coming to No. 8. Then a scorer informed him that a message was on the leader board, summoning Mrs. Faldo — Gill — back to the scoreboard area. Gill had decided to follow her husband this day, and so left their baby, 10-month-old Natalie, pram and all, with Ian Wooldridge, the noted sports columnist. The emergency, it turned out, was with Wooldridge. It seems Natalie decided to cry. Wooldridge, unaccustomed to such phenomena, did the only thing he could think of. He panicked. "When little children come unto me," Wooldridge wrote, "it seems they suffer." Gill arrived and the crisis passed.

Faldo went on to par the eighth and birdie the ninth on a 12-foot putt, having recovered his drive nicely from the right rough, and made the turn in 33. With a cross-wind blowing, the back nine was a little tougher, but Faldo came home with hardly a quiver. He made nine consecutive pars, and only twice was he forced to rescue himself, both times brilliantly — a pitch-and-run to two feet at No. 14 and a pitch to three feet at No. 16. David Leadbetter's repairs seemed to have taken. "It's nice to know that my swing is in the right direction," Faldo said. Nice, indeed.

For all of this, the hero of the day — in a manner of speaking — was former English amateur champion Roger Winchester. A week before he was scheduled to play in the final qualifier at Luffness, Winchester was making a home video from the back of a truck. He lost his balance and fell out, striking his head. Doctors warned him not to play golf, but he went to Luffness anyway and shot 63. He couldn't remember much of it. His head was much clearer the next day, he shot 68 and qualified easily. At Muirfield, then, he opened with 73, the second-best score among the 13 amateurs in the field. And to think the doctors would lay odds Winchester couldn't play.

When it came to prophecies, Rodger Davis, it would turn out, was in a class by himself. "The guy who's going to win this thing is not the guy who stays out of the rough," he said. "It's the guy who stays out of those fairway bunkers." By Sunday, that statement would ring true.

The first-round leader board:

Rodger Davis	64	Masashi Ozaki	69
Bob Tway	67	Mark Calcavecchia	69
Lee Trevino	67	Ken Brown	69
Ken Green	67	Jay Haas	69
Paul Azinger	68	Graham Marsh	69
Larry Mize	68	Tom Watson	69
Nick Faldo	68	Bernhard Langer	69
Nick Price	68	David Graham	69
Craig Stadler	69	Gerard Taylor	69

It was about 6:15 p.m. on Friday. Paul Azinger was standing at the entrance to the press tent, surrounded by reporters. Someone called to him: "Davis has just dropped a shot. You've got the lead." Rodger Davis, the first-round leader, had bogeyed No. 18, finished with a two-over-par 73. Azinger was already in with his 68 for a 136 total. He paused and smiled at the news. "Really?" he said. "Thanks." This was the calm reaction of the boyish 27-year-old. He's a man with the genuine warmth of a Cub Scout, and he approaches golf — outwardly, at least — with the intensity of a child lying on his back watching the clouds. Despite his record in the United States, he had come to his first British Open as merely one of the great unknowns from overseas.

The second round, which grew somewhat milder after starting with cold, rain and wind, was a time of good and bad news. First the bad. Craig Stadler's two-stroke penalty for lifting that embedded ball in the first round was looming bigger. Except for that penalty, he would be tied for the halfway lead. He shot his second 69 for 138, four under par. Stadler refused to cry over spilled shots. "I am completely over the two-stroke penalty," Stadler insisted. "It didn't take long. I played too well to let it bother me."

The good news was for Gerard "Gerry" Taylor. It seems part of the script that every major event must have someone rise from the depths of obscurity and take everyone by surprise. When it comes to the great unknown, few could match Gerry Taylor, 27, a diminutive Australian of about 5-feet-9 and 150 pounds. How he managed to get into this Open was storybook stuff. He had failed in three previous attempts at qualifying, and this time he found himself at North Berwick, coming to the 36th and final hole, a 270-yard par four. A friend told him he needed an *eagle-two* just to get into a playoff to qualify. Now, Taylor had won only one tournament, the New Guinea Open, and he had not distinguished himself in four years on the European Tour. His best finish this year was 20th in the Jersey Open. But this was his chance to make the Open. He reached back, drove the green, and holed a 35-foot putt for his two. That put him in a nine-man playoff for three qualifying spots at North Berwick. He was the first man through, with a birdie on the second extra hole.

Taylor was no better than a curiosity piece in the first round, when he shot 69 to join a crowd at two under and five off the lead. But suddenly, here he was, just one back at the halfway point with 68—137, and tied with the likes of Nick Faldo, Payne Stewart and Rodger Davis. Bunker trouble cost him two strokes at the first and sixth, but he birdied the second from five feet, the third from three, and the eighth from 30 to turn in one-under-par 35. He started home with two more birdies, from 30 feet at No. 10 and five feet at No. 11. His only three-putt of the day, from 30 feet, cost him a bogey-four at No. 16, but he got the stroke back at No. 18, holing from 35 feet. So the man who needed an eagle and a birdie just to get into the Open was breathing easier. He had cleared his first hurdle — making the cut. But being out front was something else. "I didn't think about leading while going around. I just tried to relax and enjoy it," Taylor said. "But toward the end," he confessed, "I saw the leader board and saw my name, and I got a little nervous. Can I handle it now? Well, all I can say is if I can settle down and get into the pattern of the previous two days, I will be fine."

The capricious Scottish weather had its say in the second round. "You just had to have patience," said Greg Norman, who started early when the weather was at its stiffest. Tom Watson was another early starter. "The wind was more from the east yesterday, and today it was from the west," Watson said. "That turned the course around." Norman couldn't get anything going. He returned a par 71 on an erratic round of five birdies and five bogeys, and stood at even-par 142. He wasn't happy, but he wasn't worried, either. "Nobody is going to shoot 63 or 64 in weather like this," he said, "so even par is a very good position at the moment. Maybe five under will be leading at the end of the day." He was very nearly right. He was finishing early in the afternoon, about the time Azinger was starting. Watson had his awkward moments, too. He started bogey-birdie-birdie-bogey, three-putting the first and fourth, one-putting the second and third. Then he settled down and came in with 69—138, joining the group two strokes back. Then he made a surprising confession. Lately, he lacked confidence and he didn't have the old desire. Shaky putting was partly to blame. "It used to be said that I never missed a four-footer coming back," Wason said. "They're a little tougher now than they used to be. Nicklaus always said to me, 'Wait till you're 37, Watson.' " Which now happened to be his age. "Nowadays," Watson added, "I don't tee it up in the tournaments with the same feeling I used to have." But Muirfield restored him. The old feeling was back, the same zip he felt when he was winning his third British Open in 1980. "I'm caught up in it," he said. "I love playing here."

If Watson's loss of spirit was a surprise, what was Payne Stewart's? Here's a man of 30, some seven years younger. "It became obvious to me at the U.S. Open that I had not been putting in a lot of time and work, and I'd become complacent," Stewart said. "It comes with all the money, and from contracts. I have almost $400,000 in the bank on the U.S. tour this year. It's obvious I had not been working on my game. I have to find the incentive to play again." Stewart was hungry now. He turned in the low round of the day (with Scotland's Ross Drummond, who improved by 13 shots over his opening 79), a five-under-par 66 that started without promise — a three-putt bogey at No. 1. Then he raced to four consecutive birdies, added another at No. 8, and made the turn in 32, and finished the day tied for second at 137. The key: He had nine one-putt greens.

It was time, not the weather, that bothered Rodger Davis. "After yesterday, we had the easiest of the weather," said Davis, who teed off at 1:30 p.m. "But we had to wait on every shot. We even went through a group on the 10th and caught a group on the eleventh green. I lost my rhythm and never got it back. I was in the rough all the time. Waiting around, you get edgy." He also admitted to a slight playing error. At some tees, he took irons when he should have used woods, and thus, he said, "I left myself too much to do." He fell one stroke behind Azinger with a two-over-par 73 that started with two bogeys — the first out of the rough, the seond out of the fairway bunker.

Faldo added 69 to his opening 68 and stood one stroke off the lead at 137. "I was just delighted to get around on a day like this," said Faldo, who started early in the teeth of the worst weather. One key to his day was a quick stop at No. 9. "I made a rush to the locker room to get a dry towel," he said. "I needed it, with the grips saturated and getting wetter."

Faldo was out in 34, with a birdie-two at No. 4 on a four-foot putt, and a birdie-three at No. 8 from three feet. Coming home was a real adventure. He birdied the par-three 13th from 12 feet, then bogeyed the next two holes after weak pitch-and-runs left him two putts to get down. Things were looking dark. But he stopped the skid with a par at No. 16, then got a stroke back brilliantly at No. 17. His tee shot ended up against the railings, and he had to go back 40 yards to the drop zone. This left him out of reach of the green. He played an eight iron short of the cross-bunkers, played another to the green, and holed from 25 feet for his birdie-four. A par at the 18th gave him 69. He trailed by one. He was playing steadily. "In playing a links course, or any difficult course," Faldo observed, "it's not the great shots you hit so much as where the bad ones go." So far, he hadn't hit many bad ones.

A par at No. 18 put Azinger into the lead. But what a par. Muirfield has about 150 bunkers, and so far Azinger had found only two — once in the first round, and now. His four-iron approach to No. 18 ended up in a greenside bunker, pin high. He took one look and his shoulders sagged. "I thought it was dead," he said. The ball was on the back upslope, and the flag was close. Just clearing the bunker lip from a downhill lie would be a triumph. Getting it close was out of the question. Except that he did. The ball came out, bumped once or twice, and rolled dead, just six inches from the hole. The spectators erupted in disbelief. "That was the greatest sand shot of my life," Azinger admitted. Which was saying something for a man who spends hours practicing sand shots, and who won a $25,000 bonus for leading the U.S. tour in sand saves in 1986, and who was leading again now in 1987. What an end to a stroll on the links course. "I was not nervous at all today," Azinger said, still surprised that the nerves hadn't hit. The draw helped. "I was trying to gear myself for the tough conditions, but I believe I got a break with the tee times," he said. "There was no wind for me yesterday, and I finished in nice weather today."

Azinger started with trouble, though. At No. 1 a drive into the rough cost him a bogey (his only bogey of the day, in fact). He shrugged it off, birdied No. 4 from 15 feet and No. 9 from a foot (after an 85-yard pitch), and turned in 35. He birdied the next two as well, the 10th from 30 feet and the 11th from 14, and cruised home in pars. "I was a little shaky the last couple of holes," he admitted. He missed the fairway at No. 15, and again at No. 17. He would remember this about No. 17: The driver was not automatically the club to use off the tee, despite the fact that the hole stretches 550 yards. In the first round, he hit a driver and birdied, and this time he hit a driver again and had to scramble for his par. So here he was leading, and so cool it was hard to believe this was his first Open, and that his best finish ever in a major was 17th in the Masters in the spring. What about nerves? someone persisted. Azinger gave a big, boyish grin. "I'll probably go throw up any minute," he said.

The 36-hole cut came at 146, four over par, and among those who made it with little room to spare was Jack Nicklaus, who won the first of his three Opens at Muirfield in 1966. Nicklaus opened with 74, not a disastrous score but not a good one, considering the weight Davis's 64 put on the entire field. There was something wrong with his swing, so after the first round, Nicklaus went to the practice tee to find out what it was. The answer came from the crowd. "I was hitting practice shots, some good, some bad," Nicklaus said. "And all of a sudden I hear a voice saying, 'You're crossing the line on your backswing.'" The voice belonged to a stranger, Doug Keddie, 52, from North Berwick. One ordinarily does not take advice from someone who carries a handicap of 23.4, which Keddie happens to have. But this was no ordinary time. "The amazing thing," Nicklaus said, "is that's exactly the fault I had been working on with my teacher, Jack Grout, just before I flew over here." Keddie's reminder worked. Nicklaus shot a 71, and was spared the ignominy of missing the cut.

In all, 78 players made the cut, and from one, at least, came a burst of the old fire. Two-time champion Seve Ballesteros, who shot a so-so 73 in the first round, birdied three of the last four holes for 70—143. Among those who didn't make it was one of the game's immortals. But he did make history in the process. A kind of history, anyway.

This was Arnold Palmer, back at the championship he revived 27 years ago. He shot 75 in the first round, but still had a realistic chance to make the 36-hole cut until he landed in a fairway bunker at No. 14, a 449-yard par four. What followed probably will not be marked by a plaque, as was his miraculous six-iron shot from the rough at Royal Birkdale in 1961, the first of his two British Open titles. But give him this — it was the same fighting Palmer spirit. The drama actually started when he bogeyed No. 13. "I decided to take it out on the next hole," Palmer said, chuckling at himself. At No. 14, after barely getting out of a fairway bunker, he hit his third into an ugly, steep-sided greenside bunker. The battle was joined — Palmer vs. the bunker. The ball was back against a bank, and he had practically no shot from that position. The prudent way out was backwards. But "prudent" is not Palmer's middle name. He was going for the flag. He swung away — five times. "I was digging a hole," Palmer said, laughing. "It just kept getting deeper." The fifth cleared the lip, and he two-putted for a six-over-par 10. Amazingly, he birdied the next two holes, then closed bogey-double bogey for a 78—153 and missed the cut by seven strokes.

Even so, he received the press in good humor. Really, someone wondered — why didn't you pitch out backward after the first try stayed in. "Because," Palmer explained, grining, "I was going to stay in there until it came out the way I wanted it to. I'm not saying God couldn't have got it out, but He'd have had to throw it out."

The first-round leader board got a good shaking out. Among those who fell off: Bob Tway with 72, Lee Trevino with 74, and Ken Green with 76. The hero of the day was amateur Ricky Willison, an English printer who came through both qualifiers to play in his first Open. He was the last man at the last hole, and he knew the awesome task he faced. The spectators let him know the cut was coming at 146. He was already at 145, and needed a 35-foot birdie putt to stay alive. He holed it. "After this," Willison said, "what's left?"

So the second round closed. The next day was waiting for Paul Azinger, the lanky American. Like Ben Hogan, Tony Lema and Tom Watson, he could win the first British Open he ever entered. Could he handle the pressure?

What pressure?

"I tried to tell myself how tough it can be, but it's not nearly as tough as I thought it would be," Azinger said. These were not words from a brash and arrogant man. No, Azinger simply was surprised that he hadn't yet felt the screws tighten, the way everyone said they would. "I want to see," he said, "what the pressure is like when you're in contention in a major." The time would come soon enough.

The second-round leader board:

Paul Azinger	68-68—136
Nick Faldo	68-69—137
Gerard Taylor	69-68—137
Rodger Davis	64-73—137
Payne Stewart	71-66—137
Tom Watson	69-69—138
Bernhard Langer	69-69—138
David Frost	70-68—138
Craig Stadler	69-69—139

As windy days go, the Saturday of this British Open was something special. It was reminicent of the 1938 Open at Royal St. George's. Back then, the wind was so strong it blew the exhibition tent away. This time, the wind blew so hard it shortened the golf course. R&A officials came out early, took one look at the situation, and knew something had to be done. Four holes, playing dead into the northeasterly, were all but unplayable. So the R&A shortened them. "This gives the players the chance to reach the fairways..." the announcement said. No. 5 was reduced from 559 yards to 506, No. 10 from 475 to 430, No. 11 from 385 to 350, and No. 17 from 550 to 501. All told, this shortened the course by 182 yards, from 6,963 to 6,781. There was more to this day than just wind, however.

"You can tell by the people wearing hats and gloves that conditions are normal here," said Sandy Lyle, grinning. "Ah, but you would expect it to be a bit warmer at this time of the year." There was, by the way, one other "normal" thing — rain. Jack Nicklaus was wondering why Seve Ballesteros didn't mind playing it. Ballesteros borrowed a line from the famous musical "My Fair Lady." Said Ballesteros: "The rain in Spain falls mainly in my part of the country." He needed that humor before long. His chances for a third Open title ended with a 77.

The morning players got the worst of it. You could practically chart the weather by the scores. Those who teed off before 11 a.m. averaged about 77, and those who teed off after, about 72. The worst part about this kind of weather, said Gary Player, is that it takes the skill out of the game. The golfer is at the mercy of the elements — just hit and hope. The gritty little veteran knows better than to fight it. Even an eight-over-par 79 couldn't rob him of his lifeboat humor. "I guess I've shrunk a little in this weather," Player said. "I'm in very good condition, physically fit. And although I'm 50, anyone who can walk 18 holes in this weather probably looks 25." Player knew what was coming when he started out double bogey-bogey-bogey. But never a whimper. "There are a lot of guys six feet under ground who would love to be playing today," he said. Scott Simpson was shellshocked after a whopping 82. "I though Turnberry (in 1986) was the worst I'd played in until this morning," Simpson said. "I finished 22 over at Turnberry. I'm already 15 over now. This isn't good for my stroke average. I've never played in anything this bad." Before he finished the front nine, his sense of humor was about all he had left. He was eight over par through six holes. "So at No. 7," Simpson said, "I told my caddy we may as well laugh and enjoy it." When the day started, Simpson had at least a glimmer of a hope of adding this Open to his U.S. Open title. Now even that was gone. The 82 put him at 228, 21 strokes off the lead.

Leave it to Sandy Lyle to spoil a good horror story. Lyle played right in the teeth of the weather, didn't even go to the practice tee (just a few warmup swings), and while everyone else was getting whipped, he came in with a remarkable par 71. His secret: He shunned the driver and the three wood like the plague. "The main thing was keeping the ball down in the wind off the tee," he said. He used his one iron like a magician, hitting it at almost every driving hole, and hitting the three iron twice and the five iron once. He also had the better of the greens, needing just 29 putts in the three-birdie, three-bogey round. "This is the best I've played in the wind for a long time," Lyle said. His 71 put him at three-over-par 216 and nine strokes off the lead. He still had hope — but just. "I wouldn't mind some more wind tomorrow," he said, grinning. Lyle's 71 was so strong that practically no one noticed the young Spaniard, Jose-Maria Olazabal.

True, Olazabal started after the worst of it. But there was still plenty of muscle in that wind, and Olazabal doesn't begin to approach Lyle when it comes to a power game. "This is the worst weather I've ever played in," he said. But it didn't keep him from shooting a 70 for a 213 total, six off the lead. Olazabal took a different route. He's not a big-hitter. He needed the driver off the tee, a risky business. It never fazed him. Golf, it has been noted, is a funny game.

An inward 39 brought Gerry Taylor, the surprise of the Open, back to earth. He began the day just a stroke out of the lead, and he made the turn at level par 36, still in fine shape. But coming home was a labor. He was just one over for the day through the 15th, then came the crash — three consecutive bogeys. "But it was still great fun," Taylor said. He stood at 212, five strokes back. Raymond Floyd shook off an outward 37 that included a double-bogey six at No. 8, and played the last seven holes in three under par for an inward 33 and a 70 that put him at 210, just three off the lead. "All my bad holes were into the wind," said Floyd, an afternoon starter. Graham Marsh came in with a 72—211, complaining about his putting, especially on the front nine — four two-putt pars from 12 feet and a three-putt bogey. "If I had putted respectably, it would have been 67 instead of 72," March said. He could have used some help at the finish, too. He closed with bogey-double bogey.

Rodger Davis, the record-setter in the first round, was an afternoon player and also got battered by the wind coming home, taking 74 for 211. He bogeyed the 10th, 12th and 13th then regained the ground with three birdies over the next four holes. At No. 18, he hit his one-iron tee shot into a fairway bunker, and as he had said, there's doom in those things. He bogeyed. "If the wind gets up like today's," Davis said, "it's in the lap of the gods tomorrow." Payne Stewart figured this had to be his day, and he didn't make the most of it. "Today was moving day," he said. "Move into contention or move out, and I stayed where I was. Still, I'm only two shots back going into the last day, and I'm tickled pink." Stewart returned a 72 for 209, two strokes off the lead. "I wasn't worried not making any putts for birdies," he said. "I was happy with pars." Also in at 209 was Craig Stadler, whose two-stroke penalty in the first round was now the difference between a tie for fourth. No complaints, though, because he actually had cause to rejoice now. "I hit it in the rough five or six times," Stadler said. He still managed a par-71.

Among the victims of the near-gale were David Graham (78), Larry Mize (76), Fred Couples (78), Howard Clark (78), Mark O'Meara (82), and even Tom Kite (81) who had looked forward to foul weather.

There was little chance of having a repeat champion, not with the disappointed Greg Norman coming in with 74—216, nine strokes off the lead. He also came in with an interesting suggestion for compensating for bad weather. "I know it's traditional at the Open, teeing off at one tee," he said. "But where possible, why not make it more fair by using a two-tee start. It just seems to be every year, half of the field gets knocked out by their starting times. Keep the whole field together and you'd make it a better tournament in the end." For a while, Norman thought he had lost a year. "The way things started out, it looked like Saturday at Turnberry for 18 holes," he said. Who could forget that horizontal rain in the third round at Turnberry the year before? Norman shot 74 then, and kept the lead. He shot 74 in this one, too, and was nowhere near it. He used a one iron off the first tee and bogeyed, used a driver off the third and double-bogeyed. But it was the shortened No. 5 he remembered the most. "That seemed like the longest hole I've ever played in my life," the long-hitting Australian said. Even at its normal length, 559 yards, it was easily within his reach in two. But now, even though it was 53 yards shorter, at 506, it was beyond him. He needed a driver, a two iron, and then a five iron to get home, and two-putted for his par. He parred two other shortened holes, the 10th and 11th, and birdied the other, the par-five 17th.

Golf is not only a funny game, it is a completely solitary game — and not only because a golfer plays alone. Consider the cases of David Frost and Tom Watson, 180 degrees apart in their thinking.

Said Frost: "I didn't know what the score was all day. I always ignore the leader board. There's nothing you can do about it — just hit your normal shots and try to play every hole as well as you can. I intend to stick to my game plan whether I am leading or not."

Said Watson: "I always look at the leader boards. I want to know how I'm doing. If I have a two-shot lead, I'll play a whole lot differently than with a one-shot lead."

Frost, playing in the "better" weather of the afternoon, returned a 70—208, and was one stroke off the lead. Watson, also a late starter, was a stroke further back at 71—209. Frost used his one iron most of the way. He hit it off 12 tees. Watson, on the other hand, mixed it up — a driver here, a three wood there. They were pretty much alike on the greens, however — outstanding. Watson's putter saved him from utter disaster. He ran off five consecutive pars starting at the third hole, and on four of them it was pure survival. After un-Watson-like first putts, he saved himself with superb seconds — one from three feet, two from seven, and one from 10. "I came out with 71 and was lucky to get that," he confessed. "It could have been closer to 81." He dodged a real disaster at No. 2, when his ball buried in a bunker. "I wondered if I could tie Palmer's 10," Watson said. But he escaped with a double-bogey six. (Langer was wondering the same thing when he got into a bunker at the par-four eighth. It took him three to get out, and he made a seven en route to a 76 that blew him out of the picture. He started the third round two strokes off the lead, and finished seven off.) Unlike Watson, Frost was getting more out of his hot putter. He birdied three straight holes and four out of six in an outward 33 on putts of four, six, 30, and 15 feet.

The weather had shaken out the field. It will be recalled that at the 36-hole cut, only 10 strokes separated the leader from the tail-end — 136 to 146 spanning 78 players. Langer's pre-Open prediction of "50 to 70" possible winners, unrealistic as it was, nonetheless was looking interesting. Langer also said that a good wind would cut that number to about 15, and that's about the way it worked out. Ian Woosnam, the European Tour leader, was not completely out of the picture. He hit 15 greens in regulation, but a balky putter got him only one birdie. He shot one-over-par 72 for a 212 total — one under for the Open but six off the lead. "I'll need a 64 tomorrow to be in contention," he said. "Maybe a 66 or 67, because if it's windy, anything can happen."

If anything was going to happen, it had to happen to Paul Azinger, who still was playing his first British Open as though it were just another day on the golf course. Just a "routine" par 71 for a 207 total, six under par, and a one-stroke lead on Nick Faldo and David Frost. He was a late starter with a 3:15 p.m. tee time, and again thanked the fates for the better of the weather — although it wasn't all that great. "I wasn't nervous on the first tee," he said. "Funny thing — the bad weather took the pressure off me. I knew everyone was going to have a hard time, and that it would be the survival of the fittest. I've played in wind like this before, but not coupled with the cold."

Azinger made what he considered his first error, three-putting No. 12 from about 50 feet for a bogey. The error — missing a 2½-footer for his par. "Really, my only mistake of the tournament," he said. "I think I made a rush at it. But I made my share of putts, and you are going to miss putts like that in the wind." He also was in his first bunker off the tee, a pot bunker at No. 18. "I hit a terrible tee shot in that left-to-right wind," he said. He had to pitch back into the fairway, then hit a poor four iron. He pitched on, and needed a 13-foot putt for his bogey. "Whew!" he said. That's what kept the lead for him. Azinger started tentatively, with a two-putt bogey on the first hole. Then he got hot, playing the last five outward holes in three under par. He birdied No. 5 from 20 feet, bogeyed No. 6 with two putts from 15, then birdied the next three. He holed from 20 feet at No. 7, from 18 at No. 8, and two-putted No. 9 for his four. Heading into the wind was a slightly different matter. His four-iron approach to No. 10 was 10 yards short, and he bogeyed. He missed that short par putt at the twelfth. A 10-foot putt got him a birdie at No. 16, then came the closing bogey for his 71.

Nick Faldo, who was paired with Azinger in the 3:15 starting time, might have caught him, but he also bogeyed the 18th. An errant approach cost him. "That was a howling left-to-right wind, and with the pin on the left, it took a hell of a two iron to get it on the green," he said. But he caught the little mound in the bunker to the right of the green. "Then I hit a chip too hard on a downslope," he said. "I wanted to make sure I got it over the hill." He calmly holed an eight-footer for his bogey and 71—208, joining Frost a stroke behind Azinger. Compared to Azinger's ride, Faldo's was steady. He enjoyed a placid front nine — a birdie at No. 3, where he holed from 15 feet, and a six-footer at No. 6 that saved par. He dropped a stroke at the 10th, where he caught a fairway bunker and had to come out sideways. But it was a good bogey. He got down in two from the back of the green after a flyer approach got away from him. He got the stroke back immediately at No. 11, holing a six-footer after a nine-iron approach. From there, it was a string of pars until the bogey at No. 18.

All told, it was a pretty good day, Faldo said. To be within a shot of the lead with one round to go — not a bad way to spend one's 30th birthday. "My present from my wife, Gill, is too big to bring in here," he told the press. "I don't know what it is. All I know is that it's wood, and specially made.

"I think," he said, with a nod toward the weather, "that it's an ark."

So — one round to go, and all eyes were on Azinger, the American newcomer. He still hadn't felt the big-time pressure. But then, he hadn't ever been in this position before — leading a major going into the final round. Who knows?

"No matter what happens tomorrow," Azinger said, "I'm going to be a better player when it is over. You cannot get this experience anywhere else. I'm enjoying it."

The third-round leader board:

Paul Azinger	68-68-71—207
David Frost	70-68-70—208
Nick Faldo	68-69-71—208
Craig Stadler	69-69-71—209
Tom Watson	69-69-71—209
Payne Stewart	71-66-72—209
Raymond Floyd	72-68-70—210
Graham Marsh	69-70-72—211
Mark Calcavecchia	69-70-72—211
Nick Price	68-71-72—211
Rodger Davis	64-73-74—211

Rodger Davis wrapped up his final round at 5:33 p.m., a two-under-par 69 that gave him a total of 280, four under par. He headed for Muirfield's clubhouse. A friend greeted him. "Hey, mate," Davis said, and he gave a big smile and a shrug that said, "Well, I've done all I can do." He paused to have his picture taken, commemorating his record 64 of the first round, then he ducked into the door and slipped into the locker room. He turned on the television set, lit a cigarette, and slumped back in a chair to watch what might be his future. Outside on the course, the Open was in its final stages. If things went right out there for him — and wrong for someone else — Rodger Davis would be the champion.

Nick Faldo was in the next-to-last group and was five under par with two holes to play, one stroke behind the leader. Paul Azinger had led since the second round, and was ahead by three at the turn, but now, coming down the stretch, he was slipping. His lead was down to one. Still, all he had to do was hold on and let Faldo run out of holes. Azinger was in the final group, and six under par coming to the 16th tee. This was where Davis picked up the thread on television. The camera turned on Azinger as he stood on No. 16 tee, his mind computing his club selection. He had little margin for error on this 188-yard, par-three hole. It is heavily bunkered all across the front and up the right side. He could not afford to waste a stroke recovering from a bad tee shot. Finally, he selected his club, a three iron, and stepped up to the ball.

"This is it! This is the shot!" Davis said, leaning forward. "It will win him the tournament. It's so hard to pick the right club on that hole." Davis had played No. 16 in three pars, and then a bogey just minutes earlier.

Azinger swung. The camera looked at his face for an instant, then reached for the ball somewhere in the air, and then the tense gallery came to life.

"They're applauding! They're applauding!" Davis said, straightening.

Azinger's tee shot came to rest about 15 feet from the hole. Davis slumped back. "Perfect," he said. "There's the golf tournament — right there."

Someone offered consoling words.

"I don't feel bad, not at all," Davis said. "I'm pretty happy, actually. I tried my best, but it wasn't good enough. I haven't enjoyed the last two days, I'll tell you. I played a lot of garbage the second and third rounds. But I gave it a go today. I tried my best."

Davis, his own chances ruined by the 73-74 in the middle rounds, figured it was over. It was Azinger's.

Not quite.

To set the stage: First, with the weather having settled down, the course was back at full length. And as the Open headed into its last hours that cool, gray Sunday afternoon, the mist the Scots call "haar" came creeping in off the sea. Soon Muirfield was shrouded. The top of a 300-foot television crane disappeared in the mist, and had to be lowered so the crew could get the overhead shots. You knew now how a sea captain felt, and you were happy to be on solid ground. It was against the backdrop of this silent, pale-gray mist that the final struggle took place.

The day started as an 11-man race. Azinger was the leader at six under par, by one stroke ahead of David Frost, his playing partner, and Faldo. Craig Stadler, Tom Watson, and Payne Stewart were next at four under, followed by Raymond Floyd at three under, and four players at two under — Davis, Graham Marsh, Nick Price and Mark Calcavecchia. Before long, it was a three-man race — Azinger, Faldo and Davis.

Price was the first victim. A double bogey at No. 1 knocked him off the leader board. Marsh was next, when he bogeyed the eighth to slip seven strokes behind. Next went Calcavecchia, on a bogey at No. 13. Floyd's challenge melted quickly. He was on his way to a 76. Watson and Stadler likewise drained away. Watson finished seventh at 74—283 (which broke a heart; someone in London that morning had placed a £10,000 pound bet on him). Frost begain sinking at No. 2. Ben Crenshaw came from the pack with a late rush, making four birdies across the last eight holes to finish at 68—281. That left him tied for fourth with Stewart (72—281), whose up-

and-down adventure was marked by a double bogey at No. 8 and eagle-three at No. 9.

Actually, it wasn't a three-man race until late in the round, after Davis had finished. A chart of their rounds would show a collision course — Davis climbing, Azinger falling, and Faldo holding rock-steady between them on a remarkable string of 18 consecutive pars. They were destined to come to a point somewhere toward the end of the day.

Davis teed off at 1:55 p.m., 40 minutes ahead of Faldo, 50 ahead of Azinger, with a four-stroke deficit. If he thought his case was hopeless, he didn't play like it. "I saw where the pins were and hit right at them," he said. After an early birdie-bogey exchange, he charged into the turn — a birdie at No. 8 from 30 feet, another at No. 9 on a tap-in after his eagle try stopped just short. He was now four under par. Far behind him, Faldo was holding steady at five under and Azinger had dropped to eight under, expanding his lead. Davis plugged away.

A birdie at No. 11, from 12 feet, got him to five under, and birdie putts at the 13th and 14th just taunted him. Then came two crippling blows. At No. 15, he caught a bunker and had to come out sideways. At No. 16 — the hole he would watch Azinger play on television in a short while — he put his two-iron tee shot over the green. He bogeyed both and was at three under. A final birdie at No. 17 and a par salvaged from a bunker at No. 18 gave him his 69—280, and he retired to the locker room, and wondered at what might have been. "I lost it early in the rain and wind the second day," he said. "I lost my rhythm. I got it back today."

The fact is, nothing short of small miracles by Davis or Faldo would have mattered, for it was this simple: This was Azinger's Open to win or lose. And he lost it.

This Open resembled the 1982 Open at Royal Troon, when Nick Price squandered his lead and dropped the old cup into Tom Watson's hands. This time, Faldo was standing there when Azinger finally collapsed.

Here's how it looked on the leader board:

Azinger	–6 –6 –6 –7 –8 –7 –7 –8 –8	–7 –6 –6 –6 –6 –6 –6 –5 –4
Faldo	–5 –5 –5 –5 –5 –5 –5 –5 –5	–5 –5 –5 –5 –5 –5 –5 –5 –5
Davis	–2 –3 –2 –2 –2 –2 –2 –3 –4	–4 –5 –5 –5 –5 –4 –3 –4 –4

"I never looked at the leader board, all the way 'round," Faldo said. "I had to play my own game. There was no point — I can't alter anything out there. I am going to play the course and play my own game. I didn't want to put any pressure on myself by thinking I was leading the Open, if that happened."

Even though he didn't know how things stood, it seemed he was doggedly playing for safe pars and waiting for Azinger to make a mistake. He was blessed with patience and a sure putter. Seven of his pars were two-putts from 20 to 30 feet, suggesting prudent approach shots to the center of the greens. But this was no cruise in the park. Faldo had to play some brilliant shots to save pars — bunker shots at No. 7 and No. 10 that left him three-footers for his pars. But if there was one shot that won for him, it was that awesome bunker shot at No. 8 that not only saved his par but steadied a game that seemed to be shaking. Faldo had hit a poor tee shot and followed that with a poor second that left him in a bunker some 35 long yards from the green. A bogey would have been a good score. But Faldo never even blinked. He splashed away, and the ball took two bounces and rolled to a stop only three feet from the hole.

"I can say my bunker shots have been the best part of my game the last 18 months," Faldo said. Perhaps it was some kind of poetic justice, but the Open had come down to the sands of Muirfield and two of the best sand players in the world. Faldo led the European Tour in sand saves in 1986, and Azinger the U.S. circuit. The difference here was that Azinger had left himself too much to do, although he figured his troubles lay elsewhere. "It was my putter that failed me down the stretch," he said, pointing to 10-foot birdies he missed at the 12th and 14th. The decline actually started at No. 10, where indecision — had the pressure finally hit? — first popped up. "I should have hit a one iron, but I hit a two iron instead," Azinger said. He caught a bunker, and bogeyed to fall to seven under and two ahead of Faldo. At No. 11, he sliced his drive into the right rough and had a bad downhill lie for his second. Somehow, he got it to the green, but about 60 feet from the flag. His first putt went 10 feet past the hole. He took two more to get down. Another bogey, and he was back to six under par and only one ahead of Faldo. He was now six under, and his lead was down to one. He held it without trouble through the next five holes. The fatal moment, then, came at No. 17.

Now Rodger Davis's prophecy, from back in the first round, echoed: The man who stayed out of the fairway bunkers would be the winner. Now Azinger committed the fatal error. At a time when accuracy and not distance was the main consideration, he elected to hit his driver at No. 17. "It was a ridiculous club to hit there," he was to say later. "It cost me the championship. If I had parred that hole, I would have been in command of the championship. There was no point in the driver. I should have hit the one iron. I don't know what I was thinking." But the driver it was, and his ball ended up in a fairway bunker at the left corner of the dogleg. There was only one way out — sideways. His next shot was well short of the green, his pitch about 20 feet above the hole, and he two-putted for his bogey six. He was now down to five under par, tied with Faldo.

And Faldo, meanwhile, was up ahead making the last of his 18 pars, and doing it with a flair. He teed off with a safe three wood at No. 18, hit a five-iron second about 200 yards to 40 feet from the hole. His first putt was too strong, going about five feet above the hole. He had a very tricky test coming back, a delicate sidehill-downhill putt for his par. He studied it thoroughly, made up his mind, then stroked it beautifully. It dropped to the accompaniment of thunder from the gallery. He had finished with a par 71 and a 279 total, five under par. Now it was Azinger's turn — one last chance.

Azinger's drive was safely in the 18th fairway, leaving him about 200 yards to the green. Now he was visibly nervous. He plucked some grass, tossed it up to check the wind, took out his five iron, bent and took some more grass, and tossed it. Finally, he hit. He watched the ball for a moment, sailing through the mist, then clenched his fist and muttered. He knew the shot had got away from him. It ended up in the long bunker to the left of the green. Worse, it ended up in an impossible position. Azinger had to bend his tall and lanky frame almost into a crouch, his left foot behind on the grassy slope, his foot right down in the sand. He laid the clubface wide open and swung the best he could. The amazing thing was that he did get the ball out. But it was about 25 feet short of the hole. He needed that putt to tie Faldo and force a playoff. But he didn't get it. His tap-in bogey gave him a 73 and a 280 total, leaving him tied for second with Davis, and leaving Faldo the first Englishman since Tony Jacklin in 1969 to win the British Open.

"Don't anybody feel sorry for me," Azinger said. "It's not the end of the world. I've had a great year. I lost a chance to win a great title, but I've proved I can play with anyone in the world. I've proved I'm a contender. I'm going to benefit from what happened to me here."

5. The PGA Championship

In the old days, you could always find a few solid favorites going into a major championship. It hadn't been like that for some time, and it sure wasn't as the PGA Championship came to PGA National in Palm Beach Gardens, Florida. Over the past 18 majors, there had been 18 different winners. "Well, you've had 18 good winners," Jack Nicklaus said, "but it's obvious that nobody has come forward to dominate."

This had, of course, led to suspicions about the quality of the modern, especially the American, golfer. As the late Casey Stengel, famed baseball manager, once lamented about his New York Mets, "Can't anybody here play this game?"

Maybe, in golf, the answer to Stengel's question would be, "Trouble is, too many can play this game."

The PGA field included Larry Nelson, the quiet man from Georgia. He won the 1983 U.S. Open and thus, it developed, became the first of the 18 different winners. Nelson also had the 1981 PGA to his credit. His last victory, however, was in the 1984 Walt Disney World Classic. He didn't seem to be a threat now. He was 39, he had gone through some injuries, he had started a golf course architecture business, he spent a lot of time off the tour in 1986, and he wasn't playing all that well this year — 101st on the money list with $59,319.

Who would have guessed that Nelson would win and break the string?

All this, however, was merely idle conversation — in air-conditioned places. The real topic was the weather. South Florida was blanketed by a suffocating combination of heat and humidity. Even the residents were smitten by it. In the majors, it seems there's always a complaint about one thing or another, but for the sheer length and depth and breadth of criticism, no event in recent memory compared with this one.

The weather aside, there was the matter of the greens which were part grass, part dirt. They had been struck by pythium blight, a fungus. The greens were a mixture of bent grass, the more delicate grass common on Northern courses, and Bermuda grass, which is more durable in the heat and humidity of the South. Course workers tried to kill the fungus with chemicals, and also reduced the amount of water they put on the greens. This left the bent grass at the mercy of the heat. Some officials speculated that the problem actually started from routine watering earlier in the month: The water is drawn from lakes and ponds surrounding the course. Copper sulfate is used to control algae in these waters, and the belief was that an unusually high concentration of the chemical was in the water at the time, and that this is what contributed to the rapid growth of the fungus.

"It's better now," said Nicklaus, who lives nearby. "I played here two months ago and there was nothing there." Said Tom Kite: "There isn't a good green on the back nine. There are patches that don't have any grass on them at all." Andy Bean, another Floridian, took a pragmatic view. "Everybody has to play them, so there's no reason to be concerned." Long before the week had run its course, it was clear that Greg Norman was speaking for a lot of golfers, and spectators, too, when he said, "It's silly to have a major in Florida in the summer."

The PGA was held in Florida just once before, in 1971, at the nearby JDM course. But that year, it was switched to February, in the season when regular tour events in Florida are also held. The weather is comparatively mild then. So why was the PGA now being played in South Florida in August?

J.R. Carpenter, president of the PGA of America, summed it up this way: A resort and real estate development company named PGA National Venture, Inc. (no relation) invited the PGA of America to locate its headquarters on the property, which the PGA did in 1981. Under the agreement, the PGA of America would stage a Ryder Cup at the course (1983) and a PGA Championship. The reason for this was the magic of golf's name in commercial enterprises. Golf sells.

Then there was the rough. It was the Bermuda grass, fluffy on top and wiry at the bottom. A ball sinks to the ground like a strawberry settling in cream. And there was no graduated cutting — shorter cut off the fairway, then deeper beyond. It was all about the same depth, some three inches. A golfer could pretty much forget about reaching the green. Just getting out would be an achievement. At stake in all this: a $900,000 purse, a $150,000 first prize, and a last chance to make the Ryder Cup team. For better or for worse, a memorable PGA was coming up.

The opening round belonged to Bobby Wadkins, younger brother of Lanny, but only on the scoreboard. Bobby, one of 15 players to break par, returned a four-under 68 to lead by one at the end of the day. But hardly anyone had noticed. A bit of golf history was going on someplace else.

It was Thursday morning, getting on to 9 o'clock, and a PGA official at the first tee was pacing anxiously. The big gallery draped around the tee and far down both sides was beginning to fidget. Off in the distance, another gallery was packed around the green, also waiting. "Where are they?" the official said. "They're going to be late." He was fretting over a historic first. In a masterstroke of theater, and for a good attraction, of course, the PGA had made up a dramatic grouping: Arnold Palmer, 57, Jack Nicklaus, 47, and Tom Watson, 37 — three eras of domination, in that order. And all they were about to do, this historic first time they were ever paired in a tournament, was miss their tee time. What theater that would be: Disqualified. But they made it. They arrived at 8:50 a.m., one minute before their tee time. Watson strode across the tee first, to a smattering of applause. ("When I first looked at us out there," Watson said later, "I thought 'Here's one guy with five PGA championships [Nicklaus], and two with none.'") Nicklaus was next on the tee. More applause. Then a voice came from the gallery: "Hey! Where's Arnie!" And Palmer appeared, as if on cue. Cheers went up as he strode across the green. The appeal of the man is amazing. He was 57 now, well past his prime, and still they loved him. It was an Arnie's Army kind of day. The threesome drew perhaps 3,000 fans, which, it turned out, seemed to be nearly everybody on the course.

Despite the magnitude of the event, the weather remained the dominant force at PGA National. When the historic threesome came to No. 1 tee at 8:50 a.m., the temperature was 95 degrees, and the humidity seemed to match it. All three were soaking wet, and when they bent to their tee shots, sweat dripped from their noses. In South Florida, the weather people issue a "Temperature-Humidity Index," a measurement that combines the two factors into an equivalency reading of what the weather *feels* like. Weather people said the THI occasionally reaches about 100 degrees at that time of the year. But this time it was above 100 from 9 a.m. to 5 p.m., the weather report said, and it was 111 from 1 to 3 p.m.

But there was golf to be played. Unsatisfactory golf for Palmer and Nicklaus. Both shot four-over-par 76s. For Nicklaus, it was a day in rough and bunkers. "Oh, this is fun," Nicklaus said, chiding himself after hitting his drive into a bunker at No. 5. This may have been the first time Palmer didn't tuck in his shirt. He didn't have to. It was plastered to his back. Things started to get almost funny. At No. 8, Palmer was leaning, one arm out on his driver, and looking miserable. "Sure you don't want a cart?" Nicklaus said, needling him. Palmer, a vigorous opponent of the golf cart, looked up and grinned. "Hands and knees first," he vowed. Palmer rocked his army with a eagle-three at 533-yard 11th — a 253-yard three wood and a 35-foot putt. Watson shot a two-under-par 70 and announced, "I felt rubbery out there."

For a while, relief — of a sort — lay ahead for everyone. At the 18th green, a large leader board was mounted on a barge floating in a lake just to the right, in full view of both the spectators in the grandstands and the golfers coming to the green. PGA National (the resort company), apparently seeking to add a festive air, or something, to the proceedings, had hired a beautiful and statuesque blonde from a modeling agency to perch visibly at that scoreboard. She was wearing a bright green bikini. It does not strain the truth to say that no one, including photographers, could miss seeing her. "How can you concentrate here?" Palmer said to no one in particular, on arriving at the green. Before long, PGA officials sent a rowboat to the floating barge. "They just came and took me away," the blonde explained. So it was back to the weather...

The pithiest observation of the day was made by Fred Funk, golf coach at the University of Maryland and one of 39 club professionals in the field, and a surprise with a 69 that left him just one stroke out of the lead at the end of the day. "The thing that's hot here," Funk said, "is the sun." He got no arguments, but he did get a lot of snickers. What he meant, actually, was that things weren't nearly so bad in the shade. But golfers do not like to play in the shade. That's where the trees are. There was nothing funny about Funk's round, though. He never missed a fairway, and he made two birdies on what he called "no-brainer" putts — a 50-footer at No. 1, and a 30-footer at No. 9. Funk said he got a thrill seeing his name on the leader board. "I thought that was pretty neat," he said. "It's been a tough name to live up to, believe me. I went through hell with it in junior high and high school. But after a while I realized it was different, and I decided I liked it." He would tee off on Friday tied for second place. How would that feel? "It hasn't hit me yet," he said.

Another club pro had a relaxing day, if one considers quiet desperation and resignation as relaxing. "Just hit it in the rough, chop it out, and keep going," said Dana Quigley, of Rehoboth, Massachusetts. "I thought I was shooting 160." Actually, it was 79, a tad better than the 80.07 average for all 39 club pros. At that, they were in good company. The touring pros were putting up some surprisingly big numbers — defending champion Bob

Tway, 78 (that included an eagle); U.S. Open champion Scott Simpson, 78; Ian Woosnam, Europe's leading money winner, 86 ("I'm embarrassed."); Australia's Rodger Davis, co-runnerup in the British Open three weeks earlier, 79 ("I just got on the bogey train and couldn't get off"); Japan's Tommy Nakajima, 78, and Paul Azinger, the leading money-winner on the American tour, 82.

Spectators understand the plight of the club pro, coming from club duties to a once-a-year pressure cooker. But how to explain the heavy scores from veterans? Woosnam, after his 86, was changing his travel plans for a quick departure. "I've never been over 80 in four years, except once, and that was in the French Open, which included a 16 on one hole," the distressed Welshman said. "I've lost my swing, and when you get on a course like this, it really shows up. I'm sick of chipping out of the rough on every hole. It's embarrassing." Said Azinger, "I didn't hit it unsolid, I just hit it 82 times." The rough was also his problem. "I didn't hit a good chip shot all day from that stuff," he said. "This just proves I have a long way to go before I get to where I need to be." Greg Norman said his 73 felt four strokes better, and he wondered if having deep rough right off the fairway was fair. "You can hit the fairway and the ball still rolls into the rough, and you're penalized," he said. "That penalizes the guy who hits the good shot more than the guy who hits the bad shot." Ballesteros' play was so erratic that he wasn't unhappy with his par 72. "Every time I made a birdie, I would bogey the next hole," he said. It was a classic yo-yo round. Starting at No. 3, he went birdie-bogey-birdie-bogey. And from No. 11, eagle-bogey-par-bogey. He would have to get moving if he wanted to add to his collection of majors.

David Edwards, a lonely voice, had no complaints after a 69 left him one stroke off the lead. "The course is in good shape and the greens putted well," he said. "The greens won't be a problem. I hit my irons good, so I feel good about that." Edwards, who started at No. 10, made six birdies but suffered three bogeys, one for each fairway he missed. He also had three excellent saves coming in. At No. 7, he chipped in for his par. He salvaged a bogey at No. 8 with a chip-in out of the rough, and at No. 9 (his final hole), he chipped to 18 inches and saved par.

Two-time PGA champion Raymond Floyd had the best score of the afternoon starters — a 70 — and credited it to his ability to adapt to conditions. "Everyone knows about playing late," he said. Late starters can always expect spiked-up and crusty greens. Still, he birdied from 12 feet at No. 10, from 10 feet at No. 13, and from three feet at No. 18. He parred the entire front nine, and the only blot on his card was a bogey at No. 16, on three putts from 25 feet. He couldn't wait for the second round. "I want to take advantage of what I've created," he said. Right with him at 70 was his old buddy, Lanny Wadkins, the 1977 PGA champion, who went after the course with his driver on all the driving holes except the downwind 16th. "I can't back off from the driver because the course is long and soft," he said. Too soft at one point. His ball picked up some mud on his tee shot at the 10th, causing his second to squirt away out of control. That cost him one of his three bogeys. An eight-foot putt at No. 18 gave him the last of his five birdies. He echoed Norman's sentiments on the depth of the rough just off the fairway. "I'd like to see a wider strip of short rough next to the fairway, because you need to penalize the guy who's hitting it really crooked," he said. He had started two groups behind his kid brother — Lanny's 37, Bobby 36 — and thus was constantly reminded of the work cut out for him. "I'm not surprised Bobby's leading, because he's been playing well," Lanny said. "No, it won't have any effect on me — except I'd like to beat him."

Also in the 70 group was Bernhard Langer. He started on No. 10 and got fooled immediately. He was expecting the comparatively slow greens he saw in practice, and so rapped his first putt 15 feet past the hole. But the greens had been well cut overnight and were much faster. Langer made the putt coming back for his par, and was four under par before bogeying his final two holes, the eighth and ninth. Langer, like Norman, has a home in Florida. And like Norman, he thought Florida was for winter golf. Two players who knew more than a little about the Far East put the weather in a global perspective. Australian Rodger Davis, who shot that 79, weighed South Florida against his stops in Malaysia, Singapore, and Indonesia, and found South Florida "stickier." Larry Nelson had been an infantryman in Vietnam, and he said South Florida's weather was only slightly better. Nelson turned in some of his best golf in a long time. He started at No. 10 and was two over par after four holes. Then he played the last five in a birdie, a par, and three more birdies. A birdie-bogey exchange coming home left him in the group tied for fourth at 70. "I can't blame any missed putts on the greens," Nelson said. "And you can't try to force anything here because each hole is bogeyable and each hole is birdieable. You have to be patient." Also at 70 was Curtis Strange, who also birdied the 16th, 17th and 18th, the last three holes on his front side. Mark McCumber, one of the pre-tournament favorites, quickly changed the odds on himself. He triple-bogeyed his first hole. He ground out a 74, though, and shrugged. "It's just one day," he said. Bobby Wadkins' day.

Bobby signed for his 68, strolled into the interview room slumped in a chair, shoved his visor back on his head, and started talking. He didn't bother to wait for the questions. "The fairways were perfect, the rough unplayable, the greens so-so, and the playing conditions perfect," he said, rapid-fire and grinning. "And in my opinion, they've made it a driving tournament." It was the rough, he said. Who can't hit the fairways can't score. "This rough is more than severe, it's brutal," he said. "In my opinion, the rough ought to be bad enough that you can't spin the ball and you don't know what it's going to do. But at least you should be able to get the ball out. I haven't hit the green yet from this rough." Bobby made two bogeys, at the first and 14th. He had hit the rough both times. But he made hay from the fairways. He birdied the par-three fourth after a six iron to two feet; the par-five fifth after just missing an eagle putt from 20 feet, and the par-four eighth from 12 feet. Coming in, he laid up at No. 11, put an eight iron to six feet, and holed the putt for his birdie four. At the par-four 13th, he holed from three feet, and he challenged the 541-yard 18th and won, hitting a three-wood second to 45 feet and two-putting for his birdie-four. Bobby, now in his 13th season on the tour, had the distinction of winning more than $1 million without having won a tournament. His chances of winning this one didn't impress him at the moment. "It's just another round of golf in another golf tournament," he said. "Unless you can go away and hide, this tournament doesn't start until the last nine holes on Sunday."

Eventually the obligatory question of the weather came up. Bobby said it was cool compared to the Memphis Classic the week before, where he shot 64 in the final round and made "a little gettin'-outta-town money."

"Lanny and I used to play 54 holes in weather like this when we were growing up in Richmond," Bobby said.

"Yeah," Lanny countered, when he came in about a half-hour later, "but we were 12, 13 years old, and we'd go swimming between rounds. I now appreciate why I live in Dallas."

For all of the stars, the surprises, the drama, this didn't seem like a major. The reason was the crowd — or rather, the lack of it. The Palmer-Nicklaus-Watson pairing drew an estimated 3,000. At one point in the afternoon, the Greg Norman-Fuzzy Zoeller-Hal Sutton pairing drew 63. They counted them. The pairing of the three majors winners — Larry Mize, Scott Simpson, and Nick Faldo — had 14 by one count. "I've seen more people at a pro-am," said Roger Maltbie. *Palm Beach Post* columnist Dave George wrote that at high noon, he saw one person sitting in the grandstands behind No. 14. Tournament officials refused to issue an attendance figure.

The first-round leaders:

Bobby Wadkins	68	Tom Watson	70
David Edwards	69	Bobby Clampett	71
Fred Funk	69	Bobby Cole	71
Raymond Floyd	70	Ray Freeman	71
Bernhard Langer	70	Dan Pohl	71
Larry Nelson	70	Mike Reid	71
Curtis Strange	70	Tim Simpson	71
Lanny Wadkins	70		

"If I stay here another month, I think I could shoot par," Paul Azinger was saying. But he wasn't staying another month. Not even another day. Azinger was "getting the weekend off," as they say on the PGA Tour. He followed his opening-round 82 with a five-over-par 77, and his 159 total missed the cut by eight strokes. This was embarrassing for the man who was leading the tour in money winnings with almost $600,000. "I played pretty horrible here, if you want to know the truth," Azinger said. "That's golf. It just happened to be the major championship after the one that I almost won." Ben Crenshaw offered his sympathy, and in the process put a wry twist on an old tale. "I've been there many times," Crenshaw said. "It's just one of those two days where nothing went right." Two double bogeys on the back nine were how things were going wrong for Azinger. Maybe it was perverse poetic justice, but Azinger's overseas counterpart, Ian Woosnam, leading money-winner on the European tour, also missed the cut, with 86-75—161. For that matter, so did one of the top Japanese stars, Tommy Nakajima — 78-74—152. When it came to an early trip home, all three were in good company.

The list of victims looked like a pretty good tournament field by itself. Also missing the cut: Former U.S. Open champion Andy North, 75-78—153; Fred Couples, 80-74—154; former PGA champion David Graham, 79-75—154; Mark O'Meara, 77-78—155; Rodger Davis, British Open co-runnerup with Azinger, 79-77—156; Masters champion Larry Mize, 75-81—

156; the young Spaniard, Jose-Maria Olazabal, 79-77—156, and Corey Pavin, a two-time winner early in the season, 78-79—157. It was probably of little consolation to them, but a few big names almost joined them. They hung on by their fingernails. Among the 16 who just made it at seven-over-par 151 were none other than Greg Norman, 73-78; U.S. Open champion Scott Simpson, 78-73, and Arnold Palmer, 76-75. Jim Thorpe also missed the cut (75-79—154) and, it was said, lost his driver in the bargain. "They take a great golf course and they make the fairways 25 yards wide," Thorpe said, clearly miffed. He had no monopoly on frustration. Home favorite Mark Calcavecchia (79-80—159) spoke for a lot of golfers when he departed with, "I'm glad it's over. That was agony."

Norman had rushed off the course, whizzed through the locker room, packed his bags, and tipped the attendants. He was dead certain he had missed the cut. No, he hadn't. The news was something of a relief — for the pride, at least. "It's been at least 18 months since I missed a cut," Norman said. Actually, it was January, 1986, in the AT&T Pebble Beach Pro-Am. So this was Norman's 29th consecutive finish in the money. But barely. The rough almost did him in. "I just kept hitting it — right rough, left rough," Norman said. So he was getting two more cracks at the course — or it at him. He didn't count himself in the running, though. "I'd have to shoot 65 to get back in," he said.

Norman, by the way, was playing in a broad-brimmed Australian hat, one of his latest endorsement products. This was not just a sales campaign, though. Seve Ballesteros was in a pork-pie hat, Palmer in a kind of plantation hat, and wristbands to stop the sweat from running onto his hands. Almost everybody had some kind of protection — if only a towel draped around the neck. The weather had not gone away. They were calling this day "Fryday." It was oppressively hot and humid. Some seemed to handle it better than others, among them, Lanny Wadkins and Raymond Floyd, a pair of very tough campaigners. Each shot another two-under-par 70 for a two-round total of four-under 140. They shared the second-round lead by one stroke over Tim Simpson (70) and Jeff Sluman, whose 69 matched Mark McCumber's for low round of the day. Bobby Wadkins, the first-round leader, slipped to a 74 and shared fifth place on 142.

"I'd be playing a lot better if I hadn't made triple bogey on my first hole of the tournament," McCumber said, his horror story finally surfacing. "I was 20 feet from the green and I hit the ball three times in the rough, and I'm telling you it didn't move a foot." He finally got it on a one-putted for his seven. Sluman, the least-known of the leaders, was runnerup in the Tournament Players Championship in the spring. That was the closest he'd come to winning in his five years on the tour. He eagled the par-five sixth after hitting a five wood to 40 feet. Ballesteros came in with a 70 to share fifth place at 142. "I missed only two fairways today. I missed six Thursday, so I'm getting better," Ballesteros said. His round included six birdies, which gave him nine birdies and an eagle so far in 36 holes. "So far, so good," Ballesteros said. Nelson, the quiet one, did not improve. But he didn't tail off badly, posting a par 72 for a share of fifth at 142. Others couldn't say the same. David Edwards, who shared second after the first round, shot 75 and drifted to even-par 144. Curtis Strange returned 76 for 146, and Bernhard Langer 78 for 148. Tom Watson crashed to 79 and plunged out of sight to 149. Jack Nicklaus improved by three strokes, 73—149 and was fretting. "I don't have a lot of years left to win a major championship," said Nicklaus, who holds a record 18 as a pro. "I'm playing very well, but dumb mistakes hurt." The second round also thinned out the club pro ranks. Fred Funk, who held a share of second after his first-round 69, came down hard with a 79 and stood at 148, eight strokes back. "I can't get back in to win, but I can make it respectable," Funk said. Still, he and Ray Freeman, driving range instructor from Greensboro, North Carolina, were tied for low club pro at 148, and only seven of the original 39 survived the cut.

Lanny Wadkins and Floyd are known as "money" players. Tuesday is "money day" on the tour, the day the pros get down some bets on the practice rounds. You may beat Wadkins and Floyd on Sunday, but seldom on Tuesday.

Only two things bothered Floyd on the Friday — the heat and the lack of a gallery. "The heat started getting to me," Floyd said. "At one point I lost my rhythm and lost my swing. I was getting so hot that the sweat was just popping out of me and running down my arms. Then I found myself rushing, trying to hit before my hands got wet. I had to slow myself down and get it back together. And once it goes for me, I usually have a hard time getting it back. But I got it back fast this time, and that's a good sign for me." There seemed to be more spectators than on Thursday, but apparently not a great many more, and Floyd shook his head at that. "It's easy to play in a mob," he said. "They give you depth. But when there are big gaps, you see every movement. The first nine holes, I don't think we had a hundred people following us, and 20 of them were camera people."

Floyd had a bumpy ride in the second round — four birdies, two bogeys — both from the rough — and five saves. Sharp iron play set up his four birdies. The shortest was 2½ feet, the longest 10. But it was a save that keyed his round. It came at the 485-yard par-five sixth (his 15th hole). He was wild with his approach, fully 40 yards to the right, and he had two trees between him and the green. This was a good time to be conservative, he said, and just knock the ball into a bunker between him and the green, and hope to get up and down for par. "But I needed to be aggressive," he said. He took the bold route, popping a shot over the 20-foot pine tree to the green, 20 feet from the hole. He narrowly missed the birdie, and saved the par. Now he was chomping at the bit. "I'm not going to let the heat bother me. I'm going to go play," he said. "But it's very difficult for me to get motivated to play anymore, after 25 years of doing the same thing — playing tournaments, corporate outings every Monday. Believe me, after 25 years, that gets old." But playing in the majors never gets old. "That's all the motivation I need," he said.

Tim Simpson returned a 70 — not the lowest score of the day, but the round of the day. That's because he had barely started before he was sinking in quicksand. He pulled himself out just in time. He began at No. 10 and parred the first two holes, then broke out in a string of three bogeys. He caught the rough at the third hole (No. 12), then water, then rough again. he was three over after five holes. It looked like a good time to throw in the towel and just play out the string. But Simpson, 31, with one victory in his 11 years on tour, pulled himself together and went back to work. He birdied two of the next four holes, one of them a near-eagle at the par-four 16th, where his six-iron approach hit two feet behind the hole and lipped the cup drawing back. He was bogey-free coming in, and birdied his 14th (No. 5) from eight feet, his 16th (No. 7) from eight, and his last (No. 9) from eight. "The big key is putting bermuda grass," he said. "I grew up on it, in Dunwoody, Georgia, and Bermuda typically breaks toward the setting sun. You always have to keep your eye on the sun." That problem solved, Simpson had one big one left. His recent pattern was to get into contention going into the final round, then fade out. It happened at the U.S. Open, Hartford Open, and Anheuser-Busch Classic. "I wasn't choking," he said. "I just had problems with my putting and my short game. Now, I have to just keep hitting it the way I have these first two days. I feel pretty good about my game."

If Simpson had the round of the day, Lanny Wadkins had the shot of the day. It was at the 533-yard par-five No. 3, his 12th hole. His tee shot ended up in the rough short of the lake, and he had to waste a shot getting back to the fairway. That left him 235 yards from the green. The green was guarded by a pair of trees that left an opening at most 20 feet wide. Wadkins studied the picture briefly, pulled out his driver, and lashed the ball through that crack between the trees and onto the green about 45 feet from the pin. Two putts later he had a sensational par. He shrugged it off. Just another day in the office. "Basically, I recovered without any double bogeys," was how he described his round. The great shot held him steady at two under par. He had an erratic outward 35, and three birdies and two bogeys. An eight iron at his 11th (No. 2) set him up for a birdie from 12 feet, then a blast to one foot from the bunker got him another at his 15th (No. 6). He was three under par then, which would have been good enough for the solo halfway lead. But he drove behind the trees at the 17th, and the bogey left him tied with Floyd for the lead going into the third round. The friendly old enemies would go at it again. "The last two times Raymond Floyd won a major, I've finished second," Wadkins said. "It's time to turn that around." That was in the 1982 PGA at Southern Hills and the 1986 U.S. Open at Shinnecock Hills. They were partners in the 1985 Ryder Cup matches, and won two of their three matches.

There was still a very strong chance the PGA would see a brother-vs.-brother finale. Bobby Wadkins was the more sentimental of the two. "Neither of us would lose if Lanny wins," he said, "because I'm his biggest fan." Lanny said he enjoyed seeing Bobby's name up on the leader board — "As long as it's under mine." They grew up in Richmond, Virginia, playing golf together and fighting like brothers. They would jump on the bicycles and pedal two miles to Meadowbrook Golf Course, and play 36 or 54 holes. "I was generally in charge until he got big," said Lanny, who stands 5-foot-9. Said Bobby with a chuckle, "When I got to be 6-foot-1, we stopped fighting."

The second-round leaders:

Raymond Floyd	70-70—140
Lanny Wadkins	70-70—140
Tim Simpson	71-70—141
Jeff Sluman	72-69—141
Seve Ballesteros	72-70—142
Ben Crenshaw	72-70—142
Larry Nelson	70-72—142

Bobby Wadkins	68-74—142
Mark McCumber	74-69—143
Bobby Clampett	71-72—143

Fuzzy Zoeller had no trouble pinpointing his problem in the third round. "I hit it lousy on the first hole, lousy on the last hole, and lousy every place in between," he said. That pretty much finished the 1987 PGA for him — a 76 for 233, seven over par and 11 strokes off the lead. Curt Byrum, a fifth-year tour pro out of Onida, South Dakota, who began the day nine off the lead, was more selective. He had a record 66 in sight until he sliced his tee shot into the water at the par-three 17th. "I was indecisive, I was unsure what shot I wanted to play," he said. There went the 66. He hit into the water again at No. 18, but salvaged his par-five with a 35-foot putt. He finished with a 68 that left him at one-over-par 217 and five strokes out of the lead. If any one shot could be called the turning point of this PGA, it was Seve Ballesteros' two-iron tee shot at the 441-yard, par-four 16th. When it splashed into the water, a horde of players rushed back into contention, crowding behind co-leaders Mark McCumber and D.A. Weibring. You could see the spectators do a double-take at the leader board. Weibring, sore-wristed one-time winner in 11 years on the tour, a likeable guy best known for playing straight man to Peter Jacobsen's comedy routines? And McCumber, looking for his first major, the guy who triple-bogeyed his first hole? Yes, them. This was becoming a most interesting PGA.

Ballesteros had played boldly in the second round, and missed only two fairways. Now he toned down his game a bit. "I hit the driver very straight," he said, "but when I hit irons off the tees, I missed three fairways." He was three under par for the day and had the lead until he watered that tee shot at No. 16. It cost him a double bogey. He got a birdie-two at No. 17 with a four iron and a three-foot putt, then bogeyed No. 18 after catching water again, this time with a one-iron second. He finished with a par 72 and a 214 total, two under par, but instead of leading he was trailing by two at the end of the day. Even so, this was a rather lighter man than the intense Spaniard everyone was accustomed to. He explained this attitude earlier, at a happier time. "People tell me I have to be more relaxed, that I put too much pressure on myself," he had said. So he was trying to ease up. He stuck to his guns, even in the face of that double bogey at No. 16 and the bogey at No. 18. "I am trying to convince myself," he said, "that I am a happy man." The press liked that so much, they almost applauded in a mixture of salute and sympathy. The gallery had good reason to suspect the cause of Ballesteros' play. He and his caddy, brother Vicente, kept pulling at a Bell's Scotch whisky bottle through the round. It seemed a strange way to combat the heat. The answer: That was water in the bottle.

It was a day of some good, rich turmoil. There would be no sixth PGA for Jack Nicklaus. He returned a 74 for 223, 11 strokes off the lead, then joined ABC as a commentator. "The greens are two different grasses and they vary speeds throughout the golf course," he told the television audience. "That makes it extra tough." Lanny Wadkins would vouch for that in spades before long. Tom Kite was still seeking his first major and was still battling the fates. At the par-three seventh, his tee shot hit the flagstick on the second bounce and stopped four feet from the hole. But he lipped out his birdie putt. "That's how I've played all week," Kite said. "I've hit the ball well but I just haven't made any putts at all." He shot 71 and was eight strokes off at 220. Jeff Sluman took himself out of the hunt with a 78. Tim Simpson started the day just a stroke off the lead, and ended up 10 behind it, thanks to an 81 that put him at 222. The 428-yard 12th gave up not a single birdie in the third round, but it was especially tough on him. He had to drop from an unplayable lie from behind a palm tree, and eventually took a triple-bogey seven. It was the sixth hole that was especially tough on a young lady from West Palm Beach. She was seated at No. 4 green, under an umbrella, fortunately, and club pro Lonnie Nielsen, from East Aurora, New York, was trying to hit the green at the par-five sixth in two. He sliced his drive about 30 yards off line, and the ball hit the young lady, umbrella and all, and left a bump on her head. "Gee," she said, "I thought Gerald Ford must have been around here somewhere."

The grand shoot out never came off. Raymond Floyd labored to a 73 and stood at three-under-par 213, one stroke off the lead, and Lanny Wadkins went through the trials of Job for a 74 that put him at 214, two behind. Bobby Wadkins, on the other hand, shook off a rising disaster to return a 71 that lifted him to 213, a stroke ahead of his brother and tied for third with Floyd.

"I wasted a heck of a round," Floyd said. "Everybody said you have to drive it in the fairway. Well, I drove it in the fairway. But..." He missed only two — the par-five 11th, which he parred, and the par-five 18th, where he made the second of two closing birdies after a nine iron to two feet. At the 17th, he put his four-iron tee shot to 10 feet and holed for his birdie-two. He also birdied No. 5, on a four-foot putt. The trouble, then? His short game was creaking. His tee shot to the par-three seventh was short, then he pitched too long, pitched back to three feet — and missed the putt. That cost him a double bogey. His six-iron approach to No. 12 was short, and his poor pitch left him 30 feet from the hole. Two putts gave him a bogey five. At No. 16, he was short again with his approach, then chipped poorly, leaving himself 30 feet to the hole. Two putts got him another bogey. The two closing birdies restored his appetite for the final round. A Ryder Cup team berth was at stake. "...and I want to make that Ryder Cup team," Floyd said.

For Bobby Wadkins, the third round opened with a sigh. "I was in a position to shoot myself out of the tournament after nine holes," he said. A birdie at No. 7 slowed the damage. He bogeyed the third and fourth, and then the eighth. He headed home with a vengeance. Except he kept hitting into the rough. But he escaped. "I played the back nine three under with the ball in the rough," he said. "Yeah, that's backwards. But I made the shots I had to make, and that makes me very positive about tomorrow." Wadkins birdied Nos. 11, 15, and 18 on putts of six, 15, and eight feet. He dropped only one shot, that at the 14th. He was hoping to be paired with his brother for the final round. "Maybe we'd inspire each other to a 65," he said. "Besides, when he's a group behind me or ahead of me, I'm always turning around trying to see what he did." There were also thoughts of a brother team in the Ryder Cup matches. Bobby would have to win the PGA to get a berth, and Lanny could make it with a good performance. It would be a nice gift, the Wadkins brothers decided, for parents who had worked so hard that they could play golf as kids.

Lanny birdied two of the first three holes and was six under par for the tournament, the first player to get that low. It seemed he was off on one of his famous tears. Then came the crash. He bogeyed the fourth, fifth, seventh and eighth, then — after four pars — the 13th. Just that fast, he was back to one under par. A birdie at No. 14 got him to two under, but he couldn't buy a putt on the crusty greens coming in and had to settle for a 74—214. Nicklaus had said the two different grasses made the greens tough to putt. Wadkins had another idea. "They've cut these things to dirt," he said, "and dirt doesn't break as good as grass."

Floyd and the Wadkins boys came in to find themselves out of the lead. There sat Mark McCumber, who had a 69, and D.A. Weibring, who vaulted over 15 players with a 67 that tied the competitive course record. They were tied at 212, four under par, and led by a stroke over Floyd and Bobby Wadkins.

McCumber had an adventure, to say the least. First, a nine iron to four feet and a birdie at No. 1. Then a save at No. 2 with a long chip to three feet. Then a scrambling bogey from bunkers at the par-four fifth. Then a save set him off. At the par-five sixth, he was 240 yards from the green. "The ball went right at the hole and I was licking my chops," he said. "Then it bounced off and went in that rough by the green, and I mean I had nothing. I'm 20 feet from the hole, and I felt I'd be fortunate to get the ball on the green." He knew the feeling. He'd been in a similar mess on the first hole of the tournament, and it took him three swipes to get the ball out. He triple-bogeyed. He didn't get to the green this time, either. His chip sailed over the green and into the rough on the other side. In disgust, he took a little swing at a drainage cap. Then he went over and got down to work. This time, he chipped to three inches. On the card, it looked like a routine par. But he had escaped the dragon. "That was the turning point," McCumber said. A birdie from 15 feet at No. 7 and a bogey out of the rough at No. 8 took him through the turn in even par. On the back nine, his only shaky moment was a save at No. 12, where he pitched to five feet and holed the putt. He bracketed that par with birdies — at No. 11 after a bunker shot to 15 feet, and at No. 13, on a 30-foot putt. At No. 18, a three wood to 30 feet and two putts gave him a birdie and a 69.

"I was nervous out there," he admitted. But it was more of a controlled excitement, thanks to a new way of thinking his young daughter had taught him. It was in 1983, and he was going to take Addison, then seven, on a roller coaster. A cautious parent, he said he wouldn't do it if she were scared. "And she told me, 'Daddy, if you're not scared, you're not having fun.'" McCumber said he would remember that the next day.

The Champion course was a roller coaster for everybody else, but for Weibring it was a pleasant stroll — a five-birdie, no-bogey 67. "I played very steady," he said. "I drove it in every fairway." That in itself may have been a record for the week. Of the top 12 finishers, it was the only bogey-free round of the entire tournament. Only twice did he even come near to making a bogey. At No. 8, he recovered from a long approach with a pitch to one foot and saved par. At No. 16, he was long again with his approach and this time pitched to eight feet and holed it. His birdies came from a masterful short game: At No. 1, a nine iron to three feet; at No. 3, a sand wedge pitch to a foot; at No. 6, another sand wedge pitch, this time to three feet; at No. 11, a bunker shot to 12 feet, and at No. 15, a 15-foot putt. Maybe his secret lay in a chronically sore wrist. "It bothered me on the practice tee," he said, "so I slowed down my swing, and I stayed relaxed all day and played within myself."

In the press room, someone mentioned two obscure items: no player leading the third round of a major this year had gone on to win it, and Larry Nelson, unassuming as ever, was being ominously steady. For a guy who made no noise on the course, he was in a surprisingly good position.

Contenders had come and gone, but Nelson "was just hanging around," as they say on tour. He began the third round at two under par and two strokes off the lead, and finished it with 73 that left him at one-under 215 and three strokes back. He had hardly budged all week. There were those who recalled that in the 1983 U.S. Open, he'd made hardly a sound early in the chase, then rushed home with the victory. Nelson was puzzled now, though. "I played better today than I did the first two days, but today I have a higher score," he said. "I don't know exactly what the difference is." Putting, perhaps? "I didn't make any putts on the front nine," he said. "The only reason I shot one under was because I reached No. 6 [a par five] in two and birdied it."

Nelson had no particular game plan for the final round. He simply hoped he could just keep on hanging around until the last few holes, to see if something might develop. "You can't really tell what you have to shoot to win," he said. "It all depends on who is leading going into the last two or three holes. The winning score might be even par. Raymond and Lanny both shot over par today, and I shot over par, so you can never tell."

You certainly can't.

The third-round leaders:

Mark McCumber	74-69-69—212
D.A. Weibring	73-72-67—212
Raymond Floyd	70-70-73—213
Bobby Wadkins	68-74-71—213
Seve Ballesteros	72-70-72—214
Lanny Wadkins	70-70-74—214
Larry Nelson	70-72-73—215
Ben Crenshaw	72-70-74—216
David Frost	75-70-71—216

Back in the 1977 PGA at Pebble Beach, Gene Littler — then age 47, and five years after undergoing cancer surgery — held a five-stroke lead going into the last round. Someone asked him whether that lead was safe. "It won't be safe," he said, "until I'm standing on the 18th green with it." Of course, he never reached that green with that lead. The unfortunate Littler ran into enormous difficulties and got caught by Lanny Wadkins, who beat him on the third playoff hole. Which is to say that going into the final round of the 1987 PGA, no one ever considered the one-stroke lead by Mark McCumber and D.A. Weibring to be safe. By the same token, no one was prepared for what happened, either. If the PGA had been the Indianapolis 500, the track would have been littered with wrecks.

There would be a survivor as much as a winner, and it could be almost anyone.

Sunday was a fitting climax to a week of steaming heat and humidity. It was another sun-struck day, this time of 97 degrees and 66 percent humidity.

Contenders fell in bunches, and only one harder than Seve Ballesteros. He started two strokes out of the lead, and after an opening birdie, he was tied for the lead at three under par through the second hole. Then he came to No. 3, a 533-yard par five, a hole he had birdied for three consecutive rounds. This time, he could find no way around, over, or through it. He drove into the right rough, chipped out sideways, hit into the rough again, then into a bunker, then into the water, and finally sank a 10-foot putt for a triple-bogey eight. He finished at 78—292, tied for 10th. "I thought I had a chance," Ballesteros said. "But nothing happened. That's really what has been happening all year. It's my destiny this year." David Frost, who started four behind, shot 76 and joined Ballesteros at 292. Others were in position to come through the wreckage, but then joined it instead, to one degree or another: Ben Crenshaw, 74; Curtis Strange, 74; Nick Price, 75, and Curt Byrum, 76, to name the principals who started on the margin.

The most gruesome crash, however, was Raymond Floyd's. He was playing with Ballesteros in the next-to-last group, and was just one stroke off the lead at the start. Then his game simply came apart, starting with three-putts on the first two greens, and he shot an astounding 80. His 293 total dropped him all the way to a tie for 14th. Bobby Wadkins was in the last group, starting out just a stroke behind his playing partners, co-leaders Mark McCumber and D.A. Weibring. He also met with disaster — 77—290 and a tie for seventh. Through the chaos of the final round, there was one parenthetical note: The collapse of the world's No. 1 player, Greg Norman. He had not broken par in his last 10 rounds of the majors. In the PGA, he shot 73-78-79-79—309. That was 21 over par and 70th place out of the 73 finishers. Five of the seven club pros left in the field beat him.

The race didn't wait for the end. It was developing early and dramatically. The last two groups had struggled over the front nine — Weibring at 38, McCumber 40, Floyd 42, Bobby Wadkins 40, and Lanny 37.

This was the perfect backdrop for the strange case of Scott Hoch. He wasn't even in the picture at the start of the day, standing at 219, seven strokes off the lead. But he soon enough forced his way in. He had teed off nearly an hour before the leaders, and was quickly on his way to putting up the "number" for everyone to shoot at. He made the turn in 34, with a bogey and three birdies. His new-found life came from a little work session before the round. "I went to the practice range today, and was really struggling," he said. "I was ready to go home. Then it started to come back to where I wanted it." On the inward nine, a bogey at No. 10 followed by three consecutive birdies suddenly inspired him with a new thought. "I realized I had a chance when I walked to the 15th tee," he said.

He came to the final hole four under par for the day and one under for the tournament. A wedge approach put him just eight feet from a birdie-four — and the lead. But he knocked his first putt a good three feet past, then missed the next coming back. "I guess I was thinking so much about the first putt that I missed the second, too," he said. It was a three-putt bogey. Still, he left the hard, sun-baked course with one of only two 69s shot that day, and a par-288 total. His hopes still weren't completely dead, however, not with what was going on behind him. But they soon would be.

Larry Nelson, playing in the third-from-the-last group, was about a half-hour behind Hoch and working doggedly. He started three strokes off the lead, and he had a lot of ground to make up. He lost a little more at No. 2, where two putts from 20 feet cost him a bogey. But he struck back with two quick birdies on an eight-foot putt at No. 3 and a six-footer at No. 4. A save at No. 5 set off a string of nine pars. Then he hit the rough at No. 14, was long with his five-iron approach, chipped to eight feet and two-putted for a bogey-five. He two-putted the 16th from six feet for another bogey after his three-iron approach came down short, and was one over par for the round and even for the championship. Now came the second-most decisive hole of the PGA. At No. 17, Nelson put his five-iron tee shot 20 feet from the flag, and calmly sank the putt. That got him back to even par for the day, and one under for the tournament. A two-putt par from 30 feet gave him a round of 72 and a one-under-par total of 287. That bumped Hock out of the winner's circle. Now it was Nelson's turn to wait.

Two more groups were coming in. Only Lanny Wadkins was left in the penultimate group, Floyd and Ballesteros already having self-destructed, and Wadkins was having a wild time. He bogeyed the first from 30 feet, double-bogeyed the second after two visits to the rough, then birdied the next two — from eight feet at No. 3, and from 12 at No. 4. After three pars, he bogeyed the eighth and ninth. The ninth really hurt. He two-putted from 2½ feet. "I never felt I was in control," Wadkins was to say later. The inward nine was not much different. A four-foot putt gave him a birdie at No. 11 and put him at two under par for the tournament. Then he crashed to his second double bogey of the day at the par-four 12th, finally two-putting from 40 feet. A 10-foot putt gave him a birdie at the par-three 15th, and two pars later he found himself at No. 18 with a chance to win. He was tied with Nelson and had 94 yards to go with his third shot. It was into the wind.

"I hit a hard sand wedge and pulled it into the wind," Wadkins said. "I tried to hit it when the wind was down, and I just pulled it left." Now he had a putt of about 20 feet for the birdie. "Not the kind you want when you're trying to win a tournament," he said. He aimed for the right edge of the hole, but pulled it slightly to the left. There went the outright victory. Next, he had a four-footer for a par five and a tie with Nelson. He got it, and pumped his fist in jubilation. "I probably muttered an obscenity at it," he said later. The 73 left him tied with Nelson at one-under-par 287.

There would be at least a two-way playoff. Weibring, one of the co-leaders at the start, had long since knocked himself out of the running with a streak of three bogeys in the middle of the back nine, then another at No. 17. A closing birdie gave him a 76—288 and a tie for third with Hoch. But one other man could still join that playoff — McCumber. He seemed to be dead after that outward 40, but he fought his way through the back nine and came to the last hole still with a chance to get into the playoff. But he needed a birdie. He was confident. He had already played No. 18 in a par and two birdies.

The 18th is a 541-yard hole with a double dogleg — left, then right. For the prudent, the second shot should be a lay-up into the neck of the right turn, then a pitch on. For the bold — or desperate — the second has to carry an elbow of the lake jutting in from the right. McCumber stood in the fairway, contemplating his second shot. He was 254 yards from the green, and the wind was in his face. He was both bold and desperate. He pulled the driver from his bag, thought a moment, put it back, then yanked it out again. "It was no bargain laying up to the left," he said. "I could have, but that wouldn't be playing to my strength. I could have hit a three wood, but that would have had no chance to get to the green." At best, a lay-up would have got him a birdie and a tie. But with a full shot with the driver, he could still get the birdie, or maybe even an eagle and an outright victory. He remembered the 1985 Doral Open. He was trailing Jack Nicklaus and Tom Kite by six strokes at No. 8. He hit a driver off the fairway 260 yards, birdied the hole, and went on to win the tournament. He had a chance to win now. He'd have to hit the green, of course.

But he didn't. "When I hit it, I didn't have that sinking feeling that it was in the water," he said. But it was. The ball faded slightly and splashed. He still didn't give up. He took his drop and aimed a 119-yard pitch right at the hole. The ball bounced on the green and rolled past the hole by just a few inches. He missed the four-foot par putt coming back. The bogey gave him a 77 and a tie for fifth at 290. The PGA now was between Nelson and Wadkins, two old Ryder Cup teammates and unalike as friends could be — Nelson a born-again Christian and as mild as could be; Wadkins feisty, sometimes argumentative.

It would be a short playoff. It would be the story of the entire PGA — tough rough and ragged, bumpy greens. They went to No. 10, a par-four, 409 yards long, a slight dogleg right. Nelson had played it in a bogey and three pars, Wadkins in a bogey, a birdie and two pars. Wadkins led off, hitting a four wood into the right rough, then an eight iron into the rough to the right of the green. Nelson drove with a three wood into the fairway, then hit an eight iron through the green and into the rough on the back slope. Nelson pitched downhill, about six feet past the hole, and Wadkins chipped sideways, to about four feet. Nelson holed his for a par four. "The greatest putt of my career, that little thing," he was to say. And Wadkins, trying desperately to stay alive, missed.

Wadkins walked over smiling, and put his arm around Nelson in congratulations. Nelson, winless for three years, had his second PGA (the 15th player to win two or more), his third major, the $150,000 first prize, and a spot on the Ryder Cup team. Wadkins, 16 times a winner in his 17 years on tour, had his third runnerup finish in the PGA, the $90,000 second money, and also a berth on the Ryder Cup team.

"He's a tough player," Wadkins said. "I've got nothing to be ashamed of. He's a hell of a competitor. When he gets in the hunt, he's very tough to shake. It came down to two guys not exactly known for their putting. Neither one of us is known for running the tables. But we both keep it in play and are strong iron players." He considered his second-place finish for a moment. "Silver's not exactly my favorite color," he said. "I'd like to find some gold somewhere. This isn't the easiest way to be flying home."

Nelson, who won for the eighth time in his 14 years, is not known for talking at length. "The tournament was won on the back nine," he said.

"It seemed that everyone backed up, and I did, too, but not as much. This was a great thrill. I won one of the greatest championships on one of the toughest courses against one of the hardest fields I can imagine," he said.

"And then after 72 holes of that, I go up against Lanny Wadkins, one of the fiercest competitors on tour."

Nelson goes again into the history books as one of the most unlikely of golfers, much less champions. The thought of golf never even occurred to him until an U.S. Army buddy nagged him when they were stationed at Fort Hood, Texas. He served a tour in Vietnam as an infantryman, was discharged in 1968, and got a job as an illustrator in an aircraft factory back home in Georgia. One day in 1969, he went to a driving range, and discovered fatal charm in a game he used to think was for sissies. He turned professional in 1971, and won his PGA Tour card in the fall of 1973. He joined the tour in 1974 — at the age of 21, just some four years after he had taken up the game.

He was reminded that his victory in the 1983 U.S. Open had started a string of 18 different champions in the majors.

"It's been all downhill since then," he said. "I was 36 then, and it was time to be thinking of other things. I needed to go out and establish myself in the business world." He did that first in building supplies and later in golf course architecture. He cut back his golf schedule. "But I said I wouldn't quit until I won again, so now," he said, with an impish grin, "if I don't win in the next four or five years — I can quit."

6. The Ryder Cup

The 1987 Ryder Cup began this way: Americans Curtis Strange and Tom Kite whipped Sam Torrance and Howard Clark, 4 and 2, in the opening foursome match. Hal Sutton and Dan Pohl came in with a 2 and 1 victory over Bernhard Langer and Ken Brown. And the third match was what horseracing bettors call a "mortal lock." Lanny Wadkins and Larry Mize were 4-up at the turn on Nick Faldo and Ian Woosnam, the two reigning powers in European golf. It was business as usual in the Ryder Cup. The 1987 edition was barely under way and already it was turning into a laugher. Then a funny thing happened to the Americans on their way to that rout...

The biennial Ryder Cup matches had come to America's heartland, Jack Nicklaus' Muirfield Village Golf Club in Dublin, Ohio, just outside his hometown, Columbus. It was an odd time and place for an important international golf event. In the United States, in late September, sports fans are swept up in baseball's pennant races, and in the collegiate and professional football seasons just getting started, and nowhere more so than in Columbus, Ohio. Everyone there lives and dies with the Ohio State University football team. There's emotion left over for professional football's Cleveland Browns to the north and Cincinnati Bengals to the southwest. But Ohio State was playing in Louisiana that Ryder Cup Saturday, and the National Football League players had gone on strike. So the Ryder Cup was the only game in town. It already had drawn terrific support on its own merits. In May, some 17,500 of the limit of 25,000 tickets were sold before they were even put on sale.

The Americans used to win with boring regularity. Back in the days of the Great Britain-Ireland side, the Ryder Cup had become, in American sports parlance, a "yawner." It occurred to someone that Spain's Severiano Ballesteros and West Germany's Bernhard Langer, could add some fire. That someone was none other than Nicklaus. And that's how the European side was born in 1979. The Americans had been under siege ever since.

Things boiled over in 1985, when the Europeans beat the Americans, 16½-11½, at The Belfry in England. This barely dented the American domination, a record of 21 wins against four losses and one tie. But that wasn't the point. The point was that the American grip was being weakened, maybe even broken. In 26 playings, that was the first time the Americans lost since 1957, and only the fourth time since the matches began in 1927. Like sailing's America's Cup, which the Australians won for the first time in 1983, no one missed the Ryder Cup until it was gone. Morever, never had the Americans lost two Ryder Cups in succession, and never had they lost on their home soil. So there was more than a ceremonial flourish to the pre-match commentary.

Nicklaus, the American non-playing captain, sounded confident, but almost defensive. "I'm not sure the Americans aren't the best this year," he said. "The European side winning last year is more of an advantage for us. Our guys are aware they can be beaten."

Tony Jacklin, the European non-playing captain, sounded cautious but not the least bit defensive. "I say this with guarded reservations because I'm an old pro and I know what can happen in this game," he said. "But I think there is a real possibility the Americans could lose." Jacklin threw more spice into the pot when someone asked about the ranking of Ballesteros, Langer and Australian Greg Norman as the best three golfers in the world. Isn't there as American who fits up there? "Day in and day out," Jacklin said, "I don't think there is an American golfer as good as they are." Then came the Earl of Derby, president of the PGA European Tour, at the opening ceremonies. "Some of you may think that our victory the last time was a fluke," he warned the American spectators. "But I would remind you that two years before (in 1983) at Palm Beach, it came down to the last two matches, and you won by the smallest of margins (14½-13½)."

"Our guys used to say, 'Gee, what a privilege it is to make the Ryder Cup team,'" Nicklaus said. "They didn't think about the match itself. Now they say, 'We want to win this thing.'"

Said Jacklin, "The main difference now is that we're not frightened anymore."

They introduced their orders of play for Friday morning's foursomes. Almost everyone missed a certain little episode. While Nicklaus was announcing his opening lineup, Ballesteros suddenly bent his head and turned slightly and muttered something to Jacklin. Someone asked about it later. "What Seve said," Jacklin reported, "was 'It worked out pretty good.' He meant that he would be playing Larry Nelson. I think he welcomes the opportunity."

Meaning that Ballesteros had a bone in his throat from past Ryder Cups. He was 0-4 against him. Nelson got his Ryder Cup berth by winning the PGA Championship early in August, his first victory in three lackluster years. Nelson, a very quiet and gentle man, and a Vietnam infantry veteran, was told about Ballesteros' reaction. He smiled. "When I heard it was Seve," he said, "I couldn't have been more delighted."

Nicklaus and Jacklin were pressed to explain the strategy behind their lineups. "It's a hunch," Jacklin insisted. Said Nicklaus, "You're trying to make great strategists out of us, and we're just a couple of old golfers." Both were laying smoke of course. Much is made of strategy in Ryder Cup play. In 1977, for example, American captain Dow Finsterwald wanted his most experienced players at the bottom of the lineup. "It's good psychology to win points at the end of the day," he said. In 1981, Dave Marr put his fastest players in front — Lee Trevino and Tom Kite were out first — so they could be comfortable playing at their normal pace. In foursomes, the object is to match up personalities or games that complement each other. Every little bit helps. Even the golfers come up with strategies. Brian Barnes and Bernard Gallacher, two veteran teammates in the days of the GBI team, had a plan. "I was better at recovery than Brian," Gallacher said. "And I wanted his strength off the tee. So I wanted him to hit first." Good thinking, except there was something Gallacher didn't know at first. Said Barnes: "I can always remember standing there on the tee, with the club behind the ball, convinced that I would miss the damned thing." At first, Gallacher was amused. "That's what Brian finally told me," he said, "but I thought he was joking." Neil Coles remembers the strategy he and Thomas Haliburton cooked up for the 1961 matches at Royal Lytham and St. Annes. The day was windy. "The idea was to jump on the Americans at the outset, give them a good shock," Coles said. "Lytham, remember, starts with a good par three. I remember Tom's two wood, falling short of the green. And then Mike Souchak hit a one iron 190 yards dead into the wind, to six inches. So much for our getting in quickly."

So Nicklaus and Jacklin had their strategy. They just weren't saying what it was.

The European team consisted of four players from Scotland, three from Spain, two from England, and one each from Ireland, West Germany, and Wales.

From Scotland: Gordon Brand Jr., 29, a Ryder Cup rookie, winner of the Dutch Open and Scandinavian Open on consecutive weeks. Ken Brown, 30, who played in the United States this year and had five top-10 finishes but no victories; he had a 4-7 record in four Ryder Cup appearances. Sandy Lyle, 29, winner of 17 tournaments, including the 1985 British Open and the 1987 Tournament Players Championship on the American tour; his Ryder Cup record was 4-8-2 in four appearances. Sam Torrance, 34, winner of 16 events, including the Italian Open this year; he was 3-7-3 in three Ryder Cups.

From Spain: Ballesteros, 30, with 51 career victories and one this year, the Suze Open; he had a 6-6-3 record in three Ryder Cups. Jose-Maria Olazabal, 21, the 1986 European Tour rookie of the year, but winless this year; this was his first Ryder Cup. Jose Rivero, 33, 1987 French Open champion; he was 1-1 in the 1985 matches.

From England: Nick Faldo, 30, winner of the British Open two months earlier, and also the Spanish Open this year, giving him 15 career victories; he was 11-6 in five Ryder Cups. Howard Clark, 33, with 11 career victories, including the Moroccan Open and PLM Open this year, was 3-3-1 in three Ryder Cups.

From Ireland: Eamonn Darcy, 35, with 11 career victories, including the Belgian Open this year. His Ryder Cup record was 0-7-2 in three appearances.

From Wales: Ian Woosnam, 29, Europe's top player with four tour victories and the Hong Kong Open. In two American appearances this year, he tied for 39th in the Memorial, on the Ryder Cup course, and he missed the cut in the PGA Championship in August. In two Ryder Cups, he was 2-4-1.

From West Germany: Langer, 30, who split his time between the U.S. and European tours. He won both the British PGA and the Irish Open, and was winless in the United States. His record in three Ryder Cups was 7-4-3.

Jacklin's team was made up of the first nine players off the Epson Order of Merit plus three "wild card" selections. Jacklin chose Lyle, Brown, and Olazabal. Nicklaus had no such latitude. The American selection process gave him the U.S. Open and PGA champions plus the 10 players who won the most points in top-10 finishes in PGA Tour events since the start of the 1986 season. It baffled Europeans that Paul Azinger, the No. 2 American money-winner and a three-time winner this year, was not on the team. The answer was simple: A golfer must be a member of the PGA of America (which is separate from the PGA Tour), and Azinger was not a member. He could have been, simply by attending a one-night instruction course on being a club professional. It had been offered three times earlier this season, but Azinger said he was unable to attend any of them. Not that Nicklaus lacked for talent.

The American team: No. 1 money-winner Curtis Strange, 32, with three victories this year; No. 2 Scott Simpson, 32, two victories, including the U.S. Open; No. 4 Ben Crenshaw, 35, one victory; No. 5 Lanny Wadkins, 37, one victory; No. 6 Payne Stewart, 30, one victory; No. 7 Tom Kite, 37, one victory; No. 8 Larry Mize, 29, two victories, including the Masters; No. 10 Mark Calcavecchia, 27, one victory; No. 12 Dan Pohl, 32, no victories this year; No. 15 Hal Sutton, 30, one victory; No. 19 Larry Nelson, 40, PGA champion, and oddly enough, No. 114, Andy Bean, 34. Injured much of this year, he actually won his berth principally on the strength of his play in 1986.

Jacklin had 10 Ryder Cup veterans and two rookies on his team, Brand and Olazabal. In contrast, the American selection system gave Nicklaus five Ryder Cup rookies — Calcavecchia, Pohl, Stewart, Simpson and Mize. They wouldn't be completely raw for long. No one would sit out the first day. "I want all of our guys to have at least one match under their belt before the singles," he said.

The schedule called for four foursomes matches in the morning and four four-ball matches in the afternoon on both Friday and Saturday, and 12 singles matches on Sunday. And when play began that Friday morning, who could have blamed the Europeans if they had been thinking, "Oh, no, here we go again..." They were down, 2-0, after the first two matches. It looked like the bad old days. In the opening match, Strange and Kite easily dispatched Torrance and Clark, 4 and 2. Kite was working carefully, taking practice putts after a hole was ended. "You want to become as familiar with it as possible," he explained, "because there are times when you may go three or four holes without hitting a putt. When you have 30-footers and 40-footers and can lag them up there stone dead so that they just give them to you, it makes it a heck of a lot easier on your partner." Kite was especially deadly. He got it so close on first putts that the Europeans conceded five times. He and Strange won the first hole on a par, the second on a birdie, the fifth on a bogey, and then after 10 halves (on one birdie and nine pars), closed out the match with a par-three at the 16th. Hard on their heels in the second match, Sutton and Pohl came from 1-down on a bogey at the first to beat Brown and Langer, 2 and 1. The hot start raised the question of a home-course advantage for the Americans, who play it each year in the Memorial Tournament.

"Muirfield Village will suit our guys more," Nicklaus had said. And he promised it would be set up the same as it was in the Memorial Tournament in May. Ballesteros had been a lonely and unpopular voice earlier in the season, campaigning in Europe for faster greens. "That is what we will see in the Ryder Cup," he warned. Nobody would listen to him. So he took matters into his own hands when he got the chance. As co-promoter of the Spanish Open, he got the greens wickedly fast. Woosnam was the most critical. Ballesteros just smiled. "They should be faster," he said.

Actually, Nicklaus had tried to offset the American familiarity with Muirfield Village. Early in the year, he invited the Europeans he thought would make the Ryder Cup team to play in the Memorial Tournament. Only a few took him up on it.

In the third match that Friday morning, the American steamroller went thud. It was easily one of the key matches of the weekend. Maybe the most crucial, if one could somehow compute psychological damage. That crash had to be demoralizing to the American team. Wadkins and Mize, were a formidable 4-up at the turn on Faldo and Woosnam, two of Europe's best. You could take this one to the bank. But suddenly the Americans went sour and Faldo and Woosnam climbed over them for a stunning 2-up victory. Wadkins, with 7½ points and a 12-4-1 record in four previous Ryder Cups, pretty much took the blame on himself. His driving went wild and left Mize scrambling. "I told Jack (Nicklaus) during the round that I wasn't swinging very sharp," Wadkins said. So much so, in fact, that he asked Nicklaus to bench him for the afternoon. He wanted to get to the practice tee. "If I hadn't hit those bad shots on the front, we'd have been 6-up at the end of nine," Wadkins said. His early hooks cost them the fourth and sixth. Woosnam and Faldo whittled away on the inward nine — winners with a birdie on No. 10 and a par at No. 12, and they were only two down. Wadkins thought the Europeans got rolling at No. 14, a wicked par four of 363 yards that calls for a delicate approach across water to a sloping, elongated green. "I hit a terrible shot," Wadkins said. "You shouldn't give that hole away to a four." Wadkins hooked his three-iron tee shot into the creek. Mize took the penalty drop and put their third shot 60 feet past the flag. They bogeyed, and Woosnam chipped to three feet to set up a winning par. In the space of five holes, the American lead had shrunk from four holes to one. Woosnam and Faldo then won three of the final four holes, with only modest golf — a birdie at the 15th, then two pars against the American bogeys on the last two holes for the 2-up victory. Faldo thought the 12th and 14th were the crucial holes (the Americans bogeyed both). "Lanny hit two bad shots," he said. "That was the first time he put himself under pressure. That opened the door to us."

The Wadkins-Mize collapse couldn't have come at a worse time because the final foursome match that Friday morning brought Ballesteros into the arena. An aroused Ballesteros is a wonder to behold, and he was aroused now. It's often been said that he can't play tight courses flanked by rough and trees, that he needs room for his wondrous recovery game. Critics say this explains his two victories at Augusta National and his failure to win the U.S. Open and the U.S. PGA Championship. Muirfield Village, a Nicklaus masterpiece, is a young course, and it first came into tournament use with the debut of the Memorial Tournament in 1976. It soon was on everyone's list of the world's great tests of golf. No wide-open Augusta, it has enough rough and trees and water for anybody. This would be the setting for one of Ballesteros's finest hours. He partnered Olazabal for this foursomes match. The pairing by Jacklin was as astute as it was obvious — the steadying, dependable hand of the older champion on the rookie, plus the comforting presence of a fellow countryman. Jacklin said Olazabal, despite his youth, was not one to shake. He compared him with a young Ballesteros. "They say you don't find an old head on young shoulders," Jacklin said, "but in Northern Spain, they made one hell of a shot at it." He sent the Spaniards out against Nelson and Stewart. A rematch with Nelson was just what

Ballesteros had been waiting for. "Larry's been struggling recently," Nicklaus said, "but he's ready when they ring the bell."

Not that Nelson and Stewart were going to roll over and play dead. The Spaniards fell two behind through the fifth on two consecutive American birdies, and it took a 30-foot birdie putt by Ballesteros to get them back to even. The struggle was on, but the Americans would not lead again. Ballesteros wedged brilliantly at the par-five 15th, leaving Olazabal only three feet for a winning birdie and a 1-up lead. Ballesteros then holed from six feet at No. 18 for a par and a half — and his first victory over Nelson. It was also Nelson's first loss in Ryder Cup play. He came in with a 9-0 record. "It's nice to beat Larry Nelson after so many years," Ballesteros said. He had been brilliant. The Ryder Cup was square at 2-2.

And if Ballesteros was brilliant in the morning foursomes, what's left to say about the afternoon four-ball. One word comes hesitantly to mind — demonic. One wonders if there has ever been such a display in Ryder Cup history. He and Olazabal went out against Strange and Kite, and the match was over almost before it began. Ballesteros started by chipping in from 40 feet for a winning birdie at No. 1. "Simple," he said. "I give it a little hit, and it went in." He made five other birdies, including a roller coaster 45-footer to win the 10th and a 22-footer to win the 17th and close out the match, 2 and 1. "I think when you play for your team, for your country, for Europe...when so many people come from Europe to see you play...," Ballesteros said, "you say to yourself, 'Hey, I better play good and don't let anybody down.'" Strange and Kite were lost in the glare of Ballesteros' brilliance. But that was hardly tepid golf they were playing. They were six under par for the 17 holes, and made not one bogey. It's just that Ballesteros made six birdies and Olazabal two — and also no bogeys — to be eight under par. The victory gave the Europeans a sweep of the four afternoon matches and a 6-2 lead at the end of the day.

Nicklaus looked drawn at the interview session. "Did I watch Ballesteros?" he said. "Unfortunately, yes. He not only played his ball, he played Olazabal's ball as well. He played beautifully."

Thus ended the longest day the Americans had ever endured. "A very large percentage of Ryder Cups we've played," Nicklaus said, "we've been behind the first day." But this was different. Not only had the Americans been torpedoed after a 2-0 start, but now the European 6-2 lead was the largest first-day deficit the Americans had ever faced in Ryder Cup history.

The Spanish victory merely wrapped up a Friday afternoon that had begun with another demoralizer for the Americans. Bean, shaking off the season-long effects of a sore elbow, and Calcavecchia, had Lyle and Langer in their pocket. The Americans were two up with five holes to play — hardly a lock, but enough to force the Europeans to go for birdies. They got two — a winner at No. 14 and a half at No. 15, and then no more. But they didn't need any more. The Americans were still 1-up with two holes to play, then collapsed. Bean blamed himself. "It was my fault," he said. "We had it — we should have had it, and I hit the ball over 17 and 18." But Calcavecchia was equally responsible. At No. 17, Calcavecchia hit his tee shot into the trees. Bean was in the fairway, but hit his approach into a back bunker, barely got out, then missed a 10-foot downhill putt for the halving par. Their match was even. At No. 18, Bean was again in the fairway, but flew his six-iron approach into the back fringe. Calcavecchia's approach ended up in the back right fringe, and his attempt at a soft lob over an elbow of rough got away from him and ended up some 40 feet from the hole, still in the rough. He was out of it. Bean's downhill chip — he barely touched it — went 10 feet past on the slippery slope. He missed coming back. Lyle, meanwhile, had put his approach about 50 feet from the hole, lagged brilliantly to three feet, and holed for his par and a 1-up victory. Another had got away from the Americans. Counting the last two morning matches, it was Europe's third consecutive victory.

In the second afternoon match, Brand and Rivero spotted Crenshaw and Simpson a one-hole lead with a bogey at No. 1, then played the next eight holes in five birdies and three pars to take a 3-up lead through the turn. Brand was dazzling on the greens, getting three of the birdies from four, 30, and 25 feet. The Europeans went to their biggest lead, 4 up, when both Simpson and Crenshaw hit into bunkers at No. 10 and bogeyed. Crenshaw's six-foot birdie at No. 12 cut that lead back to three, and that's where it stayed. They halved the 15th in birdies and the 16th in pars (Simpson missing a stay-alive birdie from four feet). The Europeans had a 3 and 2 victory, and now a 4-2 lead.

It went to 5-2 moments later when Faldo and Woosnam wrapped up a 2 and 1 victory over Sutton and Pohl, ended a gritty battle that turned on sheer luck. They were all even coming to the 538-yard, par-five 11th. With a creek cutting across the fairway to catch the long drive, and with trees pinching in at the elevated green, this is a hole that demands a layup or lures the bold. Woosnam, with all that power, is easy to tempt. He went for the green on his second. "He thought he had a terrible shot," Sutton said. "He had no idea where the ball was going." Woosnam's shot went into the trees on the right, caromed off, and ended up 12 feet from the flag. Sutton just shurgged. "Dan hits the same shot in the trees," he said, "and his ball just falls down." Woosnam sank the 12-footer for the only eagle of the day, and the Europeans were 1-up. Sutton held off the inevitable with a 15-foot birdie putt at No. 13, but that was bracketed by Faldo from 18 feet at No. 12 and Woosnam from two feet at No. 14. Two more halves at par gave the Europeans a 2 and 1 victory. Sutton and Pohl had played a bogey-free four-under round, but Faldo and Woosnam topped that with a bogey-free seven-under for a 5-2 European lead. Moments later, Ballesteros signed off the day with the long birdie at No. 17, and the Europeans went to dinner with a 6-2 lead.

A brief post-mortem revealed a startling fact. In 68 holes of golf Friday afternoon, the winless Americans made only four bogeys. But the Europeans made only one — the Brand-Rivero five on the first hole of the second match. Which is to say the Euorpeans played the next 49 holes without a bogey.

"We had several matches at the end of today that we shouldn't have lost," Nicklaus said, barely hiding the edge in his voice. "And I think we did because the European players are tougher."

Jacklin wouldn't go that far. "It was a day of superior European golf — that's what you saw," he said, elated but cautious. "But that's not to say tomorrow's going to be the same. We're all too old in the tooth to think that. This game can turn around and kick you." That was what Nicklaus had in mind when he juggled his lineup. He left one pairing intact for the Saturday morning foursomes, Strange and Kite, and sent out three new ones — Sutton with Mize, Crenshaw with Stewart, and his ace in the hole, Wadkins and Nelson. They were 3-0 together in the 1979 matches, and all three were over twosomes that included Ballesteros. The Americans had a lot of damage to repair.

Saturday morning came and just that fast, all seemed right with the Americans again. They stopped the bleeding with a quick victory, Strange and Kite taking Rivero and Brand, 3 and 1. Brand gave the Europeans an instant lead with a 45-foot birdie putt at No. 1. Strange answered from 25 feet at No. 2. They jockeyed back and forth until they headed into the turn. Rivero got into bunkers at the eighth and ninth, opening the door. The Americans parred both holes for a 2-up lead and wouldn't be headed. The 10th was a masterpiece. Rivero birdied from 50 feet, seemingly winning the hole. But Strange followed him in from 25. A bogey at the 14th cut the Americans back to one, then Strange's birdie from 15 feet at No. 16 all but locked it up. A conceded birdie at the 17th brought the Americans home, 3 and 1, cutting the European lead to 6-3.

Sutton and Mize got the Americans something of a moral victory in the second match, coming from behind for a half against Faldo and Woosnam. You couldn't tell Sutton that, though. "We should have beaten them," he insisted. "I missed two short putts there at the end of the round, and Larry missed a short one earlier." The Americans led only once, on a conceded birdie at the first when the Europeans' first putt rolled off the green. The Americans fell behind by as much as two holes through the 10th, but fought their way back. Sutton soon was kicking himself. He was up tight for a birdie at No. 15 and a par at No. 16, and he missed them both from about three feet. At the 18th, he lagged the first putt to two feet and Mize dropped it for a winning par to halve the match. Europe now led, 6½-3½.

Crenshaw and Stewart were next to feel the bite of the Spaniards, but this time it was Olazabal who led the way. "Jose-Maria made all the effort today," Ballesteros said. "He putt fantastic. He's probably the best putter from 10 feet in, I would say. He has fantastic nerves." The Spaniards led all the way from No. 2, where Olazabal holed a 35-foot putt for a birdie. He birdied No. 6 from 15 feet. It was a raw match. At the ninth, Ballesteros got up and down for a bogey that won against the Americans' double bogey. That was good for a 3-up lead that held until a bogey at No. 14 and an American birdie left the Europeans just one hole to the good. Olazabal proved himself under pressure at No. 18. Ballesteros put their second shot into a bunker. Olazabal blasted out to 12 feet, and Ballesteros ran the first putt five feet past. "I was surprised myself, this green was so quick — unbelieveable," Ballesteros said. Olazabal calmly ran the five-footer in for the halving bogey and a 1-up victory, giving Europe a 7½-3½ lead. The Americans' last hope for the morning lay in the twosome of Wadkins and Nelson, but the old magic was gone. Lyle and Langer bogeyed the first hole, and still won it when Wadkins putted to 10 feet, Nelson's return ran off the green, Wadkins chipped back, and Nelson finally got it down for a double bogey. They got back to even at No. 4 on Wadkins' 10-foot birdie, and again at No. 10 on Nelson's six-foot birdie, and that was it. At the 11th, Lyle put his second two feet from the flag and got a conceded eagle, and the Europeans rolled from there to a 2 and 1 victory, and an 8½-3½ lead through Saturday morning.

The Saturday afternoon four-ball matches will go down as possibly the most fierce competition in Ryder Cup history. Consider running off five straight birdies to start. Bean and Stewart did that in the first match. So did Woosnam and Faldo in the second. It was breathtaking, seeing the red figures trailing after their names on the leaderboard like comets' tails. Consider the Spaniards with that furious finish, almost catching the Americans with four consecutive birdies. And then consider Lyle and Langer needing four birdies and an eagle on the back nine to fight off the Americans. And all just to hold ground. Neither side could advance.

Bean and Stewart were first out with the five birdies for an outward 29 en route to a 3 and 2 victory over Brand and Darcy, making his first appearance in these matches. It was as though Bean was seeking redemption for his two closing errors in the Friday morning foursomes. He held from eight feet, then 30 on the first two holes. Then Stewart from 10 and four, then Bean again, from two. Bean holed from six feet at No. 7, and Stewart from 20 at No. 9, and they made the turn at 5-up. Woosnam and Faldo were trailing red in the match just behind, against Tom Kite and Curtis Strange. The Britons' iron play was phenomenal, leaving putts of almost nothing. Woosnam birdied from two feet at No. 1, then Faldo from 4½ and four, then Woosnam from 12, then Faldo from two to wrap up the five-birdie burst. Woosnam added another at No. 7 from 3½ feet, and Faldo from eight at No. 8. They also were out in 29 and held a five-hole lead through the turn. They closed out the Americans on a half in birdies at the 14th for the most lopsided victory of the week, 5 and 4. In all, they had five birdies each.

"We went great — we started so fast," Faldo said. "We kept hitting it close. The important thing is to come in from the right angles because of the slopes. And the thing was, we never birdied the same hole. You know the other guy is in there, so you can be more aggressive on the greens. That's the key to four-ball." For Woosnam, it was more than just a victory. It was a bid for respect. "We have so much to prove in America," he said. "We've never won in America. We do have a world-class team now, and we feel we can handle the shots you need to play here." Woosnam may have put his finger on the key to these matches — Muirfield Village's firm greens. Not their speed so much — which Ballesteros had warned of and which Nicklaus thought would be an advantage to the Americans — but their firmness. "The American players are used to pitching the ball right at the flag and having it stop," Woosnam said. "We are used to playing on firm courses and greens, and we have to pitch short and have the ball roll up."

In the third match, Sutton and Mize finally stalled the Spanish bulldozer, but not without a real fight. Marvelous iron play got the Americans off with a rush. Sutton made all four of their birdies on the outward half, holing winners from seven and two feet at the first two holes. He added a third from seven feet at No. 5, then a two-putt birdie at No. 7. Against this, the Spaniards managed just two birdies, both by Olazabal, from 12 feet at No. 3 and 13 at No. 6, to snatch two holes back from the rampaging Americans. But both he and Ballesteros hit into trees at No. 9 and made the only bogey by either side, and the Americans made a winning par for a 3-up lead at the turn. But starting at No. 12, Olazabal and Ballesteros, took turns making birdies and closed to within one. The Americans kept their heads above water on two halving birdies by Mize, from three feet and two feet at No. 14 and No. 15. Ballesteros chipped in for a par three at No. 16, and Sutton holed from seven feet for a winning birdie and a 2-up lead. A half in pars at No. 17 gave the Americans a 2 and 1 victory. After three consecutive wins, the Spaniards had suffered their first loss. The momentum seemed to be shifting. But the uprising was snuffed out in the next match, the last of the day, and perhaps the hottest.

For the second time in the day, Lyle and Langer were meeting the key American twosome, Wadkins and Nelson, who had run roughshod in previous Ryder Cups. The Europeans had cooled them off in the morning foursomes, and it seemed this one would be much easier. They were deadlocked at the turn, then the Europeans got up steam. But what happened next was best described by Lyle after it was all over. "The last nine holes," he said, "were unbelieveable!"

Langer holed a 20-yard bunker shot for a winning birdie at No. 10. "It was one of my greatest shots," he said. "I had to 'flop' it up there and onto the green, over the bunker, and it trickled left and went in. If it had dropped into the bunker, I might have made five or six." Then Lyle holed a 15-foot birdie putt at the 12th, and they led by two. Then the storm came up without warning. At No. 14, Lyle birdied from 15 feet, and Wadkins followed him in from five for a half. Lyle then made a spectacular shot at No. 11, slashing a three iron some 230 yards to about 15 feet, then holing the eagle putt to wipe out the American birdie. The Americans were now three down with four to play. That ought to do it. But it didn't. "We couldn't get away from them!" Lyle said. Wadkins, an alley-fighter if golf ever saw one, won the 16th with a birdie from four feet. Then he won the 17th from 12. Now the Americans trailed by only one. It came down to the last hole. Wadkins nearly holed his approach. The ball rolled away. Then Lyle put his about four feet from the hole. The Americans conceded the birdie, received one in return, and the match ended with a half in birdies, a 1-up victory for Lyle and Langer, and a 10½-5½ lead for the European side. It should be noted that Wadkins and Nelson had played in eight under par — and lost. Golfers, spectators, writers — the afternoon left everyone limp.

"The 18th, every year, is one of our toughest holes," an admiring Nicklaus said, "and these guys are playing up there to gimmes. They're not even bothering to putt out."

Tony Jacklin slumped in a chair in the interview room. It was a while before he could speak. Finally, he did. "I never thought I'd live to see golf played like we saw it today," he said. "It was pure, unadulterated inspiration on both sides."

It was a perplexed Nicklaus who contemplated the Americans' last chance, in the singles on Sunday. "Some of the golf I saw this morning..." he said in disbelief. "I had a team of Strange and Kite out there, playing very well, and they probably would be in there right to the end with anybody else. But they weren't even in the match. They have been six under and five under, and hit by Ballesteros' blitz yesterday and Woosnam and Faldo today. Our guys feel they haven't played that badly. They've just been beaten. They know they can't be losing anything tomorrow. We lose four matches, and it's history. If they win it, it will be one of the most unbelieveable comebacks in golf. They believe they can do it. And I do, too."

Come Sunday and the 12 singles matches, and Nicklaus was up against it. You think of those old slapstick comedy movies, where the car is teetering on the brink of a cliff, and one false move will send it crashing over. The Americans were in that car, just four little points from extinction. Now for the strategy. Surely Jacklin would send his big guns out early and go for the quick kill. They already had turned back the best the Americans could throw at them for two days. Would Nicklaus counter with his strength at the top and hope for the best in the later matches? Or reverse that — hope his rookies could hold the line early, leaving the veterans to clean up later? It was a devilish choice. Wadkins and Nelson, who had such great success in previous Ryder Cups, had been out three times so far — they were even paired twice — and had not a solitary point to show for it. Nicklaus elected to hop early. He sent out one veteran, Bean, in the first match, then packed his five rookies into the next six, and saved his strength for later. Jacklin, as expected, went for the quick kill. But he saved an ace-in-the hole, just in case. He put Ballesteros in the 10th match. It proved to be the crucial move. If Saturday afternoon's four-ball was the Ryder Cup's greatest hour, the Sunday singles weren't far behind.

This is the way it went, in the order in which they finished:

— In a complete mismatch of size, Bean, 6-foot-4 and 225 pounds, met Woosnam, 5-foot-4½ and 147 pounds, in the first singles. But this wasn't boxing. "Shoot," the long-hitting Bean said later, with a grin, "it hurts when a little bitty fella outdrives you." In fact, Woosnam outdrove Bean on all but one hole. But this wasn't a driving contest, either. Woosnam fell behind immediately when he missed the first green. Bean led all the way, his biggest edge being two holes. He lost the 13th on a three-putt bogey from 25 feet. They halved on in — par-birdie-par-bogey-par — and Bean had a 1-up victory. Europe's lead was cut to 10½-6½.

— Pohl and Clark dueled all the way. Neither led by more than one hole. They fell to even when Clark bogeyed the 16th. It was settled at the last hole. Pohl crashed into rough and bunkers, and Clark made a routine par four for the 1-up victory. "It was like drawing teeth," Clark said. "But really, I'm sorry the game ended like that, in such fashion." Europe, 11½-6½.

— Mize all but had the match in hand when Torrance bogeyed No. 17. Then Mize also stumbled at No. 18, having to take a penalty drop off his drive. Torrance parred for a half, and Europe inched a half-point closer to the cup, 12-7.

— Nicklaus's strategy bore some fruit when Faldo couldn't shake Calcavecchia. Faldo led by one through the 10th, then bogeyed the 11th and 14th. Calcavecchia held that one-hole lead on halves the rest of the way and cut into the European lead with a 1-up American victory. Europe, 12-8.

— The Americans took another bite in a rookie-vs.-rookie match. Stewart edged ahead of Olazabal with a birdie at the 10th from six feet and held the lead until Olazabal drew even with a birdie at No. 15. Stewart went back out in front and stayed there for a 1-up victory when Olazabal bogeyed No. 16. Europe, 12-9.

Suddenly, the impossible seemed possible. The pace quickened:

— At 2:17 p.m., Simpson, playing in the seventh match, closed out Rivero on the 17th for a 2 and 1 victory. Rivero did not lead in the match, but he came from two down at the turn and got back to even with a birdie-two at No. 12. Simpson moved back in front with a birdie at No. 15, picked up another hole when Rivero bogeyed No. 16, and ended it with a half at No. 17. The Americans were in full swing. Europe, 12-10.

— At 2:25 p.m., the Americans got another point in the ninth match, and perhaps an unexpected one. Length is vital at Muirfield Village, and Lyle had used his superior strength to excellent advantage. He had shared in three victories and had not lost. Kite is an average hitter, but one of the grittiest players in the game. Kite disposed of Lyle with ease. He shrugged off an opening bogey that put him one down and took the lead with an eagle-three at the 531-yard fifth. Three birdies in the span of four holes put him 4-up through the 14th. He dropped one hole, then closed out Lyle in halves at No. 16 for a 3 and 2 victory. Europe's lead was down to a point, 12-11.

— At 2:29 p.m., it went back up in a strange match, the sixth on the schedule. Darcy, after losing the first hole to Crenshaw's 40-foot birdie, led by three at the turn. Crenshaw, that master on the greens, had broken his putter after three-putting the sixth from 50 feet to drop his second consecutive hole. Some say he slammed the putter into the turf in considerable anger. Crenshaw said he merely was tapping at an acorn, and that the putter, weakened after some 15 years of use, snapped near the head. At any rate, Crenshaw putted with his one iron most of the way after that. And to deadly effect. He was three down through No. 7 and again through No. 11, then won three consecutive holes with two pars and a birdie. He went one ahead when Darcy bogeyed the 16th. At No. 17, he opened the door when he took two to escape a fairway bunker and Darcy birdied from three feet. Now the 18th would strike again. Crenshaw drove into the water, dropped, and hit his third into a bunker. Darcy bunkered his second but got up and down for his par and a 1-up victory. Europe, 13-11.

— At 2:46 p.m., in the eighth match on the schedule, came perhaps the strangest halve in Ryder Cup history. Nelson led Langer by three with seven to play and the Americans were all but pocketing the point. Then Nelson bogeyed the next three, against two pars and a birdie by Langer, and they were even at No. 14. They they were on the 18th green, still even and both facing par putts — Nelson from about two feet, Langer from a little less. Langer said something to Nelson, then they shook hands and left the green. "He said, 'Do you want to pick up?'" Nelson said. "And I said sure." It was a critical halve. In a way, it was reminiscent of Nicklaus' conceding a two-foot putt to Jacklin on the final hole of the Ryder Cup at Royal Birkdale in 1969. That resulted in the only tie in Ryder Cup history. Jacklin recalled the incident. "Jack understood my place in British golf that year," he said. "And he told me, 'I don't think you would have missed that putt, but I wouldn't want to give you the opportunity under the circumstances.'" The circumstances were somewhat different this time. This was the eighth match, not the last, and the Americans were trailing by two points. Not only did the championship still hang in the balance, but a tie would keep the cup in Europe. "I just didn't feel he'd miss," Nelson said later. "Besides, it's still a gentlemen's game." The double concession left the Europeans on the verge of victory. Europe, 13½-11½.

— At 2:48 p.m., the matter became academic. Ballesteros, after wobbling briefly, closed out Strange with a halve in pars at No. 17 for a 2 and 1 victory. That was the magical point. Europe — 14½-11½, and for the first time in history not only a second consecutive Ryder Cup victory but the first on American soil.

The rest was formality. Wadkins beat Brown, 3 and 2, in the next-to-last match to come in, and as if to punctuate the Americans' frustration, Sutton caught Brand with a birdie at No. 17, then failed to close him out at No. 18. They halved their match for the final score: Europe 15, United States 13.

The Europeans, of course, whooped it up. They even danced a kind of team jig on the 18th green, with Jacklin in the middle. Jacklin apologized. "We do get carried away at times," Jacklin said, "But it's largely because we got our brains beat out for so long." Nicklaus shrugged. "Don't worry about it," he said. "The way we played it this week, I think I'll dig it up." The barb was aimed at his own men. Nicklaus was not a happy man. In the team matches, the Americans lost twice at the final hole. The toll was worse in the singles — two matches lost there, and two halved when victory slipped away. "I don't want you to single any one man out," Nicklaus told the press. "It's not that they lost there, but that the Europeans won there." Nicklaus was a bit like a parent asking, "Where did I go wrong?" He took some blame on himself. "I think I left just a little too much to do," he said. "Obviously, that Friday afternoon match (the European sweep) killed us."

Jacklin had little to add to what his team had just said in three days of competition, except to say, "I'm the happiest man in Europe."

It wasn't just a victory, but a sense of fulfillment. This goes to the core of the post-match analysis. It had seemed clear enough, in all kinds of international competition, that the Americans no longer had a stranglehold on golf. This proved it beyond all doubt. But this victory meant more than that. It also proved that European golf had truly come of age.

7. The Dunhill Nations Cup

Someone with a gift for putting a wry twist on the obvious once observed that politics makes for strange bedfellows. Golf is a lot like that. For much different reasons, happily. So when the third Dunhill Nations Cup dawned at the Old Course at St. Andrews the first week of October, men who were such inspired allies the week before in Europe's Ryder Cup victory were now opponents. Broad allegiances suddenly narrowed, and not only that, but two impressive principles were at stake: national pride, same as in the Ryder Cup, but this time money as well — $1 million, the richest team event in golf. Sixteen three-man teams from around the world converged on St. Andrews. Prize money ranged from $100,000 to each member of the winning team down to $7,500 each for first-round losers.

Scotland sent a solid front of Ryder Cuppers — Sandy Lyle, Sam Torrance, and Gordon Brand Jr. The three showed up in kilts for opening ceremonies Thursday evening. "It was my idea," Lyle said. "It's sure to get us fired up with patriotism." Some wondered whether jet lag plus post-Ryder Cup celebrations might have left the Europeans off their game. "You've got to be kidding," Torrance said. "Playing for Scotland is the only incentive I need. And besides, this week we are getting paid!" From England came two — Nick Faldo, the British Open champion, and Howard Clark, joined by "the other Brand," Gordon J. Brand. From Spain came two more Ryder Cuppers, Jose-Maria Olazabal and Jose Rivero, with Jose-Maria Canizares the third man. Ireland sent Eamonn Darcy, who beat Ben Crenshaw on the last hole in the Ryder Cup, along with Ronan Rafferty and Des Smyth.

Only four Ryder Cuppers were not in the Dunhill field. Spain's Seve Ballesteros did not play. West Germany's Bernhard Langer was playing on the American tour at the time of the qualifier in the spring. Ken Brown was not selected for the Scottish team, and Ian Woosnam of Wales was absent against his will. Woosnam was part of the Welsh team, with Philip Parkin and Mark Mouland, that was eliminated in the European qualifier by the Danes, who then were ousted by Sweden and France.

Only one Ryder Cupper was on the American team, and that was Curtis Strange, the leading money-winner on the American tour. He was joined by Mark O'Meara, who had won the Lawrence Batley International, and D.A. Weibring, winner of the Western Open. The hot subject, of course, was the American defeat in the Ryder Cup. "Forget all about that," Strange said, shrugging off any weighty international implications. "This is a different format, a different event, and a different team. D.A., Mark and I have nothing to prove this week."

All eyes, however, were on the marauding Australians. They had won the first two Dunhill Cups, and looked no less formidable with Peter Senior, making his first appearance in place of David Graham from the 1986 title team. Two powerhouses returned — Rodger Davis and, of course, Greg Norman. But this was not the devastating Greg Norman of a year ago. In 1986, Norman won twice in the United States, four times in Europe, including the British Open, and four times in Australia. He came to the 1987 Dunhill Cup as No. 1 on the Sony World Rankings, but still looking for his second victory of the year. He had won only the Australian Masters.

Norman also arrived looking something like a Viking. He had just spent two weeks hunting and fishing in Australia, and hadn't bathed or shaved during the sojourn. He was still wearing a shaggy reddish-brown beard, an unexpected contrast to his blond mane.

Lyle picked up Strange's theme. "I suppose we're still on a high after what happened Sunday," he said. "But that's in the past now, and walking out on a golf course thinking you've won the Ryder Cup won't do anything for you. A Scotland-England final would be great for the fans, but the Americans and Australians won't be pushovers." Faldo wasn't quite so reserved. "I see no reason why it shouldn't be an England-Scotland final."

It wasn't merely possible, it was inevitable if they kept winning. The seedings and draw would see to that. This was the seeding: 1-Australia, 2-United States, 3-Scotland, 4-England, 5-Spain, 6-Ireland, 7-Japan, 8-Canada. Six teams came in through qualifiers: France, Italy, New Zealand, the Philippines, Sweden, and Malaysia; and two were invited, Mexico, representing Latin America, and Zimbabwe, representing Africa.

For the order of play, the higher seeded team got the first choice, the lower seed the other two. The play consisted of three two-man games at stroke play. The winner of each game won one point for his country. Tied games were settled by a sudden-death playoff, but only if the result would determine the outcome of a match.

When play began, even the British press, some of which had panned the format the first two years, were converted. This was the hottest Dunhill Cup yet, and the format seemed tailor-made for the Old Course, for one big reason.

Every quality golf course has at least one pivotal hole. But when it comes to sheer domination, No. 17 at the Old Course stands supreme in all the world. This is the notorious Road Hole, a 461-yard par four with a road a few feet to the right of the green, and the Road Bunker on the left, nudging the green where it is only 15 paces wide. The hole is a slight dogleg left that plays over the edge of the Old Course Golf and Country Club that juts out into the fairway. No. 17 is like one of those ship graveyards that terrorize mariners even from a distance. It takes luck as well as skill to get past them alive. Norman was to suffer at that hole, but he forgave it. "I don't know how you play that hole, I really don't," he said. "But I think it is a great hole, and I enjoy playing it every time, whether I walk off with a nine or a three."

Domination? No. 17 played to an average of 4.72 strokes, decided the outcome in five of the 30 games, and figured heavily in four others. In 90 playings, there were 41 bogeys, 11 sixes, one seven, and — the poor soul — a 10. It yielded only three birdies.

Only one of them was "routine." That was the 40-foot putt by Weibring in the second round. Then there were two of the "other" kind. Zimbabwe's William Koen, in the process of falling to Torrance in the first round, hit a one-iron approach that caromed off the old stone wall and came to rest 15 feet from the cup. He didn't look at this gift horse for very long. He holed the putt. In the second round, Canada's Richard Zokol, in a real battle with Norman, lay 90 feet from the hole. Norman looked on in awe and maybe a touch of horror as Zokol sank that cross-country putt for his three.

It didn't take long for No. 17 to rear its formidable head. It happened on opening day, Thursday, Canada vs. New Zealand. Canada's Dave Barr led off with a 71-75 victory over Bruce Soulsby. Then came a 74-74 tie when Dan Halldorson's four-stroke lead on New Zealand's Greg Turner began to disappear with a double bogey at No. 17. A playoff became unnecessary when Zokol, with a bogey-birdie finish, scored a 72-74 win over Frank Nobilo, who fell out of a tie with a double bogey at the 17th. Canada advanced, 2½-½. The second match of the first round was notable first for having six players almost completely unknown outside the Far East — the Malaysians against seventh-seeded Japan, whose familiar names had stayed home for the Japan Open the following week. Surprisingly, Malaysia jumped out to a 1-0 lead on Marimuthu Ramayah's 74-75 victory over Koichi Suzuki, who bogeyed No. 17. Nobuo Serizawa evened things for Japan with a 70-76 win over Sahabudin Yusof. So the outcome hung on the last match. The Road Hole was about to strike like an assassin.

Malaysia's golf-happy Crown Prince of Pahang was in the stands at No. 17, and he had to be proud. His unheralded countrymen were about to defeat the mighty Japanese. Just one more win would do it, and Zainal Abidin Yusof, brother of Sahabudin, was leading Japan's Nobumitsu Yuhara by a stroke coming to the 17th. Then unfolded one of the cruelest episodes in Old Course history. Crueler even than the nine suffered by Japan's Tommy Nakajima in the 1978 British Open, when the Road Bunker swallowed his first putt. To put it bluntly, Yusof took 10. But what a 10. He did it without getting into the bunker. His approach shot rolled onto the road, which is in play. He tried to chip on, but the ball failed to clear the three-foot bank and rolled back to him. He wouldn't risk that again. He took his putter this time. The crowd watched in silent horror as it took Yusof four tries to climb that little bank, then three more putts to get down. He had come to the hole at two over par and leading by one. He left at eight over and trailing by five, and lost, 75-80. Japan advanced, 2-1.

Somehow, the shattered Yusof found the ability to smile. "I do one better than Nakajima," he said.

Yusof was merely the bloodiest victim. The cruelest blow fell on Sweden's Mats Lanner. Call it mental lapse, pressure, or whatever, but Norman and the Australians breathed a collective sigh of relief. Lanner was on the verge of knocking the Aussies out when he crashed at No. 17.

The Swedes, who are rising fast in European golf, were leading Australia by 1-0 in the first round on Ove Sellberg's 69-75 defeat of Davis in the first game. Lanner, winner of the 1987 Epson Match Play, was three under par and leading Norman by one stroke coming to the 17th. The upset of the tournament was about to happen. Lanner's approach shot came to rest on the front of the green, in a little depression lined in white as ground under repair. Now the infamous Road Bunker came into the picture. Old Course lore is full of tales of golfers who have putted into the bunker from the front of the green. A ball just slightly off line to the left will be pulled into the bunker, as though some capricious magnet were at work. No doubt that was working on Lanner's mind. But first, he took relief from the ground under repair, then found he was standing in the depression he had just lifted the ball from. So he took relief again. But he had agonized long over this process. Norman, watching, could practically read his mind. "When he lined it up straight with the hole," Norman said, "he looked at the bunker, then decided to putt farther to the right. All the time, the pressure built up. When he changed his mind, it threw him all out." So much so that in trying to steer clear of the bunker, Lanner putted too far to the right. The ball ran off the right side of the green and onto the road. His first return didn't make it, his second did, and he had to sink an 18-foot putt just to save a six. Norman, safely on the green, parred. The two-stroke swing lifted him into a one-stroke lead, and he went on to win, 70-71. Australia had life, and then it had the match, 2-1, when Senior beat Anders Forsbrand in the final game, 67-70.

"I'm glad we won, but I am sad at what happened at No. 17," Norman said, "Unfortunately for Mats, he may have been caught up in a wrong situation at the wrong time. I'm impressed with his talent, but he didn't have the experience of settling himself down and making the right decision."

So the Aussies advanced, and so did the possibility of a Scotland-England final.

Scotland ousted Zimbabwe, 3-0, but not without sweating a bit. Lyle was one under par for five holes, yet tailed Tim Price by two before winning, 71-73. Brand birdied four of the last five outward holes, and came home with a 70-72 win over Anthony Edwards. But Brand was still at work while Torrance, in the game behind, was struggling with Koen. Torrance eagled the fifth from four feet, but didn't get real breathing room until Koen took three consecutive bogeys on the front. Torrance looked safe, but then staggered through the Road Hole with a double-bogey six to Koen's miracle off-the-wall birdie. Both parred No. 18, and Torrance mopped his brow, a 72-73 winner. Scotland had a 3-0 sweep. "That was a real tough one — a lot harder than I expected," Torrance said.

England had only one uncertain moment in its 2½-½ victory over Mexico — the 71-71 tie between Ernesto Perez Acosta and Clark in the opening game. Faldo breezed past Carlos Espinoza, 70-75, and Brand past Feliciano Esparza, 74-81, for the victory. The United States swept Italy after an early scare. "I was three under at one point," Strange said, "but in these matches you're not going to have a walk in the park no matter who you're playing." That said it all in his 71-72 victory over Costantino Rocca. Strange eagled the fifth from 12 feet to go to three under par and three ahead, but Rocca aced the 178-yard eighth with a five iron to get within one. The other two American victories came easier, Weibring over Sylvio Grappasonni, 69-77, and O'Meara over Giuseppe Cali, 70-75.

Spain had no difficulty with the Philippines. Rivero led off with a 68-75 win over Frankie Minoza, Olazabal followed, 71-80 over Rudy Lavares, and Canizares wrapped it up against Eddie Bagtas, 72-77. Ireland trailed in only one match in sweeping France. That was in the second game, when Darcy took seven at No. 9 to slip one stroke behind Gery Watine. Watine then came home in 40, and fell 72-76. In the first game, Rafferty dismissed Michel Tapia, 71-76, and in the last — the only game of the week in which neither player had a birdie or eagle — Smyth beat Emmanuel Dussart, 74-76.

The Dunhill Cup began in 1985 and had managed to go 122 matches without a playoff. And then there were three in succession.

First, O'Meara of the United States vs. Japan's Serizawa. They were the 123rd match in Dunhill's young history, and the deciding match after a 1-1 split in the first two games. Strange had got the Americans off and flying, 68-70, against Suzuki, running up a four-stroke lead at the turn that included his second eagle-three at No. 5, where he put a four-wood second shot to 25 feet. Japan got back to level in the next match when Yuhara came from behind to beat Weibring, 69-75. So it all came down to Serizawa and O'Meara.

"I hadn't played him before and didn't know who he was," O'Meara said later. But he got a convincing introduction. He made the turn in 34 and found Serizawa right with him. The lead changed hands four times before they tied at 70-70. Back to square one for the first playoff in Dunhill history.

O'Meara narrowly missed a quick victory at No. 1 when his 12-foot birdie putt lipped out. At No. 2, he pitched brilliantly to 18 inches but before he could tap in for the win, Serizawa rammed in a 40-foot birdie putt from the front of the green. Finally, the fatal crack: Serizawa came up short of the green at No. 3, sent his first putt eight feet past, and two-putted from there. O'Meara two-putted from 12 feet for his winning four and a 2-1 American victory.

"I don't need it any more exciting than that," O'Meara said with a tight smile. "I realized Weibring was going to lose and that Strange would win. That's pressure — playing for two other guys as well as yourself." Which pretty much captures the essence of the Dunhill format.

Then came the question of the status of American golf, brought into sharper focus by the Ryder Cup loss. "Watson, Nicklaus, and Trevino dominated for so long," O'Meara replied. "Now we realize that throughout the world, players have reached top caliber and are now capable of winning."

Meanwhile, the Canadians and the defending Australians were locked in the tensest match in the three years of the Dunhill Cup. No sooner had O'Meara and Serizawa wrapped up the first-ever playoff than two more followed in succession.

First came Barr and Senior. They tied at 73-73. Barr birdied No. 1 in the playoff, and Canada had a 1-0 lead. What followed was a kind of time warp. In the second game, Norman and Zokol dueled for five extra holes. But before they could settle it, the third game was decided. Little wonder. Davis threw a stunning course-record 63 at Halldorson (73) in the final game. The match was then square, 1-1, so everyone had to sweat out the Norman-Zokol playoff. On paper, it was a mismatch. Zokol was not even in the top 200 of the Sony World Rankings, and he was going head-to-head against No. 1.

If Zokol was intimidated, it didn't show. He battled Norman even through the turn, both at one-under-par 35. Norman charged with three birdies over the next seven holes, and he was leading by three coming to — where else? — No. 17. Later, Norman could only shrug and grin. "There I was, cruising with a three-shot lead, thinking of no danger at all," he said. "And all of a sudden I'm walking out tied with Zokol at two under." It was this quick: Zokol rolled in the 90-footer to pluck the third and last birdie from the

Road Hole in this Dunhill. Norman was on the road with his second shot, failed to get on the green with his putter, then chipped. That put him five feet from the flag. Then he two-putted for a six. The match was all square, and stayed that way when both bogeyed No. 18 for a 71-71 tie.

As they headed for the first tee, Davis was wrapping up his 10-stroke victory over Halldorson to even the match at 1-1. Now Davis would have to squirm for about an hour during the playoff — was his 63 the winner, or merely a record? The Norman-Zokol playoff would decide. But not so fast. Zokol and Norman halved the first three holes in pars, then crossed over and halved No. 16 in pars. And now what could be more fitting? — the Road Hole. "I respect that hole more than any other in the world," Norman had said. And he proved it. This time, he laid up short of the green with a five-iron, some 140 feet from the flag. Zokol went for the kill, and ended up the victim instead. His second ended up on the road, and while he was taking two to get back to the green, and two-putting for a six, Norman rolled that 140-footer to within a foot and tapped in his winning four. Australia survived, 2-1.

Now Davis could celebrate. His 63 began quietly, with a par at No. 1. Then he ran off four consecutive birdies on putts of 30 feet, eight feet, 18 inches, and five feet. He holed from three feet at No. 7 and from four at No. 9. He eagled No. 10 from eight feet, and birdied No. 14 from four. He said his putter was hot. Talk about understatement. The 63 included two-putt pars that ranged from 23 feet to 80 feet.

Here was a card for the books:

```
Par out    4 4 4 4 5 4 4 3 4 — 36
Davis out  4 3 3 3 4 4 3 3 3 — 30
Par in     4 3 4 4 5 4 4 4 4 — 36 — 72
Davis in   2 3 4 4 4 4 4 4 4 — 33 — 63
```

"With the pin positions the way they were today," Norman said, "that score was worth a 59."

Davis wasn't quibbling. "It's a great thrill to hold the record at St. Andrews," he said. "But today, it was team more than my score."

Davis' 63 broke the previous course record of 65 set 27 years earlier by Neil Coles in the 1970 British Open and tied by Faldo in the 1979 British PGA, Norman in the 1985 Dunhill Cup, and Davis himself in the 1986 Dunhill Cup. It figured to last a long time. In fact, it wouldn't last more than 48 hours.

What with the playoffs and Davis' 63, it was almost anticlimactic that Scotland and England continued to roll.

Scotland jumped into the lead over Ireland on Torrance's 69-74 win over Rafferty. The game was tight briefly when Torrance bogeyed No. 11 and fell into a tie at par, but he regained the lead with a birdie-bogey exchange at No. 13. Lyle wrapped up the match for Scotland with a back-nine 32 for a 67-72 victory over Darcy. Smyth saved a point for Ireland, breaking from a tie on two birdies at No. 1 for one-bogey 67 to a 73 by Brand. It wasn't that easy for England. After a tie at par 36 at the turn, Howard Clark bogeyed the 13th and double-bogeyed the 14th, then double-bogeyed the 17th for an inward 41, and lost to Rivero, 72-77. England got square in the second game, with Faldo turning in a relentlessly steady one-birdie

71 while Olazabal staggered down the last three holes for an inward 41 for a 77. Olazabal was at even par and just a stroke behind when he drove into the Principal's Nose bunker at No. 16. Trying for the green, he knocked his second shot out of bounds and took six. He drove out of bounds at the 17th and took seven. The decisive game, and the last one of the day, gave England the match. It was effective, but not pretty. Brand led by a stroke at No. 12, made three bogeys and only one birdie over the next six holes, and won by three over Canizares, 71-74. Canizares, two under par through No. 11, proceeded to double bogey No. 13 and take bogeys at the 15th and 17th for an inward 39.

In the semi-finals Saturday, then, it was Scotland against the United States for the third consecutive year, followed by England against Australia. But an England-Scotland final looked doomed. While Scotland was doing well against the Americans that gray, breezy Saturday morning, England was getting mauled.

Coming down the stretch, the England-Australia match was shaping up as a mere formality. The Aussies were collectively 13 under par and rolling. Senior was five under par and four ahead of Clark with four holes to play. Norman was five under and three ahead of Brand with two to play. And Davis was three under and three ahead of Faldo with three to play. In gamblers' parlance, that's called a mortal lock. What happened next has a different name: Myth.

Incredibly, despite those leads, Norman was the only Aussie able to win. He came from one behind at the turn, he went three ahead, then bogeyed No. 17 and parred No. 18 to Brand's par-birdie finish to win by one, 68-69. That evened the match at 1-1. Senior had already fallen into a nightmare and lost to Clark, 73-74, in the first game. Senior was sitting pretty, five under and four ahead through the 14th. He bogeyed No. 15, but his lead was still a very comfortable three strokes with three holes to play. But next came an episode that belongs in Madame Tussaud's. The scene was No. 16, a 382-yard par-four.

Senior drove into the bunker; failed to get out on his first try; sliced his third out of bounds; took a penalty drop in the bunker; finally exploded out; hit a nine-iron to 30 feet; and three-putted for a nine. "How can you do that?" the shaken Senior muttered, leaving the green. Clark couldn't believe his luck. He had driven out of bounds and made seven, and still picked up two strokes. Now he was only one behind. A moment later, Senior bogeyed No. 17 to Clark's par, and they were tied. At the decisive 18th, Clark wrecked his nine-iron hitting his approach off the road, but still got the ball to seven feet, and holed the putt for a winning birdie. Norman was right behind, with his narrow victory over Brand for the 1-1 tie, and now it was all up to Faldo and Davis in the last game.

"It's just the sort of thing you dream of," Faldo said later, "and when it happens, it just seems not possible."

Davis holed from 10 feet for a birdie at No. 13 to go four under par and take a four-shot lead with just five holes to play. Then while Faldo ground along in pars, Davis lost his touch on the approach shots. He bogeyed No. 14, three-putting from 65 feet; saved par at No. 15 with two putts from 70, then bogeyed No. 16 with two putts from 55. His lead was down to two strokes. At the Road Hole, it disappeared completely. His three-iron approach was wide to the left, his sand wedge pitch left him 40 feet from the flag, and he three-putted for a six. Faldo parred, and they were tied. Then Faldo birdied No. 18 from 15 feet, and the Australian grip on the Dunhill Cup was broken. Faldo won, 71-72, giving England a 2-1 victory. An England-Scotland final it would be.

The Scots had had no trouble with the Americans in the earlier match — no heroics, no fireworks, no suspense. Just workmanlike golf. Torrance led off against Strange, went three ahead at the turn, and coasted to a 69-73 victory. Lyle spotted O'Meara a stroke with a bogey at No. 1, then birdied four of the next seven holes to go three ahead through No. 8. He won, 70-71, and Scotland had the match, 2-0. The final game was a formality, then, Brand edging out Weibring, 73-74, for a Scottish sweep. "You learn something everyday," said the personable Weibring, on discovering the hidden charms of the Old Course in his first visit. He was referring to the 13th, where a par would have put him a stroke ahead. He took a double-bogey six instead. "I drove into the Coffins bunker, but I got it out just where I wanted it, about 50, 60 yards ahead," he said. "And when I got to my ball, there it was — in another bunker."

So the Americans were out for the third year running, and the new strength of European golf was underlined once again. The British press was crowing on Sunday.

The Americans saw it another way. "People don't give other golfers enough credit," Strange said. "I've known these European players for 12 years. I know they can play. But the (American) press doesn't know it."

An Englishman approached Clark on Saturday night. "If you think you were playing away from home last week (in the Ryder Cup)," he said, laughing, "wait till tomorrow!"

"When it's a confrontation between England and Scotland," the man said to an outsider, "it could be tiddlywinks — it doesn't matter." So forget the United States, forget Spain, forget anybody else. Now it was Scotland against "the Auld Enemy." Bannockburn revisited — with putters. But before the grand battle could begin, something else grabbed the attention of the nearly 9,500 who came out on that gray Sunday.

When it came to course records, Davis' 63 on Friday had seemed as safe as the Bank of Scotland. So safe, in fact, that Dunhill, the sponsor, awarded him a wristwatch the very next day. That watch had ticked away less than 48 hours before a Dunhill spokesman sighed and said with a grin on Sunday, "Well, I suppose now we'll have to give Curtis Strange the entire factory!" If Davis was playing a different game on Friday, Strange was playing in another world on Sunday. How else do you explain a no-bogey, 10-under-par 62 on the Old Course?

"There is no greater place in the world to have a course record," Strange said. "I have a few course records at home — maybe seven or eight — but this is more exciting than any other course record or low score."

Poor Norman. He had gone undefeated through 11 previous Dunhill Cup matches. But this one, the final match of the battle for third place, was hardly under way before he knew it was not his day. Strange went around the loop like an Indianapolis racer going through a turn. Starting at No. 7, he ripped through six consecutive birdies to go to eight under par with six holes to play. He added another birdie at No. 15, dodged a sure bogey at No. 17, and birdied No. 18.

Strange needed only 27 putts overall, and had 10 one-putt greens, all for birdies. He had only one three-putt on those immense carpets, and that was for a par five from about 80 feet at No. 5, a hole he had eagled in the first two rounds. For posterity's sake, this is Strange's 62:

No. 1 —Birdie three: Driver, sand wedge, 18-foot putt.
No. 2 —Par four: Driver, eight-iron, two putts from 14 feet.
No. 3 —Birdie three: Driver, wedge, seven-foot putt.
No. 4 —Par four: Driver, four-iron, two putts from 28 feet.
No. 5 —Par five: Driver, five-wood, three putts from 80 feet.
No. 6 —Par four: Driver, sand wedge, two putts from 26 feet.
No. 7 —Birdie three: Driver, sand wedge, five-inch putt.
No. 8 —Birdie two: Five iron, 16-foot putt.
No. 9 —Birdie three: Driver, nine-iron, 12-foot putt. (Out in 31)
No. 10—Birdie three: Driver, sand wedge, four-foot putt.
No. 11—Birdie two: Seven-iron, 15-foot putt.
No. 12—Birdie three: Driver, wedge, 25-foot putt.
No. 13—Par four: Driver, two-iron, two putts from 81 feet.
No. 14—Par five: Driver, three-iron, five-iron, two putts from 28 feet.
No. 15—Birdie three: Driver, five-iron, 16-foot putt.
No. 16—Par four: Driver, seven-iron, two putts from 14 feet.
No. 17—Par four: Driver, four-iron, two putts from 72 feet.
No. 18—Birdie three: Driver, wedge, 14-foot putt.
(Back in 31. Total — 62)

Strange credited his 62 to a number of things — to the condition of the course, the work of the superintendent, the wet summer and the watering system that made the greens uncharacteristically receptive to shots, and to the absence of wind. And to himself. "We did catch St. Andrews on a calm day," he said. "But there must have been other calm days here — the course is a *few* years old — and nobody ever shot 62 before."

Norman was shooting a strong round, a one-bogey 70, but it paled against Strange's 62. He was just along for the ride and he knew it. "If a man's got to go," Norman said, "let it be to a 62 on the Old Course. It was great just to see such a round at close quarters." Strange's outburst ruined what might have been a tight finish. The Americans had taken a 1-0 lead on O'Meara's 71-72 victory over Senior. Davis squared it for the Australians with a 70-71 victory over Weibring, who win or lose had something besides golf on his mind. His wife, Kristy, had just given birth to their third child back in Dallas. Good theater, then, said that Strange and Norman should have had a great shootout in the deciding game. But Strange hadn't read the script. His rampage gave the Americans third place, 2-1, with a sweat.

Records notwithstanding, the stage belonged to the England-Scotland finale. Two British Open champions were matched in the first game — Faldo against Lyle, strength vs. strength. The Scottish pick struck many as odd, including Faldo. "It was the obvious choice, but still I was surprised when they came up with it," he said. Ordinarily, each side would send its strongest player against a lesser player in hopes of nailing down one point, and hope for the best in the other match. But Scotland went for the kill early, counting on Lyle to knock out Faldo. Strategy didn't matter this time. It was a question of who was hot, and that was Faldo.

Lyle made only one bogey, but the last he saw of Faldo was at the sixth tee. Faldo had birdied No. 1 from two feet, Lyle from six. They traded pars to the fifth, where both birdied again, Faldo two-putting from 60 feet, Lyle from 32. So they came to No. 6 all square. Then Faldo took off. He birdied the sixth from eight feet, and Lyle took his only bogey, two-putting from 14 feet after bunker trouble. Faldo went ahead by three with a birdie from 12 feet at No. 8. He dropped his only stroke at No. 10, on three putts from 45 feet, and got it back immediately with a 12-foot birdie at No. 11. Lyle answered him at No. 12 with a birdie from one foot. Then Lyle settled into a run of five pars, and Faldo stretched his lead — three ahead with a three-foot birdie at No. 14, then four ahead from 12 feet at No. 15. Lyle's struggles were finally rewarded at the 18th, where he birdied from three feet. Too late. It was Faldo, 66-69, and England, 1-0.

Not to worry, as the popular expression put it. Scotland would get that point back in the next pairing, a clear mismatch: Torrance, a 17-time winner, including the 1987 Italian Open and a Ryder Cup hero, against England's Brand, best known for winning in Africa and for a runnerup finish to Norman in the 1986 British Open. According to the script, Torrance would win here, and the championship would be decided in the last match — Clark vs. "the other Brand," Scotland's. The Dunhill Cup was building to a feverish finish.

But England's Brand hadn't read that script. He was two ahead through the fourth, on his eight-foot birdie at No. 1 and Torrance's three-putt bogey at No. 4. Torrance birdied No. 5 from 15 feet, but still lost ground because Brand eagled the hole, firing a four-wood to 15 feet and dropping the putt. Brand was now three ahead. He went to four under par and four ahead with a birdie from two feet at No. 7, and took a 32-36 lead through the turn. Torrance caught fire coming home, getting three birdies in four holes — from four feet at No. 13, from four at No. 14, and from 10 at No. 16. It wasn't enough. Brand was even hotter. He went to six under par with birdies at No. 10, from eight feet, and No. 11, from 25. At No. 13, he fired the killer.

Clark, playing in the match behind, heard a huge roar up ahead. "I didn't know what it was," he said. "Then I found out Gordon had holed out a five-iron. In fact, Gordon didn't know he had holed it." Brand laughed at himself. "I thought Nick had made an eagle up ahead," he said.

Poor Torrance. There he was, trailing by six strokes with six holes to play, when suddenly, "There was a glimmer of hope for me at No. 13," he said. Brand's tee shot found a fairway bunker. That ought to hurt, maybe open the door. Brand had to blast his ball out, and he still had 175 yards to the green. Maybe he could salvage a bogey. He slashed away with his five-iron. Seconds later, a roar erupted ahead.

"When I got to the green and saw only one ball, I thought I had hit mine in the bunker. Then I found it in the hole," Brand said, with a big grin. "It's just as well. I hadn't read that green all week."

"That was it," Torrance said.

Brand added another birdie at No. 15, from five feet, had no trouble parring the 17th, and came home in 32 for an eight-under-par 64 — the second-best round of the day, third-best of the tournament, and a five-stroke victory over Torrance. And England's first Dunhill Cup.

Scotland's Brand then defeated the struggling Clark in the final match, 68-73, to win a point and avert an English sweep.

"It's great to be on a winning team," Brand said. "I've never been on a winning team. I have always been a jinx."

The 2-1 decision didn't tell the complete story of the English victory. Torrance did. "All the Scots have broken 70 today," he said, "and we have been beaten. What can you say? They played great golf in perfect conditions. We just got hammered, Sandy and I."

Someone noted that Scotland had three Ryder Cuppers and England two. Brand turned his self-deprecation into a laugh. "But we," he said, giving that self-conscious grin of his, "had the Nigerian Open champion."

8. The World Match Play Championship

One of the mysteries of the Suntory World Match Play Championship, first held in 1964, was that a British player had never won. Neil Coles got to the final that inaugural year but lost to Arnold Palmer, and in subsequent years Sandy Lyle three times and Nick Faldo once went all the way before being beaten on the last day. Thus a victory by Ian Woosnam, the son of a Welsh farmer and already the leading money winner on the European Tour, was a very special landmark. Yet it is arguable whether the 1987 championship will be remembered more for Woosnam's victory or the Great Storm.

The Great Storm struck the night after the first round had been suspended in the latter stages. A fine Thursday morning had gradually turned into rain as Mark McNulty and Howard Clark, Lyle and David Ishii, Seve Ballesteros and Katsunari Takahashi, and Woosnam and Sam Randolph battled to see who would meet the four seeded players: defending champion Greg Norman, Larry Mize (Masters champion), Scott Simpson (U.S. Open champion) and Faldo (British Open champion).

It already was a wet autumn, two inches of rain having been absorbed during the previous week. Although in spendid condition, Wentworth was unable to take any more prolonged downpours. It was not long before the staff was facing a losing battle. Pools formed all over the greens as fast as they were removed. The impassable point proved to be the 13th green, and one after another the four matches came to a halt. McNulty was two up on Clark, Lyle was tied with Ishii, Ballesteros was two up on Takahashi and Woosnam was four up on Randolph. These positions reflected a great deal of recovery work, but more of that later.

Failing to complete the opening matches, the schedule had to be reconsidered. Matches would be resumed, it was decided, at 8 a.m. the following day, and the second round would be reduced to 27 holes. It was not a totally satisfactory arrangement, but the championship would be back on schedule by nightfall Friday.

No one had bargained for what the early hours Friday would bring. Not even the weather forecasters gave any warning, having misread two merging depressions in the Bay of Biscay. In the south of England it proved to be the worst storm in not only living memory, but the worst for just over 300 years. Fifteen lives were lost, hundreds of thousands of trees uprooted, cars smashed, roofs blown off, and sheds lifted from one garden to another. The trail of destruction was reminiscent in its way of the Blitz during the Second World War. People were advised not to go to work and in many cases it was impossible to get there anyway.

Ballesteros was expecting a car to pick him up at 6:45 a.m. When it failed to arrive, he tried to telephone the club but the lines were down. Roads on the estate were blocked by fallen trees and Ballesteros had to climb over them. "It was," he said, "like Vietnam but without the guns." When he got to the clubhouse there was no one there and he decided to give it another two hours before trying again. Clark began his four-mile journey by car but had to abandon it half way and did the rest on foot. Vicky Richards, the tournament secretary, took seven different forms of transportation to get to the club. It took her two and a half hours instead of 30 minutes.

The golf course did not escape damage. Many trees bordering the fairways were down and a local rule was introduced so that any ball that came to rest among the fallen branches was considered to be on ground under repair. A giant pine lay across the 14th hole, another had keeled over by the 15th tee, and next to it was a silver birch. Yet, almost miraculously, the course was still emminently playable and out of the mayhem, order was restored.

The re-start was scheduled for 2:30, time enough only to complete the interrupted matches. A decision had to be made over the rest of the format. This took some time because BBC television was not enthusiastic about continuing to a Monday finish. The opinion of the players was that the Suntory World Match Play is a 36-hole event and to cut the second and third days to 18 holes would be a mistake. An extra day, the first since 1978, was the right decision.

The first shot of the afternoon was by McNulty, a chip over a bunker beside the 13th green against Clark while, behind them, Lyle waited in a fairway bunker for the green to clear in his match with Ishii. Ballesteros and Takahashi, Randolph and Woosnam were all on the 13th tee. With McNulty and Ballesteros both two up and Woosnam four up, attention was focused on the Lyle-Ishii match, since that was tied.

Not many had heard of Ishii, an American and a native of Hawaii, but with a good record in Japan, including three victories so far this year. It was widely assumed that Lyle, the winner earlier in the year of the American Tournament Players Championship and of the new German Masters the week before, would have no trouble. Far from it.

On the Thursday morning Ishii went two up with birdies at the fourth and eighth holes, but this was not regarded too seriously, particularly when Lyle struck back with his first birdie at the ninth on a putt of around 20 feet. This was followed by an even longer putt, and the match was tied. The slim, bespectacled Ishii then took four holes in a row, the first two with birdies and the next two with pars. Lyle came back with a birdie at the 15th but still went into lunch four down, when Ishii saved par from a bunker beside the last green.

Lyle won the first hole in the afternoon with a four, the second with a birdie-two and then the fourth with a birdie-four. He was on his way. Ishii came back with a two of his own at the fifth, and when Lyle took three putts at sixth, the difference between them was three holes again. It was short-lived. Lyle won the next three holes, two with birdies and they were tied with nine holes remaining.

When play was abandoned they were still tied, and on Friday Ishii quickly forged in front once more with a fine tee shot to the 14th and short putt for a two. Three putts by Ishii at the 15th levelled the match before Ishii made up for it with a good approach to the 16th and took the lead once again.

Many have faltered at the 17th and Ishii joined them with a lost ball from the tee into the gardens on the left. After two fives at the 18th, they were into extra holes. The first two were halved, Ishii with the better chance at the first, Lyle with the advantage at the second, but the Briton prevailed at their third extra hole, the 17th. From an unpromising situation below the bank and close to a fallen tree, Lyle somehow got the ball to four feet and sank the putt.

Just as Lyle survived a tough time, so did Woosnam against Randolph, who played on the 1985 American Walker Cup team and this year won his first tournament, the Bank of Boston Classic. Randolph shot 69 for a one-up lead on Thursday morning. Woosnam came back to even twice over the first seven holes but went behind again at the eighth on Randolph's birdie. It was the American's first birdie, but he had another at the 12th for a two-up lead that was not cut until the 17th when Woosnam made a 15-foot putt for a birdie. Only sound putting, particularly some difficult return putts, kept Woosnam in the match.

A further turning point came at the first hole in the afternoon. Woosnam's second shot seemed bound for the second tee, but it hit a spectator and rebounded so close to the flag that the Welshman had the unexpected bonus of a birdie. That tied the match, then the picture rapidly changed.

Randolph fell victim of the famous step in the third green, which was to be dug up the week after the tournament and made less eccentric, to go one down, and birdies by Woosnam at the fifth and sixth holes accelerated him into a swift lead of three up. When Randolph missed the 10th green, he was four down and the position was unchanged as the flooding greens brought play to a halt. The following afternoon Woosnam had only to coast along with three pars and he was into the second round where he faced Faldo, with whom he had been unbeaten in the Ryder Cup.

Ballesteros, whose four Suntory World Match Play titles have been exceeded only by Gary Player, was also in some trouble against Takahashi, for whom the Spaniard had an abundance of praise. This was reflected in the fact that Ballesteros, who had played so well in the Ryder Cup, had seven birdies in his first 12 holes and yet was still only even. Takahashi was two up after three holes and three up after eight, where the Japanese had his fourth birdie.

Ballesteros answered with birdies at the ninth and 10th, and drew level with his seventh birdie at the 12th. After losing the 13th to a four, Ballesteros drew level again at the 16th, when Takahashi three-putted. The signs were by now clear and with a good pitch and putt at the 17th, Ballesteros took the lead for the first time. He was not caught again, shooting 68 to 69 in the best golf of the morning. A birdie three at the first hole in the afternoon made Ballesteros two up and the next eight holes were halved, Ballesteros out in 33, Takahashi in 34. The 10th and 11th holes were exchanged and when they resumed on Friday afternoon, Ballesteros forged further ahead when Takahashi went into the trees with his second shot to the 13th. The door was shut three holes later, with Ballesteros 10 under par for the 34 holes.

McNulty had been consistent all year on the European Tour, and Clark faced a difficult task. Yet the British player came leaping out of the starting gate, and was three up after three holes as the Zimbabwean made bogeys at each hole. It was a violently fluctuating match. McNulty took the next three holes, two with birdies, but lost the seventh, ninth and 10th to go three down again. Another six holes and they were tied once more before Clark stole the lead again at the 17th, where a par-five was good enough.

The reprieve was brief. McNulty won the first five holes in the afternoon, only two with birdies. Although Clark was back within two again when the rain intervened, his chances were running out. Had he holed from around 15 feet on the re-start Friday, it could have been interesting. He didn't, and McNulty coasted home.

Expectation was high as the Suntory World Match Play entered its third day, even if for only the second round. What happened then was without precedent. All four seeds — Norman, Mize, Simpson and Faldo — were beaten. Norman went down by one hole to McNulty, Mize by 7 and 6 to Lyle, Simpson by 5 and 4 to Seve Ballesteros and Faldo by one hole to Woosnam. It was the first time in the 24 years of the championship that the four semi-finalists were all members of the European Tour even if one of them, McNulty, was not European, although he was the second-leading money winner. Such strong European involvement did not escape the notice of Ballesteros. "I've been saying for four or five years that the Europeans are getting better and better," he pointed out. "People used to laugh at me. It's nice to be proved right after all."

To some extent the seeds were at a disadvantage, left waiting to play until the Saturday after the intervention of the rain and then the Great Storm. It was difficult to practice and they came in cold. Norman, always one to speak his mind (a year earlier he had threatened never to come back because of biased crowds), said the format should be changed. He did not think it was right that some players should be asked to play only three matches and others four. He would rather see the Suntory World Match Play go back to its original format of eight players or increase the field to 16. That way everyone would play the same amount of golf.

The Woosnam-Faldo match, the leading European money winner of the year against the British Open champion, offered the most intrigue. In the Ryder Cup they were partners and didn't lose in four matches together, only in their respective singles. No one was disappointed. It was a gripping struggle, with seldom more than a hole between them. Faldo shot 66 against 68 in the morning and was one up. Woosnam shot 66 in the afternoon against 67 and was the winner on the last green. It could hardly have been closer.

Faldo made two early errors, losing the first and third holes to par-fours. In between Faldo had a birdie at the second hole with a seven iron to 12 feet. Birdies were exchanged at the fourth and Faldo was in full stride. He had another birdie at the fifth with a five iron to not much more than three feet, holed a putt of 10 feet for his fourth birdie at the seventh to go one up, then demolished the ninth with a drive, three iron and 15-foot putt. He was out in 32 and two up.

Woosnam did not falter. After they halved the 12th with birdies, he struck what seemed an important blow when he hit a seven iron to six feet at the 13th. Faldo was at least twice that far away but made his putt. Then Woosnam holed as well. At the 16th, after taking a one iron from the tee, Woosnam followed with a wedge to six feet for a birdie to get back to one down and then pitched virtually dead at the 17th to draw even. Still, Faldo went into lunch one up. At the 18th he missed the green on the left, and chipped close enough to hole the putt. Woosnam, from the right side, with the slope running away from him, took three to get down.

If that seemed an important blow psychologically, Woosnam bounced straight back. He was assisted in winning the first hole in the afternoon when Faldo three-putted, then went ahead for the first time since the third hole in the morning, dropping his seven iron across the valley to the raised second green 15 feet from the flag and holing the putt. Immediately Faldo drew even again, getting up and down from a bunker at the third and by the seventh, he had resumed the lead, finding the top ledge with his second shot and his putter doing the rest.

Again, the lead was short-lived. At the eighth Woosnam had a birdie with a five iron to 10 feet and they remained tied at the turn. Two holes later Faldo was in front once more, although as it happened for the last time. More birdies followed at the 12th, then Woosnam struck what seemed the telling blows, birdies at the 14th and 15th to go to one up with three to play. It is then that the golfer has to dig deep into his reserves, and Faldo came up with what he must have felt was a possibly winning thrust. A drive and fairway wood found the green 571 yards away at the 17th and he capped it with a single putt for an eagle three. They were tied, with one to play.

Adrenalin flowing, Woosnam reduced the 502 yards of the 18th to two strokes with a drive and one iron while Faldo was just short. It was the sort of chip that he ought to have laid closer than he did. Instead, it came up short and he missed for his birdie. Woosnam got his four, but only just. Not for the last time this week, he faced a five- or six-footer for the match and, not for the last time, he made it.

This was not the only match to go all the way. So did the one between McNulty and Norman. The Australian was the much stronger player, outdriving McNulty again and again and often by so large a margin that there was a four-club difference between them for their second shots. This was no surprise to McNulty. He was prepared for it and by still hitting the greens he was able to keep the pressure on. So effective was McNulty's game that he was down only once, after the third hole in the morning, and he drew even straight away as Norman strayed right with his second shot and ultimately had to concede the hole. From that point McNulty, reminiscent in many ways of Peter Thomson with his quiet, methodical swing, held control.

McNulty went ahead with a birdie at the fifth hole and another at the seventh, where he was hitting a five-iron second shot against an eight iron, put him two to the good. Over 36 holes there was of course still plenty of room for error, and when Norman came back with birdies at the ninth and 10th, the suspicion was that McNulty might be on his way out. McNulty drew ahead again at the 11th with an eight iron closer to the flag than Norman could hit his wedge. A five wood to the 12th was just as effective as Norman's four iron, and they halved that in birdie-fours. Nor was distance any advantage at the 17th. Norman was close enough to the green in two to be able to use his putter and he still took three to get down, while McNulty pitched within single-putt range to go two up for the second time. Norman regained his appetite for lunch by chipping in for an eagle-three at the 18th to cut his deficit.

McNulty went two up at the second hole in the afternoon with a birdie, lost the third, where he took three putts, but moved two clear once more at the eighth where, for once, he was hitting a shorter iron to the green but, ironically, sank the longer putt.

There was still life in Norman, and a much longer drive to the 13th led to a birdie-three to close the gap to one again before he slipped by finding a bunker with his approach to the 15th. This was offset by a birdie at the 16th but McNulty had a matching birdie at the 17th to retain his lead. With two fives at the 18th, Norman failing to make the green with a two-iron second, McNulty was through to a semi-final against Lyle.

The outcome of this quarter-final was never in doubt. Lyle won four holes in a row from the third, the last three with birdies, and was five up after nine. Mize was far from doing himself justice. He was struggling for length off the tee and, with Lyle striking the ball effortlessly into the distance, it rapidly became no match at all. Lyle went six up at the 15th with his sixth birdie and seven up at the 17th with his seventh. He shot 67, nine strokes better than the Masters champion. The pattern did not change in the afternoon. Although Lyle lost the first hole to a par, he advanced to nine up with 11 to play. At this point Lyle was in line to equal Tom Watson's 11 and 9 defeat of Dale Hayes in 1978. Only then did Mize find some vestige of form, but not even three birdies in his next five holes were enough to stop Lyle winning by 7 and 6, eight under par for 30 holes.

We had not seen the best of Mize, nor did we see the best of Simpson, the U.S. Open champion. He found Ballesteros too hot, and was trailing from the start, able to draw level only once, at the second hole, which the Spaniard three-putted. It was a short reprieve. By the fifth Ballesteros was two up. The avalanche came on the second nine. Ballesteros started back with three birdies, although a rare error led to him losing the 13th. A birdie at the 14th and Simpson's bogey at the 15th made the difference four holes. At lunch it was five, with Simpson making a mess of the 18th and not even asking Ballesteros to putt. When Ballesteros took the first two holes in the afternoon, he was racing towards an early finish. Successive birdies by Simpson at the eighth and ninth cut the margin to five, and there was just the possibility that Ballesteros might be losing his concentration, but a succession of halved holes brought the match to a quiet conclusion, by 5 and 4.

Considering all the bad weather, Wentworth made a remarkable recovery and praise cannot be too high for the course superintendent, Kevin Munt, and his staff. The greens were quick and testing and the fairways, criss-cross cut with the triplex, were reminiscent of those at Muirfield Village for the Ryder Cup. They were also firm enough that there was no need for preferred lies, other than in casual water. All told, Wentworth looked as well as ever.

For all Wentworth's splendid holes, there are also some controversial ones. High among them is the third, a brute of a par-four, 452 yards long to a two-tiered green so severe now as to be unfair. The only realistic place for the flag is on the top step but the slightest misjudgment can lead to a player watching his ball just about mount the crest, hesitate and then roll down the slope with ever-increasing momentum until it is not only off the green but 10 to 15 yards down the fairway again. Many a famous player has suffered this anguish and the last was Ballesteros in his semi-final against Woosnam. It happened in the afternoon round and had a crucial bearing on the match — Woosnam went on to win by one hole. In the other semi-final, Lyle, for the second time in three days, had to go to the 39th before beating McNulty.

No sooner was the tournament over than the curtain was brought down on the third green. It was being dug up and re-laid with much more subtle contours. While this will be of little consolation to Ballesteros, the third hole at least made a contribution to the first all-British final in 24 years. Lyle and Woosnam had been rivals as boys and it was typical of their friendship that Woosnam's reaction to their meeting in the final was merely to say, "After 24 years we're going to have a British winner and it doesn't matter who it is." Lyle, through to his fourth final, added that he was convinced it would be close "with probably never more than a hole between us."

What ever the following day would present, it was difficult to believe that anything could cap these two semi-final matches, each so close that it is hard to separate them for drama and excitement. Lyle, three down and five to play against McNulty, survived at the third extra hole while Woosnam, three up with six to play against Ballesteros, found himself even coming to the last, which he won by no more than the diameter of a golf ball.

If Lyle had been expected to assert himself through his much more powerful game and on a course he knows so well because he lives on the estate, it did not happen that way. McNulty was in control for most of the day. McNulty shot 73 in the morning and was two up since Lyle could do no better than 76. In the afternoon McNulty shot 73 again, but Lyle improved with 72 and that was sufficient to give him a reprieve that led to the final. When Lyle won at the 39th, it was only the second time all day he had been ahead.

McNulty went one up in the morning with a birdie at the fourth and was two holes clear when Lyle took three putts at the fifth. Pars followed until the ninth, where McNulty was in trouble most of the way and lost. He also lost the 10th to go back to even, but quickly recovered with a nine iron to the 11th, which he holed from 30 feet. Lyle's hunt for a birdie was at last rewarded at the 12th. Both missed the green at the 13th, but Lyle got up and down, and was in the lead for the first time. Not for long, however. He was short with a seven iron to the 14th and took three putts and at the 15th, McNulty struck a near unanswerable blow with a five iron to five feet for a birdie. Lyle could not get going at all and, with three putts at the 17th for a six, he went into lunch two down.

McNulty dropped strokes at both the second and third holes in the afternoon to go back to even again. Then suddenly he was clear, taking three holes in a row from the sixth. He won the first with a par and the next two with birdies, a drive and five iron to the seventh and a drive and four iron to the eighth. Although Lyle got back the ninth, where McNulty hit his second shot into a ditch, he went three down again at the 10th to a birdie and was lucky to be only that. In 28 holes so far, Lyle had still had but one birdie and was six over par.

One can never tell with Lyle. There was a glimmer of hope when he reduced the 11th to a one iron, wedge and single putt, but it seemed to fade when he hit into the trees at the 13th. He was three down with six to play, and later three down with four to play. The three putts McNulty took at the 15th tipped the scales. At once Lyle came off the ropes. He hit a one iron and nine iron down the 16th for a birdie, then two majestic blows along the narrow confines of the 17th. A drive and one iron found the green, and for once McNulty could not rely on a pitch and one putt. He took two putts missing from seven feet. At the 18th Lyle was in the rough off the tee. He had to play two six irons and was still not on the green, but he chipped close to get his par, the halve, and extra time.

The first two extra holes were halved but at their third, the 17th, Lyle found the knock-out punch, a wedge from the rough to eight feet. His putter did not let him down.

Woosnam's defeat of Ballesteros was no less griping and one had to admire the quality of the Welshman's game againt someone who has frequently reserved his best golf for the Suntory World Match Play. Both shot 70s in the morning and it took a 67 from Woosnam in the afternoon to get him home. Ballesteros won the first hole in the morning with a four, Woosnam taking three putts. When Ballesteros won the sixth to go two up, it seemed he might be taking control. However, Ballesteros' three putts from less than six feet at the seventh let Woosnam back in. Woosnam made par at the ninth, where Ballesteros was in trouble off the tee, and they were tied again. Woosnam took the lead for the first time at the 13th where an enormous drive, followed by a wedge, yielded a birdie-three. He led until the 18th were Ballesteros cut loose with two drivers, made the green in two and got his birdie.

Woosnam took charge in the afternoon. A birdie at the second put him ahead, then came Ballesteros' mishap at the third. On the bottom tier of the green in two, he putted up, just failed to negotiate the crest and was left playing his third with a wedge from the fairway. Woosnam, through the green in two, meanwhile had played a deftly-lofted chip and would probably have made his four.

He made it three up at the seventh hole, where Ballesteros was short off the tee and needed a four iron for this second. Ballesteros closed the gap with a birdie at the 10th but was out of bounds at the 12th, and time was beginning to run out. Sure enough, the match was not over yet. A drive and seven iron by the flag at the 13th cut Woosnam's lead to two holes. A nine iron to five feet at the 16th reduced the deficit further, then at the 17th Ballesteros drew level, reaching the green with a huge drive and two iron and two-putting. It was a splendid recovery, so typical of Ballesteros, and the odds against his now winning must have been remote.

This became even more certain as Ballesteros lashed his drive down the 18th fairway, Woosnam following with a shot that had him turning away in disgust. It flew into the trees and he immediately called for another ball. As luck would have it, the Welshman's first ball caught a branch and came down on a muddy path from which he got a free drop. He was able to belt a one iron towards the green, although still an eight-iron distance away.

For Ballesteros, there were no half measures. He reached for his driver once more, and paid the penalty. He came off the shot marginally and his ball clattered among branches short and just right of the green. It fell among debris from the storm and Ballesteros got relief, dropping his ball on muddy ground littered with pieces of straw which helped give some stability to the morass that can be the consequence of heavy rain. Ballesteros did not like the lie and asked for further relief. Andy McPhee, the referee, refused. Ballesteros became quite heated, and pointed out that Woosnam — who was all the time minding his own business and keeping well away from the exchanges — had had relief from a similar area, and why couldn't he? He wanted a second opinion from Tony Gray, the senior referee, who would be officiating at the final.

By now the crowd was suggesting that Ballesteros drop his ball on the fairway, and one even suggested that he throw it on the green. Gray did in fact grant further relief, in the rough. When Ballesteros chipped on the green to six feet, it looked very much like extra holes or even a Spanish victory. Instead, Ballesteros missed the putt. Woosnam, whose third shot had been so perfectly judged that it came to rest some five feet from the hole, made his putt.

By defeating Lyle in the final, Woosnam capped the greatest year in his career. Still six months short of his 30th birthday, he had already established himself as Europe's leading money winner. Whether this gave him the most satisfaction, or becoming the first Briton to win the Suntory World Match Play, would be hard to decide. Woosnam could do little wrong from the moment he also became the first Briton to win the Hong Kong Open in March. He also won the Jersey Open, Cepsa Madrid Open, Bell's Scottish Open and Lancome Trophy and was runner-up three times, in the Suze Open, Belgian Open and Dunhill British Masters. He had 14 top-10 finishes in 22 starts and missed only two cuts.

What one most admires about Woosnam is the effortlessness of his long game, hands quite low at the address, the toe of the club slightly raised, then a full shoulder turn and a healthy crack into the ball that, on occasions, seems to fly forever. He is certainly one of the longer hitters in the game. If he could ever putt as well, there is no saying what he might do, but that is one aspect of the game that bothers him. He is always trying new methods and different putters.

Rewarding though it was to see Woosnam scale this peak, in terms of British golf, there had to be sympathy for Lyle, who has reached four finals and lost them all. Two have been on the last green, one in extra holes and the other at the 35th. Such a tantalizing quartet of near-misses. For Lyle, it already had been a difficult year, promising though it began with victory in the U.S. Tournament Players Championship. An unexpected broken marriage heralded the beginning of a slump and at one stage there were even doubts that he would be on the Ryder Cup team. He had to rely on one of the three invitations from Tony Jacklin, but in four matches he was on the winning side three times (each time with Bernhard Langer). Then, a week before the Suntory World Match Play, Lyle won the German Masters. The bad times may now be behind him.

The match between Woosnam and Lyle was wonderfully close, with golf of the very highest order. Both shot 68s in the morning, and Woosnam edged ahead in the afternoon, 67 to 69, winning on the last green. Woosnam was eight under par for the day and 32 under par for his four matches, unquestionably the best golf of the week.

Lyle drew first blood at the third hole, where he saved par from off the green. His three putts at the fifth tied the match, then Lyle got into trouble at the seventh, conceding the hole. Woosnam went two up by holing a monster putt at the eighth, only for Lyle to come back with a birdie at the ninth. Woosnam's birdie putt from 12 feet at the 11th restored his two-hole advantage, but again it was quickly lost when he took three putts at the 12th for a par.

The impression was that Woosnam might be getting the upper hand, particularly at the 14th, when Lyle had the misfortune of having his six iron hit the green and spin back so sharply that it ran down the slope, leaving a 40-yard wedge shot instead of a putt. Unsettled, Lyle drove too far right with a one iron at the 15th, then having a blind shot he had to fade around the trees to reach the green. Woosnam was dead-center and very much in the driver's seat. But Lyle played a brilliant shot to the green and Woosnam, possibly disturbed when he had to wait for a Concorde to pass overhead, slightly pushed his four iron and could not get down for a par.

Lyle played the 16th beautifully, but Woosnam matched him, both scoring birdies before Lyle struck again, drawing level with a birdie at the 17th. Woosnam should have had one, too, but he was not confident about a putt of four feet, and missed it. Suddenly the match was transformed, and at the 18th, Lyle struck two great blows, a drive and three iron to around 20 feet. His putt went in for an eagle-three, and he was one up at lunch. Since Woosnam had hit a three wood even closer, it was hardly surprising that he described himself as putting "like an idiot."

After a quick sandwich, Woosnam spent a long time on the practice green, but to little or no benefit. By the fourth hole of the afternoon Lyle was two up, reaching the par five with no more than a five-iron second shot for his birdie. At the sixth, Woosnam pitched to within three feet of the flag, but missed the putt. Such fallibility seemed to be the difference, and when Woosnam's approach to the seventh spun back down the slope, it looked like he would be three down. Woosnam's approach putt ran well past the hole, but he experimented by standing a little more upright, sank the next putt, and the crisis was over. At the eighth he sank a putt from off the green for a birdie to get back to one down, and at the 10th he holed another, this time just as Lyle seemed to have saved himself with a delicate chip from well left of the green.

It was thrust and counter-thrust all the way down the finishing stretch, with no error on either side until the 15th. There, Lyle got a flier from the fairway and his four iron skipped through the green into a rather bare lie. A bogey resulted. This was an important break, although Lyle made up for it at the 16th, where he hit a nine iron to five feet and sank the putt for a birdie. The match was even again.

In the mounting excitement, both were just short of the 17th green in two, Woosnam in the rough and Lyle on the fairway. Woosnam's pitch, from a lie in which the ball was barely visible, was so close that Lyle conceded the putt. Lyle's retort was just as stunning, the slightly shorter pitch biting on impact four feet away. There was never a doubt about the putt.

Both hit perfect drives down the 18th, Lyle's slightly the longer. Woosnam had to play first to the green and as soon as he had struck it, he knew it was good. "Turn, turn," he shouted and turn it did to the middle of the green. Then it was Lyle's turn, with a two iron. His ball stayed marginally right and hit the second of the right-hand bunkers beside the green. From there, Lyle came out short and when he putted short again, Woosnam could not bring himself to look. Woosnam's try for a eagle-three had run five or six feet past, and so it was that for the match, as it had been earlier against Faldo and Ballesteros. For the third time, he holed it.

9. The U.S. Tour

Ever-rising purses produced more big-money winners than ever before on the U.S. PGA Tour, and one of them — Curtis Strange — nearly hit the $1 million mark. Four players earned more than did Sam Snead in his 50-year career ($620,126) and a fifth nearly matched Snead's total.

They did it not by winning a lot of tournaments, but simply winning a few and finishing high in a few others.

It took $65,695 — by Aki Ohmachi — to land the 126th, and last, exempt spot. The all-exempt list includes only the first 125 places, but Seve Ballesteros placed 32nd with $305,058 (in only eight tournaments). Since Ballesteros is not a member of the tour, his spot was discounted.

Strange set a money-winning record with $925,941, including $175,000 in bonus money from Nabisco. He won the Canadian Open, Federal Express St. Jude Classic and NEC World Series of Golf, and collected more than $382,000 for those three victories alone. Strange had six other finishes in the top six and two more in the top 10, but most of his success came after mid-season.

Larry Mize came up with the shot of the year in the Masters, when he sank a 140-foot pitch at the second playoff hole — Augusta National's dangerous 11th hole — while Greg Norman watched awestruck. Ballesteros had dropped out of the playoff by three-putting the first hole.

It was the second straight major championship in which Norman had been beaten by a sensational shot at the last hole. In the PGA Championship, he was denied victory when Bob Tway holed a bunker shot at the 72nd hole. The double dose of nerve-shockers obviously had an effect on Norman. He didn't win a tournament in America. Tway, who had shown such promise, didn't win until the last tournament of the year, when he teamed with Mike Hulbert to take the Chrysler Team Championship.

Among the players advancing among the tour's stars were Paul Azinger, Mark Calcavecchia and Corey Pavin. However, Calcavecchia and Pavin faded after starting well. Azinger, on the other hand, had a solid season in his fifth year on the tour. He won three times — Phoenix, Las Vegas, Hartford — and tied for second in the British Open after having victory in his grasp with two holes to go.

Azinger was PGA Player of the Year and finished second to Strange with $822,481. Ben Crenshaw, who won only the USF&G Classic and was beaten by T.C. Chen in a playoff for the Los Angeles Open title, was third with $638,194. Scott Simpson, the U.S. Open champion, was fourth with $621,032 and Tom Watson, outplayed by Simpson in the stretch in the Open and a winner for the first time in more than three years in the rich Nabisco Championship, was fifth with $616,351. Strange and Azinger both broke Norman's one-year record of $653,296, set in 1986.

Larry Nelson, planning to play all-out for one more year before turning to designing courses, had the greatest one-month stretch, winning the PGA Championship for the second time in a playoff with Lanny Wadkins, placing second in the rain-ravaged Western Open and tying for fourth in the World Series of Golf. Late in the season, he added the Disney World title.

Keith Clearwater emerged as the most successful of the newcomers. Clearwater won the Colonial Invitation by shooting 64-64 in a 36-hole windup, shook up the field with another 64 in the third round of the U.S. Open, and won the final official tournament of the year, the Centel Classic. He placed 31st among the money winners with $320,007. Other rookies who won were John Inman, in the Provident Classic, and Sam Randolph, in the Bank of Boston Classic.

Mike Reid, who had played 10 years without a victory, finally ended that drought with an emotional triumph in the Tucson Open. That left only Chip Beck and Bobby Wadkins as those who have won more than $1 million without placing first. Beck placed ninth in money winnings with $523,003.

Spalding Invitation—$250,000
Winner: Ken Green

Despite a couple of obstacles — the flu and rain in the final round — Ken Green won the Spalding Invitation non-PGA Tour event by one stroke over Willie Wood and Don Pooley with a 10-under-par 274 at the Carmel Valley Ranch, Pebble Beach and Quail Lodge courses in California.

Green's four-foot par putt at the final green avoided a playoff after Wood had finished with 64 and Pooley, 66. Green caught the flu while shooting 67 in the first round, but took the lead with 66 in the third round, then won by shooting 71 in the rain.

The Spalding is the only tournament in which PGA Tour and LPGA players compete against each other head-to-head (the women use different tees.) Jan Stephenson and Patty Sheehan came close to winning. They tied for fourth place at 276 with Lennie Clements and George Archer.

↑ Professionals — not ProAm

FILA Invitational—$250,000
Winner: Hale Irwin

Just as in 1986, Hale Irwin began the year with a victory in the FILA Invitational, a non-PGA Tour event, at Fiddlesticks Country Club in Fort Myers, Florida. Irwin shot 68, 69, 70 for a 207 total and won by five strokes over Scott Verplank and Calvin Peete.

Verplank, a disappointment in his first year in 1986, got off to a fast start with 66. Irwin made five birdies on the second nine the second day, tying Verplank at 137. "I'm trying to get my game back to what I used to have when I was playing my best," Irwin said. He gave indications that he was on the right track in the final round when he opened with a bogey, then won going away.

MONY Tournament of Champions—$500,000
Winner: Mac O'Grady

The official PGA Tour opener for 1987, the MONY Tournament of Champions, ended with players in the top four places who epitomized the 1986 Tour:

Mac O'Grady, who won by one stroke with a 72-hole total of 278, was the "bad boy" the year before. After a battle with Commissioner Deane Beman, the colorful O'Grady scored his first victory in the Greater Hartford Open, gave up his struggle with the authorities, paid his fine and served a suspension.

Rick Fehr gained his first victory in the 1986 B.C. Open. He represented the young men with stars in their eyes.

Mark Calcavecchia played so poorly in 1985 that he lost his players' card. He had to win one of the four berths available each week, and regained his players' card, winning the Southwest Open.

Greg Norman, who tied Calcavecchia for third place at 280, was the greatest golfer in the world in 1986.

The event at LaCosta Country Club, in Carlsbad, California, brings together the PGA Tour winners of the previous season and all played except Jack Nicklaus. O'Grady led for all but the second round with scores of 65, 72, 70 and 71. He ran in and out of trouble, because of what he called "anterograde amnesia" (to instantly forget three-putt greens) and "focal dystonic myotonia" (the yips). He three-putted the 10th and 12th holes in the last round, birdied the 13th with a chip to within a foot of the hole and birdied the 14th with a 48-foot putt. Calcavecchia tied O'Grady with a 12-foot birdie putt at the 13th hole, but after O'Grady birdied No. 14, the demons in his game had been exorcised. *restricted to PGA winners from previous season*

Bob Hope Chrysler Classic—$900,000
Winner: Corey Pavin   *celebrity Pro Am*

The course for two of the five rounds of the Bob Hope Chrysler Classic — including the final round — got as much attention as the players. It was the PGA West layout designed by Pete Dye, a 7,000-yarder so tough that some pros called it too severe and asked that it not become a regular venue.

When Dye was signed to build PGA West, he was told to make it difficult. The degree of difficulty was not spelled out. Dye came up with some of the deepest bunkers this side of the moon.

Corey Pavin played PGA West better than anyone and was rewarded with a one-stroke victory over Bernhard Langer. On the final hole, Pavin sank an 18-foot birdie putt for 67 and 341 total for 90 holes. Pavin's 67 was the lowest score at PGA West in the five rounds.

Andy Bean, who entered the tournament because he wanted to play the much-heralded PGA West, shot 68 at Indian Wells and took the 36-hole lead at 131 after opening with 63 at Tamarisk. The third day was cold and wet, compounding the problems for those at PGA West. One of them was Bean, who tumbled out of contention with 75. Another was Langer, who shot 68 for the lead at 202. Raymond Floyd, with 68 at Indian Wells, was second, and Pavin began his charge after opening rounds of 72, 71 and 65 at Tamarisk.

Pavin shot 66 at Indian Wells in the fourth round and Langer took 70. Now Pavin trailed by two strokes. Langer finished with 70, which before the round looked as if it would be good enough to win. But Pavin wouldn't be denied.

Phoenix Open—$600,000
Winner: Paul Azinger

Paul Azinger credited a tip from Andy Bean for his first PGA Tour victory in the Phoenix Open. But to hear Azinger relate his final round, two of the greatest shots he ever hit also contributed heavily to his one-stroke triumph over Hal Sutton.

At the 16th hole, Azinger came out of a bunker and sank a 12-foot putt for par. "That was my best sand shot ever," he said. At the 18th hole, his tee shot cleared a bunker next to the lake and landed in the fairway. "That was my best drive ever," he said. "I was shaking like a leaf when I handed by club back to my caddy."

Azinger hit a seven iron to within 22 feet of the cup, then rolled his approach putt to within tap-in distance to finish a 67 for a 268 total that ruined Sutton's magnificent bid to win the tournament for the second straight year. Sutton blazed in with 64, the decisive shot being a five-foot par putt at No. 18 after his drive landed in a fairway bunker. "People will remember that putt, but I missed so many putts the first three days I could have been 25 under par," Sutton said.

The Phoenix Open was played at a new site, the Tournament Players Club of Scottsdale, designed by Tom Weiskopf and Jay Morrish, with consultancy by Howard Twitty. True to TPC standards, it was a spectator's delight and the fans flocked to the course.

The huge crowd on Saturday had a lot to cheer about. Doug Tewell shot a course-record 62 and vaulted into a tie for third place with Fuzzy Zoeller and Jay Haas at 202. Corey Pavin, still on a high after his victory in the Bob Hope Classic, took the lead with 66 for 200, and Azinger took his position behind Pavin with 65.

At one point in the final round, Azinger, Tewell and Pavin were tied. But Azinger didn't notice. He was following the advice he received from Bean at the Kapalua International. Azinger said nervousness and a penchant for playing match play had hurt him. "Andy said, 'Just go play your own game. Go for the middle of the green, take what that will give you and go,'" Azinger recalled afterwards.

AT&T Pebble Beach National Pro-Am—$660,000
Winner: Johnny Miller

Thoughts of retirement had flitted through Johnny Miller's mind before the AT&T Pebble Beach National Pro-Am. He was nearing 40, the intensity that he had in the mid-1970s was no longer there and his putting was driving him crazy. Maybe he wouldn't retire until the end of the year, but in the third round he considered withdrawing.

"I shot a 69-68 at Phoenix and withdrew because of a groin pull," Miller said. "At the eighth hole at Pebble Beach in the third round I felt it pull and told my caddy we might have to go in after that hole. Then I chipped in. So I said, 'What the heck.' I guess there's a reward for sticking with something."

The reward, Miller's first victory since 1983, came at the expense of Payne Stewart, the runner-up here for the second straight year and for the fourth time in 13 months.

All the excitement was packed into the final two holes at Pebble Beach. Miller, who started the final round five strokes out of the lead, had an 18-foot birdie putt at the final green to tie Stewart, who was playing several groups behind. Miller's putting had been so bad in recent years that he had gone to a 50-inch putter. He tucked the end of it under his left armpit and rested the shaft against his arm, preventing him from bending his wrist on a putt.

Miller's putt ran unerringly for the cup and dropped for a birdie that gave him 66 and a 278 total.

No. 17 is a difficult par-three and No. 18 is a par-five that yields a number of birdies. If Stewart could get past No. 17 safely, a winning birdie at No. 18 was not out of the question. But Stewart's tee shot at the 17th went into a bunker and he missed a par putt from about six feet, falling one stroke behind.

The long-hitting Stewart played to get in position for a wedge shot that could set up a birdie at No. 18, but left himself with a 20-footer. His putt was too far right.

"I thought my years of winning were over — unless a miracle happened," Miller said. Few could have envisioned it happening at Pebble Beach after Miller's first three rounds. Stewart's third consecutive 69 gave him a two-stroke lead, and an edge of five over Miller, who had shot 72, 72 and 68. Miller slowly crept close to the lead in the last round, gained a share with his final putt and soon found himself holding it alone.

He later noted the source of some of his inspiration — the showings of Lee Trevino in 1984 and Jack Nicklaus and Raymond Floyd in 1986: "Trevino won the PGA. Jack won the Masters. Floyd won the Open. And, hey, Hubert Green won the PGA (in 1985). I said to myself, 'I can play better than Hubert Green, can't I?'"

Hawaiian Open—$600,000
Winner: Corey Pavin

Corey Pavin gave the impression he might become one of the giants of professional golf in the early part of 1987. Pavin, 27, scored his second victory of the year in the Hawaiian Open. He shot an eight-under-par 64 to catch Craig Stadler at 270, then won on the second playoff hole with a 22-foot birdie putt. It was the second year in a row Pavin won the tournament and was his sixth career triumph.

Pavin was just as impressive in the first round as he was in the last, but his middle rounds were another matter. With the wind whipping across Waialae Country Club in the first round, the lightweight Pavin kept his balance for a seven-under 65 that gave him a one-stroke lead over Mac O'Grady and Jack Renner. When the wind calmed in the second round, Pavin did no better than 75 as Fred Couples (69-65) and Bernhard Langer (70-64) moved into the lead.

Saturday was Stadler's day as he carved out a 10-under-par 62 that tied the course and tournament records, putting him one stroke ahead of Paul Azinger, who had 65. "I feel great to be in contention and I'll go for the win tomorrow," Stadler said. "I hope to be four under on the front nine, that's my objective."

Stadler didn't reach his mark, going out in even par enroute to a 70. He did have a chance to avert a playoff. After Azinger missed a 12-foot birdie putt at the 18th hole that would have tied Pavin, Stadler faced an eight-foot putt for birdie. He missed it on the same line as Azinger's putt. "I couldn't believe Paul's putt didn't break left. I hit mine on the same line and it didn't break either," Stadler said.

Pavin recovered from his second-round 75 for 66 in the third round, but still trailed Stadler by six strokes. After finishing with 64, Pavin had a long wait to see if anyone would beat or match him.

Shearson Lehman Brothers Andy Williams Open—$500,000
Winner: George Burns

The Shearson Lehman Brothers Andy Williams Open will be remembered not because George Burns won with a record score, but because Craig Stadler didn't tie for second place. Sounds crazy, but it was a crazy week on the Torrey Pines North and South courses in San Diego, California.

Burns won by making two eagles in the final round, shooting 65 for a 266 total, four better than the runners-up, J.C. Snead and Bobby Wadkins.

Stadler, and millions of television viewers, thought he tied for second. But television did him in. During the final round, NBC showed a tape of Saturday's play. In one segment, Stadler was shown placing a towel under his knees as he knelt to hit a shot from under a pine tree at the 15th hole. Several viewers called to question whether Stadler should have been penalized for "building a stance." Officials agreed. Since Stadler had not added the penalty to his third-round card, he was disqualified.

It was a bitter pill for Stadler to swallow, but he did so without complaint.

Burns' nine-under-par 63 in the first round gave him a one-stroke lead over Snead and Lon Hinkle. Stadler, with nine birdies and an eagle, and Andy Bean, with 10 birdies, each shot 62 in the second round. Stadler was tied with Burns for the lead and Bean was one stroke behind.

An overnight rain softened the greens for the third round and the result was that only 11 players failed to match or beat par. Snead and Raymond Floyd both turned in 66s and were deadlocked at 199. Burns slipped two strokes behind with 70.

Rain, wind and mist formed the backdrop as Burns stepped out to his fourth career victory. Burns said he was concerned about Floyd, a noted front-runner, but George sank a 50-foot putt for an eagle-three at the fifth hole and holed a 129-yard nine iron for an eagle-two at the 15th hole to break away from Floyd, Wadkins, Snead, Stadler and Buddy Gardner. He had as many eagles in one round as he had bogeys in the tournament.

Los Angeles Open—$600,000
Winner: T.C. Chen

Oper

When Ben Crenshaw sank a 16-foot birdie putt on the last hole at Riviera Country Club, Crenshaw and the roaring crowd thought he had won the Los Angeles Open. When T.C. Chen made a breaking birdie putt from a foot closer a minute later, they knew Ben hadn't won, and possibly wouldn't.

Crenshaw was 0-5 in playoffs and that figure became 0-6, the worst among active PGA Tour players, when he lost to Chen on the first playoff hole. "I thought my chances were gone when I missed my short putt on the 17th hole," said Chen, who scored the first U.S. victory by a Taiwan native. "When Ben made his putt at 18, I thought he had won."

The tournament came down to the final threesome of Chen, Crenshaw and Danny Edwards. Any could have won and all three could have been in the playoff. Edwards led by two strokes with four holes to play, but couldn't maintain his advantage. When they teed off at No. 18, they were tied for the lead and all hit the green. After Crenshaw made his dramatic birdie putt, Edwards just missed on a tying 15-footer. Then Chen forced the playoff, as he and Crenshaw finished at 275, Chen with 71 and Crenshaw with 69.

The playoff began at the 449-yard No. 15, and Chen hit his drive down the right side of the fairway. Crenshaw pulled his drive left, onto a gravel path, 192 yards from the flag. He was faced with a dilemma: take a drop and try to hit a draw from a downhill lie or hit it off the path? When Chen hit a four iron 15 feet below the hole, Crenshaw decided to play from the path and hit into a bunker. His bunker shot stopped within a yard of the hole.

Chen's birdie putt grazed the hole and he tapped in for par. Crenshaw had only a three-footer to continue the playoff, but he missed it. "I've had that putt many times and it breaks sharply left to right. I just hit it too hard and it missed on the high side," he said.

The last straw: Crenshaw was informed that he had taken 68 seconds to hit his putt at the 18th hole, making him liable for a $1,000 fine for slow play.

Bobby Wadkins, the first player off the front nine, gained the first-round lead with a five-under-par 66, then Bill Sander took over after 36 holes with 70-66. Edwards, who had 64 the second day, took the lead in the third round but Chen just as quickly took it from him. Chen chipped in for birdie at the fifth hole, hit a six iron into the hole for a hole-in-one at the 171-yard No. 6 and sank a 45-foot birdie putt from the fringe at No. 7. After 10 holes of the third round, Chen was 11 under par and led Rick Fehr by four strokes. But Chen played the last eight holes in two over, bogeying Nos. 15 and 18. After 54 holes, Chen led Edwards by one stroke and Crenshaw and Wadkins by two.

Doral Ryder Open—$1,000,000
Winner: Lanny Wadkins

A change in venue, from California to Florida, was just what Lanny Wadkins needed. After finishing third and fourth twice in his last three California appearances, Wadkins scored his first victory since 1985 in the Doral Ryder Open.

He won by three strokes over Tom Kite, Don Pooley and Seve Ballesteros with a front-running exhibition after a start that put him in position to miss the 36-hole cut. Wadkins said "I putted horrendously, but I didn't want to go home Friday night," as he struggled to an opening 75. He recovered for two straight 66s and breezed in with a 277 total.

Bernhard Langer, with 65, and Larry Rinker, with 66, were one-two after the first round and forgotten after the third. Langer failed to break par on Doral Country Club's Blue Monster course in the last three rounds and Rinker withdrew before the final round because of flu.

Wadkins' 66 in the second round got him to within four strokes of a host of players tied for the lead and his second 66 put him two strokes ahead. Mark Calcavecchia trailed by one stroke with one hole to play in the third round, then hit two balls into the water at the 18th and took an eight that finished his hopes.

Wadkins led all the way in the final round, gaining impetus with a 91-yard wedge shot for an eagle-two at the 371-yard fifth hole. With nine holes to play, he led by five and even though he bogeyed the 10th, those closest to him never threatened. Ballesteros birdied Nos. 15 and 16, but a birdie putt at the 17th spun out of the hole. Kite birdied Nos. 17 and 18 for 68, but that was not enough. Pooley fell back then finished with birdies at Nos. 16 and 17, but all that got him was a tie for second place.

Honda Classic—$600,000
Winner: Mark Calcavecchia

Mark Calcavecchia, struggling to win back his PGA Tour card, caddied for Ken Green in the 1986 Honda Classic. Green missed the cut. "There were times I wanted to take the club out of his hands and hit the ball myself," Calcavecchia said. A year later, Calcavecchia did just that. He came back and won the tournament himself, beating Bernhard Langer and Payne Stewart by three strokes with a nine-under-par 279 total.

Wind the first two days and a heavy rain Friday night that delayed the start of the third round for three hours and caused the lift-clean-place rule to be put into effect made the TPC at Eagle Trace in Coral Springs, Florida, play at its most difficult.

Langer, who led Calcavecchia by two strokes after three rounds, dropped into a tie with Calcavecchia with bogeys at the sixth and seventh holes. Calcavecchia took the lead for the first time with a birdie at eight. He promptly bogeyed the ninth, putting them in a deadlock again, but after Calcavecchia birdied the 12th he was in front to stay as Langer's putting stroke went sour.

Stewart made a determined charge with birdies at the 10th and 15th holes, but had putts lip out on Nos. 11, 12, 13, 14 and 16, and his hopes sank when he hit his tee shot into the water at the par-three 17th and took a double bogey. Bruce Lietzke, the defending champion, suffered a similar fate, taking a triple-bogey six at the short seventh and placing fourth at 284.

Mike Sullivan overcame the windy conditions to take the first-round lead with 65, but quickly dropped out of the race with 77 the next day. Langer tacked 67 onto his opening 70 for the lead after 36 holes. Calcavecchia trailed by four strokes. Langer maintained his two-stroke lead with 70 in the third round, as Calcavecchia pulled to within two strokes with 68 and Lietzke went alongside Calcavecchia with 70. Stewart, with a second successive 68, was four back.

Langer held on as long as his putting stroke would let him and Stewart staged an aborted rally in the final round as Calcavecchia won for the second time in his career. A large group of his fans whooped and hollered. Calcavecchia was born in Laurel, Nebraska, but he has lived in North Palm Beach, Florida, since he was 13. That's only 55 miles from Eagle Trace and Calcavecchia commuted to the tournament. So did his fans, their number a surprise to the hometown-boy-makes-good, caddy-makes-good hero.

Hertz Bay Hill Classic—$600,000
Winner: Payne Stewart

The Hertz Bay Hill Classic was a great tournament for Payne Stewart, Don Pooley and charity.

Stewart, so often a runner-up and so seldom a winner — his only victories in his first six years came in 1982 and 1983 — ended more than three years of frustration by winning a sizzling duel with David Frost for a three-stroke triumph at Arnold Palmer's Bay Hill Club in Orlando, Florida. Then he donated his $108,000 check to an Orlando hospital in memory of his late father.

Pooley made his first hole-in-one a momentous one when he sank his four-iron shot at the 192-yard No. 17 in the final round. It was a million-dollar ace — $500,000 for Pooley and $500,000 for The Arnold Palmer Children's Hospital and Perinatal Center.

"I was shocked. I couldn't believe it," said Pooley, who will receive $2,083.33 a month for 20 years. The hole-in-one was the capper to a 67, but Pooley was never in contention for the title, placing 20 strokes behind.

Even though he finished third on the money list in 1986, some people had branded Stewart a "choker." His time came at Bay Hill, just the way he hoped it would. Frost shot 65-67 the last two rounds and lost ground to Stewart, who had 63-65 for a 264 total, a tournament record. "This was the way I wanted to win," Stewart said.

"I would have won any other week," Frost said.

It was also the place where Stewart wanted to win. He has a home next to the course and every day, after hitting his drive at the 12th hole, he would hurry to his backyard fence to receive a kiss from his 16-month-old daughter Chelsea.

Another Orlando resident, Brad Faxon, grabbed the limelight first, taking the opening-round lead with a five-under-par 66. As Faxon vanished with 76 the next day, Frost stepped in front with 68 on the heels of his 67. Stewart pulled in behind Frost with 67 that tied him for second place, one stroke behind, along with Tim Simpson.

Then the tournament really got hot. Stewart had an eagle and eight birdies in the third round and missed tying the course record by a stroke with 63. That gave him a 54-hole total of 199, but Frost stayed on his heels with a 65 for 200. "I putted well, but he putted better. He just made everything," Frost said. And neither was finished.

Frost caught Stewart with a birdie at the first hole in the final round and played the front nine in a three-under 33...and lost ground. Stewart went out in 31. He clutched his lead throughout the back nine and when they got to the 456-yard 18th hole he was two ahead. With the second shot over water, it was not a comfortable two strokes, but it was two strokes nevertheless. It became less comfortable when Frost hit his approach to within 12 feet of the hole. Stewart reviewed how well he had hit the ball all day and went for the green with a seven iron. He hit it eight feet from the hole and, after Frost missed his birdie putt, Stewart rolled his in.

USF&G Classic—$500,000
Winner: Ben Crenshaw

His victory in the USF&G Classic at Lakewood Country Club in New Orleans was vintage Ben Crenshaw: Hit the ball all over the lot, then sink a putt for par or birdie. And Crenshaw was able to do that while trying to keep his temper from boiling over.

Crenshaw was fined $1,000 for slow play after he lost a playoff to T.C. Chen in the Los Angeles Open a month earlier. So when Crenshaw, Ronnie Black and Keith Clearwater were warned about playing too slowly at the ninth hole of the final round, the warning struck a nerve. Crenshaw thought it was unfair. At the second hole, all three had needed rulings, causing them to fall behind. Crenshaw showed what he thought about the warning when, after he had holed a 25-foot putt for birdie at the ninth hole, he slammed his putter into the bag.

The warning continued to trouble him for a few holes...and the putts kept dropping. Crenshaw had 12 one-putt greens and 24 putts in all as he shot a five-under-par 67 and won by three strokes over Curtis Strange with a 268 total. Strange, putting nearly as well as Crenshaw, got within two strokes of the lead with a 30-foot birdie putt at the 16th hole, but no closer, as he matched Crenshaw's 67 for 271.

"I knew if I kept the ball safe it would be tough to catch me," said Crenshaw.

First, Crenshaw had some catching of his own to do. Dick Mast, a veteran of the mini-tours, opened with 64. Crenshaw had 66 from which he drew encouragement. In eight previous tournaments he had an average of 73.75 for his first round score. "It makes Friday a heckuva lot of work," he said. He matched Mast's 68 in the second round and stayed two strokes behind Mast and one behind Bob Gilder.

Gilder took the lead in the third round, but hit into water at the 14th and 15th holes and never recovered. Mast also went backward, as Crenshaw slipped into a two-stroke lead over Black, who had 69. His lead all but disappeared when Crenshaw opened the final round with a bogey after his tee shot hit a tree and rebounded, traveling only 120 yards. At the second hole, a 560-yard par-five, Crenshaw's three-wood second shot hit a tree limb and dropped into a lake. He hit a wedge to within a yard of the hole and made the putt for par and "that really settled me down."

Then came a succession of one-putt greens that maintained his edge, and even the irritation caused by the slow-play warning failed to take away his putting touch, which kept Strange from making any headway despite birdies at the second, third and fifth holes. When Strange sank a 25-foot birdie putt at the 11th, he was still three strokes behind. Every time Strange thought he might erase the difference, Crenshaw would make a par-saving putt — a 10-footer at the 12th, a 20-footer at the 13th. At the par-three 17th, Crenshaw's tee shot hit a spectator on the head and bounced into the rough, but he got a good lie and sank an eight-foot putt for par. He capped his day with an eight-foot birdie putt and said, "I'm just glad it's over."

Tournament Players Championship—$1,000,000
Winner: Sandy Lyle

One of the toughest courses on the PGA Tour was transformed into one of the easiest by steady rain and little wind in the Tournament Players Championship. It took an under-par score to survive the 36-hole cut, and Sandy Lyle and Jeff Sluman equaled the course record with 72-hole totals of 274, 14 under par. Lyle, the 1985 British Open champion, won the playoff on the third hole with a par.

Lyle's victory, his first since the Greater Greensboro Open a year earlier, capped what had been an often-confusing tournament. The rain that softened the course was so heavy it caused suspensions of play the first two days, leaving the late starters to finish their rounds the next day and causing doubt as to who was the leader.

Lyle attracted little attention after opening with 67-71-66 that left him two strokes out of the lead. Then, for a while, it looked as if Lyle, Sluman, Scott Simpson, Mark O'Meara and Greg Norman might be involved in a playoff. But Lyle ended that possibility by rolling in a birdie putt of more than 30 feet at the last hole for a 70, and Sluman matched that birdie with a gutsy 12-footer for 69.

The first round was held up by rain for 1:20 early in the afternoon and was suspended at 3:55 p.m. with 72 players still on the course. Norman was low among the Thursday finishers with 67. Steve Jones, made two birdies and an eagle Friday morning for 66 and the first-round lead. Jones then teed off in his second round and maintained his touch as he birdied three of his first four holes — one a 50-foot bunker shot — and scored 67 for 133, breaking the course record for 36 holes by one stroke. The next morning, O'Meara completed his second round with 65 that tied Jones, a stroke in front of Simpson and Dan Pohl. Jones' demise began at the ninth hole in the third round, where he double-bogeyed. He fell out of the race with 76.

O'Meara and Simpson took over at 202 with 69 and 68, respectively.

The lead was in doubt almost from shot to shot in the final round. O'Meara led by a stroke with nine holes to go, but Simpson was coming on strong. Sluman took the lead with a birdie at the 10th, as O'Meara bogeyed. Simpson tied Sluman with a birdie at No. 11, Norman made it a threesome at the top with birdies at Nos. 12 and 13, and O'Meara made it a four-way tie with a birdie at the 12th. Simpson had the lead to himself as O'Meara and Sluman bogeyed No. 13 and Norman bogeyed No. 14.

Lyle, lurking in the shadows while playing even par, jumped into a share of the lead with Simpson with a chip-in birdie at the 15th hole. Norman left the chase with a bogey at No. 16, and O'Meara birdied the par-five to climb into a tie with Simpson, Lyle and Sluman. But O'Meara and Simpson couldn't match the birdie putts of Lyle and Slumann at the final green.

Greater Greensboro Open—$600,000
Winner: Scott Simpson

Scott Simpson, who faltered at the end in the Tournament Players Championship the week before, grabbed the lead after 54 holes with 70-73-69 and shot a steady two-under-par 70 in the final round for two-stroke victory in the Greater Greensboro Open, his first win since 1984. Clarence Rose placed second at 284, but it was Payne Stewart, who tied for third with Tom Byrum and Kenny Knox, who gave Simpson the greatest scare.

The weather was cold when the tournament began and it didn't get any better. Even though the thermometer got up to 60, the wind-chill made it feel closer to freezing. Under stocking caps, turtleneck sweaters and mittens, there was only one player with a smile on his face. T.C. Chen had never seen snow, and when the Saturday forecast called for snow, he was delighted. He was not disappointed.

Only 14 players broke par in the first round, led by Chen and Roger Maltbie with 68s. The second round was miserable for those who teed off late. Only half the field had finished when play was called off because of lightning. Those caught on the course had to complete their rounds the next morning, when it was really cold, before playing their third rounds.

Danny Edwards, with 70-69, led after 36 holes, then slipped away. Simpson had to play eight holes to complete his second round, then came back with 69 for a one-stroke lead over Byrum. Simpson played his 26 holes Saturday without a bogey.

Byrum took the lead early in the final round but couldn't maintain it as he put together a string of pars for 72. Stewart chipped in three times, his third a birdie at the par-three 17th. But Stewart and Rose, who had a 69, could not overtake Simpson. Simpson saved par after driving up against a fence at the 13th hole, then three-putted No. 14 for a bogey. But he did not crack. He birdied No. 16 to take the lead for good, and doubled his margin of victory with a 15-foot birdie putt at No. 18.

Deposit Guaranty Classic—$200,000
Winner: David Ogrin

In more than four years on the PGA Tour, David Ogrin had come close to winning only once, losing to Hal Sutton in a playoff in the 1985 St. Jude Classic. Victory finally came in the Deposit Guaranty Classic at the Hattiesburg Country Club when Ogrin won by one stroke over Nick Faldo.

For three rounds, Ogrin stayed in contention with scores of 66, 68, 69. Mike West opened the tournament by tying the course record with an eight-under-par 62. Robert Wrenn matched West's record in the second round as he jumped to a two-stroke lead at 131. Wrenn maintained a one-stroke lead with 68 in the third round and West stayed on his heels with 67.

Faldo strung together three straight 67s and trailed by two. Ogrin was four strokes back and predicted "somebody will shoot in the mid-60s all week and then they'll have that one good round where they put it all together." He was talking about himself.

Ogrin started an hour before the leaders in the final round and that was an advantage. He birdied the first hole and three more as he went out in 31. He made two more birdies on the back nine for 64 and a 267 total. Then he went into the clubhouse and watched the Masters on television, as friend John Adams kept him informed about how his pursuers were doing. Wrenn faded to 72 and Faldo ran out of holes, as he birdied the final four for another 67 and 268.

MCI-Heritage Classic—$650,000
Winner: Davis Love III

Davis Love III, in his second year on the PGA Tour, proved something to those who view him as a one-dimensional player by winning the MCI-Heritage Classic at the Harbour Town Golf Links on Hilton Head Island, South Carolina. While winning by one stroke with rounds of 70, 67, 67, 67 for a 271 total — 13 under par — Love showed he is not just a young man who can hit golf balls prodigious distances.

Harbour Town, at 6,657 yards, is a short course by modern standards, but places an emphasis on accuracy and its smallish greens make the Heritage Classic less a putting contest than many other events.

That Love won because of a mistake by another player diminished his first victory in his eyes.

Love, playing in the group just in front of Steve Jones, was on the 18th green facing a 40-foot putt, as Jones prepared to tee off on that hole. Jones led by a stroke. He needed a par to win — Love two-putted for his par — and a bogey to go to a playoff.

"I've never been in this position before," said Jones, who led the 1986 Tour qualifier, "and when I got to 18 I kind of rushed things." In the first three rounds, Jones had used a three wood off the tee at 18 so he wouldn't hit his drive through the fairway and into the marsh beyond. But this time there was a wind in his face, and he hit a drive off the tee. Just as he readied to swing, the wind died and indecision took over. "If I turned over on the driver with no wind, it would be gone. I let up and blocked it and I knew it was gone." Out of bounds. Now he needed a bogey desperately. But he failed to reach the green at the par-four hole with his fourth shot and his chip shot failed to drop. Jones finished second with 72 for 272.

Until he made his fatal mistake, Jones was in control. Gene Sauers had faded, Mark Wiebe had made a late move with 67 and it looked as if it were Jones' time to win. At the par-five 15th, Jones drove left, hit his approach into the trees on the right, then plunked his third shot within tap-in range for a birdie. With one hole to go, he was 13 under par and Love, at 12 under, was his only threat. Sauers, with 73, tied Wiebe for third place at 273.

Big I Houston Open—$600,000
Winner: Jay Haas

Buddy Gardner may never forget two putts in the 1987 Big I Houston Open — a 50-footer by Jay Haas and his own 30-incher. Haas' putt put him in position to win the tournament; the other putt lost it for Gardner, a non-winner in his 10th year on the PGA Tour.

Trailing Gardner by a stroke, Haas was confronted by a 50-foot birdie putt at the 18th hole. He needed the putt to keep his hopes alive. "I was trying to make it, but I also knew I needed a par because Payne was already in at 11 under," Haas said. It meant another Texas disappointment for Payne Stewart, who has been short by a total of six strokes in five tournaments in the state.

Haas' birdie finished off a 67 that gave him a 72-hole total of 276. Instead of needing par to win, Gardner suddenly was faced with par to tie. Gardner hit his tee shot into the right rough. To reach the green he had to hit between two pines and over a menacing lake. He got to the green, but was 90 feet from the hole. He would do well to two-putt, and it looked as if he might not do that when he left his first putt 15 feet short.

"I knew what I had to do," Gardner said. And after he did it, he jumped with joy. "I was so darned excited I didn't even know who I was playing off with."

Gardner's emotion went from cloud-high to bedrock-low on the first playoff hole, the par-three 16th. Haas hit his tee shot into the right rough, Gardner put his into a bunker left of the green. Haas chipped to within two feet of the hole. Gardner nearly holed his blast, his ball stopping less than three feet from the hole. "I was getting ready to go to the 17th," said Haas, whose thoughts were interrupted when Gardner missed his putt. Instead, Haas tapped in his two-footer and it was over.

Panasonic Las Vegas Invitational—$1,250,000
Winner: Paul Azinger

Because of a thunderstorm in the first round, the Panasonic Las Vegas Invitational was cut from 90 to 72 holes. But it couldn't have produced more excitement than was generated by Paul Azinger's second victory of the year.

Azinger came out of the pack with an eight-under-par 64 in the final round and, just as he had done in the Phoenix Open earlier, he won by one stroke over Hal Sutton. This victory, worth $225,000, was more dramatic.

Curtis Strange sank long birdie putts at the 16th and 17th holes and Sutton birdied No. 16 and saved par at No. 17 as they pulled into a tie with Azinger, playing ahead of them.

The 18th hole at Las Vegas Country Club, one of three desert courses used in the tournament, is a par-five that is reachable in two strokes.

Azinger hit a perfect drive, leaving him with 183 yards to the green. A birdie probably would mean playoff; Azinger was thinking eagle. He hit a five iron that caught the front of the green, 25 feet below the hole. The putt was up over a rise to a hole cut near the back of the green. "Reading it was easy. It was the speed I was thinking about," Azinger said. He got both right, and the ball dropped for an eagle-three. The crowd let out a whoop that carried back to Sutton and Strange at the 17th hole.

"I thought someone would make eagle and win. In fact, I thought it would be me," Sutton said later. Sutton went for the flag with a four iron. His ball stopped in the fringe behind the green, about 15 feet from the hole. He hit the putt well. It touched the left side of the cup, but refused to drop. "I played it where I wanted to. It just didn't break," Hal said. He tapped-in for 67 and 272. Strange, who took himself out of contention by hitting his approach into a bunker, also had 67 for third place at 273.

Azinger was virtually unnoticed for three rounds. Ken Brown was in the first-round lead with 64, then Larry Rinker took over with 131 and a two-stroke lead. The third round produced a jam at the top, involving Brown, Sutton, Kenny Perry, and Dan Pohl at 205. Azinger was at 207, and also behind Strange, David Frost and Andrew Magee. Defending champion Greg Norman was four strokes behind. Norman eagled the first hole and birdied the second in the final round, but couldn't keep it going. Azinger got going with a birdie at the first hole and kept it going.

Azinger won more than $250,000 without a victory in 1986. His coach, John Redman, told him he would be the leading money winner in 1987, much to the surprise of a lanky young man who couldn't break 40 for nine holes when he was in high school. But with his big Las Vegas payday Azinger took over the money lead with $442,460 and the season wasn't even half over.

Byron Nelson Golf Classic—$600,000
Winner: Fred Couples

What might Fred Couples accomplish if he took golf more seriously? He's a young man, age 27, who abstains from excessive practice, has talked about retiring and takes off for long periods in midseason. Nevertheless, he had managed to win two tournaments before the Byron Nelson Classic and for four years in a row had made a comfortable living.

Couples planned to play in the Houston Open two weeks before, and arrived a week early to practice. He was surprised to find he was not officially entered. So Couples spent 10 days working with two teachers and "hit more practice balls than I had ever hit in my life. The practice was fun because I usually don't do it."

Couples was eager to play, and he scored a playoff victory over Mark Calcavecchia, who launched a great comeback to get to extra holes. One stroke away from the cut after 36 holes following his 73-66, Calcavecchia came in with 63-64 to tie Couples at 266, 14 under par at the TPC course at Las Colinas in Irving, Texas.

The playoff nearly ended as soon as it began. Couples hit only five of 16 fairways in the final round — he hit little more than half in the tournament — but a good short game kept him on track. At the first playoff hole, No. 16, Couples hit his drive into the right rough. It was merely four inches from being out of bounds. Given the break, Couples matched Calcavecchia's birdie. Both scrambled for pars at the second extra hole. Both hit good drives at No. 18, but after Calcavecchia's nine iron went into a grass gully behind the green, Couples hit a wedge to the front of the green. Calcavecchia had a difficult lie, and his chip went 20 feet past the hole. His putt was six inches short. Couples two-putted from 35 feet for par and the victory.

The playoff ended a week of low scoring and a three-year victory drought for Couples. Las Colinas was in superb condition and the greens were softened by a brief rain Friday. And the usual Texas wind was virtually absent. Payne Stewart and Greg Norman opened with 64s. Norman hung around to take a share of fifth place, but Stewart never was a factor. Bob Lohr shot a tournament-record 62 in the second round, and missed several short putts. Lohr's 131 was a 36-hole record for the tournament. The next day, Couples set the 54-hole mark with 64 for 196. Calcavecchia then trailed Couples by six strokes. In the final round, Calcavecchia cut into Couples' lead on the closing holes, birdieing Nos. 14, 15, 16 and 17 while playing four groups ahead. The key hole for Couples was the par-five 16th. He chipped to within three feet of the hole and birdied to tie Calcavecchia. It also proved to be a key hole later, when his tee shot almost went out of bounds.

Colonial National Invitation—$600,000
Winner: Keith Clearwater

Keith Clearwater posted 64-64 in a 36-hole windup of the Colonial National Invitation to score his first PGA Tour victory by three strokes over Davis Love III. "It sure is hard to beat a pair of 64s in one day," said Love, whose 65-66 finish gave him second place at 269. Clearwater tied the tournament record at 266 as he became the first rookie to win the Colonial.

Bill Rogers showed some flashes of his former brilliance when he took the first-round lead with a 65. Four inches of rain fell on the Colonial Country Club course Friday, postponing the second round to Saturday and setting up a 36-hole finish. Scott Simpson, Chip Beck and Steve Elkington tied for the 36-hole lead at 133. At this point, Clearwater was five behind after his 67-71 start.

Clearwater's 64 in the morning round Sunday moved him within a stroke of Ben Crenshaw, who had 65. Crenshaw faded with a 72 in the afternoon, but Clearwater continued his birdie binge. "After that 64 in the morning, I knew I had a shot at it," said Clearwater. "Then those quick birdies (two in the first three holes) in the afternoon convinced me, and I just tried to keep the ball in play."

Georgia-Pacific Atlanta Golf Classic—$600,000
Winner: Dave Barr

Dave Barr, that big, mustachioed Canadian, won only once in his first nine years on the PGA Tour. But Barr showed steady improvement, and in the Georgia-Pacific Atlanta Classic, his career reached a peak. He shot a tournament record-tying 265, 23 under par, and won by four strokes over Masters champion Larry Mize.

Although he played well, Barr drew little attention through the first three rounds. There were many players from the Atlanta area in the field and they were in contention. Davis Love III opened with 65-65, was hit by the flu Friday night and weakly turned in 72-73 the last two rounds. As Love slipped, Virginian Bobby Wadkins took over, opening a one-stroke lead with 65. Wadkins shot a disastrous 73 in the final round.

Barr started the last round with two birdies and made two more at the fifth and sixth holes. He was 20 under par and had a three-stroke lead. Mize birdied Nos. 7, 8, 9, 10 and 11, and when Barr bogeyed the ninth hole, only one stroke separated them. Then Barr birdied Nos. 13, 14, 15 and 16, and only one of his putts was longer than six feet. "That stretch of holes won it for me," he said. Mize matched his 65 for second place.

Memorial Tournament—$849,290
Winner: Don Pooley

For three days, Scott Hoch had the Memorial Tournament in his pocket. A head cold and a drastic change in the weather stole it from him. In stepped Don Pooley for his second victory in 12 years, his first since 1980. Pooley finished with 272, one off the Muirfield Village record he throught Hoch was going to break.

The wind didn't blow and a downpour on Saturday made the course play easier. A total of 52 players finished under par.

Curt Byrum tied the tournament record with 64 in the first round. Hoch matched it in the second round for a tournament-record 131 that put him four strokes ahead of Byrum, who had 71.

Hoch had just birdied the seventh, eighth and ninth holes to go 15 under par — an unheard-of figure for Muirfield Village — when the clouds let loose, ending play in the third round for the day. Hoch completed his round the next morning for 67 and a four-stroke lead over Pooley. After a three-hour wait, Hoch began the final round at 18 under par. Pooley was 14 under, Byrum 12 under and John Mahaffey 11 under. "I thought Scott was going to break the tournament record by a bunch," said Pooley, who had 65.

But Hoch was a different player that afternoon. He bogeyed the second, third and fourth holes, and when Pooley sank a 15-foot birdie putt at the third hole, they were tied for the lead. "I had no expectations. It was totally up to Scott. If he shot a good score, there was nothing I could do," Pooley said. Hoch bogeyed the ninth hole and double-bogeyed the 10th. Pooley also bogeyed No. 10 and David Frost pulled into a tie with him, one stroke ahead of Byrum. Half a dozen others were in the chase. The last of these to go was Tom Watson, with a bogey at No. 18.

It was down to Pooley and Byrum as they stood on the No. 17 tee. Pooley hit an eight iron to the back fringe, 15 feet from the flag. He holed it. Byrum parred from 20 feet. Byrum's approach to the 18th green left him 35 feet short; Pooley's landed a comfortable 12 feet away. When Byrum missed his birdie putt, Pooley was assured of a victory and he holed his second birdie putt in a row.

Kemper Open—$700,000
Winner: Tom Kite

When Tom Kite won the Kemper Open, it marked the seventh year in a row he had won, a streak that is currently the longest on the PGA Tour. He won by seven strokes with a 270 total, 14 under par. Howard Twitty and Chris Perry tied for second place.

The Kemper was held at a new venue, the TPC at Avenel in Potomac, Maryland. Whether the players saw the course at near it toughest remains to be seen. At 6,864 yards Avenel is almost 300 yards shorter than Congressional, a course defending champion Greg Norman called "a true classic," and Avenel was hit by rain for five of six days before the tournament.

Kite and Norman jumped out with 64s, for a one-stroke lead over Scott Hoch. As the course began to dry Friday, Perry turned in his second straight 66 for 132. Kite and Twitty trailed by a stroke.

As the strength of the course began to show in the third round, Kite took charge. At one time Kite led by five strokes. Poor tee shots cost him bogeys at Nos. 15, 16 and 17 and permitted Perry to catch up. Kite sank a 20-foot birdie putt at the 18th for 68 and 201, and led Perry by one stroke.

After playing the first five holes in two over par in the final round, Kite saw his lead doubled from one stroke to two strokes. Twitty, who trailed by five after 54 holes, came to within a stroke a couple of times, but each time Kite pulled away. The final pullaway began at the 11th hole, where Kite sank a six-foot birdie putt. He sank a 40-foot putt for an eagle at the 13th hole that all but settled matters. Kite thought the birdie he made at the 454-yard No. 12, a very difficult par-four, was the key "because it was the first time today I backed up a birdie with a birdie." Given the big edge, Kite parred in for the $126,000 payday.

Manufacturers Hanover Westchester Classic—$600,000
Winner: J.C. Snead

The press would not have been surprised after the Westchester Classic if the winner and runner-up, J.C. Snead and Severiano Ballesteros, had vanished from their sight. Snead has been inaccessible for years, and Ballesteros has often hurried away to hide his emotions after losing.

So it was no great shock that Ballesteros left quickly. What was a little surprising was that Snead declared that his "feud" with the press was over after beating Ballesteros on the first playoff hole. "As far as I'm concerned, that is a thing of the past," Snead said.

The last time that Snead had won in his 20-year career was in the Southern Open in 1981.

Ballesteros used his driver in the playoff at the 304-yard No. 15 and hit into the woods below the green. Snead, aware of the trouble facing Ballesteros, played more conservatively, hitting a four iron off the tee. Ballesteros hit two trees and finally got on the green with his fifth shot, at which point he conceded to Snead, who two-putted for par.

That Ballesteros made the playoff was a credit to his short game. Westchester Country Club rewarded the conservative players and penalized the gamblers. Mike Reid, one of the most accurate drivers on the PGA Tour as well as one of the most conservative, led Ballesteros by one stroke and Snead by three with one round to play.

Reid's plan seemed to be just to play for pars and let everyone else self-destruct. It worked for 11 holes. Reid bogeyed No. 12, but so did Ballesteros. The Spaniard birdied No. 14, hitting a nine iron less than a foot from the hole, then he and Reid both bogeyed No. 15. Reid flew the green with a wood shot at the 204-yard No. 16 and took a double bogey.

Now Roger Maltbie was in front, but when Maltbie bogeyed No. 17, Snead took over with a birdie at that hole and had a birdie at the par-five 18th. Only Ballesteros had a chance to catch him. Seve did it dramatically, sinking a 10-footer for birdie at No. 17 and knocking in a 12-footer for birdie at No. 18.

When the playoff was over, Ballesteros headed to San Francisco and the U.S. Open. Snead had more time to savor his triumph. He hadn't qualified for the Open.

Canon Sammy Davis Jr. Greater Hartford Open—$700,000
Winner: Paul Azinger

Paul Azinger had won at Phoenix and Las Vegas by coming from behind; at the Greater Hartford Open, he held onto a lead and nailed down the triumph with an eight-foot par putt at the 72nd hole. He had rounds of 69, 65, 63 and 72 for a 269 total at the TPC of Connecticut and left Wayne Levi and Dan Forsman holding their breaths for a playoff before his last stroke dropped.

The 17th hole has a lake on the right side of the fairway, but Azinger wasn't about to play safe. He hit his driver into the water. "I hit a driver off that tee every day because I figured even if it did go into the water I'd have a short shot to the green," Azinger said. He had a nine-iron shot and walked off with a bogey and a one-stroke lead.

His drive at No. 18 went into the right rough and the ball bounded from the crowd back to the fairway. His seven-iron approach stopped on the back fringe. "When I hit the putt, I knew it was going past the cup, but I never expected it to go that far," Azinger said. It went eight feet beyond, and Azinger's nerves, already quivering, fairly rippled. But Paul hit the winning putt perfectly and said, "I can always look back on that putt and the one I made to win at Las Vegas and say, 'I made a tough putt to win. People can't say I'm a choker.' "

Levi was around the lead all week. He opened with 64 and 68, and was two strokes behind Bernhard Langer, who started with two 65s. Langer didn't break par again. Azinger, four strokes behind after 36 holes, took command with a 63 in the third round for a three-shot lead.

Crosswinds made the course play more difficult in the final round and the scores went up. Gene Sauers birdied the ninth hole and sank a wedge shot for an eagle at the 10th to pull to within a stroke. But Sauers bogeyed Nos. 11 and 14. Forsman closed with 67 and Levi sank a 20-foot chip shot at No. 16 and holed an 18-footer for birdie at the 17th. When Azinger bogeyed No. 17, they had chances to win. But with the heat on, Azinger dropped the putt that drained their hopes.

Canadian Open—$600,000
Winner: Curtis Strange

Richard Zokol, Dan Halldorson and David Barr made Canadian hearts beat faster with the prospect that a native son might win the Canadian Open for the first time since Pat Fletcher did it in 1954, and for only the second time in 73 years. But Curtis Strange won with a tournament record 12-under-par 276 on rounds of 71, 70, 66, 69. It was his first victory since the 1986 Houston Open.

A record score was not on Strange's mind after a first round played amid swirling winds. Only 14 players broke par, led by Joey Sindelar with 68. Five of the 21 Canadians in the field were in contention — Zokol at 70, Jim Nelford, Ray Stewart and Daniel Talbot at 72 and Halldorson at 73.

Late on the second day, an inch of rain fell in two hours, forcing those who had not yet completed their rounds to return early the next morning. David Frost, with 71-67—138, was the leader when play was postponed. On Saturday morning, Zokol sank an eagle putt at the 18th hole for a share of the lead.

Mike McCullough, who got into the tournament as an alternate, played the first 53 holes without a bogey and when he teed off at the 18th hole in the third round, he had a two-stroke lead. He then made a double bogey and dropped into a tie at 207 with Zokol and Strange. Zokol had to play 36 holes on Saturday and turned in scores of 68 and 69. Barr, with a second straight 67, was at 212 and Nelford, with a 69, was at 213. Strange kept pumping out pars in the final round, and made three birdies as well, pulling away for a three-stroke victory over Frost and Jodie Mudd. Frost got within one stroke of Strange after seven holes, but then missed numerous birdie opportunities.

Nelford finished 10 strokes behind, but scored a personal triumph. Less than two years before, on September 8, 1985, he received numerous injuries in a ski-boating accident in Phoenix, Arizona, the most serious to his right arm, which was broken in nine places and had to have a plate and 13 screws inserted. "All I had to worry about this week was that the screws didn't fall out," he said.

Anheuser-Busch Golf Classic—$612,000
Winner: Mark McCumber

Mark McCumber has been on the PGA Tour since 1978. The years of experience should make it easier for him to control his emotions. But McCumber still gets excited when he's in contention, and on the final holes of the Anheuser-Busch Classic, "you could have lighted the city off my nervous system." With the help of caddy Chico Fernandez, McCumber was able to keep his nerves under control and he beat Bobby Clampett by one stroke at the Kingsmill Golf Club in Williamsburg, Virginia.

"I was determined to dwell on the good things and not the bad things," McCumber said. He had to forget about the birdie putts he missed at the first two holes and concentrate on birdieing from 15 feet at the third. He also birdied No. 7, and at the next hole came the first of three breaks, if a bogey can be called a break. In this case it could, because after missing the green he faced a double bogey.

His second break came when shortly after that play was stopped for 85 minutes because of lightning. John Cook had a two-stroke lead before the delay; when play resumed, he quickly lost his advantage with two bogeys. Then came break No. 3. McCumber hit his second shot 25 feet from the hole at the par-five No. 15. Clampett's shot was 20 feet away. McCumber holed his eagle putt, Clampett missed his, and McCumber was in the lead to stay.

"I expected to make the putts at Nos. 1, 2, 12 and 14 and didn't," McCumber said. "On No. 15 I expected to two-putt. I was just trying to get the speed right...and it went right into the cup." The eagle capped a five-under-par 66 for a 267 that tied the tournament record. Clampett finished with a 68 for a 268 and a two-stroke edge on Scott Hoch.

Hardee's Golf Classic—$500,000
Winner: Kenny Knox

Kenny Knox, who scored his first victory in the 1986 Honda Classic, notched triumph No. 2 in the Hardee's Classic, winning by one stroke over Gil Morgan with rounds of 67, 66, 66 and 66 for a 265 total. That broke the tournament record, which figured. It seemed that everyone was shooting for records at Oakwood Country Club in Coal Valley, Illinois.

Mike Smith, in danger of missing the cut after an opening 71, bounced back with a nine-birdie 61 that broke the tournament record by a stroke and was just two off Al Geiberger's PGA Tour record. The next day, Smith shot 74 that ended his title aspirations.

Morgan, a 15-year veteran, had undergone rotator cuff surgery in the autumn of 1986, and was making only his eighth appearance of the year. After shooting 66-69, he trailed Brad Fabel by six strokes, but Fabel slipped in the third round and Morgan went into the lead with 63 for a one-stroke margin over Knox.

Morgan and Knox fought it out until the 15th hole in the fourth round. There Knox made a two-footer for a birdie and the lead. At the final green, after Morgan missed a birdie putt, Knox was faced with a clutch five-footer.

Carefully, he holed it. Anyone can win one tournament, Knox noted, but a second victory removes any doubt that the first was a fluke.

Buick Open—$600,000
Winner: Robert Wrenn

Before the Buick Open in Grand Blanc, Michigan, Robert Wrenn had played so poorly that he had received an entry form for the PGA Tour qualifying school.

Some of the statistics seemed to say that Wrenn did not play very well in the Buick Open, either. He was 113th in driving distance, tied for 40th in fairways hit, tied for 32nd in greens in regulation.

So much for statistics.

Just as improbable as Wrenn's victory was the way he achieved it — going away, by seven strokes, with a tournament record 26-under-par 262. He took a four-stroke lead with his 63 in the second round for 128 — the lowest 36-hole total of the year — and stretched his margin to six strokes with 67 in the third round.

Everyone was cheering for Wrenn to break the PGA Tour's 72-hole record for strokes under par. He then was 21 under par and the record was 27 under, by Ben Hogan in the 1945 Portland Open and Mike Souchak in the 1955 Texas Open.

"I told my caddie, 'Let's get 30 under.' As long as I'm living a fantasy, I might as well take it all the way," said Wrenn, another of the Wake Forest University graduates. Wrenn got to 27 under at No. 13, but then bogeyed the 14th and 15th holes. He got one stroke back by sinking a five-footer at the 17th hole, and needed a birdie at No. 18 to tie the record. He missed the green and his 25-foot chip shot slipped inches past the hole.

The only day Wrenn wasn't in the lead was Thursday. Ed Dougherty, the PGA Club Pro champion, opened with a 64 and led Wrenn, Jay Haas, Bob Murphy and Dewey Arnette — who tied the PGA record with eight straight birdies — by one stroke. After that it was all Wrenn. After his 63 in the second round, all that remained was the scoring record, and he gave it a good try.

Federal Express St. Jude Classic—$600,000
Winner: Curtis Strange

The Federal Express St. Jude Classic in Cordova, Tennessee, almost wound up in a five-man playoff, which would have been like punishment, considering the 100-degree heat and the humidity.

Mike Donald, Russ Cochran, Tom Kite and Denis Watson weren't thinking about that as Curtis Strange walked down the 18th fairway. For a chance at a more than $130,000 prize, they would have played anywhere, any time. Then Strange ended their hopes by birdieing the hole for a one-stroke victory, his second of the season. The difference between first place and a tie for second was more than $81,000.

After just missing a fairway bunker with his drive at No. 18, Strange heard a roar at the green. Strange thought Cochran had made a birdie and that he needed a birdie to tie. But Cochran had hit his drive into the lake, and his putt was for par.

Strange's ball was 80 yards short of the green and as far as he was concerned, it might as well have been eight feet. "I wouldn't want to be standing around the scorer's tent waiting for Curtis Strange when he had only 80 yards left," he said.

He hit the ball within seven feet of the hole, and sank the putt for 69 and a 275 total.

Cochran, a lefthander, shot six-under-par 66 to lead the first round; Strange trailed by four strokes. Cochran fell back with a 73 in the second round as Trevor Dodds, a South African, took over with 68-67; Strange, with a 68, was three back. Dodds crashed with a 74 on Saturday; Strange and Andy Dillard shared the lead at 206. Cochran, Donald, Hubert Green, Fuzzy Zoeller and Jay Don Blake were one stroke behind.

On that steamy Sunday, Donald and Cochran shot 69s, Kite 67 and Watson 66 to tie at 276. Zoeller three-putted the 18th and finished a stroke further behind.

The International—$1,115,190
Winner: John Cook

John Cook, who plays with a painful left elbow and wrist, is not one of the PGA Tour's longer hitters. Until the International at Castle Rock, Colorado, he had made only one eagle in 1987. At the 17th hole on the final day he collected his second, vaulting past defending champion Ken Green for a two-point victory under the modified Stableford scoring system.

Cook barely got through the first three rounds. The field was split for the first round, half playing Wednesday and half Thursday, with the survivors moving on. The scoring was not cumulative. Cook made five points Wednesday; seven who tied at four points played off for one spot. In the second round, he had no points and minus-two played off. In the third round, Cook and six others tied at plus-four, and one was eliminated in a playoff.

The final two holes were decisive. No. 17 is a 492-yard par-five that was the easiest hole in the tournament, an almost-certain birdie hole. No. 18 is a 480-yard par-four, a possible bogey hole. Green reached No. 17 in two strokes and two-putted, giving him a total of nine points. Cook was the only one with a realistic chance to catch him. When Green finished with a par and still nine points, Cook's chances were slim. He might birdie No. 17, but he also might bogey No. 18.

A good drive at No. 17 left Cook 210 yards from the pin, for some in the thin air a seven iron, for Cook a four iron. He hit a magnificent shot and faced a six-foot putt for eagle, the lead and probably the victory. "I felt very comfortable over that putt. I knew what it meant," Cook said. He stroked it unerringly. That gave him a three-point lead over Green, and as long as he didn't double bogey the 18th the title was his. He hit the green and that was it, even though he three-putted for bogey.

Beatrice Western Open—$800,000
Winner: D.A. Weibring

D.A. Weibring picked up the $144,000 first-place check in the Western Open, but the co-champions were Oscar Miles, superintendent at Butler National Golf Club, and numerous volunteers who helped to avert the first postponement on the tour since 1949. The Western Open was the tournament that almost wasn't. It ultimately was played on a course that never was used before and probably will never be again.

A week before the tournament, Butler National was inundated by 8.3 inches of rain. About one-third of the course was flooded. Salt Creek, which meanders through the course, kept spilling over from rains upstream, forcing postponement of the Monday and Thursday pro-ams until the autumn, and pushing the start of the tournament back a day, until Friday. Some thought was given to moving the tournament 30 miles south to Olympia Fields, but that was ruled out "because Butler National is our course," said tournament director Peter de Young.

With the help of two helicopters and water hogs (portable pumps) much of the water was removed by Thursday. Officials were confident play could begin Friday, but the rain resumed early that morning and continued for eight hours. That led to one of the most bizarre emergency plans in tour history. The tournament was reduced to 54 holes, with a cut after the first round, and 36 holes on Sunday. Only nine holes would be played at Butler National. The back nine at adjacent Oak Brook Golf Club, a public course, would serve as the front nine. The tournament course back nine would be a mixture of nine holes at Butler National. The back nine at Oak Brook measured 3,286 yards, none of the par-fours were longer than 400 yards and the two par-fives were reachable in two. The finishing holes were to provide much of the drama, as Larry Nelson made a futile attempt to beat Weibring.

Seven players led the first round with 69s. It took an even-par round of 72 to survive the cut. With players starting at both nines at 6:30 a.m. Sunday, Nelson shot a 67 — the low round for the tournament — in the second round to join Weibring, Greg Norman and Lennie Clements at 139, a stroke behind Brian Fogt and Dave Barr. The field was so jammed it seemed that any of the 75 who survived the cut could still win.

Weibring birdied the ninth hole at Butler to tie Clements, Norman and David Frost for the lead and appeared to open the door for a runaway on the nine holes at the easier Oak Brook course. But Weibring missed birdie opportunities at three of the first four holes, and with three holes to go he said "I felt I needed a birdie," after television commentator Ed Sneed informed him he was tied for the lead. He got it at the 17th hole, converting a possible five into a three. He drove into a fairway bunker, hit a 131-yard nine iron to the green and sank a five-foot putt. "I began to feel emotional when I walked to the green," said Weibring, a native of Illinois whose only other tour victory came at the 1979 Quad Cities tournament in Coal Valley, Illinois.

Weibring finished with 68 for 207. After Norman failed to catch him, shooting a 69 for 208, only Nelson had a chance. Nelson's birdie at Oak Brook's fifth hole cut the margin to one stroke. Weibring went to the practice range in anticipation of a playoff. But Nelson got only one more chance at a birdie. That came at the par-five 18th hole, Oak Brook's 16th. Nelson tried to cut the dogleg off the tee and hit a tree. The ball ricocheted into the fairway, and he was able to hit his second shot to where he could hit a wedge to the green. A birdie and playoff seemed likely, but his approach was 15 feet away. Nelson missed on the high side, and tied Norman for second place.

"I don't care if we only played 54 holes. I don't care if we played two different nines. I just really feel good to have won a golf tournament again," Weibring said.

NEC World Series of Golf—$800,000
Winner: Curtis Strange

Everyone agrees the PGA Tour could use a dominant player. Maybe Curtis Strange isn't, but when he won the NEC World Series of Golf, he gave the appearance of being one. It was his third victory of the year and his seventh in three years, the most by any tour player in the span.

Strange's $144,000 check pushed his official tour earnings to $653,296, a one-year record with more than two months remaining. It was the third straight year in which the money record was shattered, and Strange had done it twice. Strange's $542,321 in 1985 broke the record of $530,808 by Tom Watson in 1980. Greg Norman topped Strange's mark with $653,296 in 1986.

It was curious that Strange would break the record at Firestone Country Club, a long, demanding course that caused him trouble in the past. In five previous World Series, he had broken the par only four times. "It's a long course for me," he said. "If I hit 13 or 14 greens, it's good for me." Despite damp weather that made the course play longer than its 7,173 yards, Strange broke par twice and matched it once in a 70-66-68-71—275 performance that gave him a three-stroke margin over Fulton Allem, the South African golfer appearing in only his fifth U.S. tournament.

Allem won $86,400, "more money here in one week than I did on the whole tour back home." His final-round 70 gave him second place by one stroke over Mac O'Grady, who shot 69 in every round but the second.

Bobby Wadkins shot 64 and took the first-round lead by three strokes over Larry Mize and Kenny Knox. Wadkins was 10 strokes higher in the second round, as Strange leap-frogged past him to a two-stroke lead over Wadkins, Paul Azinger and Fred Wadsworth.

Strange was in the lead to stay. A 68 in the third round gave him a 204 total, and a two-stroke lead on Davis Love III, who had 66. Tom Kite made the first eagle in 21 years at the 625-yard No. 16, sinking a 150-yard seven iron shot en route to a 65 that tied him at 208 with Wadkins and Allem.

All the pursuers except Allem faded in the final round. Allem moved within two strokes with birdies at the second and sixth holes, but nullified them with bogeys at the seventh and ninth. With nine holes to play, Strange was five strokes in front, and one was about to catch him. "It wasn't as exciting as some tournaments, but a lot of that has to do with Firestone being such a tough course," Strange said.

Provident Classic—$450,000
Winner: John Inman

It seems that everyone has a nemesis. For Rocco Mediate, it may be John Inman. In the 1984 Western Amateur, Inman won by beating Mediate. For his first professional victory, Inman beat Mediate again.

With two holes left in the Provident Classic in Hixson, Tennessee, Mediate led Inman by one stroke. At the par-four 18th, Inman, playing one group ahead of Mediate, hit a seven iron just on the green, but near the pin, which was cut on the front right. He sank the birdie putt for 66 and a 15-under-par 265. Mediate's drive landed in a divot and his six-iron approach was 35 feet left of the green. He chipped to within four feet, but played too much break on the putt and had to settle for 66 and a tie for second with Bill Glasson at 266. Glasson, who shot 66, also had several opportunities to send the tournament into extra holes.

Joey Sindelar tied the course record with an eight-under-par 62 in the first round and Robert Thompson, whose highest finish in two years on the tour was 16th, matched the score in the third round. Mediate, who opened with 66, took the 36-hole lead with 63. Thompson, who birdied eight of the last 11 holes and played the back nine in a record-equalling 29, tied Mediate, who had 69, for the 54-hole lead.

Thompson began the final round with a birdie, but two bogeys dropped him three strokes behind Mediate, who led Glasson by one stroke and Inman by two at the turn. Inman sank a 25-foot putt for birdie at No. 10, but Mediate also birdied the hole, maintaining his two-stroke edge. Inman got a break when his tee shot took a good bounce at No. 13 and he birdied from 25 feet. A 12-foot birdie putt at No. 15 tied Mediate, but Inman bogeyed No. 16, setting up the 18th-hole dramatics.

Inman, brother of Joe Inman, became the second first-year player to win in 1987 — the other was Keith Clearwater in the Colonial. "I had two goals this year — to make the top 125 and win a tournament," he said.

B.C. Open—$400,000
Winner: Joey Sindelar

Joey Sindelar's second victory in three years in the B.C. Open at Endicott, New York, was rooted in a dismal showing in the PGA Championship a month earlier. Sindelar shot 80-79, a performance that made him realize his game needed some tailoring. He is a right-to-left player who shoots for the flag. When the flag is on the right side, he has problems. So Sindelar went home to Horseheads, New York, and consulted his pro, his father, who recommended reducing his upright swing and weakening the grip with his left hand.

In the Provident Classic, Sindelar opened with 62 and tied for seventh place. Then came the B.C. Open, a tournament played virtually in his back yard. The result was a wire-to-wire victory that left the rest of the field playing for second place after the second round. Sindelar shot 65-63-69-69—266, one above the tournament record. Jeff Sluman, another New York native, place second at 270, four strokes behind Sindelar and five ahead of Mike McCullough and Tony Sills.

Sindelar's father walked with him as Joey scored his third victory in four years on the tour. After Sindelar's opening 65 gave him a one-stroke lead, his caddy had to leave because of his father's illness. Joe, Sr., picked up his son's bag and saw him play one of his finest rounds, an eight-under-par 63 in which thoughts of a score in the 50s popped into their minds. Sindelar had five birdies and an eagle as he went out in 30. He began the back nine with birdies at Nos. 10 and 12. "If you can't think about 59 when you're nine under after 12, when can you?" Sindelar said.

The 59 was not to be, but the 63 gave him a 36-hole total of 128 and a seven-stroke lead, the largest two-round lead on the tour since 1975. His 69 in the third round extended his advantage to eight strokes over Sluman, and Sindelar's only problem then was how to handle the big lead. "My purpose was not to get into the mid-60s; it was to get into the 60s." His 69 was more than enough.

Bank of Boston Classic—$500,000
Winner: Sam Randolph

It had been dry for so long in Massachusetts, when rain came in torrents during the fourth round of the Bank of Boston Classic, Sam Randolph joined the natives in giving praise. With a four-stroke lead after three rounds, Randolph didn't mind a final-round washout. "I did my rain dance this morning," Randolph said, as players slogged in from the course before he was scheduled to tee off.

Play was halted with only four of the 82 players in with complete rounds and was cancelled four hours later. So Randolph, in his rookie year, won his first tournament as a pro, and who is to say he wouldn't have won had the tournament gone 72 holes? Randolph had a 67-68-64—199 total, and a four-stroke edge over Wayne Grady, Ray Stewart and Gene Sauers. The most disappointed were Grady and Stewart, fighting to keep their tour cards, but their shares of second place helped their quest.

Randolph, figuring he needed a break, took the three weeks off before the tournament, and the rest seemed to help. His opening-round 67 left him two strokes behind Curtis Strange, John Mahaffey and Stewart. Lee Trevino then shot 66-67—133, tying the tournament 36-hole record and giving him a one-stroke lead. A 72 in the third round dropped Trevino six strokes behind and he never made up the lost ground. Saturday, calm and overcast, was Randolph's day. He took only 24 putts — 14 on the first 12 holes — as he carved out 64, one above the tournament record, for the four-stroke lead.

Greater Milwaukee Open—$500,000
Winner: Gary Hallberg

It rained every day during the Greater Milwaukee Open, but not bad enough to reduce the tournament to less than 72 holes. Gary Hallberg played the best in the inclement conditions, gaining his first victory in four years. Hallberg made a 50-foot chip-in at the 71st hole that ended the aspirations of Robert Wrenn. He won by two strokes over Wrenn and Wayne Levi with a 70-66-67-66—269 total.

Tommy Nakajima shot a 10-under-par 62 in the first round that included 10 birdies and an eagle on the Tuckaway Country Club course in Franklin, Wisconsin, despite a rain delay of 2½ hours. But Nakajima shot 76 the next day and never recovered. Veteran Larry Ziegler, age 48, finished off his first round for a 64 Friday morning, then tacked on 68 in the afternoon. That gave Ziegler a four-stroke lead when darkness stopped play. Wrenn, one of those forced to complete their second round Saturday morning, played his final five holes in one over par for 68 that left him one stroke behind. Ziegler slipped to 72 in the third round while Wrenn and Hallberg, former teammates at Wake Forest, tied for the lead. Hallberg ignored the persistent rain for 67 and Wrenn had 68 as the field bunched up behind them.

It rained again Sunday, and only 15 of the 29 groups finished before play was postponed for the day. The delay was welcomed by Wrenn, who said he did not feel comfortable over the ball. Hallberg had birdied four of his first eight holes and was tied at 15 under with Levi, Bill Kratzert and Dan Pohl. The next day, Hallberg completed his front nine in 32 and came back in 34, shaking off Wrenn, who birdied the 13th and 14th holes, with his chip-in birdie at the 220-yard No. 17. "I thought I would jump into the lead at the 17th, but he hit a Larry Mize-like chip," Wrenn said.

Southwest Golf Classic—$400,000
Winner: Steve Pate

Two years ago, in his first year on the tour, Steve Pate was tied for the lead in the Atlanta Classic with six holes to play and lost to Wayne Levi in a playoff. In a charity tournament in Pittsburgh 10 weeks before the Southwest Classic, Pate came from behind with four birdies on the last six holes to tie Mike Nicolette, then beat him in a playoff.

Those experiences perhaps contributed to Pate's first victory in the Southwest Classic at the Fairway Oaks Golf and Racquet Club in Abilene, Texas. Involved in a large battle in the last round, Pate faced a five-foot par putt at the final green for 67 and 15-under-par 273. There was no hesitation; Pate sank the putt. Mark O'Meara then missed a tying six-footer, and Pate won $72,000, pushing his career earnings past $500,000.

Pate opened the tournament with 67, but was two strokes behind Bob Eastwood. Dan Halldorson shot a second straight 66 in the second round for a two-stroke lead over Frank Conner and Eastwood, six ahead of Pate.

Saturday, it was David Edwards' turn. He shot 65 for a 202 total, moving from five back to one ahead of Eastwood (69) and Hale Irwin (65). Pate's 68 left him four behind. The final round quickly turned into a dogfight. Pate had the best round among the leaders, 67, leaving Halldorson (70), Eastwood (71), Edwards (72) and O'Meara (69) to contemplate the shots they missed as they tied for second place.

Southern Open—$400,000
Winner: Ken Brown

In two Ryder Cup matches, Ken Brown was winless, leaving him with the feeling he had let his team down. Two weeks later, Brown's spirits were lifted when he scored his first U.S. victory in the Southern Open in Columbus, Georgia. He did it impressively, winning by seven strokes over Larry Mize, David Frost and Mike Hulbert.

"My goal has always been to win here and at times I thought I played well enough to win, but someone always seemed to sneak past me," the Scotsman said. "It's satisfying to win over here because it's so hard to do."

Frost gained a two-stroke lead in the first round with 63, while Brown, Hulbert and Vance Heafner shot 65s. Frost struggled to 71 in the second round, and Brown took a two-stroke lead over Hulbert with 64. He shot 69 in windy conditions Saturday for a five-stroke lead over Hulbert and Irwin. "I think Ken Brown might have won the tournament today," Irwin said. No one made a run at Brown as he strolled to 68 for a 266 total. "The idea was to start well today and not give anybody a glimmer of hope," Brown said.

Pensacola Open—$300,000
Winner: Doug Tewell

There had been some high moments in Doug Tewell's career, including a course-record 64 in the 1985 PGA Championship, but for the most part his 12-year record had been one of unfulfilled promise. He had won three times, the drawbacks being other interests, which cut into his tour time, and a herniated disc.

After giving his back a rest, Tewell demonstrated in the Pensacola Open how well he can play with a three-stroke victory built on power as much as putting ability. Tewell had three eagles, the last igniting a torrid final nine as he shot 69-66-66-68—269, 15 under par at the Perdido Bay Resort. Phil Blackmar and Danny Edwards tied for second place.

John Mahaffey, sinking three putts of 30 feet and another of 20 feet, led the first round with 66, then watched the parade go past. First came Edwards, returning after a two-month layoff after working on a public course he joined in buying, and Trevor Dodds, who went 67-67. Then came Tewell, whose second 66 gave him a one-stroke lead.

Edwards and Blackmar kept up the pressure as Tewell played the front nine in even-par in the last round. Then Tewell hit a four iron to within 18 feet to set up an eagle putt at the 11th hole. A birdie from six feet after another four-iron approach at the 12th hole and a 15-foot birdie putt from the apron at the 14th hole put him in position for the coup de grace — an 18-foot birdie putt at the 16th hole after a nine-iron approach. "After the birdie at 16, it was the first time I felt I had the tournament won," he said. Even bogeys at the final two holes couldn't deny him that.

Walt Disney World/Oldsmobile Classic—$500,000
Winner: Larry Nelson

Larry Nelson has been viewed as a good, steady player, but not a great one, despite his three major triumphs. That probably won't change, even with Nelson's final-round 63 to overcome a six-stroke deficit and pass nine players to win the Walt Disney World/Oldsmobile Classic.

Morris Hatalsky and Mark O'Meara had a chance to catch Nelson, who teed off an hour before them, and was in the press tent recounting his round as they reached the 18th green. Nelson held his breath as he listened for the reaction from the crowd as Hatalsky and O'Meara hit their putts in an attempt to tie him. He heard only welcome silence. O'Meara missed a 25-foot birdie and Hatalsky failed on a 15-foot birdie, tying them for second place.

O'Meara, winless since 1985, opened with 63 at Lake Buena Vista, Florida, one of the three courses used in the tournament, and stayed a stroke in front with 68 at Disney's Magnolia course the next day. Nelson, with 68-69, trailed by six strokes. Steve Pate burned up Disney's Palm course front nine in the third round, eagling two holes, playing the first seven holes in six under par, despite a bogey, and cruised in with 65 for a 199 total. Nelson had 68 and still trailed by six. Nelson began the final round with 33 on the first nine at Magnolia. The adrenaline was starting to flow. A 35-foot eagle at the 10th hole made him five under par for the day. At Nos. 13 and 14, he sank birdie putts of three feet. Nelson finished with a six-under 30 on the back nine, then waited to see if he had won. The silence after the putts by O'Meara and Hatalsky was joyous.

"That's certainly my best competitive round on a Sunday," he said. "To shoot 63 when you have to do it, that's really something."

Seiko-Tucson Open—$600,000
Winner: Mike Reid

For more than 10 years, Mike Reid made a good living on the PGA Tour while enduring the constant observation: "You've never won as a pro." As an amateur, Reid briefly led the 1976 U.S. Open, and from the time he joined the tour in 1977 he displayed the ability to hit fairways with monotonous regularity, constantly placing near the top in driving accuracy. But he never won. He earned more than $1 million, but he didn't win.

Finally, he did. Victory came in the Seiko-Tucson Open. After Reid came from behind to win by four strokes, he said, "For 11 years there has never been a point that I didn't believe I could win. If it takes 11 years to win, I guess it takes 11 years."

When Reid collected his first winner's check, he passed the label of making a million without winning a tournament to Chip Beck, who tied with Mark Calcavecchia, Fuzzy Zoeller and Hal Sutton for second place. Beck had passed the million-dollar mark in nine years with his $39,600 check.

Reid opened with a 64 at the new TPC at StarPass course, giving him the first-round lead. But Reid had been in first place after 18 holes many times before. Sutton scooted past him with a 62 in the second round, then

Zoeller took the lead with a 64 in the third round.

Trailing Zoeller by four strokes entering the final round, Reid quickly narrowed the gap by birdieing the first hole and sinking a 20-foot chip for eagle-three at the third hole. He played the next six holes in one under par, and watched as the leaders came back to him.

The wind, which had been absent for the first three rounds, kicked up and the four players whom Reid was battling for the lead have never been known for keeping their drives on the fairway. With StarPass' narrow fairways, that can be disastrous. Reid kept hitting his drives where he could play them and the others struggled. When Reid began the back nine with two birdies, he had a three-shot lead over Calcavecchia and played the final seven holes in one over par. His only mistake was a bogey at the 17th hole, for 67 and a 267 total. Zoeller, after almost sinking a long birdie putt at the 18th, three-putted for a 75 and had to share second place with the other three.

Centel Classic—$200,000
Winner: Keith Clearwater

Despite winning in his rookie year, Keith Clearwater found himself in Tallahassee, Florida, instead of at the Nabisco Championship in San Antonio. Second-best was not so bad, Clearwater discovered. He won the Centel Classic by one stroke over Joey Sindelar, Bill Glasson, Bill Kratzert and Bob Lohr and the $90,000 first prize gave him $320,007, the most ever for a first-year player.

Tom Sieckmann led the opening round with 66 and stayed in contention until he crashed with 75 in the fourth round. Kratzert, with 69-67, tied Sieckmann for the lead at the halfway point, one stroke ahead of Buddy Gardner, who made a hole-in-one at the 11th en route to a 68. Sindelar, bidding for his second victory of the year, shot 67 and Clearwater, with his second straight 68, tied Sieckmann (71) and Gardner (72) for the third-round lead at 207.

It looked like it was to be Sindelar's tournament when he played the front nine at Killearn Golf and Country Club in two under par. But Sindelar hit his tee shot into the water at the 12th hole for a double bogey. He also bogeyed the 15th and watched as Clearwater struggled for pars for 71 to win.

Nabisco Championship—$2,000,000
Winner: Tom Watson

Only 30 players were in the field for the Nabisco Championship at Oak Hills Country Club in San Antonio, Texas, but it was not astounding that a player who hadn't won in more than three years would finish on top — not when that player was Tom Watson.

Watson hadn't won in the U.S. since the 1984 Western Open, but he had the 1987 U.S. Open in his grasp until Scott Simpson took it from him. That weekend in San Francisco was a prime indicator that, at 38, Watson was not finished yet. When he won, it wasn't the $360,000 winner's check that fueled his exhilaration as much as the fact he finally had won again: "This ends three years of frustration, three years of questions. There were questions internally, too, but it turned out to be worth the wait."

A total of $5 million was distributed — $2 million to the 30 contestants (last place paid $32,000), $1 million in year-long performance bonuses to the same 30 players, and another $2 million in the team charity competition, which involved the other tour events.

Curtis Strange was both a winner and a loser, if there was a loser. He picked up $175,000 for winning the yearly competition, but was a distant last in the tournament, 25 strokes behind Watson. Including the bonus, which was considered official money, Strange shattered the money record with $925,941, more than $100,000 ahead of Paul Azinger, who had a fourth-place finish in the tournament. But Azinger overtook Strange in the Player of the Year points race.

Those figures were secondary to Watson's return to glory. He left nothing to chance for the Nabisco Championship. Driving had been the troublesome part of his game, but he knew it was the short game that produced victories. He took six weeks off, starting in late August, and spent much of that time working on his short game. "You should spend a third of your time on the long game and two-thirds on the short game, and I wasn't doing that," he said.

Watson opened with 65 for a one-stroke lead over Larry Mize and David Frost. A 66 expanded his lead to four strokes. In those two rounds he hit only 25 greens and one-putted 19 times, which is the way he used to play.

He shot a steady 69 in the third round to keep his lead at four strokes over Mark Calcavecchia and Mark O'Meara. Four or five years before, everyone would have been playing for second place. Now they weren't certain.

Corey Pavin got within three strokes in the last round with an eagle at the 10th hole, then made birdie at the 11th, but negated that advance by bogeying the next two holes. Calcavecchia and Azinger kept their hopes alive until the 16th hole, where Calcavecchia bogeyed and Azinger double-bogeyed. Greg Norman started the day five strokes behind, and the best he could manage was 66 after two bogeys on the first three holes.

The only one who put any pressure on Watson was Beck, six behind at the start of the round. Watson had just missed the green at the 17th hole when his caddy informed him he held only a one-stroke lead over Beck, who had completed his round with 64 for a 270 total. "I thought I led by two," Watson said later. Up ahead, the crowd roared as Norman hit his tee shot at the par-three 18th hole to within seven feet of the hole, as Watson looked over his chip shot at No. 17. He hit it to within four feet of the cup and made the par-saving putt. His lead was still one stroke.

The 18th at Oak Hills is not a difficult hole, a 198-yarder that can be reached with a six-iron. But when a person hasn't won for a long time, any shot under pressure can be terrifying. But Watson hit his shot true, to within eight feet of the hole, an almost certain par for a one-stroke triumph. "Let's just two-putt," Watson told himself as he walked to the green. When he got to the ball, he said to himself, "What the hell are you trying to two-putt this for?" He sank it for 68 and a 268 total. When he flung his visor high in the air, it was if he had just lifted a load from his mind. Which, of course, he had.

Isuzu Kapalua International—$600,000
Winner: Andy Bean

The year ended on an upbeat note for Andy Bean. Gone was the tendinitis in his elbow that caused him to finish 120th among the money winners with $73,808 — a considerable drop from his $491,000 in 1986 — and the result was two victories in a row. Not official PGA Tour victories — but the money spends. Two weeks after winning low individual honors in the U.S. vs. Japan tournament, Bean repeated as champion of the Isuzu Kapalua International at the Kapalua Bay course in Maui, Hawaii.

Sandy Lyle, who won in 1984, took the first-day lead with 65. Bean led in the second round with 65 following 66. It was then a three-man tournament — Bean, Lyle and Lanny Wadkins. Bean shot 69 in the third round, and was one stroke ahead of Lyle, who had 67. Wadkins, after two straight 67s, added 69 that placed him three strokes back.

In the last round, Wadkins missed a 3½-foot birdie putt at the second hole and Bean bogeyed. Bean birdied the fourth and fifth holes, negating an eagle by Wadkins at the sixth. Bean stayed comfortably ahead after that, as Lyle and Wadkins battled for second place. Wadkins bogeyed Nos. 9 and 11, but birdied four of the final holes for 67 and 270. Bean matched his 67 for 267, with birdies at the 10th and 13th holes easing the way. Lyle never got started, posting a steady 71 that gave him third place at 272, one stroke ahead of Ben Crenshaw, who closed with 66.

World Cup—$750,000
Winners: Ian Woosnam and David Llewellen, Wales

After a year off, the World Cup returned for its 33rd showing at the Kapalua Bay course, site of the Kapalua International. Seven of the 64 men — 32 two-man teams — in the World Cup were judged to have an edge in course knowledge from the week before. But it was a different Kapalua course on which the World Cup was played. For all four days, there was wind and rain.

It seemed reasonable that players from Great Britain would have the least trouble with the weather, and that proved true. Ian Woosnam of Wales, with rounds of 67-70-65-72, shot a 14-under-par 274 and won the individual title by five strokes over Sandy Lyle of Scotland. Woosnam's 274 and David Llewellen's 300 gave Wales a score of 574, tying Lyle (279) and Sam Torrance (295) for the team championship.

Holes No. 10 and 18, both par-fives, were used for the playoff. A short putt decided the outcome. Lyle and Torrance both missed birdie putts of about 12 feet at the first hole, as everyone made par. At the second hole, Llewellen and Torrance both had six-foot putts for par. Llewellen made his; Torrance missed.

The U.S. team of Ben Crenshaw and Payne Stewart stumbled to a third-place finish at 576, Crenshaw with 286 and Stewart with 290. The Americans took the first-round lead with both shooting 70s, a stroke better than Ronan Rafferty and Eamonn Darcy of Ireland. That was their last time in front. Lyle shot 69 and Torrance, 71, the second day to give Scotland a three-stroke lead over the Americans, who both shot 73s. Scotland's lead might have been bigger had not Torrance hooked his drive out of bounds at the 18th hole.

Only three players broke 70 in the third round, as Woosnam moved Wales to within a stroke of Scotland with a remarkable 65. Llewellen birdied the last two holes for 73. Torrance and Lyle both turned in 71s. The Americans were three strokes behind.

Scotland's edge quickly disappeared when Torrance four-putted the first green in the final round. With the winds blowing at their hardest of the week, the pivotal holes were expected to be the ocean holes, Nos. 3, 4 and 5. The Scots played them in three over par, the Americans in two over, and when the Welshmen negotiated them in one over, they had a two-stroke lead.

Woosnam bogeyed the eighth hole and Llewellen the ninth, setting up a final-nine dash that had the Scots and Welshmen tied and the Americans two strokes behind. Stewart drove into the hazard at the 16th hole and failed to par after missing the green at the 17th hole, all but ending the U.S. hopes. Torrance once again hooked his drive out of bounds at the 18th hole, but managed to make a bogey. When Lyle birdied, and Woosnam and Llewellen parred, the teams were tied at 574. Shortly thereafter, Wales, which had never finished higher than fourth place in the past, had its first World Cup title.

J. C. Penney Classic—$650,000
Winners: Jane Crafter and Steve Jones

Neither Steve Jones nor Jane Crafter had won by themselves on the tour but got their first taste of victory in the J. C. Penney Classic, winning by two strokes over Mark McCumber and Debbie Massey with 65-69-66-68— 268.

Jones had been earning a reputation for throwing away advantages in the Phoenix Open and Tournament Players Championship, and he hit his drive out of bounds at the last hole with victory in his grasp in the Heritage Classic. Crafter, a native of Australia, had a career-low 64 in the final round of the S&H Classic, but all it got her was a second-place finish.

In the J. C. Penney Classic, Crafter came up with the clutch shots. She chipped in three times for birdies in the last 25 holes, the most important one a 35-footer at the 71st hole that broke a three-way tie for the lead. Doug Tewell and Betsy King missed short par-saving putts at the last two holes as they tied Morris Hatalsky and Donna White for third place at 271, and McCumber missed a 15-footer at the final hole.

Ken Perry and Sally Little blazed to the first-round lead with 62, three strokes ahead of four teams, but they failed to break par in the last three rounds. A jam developed in the second round, led by Ronnie Black and Dawn Coe with 66-66. Saturday was the day for McCumber and Massey, whose 65 gave them a 54-hole total of 199 and a one-stroke lead on Jones and Crafter.

Jones and Crafter made their move early in the final round, taking a three-stroke lead with birdies at the first, fourth — where Crafter chipped in —

The **EBEL** Shot of the Year: Larry Mize won the Masters with a miracle.

Major Champions

Larry Mize (Masters) with Jack Nicklaus.

Scott Simpson (United States Open).

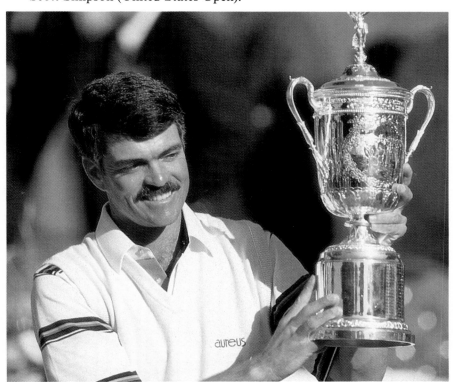

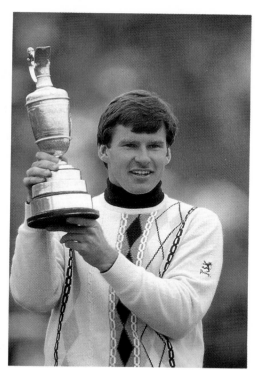

Nick Faldo (British Open).

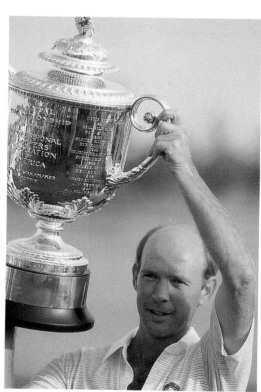

Larry Nelson (PGA
Championship).

Stretched like the Georgia pines, Seve Ballesteros lets loose on Augusta National.

The Masters

For Greg Norman, the Masters was a painful experience.

Frequent contender Curtis Strange led after 36 holes.

Ben Crenshaw came close here, and in the other majors.

Almost unnoticed, Bobby Wadkins tied for fourth.

Bernhard Langer also shared fourth.

U.S. Open

Crucial for Scott Simpson was his bunker shot at No. 17.

Tom Watson's last chance was this putt on the final hole.

From the misery that was Muirfield came a happy result for Nick Faldo.

British Open

Until the final holes, Paul Azinger's short game kept him in the lead.

Australian Rodger Davis tied Azinger in second place.

Lanny Wadkins congratulates Larry Nelson at the PGA Championship.

Hapless Scott Hoch couldn't get past the 72nd hole.

PGA Championship

Tied for the lead, D.A. Weibring then slumped with 76.

Raymond Floyd was a contender until he finished with 80.

Seve Ballesteros points the way for Jose-Maria Olazabal.

Europe's Mutt and Jeff duo, Nick Faldo and Ian Woosnam.

The triumphant European team with captain Tony Jacklin.

Ryder Cup

Eamonn Darcy won the praise of Jack Nicklaus.

Britain's worst storm in over 300 years toppled thousands of trees in southern England and delayed the World Match Play one day.

Once again Sandy
Lyle lost in the
final.

World Match Play

Ian Woosnam concluded a fantastic European season by becoming Britain's first World Match Play champion.

England's team of Howard Clark, Nick Faldo and Gordon J. Brand.

Dunhill Cup

Curtis Strange and his caddy pose after his course-record 62.

and sixth holes as McCumber and Massey bogeyed No. 4. They gave two strokes back with a double bogey at the eighth hole. Crafter sank a birdie putt at the ninth and they birdied No. 13, too. A bogey at No. 15 left them a stroke behind King and Tewell, with McCumber and Massey alongside them. The only good shot on the final three holes was Crafter's chip-in at No. 17.

Chrysler Team Championship—$600,000
Winners: Bob Tway and Mike Hulbert

In the final round of the Chrysler Team Championship in Boca Raton, Florida, Bob Tway and Mike Hulbert bogeyed the par-three fourth hole. It was their only bogey in two years of the better-ball event, but it sent a shiver up their spines. "We felt no lead was too big," said Hulbert, the memory of their showing in the tournament the year before still fresh. Then, they led for three rounds only to have Gary Hallberg and Scott Hoch overtake them on the last day. And Hallberg and Hoch were on their trail again.

This time, Tway and Hulbert had a five-stroke lead at the beginning of the round, instead of one stroke, and that was the cushion they needed. They won by one over fast-closing Fred Couples and Mike Donald with a 38-under-par 250. Hallberg and Hoch placed third. Couples and Donald made an eagle and six birdies on the final nine, but a poor showing on the previous 15 holes — the final six the day before and the front nine on the final round — on which they made only three birdies, proved the difference. Still, they made it interesting.

Tway and Hulbert parred the next four holes after their bogey, then Tway eagled the eighth hole with an 85-yard wedge shot. Birdies by Tway at the 11th, 12th and 13th holes were enough to keep Couples and Donald at bay.

The Chrysler Team Championship is played on three different courses in Boca Raton. Tway and Hulbert opened with 61 at Greenview Cove, turned in a sensational 59 at Polo South and came in with a 64 at Wellington. Hallberg and Hoch matched their 61 and 62, but 66 in the second round gave them too much ground to make up. Couples and Donald had steady scores — 62, 63, 64, 62 — but the 15-hole stretch starting in the third round put them in a hole.

10. The U.S. Senior Tour

Sounds incongruous, but youth, of its sort, continues to be served in the arena of senior golf. It's not the liability so apparent on the regular tours of the world where victory and real success almost always comes with age and experience. The youth of senior golf is age 50 or 51 or 52. Almost from the beginning of the formal Senior PGA Tour in the early 1980s, the men who had just passed that 50 mark and had remained competitively active were the dominant players — Miller Barber, Don January, Gene Littler, Arnold Palmer. For a brief period in the mid-1980s, this same group with the notable addition of Peter Thomson held sway, perhaps in part because the new seniors of that time did not come with very distinguished credentials. Then, the dam broke. The newcomers came in takeover waves — Bruce Crampton, Gary Player, Dale Douglass, Bob Charles and, in 1987, Chi Chi Rodriguez and Al Geiberger among other tour freshmen and sophomores.

Rodriguez, 51 during his 1987 exploits, piled up seven victories in official events on the Senior PGA Tour and swashbuckled his way to a record $504,995 in earnings, half of what he earned in two decades on the regular circuit. Chi Chi won a "major" — the PGA Seniors — and at one point in mid-season was the winner in four consecutive starts. Crampton, an exception to the others in a way because he returned to tournament golf after a long absence, had a second straight strong season, following up his seven-victory 1986 season on the tour with four official wins and three others in unofficial events in the United States and Australia. Player, as Palmer has been, does not play a full Senior Tour schedule, but in his second season added three impressive titles — USGA Senior Open, Senior TPC and PaineWebber World Seniors — and a non-tour victory to the four he scored during his first 14 months. Charles won three times in the early season and in an unofficial event in Hawaii in December.

Geiberger made a terrific impact. Although he didn't turn 50 until the first of September, Al won three of his first six starts, including the lucrative Vantage Championship, and banked more than a quarter million dollars. Little-known Larry Mowry, with late-season wins at Richmond and Atlanta, and Dave Hill, with victory at Suntree in Florida later in the season, also were first-season titlists.

The older seniors certainly were not swept aside, it must be hastily added. All the earlier-year stars except Palmer scored victories, Barber nailing two individual titles well into the season, then teaming with Nancy Lopez to claim the whopping $250,000 first-prize share of the end-of-season Mazda Champions purse. Littler, Orville Moody and Billy Casper each scored a pair of victories, Littler also winning the rich Coca Cola Grand Slam in Japan and Moody teaming with Crampton to take the Legends of Golf title. Don January, the year's oldest winner at age 57, played a limited schedule by design and added his 24th individual victory at the year-opening Tournament of Champions. That kept him one ahead of Barber in the count of official titles on the circuit.

In keeping with the general pattern in world golf in 1987, the International team completely turned the tables on the Americans in the Chrysler Cup matches, which were played in the early spring in Sarasota, Florida, seven months after the U.S. team had won in a rout in the inaugural at the TPC at Avenel at Washington, D. C. Furthermore, a potential new addition to the "majors" category in senior golf was launched with the playing of the first British Senior Open at Turnberry and that title went to Neil Coles, the fine English pro who has thus far disdained the Senior Tour in America because of his extreme dislike of flying.

Overall, senior golf flourished in 1987 with a minimum of internal fuss over cart use, pace of play and the institution of a Super Seniors program intended to deal with the "youth" problem. Vantage and Mazda, the circuit's biggest commercial supporters, were joined by GTE, which sponsored tournaments in Los Angeles, Seattle and Hawaii in 1987 and will add Tampa and Indianapolis in 1988. The year ended on a sad note, however. Dan Sikes, a multiple winner and consistent money-maker over nearly three decades of tour golf, died in December following surgery.

MONY Senior Tournament of Champions—$100,000
Winner: Don January

Don January scored his 12th and last victory on the PGA Tour in 1976 when he was still four years away from senior golf, an impressive victory as the elder statesman in the elite field of the MONY Tournament of Champions at Southern California's plush La Costa Resort. Nearly 11 years later, January won the Tournament of Champions again, this time in January of 1987 in the fourth staging of the event as a Senior PGA Tour adjunct. He became the first player with both Tournament of Champions titles on his record.

It was a hard-earned victory as Butch Baird, in his first year on the circuit, forced him four holes into overtime before yielding the title with a bogey at the par-four 15th hole. The two Texans (Baird a transplant for most of his adult life) had finished the 72-hole tournament with one-under-par 287s, neither particularly auspiciously. January shot 75 in the final round and gained the tie when Baird three-putted the 18th green for 77.

The 57-year-old January launched his move toward his 24th individual title in senior golf with an opening-round 67, which staked him to a three-stroke lead over Baird and Gene Littler. He capped the round with a 35-foot birdie chip-in. Baird made the birdies Friday. He shot a 68 that included six birdies and gave him a one-stoke margin over January, 138-139, with Littler the only other player under par at 142. It remained a Baird/January dogfight Saturday, Butch widening his lead to two with 72—210 to Don's 73—212. Chi Chi Rodriguez moved a shot ahead of Littler into third place at par 216.

Baird never trailed in the final round, although January caught him in a birdie/bogey swing at the 12th hole before double-bogeying the par-three 14th. Don got one back when Butch bogeyed at the 15th and the decisive one with the Baird bogey at the 72nd. January missed a chance to end the playoff at the second extra hole when he failed on a two-foot birdie putt, but closed it out easily two holes later when Baird visited rough and sand enroute a bogey before January even had to try the eight-foot birdie putt that he made to capture the $30,000 first-place prize.

Seniors Classic—$300,000
Winner: Harold Henning

Harold Henning overcame a weak start and won the first playing of the Seniors Classic at the Gary Player Country Club in Sun City, Bophuthatswana in late January. Henning, who had ranked sixth in the 10-man field at the southern Africa resort and gambling mecca after an opening 75, recovered with rounds of 69 and 70 to catch Billy Casper, then defeated him with a birdie on the first extra hole to take the $90,000 first prize.

Doug Sanders and Orville Moody were the first-round leaders with 70s, but Casper and Henning took over in the second round, Casper with his second straight 72 and Henning with the 75-69 on a blisteringly-hot, 104-degree day. Casper took the lead in Sunday's final round at the fifth hole and kept it until Henning made a seven-foot par putt as Casper bogeyed at the 18th hole for the matching 70s. In the playoff at the par-three 16th, Casper put his tee shot inside that of Henning, but Harold holed from 16 feet and Billy missed the matching attempt. Still, he collected $47,000. Peter Thomson, who closed with 67, was third at 218, four strokes behind Henning and Casper. Gary Player did not play in the event.

General Foods PGA Senior Championship—$260,000
Winner: Chi Chi Rodriguez

If Chi Chi Rodriguez had any drawbacks during his fine career on the regular PGA Tour, it was the absence of a major title among his eight victories. Such will not be the case when he looks back on his performances on the Senior PGA Tour. In little more than a year on that circuit, Rodriguez had picked off two senior "majors" — the Senior TPC Championship in Cleveland in the summer of 1986 and, with a brilliant finish, the General Foods PGA Senior Championship at Palm Beach Gardens in February of 1987.

The chipper Puerto Rican, disconsolate after giving away the tournament lead in the third round of the PGA Senior on the Champion course, rallied from six strokes off the pace on the final Sunday to nip Dale Douglass by a stroke with a 67 and 282. It was the same sort of disappointment Douglass had felt 19 years earlier when Chi Chi staged the same sort of comeback and beat him in a playoff in the old Sahara Invitational at Las Vegas. Dale had come back from an opening 74 to take a five-stroke lead at 209 after 54 holes (74-66-69) over Harold Henning and Bobby Nichols as Rodriguez, the 36-hole leader with 70-69—139, encountered a disastrous, third-round 76 during which he even broke one of his irons.

Chi Chi liked the replacement iron from a set in the PGA National golf shop so much that, after a session on the practice range with old mentor

Pete Cooper, he put the entire set into his bag Sunday. "They felt better than the ones in my bag and they'd won me about $500,000," he explained after his sparkling final round. He made up two of the six-stroke deficit on the front nine Sunday. He birdied the second and Douglass went one over par with a bogey at the eighth. Then, the affable Latin gained three more in a hurry with birdie putts of 10 and 20 feet at the 10th and 11th while Dale was going par-bogey on the holes. Rodriguez finally moved back into the lead with five-foot birdie putts at the 15th and 16th holes and clung to the one-stroke margin through the final two holes.

The victory, Chi Chi's fourth as a senior, paid $47,000. At 283, Douglass finished three shots in front of Nichols and Bob Charles.

Australian World Senior Match Play Championship—A$165,000
Winner: Bruce Crampton

Australian golf fans got an opportunity to see one of their own who had long been absent from the events in his native land but had made such a big impression in his first season as a senior player when Bruce Crampton returned home for the first World Senior Match Play Championship at the Coolangatta-Tweed Heads Golf Club at Coolangatta, Queensland at the end of February.

The eight-man international field displayed high-quality golf as Crampton, Miller Barber, Bob Charles and Arnold Palmer won opening-round matches, defeating Christy O'Connor, Doug Sanders, Bobby Nichols and Bob Rosburg, respectively. Crampton worked hard for a 1-up victory over Charles and Barber took out Palmer in another tough match, 2 and 1. In the final, Barber jumped off to a three-hole lead over the first five holes, but Crampton fought back, eventually taking the lead with a 12-foot birdie putt at the 17th hole and clinching the victory with a 15-foot putt at the last hole.

Elsewhere in Australia that week, Orville Moody won the Australian PGA Seniors in a runaway, his 281 beating Harry Berwick by 10 strokes, Ken Still by 14 and Peter Thomson and two others by 16. The event was staged at Rich River Golf Club in Victoria.

Del E. Webb Arizona Classic—$200,000
Winner: Billy Casper

That Billy Casper would break a three-year victory drought on the Senior PGA Tour at Hillcrest Golf Club in Sun City West, Arizona, came as no real surprise, particularly to such as fellow competitor Orville Moody. Back in 1984, Moody had sized up Hillcrest when the event was founded and predicted a Casper victory there that year. Noting Billy's normal big looping hook with his woods, Orville observed that "all the par-fives are dogleg left around the lake." He was right. Casper scored his fourth Senior Tour win there that year.

Nobody polled Moody when the 1987 circuit resumed action with the Del Webb Arizona Classic at Hillcrest in March, but he probably would have called it again. Casper, whose only victory in the three years since the

Sun City win in 1984 had been in the Legends that year with partner Gay Brewer, handled a cold, blustery Sunday better than the rest of the contenders and zipped to a five-stroke victory. He closed with a 68 for 201, five shots ahead of Dale Douglass and Bob Charles.

Until Sunday, the Arizona weather was excellent. So was the golf, particularly that of Charles, who opened the tournament Friday with a course-record-tying 64, which, in turn, was just a stroke better than the rounds of Chi Chi Rodriguez, Miller Barber and Bobby Brue. Casper lingered at 68, then came up with a 65 Saturday that propelled him into a first-place tie with Barber at 133. Billy birdied four of the last seven holes for the 65 as Barber shot 68. Charles shot 70 and was just one back going into the final round.

Casper carried his bogey-less golf through the foul weather Sunday in remarkable fashion. However, Barber made three birdies on the first seven holes, threatening a runaway. However, he bogeyed the eighth, losing momentum, and Capser took advantage when his famed putting stroke produced birdie putts of 18 and 30 feet at the 10th and 11th holes and a tie for first. He birdied again at the 12th, from 15 feet, as Barber missed a short par putt when the wind blew off his cap. A two-stroke swing and a rattled golfer. Two holes later, Miller put his tee shot at the par-three 14th over the green and into the water, taking a double-bogey five. Barber wound up shooting 74, dropping into fourth place at 207, a stroke behind Douglass (70) and Charles (72).

Vintage Chrysler Invitational—$270,000
Winner: Bob Charles

Bob Charles, who went through a series of near-misses all 1986 season long before finally picking off the richest first prize of the year in December, found the winners' circle early in 1987 when he captured the exclusive Vintage Chrysler Invitational, the fourth event on the season's schedule and one of the most prestigious with its selective field and posh surroundings.

Charles pulled away to a four-stroke victory with his 285, the highest total in the seven-year history of the tournament at the Vintage Club in Indian Wells, one of the rich communities in the Palm Springs area of desert Southern California. The New Zealander's win was no surprise. After his $250,000 victory with Amy Alcott in the season-ending Mazda Champions tournament in Jamaica, Charles had begun the 1987 campaign with a third in the PGA and a second at Sun City, priming for the Vintage.

The weather and confusion reigned in the opening round. Bitter winds roared through the Coachella Valley that Thursday and only two players broke par. Howie Johnson, 61, who lives in Palm Springs, led the field with 70 — but didn't. He had opted for the new Super Seniors category for 60-year-olds and over, which made him ineligible for an official position in the tournament proper. So, Miller Barber, who had a 71, was the actual front-runner on that miserable day. Charles, Bobby Nichols and Gary Player matched par.

Dale Douglass, whose sensational start as a senior was highlighted by his initial victory in the 1986 Vintage with a 272 score, moved into a first-place tie in benign weather Friday with a 67, his 142 deadlocking him with Charles and Nichols, who both had 72-70s. Barber shot 77. The winds came up again Saturday and Charles made the best of the conditions. The left-hander managed a 73 despite an absence of birdies for 215 and a two-shot lead over Douglass (75), with the ubiquitous Johnson in between with his no-count score at 216. Bruce Crampton, Walt Zembriski, Butch Baird and Nichols were still in the running at 218. As it turned out, Crampton and Zembriski had a chance until shots into the water at the pivotal and treacherous 16th killed their chances. Charles birdied there and finished with 70, while Douglass three-putted an eagle try at the 18th to fall into a second-place logjam with Player, Baird, Crampton, Nichols, Johnson and Chi Chi Rodriguez at 289.

GTE Classic—$275,000
Winner: Bob Charles

The victory of Bob Charles in the GTE Classic should have surprised nobody. After all, he was merely following suit. Just as Peter Thomson did in 1985 and Dale Douglass in 1986, Charles put a victory in the seniors tournament in Los Angeles back to back with the one he had acquired the week before at the Vintage Club over in the Palm Springs area.

In 1987, GTE had taken over as the tournament sponsor and moved the event to the new Wood Ranch Golf Club in Simi Valley northwest of Los Angeles. Except for Charles, Wood Ranch proved a tougher test than the site of the first two seniors events at Mountaingate, although Bob's 208 total was, by three strokes, the highest of the three winning scores. However, only two other players broke par in the 54-hole tournament, Bruce Crampton four strokes behind the winner at 212 and Harold Henning another three back.

The New Zealander led from the start, opening with a 67 and a two-stroke advantage over Tommy Aaron, the newest 50-year-old on the Senior PGA Tour who was making his third appearance. Charles birdied five of the last eight holes, just missing a 10-foot eagle putt at No. 15. Crampton was at 70, Arnold Palmer and Bob Rosburg the other two players under par the first day at 71. Charles started slowly again Saturday, taking bogeys at the first and third holes on a windy day with gusts up to 35 mph, then fashioned seven birdies on the final 13 holes for another 67 and a seven-stroke lead over Crampton and Henning. He flashed some of his career putting magic with birdie putts of 50, 25 and 20 feet. Crampton had 70-71 and Henning 72-69 for their 141s, setting up an apparent battle for second place.

However, Charles lost his sharpness Sunday and Crampton made a game of it. He got two strokes back with an outgoing par 36 to Bob's 38 and three more in a hurry at No. 10, where he birdied and Charles double-bogeyed with a shot in the water. Bruce holed a sand-wedge pitch for an eagle at the 12th and had made up all seven shots. Crampton promptly lost the momentum when he bogeyed the 13th and Charles took quick advantage with a birdie at the 14th and a chip-in eagle at the 15th. He went on to a 74 and the final four-shot edge as Crampton finished bogey-bogey for 71.

Chrysler Cup—$600,000
Winners: Internationals

Arnold Palmer knew what he was talking about. Palmer, who had just captained an all-star squad of eight United States seniors to an overwhelming victory against a like team of International standouts in the inaugural Chrysler Cup matches in the fall of 1986, cautioned against "drawing any long-term conclusions based on just this week." He felt his team had played over its head, the Internationals under theirs.

What the American captain didn't expect was the complete turn-around that occurred when the second edition of the Chrysler Cup was staged seven months later at its new Florida site — the just-opened TPC at Prestancia Club at Sarasota. Just as the Yankees had done the previous autumn, the Internationals had virtually closed out the competition going into the final day. The final score was somewhat closer than the first time only because of some adjustment of the format and the one-two medal finish of Chi Chi Rodriguez and Dale Douglass that Sunday. Between them that day, they picked up 18 of the 40.7 U.S. points in the loss to the International team with its 59.5 points.

The winners, who collected $50,000 apiece, broke it open on a windy and abnormally chilly Florida Saturday in early April, picking up 26 of the available 34 points and moving within five points of clinching victory. Too late, the aforementioned Rodriguez and Douglass made amends Sunday for earlier misdeeds which contributed mightily to the 20-12 International lead after the first two days. The points should have been split evenly in the better-ball match play Thursday. The Internationals had two victories, the U.S. one and Douglass and Gene Littler were accepting congratulations from Gary Player and Bob Charles on the 17th green when it dawned on the four that Dale had holed the winning short putt from the wrong spot after marking it a putterhead away from the right position and failing to return it there. Loss of hole. Player and Charles then won the 18th to salvage a tie.

The Internationals won five of eight singles, stroke-play matches Friday as Rodriguez blew a one-stroke lead on the last hole and lost to Bruce Crampton, 69-70; Palmer frittered away a four-stroke lead in a 72-73 setback to Harold Henning and Christy O'Connor overcame Billy Casper, 69-72, with the help of a hole-in-one at the 16th. Saturday's competition was better-ball with the scores going into a points-rewarding standings. The Internationals took four of the first five places, Player-Charles and Crampton-Henning showing the way with 66s for 18 of the day's 34 points. The score then was Internationals 46, U.S. 20.

Which meant that, with a points structure for Sunday's individual stroke play that rewarded only the top eight finishers, the Americans had to take all of the first five places or the first four, sixth and seventh. Rodriguez and Douglass did their share with a 68 and a 69, but Charles, Roberto de Vicenzo, O'Connor, Player and Henning all shot 70s along with Billy Casper to insure the decisive victory.

Doug Sanders Kingwood Celebrity Classic—$198,296
Winner: Bruce Crampton

Until he returned to the scene of his first victory as a senior, Bruce Crampton was off to a slow start on the 1987 Senior PGA Tour after the outstanding freshman year he had in 1986. When he came back to defend his title in Doug Sanders' Celebrity Classic, Crampton had only his capture of the small-field World Match Play tournament in Australia at the end of February to show for his efforts for the early months of the year.

In 1987, seeking an official spot on the Senior Tour in 1988, Sanders moved his six-year-old tournament in Houston from the municipal Memorial Park course to the more demanding Deerwood Golf Club, obtained corporate sponsorship help from Kingwood and enhanced his pro invitation list. It didn't make much difference to Crampton, although he needed a dazzling finish and a long birdie putt in a playoff to win the Sanders Classic again.

The Australian trailed Charlie Owens by three strokes with just three holes remaining in Sunday's final round. He had just lipped out a six-foot birdie try on the 15th green, another example of the balky putter that had seemingly doomed him to second place at the end. However, he then went birdie-birdie-birdie, holing a 40-footer at the 17th, and he had overtaken Owens, who had parred the last three holes for 70 after coming back from a four-putt double-bogey on the first hole that day. Crampton, who had opened the final round with a one-stroke lead at 70-69—139, shot 72 for his 211 that forced the playoff. It ended quickly on the par-five 16th when Bruce rolled in another 40-footer, this time for an eagle and the victory.

Bobby Nichols had his day Friday. Another of the new seniors, Nichols put a six-under-par 66 on the board and took a three-stroke lead over Owens and George Bayer, but his 74 on Saturday enabled Crampton to move into his one-shot lead. When it was over, Bruce considered himself fortunate to have edged Owens for the $30,000 first prize. "I'll be honest. I may have had a fantastic finish, but I didn't deserve to win. I made far too many mistakes out there today."

Coca Cola Grand Slam Championship—$300,000
Winner: Gene Littler

While most of the senior tourists were playing at the Doug Sanders Celebrity in Houston, Texas, sixteen of them were in Japan, where they were joined by a like number of seniors from that part of the world in the annual Coca Cola Grand Slam tournament at Oak Hills Country Club near Tokyo.

One of the attractions for that April trip to the Far East was the size of the first-place check — $60,000. This year, it went to Gene Littler, who came from a stroke off the pace of Harold Henning in the final round, shooting a 69 for 204 and a two-stroke victory over Miller Barber, four over Lee Elder, the defending champion and two-time winner of the event. Americans took the first seven places. Then, eight shots behind Littler, came Tadashi Kitsuda, one ahead of better-known Oriental pros Shigeru Uchida of Japan and Taiwan's Lu Liang Huan and Hsieh Yung Yo.

Orville Moody, who spent much of his Army time in the Far East many years ago, seized the first-round lead at Oak Hills with a six-under-par 66, but had only a stroke on Henning and Bobby Brue. Henning made seven birdies Saturday, shot another 67 and took a one-stroke lead over Littler and Barber with his 134. Moody struggled to a 71. It came down to a battle between Littler and Barber Sunday as Henning quickly began to fade to his eventual 80. Elder claimed the third spot when he came up with the best round of Sunday's play — 66 — for 208.

Legends of Golf—$600,000
Winners: Bruce Crampton and Orville Moody

The reign of Don January and Gene Littler in the Legends of Golf ended in April of 1987 when Bruce Crampton received unlikely help from the weird putter of Orville Moody and the two posted the best victory score ever in the tournament that ignited the Senior PGA Tour. In their second season as a pair in the TV-hatched team tournament, the two men, whose personalities will never be described as outgoing, methodically cut down the opposition the last two days and rolled to the record 251 winning total, finishing four strokes in front of runners-up Bobby Nichols and Butch Baird.

Astonishingly, it was the on-the-greens success of Moody, a notoriously-bad putter, rather than the play of Crampton, 1986's most-prolific winner, that brought them to the fore in Saturday's third round. The Moody/Crampton combo birdied the last six holes for a tournament-record 59, 11 under par, and took a one-stroke lead over Miller Barber and Bob Charles, 187 to 188. They went from there with five more consecutive birdies at the start of the final round, their eventual 64 creating the four-shot margin. Moody, wielding a putter with a head resembling a square horseshoe and a 50-inch shaft that poked into his breastbone, had seven of the birdies Saturday and three of the first five Sunday.

Barber and Charles created most of the excitement the first days in the 10th edition of the classic event at Onion Creek in Austin, Texas. They birdied the last three holes in the opening round for 61 and a tie for the lead with Nichols and Baird, then followed with a 62 that sprung open a five-stroke lead over the co-leaders, Crampton/Moody and January/Littler. The eventual winners still trailed Barber and Charles by five after nine holes Saturday, birdied the 10th and 11th, then delayed their charge when they both three-putted the 12th green. However, the all-birdie finish from there accounted for the 59 and the one-shot lead when Barber/Charles failed to birdie the par-five 18th.

They also failed to score more than a single birdie during the early Crampton/Moody streak Sunday and fell five behind quickly. Their last hopes died when they bogeyed the 13th hole. Nichols and Baird made a late run to pick off second place, shooting 62, but missed birdie putts on the last two holes. Ironically, their 255 score matched the Legends record that Crampton and Moody demolished.

Sunwest Bank/Charley Pride Classic—$250,000
Winner: Bob Charles

The Senior PGA Tour returned to its normal, 54-hole individual competition in Albuquerque, New Mexico, after a gap of more than a month, but the variety of competitions that followed the GTE Classic in Los Angeles in late March did nothing to affect the early-season spurt of Bob Charles. The New Zealander picked up where he left off in California and scored his third straight Tour victory in the Sunwest Bank/Charley Pride Classic.

However, the Charles victory came harder than did the win of Gene Littler in the 1986 inaugural of the tournament. Gene eased to a two-stroke victory with a closing 71, but Charles needed a birdie on the final hole at Four Hills Country Club to nose out Dale Douglass for the title. He shot a closing 68 for an eight-under-par total of 208, a stroke ahead of Douglass and two in front of Bobby Nichols.

The early leaders — Bruce Crampton and Lee Elder at 68, Littler and Orville Moody at 69 — fell back in Saturday's second round as Douglass, Nichols and Jimmy Powell shared the lead at 139 with identical 71-68 cards, Charles sitting at 140 (70-70) with Ralph Terry, the old New York Yankees pitcher who had always aspired to a pro golf career like his Gotham baseball predecessor, Sam Byrd. Terry was unable to maintain the pace Sunday, but the other four battled it out to the finish with Chi Chi Rodriguez mounting a short-lived challenge before a double-hit led him to an eight at the 10th hole.

Charles forged three shots ahead through 15 holes, but gave the others an opening when he bogeyed the 16th. Nichols and Douglass birdied that hole to draw within a shot of the leader, a futile effort, it turned out, when the left-hander lofted a nine-iron approach three feet from the hole at the 18th and put his 68 on the board with that birdie. A matching birdie there moments later by Douglass merely gave him second place to himself. Dale, who had been second in three earlier 1987 tournaments, birdied three of the last four holes for his 70. Nichols shot 71 for 210, a stroke in front of Powell (72) and Bruce Crampton, who finished with a 69 for his 211.

Vantage at the Dominion—$250,000
Winner: Chi Chi Rodriguez

Chi Chi Rodriguez, who had been running in idle on the Senior PGA Tour since his February victory in the PGA Seniors Championship, launched an explosive spring in San Antonio at the scene of the Vantage at the Dominion tournament. With three solid rounds in the 60s, Rodriguez rolled to a three-stroke victory that did not bode well for the other circuit riders in the immediate future. He shot 67-67-69 for 203, 13 under par at the new club and course in South Texas in early May.

J. C. Goosie, a journeyman on the regular PGA Tour back in the late 1950s and early 1960s whose greatest contribution to the game came instead with his founding of the "mini-tour" concept for the fringe professionals and neophytes, had a moment of playing glory in the first round. Goosie opened the tournament with a bogey-free 64 and a three-stroke lead over Chi Chi and Bob Charles, who was going for a fourth straight Senior Tour victory.

Goosie slipped to a one-under 71 Saturday and yielded the lead to Rodriguez, when Chi Chi posted the second 67 that was highlighted by a birdie at the ninth hole that could have been a double-eagle had his three-iron approach not missed the cup by inches. Billy Casper took over third place that day as Charles dealt his victory string a fatal blow with a 73.

Even though sitting in the catbird seat, Chi Chi was not a fired-up leader when he reached the course Sunday. "I really didn't feel like playing," he admitted later. "I couldn't sleep last night." Once on the course, though, he shook off that lethargic feeling and maintained his command of first place through the round and built his final three-stroke margin. Butch Baird, who had trailed by five strokes going into Sunday's round, jumped into second place with the day's best score — 67 — for 206. He finished two strokes in front of Miller Barber, Charles Owens and Goosie. Rodriguez collected $37,500 for the victory, his fifth PGA Senior Tour win.

United Hospitals Seniors Championship—$225,000
Winner: Chi Chi Rodriguez

Chi Chi Rodriguez took a different route but the result was the same as the Senior PGA Tour jumped from Texas to eastern Pennsylvania for the United Hospitals Seniors Championship. He put that title back to back with his championship the previous Sunday in San Antonio and took over first place on the circuit's money list.

The Puerto Rican never really got things going through the first two rounds, but what a final round he produced that May Sunday. He came up with a 63, which set a tournament and Chester Valley Country Club record and was just enough to give him a one-stroke victory over second-round leader Lee Elder. Chi Chi's cards: 70-69-63 for 202. The $34,000 first-place check improved his 1987 earnings to $174,790. The defeat surprised Elder, who noted that "69 or 70 were my target scores and I shot 70. But what can you do when a guy shoots 63 in front of you."

Elder has wrested the lead away from Dale Douglass the second day, posting birdies on the last three holes for 66 and 133. That gave him a four-stroke lead over Douglass, who had opened the tournament Friday with a 64 that broke the former course/tournament record at the suburban Philadelphia (Malvern) club and provided a three-stroke margin over Miller Barber, Gary Player, Tommy Aaron and Elder. Douglass slumped to 73 Saturday, giving Elder the opening he wanted. He looked comfortable with the four-shot lead over Douglass, five over Player and six over Rodriguez, Paul Harney (66 Saturday), Aaron and Barber.

Chi Chi came out firing Sunday. He birdied four of the first six holes, had seven in all over the rather-hilly course as he broke par by seven strokes. Yet, he was not satisfied. He has always had a goal of shooting in the 50s and remarked at Chester Valley, "If I didn't do it today, I don't know if I ever will." He was referring to five birdie putts he missed from inside the 10-foot range. Still, "I can't remember playing any better."

Elder still had a chance to tie when he came to the 18th. He needed a birdie, but put his approach in the trap and the par for 203, while it didn't help him catch Rodriguez, gave him a two-stroke margin over Gary Player, who finished third at 205.

Silver Pages Classic—$250,000
Winner: Chi Chi Rodriguez

Chi Chi Rodriguez provided a special touch to his third consecutive victory on the Senior PGA Tour when it visited an old regular tour locale for the Silver Pages Classic in Oklahoma City — Quail Creek Golf and Country Club — in late May. In running to a four-stroke lead in the second round, Rodriguez dashed off eight straight birdies on his way to a 65. That feat broke by one the Senior Tour record Gene Littler set in 1983 and matched the PGA Tour record held jointly by Bob Goalby (1961) and Fuzzy Zoeller (1976).

For the record, Chi Chi did it this way: No. 6 — seven feet; No. 7 — seven feet; No. 8 — nine feet; No. 9 — three feet; No. 10 — 12 feet; No. 11 — 15 feet; No. 12 — 35 feet and No. 13 — one foot.

Rodriguez closed with a 69 Sunday at the site of the old Oklahoma City Opens in the early 1960s, his 200 total giving him a three-stroke victory over Bruce Crampton. It was the lowest 54-hole winning score of the season and added $37,500 to Chi Chi's 1987 bankroll, although he figuratively peeled off $10,000 for the victims of a killer tornado that week in south Texas.

The wet weather also plagued the tournament, rain delaying play the first two mornings, drenching the course overnight prior to the final round and catching the final groups before they finished Sunday. Preferred lies were played through the tournament and doubtlessly contributed to the excellent scoring. Five men, including Rodriguez, shot 66s in Friday's first round as 32 players broke Quail Creek's par 72. Joining Chi Chi at the top were Miller Barber, Harold Henning, Don Massengale and Jim King.

When his fireworks had ended Saturday, Rodriguez was four strokes in front of Crampton and Henning with three others another stroke back. However, on Sunday, Crampton was the only challenger and he never got closer than the final three-shot margin. Chi Chi felt he insured the victory when he put his confidence in his driver at the tight, par-five eighth hole and converted his perfect drive into a padding birdie. Rodriguez did not have a bogie in the final two rounds.

Denver Champions of Golf—$250,000
Winner: Bruce Crampton

Just as in 1986, Bruce Crampton went through a sizeable portion of the early 1987 season on the Senior PGA Tour before posting his first official title. Not that he wasn't heard from frequently during the first five months — two seconds and heavy earnings, plus unofficial wins in the Doug Sanders Celebrity at Houston and in the Legends of Golf the next week with Orville Moody in Austin, Texas along with the title in a senior match play event in Australia.

It may not have made any difference, but Chi Chi Rodriguez, riding a hot streak that saw him beat Crampton for three in a row the previous week in Oklahoma City, passed up the Denver Champions of Golf stop on the Senior Tour. Regardless, Crampton seized control of the Denver tournament at the TPC at Plum Creek with an eight-under-par 64 in the second round and held on for a one-stroke victory, shooting 67 in the final round for a 12-under-par total of 204.

Aside from Crampton, who nailed the big money of $37,500, Plum Creek proved a good week for several of the circuit's lesser-known players. Ben Smith, who didn't even turn professional until he was 48, led the first day with 67 before disappearing from view with an 80 the next day. John Brodie, the old pro football star and telecaster, shared second place that Friday with Bob Brue at 68 and Walt Zembriski, another late-blooming pro, was among three players at 69. Crampton opened with 73.

Actually, the 64 on Saturday merely tied Crampton with Zembriski, but it created the momentum he needed. Bob Charles and Dale Douglass also moved into the picture Saturday at 138 and 139, respectively, with Brodie slipping to 140 and into a tie with defending champion Gary Player. Although Bruce got in front on the front nine and never lost the lead, the back nine was exciting. Crampton reached his winning 12-under total with a birdie at the par-five 15th and parred in. A shot in the water at No. 16 finished Douglass, Charles couldn't muster a birdie, Brodie bogeyed the par-three 17th after making his second eagle of the day at the 15th and Zembriski slipped into second place when he holed an 18-foot birdie putt on the final green for 68 and 205. His runnerup check of $21,500 was the biggest ever for non-winner Zembriski.

Senior Players Reunion Pro-Am—$200,000
Winner: Chi Chi Rodriguez

Chi Chi Rodriguez never missed a beat when he returned to Senior PGA Tour action at the Senior Players Reunion Pro-Am in Dallas, much to the consternation of Bruce Crampton, who was fast becoming an arch-rival of the Puerto Rican star. When Chi Chi sat out the Denver Champions of Golf tournament on the heels of three consecutive victories, Crampton jumped in to nail his initial official victory of the Senior Tour season.

Bruce was on his way to two in a row at Dallas' Bent Tree Country Club when Rodriguez came up with another of his strong finishes and made it four straight in the Reunion Pro-Am. Not only did Chi Chi keep his string going but he also prevented Crampton, a Dallas resident (though Australian citizen) for many years, from scoring a hometown victory to go with seven wins in other Texas cities over those years. Another Dallas resident, Don January, was the defending champion, but withdrew when his father-in-law died on the eve of the tournament.

Crampton, coming in hot off his Denver victory, blazed a tournament-record 64 in the first round Friday, jumping off three strokes in front of Rodriguez and John Brodie. Both Crampton and Rodriguez shot 69s Saturday to set up the final-round confrontation between the loquacious Chi Chi and stolid Bruce, about whom Rodriguez remarked: "Playing with him is a little like playing with Ben Hogan. He only talks to you to tell you when you are away."

They both played so strongly Sunday that even a 65 by Gary Player, who had started the day just five strokes back, only moved him into third place. Chi Chi still trailed Bruce by three at the turn Sunday, but he birdied four of the last nine holes for 65 and the one-stroke victory at 201. He finally took the lead when he holed a 12-foot birdie putt on the 17th green and watched as Crampton made a final bid for a tie from 30 feet on the final green and missed. With that, Rodriguez had his fifth Senior PGA Tour victory of the season and another $30,000 in official prize money.

Senior Tournament Players Championship—$400,000
Winner: Gary Player

Gary Player illustrated once again that he is usually at his best in the most important tournaments when he outfought streaking Chi Chi Rodriguez and domineering Bruce Crampton to capture the Senior Tournament Players Championship in mid June. Flash the word — major — in front of Player and he is hot on the trail of another prestigious title. Among the remarkable 131 victories on Gary's record from his regular tour days are three Masters and British Opens, two PGA Championships and the 1965 U.S. Open and a whole string of South African and Australian Opens, among other top-shelf events. He is one of only four men to have won all four of the golf world's major championships.

Player picked up where he left off a few months into his Senior PGA Tour career by winning the PGA Seniors Championship, then added the Senior TPC in its initial staging at Jacksonville's Sawgrass, hard by the home of the PGA Tour.

Gunning for his fifth consecutive victory, Rodriguez quickly took command Thursday with a tournament-record 65, making six birdies and an eagle to start a stroke ahead of Billy Maxwell. Six other players, including Player and Arnold Palmer, broke 70. Chi Chi slipped to par 72 Friday, but retained first place, then over Billy Casper, who had 70-68 for 138. Crampton posted his second straight 70, Player had 69-73 for 142 and Palmer, of whom little had been heard all year, challenged for the lead until he double-bogeyed the 17th and had to settle for 141.

Casper had an up-and-down round Saturday, winding up in front by a stroke over Rodriguez, Crampton, Player and Charles Owens. Billy birdied two of the first three holes and had a four-shot lead after Chi Chi bogeyed the fourth and double-bogeyed the fifth. However, Casper couldn't maintain the pace and drifted back to the other contenders. He was six under par at 210 after 54 holes.

Sunday was not his day, however. Player, Rodriguez and Crampton battled it out all afternoon, arriving at the 18th green in a three-way deadlock. After Chi Chi and Bruce had made scrambling pars, Gary ran in a seven-foot birdie putt for the victory and the year's second largest first prize — $60,000. With 69, he finished with an eight-under-par 280. It was Player's first victory on the Senior Tour since the Denver Champions of Golf 12 months earlier. Rodriguez and Crampton tied for second at 281 as Casper shot 73 and placed fourth at 283. Palmer, Owens and Doug Sanders were next at 284.

Northville Invitational—$300,000
Winner: Gary Player

While most of the golf world's attention focused on the other coast and the U.S. Open, the seniors flocked to Long Island where the sponsors of the event called the Northville Invitational filled an intentional gap in the Senior PGA Tour schedule with a $300,000 tournament that drew most of the circuit's players. The $100,000 first prize attracted most of the interest and it wound up in the pocket of Gary Player on the heels of his Senior TPC victory in Florida.

Player scored the victory in uncharacteristic fashion — in a playoff. Gary, who had a 3-11 playoff record on the PGA Tour and only a single victory in sudden-death, ran in a 35-foot birdie putt on the second extra hole to defeat Bruce Crampton, who had come from three strokes off the pace Sunday with a 70 to Player's 73 to force the playoff. Both had 10-under-par 278s at the Meadow Brook Club at Jericho, Long Island.

The South African Hall-of-Famer was never out of the lead in the unofficial tournament. He opened with 67 and led Charles Owens, Gene Littler and Billy Casper by a stroke. A 70 the second day maintained that margin as Orville Moody moved into the runnerup slot with a 66 for 138. Crampton moved into the No. 2 spot Saturday with 67 for 208 as Player added a 68 for 205. Chi Chi Rodriguez was a shot behind Crampton, but mounted no challenge Sunday. Bruce overtook Player at the 13th hole Sunday with a par, then dropped back a shot when Gary birdied the next hole. However, Player was bunkered off the tee at the par-five 17th and took a bogey to Crampton's par. Both two-putted the 18th to set up the playoff.

Player collected the $100,000 and Crampton $40,000 as runnerup, but the most significant payoff was the $25,000 to Ben Smith, who had never won anything close to that kind of money in his brief pro career. The $100,000 was the most Player ever claimed at any of the zillion tour stops he has made over the years.

Greater Grand Rapids Open—$250,000
Winner: Billy Casper

Billy Casper hadn't done it since 1982, his first full season on the Senior PGA Tour — win more than once during the year, something that was rather commonplace for him in his great years on the regular PGA Tour. In 1982, Casper won at Jeremy Ranch and Newport, but in subsequent years failed to land more than a single victory during a season. Early in the 1987 campaign, the hefty Casper ran away with the Arizona Classic, his first individual victory in three years. He continued to play well during the next three months and added the Greater Grand Rapids Open to his record, his ninth senior title, in late June.

Although Billy won the Grand Rapids title by three strokes at the 6,453-yard Elks Country Club, the victory did not come without a scare. Miller Barber threw an eight-under-par 63 at him in ideal conditions Sunday, at one point closing within a shot. However, Casper fired a 64 himself for the victorious 200. At 203, Barber finished three strokes in front of Jim King and four in front of neophyte senior Dave Hill, playing in home country.

Casper put together a pair of 68s in windy conditions the first two days. The first one placed him in a three-way tie for second behind another first-year senior, Tommy Aaron, who opened with 65. Casper shared second with Orville Moody and Bob Charles Friday, then surged into a two-shot lead with the second 68 Saturday as Aaron took a 73 for 138 and a tie for second place with Hill (69-69). The leader virtually put things away on the front nine Sunday as he birdied the first, second, fifth and ninth holes. Barber had become his only challenger with five birdies on the front nine after starting the tournament with a pair of 70s, but Miller never got closer than one stroke as he missed five-foot birdie putts at the ninth and 10th holes. His 63 matched the tournament record, set in 1986 by Bruce Crampton, but Casper, with just three bogeys over the 54 holes, collected the $37,500 first-place check.

Greenbrier/American Express Championship—$225,000
Winner: Bruce Crampton

The way Bruce Crampton played, the rest of the field might as well have taken the holiday off that Fourth of July weekend at West Virginia's Greenbrier Resort. The Australian picked up his second official Senior PGA Tour title — and fifth overall victory — of the 1987 season with ease in the third playing of the Greenbrier/American Express tournament, breaking Don January's stranglehold on that title in the process.

The victory, the circuit's second wire-to-wire triumph of 1987, came this way on the 6,709-yard resort course in the mountains of southern West Virginia:

Crampton birdied four of the first five holes he played Friday and went on to a nine-under-par 63. That gave him a four-stroke lead on the field with Billy Maxwell and Orville Moody the closest at 67. Bruce was out in 30 and finished the splendid round with 10 birdies and a bogey, remarking that "the only thing wrong is that it's not Sunday night."

Crampton added a stroke to his lead Saturday, when he shot 70 for 133. He birdied three of the par-five holes and lipped out a five-footer for another at the fourth long hole. Four men, including defending champion January, were at 138. The most interesting story among them was that of Kel Nagle, who at 66 came within a stroke of shooting his age. Nagle, 14 years the senior of fellow Australian Crampton, had done little on the senior circuit the last few years, but he mounted a brief challenge to Bruce with five birdies on the first 12 holes. He was only able to par in from there and joined January, Bobby Nichols and Moody at 138.

After his second-round 68, January noted that "he (Crampton) is in control of things." He was right. Bruce coasted to a six-shot victory with a closing 67 Sunday. His 200 total matched that of January in the inaugural tournament in 1985. Moody broke from the second-place logjam to take the runnerup position at 206 with his 68, finishing three ahead of January, Nichols and Lee Elder. Crampton collected $34,000 for his wire-to-wire performance, matching that of Bob Charles in the GTE Classic at Los Angeles in late March.

USGA Senior Open—$300,000
Winner: Gary Player

Like all of the great champions of golf, Gary Player seems able to bring his game to its peak at the tournaments of special significance. This was the case when he was winning one important championship after another through the years and continued to be the pattern in his first two seasons on the PGA Senior Tour. First, it was the PGA Seniors in his fourth month. Next, it was the Senior TPC Championship midway through his second full season. Perhaps more impressive than either of those fine victories, though, was his runaway triumph in the USGA Senior Open.

Records fell in all directions as Player rolled to his 270 total and a six-stroke victory. It was by nine shots the lowest score in the Senior Open's eight-year history, easily surpassing Dale Douglass' 279 in 1986, when Gary was runnerup by a stroke. No earlier victor had won by more than four shots nor had any of them shot four rounds in the 60s in probably the toughest of the senior events. Player lowered his score a stroke a day with rounds of 69, 68, 67 and the crushing 66 Sunday, when he broke away from a two-stroke lead over Chi Chi Rodriguez and was never remotely threatened.

Opting for the one-iron rather than the driver much of the way over the 6,599 yards of the Brooklawn Country Club course at Fairfield, Connecticut, Player kept the ball out of the USGA rough and the course's trees most of the time, at one point going 31 holes without a bogey. When the last one came to break the streak at the ninth hole in the final round, Gary had built a four-stroke lead over Rodriguez — and Chi Chi bogeyed the same hole. A fine par from trouble at the 11th and birdies at the 14th and 15th wrapped it up for the South African, his third victory (one lucrative but unofficial) of the year and the 134th of his remarkable, globe-circling career. A bogey at the 17th by Rodriguez enabled Doug Sanders to slip into second place with the week's best score — 65 — for 276.

Player moved into the lead for good at the 17th hole in Saturday's third round when he sank a 10-foot birdie putt and carried a two-shot margin into Sunday's head-to-head meeting with the five-time-winning Puerto Rican when Chi Chi three-putted the final green. Rodriguez had taken the halfway lead with a pair of 68s as John Brodie faltered at the finish of the second round bogey-double-bogey for 137 and a runnerup tie with Player. First-round leaders Peter Thomson and Gordon Jones, with 66s, were never factors after that.

MONY Syracuse Classic—$250,000
Winner: Bruce Crampton

Most of the winners' names had been the same as in 1986, but Bruce Crampton's victory in the MONY Syracuse Classic in mid-July marked the first successful title defense of the 1987 season on the Senior PGA Tour. Scoring his sixth triumph of the year — third in an official Senior Tour event — Crampton did it with a record-tying assault on par that left the rest of the field well back in his wake. Bruce led from start to finish, winding up at 197 with a six-stroke margin. He was 19 under par over the 6,540 yards of the Lafayette Country Club course at the New York town, equalling Don January's par-breaking in 1984 in the now-defunct du Maurier Champions tournament at Vancouver, British Columbia.

Crampton attributed an address-position adjustment suggested by Legends partner Orville Moody to getting him back on track after a poor performance the previous week in the Senior Open. It produced 10 birdies and a seven-under-par 65 in the Thursday pro-amateur and he repeated that score in the opening round Friday, that time with eight birdies. It staked him to a one-stroke lead over, ironically, Moody. When Crampton followed with a 67 Saturday to go 12 under par at 132, he moved to a three-shot lead over Chi Chi Rodriguez, who produced a matching 67, with Peter Thomson at 136 and Miller Barber at 137.

Rodriguez was the only challenger at all Sunday and he observed afterwards that Crampton "beat my brains out...He played extremely well." Indeed he did. He fired yet another 65 for the $37,500, six-stroke margin over Rodriguez. Bruce dispelled any doubts Sunday when he ran off consecutive birdies on the last three holes of the front nine, then rolled in a 30-foot eagle putt at the par-five 12th. In different words, the transplanted Australian concurred with the Rodriguez appraisal of his tournament. "It's probably the finest three rounds I've ever played, even if I do say so myself," observed Crampton, whose margin of victory matched the year's best — Gary Player in the Senior Open and his own when he scored his earlier wire-to-wire triumph at Greenbrier. Bruce then took his first break — two tournaments — after playing in 52 straight events for which he was eligible.

Seniors British Open—$240,000
Winner: Neil Coles

Neil Coles completed an unprecedented two-week period in the modern history of English golf, joining countryman Nick Faldo in repelling the powerful invaders of British soil in mid-July. On the heels of Faldo's triumph in the British Open at Muirfield, Coles defeated a strong international field and bitter wet weather at Turnberry to capture the first Seniors British Open. Coles' victory, though, was almost predictable.

The 52-year-old Ryder Cup veteran has remained an active player on the PGA European Tour, keeping his game sharp, and upon passing his 50th birthday, won the British PGA Seniors the first three times out, the third just a few weeks before the joust with Turnberry and the rugged Scottish weather of that week. At the end, Neil's one-under-par 279 enabled him to edge late-challenging Bob Charles by a stroke. He closed with a two-over 73 as Charles, with 67, and Harold Henning, with 70, had the only sub-par rounds in cold, driving rain that Sunday at the 6,558-yard Ailsa course at Turnberry.

Even on the benign opening day, just five players shot in the 60s. Coles, with four birdies and 14 pars, began in front at 66, a shot ahead of Charles, two in front of Arnold Palmer and Harold Henning and three atop Gary Player. "I don't think I can play better than that," reflected Coles, who was putting for birdies from 15 feet or closer on eight of the nine holes on the back nine. He had a triple-bogey seven on the card and shot 73 Friday, yet widened his lead to two strokes over Palmer, Henning and Charles. The winds kicked up strongly, making the seven holes along the shore extremely difficult. It blew many scores well up into the 80s and Peter Butler and Brian Huggett, with 72s, had the best rounds of the day.

Coles bounced back Saturday in still-difficult conditions to virtually put it away. With his three-under-par 67, Neil jumped five strokes ahead of Palmer and seven in front of the rest of the field. He was out in 32 with an eagle at the seventh and parred the back nine with a birdie and a bogey. Palmer, who was paired with Coles on the miserable final day, twice closed to within two strokes of the leader, but a double-bogey at the 12th quenched his bid. Charles was barely too little, too late. He birdied the 15th, 16th and 17th for the 67 and Coles needed par at the 18th for the victory. He came up short of the green, but chipped to 18 inches to insure his capture of the title.

NYNEX/Golf Digest Commemorative—$250,000
Winner: Gene Littler

The reliability of Gene Littler's competitive game showed through once again at the NYNEX/Golf Digest Commemorative tournament. In his first seven years of senior golf, Littler never went a season without a win or two in America as he put 12 titles on his record. He kept that string intact in 1987 with a brilliant finish and a one-stroke victory in the Commemorative. Actually, it was Gene's second win of 1987, since he won the Coca-Cola Grand Slam in Japan for a second time earlier in the year.

Little-known players attracted the headlines in the early rounds over the 6,545-yard Sleepy Hollow Country Club course in New York's Westchester County. Larry Mowry, who had last played regularly on the PGA Tour in 1972, made the best start of his initial year on the Senior PGA Tour in the opening round. His 66 that Friday gave him a one-stroke lead over seven players, including Littler. The others were Dale Douglass, Fred Hawkins, Don Massengale, Miller Barber, John Brodie and Bill Collins.

Next to emerge from obscurity was Roland Stafford on Saturday. Stafford, a club professional most of his career, put a 65 with his opening 69 for 134 and a share of the second-round lead with Douglass (67-67). Littler and Miller Barber, with identical 67-68s, trailed by a stroke as Mowry slipped to 73 and 139. Mike Souchak, who has had little success in senior golf, bogeyed the last two holes but still shot 66 for 136.

Littler's winning 65 finish was a wild one. He made just three pars all day, negating half of his 10 birdies with five bogeys. The final total of 200, 10 under par at Sleepy Hollow, gave Gene a one-shot victory over Douglass, who finished second for the fifth time in 1987. Playing with Littler, Dale noted: "Gene kept putting the ball into position to make birdies. Every putt he hit looked like it was going in, even if it didn't." Douglass had three 67s for his 201. Barber also shot 67 for 202 and Stafford won his biggest seniors check — $14,800 — with his 70 for fourth place at 204.

Digital Classic—$250,000
Winner: Chi Chi Rodriguez

Chi Chi Rodriguez would have to include Nashawtuc Country Club at Concord, Massachusetts, among his favorite golf courses. He has certainly fared exceptionally well at the site of the Digital Classic on the Senior PGA Tour in his first two appearances there — consecutive victories with scores of 16 and 18 under par. The win in 1987, with the 198 score for the 54-hole distance, was in sharp contrast to the 1986 victory in terms of degrees of difficulty. Chi Chi went from a tight squeeze to a runaway. He broke from a first-place tie on opening day to an eight-stroke victory, the biggest of the 1987 season up to that point.

Rodriguez birdied the last two holes Friday for an opening 65, matched by South African Harold Henning, who shot a front-nine 30 enroute to his 65. Jimmy Powell and Orville Moody were next at 67. Chi Chi fashioned the 65 with a new set of clubs he had just received the previous day. Athough his score was a stroke higher Saturday, he jumped four shots ahead of Henning, doing most of the damage at the end of the day with birdies on the last three holes. His 131 was a tournament record. Henning was at 135, Moody at 136 and Peter Thomson at 138 after 36 holes.

Chi Chi didn't coast Sunday. With birdies at the first, third and sixth holes, he widened his lead to seven strokes over Henning. Moody then moved ahead of Harold with birdies at the 10th and 12th, but that merely closed the gap to six and Rodriguez birdied the 14th and 16th holes for his final-round 67 and his eight-shot margin over Moody. Orville had a 70, Henning a 73 for 208. Thomson and Larry Mowry were next at 209.

The victory, Chi Chi's sixth of the season and ninth in his 21 months on the Senior PGA Tour, increased his earnings in the over-50 action to more than $760,000. That constituted more victories than he collected in his 25 years on the PGA Tour and some three-quarters of his total winnings.

Rancho Murieta Gold Rush—$300,000
Winner: Orville Moody

Victory in golf can turn on many single factors — a long putt, a stoney approach, perhaps, as in recent major championships, a holed sand shot or long chip. Though often stunned, the victims usually can accept defeat under these terms. Not so easy to take is a loss that can be blamed primarily on an inadvertent rules infraction. Such was the fate of Butch Baird in the Senior Gold Rush at Rancho Murieta, a new event on the Senior PGA Tour near Sacramento, California, and Orville Moody was the beneficiary of that misfortune.

Moody might well have won without an assist from the rules. He shot three solid rounds — 69-67-69 — for his 11-under-par victory total over the Arnold Palmer-designed course and fended off the last rush of Baird, who shook off the onus of a two-stroke penalty to overhaul Orville before taking two bogeys on the last three holes. He finished second with 207, two shots behind the winner.

The peculiar rules situation that damaged Baird's bid occurred in the opening round and involved a lift he took in the 10th fairway, one he thought he was entitled to because of the rules sheet he had in his possession. The trouble was it was the wrong rules sheet, one that had been prepared for the Monday qualifying round and wound up being handed to him and few others on the first tee that day by tournament volunteers. The correct ones had no provision for a free drop at the 10th hole.

Butch shot 70, Moody 69 in that first round in which Bill Collins had taken the lead with 67, a shot in front of Dale Douglass and Bob Brue. The rules sheet mixup was not yet realized, but came to officials' attention during Saturday's round. After long deliberation, they decided on a two-stroke retroactive penalty, changing Baird's opening 70 to 72. Those two shots prevented Butch from sharing the second-round lead with Moody, who shot 67 for 136. Baird eagled the 18th hole for 66 — 138 as Douglass and Brue both had 72s for 140 and Collins skied to 79—146. Moody, who hadn't won an individual title since 1984, threatened a runaway Sunday, opening his lead to five strokes on the front nine. But Baird birdied five of the next six holes to catch Orville at the 15th. However, Butch three-putted the 16th green and bogeyed the final hole, too, to establish the final margin.

GTE Northwest Classic—$300,000
Winner: Chi Chi Rodriguez

The Senior PGA Tour gave the golf fans of the Northwest an illustration of what had been happening as a general rule during the earlier months of the season. Chi Chi Rodriguez, the year's predominant player, showed them how and why he came to Seattle for the GTE Northwest Classic with six victories and the lead in the seasonal money-winning race in his possession. He put together three solid, sub-par rounds and annexed his seventh win that August week at Inglewood Country Club in suburban Kenmore, posting a 10-under-par final score of 206.

For the second week in a row, it was close but no cigar for Butch Baird, who missed a four-foot birdie putt at the 54th hole that would have given him a tie and forced the official tour's first playoff since he bowed to Don January in one in the season's opening Tournament of Champions. He had a final-round 69 and Rodriguez a 68 in the tight finish. Both they and Arnold Palmer overtook Miller Barber, who led at the end of the first two rounds. Palmer shot 66, Barber 72 Sunday to tie for third at 209.

The field was rather bunched up the first two days. Barber's opening 68 put him a stroke ahead of Larry Mowry, Gordon Jones, Jack Fleck and Bob Brue as Chi Chi and Butch opened with 70s. Miller followed with 69, retaining his one-stroke margin over Rodriguez and Baird, with 68s, and Orville Moody, with 71-67 for his 138.

Rodriguez jumped in front quickly Sunday. He birdied the first hole, eagled the second and birdied again at the fifth, but out in front of him a surprising Ben Smith had unloaded even more fireworks. The Georgia native, an amateur until 1982, also started birdie-eagle and made three other birdies on the front nine to move two shots ahead of Chi Chi, who bogeyed the eighth hole because of a missed green. However, the rarified atmosphere of first place felled Smith on the back nine. He bogeyed seven of the last nine holes. Rodriguez also bogeyed the 11th, but his birdie at the 14th gave him a one-shot lead over Barber. Baird mustered another final-round rush. He birdied the 15th and 16th holes, missed a 12-footer for another at the 17th and then failed on the four-footer on the final green.

With the $45,000 check, Rodriguez increased his Senior Tour earnings in his first 21 months to $815,304.

Showdown Classic—$325,000
Winner: Miller Barber

Doubt, a dangerous mental hazard for a golfer, had been creeping into the mind of Miller Barber as the 1987 season of the Senior PGA Tour had progressed. Barber, a domineering figure in the early years of the circuit with 21 individual victories, hadn't won since the season-opening Tournament of Champions in January of 1986 and was beginning to think he might be headed for his first winless season in senior golf. "When you get to be 56 out here, those 50-year-olds will run over you like a Mack truck," Miller observed. "You start thinking negatively and that's never good. I'd come close two or three times this year (including the previous week in Seattle), but the younger fellows always won."

Barber did get into the barn with his 22nd victory in the remodeled Showdown Classic, but barely stood off one of those "younger fellows" — Bruce Crampton — in scoring a one-stroke triumph at Jeremy Ranch, the fine course in the Wasatch Mountains outside Salt Lake City, Utah. His closing par 72 gave him a final 210 and the $45,000 winner's check.

His opening 71 left him two strokes off the first-round lead, held by Crampton and first-year-senior Charles Coody, but he took charge Saturday. Six birdies in an eight-hole stretch sparked him to a five-under 67 and his 138 put him three strokes in front of Don Massengale and Bobby Nichols, who had won at Jeremy Ranch in 1986 with junior partner Curt Byrum in the last of four editions of the tournament as a team affair. Crampton was at 142 with Butch Baird after a 73.

Barber was on the verge of putting the victory on ice Sunday, making four birdies on the first 10 holes to widen his lead to five strokes. But near disaster struck. Miller three-putted the par-five 13th and found a trap at the 14th for another bogey. Then followed a double-bogey, as he left a long-iron shot in a fairway bunker. His lead had gone from five to one. Perhaps fortunately for him, though, Crampton didn't know all of this had happened. Playing just ahead of him, Bruce pulled his drive into the water at the par-five 16th and wound up with a six. Barber followed with a birdie there and the three-shot margin gave him the cushion he needed to get in with the one-shot win. The five third-place finishers — Nichols, Coody, Chi Chi Rodriguez, Gary Player and Orville Moody — were four strokes farther back.

Bank One Classic—$225,000
Winner: Bruce Crampton

A pattern seemed to be developing. Miller Barber had won the previous week in Utah after a near-miss the week before at Seattle. Bruce Crampton had been the challenger to Barber at Jeremy Ranch and he followed suit with a victory the next week when the Senior PGA Tour moved east for the Bank One Classic at Lexington, Kentucky. He made no bones about it, either, racing to a six-stroke victory with a 13-under-par 197, the best score in the five-year history of the tournament at the Griffin Gate Golf Club.

The remarkable senior players made a shambles of the rather-prosaic Griffin Gate course that first week of September, especially Crampton. Twenty-one pros broke par 70, Crampton and Jim King leading the way with 63s in perfect weather in the first round. Bruce then settled matters for all intents and purposes Saturday. His follow-up 64 and 36-hole total of 127 staked him to a seven-stroke lead over Barber, making Miller's pair of 67s appear rather mundane. The 127 broke the Senior Tour's all-time record for that distance — Don January's 128 in the du Maurier Classic in Canada in 1984. King tumbled out of contention with a 74 as Dale Douglass, Ben Smith and Harold Henning generated some hope for themselves by moving into a third-place tie a shot behind Barber at 135.

Although his putter wasn't as effective Sunday, Crampton was never in serious trouble. "I struck the ball almost as well as I did Saturday," he remarked. "I just didn't make as many putts." What hopes Barber, Joe Jimenez and Bob Charles, the eventual runners-up, had of catching the Australian died as Crampton zeroed in approaches to tap-in range for birdies at the 15th and 16th holes. Charles could have been more of a threat, since his fine 66 would have been an even-finer 64 had he not absorbed a two-stroke penalty for a late start.

The victory was Crampton's 15th as a senior, 11 of them in official individual events. Following unofficial wins in the Senior World Match Play in Australia, the Doug Sanders Celebrity and the Legends of Golf with partner Orville Moody in the early season, Bruce scored Senior Tour victories at Denver, Greenbrier and Syracuse before picking up the Bank One title. He was the fifth different winner in the event.

PaineWebber World Seniors Invitational—$250,000
Winner: Gary Player

Winners have come up with a variety of ways of celebrating their golf tournament triumphs over the years. Champagne or other beverages in the press room, hastily-arranged parties on the scene or back home, Jerry Pate's memorable dives into water hazards after holing out at 18th greens at Memphis and the TPC at Jacksonville.

Gary Player came up with a new wrinkle at Charlotte, North Carolina, after his hard-fought playoff victory over Bob Charles in the eighth PaineWebber World Seniors Invitational at Quail Hollow Country Club. The club pool beside its cabana, which serves as the tournaments's media headquarters, was so inviting to Player that, after going through the usual interviews, he neatly stripped to his undershorts and swam a victory lap to the astonishment of the assembled reporters and photographers.

Player's dip figuratively punctuated the week at Quail Hollow, which was a wet track from start to its exciting finish. Heavy Wednesday rains and early morning fog jeopardized the first round, but all but one group finished before dark, Chi Chi Rodriguez jumping off to a one-stroke lead over Player with a 67 that he fashioned with two of his five birdies on his last two holes. Only that last group saw action Friday at soggy Quail Hollow after more heavy rains hit Charlotte over night. The scheduled second round was cancelled and, for the first time since the inaugural World Seniors in 1980, the tournament was set for a 54-hole finish. Player surged in front on the first hole Saturday in a birdie-bogey exchange with Rodriguez and at day's end as his 67 and 135 gave him a two-stroke lead over Charles, who also shot 67, and three over Rodriguez, who had a 71.

Gary built his lead to three strokes over Dave Hill on the front nine Sunday, but in a rarity he let it get away on the back nine. He bogeyed the 11th and 12th, missing a short putt at the latter hole. Charles, who also bogeyed the 11th, birdied the 14th, 16th and the tough 17th from 10 feet to catch the par-making Player. Gary missed another short putt at the 18th green after Bob made a fine par from a greenside bunker to force the tournament's first playoff and the Senior PGA Tour's initial one since the opening Tournament of Champions in January. Gary had a 72, Bob a 70 for 207s.

Player has a poor playoff record and particularly dislikes the sudden-death variety, but he survived a brilliant, scrambling par by Charles at the starting 16th hole to win his third important tour title and fourth overall in 1987 when he ran in a 10-foot birdie putt.

Crestar Classic—$325,000
Winner: Larry Mowry

Unlike the regular PGA Tour, where first-time winners abound every year, the Senior PGA Tour's victory circle is filled week after week by men who have been there before on the main circuit in years gone by. Almost without exception. The first exception came early in the 1986 season when Charles Owens won twice. It didn't happen again until the Crestar Classic, the renamed Senior Tour event at Richmond, Virginia, was played in mid-September.

That was when Larry Mowry, a regular tour player of no great distinction back in the 1960s who collected a variety of minor-league titles in the subsequent years while admittedly battling and eventually overcoming a drinking problem, fended off the fearsome challenges of Gary Player and Bob Charles to win by a stroke at the Hermitage Country Club. He was 13 under par with his 203, this man who got into the tournament from the non-exempt ranks and the qualifier.

Mowry, who just turned 50 in October of 1986, had made one stir earlier in the year when he shot a 62 at Albuquerque and he was the first-round leader in the Commemorative, but Richmond saw him in the midst of things throughout the three rounds. He was three strokes back after 18 holes as Player and Orville Moody opened with 66s, Gary holing from 35 feet at the 18th hole. Both birdied five of the last seven holes. Charles put a 66 with his starting 68 to move two shots into the second-round lead, heading Chi Chi Rodriguez, Dale Douglass and Mowry, who were at 136. Mowry was comfortable in his position. "I'm playing that good," he explained.

It was a blanket finish Sunday. After 16 holes, five players shared the lead. Then, Miller Barber self-destructed with a ball in the water at the 17th and triple-bogey. Douglass bogeyed the last hole, Player and Charles made pars and Mowry won it all when, though doubtful about it, he went with his caddie's read of a 25-foot birdie putt and watched it take a five-inch break right into the cup. It was his fifth birdie of a bogey-less round, giving him a 67 and the 203. Besides the victory and the first-place money of $48,750, Larry automatically became an exempt member of the Senior Tour for at least the next year.

Newport Cup—$200,000
Winner: Miller Barber

The golf tradition still weighs heavy at Newport, Rhode Island, where the American tournament game really got its start in 1895, when the first U.S. Amateur and first U.S. Open were played at Newport Country Club. The powers-that-be at Newport, not content to abandon things there when the sponsors of the Commemorative moved the tournament to Westchester County in metropolitan New York, reclaimed their spot on the Senior PGA Tour and inaugurated the limited-field Newport Cup at the famous old club on Rhode Island Sound.

They invited 36 seniors, the smallest field of the season other than that of the Tournament of Champions, but, as matters turned out, 34 of them played supporting roles to one of the best tournament duels in a long time. Miller Barber and Bruce Crampton were one-two in the standings through the three rounds and traded the lead back and forth Sunday before Barber pulled away to a three-stroke victory on the final holes, scoring the 23rd individual win of his senior career, one short of record-holder Don January.

After the first round, the leaders were Barber 67, Crampton 68. After the second round, the leaders were Barber 137, Crampton 138. After the first hole Sunday, the leaders were Barber and Crampton, both eight under par as they launched their exciting battle on the 468-yard, par-five first hole with a birdie and an eagle, respectively, Bruce reaching the green in two and dropping a 15-foot putt. He bogeyed the second, parred the third and fell two strokes back when Barber aced the 209-yard fourth hole with his two iron. Crampton came right back with a birdie at the fifth, Miller bogeyed the sixth and Bruce took the lead alone for the first time with a birdie at the seventh. The barrage continued when Barber birdied again at the eighth and both birdied the ninth to make the turn all even. Crampton had shot 31 and Barber 32 on the front nine.

The final swing came at the par-three 14th, where Barber birdied and took a one-stroke lead when Crampton bogeyed. Bruce bogeyed again at the 16th and Miller created the final margin when he holed his sixth birdie putt of the day on the 18th green for 65 and his 14-under-par 202. Crampton finished with 67 and 205, two in front of Bob Charles, who made a too-late bid with the week's best score, 64, for 207.

Vantage Championship—$1,000,000
Winner: Al Geiberger

Al Geiberger, whose life has had more highs and lows than a television weatherman's logbook, was at the top of the scale in Winston-Salem, North Carolina. The 50-year-old Californian, playing in just his fourth Senior PGA Tour event and feeling beforehand that "I'm not sure that I'm ready to win yet," had just won the Vantage Championship, by far the richest tournament in circuit history, and a first-place check of $135,000, almost 36 times more than he collected in Ontario, California, when he won his first of 11 regular tour events in 1962.

What transpired in the life of Al Geiberger in the ensuing 25 years would test the imagination of a soap opera scripter. On the happy side, an outstanding playing career studded with big victories — 1966 PGA Championship, 1975 Tournament Players Championship and Tournament of Champions among them — and capped by the unforgettable record 59 at Memphis in 1977. The other side of the coin saw him through two failed marriages, the death of his father in the Tenerife airline disaster, serious financial problems and a series of severe physical ailments that led to career-threatening knee and intestinal surgeries.

With the promised land of the Senior Tour looming, Geiberger remained active, though struggling, on the regular circuit in preparation. It paid off in spades at Tanglewood Golf Club in the inaugural Vantage Championship at the site of the 1974 PGA Championship as he seized the lead early in the final round and went on to a two-stroke victory, closing with a 67 for a four-under-par score of 206.

Al's opening round of 72 left him six strokes behind leader Orville Moody, five behind Gay Brewer and Dave Hill, the latter, also a first-season senior, to be his closest pursuer Sunday. Gene Littler entered the picture Saturday, shooting 67 for 137 to lead Brewer (67-71) by one and Geiberger (72-67) by two. Al's decisive front nine Sunday really won the tournament. He birdied the first two and last three holes on the front side for a 31 and a two-stroke lead. Eight pars and a bogey at the 17th were more than enough to handle Littler's two-over 72 and Hill's charging 65 when Dave bogeyed the 18th hole ahead of him for his 208. That Hill bogey at the last hole made Geiberger's concluding, five-foot par putt a lot easier. Hill's $81,000 runnerup check also was by far his largest ever.

Pepsi Challenge—$250,000
Winner: Larry Mowry

The circumstances were quite different for Larry Mowry in the Pepsi Challenge at Atlanta from those three weeks earlier when he became the surprise winner of 1987 on the Senior PGA Tour. He had the confidence of knowing that he could win in the company of players he never beat in his younger days, but the win had come suddenly in the Crestar Classic when he holed a long putt on the final green to emerge the victor in a blanket finish.

Mowry really proved himself and his ability in the Pepsi at Horseshoe Bend Country Club when he found himself paired in the last group in the final round with two of the game's all-time greats, Arnold Palmer and Gary Player. In similar circumstances, many other pros have succumbed to their nerves and the awe of the situation, seemingly just getting out of the way so that one of the others could win. However, Larry had won with Player, Miller Barber and Bob Charles in the fray to the end at Richmond and had played well earlier in the season when he was paired with Palmer in the Senior Open.

"I didn't feel like getting out of the way today. I wanted to push Arnie," Mowry said of his attitude Sunday in the Atlanta suburb of Roswell. He and Player started that final round four shots behind leader Palmer, who was gunning for his first victory of 1987 and had been the central figure through 36 holes for the first time in the season. He had opened with 66 for a one-shot lead over Buck Adams and Dave Hill. With eagle-threes on the first and last holes, he shot 67 Saturday to establish the four-stroke lead. Player, who had opened with 72, birdied five of the first eight holes for his 137 while Mowry had a back-nine 31 for 67 to go with his opening 70. Ironically, Larry remarked in Palmer's presence in the media interview that it would be "a wonderful thing for the Senior Tour if Arnold wins" and Palmer responded that "I'll try to accommodate."

Each had an early birdie Sunday and Arnie missed a short putt for another at the fourth hole, probably the turning point. Two holes later, the Atlanta resident, Mowry, launched a blitz that produced five birdies on the next eight holes and put him in the lead to stay as Palmer three-putted twice. Larry parred in from the 13th for 66 and the winning 203 while Palmer continued to fade to a back-nine 41 and a 77 for the day, finishing fifth behind Gene Littler, who closed with 66 for 205, and Bruce Crampton and Bob Charles at 209. Player's 75 dropped him to eighth place with 212.

Hilton Head International—$200,000
Winner: Al Geiberger

It worked for Nick Faldo in the British Open and almost did, too, for Al Geiberger in the Hilton Head International several months later in America on the Senior PGA Tour. Faldo ran off 18 straight pars at Muirfield and watched as Paul Azinger bogeyed the 72nd hole to lose by a stroke. Geiberger parred the last 18 holes of the testing Harbour Town Links, which handled everybody in that final round except one — Jim Ferree, the dapper pro at the Long Cove Club on the resort isle. Ferree, a one-time winner on the senior circuit, birdied the last two holes to catch Geiberger at 209 and force the season's third playoff. Al finally made a birdie at the second extra hole to win his second title in three weeks and in his sixth senior appearance.

Geiberger, whose rich victory in the Vantage Championship in the other Carolina two Sundays earlier had given him a winning attitude, positioned himself well the first day at the Harbour Town course, the par-71 seaside links used by the seniors for the first time but the permanent site of the prestigious Heritage Classic on the regular circuit. He shot 70, one of seven players led by Bruce Crampton's 67 who broke par in the opening round, then, with a 68, moved into the lead with 138, a shot in front of Charles Coody (70-69) and three ahead of five others, including Crampton and Ferree, whose presence at that position was rather remarkable since he had shot 86 Thursday in the pro-amateur. A lesson from his golf pro wife, Karen Shapiro, and a change of 50-foot putters turned things around, though Jim started with 73.

It wasn't as routine as 18 straight pars might seem for Geiberger. Four times he scrambled for pars and both Coody and Crampton caught him at one point or another on the front nine. Bogeys in the middle of the round dropped them behind and they never overtook him again. Then, Ferree emerged with his birdies at the 17th and 18th, sending the players and gallery to the 10th hole to start the playoff. Geiberger gave Ferree a chance to win it all there when he hit a wild second shot, but Jim also missed that green and both scrambled for pars. Then Al closed it out with a brilliant approach to 18 inches at the next hole (the 16th) as Ferree again missed the green and ultimately a five-foot par putt before Geiberger tapped in for the win and the $37,500 victory check.

Las Vegas Classic—$250,000
Winner: Al Geiberger

Al Geiberger took a different approach in scoring his third victory in four weeks on the Senior PGA Tour. He tried to duplicate his fabulous 59 in the final round of the Las Vegas Classic and didn't miss it by much. He shot 62, which was a good bit more than enough to insure the win that jumped his earnings in seven weeks of senior golf well over the $200,000 mark. Although he fell short of his all-time tournament record 59, Geiberger still shot the lowest round ever at the respected Desert Inn Country Club course, scene of many memorable Tournaments of Champions back in the 1950s and 1960s. It gave him a 13-under-par 203 and a four-stroke victory over Chi Chi Rodriguez, the year's leading senior money-winner.

Geiberger's prospects for the third win didn't seem good after 36 holes. He had opened with 68 and was just a shot behind Bob Charles. Arnold Palmer, Orville Moody and Bobby Nichols were at 69. Steady rains swept into Las Vegas Saturday and the scores were generally higher. The wet weather didn't bother Charles, though. He shot 69, one of only three scores under 70 Saturday, and widened his margin to three strokes over Charles Coody (71-68) and four over Palmer and Nichols (69-71 each). It appeared that Geiberger had shot away his chances with a 73 Saturday, falling five strokes off the lead.

The weather turned benign Sunday and Geiberger turned on the gas. With only one putt shorter than 10 feet, Al birdied the first five holes and caught Charles, who had made five pars. He held the lead for a hole when he birdied the eighth, but Coody caught him with a birdie at the ninth and Charles went ahead with another birdie at the par-five 10th. He bogeyed the 11th and Geiberger regained the lead with a birdie at the 13th, made a crucial par save from a trap at the 14th and virtually sewed things up when he ran in a 10-foot eagle putt at the par-five 15th, his third of the week there, including one in the pro-amateur. He grabbed the tournament record when he made his eighth birdie of the day with an eight-foot putt in front of an admiring gallery at the last green. Rodriguez, who had started almost as torridly as Geiberger with birdies at the first three holes, shot 66 for 207 to nose a stroke ahead of Charles and Coody in the final standings. Palmer shot 69 and finished fifth at 209.

Fairfield Barnett Classic—$200,000
Winner: Dave Hill

For a variety of reasons, "golf hadn't been much fun for a long time" for individualistic Dave Hill, but the talented pro never really lost the game that brought him 13 titles in his earlier career even though he only dabbled in it in the last years before he reached age 50 and the Senior PGA Tour. In fact, Hill maintained that he resumed competition primarily because he needed the money.

Well, when he ran his earnings in his first six months of senior golf over the $200,000 mark with the $30,000 first prize money of the Fairfield Barnett Classic (the new name for the eight-year-old Suntree tournament at Melbourne, Florida), he certainly was taking care of his financial shorts. And he had to agree that it was fun to win again after 11 years. With the five-stroke victory at Suntree Country Club, Dave joined Al Geiberger and Larry Mowry as "rookie" winners on the 1987 tour with six wins in the seven previous events.

Hill was in contention from the start. He was among six players who shot 68 in the opening round and trailed leader Bobby Nichols by a shot. Then, he took over Saturday with a six-birdie 66 and 134 that gave him a two-stroke margin over Nichols and three over Mowry and Bruce Crampton, who also fired 66 that day. "I didn't know if my game would hold up," Hill remarked, but had good reason to feel confident because he had always been a strong finisher and never blew leads in the final round.

Concentrating on keeping a steady tempo, Dave maintained his two-stroke lead through 12 holes. Then, a sudden series of developments put him clearly in the driver's seat. Mowry, his closest pursuer playing just ahead of him, hooked out of bounds at No. 13 and took a double-bogey. Hill followed with a birdie there and another with a monster putt at No. 14. It was a breeze from there in as he finished with a second 68 and a 14-under-par 202 for the distance. Geiberger and Lee Elder also shot 68s Sunday and tied for second at 207, a stroke in front of Mowry and Crampton. Nichols faded with a closing 76 for 212.

Gus Machado Classic—$300,000
Winner: Gene Littler

Everybody was asking, "Who the devil is Gus Machado?" but they had no identity problems with the tournament winner — the redoubtable Gene Littler — who captured the event Machado rescued for the Senior PGA Tour in south Florida at season's end. In fact, Machado, a Miami car dealer who is a long-time friend of Chi Chi Rodriguez, picked up the sponsorship of the tournament when it was moved to the par-71 municipal Key Biscayne

Golf Club in suburban Miami after the bankrollers of the 1986 tournament at Delray Beach bailed out.

Littler had to be happy about the "save". It enabled him to add $45,000 to his bankroll with the victory and he became the ninth multiple winner of official titles during the season. Gene had won the Commemorative in August as well as the non-tour Coca Cola Grand Slam in Japan earlier in the year. He outfought Orville Moody in the final round at Key Biscayne, posting a 69 for 207 and three-stroke victory.

The Von Hagge/Devlin course provided a strong test for the seniors. The best they could do in the opening round was 69, a score posted by Bob Brue, Bill Johnston, Lee Elder and Pat Schwab. Littler began with a 71, then seized the lead Saturday with a 67, going a stroke in front of Moody and Bob Charles as none of the first-day leaders did better than 72 (Elder).

Moody's old bugaboo — putting — betrayed him in the clutch Sunday. Even though his use of the elongated, 50-foot putters the last couple of years has helped Orville, his putting always has remained suspect. He and Littler were even after 14 holes and he had a tap-in of only a foot in length to take the lead on the 15th green. But, he missed it. Obviously unnerved, Moody missed the green and bogeyed the 16th. Littler ran the victory margin to three when he fired a seven-iron approach a foot from the hole at the final green for a concluding birdie. Moody finished with 71 for 210, taking second place by a shot over Bob Toski, Larry Mowry and Bob Charles. The $45,000 check jumped Littler's senior tour earnings since 1971 over $1 million. It was his seventh official individual victory, but his 13th overall in senior competition along with two triumphs in the team Legends of Golf.

GTE Kaanapali Classic—$300,000
Winner: Orville Moody

The 1987 Senior PGA Tour came to its official end in Hawaii on a wet note in early December, but the weather put no damper on the play of Orville Moody. The loss of the second round of the inaugural GTE Kaanapali Classic to heavy rains didn't seem to faze first-day leader Moody a bit. He was in control all the way Sunday, playing flawless golf as he rolled to a three-stroke victory over the soggy North course of the Royal Kaanapali club, site of the 1964 World Cup won by Arnold Palmer and Jack Nicklaus and more recently the Women's Kemper Open for four years.

It really was hard to tell which of Moody's two rounds was the better one. The Sarge, apparently oblivious to the strong winds, tied the course record Friday with a 65, missing two other makable birdies but three-putting twice. The seven-under-par score gave him a two-stroke lead over Bobby Nichols and Charles Coody. Then, the weather turned foul and virtually flooded the 6,700-yard course Saturday, forcing the cancellation of the round and the shortening of the tournament to 36 holes, the first loss of a round on the Senior PGA Tour since the PaineWebber World Seniors at Charlotte in September.

The course was still very wet, but, with a three-hour delay of the start Sunday, course personnel were able to get it in adequate shape for an "improved-lies-allowed" round. Orville found it to his liking, starting fast with birdies at the first and third holes. Although he made only three more during the day, his game was solid all the way. "This was the best round of golf I've played this year," he said afterward. "I never came close to a bogey." John Brodie and Dave Hill, who had opened with 68s, were the closest to being threats to Moody. Brodie matched Orville's 67 to edge Hill for second by a shot with his 135. It was the old San Francisco quarterback's best finish on the Senior Tour in his three seasons.

Most of the name players arrived in Hawaii the preceding week and played in the non-tour Mauna Lani Challenge. Bob Charles, who hadn't won on the Senior Tour since early May in Albuquerque, picked up his fourth victory of the year and a $45,000 first prize the equal of that claimed by Moody a week later. Charles shot 68-70-69—207 at the Mauna Lani course for a two-stroke win over Dale Douglass, who finished the season with six second-place finishes but no victories. Douglass rebounded from a 77 start with 65-67 for his 209.

Mazda Champions—$850,000
Winners: Miller Barber and Nancy Lopez

Miller Barber and Nancy Lopez teamed so well that, for the first time, the rich, season-ending Mazda Champions tournament in Jamaica was almost a "laugher." Playoffs had decided the first two stagings of the unique event pairing the leading players on the Senior PGA and LPGA Tours, the big money — 12 teams competing for a $500,000 first prize and $850,000 in all — creating an electric air of excitement in the tropical island setting at the Tryall Golf and Beach Club near Montego Bay. That edge was not present in the pre-Christmas atmosphere in 1987, but the victory of the Barber/Lopez combine was perhaps the most impressive yet. They "ham-and-egged" a pair of 63s after an opening 65 and coasted to a three-stroke victory with a record 22-under-par 191.

The first-round 65 set them just a shot off the lead, held that windy Friday by Butch Baird and Chris Johnson. They remained just a stroke behind after the Saturday round as Barber struggled with his game and Lopez carried the bulk of the load. The leaders after 36 holes were Arnold Palmer and Colleen Walker, perhaps the least known of the women pros who had scored her first LPGA victory and placed 11th on the 1987 money list. Colleen made seven birdies and Arnie the other two as they posted a 62 for 127. Baird and Johnson slipped to third with their 65 and 129.

A post-round session on the practice tee cured Barber's swing problems and he was the major front-nine contributor Sunday as they battled Palmer/Walker on the outgoing side and took charge when both Arnie and Colleen double-bogeyed the ninth hole. Through 11 holes, they had moved two strokes in front and they made four more birdies on the way home. Nancy had three of them, her 12-footer at the 15th virtually sewing up the victory. Palmer and Walker fought back from their ninth-hole disaster with four birdies on the back nine, including two on the final two holes for 67 and 194, three back of the winners but two strokes ahead of Orville Moody/Jan Stephenson and Bruce Crampton/Betsy King in second place, worth $50,000 apiece.

11. The European Tour

A record purse, a new giant (this one five feet, four and a half inches tall), the surge of the Swedes, and in general a strength shown in international competition with a European winning the British Open, and European victories in the Ryder Cup and the Dunhill Cup. Any one of them would make for a good script, and 1987 had them all. Despite all this, something else commanded center stage. Here it was in a nutshell:

Was the balance of power shifting, or were the powers-that-be merely off line for the moment?

The new giant was "Little Woosie" — Ian Woosnam, the diminutive Welshman — with four official tour victories and the No. 1 spot on the Epson Order of Merit. Of his more than $1.8 million worldwide, Woosnam won a tour-record £253,717 on the European circuit. And No. 2, on the money list, although a distant £64,000 behind, was not a noted European at all. It was Zimbabwean Mark McNulty, who seems just a major victory away from gaining a reputation to match his formidable record. And a bunch of others helped set the pot bubbling, but not the ones you would expect.

In the eye of this little hurricane were the Big Three of the whole world — Seve Ballesteros, Bernhard Langer and Greg Norman. But mostly Ballesteros, because he's been the focal point of European golf since 1976. This was a far different Ballesteros than the one who used to move from crash to stunning triumph with seeming impunity. Even in 1976 he won twice. This time, he won only once. Ballesteros doesn't have to win every time out to keep tongues from clucking. He's permitted to catch his breath with a second or fifth, or something. Then back into the fire. But it didn't happen this time.

It will be recalled that in 1986, Ballesteros crashed at the Masters late in the final round, but before the doomsayers could start the funeral, he was tearing up the European Tour. He won six times (or five and a half, counting a tie in the Lancome Trophy, conceded because of darkness). The parallel for 1987 also began at the Masters. He fought his way into a playoff with Norman and Larry Mize, then most uncharacteristically three-putted from medium range to bow out on the first extra hole. The clucking started. Then bang! The very next week, in his first European outing, the Suze Open, he was a winner. Ballesteros was back. Or was he?

That turned out to be his only win in 13 European events in 1987. It was his smallest harvest in a 12-year career. He did have eight other top-10 finishes, which helped put him No. 6 on the Order of Merit, a big drop from No. 1. Now, some golfers might resort to witchcraft for that kind of success. But this was Ballesteros.

And if Ballesteros was slumping, what was Norman doing? He's not a member of the European Tour, but he touches down from time to time, and much is expected of him when he does. But he was disappointing in three 1987 outings — 35th in the British Open, where he was defending, a joint sixth in the Panasonic European Open, and a joint fifth in the German Masters. In 1986, he had won around the world. In 1987, by the end of the European Tour, he had won only once — in Australia.

Of the three, Langer was holding the line. He divided his time between the American and European tours as a member of both. He won twice in 10 European events, the Whyte & Mackay PGA Championship and Carrolls Irish Open, the latter by 10 strokes at 19 under par at tough Portmarnock. He also had five other top-10 finishes, and was no worse than 19th for the year.

Time will tell whether 1987 was just a bump on the seismograph of golf or a change in the order of things.

The tour was its richest ever, with a total purse of £7.5 million and a record bonus pool of £175,000 to be shared by the top 15 players on the final Epson Order of Merit. Money was one attraction but there was another that no one could put a price tag on. This was a Ryder Cup year. The taste of the victory over the Americans in 1985 was still sweet and fresh. So the rush was on for money and Ryder Cup points.

There's a key point here for the uninitiated. All this talk of a European winning the British Open, of Europeans winning the Ryder Cup and the Dunhill Cup, meant more than just the victories. It meant that the Americans' world-wide domination of golf for, oh, 60 years, had pretty much ended. That's easy enough to say, but it's the feeling that counts. European football fans would feel it if America suddenly started winning the World Cup.

What a year.

The tour started with the Moroccan Open in March and Woosnam — already the winner of the Hong Kong Open — was thinking of a year of three or four victories. His words had hardly cooled when, in a three-week stretch in April, he won the Jersey Open, finished second to Ballesteros in a playoff for the Suze Open, then won the Cepsa Madrid Open. He added the Bell's Scottish Open in July, the Lancome Trophy in September and the Suntory World Match Play Championship in October. Observers had been predicting for years that Woosnam would be a force some day. The day had arrived.

Nick Faldo, who had spent two uncertain years rebuilding a swing that had served him fairly well — but not well enough, he felt — broke through in the Peugeot Spanish Open in May, then took the British Open. That victory shut out the Americans for the fourth year running. The Swedes were heard from again, stronger than ever. Mats Lanner succeeded countryman Ove Sellberg as the Epson Grand Prix champion, reviving talk that a Swede at last would make the Ryder Cup team. That was delayed when Lanner faded. Then came Magnus Persson, challenging in the Scandinavian Enterprise Open before losing to Gordon Brand, Jr., in a playoff, and Sellberg was second in the Benson and Hedges International. And then the Swedes got their first European stroke-play victory when Anders Forsbrand swept to the Ebel European Masters-Swiss Open title at a stunning 25 under par.

Two other surprises made 1988 a year to be watched. Paul Way, the young Briton who fell into a deep slump after exciting success two years earlier, resurfaced with a victory in the Panasonic European Open. And a new face appeared from a most unlikely place. This was Oliver Eckstein, 18, of West Germany. He played in five events. He tied for 62nd in the season start, the Moroccan Open, and tied for 13th in the finale, the Portuguese Open. He missed the cut in two other tournaments, but caught everyone's attention with a tie for sixth in the German Open, where West Germany's "only" golfer, Bernhard Langer, finished ninth. That helped boost Eckstein to 109th on the final Order of Merit, well into the top 125 exempt places for the 1988 tour.

The irrepressible McNulty continued his rampage. The master of South African golf proved that his victory in the 1986 Portuguese Open was no fluke by winning three times — the London Standard Four Stars National Celebrity Pro-Am and the Dunhill British Masters, back-to-back, and the German Open.

By all accounts, however, it was Ian Woosnam's year. But oddly enough, not by his account. The four European Tour victories plus the Hong Kong Open, Suntory World Match Play, World Cup, Sun City Million Dollar Challenge, the record winnings, the top spot on the Order of Merit — all well and good. But no matter. One thought gnawed at him all year, perhaps drove him: He had been snubbed by the U.S. Masters. He felt he had played well enough in 1986, but the invitation from Augusta National Golf Club never came. Getting to the Masters was a consuming goal. He had said as much at the start of the season, and was still saying so at the end.

Moroccan Open—£165,000
Winner: Howard Clark

The Moroccan Open marked the start of the 1987 PGA European Tour, and the golfers welcomed it with something akin to a New Year's resolution combined with a dream. As Ian Woosnam put it, "A decent year could well earn you £200,000, and if you manage to win four or five events, you could end up with over £300,000." This was the richest European Tour ever, with over £7.5 million in the 30 tournaments. There was another kind of riches at stake — Ryder Cup points. A berth on the Ryder Cup team was always highly coveted, but after the historic European victory over the Americans in 1985, a place on the team was a treasure.

Woosnam's ambitions were commendable, but this was Howard Clark's week at Royal Dar-es-Salam near Rabat. Clark, No. 3 on the 1986 Epson Order of Merit, started slowly, then shot past Mark James with a record 66 in the third round en route to a three-stroke victory. It was a complete reversal from his first visit.

"The last time I was in Morocco was nine years ago, for the Hassan II Trophy," Clark said. "I finished last. This is the kind of confidence-booster I needed just before the Masters." Clark, who would be playing in his first Masters two weeks later, was hardly to be found when the Moroccan Open began. His first-round 73 left him six strokes behind leader Eamonn Darcy, whose 67 tied the record that was to last only two more days. Darcy, switching to a favorite old set of clubs and using a shorter putting stroke, made seven birdies and only one bogey on the 7,362-yard course.

The scene changed rapidly after that. Darcy drifted into the mid-70s, and James, the 1986 Benson & Hedges International champion, moved into the halfway lead at 70-141, five under par. Clark inched up a stroke with another par-73 for 146.

Clark, winner of the Cepsa Madrid and Spanish Opens in 1986 (two of his first four starts), made his move in the third round, a course-record 66. He made only two bad shots, both off the tee, and recovered each time. He birdied the third through the fifth, and eagled the par-five 10th from six feet. He birdied No. 13 from eight feet, and rolled home a 23-foot putt for a birdie on the final hole to set the record. It carried him a stroke clear of James, 212-213. "One shot is nice, but it doesn't mean too much," Clark said. "Even a five-shot cushion on a course as tough as this would be no insurance."

In the final round, James crept ahead with birdies at the ninth and 10th. Clark caught him with a birdie-four at No. 12. A plugged lie in a bunker cost James a stroke at the par-three 14th. Then came the decisive moment. At No. 16, Clark saved par from a bunker while James three-putted from 20 feet. Clark, locking up his ninth career victory in 14 years on the tour, increased his winning margin with a birdie-four at No. 18, then said of beating his good friend, "It could easily have gone the other way, and I'd have been just as pleased if Mark had won as I know he is for me." Clark shot 73-73-66-72—284, eight under par, to James' 71-70-72-74—287.

Jersey Open—£97,000
Winner: Ian Woosnam

Ian Woosnam was hardly in a mood to play golf. First, there was the embarrassment of just a week earlier in Rome. He and his Welsh teammates were favored to win the Dunhill Cup European Qualifier, but were beaten. He was already smarting from two earlier disappointments. He was not among the victorious 1985 European Ryder Cup team invited to the Memorial Tournament in Columbus, Ohio, the site of the 1987 Ryder Cup Matches. Worse, he had hoped to be playing in the Masters this week. But he had not been invited. And so here he was in the Jersey Open at La Moye. And his back was still hurting.

But then Woosnam is a battler. Perhaps because of all these reversals rather than in spite of them, he took a grip on the Jersey Open and wouldn't let go until he had the fifth European victory of his 10-year career. Woosnam scored 68-67-72-72—279, nine under par, and won by one over American Bill Malley, who shot 69-72-69-70—280.

Woosnam opened with a 68, and the next day posted a 67 that left his caddy, John Davidson, saying, "This is as well as I've seen him or anyone else play." He had missed only two greens in two days, and only his putter kept him from burning up the course. The 67—135 gave him the lead by one over David Russell.

In the third round, Russell (71) and Mark Mouland (67) caught Woosnam (72), leaving the three deadlocked at nine-under-par 207 for the final. Then while Russell was working on a 74 and Mouland on a 78, Woosnam put together a makeshift 72 that would have been a lot safer had not Malley caught fire. Malley, 106th on the Order of Merit the year before, began the final round three strokes off the lead, and birdied four of the final six holes for his 70.

Woosnam, out in an uneventful 35, struggled coming home. He three-putted the 10th, had to hole a dangerous downhill six-footer for a birdie at No. 11, and needed another six-footer to save par at No. 12. He birdied No. 16, then escaped disaster at the 17th after what he termed "the worst shot I have ever hit under pressure" — a five-iron second into a grassy pit. He stayed in trouble, hitting his third into a greenside bunker, then coming out anemically to 30 feet. Then he holed that 30-footer to escape with just a bogey. At that point, the Masters seemed very far away.

Suze Open—£159,905
Winner: Severiano Ballesteros

To borrow a bit of literary license, Seve Ballesteros either strikes lightning or is struck by it. Take the Suze Open, his first European outing of the season. He arrived at Cannes Mougins, in the hills above the Mediterranean, criticizing the sudden-death playoff. Just the week before he had lost in one at the Masters. This time he won in sudden-death, and he left Cannes still criticizing it. In between, Ballesteros was the author of some electrifying golf, the victim of some, and if there was one other way for controversy to find him, it did. He was fined for, of all things, using his brother as a caddy.

"It is wrong to settle major championships by sudden-death," Ballesteros said on arriving at Cannes. "I don't want to take anything away from Larry Mize, but I think it is more likely that the real champion will win in an 18-hole playoff." That out of the way, he got on with the Suze Open. Ballesteros was to shoot 69-70-68-68—275, 13 under par, and not lead a round until the 72nd hole, when he shared it with Ian Woosnam (73-64-68-70).

First, however, came Mark McNulty, the scourge of the South African circuit. He had won nine of his last 13 tournaments, beginning with the Portuguese Open in the final week of the 1986 season. He also won the 1986 Sun City Challenge, lifting his earnings in that hot spell to over a half-million dollars. "I must be catching up, Seve," McNulty cracked. He took the first-round lead at four-under-par 68, one ahead of Ballesteros and Gordon Brand Jr. At the eighth hole, where McNulty was about to score his fourth straight birdie, Ballesteros grinned and plucked a cigarette from McNulty's lips. "This is a no-smoking zone," Ballesteros said. "You won't win majors if you do that."

It was McNulty's putter that was on fire. He made seven birdies on putts from between six and 25 feet, drawing praise even from the bold Ballesteros. "I've never seen anybody putt so aggressively on such quick greens," Ballesteros said. He came in for some applause himself, turning wizard to hit left-handed from against an out-of-bounds fence, thus saving par at No. 14. Both men also praised the tough set-up of the course. "Only by playing tight pin positions on fast greens," Ballesteros said, "will European golfers catch up with the Americans."

A 74 in the second round would take McNulty out of the chase (he finished a solid third at 283). But Woosnam, winner of the Jersey Open the week before, came hurtling into the picture with a record 64. He made nine birdies, six in the last eight holes. He enjoyed an awesome combination of iron play and putting. He had 10 one-putts, and only one was longer than 12 feet.

At the halfway point, he stood at nine-under-par 137, two ahead of Ballesteros, who manufactured a 70 from a typical Ballesteros adventure — seven birdies, one bogey, and two double bogeys. He also discovered a difference between European and American rules. His caddy was his brother, Vicente, who also is a golf pro. Vicente had caddied for him in America, where it is legal to have a fellow pro for a caddy. But it is not under European rules, and Ballesteros was fined £50. "It is a stupid rule," Ballesteros said. And he added Vicente would continue to be his caddy.

Woosnam held his two-stroke lead through the third round, 205-207, after both shot 68s. Woosnam got the edge with two stunning shots. He holed out of a bunker for an eagle-three at No. 16 and chipped in for a birdie at No. 18. In the final round, Ballesteros loosed some typical Ballesteros lightning to catch Woosnam. First he flirted with disaster, taking a triple-bogey seven after driving out of bounds at No. 10. He shook that off like a minor irritation and proceeded to birdie four of the last eight holes. His 68 to Woosnam's 70 left them tied at 275. Compared to the fireworks of the week, the playoff was sedate. Ballesteros made a routine par four at the first extra hole. Woosnam, going from thick rough into a stream, made six.

Ballesteros, in victory, was as consistent as he was gracious. "We are both champions," he said. "I said after the Masters when I lost that sudden-death was unfair, and I still say it now. I have won — but it's like tossing a coin and guessing which way it will fall."

Cepsa Madrid Open—£165,000
Winner: Ian Woosnam

The Cepsa Madrid Open, at Puerta de Hierro, began on a royal note for Seve Ballesteros — lunch on Wednesday with King Juan Carlos of Spain and Britain's Prince Charles and Princess Diana. The engagement forced him to miss a meeting of a tournament committee in which he played the odd role of both rule-maker and rule-breaker. The committee was to discuss the £50 fine levied against him at Cannes the week before for using a professional golfer — his brother Vicente — as a caddy. Ironically, Ballesteros, as a member of this committee, helped to draw up the very rule he was charged with violating. After due deliberation, the committee restored an escape clause that was omitted from the rule book a year earlier: That only PGA European Tour members may not caddy. Vicente has never been a member. So the matter was resolved happily for all. On with the golf.

If Ian Woosnam was still aching from having lost to Ballesteros in a playoff at Cannes just a few days before, he didn't show it. Once American Brad Bell had his day, an eight-under-par 64 for the first-round lead by three strokes, Woosnam breezed to the front and took his second victory of the season and, with the Hong Kong Open in March, his third of the year. Woosnam, who won the Jersey Open two weeks earlier, posted 67-67-69-66—269, a tournament-record 19 under par. Woosnam led Ballesteros and Gordon J. Brand by two after 36 holes, led Ballesteros by four after 54, and won by three over Australia's Wayne Grady.

Bell's opening 64 included a double-eagle two at the 530-yard fifth, his 14th hole of the day (he started on No. 10). He was nearing Ballesteros' record 63 until he missed his only fairway of the day at No. 9, his last hole. It cost him a bogey-five. Bell was to fade quickly to a 77 in the second round (and finish tied for 55th) while Woosnam ignored a blustery wind to card his second 67. Putting lapses kept him from going lower. He missed a birdie from four feet at No. 5 and took three putts at No. 15. It became clear with each passing hole that someone was going to have to get very hot to head him off.

Grady gave it a try, surging to a 64 in the final round. He wasted an opportunity for a 63 when he three-putted after driving the green at the 310-yard 13th. Woosnam had figured that a 69 would win for him, and except for Grady, he was right. But only just. Nick Faldo, returning to the European Tour from America, shot a 64 for fourth place at 274. Ballesteros came to life with a streak of four birdies starting at No. 10. But Woosnam never flinched. He all but locked up the victory with two spectacular shots — a seven-iron second that stopped just inches from the hole at No. 12, and a drive to the 13th green, matching the one by Ballesteros. Woosnam had begun the year at the Moroccan Open speaking of how a "decent year" could be worth perhaps £200,000. Only time would tell, but is seemed Woosnam, already with two victories in four tournaments, may have understated the case.

Italian Open—£141,045
Winner: Sam Torrance

To call a golf tournament a dogfight might strike some as hyperbole, but if the Italian Open at Monticello, near Milan, wasn't a dogfight, it will do until one comes along. Examples: Nick Faldo's highest score was two-under-par 70, and he finished third. Jose Rivero shot all four rounds in the 60s, and he finished second. Sam Torrance had the highest single round of the top four finishers, a 71 in the third round, but it was well offset by his opening course-record 64. Torrance, the mustachioed Scot, picked up his 16th career victory, but only after a 15-hole duel — the last nine holes of regulation and a six-hole playoff with Rivero.

"It is two years since my last victory in the Monte Carlo Open, but I never gave up hope of winning again," Torrance said. He might well have, though. After leading the first three rounds by four, then five, then two strokes, Torrance had to birdie three of the last four holes just to stay alive. The raw figures: Torrance, 64-68-71-68; Rivero, 68-69-68-66, the two tying at 17-under-par 271. They barely escaped having Faldo crash their party. Only a bogey at No. 16 kept him out. He settled for third place at 272.

Torrance and Rivero set out for their playoff with evening falling fast. They halved the first five holes in 4-2-4-4-3, each man missing opportunities to win, Torrance from four feet at No. 3 and Rivero by no more than five at No. 4 and No. 5. By the time they came to the sixth extra hole, there was thunder and lightning, and the Alps were obscured by a mist. Then a heavy rain began to fall. It was doubtful the playoff could have gone to a seventh hole. Suddenly, it didn't have to. At the sixth extra hole, Rivero drove into the trees, then bunkered his recovery and took a five to Torrance's winning four.

Torrance had set the course record with a 65 in Wednesday's pro-am, then broke it the next day with his 64 in the first round. His putter was a big help. "I have simply edged about an inch nearer to the ball in order to get a little more upright, and I've gripped the putter a wee bit more firmly," he said. He needed only 26 putts the first day, and only 11 through the first nine holes the second day. The putter had saved him, because suddenly his driver was running amok.

Epson Grand Prix of Europe—£250,000
Winner: Mats Lanner

The Epson Grand Prix of Europe, only two years old, has made a name for itself — the Tournament of Surprises. The 1986 Epson ended in one, with Ove Sellberg becoming the first Swede ever to win a European Tour event. If that set the pattern, then the 1987 edition was faithful to it. This one was full of them, especially the finish: A Swede would win again. This time, Mats Lanner, age 26, scoring his first Euorpean victory.

The tip-off to the kind of tournament this would be came in the first round when Nick Faldo, fast returning to form, was rudely interrupted by a relative unknown from Australia, Vaughan Somers, and by the healthy margin of 4 and 2. Not that the battle-tested Faldo was playing badly. He played St. Pierre, at Chepstow, in solid par for the 16 holes the match went. The problem was, Somers, played in five under par.

And so it would go in the European Tour's only match play event. Not one of the eight seeds in the 32-man field would survive to the final. Australia's Peter Senior pulled the biggest of the early upsets in the second round when he rallied from three down with eight to play to beat Bernhard Langer on the last hole. "I didn't think I was going to lose when I was three-up after 10 holes," said Langer, making his first European appearance of the year. "But then the greens got slower and slower as the day went on, and they are not all that good." That was merely the first complaint against the greens. Sellberg also fell in the second round, to Tommy Armour III at the 20th.

Seve Ballesteros, No. 1 seed, entered in the second round and had clear sailing until meeting little-known Jeff Hawkes of South Africa, who got into the tournament when Sandy Lyle decided not to play. Hawkes rolled over David Feherty, 1-up; Howard Clark, 3 and 2; Armour, 3 and 1, and Sam Torrance, 1-up. Against Torrance, he came back from 3-down with four holes to play, capping the rally with a sensational one-handed backward shot from near a wall. The ball hit the flagstick and stopped about four feet away. "In the circumstances," Hawkes said, "that has to be the best shot I have ever hit in my life." He holed the putt to end it for the startled Torrance.

Then Hawkes delivered the crusher in the semifinals. One-putting 11 times in 15 holes, he thrashed Ballesteros, 4 and 3.

Hawkes' unexpected march through the draw put him on a collision course with an equally surprising Lanner. This was Hawkes' 12th year on the tour, Lanner's sixth, and neither had yet won. Ironically, they were tied for 251st on the Sony Rankings, and between them they had won only some $9,000 this season. Yet they left some impressive bodies in their wake. Lanner beat Ian Baker-Finch, 5 and 3; Gordon J. Brand, 4 and 2; Des Smyth at the 19th; Greg Turner, 3 and 2, and Senior, 1-up.

In the final, Lanner jumped out front by two holes then just as abruptly slipped to one behind when he lost three out of four holes from the eighth. Lanner squared the match at the 15th, then turned back a stiff challenge at No. 17, halving the hole on a 10-foot putt after Hawkes got his birdie from 16 feet.

Hawkes' error at the 18th settled the issue. Lanner put a one-iron just off the back of the green of the 237-yard par three. Hawkes missed the green, chipped too strongly over a bunker, and missed the putt coming back. Lanner holed for his par and his first victory.

Peugeot Spanish Open—£175,000
Winner: Nick Faldo

This was the position Nick Faldo found himself in: he won five times in Europe in 1983, and he won once in Europe and once in America in 1984. No matter. He felt there was a flaw in his swing that kept him from fulfillment. So in 1984, he made a decision that many observers considered suicidal: He decided to re-build the swing. For two frustrating years he worked with Florida-based David Leadbetter. And for two years, despite some improvement, he could not win.

Finally, deliverance. Faldo broke out of the long doldrums in the Peugeot Spanish Open at Las Brisas with 72-71-71-72 for the two-under-par 286 total, coming from behind for a two-stroke victory over Seve Ballesteros and Hugh Baiocchi. It was his first victory since 1984. But it did not come easily.

The tournament opened with controversy. Ballesteros had been complaining and warning for weeks that the slow, soft greens on the European Tour would take their toll on the European team at the Ryder Cup Matches in September. Ballesteros leapt to his opportunity this time. As co-promoter of the Spanish Open, he thrust slick greens at the field at Las Brisas, and proved his point — to his content, at least — with a course-record eight-under-par 64 in the pro-am.

Many remained unconvinced. Chief among the critics was Ian Woosnam, who dreams of playing some day in the Masters, where he will again find fast greens. He said Ballesteros's 64 was a "freak round," and criticized Ballesteros for setting up the greens too hard and too fast.

In the second round, despite high winds and hard greens that lifted scores, Dennis Durnian posted a 69 to move into the halfway lead at 140, two ahead of Ballesteros and Baiocchi. Ballesteros complained that the greens had been watered after all the furor. "It is wrong," he said. "They should have stayed consistently quick throughout the week." All the bother was lost on Durnian. "I don't know what all the fuss is about," he said. "I had 10 single putts today." (His joy was short-lived. He finished 81-76—297, in a tie for 14th that included Woosnam.)

Faldo broke through in the third round, his 71-214 tying him with Baiocchi for the lead, two ahead of Ballesteros. A buffeting wind came up in the fourth round and sorted out the field. Faldo made the turn in even par, scambling to a par five at No. 8 on a 20-foot putt after dumping a shot into the lake. He fell behind Baiocchi twice. But Baiocchi crashed with three straight bogeys, beginning at No. 14, and Ballesteros hooked his drive into the lake and took a double-bogey six at the 15th. Faldo jumped at his chance, holing from 12 feet for a birdie-three at No. 14. So on a course toughened by Ballesteros and the weather, Faldo, at 286, was the only player to finish under par. He had his first victory in three years. Was it a "freak," as Woosnam had said of Ballesteros's pro-am 64? Or had the "new" Nick Faldo arrived? Time would tell.

Whyte & Mackay PGA Championship—£220,000
Winner: Bernhard Langer

The most revealing way to veiw Bernhard Langer's victory in the Whyte & Mackay British PGA Championship is through the frustrations of the runnerup. This was none other than Langer's longtime nemesis, Seve Ballesteros. To put this into proper context, it should be noted that for the past few years and up to this time — May, 1987 — Ballesteros, Langer, and Greg Norman were acknowledged as the three best golfers in the world. Of this group, Langer was usually second or third.

Ballesteros certainly proved himself again in this PGA at Wentworth, site of his four World Match Play victories. In this PGA, he posted four sub-par rounds; 70-67-68-69, for a total of 274, 14 under par. That was even 12 strokes better than his winning total in the 1980 Martini, also at Wentworth. Which is to say that Ballesteros put on a very strong showing in this PGA, and could only finish second. "No one could have beaten Langer this week," he said, shrugging. "Those four rounds were unbelieveable."

It was Langer's first victory of the year, and his four rounds were 66-69-68-67, for an 18-under-par total of 270, the championship record by one stroke under the previous record set in 1967 by Brian Huggett over the less-demanding Thorndon Park. While Langer's play was impressive enough in its own right, it was even more so considering that the first two rounds of the PGA were played in cold weather that ranged from foul to downright nasty, complete with hail and thunderstorms in the first round. Such brilliant play is not uncommon at Wentworth's West Course, but it's usually seen in the World Match Play in the autumn, when the weather and the grounds are more agreeable.

At any rate, Langer was bundled against the cold in the first round, wearing two sweaters under his rain suit. Despite such restrictions, he came home in 32 with five birdies and three pars, one-putting six times, to complete his six-under-par 66. That left him two strokes ahead of Jose-Maria Canizares and American Rick Hartmann, both at 68, and four ahead of Ballesteros, who wrapped up his 70 by hitting a four-iron 200 yards to 30 feet and holing the putt for an eagle-three.

Langer kept putting daylight between himself and the field, except for Ballesteros, and it seemed the PGA would become another of their famed confrontations. Through the third round, Langer was at 203 and Ballesteros at 205, and Canizares was a distant third at 209. The last time Langer and

Ballesteros came head-to-head in the final round was in the Lancome Trophy at St. Nom la Breteche in October, 1986. After four extra holes they remained tied, and falling darkness that day and previous commitments the next left them unable to settle it, thus creating a tied finish. Ballesteros had won all of their other battles.

Not this time. Langer's closest call came in the third round, when a bogey at No. 15 reduced his lead to one stroke. He got that back with a birdie at No. 18 after a three-wood second shot to the green. In the final round, a three-stroke swing at the 10th and 11th settled things. Ballesteros, trying to come up a bank at the par-three 10th, hit a branch and took five. At No. 11, Langer was outside him but holed his putt for a birdie-three, and was six strokes clear. Buried in the detail of the tournament was perhaps the real story of Langer's superior play: He made only two bogeys in 72 holes, and he did not three-putt once. Ballesteros contemplated his recent near-misses — third, third, second, and second in successive tournaments. "You'll see," he said, grinning. "One day I will break through." The struggle for supremacy rolled on.

Four Stars National Pro-Celebrity—£138,500
Winner: Mark McNulty

With some of the European headliners playing in the Memorial Tournament in the United States and others taking the week off, pencil-thin Ken Brown, the winner two years ago, found himself the favorite in the London Standard Four Stars National Pro-Celebrity. The role didn't make him uncomfortable, but something else did: the impending arrival of his first child. His home was only a half-hour from Moor Park. "So if I get a phone call saying the baby is coming..." he said bravely before the tournament, "I'll be off — even if it means missing my tee-off." But as any new father could have told him, the call of the stork easily drowns out the call to the tee. And so, after an opening 69 that left him just two strokes off the lead, and after nine holes of the second round, he was off. "It was impossible for me to concentrate," Brown said. "Our first child is much more important than golf."

That's as it should be. No telling what might have happened, but what did happen was that Mark McNulty, the irrepressible Zimbabwean, came from behind in the final round, caught Sam Torrance, then beat him in the playoff. The man's record is hard to believe. It was his 10th victory in 18 starts spanning the South African and European Tours, and it was, incredibly, his 13th victory in 13 playoffs since his junior days.

Torrance opened with a seven-birdie 67, five under par, to share the first-round lead. It was an odd round. He three-putted twice going out, then made five consecutive threes — three of them birdies — starting from No. 11. Torrance was in interesting company. His amateur partner was actor Sean Connery, who as James Bond outsmarted the evil Goldfinger at Royal St. Georges (St. Martins in the Ian Fleming spy novel).

Torrance was not about to be budged. He was second by a stroke at the halfway point, behind England's Derrick Cooper, age 32, the surprise leader with 66—135, nine under par. Cooper also led after three rounds, with 69—204, and it was here that the dangerous McNulty finally surfaced.

His 69—206 left him only two strokes behind.

Cooper's final-round 75 (he finished tied for eighth) left the stage to Torrance and McNulty for a furious finish. Torrance, who started the final round four behind Cooper and two behind McNulty, birdied the second, third, and fourth holes on the way to the best score of the week, a seven-birdie 65. That gave him a total of 15-under-par 273 that put him three strokes clear of Tony Charnley (67) in third place. But McNulty was on the prowl. His only error in an outward 34 was a three-putt four at No. 5. He caught Torrance with birdies at the par-four 15th and the par-five 17th, then escaped trouble at No. 18. He missed the green to the right with his approach, but chipped brilliantly to within inches of the flag and saved his par for a 67 to force the playoff. They halved the first playoff hole in birdie fours. Then McNulty holed a 40-footer for a birdie three at the next to end it. The first prize came just in time. "It will go a long way," he said, "toward paying for the new Mercedes I bought myself a couple of days before the tournament."

Dunhill British Masters—£200,000
Winner: Mark McNulty

It's beyond dispute that the South African Sunshine Circuit is not in the same league with the American PGA Tour, not even as it existed in the 1940s. Point conceded. Now it is safe to address the remarkable accomplishments of Mark McNulty, for one has to go back to Byron Nelson and his awesome record to find a benchmark for comparison. In 1945, the effects of World War II notwithstanding, Nelson won 11 tournaments in a row and 18 in a single season on the American tour — the greatest performance in the history of golf. Such a performance today may be possible, but the odds against it are astronomical. So give McNulty his due. One has to go back to Nelson to find anything comparable. In taking the Dunhill British Masters at Woburn, McNulty not only won his second in a row but his 11th in his last 19 starts over the South African and European circuits. That would be a stunning record even in a pitch-and-putt league.

Granted, the Masters field was not at full strength, not with the absence of defending champion Seve Ballesteros. And this drew a mild rebuke from Bernhard Langer. "There is an unwritten rule among golfers," Langer noted, "that you always defend a title." There was no firm explanation for Ballesteros's absence, but the field was strong, nonetheless. It included Craig Stadler and, back from the Memorial Tournament in the United States, Ian Woosnam (seeking his third victory of the season), Howard Clark, and Nick Faldo. The only other notable absentee was Sandy Lyle, who stayed on the American tour. There was nothing cheap about McNulty's victory.

Woosnam and Hugh Baiocchi shared the first-round lead on five-under-par 67s. Woosnam birdied all four par-five holes, and Baiocchi birdied two of them and eagled another. Stadler, one of four at 68, made seven birdies, none of them at the par fives. (Stadler was to come to a sudden and surprising grief. He finished bogey-bogey-double bogey in the second round for an 80, and missed the cut with 148.)

Woosnam inched ahead in the second round with a 68 for 135. He gave up three bogeys, but putted beautifully to recover. He eagled No. 4 from

20 feet, birdied the seventh, then escaped No. 14 with only a bogey by sinking a 12-foot putt. McNulty followed his opening 71 with a 65 and rushed to a joint second at 136, a stroke off Woosnam's lead. Paul Way, one of the heroes in the 1985 Ryder Cup Matches, scored five birdies in eight holes to move into a share of the early lead, then was ambushed at the par-five 18th. He sliced his drive into the rough, shanked his next into deeper rough, then lost his ball. He ended up with a 10 for 73-145 and did not threaten again.

A third-round 71 moved McNulty into a tie with Woosnam (72) at 207 through 54 holes, the two of them one stroke clear. McNulty slipped behind immediately at the start of the fourth round, three-putting the first hole. Woosnam failed to hold his edge, three-putting the second while McNulty birdied from 10 feet, triggering a streak. McNulty birdied the next two from about 10 feet each, parred the par-three fifth with one putt, then birdied No. 8 from 20 feet and No. 9 from 25 to make the turn in 30. The surge lifted him four shots ahead of Woosnam.

But he wasn't home free. Christy O'Connor, Jr., made his bid with birdies at the 11th and 13th, then fell back with two consecutive bogeys. He finished with 70—278 for a share of third place. Woosnam came charging back with a birdie-three from 15 feet at No. 14 to get within one stroke when McNulty bogeyed No. 15. Woosnam then caught him with a birdie at the 17th. The time came, then, for McNulty to prove himself at the 514-yard 18th. Woosnam was wide with his third shot, but McNulty ran his 50-yard chip shot to 18 inches and sank the putt for his birdie-four and the victory. His 71-65-71-67—274, 14 under par, gave him a one-stroke victory over Woosnam. If there had been any doubts about McNulty before, there weren't now.

Peugeot French Open — £250,320
Winner: Jose Rivero

Joey Sindelar, the personable young American with the graceful swing, turned prophet after the third round of the Peugeot French Open. Sixty out of 79 players posted sub-par rounds under ideal conditions that day at the par-72 St. Cloud course near Paris. "If you had told me I'd be 16 under after three days, with a crowd like this around me, I'd have laughed at you," said Sindelar, whose 66—200 left him just two strokes off the lead. "It's going to be an incredible finish tomorrow." The crowd around him included Sam Torrance, the leader by two strokes on 65—198, and sharing second at 200 with Sindelar: Nick Faldo (64), Hugh Baiocchi (66), and Gordon Brand Jr. (65).

Sindelar was dead-on about the incredible finish. Who could possibly have believed — Jose Rivero? The 31-year-old Spaniard turned professional in 1973, joined the tour in 1976, and had only one victory to his credit, the 1984 Lawrence Batley International. His best 1987 finish to date was a second in the Italian Open seven weeks earlier, only the second runner-up finish of his career.

Rivero definitely was not part of the "crowd" Sindelar had in mind. Only two of the top 21 finishers failed to break 70 in the third round, and Rivero was one of them. He opened the tournament fairly well, then proceeded to drift: In the first round, his 68 left him in a crush of seven players four strokes behind leader Howard Clark (64); in the second, his 67—135 left him three behind Clark (68—132); and in the third, his 71—206 put him eight behind Torrance (198). Sindelar's crowd stood between him and the top. Some of them could be counted on to falter, but not all. There was only one way to get to the top, and Rivero did it. Ignoring a relentless rain, he shot 63 in the final round for a 19-under-par total 269 to vault over 12 players and edge Clark (69) by one stroke.

Golfers say they like to "put up a number" for the field to shoot at. Rivero certainly did that. Playing well ahead of the leaders from his eight-stroke deficit, he left the course in ashes, despite the rain. He birdied four holes in a row, beginning at No. 3, then closed like a champion with five consecutive birdies.

Volvo Belgian Open—£150,000
Winner: Eamonn Darcy

The pun-makers were in their element for the Belgian Open. It was played at Royal Waterloo, and water is what it had more than enough of. The event was revived after a seven-year hiatus, and drew a strong field despite the absence of some European stars who were playing in the U.S. Open the same week. Rains forced a premature end after three rounds, leaving Eamonn Darcy with well-earned victory, his first after a four-season drought.

Also premature was Ian Woosnam's outlook. He was already looking ahead to the British Open, a month away, after taking the first-round lead on a five-under-par 66 in heavy rain and strong winds. "Get your money on me for the Open if I continue to putt like that," Woosnam said. He holed from 12 feet twice, and from 18 and 20 feet for four of his birdies, and one-putted for two pars. He was one ahead of England's Brian Evans, a rookie in his second event, and American Billy Andrade, who turned professional and stayed in Europe after helping the U.S. Walker Cup team to victory a month earlier. Among those two strokes behind, at 69, were Darcy and Spanish Open champion Nick Faldo.

Darcy (67) and Faldo (67) moved into a tie for second at 136 through 36 holes, but Woosnam seemed bent on leaving no room for anyone else. He put up another 66 for a 10-under-par 132 and a four-stroke lead after an amazing finish. He had slipped out of the lead through No. 11 when England's Barry Lane returned a course-record 64 and Ronan Rafferty a 65. But he exploded down the stretch, getting birdies at No. 12, No. 15, No. 16, and an eagle-three at No. 17 from 20 feet for an inward 30.

The third round belonged to Darcy and the rain, and it turned out to be the final and decisive round. The weather touched off a weird situation. Howard Clark complained that the hole at No. 11 was egg-shaped and smaller than the stipulated 4¼ inches as a result of the downpour and the squeegee work of the ground crew. He refused to putt. After a half-hour wait in the rain, the players were allowed to go to the warming shelter of the clubhouse. Play was suspended for nearly three hours.

If Darcy was bothered by Woosnam's four-stroke lead and the weather, it didn't show. By the time play was suspended, he had caught the suddenly struggling Woosnam, his playing partner, with a barrage of six birdies and made the turn in an amazing 31. His putter, balky the first two days, had become his friend. He birdied No. 1 from 15 feet, and got five more birdies in a span of six holes. These included a just-missed hole-in-one at No. 4, and putts of five, 10, and 12 feet. He dropped just one shot, bunkering his drive at No. 6. Darcy got two more birdies after play resumed for his record-tying 64 and a 13-under-par 200 total. When the final round was washed out, Darcy was declared the winner. It was the third solo victory of his career (he had won twice in better-ball tournaments), and his first since the 1983 Spanish Open. The consistent Woosnam, a two-time winner this season, was now runnerup for the third time. He shot a 69 to join Rafferty (64) and Faldo (65) at 201.

Johnnie Walker Monte Carlo Open—£204,400
Winner: Peter Senior

Seve Ballesteros arrived at Mont Agel in a fine mood, despite a rigorous 21-hour trip and the disappointment of another near-miss in the U.S. Open. "I got a bronze medal for third place in San Francisco to go with my silver for losing in the playoff in the U.S. Masters," Ballesteros joked. "Maybe I'll win a gold in the British Open at Muirfield."

It would be several weeks before that dream could hatch. Meanwhile, there was the Monte Carlo Open to contend with. And as the fates would have it, Ballesteros, the defending champion, was not a factor in the tournament. He finished tied for fourth. It ended up an all-Australian affair, with Peter Senior edging Rodger Davis by one stroke. It was his sixth top-five finish in eight European starts this season. It also was his second European Tour title, following his PLM Open victory in 1986.

But this one looked like anything but a victory for Senior at the start. He opened with a 66, but Scotland's Brian Marchbank, age 29, posted a six-under-par 63 and took the first-round lead by two strokes.

It is sometimes said that golfers play in a fog. This time, it was literally true. Fog is a common hazard at Mont Agel, which sits in the Alps some 2,700 feet above the principality of Monaco, and it was to plague play several times during the tournament. In fact, it brought the second round to a halt, leaving Marchbank to complete a 70 the next day and find himself four strokes behind Senior, who added a 63 to his opening 66 to take a two-stroke lead at 129.

The fog forced officials to change the character of the course. In order to allow players to see two of the holes, they not only shortened one par three to 178 yards, but transformed a par four into a par three, thus reducing the course par to 68. It was not a good tournament for bookkeepers.

The third round also was interrupted by fog, but Senior was not about to let that sidetrack him. He dropped one stroke going out, then scored three birdies in a five-hole stretch coming home for 65 to move to 11 under par at 194. Davis shot a 65 and stood in third place, five strokes behind Senior going into the final round. Then Davis made a real battle of it.

He eagled No. 17 and birdied No. 18 for a closing 62, leaving Senior needing a birdie of his own at No. 18 to win. He got it on a six-foot putt for a 66 and the one-stroke victory. The key to Senior's win was his wizardry over the last four holes. He played them in 11 under par for the four rounds. His 14-under-par 260 total, which included 17 birdies and one eagle, matched the European record set by countryman Kel Nagle in the 1961 Irish Hospitals tournament at Woodbrook, in Dublin.

Carrolls Irish Open—£215,032
Winner: Bernhard Langer

They badly needed some comic relief at Portmarnock, and it came too early and too little in the form of a weird misfortune committed on and by Ross McFarlane, age 26, a little-known English pro. It happened in the first round. McFarlane's second shot to the sixth hole finished so close to the pond that he would have to stand in it to hit his next shot. Prudently, he wanted to know how deep the water was. Imprudently, he probed the water with a stake. There is a rule against testing the conditions of a hazard, and so he was penalized two strokes, which made his six an eight and his 74 a 76. Not that it mattered. McFarlane was to miss the cut badly. And so did everybody else in the field, it seemed, the way Bernhard Langer was playing.

This was a different form of comedy. Langer turned the Carrolls Irish Open into what the American sportswriters term a "laugher." He was simply playing some other game, somewhere else. It would be priceless to read the mind of a golfer at a time like that. Better yet, to read the minds of the others. Understand that Sandy Lyle turned in some superb golf at the tough 7,102-yard, par-72 links course — 70-70-71-68—279, which is nine under par. That would have won seven of the previous eight Irish Opens at Portmarnock. Seve Ballesteros won there in 1986 with 285. Yet Lyle was merely second — by 10 strokes.

Langer shot 67-68-66-68—269, a record 19 under par. That cut seven strokes off Sam Torrance's previous record of 276 in 1981. The post-mortem looked like this: Langer's opening 67 tied him with Gordon J. Brand, his 68 moved him five strokes ahead of Lyle through 36 holes, and his 66 nine ahead of Rodger Davis through 54. It was Langer's second European victory of the season, and it seems mere victory is not enough. He has to do it with records. Just five weeks earlier, he roared through the Whyte & Mackay British PGA with an 18-under 280 at Wentworth.

Langer seeks that certain putter the way Sir Galahad sought the Holy Grail, and thereby hangs a curious tale. Early in the second round, Langer realized there was something wrong with the putter he had bought earlier in the week. "I left an uphill 15-foot putt short at the seventh, and there's no way I should do that," he said. "The club felt soft when I hit the ball. I hadn't realized the head was loose." Under the rules, he could not fix the club during the round, so he plugged away with the wobbly-headed putter and still came in with a 68. He went immediately to have the putter fixed, leaving the others to contemplate his five-stroke lead.

It was a fruitless exercise. After a 66 in the third round, Langer still would not so much as quiver. In the final round, he didn't make his first birdie until the seventh, but he did not made a bogey or even threaten to. He coasted to his 68. The only excitement came from Ireland's David Jones, who tied the course record with a 65 and finished seventh. Then came the best news of the tournament: Langer would take the following week off, leaving the Scottish Open to someone else. He needed to recharge his batteries for the British Open two weeks later.

Bell's Scottish Open—£200,000
Winner: Ian Woosnam

There was nothing subtle about Ian Woosnam in the Bell's Scottish Open — no frills, no chills, no mysteries. Like Bernhard Langer in the Carrolls Irish Open the week before, he simply ran it to earth. He returned 65-65-66-68 for an intimidating 20-under-par total of 264, stretching his lead round by round — one stroke, two, three, and finally winning by seven over Peter Senior. This was his third victory of the season, following the Jersey Open and the Cepsa Madrid Open. Add to that three runnerup finishes, and that's a brilliant season's work by anybody's standards. And the season was only about half over. This one came against a strong cast at Gleneagles' famed King's Course.

King's, generally considered too short for the modern game, was lengthened by 500 yards to 6,823 yards. And since it was near Muirfield, site of the British Open the following week, the Scottish Open suddenly became an attractive event for some who might have passed it up otherwise. On hand were Seve Ballesteros, Nick Faldo, Tom Kite, and Fred Couples, to say nothing of Deane Beman, commissioner of the American PGA Tour. Beman decided to give tournament golf another try, as he had in 1986 after a 13-year absence. (He would shoot 79-71—150, and miss the cut.)

But it was all purely academic. Woosnam saw to that. Brian Marchbank took the early first-round lead with 66 on a blustery, cloudy day. That was the course record, but Marchbank had little time to enjoy it. Woosnam came along about 8 p.m. with his 65. That included bogeys at the 10th and 11th, strokes he grabbed back, and then some, with birdies at Nos. 13, 15, 17, and 18. Ironically, Woosnam had almost withdrawn in the morning because of a chronic back problem. But he took some pain-killing medication and hit away.

Woosnam's course record lasted about a day. First, Roger Chapman lowered the record by a stroke, with the help of two eagles, to 64. Sam Torrance, playing despite a throat infection, equalled it a short time later. Then later in the day, Jose-Maria Olazabal, the Rookie of the Year in 1986 but struggling now, set a record that ought to stand for some time. He went out in 31, birdied three of the next five holes, then closed with an eagle three from about 45 feet at No. 18 for a nine-under-par 62. It moved him into contention at 136. Woosnam, playing earlier, had already posted another 65 and stood at 130, 12 under par. He was two ahead of Chapman (132). Ballesteros played late, with Woosnam's score there to tempt him, and shot a 65 for 133, three behind. His round included two birdies and an eagle in the first six holes, and a brilliant saved par at No. 10, where he holed a putt of about 25 feet after being unplayable in a bush. Woosnam set a fierce pace. With a birdie at No. 1 and an eagle-two at No. 3 (an eight iron from 118 yards), he was three under par through the first three holes. The fifth slowed him, but then he ran off three straight birdies from the sixth and made the turn in 30.

Woosnam encountered his only serious challenge in the third round, after he took an embarrassing four-putt bogey six on No. 10, letting Peter Senior slip into the lead. Woosnam reached the 499-yard hole with no difficulty, but his three-iron shot from the rough rolled back off the tier. His first putt, for a possible eagle, did not clear the crest, and the ball came back to him. In fact, it finished behind where he started. His next try just did stay up, and it took him two more putts to get down. Senior, winner of the Monte Carlo Open two weeks earlier, had five birdies and a bogey going out to tie Woosnam, who made the turn in par 35 after two birdies and two bogeys. Senior's lead after the 10th was brief.

Woosnam surged back in front with inspired golf. He birdied No. 12 from five feet and No. 13 from six. He got an eagle two at No. 14 after a one-iron to 20 feet, then birdied No. 17 and No. 18. That gave him a 66 and a three-round total of 196, 17 under par and three ahead of Senior.

KLM Dutch Open—£180,000
Winner: Gordon Brand Jr.

Pity the American visitor at the British Open when the Brands get to the leader board. Is it Gordon Brand, Jr., or Gordon J. Brand? They're different? Okay, then Gordon Brand, Jr. is Gordon J. Brand's son, right? No? Well, which is which?

This might help sort things out: It was Gordon Brand, Jr. — age 28, a Scot, and no relation to Gordon J. Brand, 31, an Englishman — who chalked up his third career victory and his first in three years in the KLM Dutch Open at Hilversum, It's not many who can shake off a challenger's closing eagle and get a birdie of his own to win by one. And that's what Brand did in nipping David A. Russell. Brand, who took the lead at the third round, posted scores of 69-67-67-60—272, 16 under par.

David Feherty bolted into the first-round lead with a record-tying 65, despite a two-hour rain delay, and credited the inspiration of Tony Jacklin, the European Ryder Cup captain. During the British Open, Jacklin accused some young European pros of being too easy-going. "Tony didn't name names, but I took it personally," he said. "I'm as ambitious for success as anybody." Feherty was in the process of changing his swing from left-to-right to right-to-left. "It's a painful process," he said. Seve Ballesteros birdied the last four holes for a 67, but was not a factor. He finished tied for ninth.

Feherty's second-round 72 carried him out of the picture (he also would share ninth), but a new face popped up. Canadian Jerry Anderson, age 31, the 1984 Ebel European Masters-Swiss Open champion, soared into the halfway lead with a nine-under par 63 for a 12-under-par 132. The fireworks included the fourth hole-in-one of his career, at the 125-yard fifth, and four straight closing birdies. That left Anderson two ahead of Tony Johnstone (68), Mark Roe (66), and David A. Russell (68).

While Anderson faded — a pair of 75s would leave him tied for 19th — Brand surged to a three-stroke lead after 54 holes on 67—203, 13 under par. Jammed behind him at 206 were Roe, Antonio Garrido, Bob Smith, Mangus Persson, Ronan Rafferty, and Jose-Maria Olazabal. Olazabal was the chief threat in the final round. He had three birdies and an eagle in an outward 33, then inched into the lead by one stroke with birdies at the 12th and 15th. Then trouble.

Brand came to the last hole believing he needed a birdie to tie, unaware that Olazabal had bogeyed No. 16. Brand hit his drive at No. 18, and from the fairway watched Olazabal — on his way to a 69 and a tie for fourth — chop his way through trees and thick rough to a double-bogey seven. But that was no real comfort, for at that moment Brand learned that Russell had chipped in from 50 yards for an eagle-three and a 66—273. Now Brand needed a birdie to win. He got it like a champion. He hit a two iron some 240 yards to the green, and two-putted for his birdie-four and the victory.

Scandinavian Enterprise Open—£193,236
Winner: Gordon Brand, Jr.

Perhaps it's sometimes as simple as being battle-tested. Gordon Brand, Jr., summed it up this way: "I knew I had to birdie one of the last three holes, but I didn't panic." Not that others did panic, but it was Brand's ability to keep his head that brought him the Scandinavian Enterprise Open at Ullna, near Stockholm. He beat Magnus Persson with a birdie on the first playoff hole for perhaps the biggest victory of his seven-year career. It was his second successive victory.

Brand returned 64-71-71-71—277, 11 under par, to tie Persson, who had closed with 68. But for a while, it seemed he had squandered a big chance.

The first round opened in warm, calm weather. It was very much to Brand's liking. He served notice with a nine-birdie 64, eight under par. That put him into the lead, one ahead of Des Smyth, who also carded nine birdies, but who offset two of them with a badly judged nine-iron recovery from the rough. He caught the lake, and took a double-bogey six. The course record of 62, set in 1986 by champion Greg Turner of New Zealand, escaped untouched, but Ullna took a fearful beating nonetheless. Fully 33 players scored in the 60s in the first round.

The second-round attack was nearly as impressive, with 27 players in the 60s. Brand was not quite equal to the pace. His one-under-par 71 dropped him four strokes out of the lead. It was a jumbled 71: he suffered two sixes, but birdied three of the last 10 holes. Smyth jumped through the opening with a 66, including five birdies in a nine-hole stretch, for a 13-under-par 131. That put him two ahead of Ronan Rafferty, whose 65 was the best of the day.

Smyth closed with 72-79 and dropped to a tie for ninth at 282. He was not alone in that pressure-cooker. Rafferty repeated his error of a week earlier, when his first tour victory slipped away on a final-round 77 in the Dutch Open. This time, he led by one after three rounds in the 60s, then closed with 77 again. He shared fourth with 279.

It was Persson who thrilled the home crowd. Seven off the lead through the third round, Persson solved the heavy rains and high winds on the final day for a 68 and the early lead at 277. He seemed to have the victory locked up when Brand pushed his drive at No. 14 into the trees. That cost him a bogey six. Then he bogeyed No. 15 after playing a recovery shot from the lake. Now he had three holes left, and needed one birdie. He just missed from 10 feet at No. 16, then got it at No. 17 on an 18-foot putt for a three. A birdie at No. 18 would have given him the victory, but his long putt taunted the hole and stayed out.

Brand made short work of the playoff, at the 363-yard sixth. He hit a one iron off the tee and a 102-yard wedge shot to eight inches.

PLM Open—£145,210
Winner: Howard Clark

With summer rushing toward that September appointment with the Americans, the Ryder Cup — never far from anyone's mind — had become the focal point. That was the case at the PLM Open at Ljunghusen, on Sweden's southern tip. Eight of the nine automatic places were already taken, and with several other candidates absent, the eyes were on three players knocking at the door — Mats Lanner, Ronan Rafferty, and Magnus Persson, 10th, 12th, and 14th, respectively, on the Order of Merit. Of the three, Lanner was the strangest story. He had a Ryder Cup position all but locked up with his Epson Match Play victory early in May, but he had been struggling ever since. So more than just a tournament title and a £24,000 first prize were at stake here.

As the fickle gods of golf would have it, not one of them would be a real factor. The prize, instead, went to Howard Clark, winner of the first event of the year, the Moroccan Open. He took this title, the 10th of his 14-year career, with one of the most dramatic finishes of the year. He was three behind after the first round with 68, five behind after the second round with 73, and five behind after the third round with 67. Then came the charge — a final-round 63 for a 17-under-par 271 that overran Ossie Moore by two. The unfortunate Moore, himself with a 63 in the second round, had not exactly backed up. His closing 68 would have won most times.

David J. Russell, limping with a severe right ankle injury suffered five weeks earlier in the Bell's Scottish Open, took the first-round lead with a course-record 65. He put on a dazzling mix of accurate irons and putting. He needed just 26 putts, and one-putted six of the last seven holes, four of them for birdies. He led by two over Peter Senior and David Feherty.

In the second round, Senior shot 69 and Moore 63 (not a record because players were permitted preferred lies due to the soggy fairways). They shared the lead at eight-under-par 136. Senior moved ahead by two through the third round with a 67 to Moore's 69. This merely set the stage for Clark's sprint. Senior was at 13-under-par 203 to start the fourth round, and Clark was an unpromising five back at 208.

It was another case of the walking wounded coming through. Clark's problem was a stiff neck, and the solution was Jan Blomqvist, a Swedish golf coach. "Jan came in every day and put his magic fingers on me," Clark said. "He said it was muscle tension. I tend to get uptight."

Clark literally exploded into the victory. He made nine birdies in the fourth-round 63, and five of them came in the first six holes. The length of the putts didn't seem to matter. He made practically everything he looked at. He birdied No. 1 from 10 feet and No. 2 from 20. He missed from four feet at No. 3, then holed from three feet at No. 4, a near hole-in-one. He followed that with a 20-foot birdie at No. 5, and was out in 30. He tied for the lead with a birdie-two at No. 11, and edged ahead with a birdie-four at No. 14. Ljunghusen was reeling by now, but Clark didn't let up. He wrapped up the title with birdies from 18 inches at the 17th and from 10 feet at the last.

Benson & Hedges International Open—£200,000
Winner: Noel Ratcliffe

Nearly all the marquee names were on hand for the Benson & Hedges International at Fulford Golf Club. There were Nick Faldo, in his first European appearance since winning the British Open a month earlier; Howard Clark, winner of the PLM Open the week before, and Sam Torrance, Ian Woosnam and Bernhard Langer. It looked like a shootout of the first order. The name Noel Ratcliffe certainly never came up, but Ratcliffe became the surprise winner of the season.

Ratcliffe had won only once before in his 11 years on the European Tour, and that was nine years earlier, in the 1978 Belgian Open. His only other victories were in the 1976 Huon Open, in New Guinea, and the 1977 South Australian Open. Beset by injury, illness, and a sagging game, he had flirted with the idea of quitting, but he plugged on.

Although under par for the first three rounds, Ratcliffe gave no indication he was about to break through. A 69 in the first round left him four strokes back, with 15 players ahead of him. In the second, 70—139 left him four back with 11 players in the way. And in the third, 70—209 found him three behind with seven ahead of him. He would have to pole-vault over that crowd, and that he did — with an eagle on the final hole for a six-under-par 66, a 13-under-par total of 275, and a two-stroke victory over Ove Sellberg.

Little wonder he went unnoticed. Some furious golf was going on in front of him. Sam Torrance needed an eagle-three at No. 18 to take the lead in the first round. He hit a three iron 216 yards from the light rough to within six inches of the hole for a 65. Langer surged into the spotlight in the second round. He needed an eagle from a bunker at the last for a share of the lead. His attempt was dramatic. He had the flag removed to give himself every chance. He missed, but he got his birdie for 67—136 and a share of third place with Barry Lane. The co-leaders were Torrance and Bill Longmuir at 135. Then it was Peter Senior's turn. "I have won in Europe," the stocky Australian said, "but it has always been my big ambition to win in England because my father is English." Senior made his bid with a 69—206 and a one-stroke lead over Langer.

Suddenly, there Ratcliffe was. Two obstacles were removed from his path. Langer closed with 73—280, tied for sixth. Senior suffered a gruesome 45 on the back for 79—285 and plunged to 35th. Ratcliffe, meanwhile was enjoying the fast greens he likes so well. He one-putted nine times, then got his crowning glory, an eagle-three at No. 18. "I put my best swing of the week on it," he said. His three-iron shot stopped 13 feet from the hole. One putt, and the 66 was his. Sellberg, playing behind him, was the final threat. He had drawn level with a long birdie putt at No. 17, and now needed a birdie at No. 18 to tie. But he drove into the trees and had to pitch back to the fairway, then missed the green. A bogey-six gave him 69—277 and second place by two. Ratcliffe now could go have his rest.

Lawrence Batley International—£140,000
Winner: Mark O'Meara

The Lawrence Batley International was shaping up as a pivotal tournament. Ian Woosnam was trying to hold on to first place in the Order of Merit. Nick Faldo was pressing him. Eamonn Darcy had come to Royal Birkdale clinging to the ninth and final automatic Ryder Cup team spot off the Order of Merit, and Ove Sellberg had come to stomp on his fingers. It would be a dramatic week. Suddenly, it got more dramatic. A lightning bolt named Mark O'Meara saw to that.

It went this way: Carl Mason, 34 and still looking for his first victory after 14 years on the tour, beat Birkdale's old British Open record with a 274. All that got him was second place by three strokes. O'Meara won going away, a landmark victory — his first in Europe, his first since the 1986 Australian Open, and the first American win in Europe in more than two years. It was neat and quick. O'Meara, taking advantage of generally favorable weather, simply blitzed the old course (altered somewhat now) with 71-64-70-66 for a 17-under-par 271, four strokes under the previous record set by Tom Watson when he won the 1983 British Open there. O'Meara's closing 66 included, amazingly, two eagle-deuces, both with the seven iron.

O'Meara trailed only once. His 71 left him four strokes off the first-round 67 lead shared by the ill-fated David Feherty. O'Meara took the lead for good in the second round with the 64, a record for the altered course. Mason had a glimmer of hope in the final round, but O'Meara snuffed it out with those two eagles.

In the second round, it looked like Faldo's day. He was out in a blistering 29. O'Meara's record 64 seemed doomed to a very short life. But Faldo's tee shots betrayed him coming home, and he had to hole from off the green at No. 18 for 65. O'Meara, playing the back nine first, had four birdies and an eagle, and was out in 31. He also had nine one-putt greens overall. His halfway total of nine-under-par 135 put him one ahead of Feherty (69) and Andrew Oldcorn (68), who were part of a heavy attack on Birkdale. Of the 73 players who made the cut, 27 shot in the 60s, helping put the cut at the demanding figure of only 145, one over par.

Mason kept the pressure on with a third-round 65 that included only 23 putts. Feherty could have used some of his touch. Feherty's chance for the outright lead died with three three-putt greens, all from about two feet. His 70 left him tied for second with Mason at 206. O'Meara, starting with three birdies in his first seven holes, stayed on ahead with a 70—205.

The time for catching him had passed. The two eagles settled things. The first, from 152 yards at No. 11, was bad enough for Mason. The second was a heartbreaker. He birdied No. 16, but the gap only got wider. O'Meara eagled the hole from 145 yards. That sapped the drama from the satellite issues. Faldo tied for fourth and drew closer on the Order of Merit to Woosnam, who tied for 18th. And in the Ryder Cup scramble, Darcy was safe from Sellberg. Darcy tied for 23rd, and Sellberg, 46th.

German Open—£271,185
Winner: Mark McNulty

This was the week for completing the European team for the Ryder Cup matches, and it perhaps was fitting that the final choices be made at the German Open at Frankfurt, underlining the "European-ness" of the side. The big day would be Sunday. Tony Jacklin, the European non-playing captain, would be flying in to announce his three wild-card selections, adding them to the nine who won their places through the Epson Order of Merit. Ireland's Eamonn Darcy said he had a "few knots in the stomach" since he was sitting tentatively in the ninth and final Order of Merit spot. He did not have it locked up yet, even though he was more or less comfortably ahead of his nearest competitors — Mats Lanner, Jose-Maria Olazabal, and Ove Sellberg. Pre-tournament speculation held that Olazabal would make it anyway, as one of the wild cards, along with Ken Brown and Sandy Lyle.

The par-71 Frankfurter Golf Club, softened by a summer of rain, invited attack. The field was quick to oblige. Lanner, off form since winning the Epson Match Play earlier in the season, staked his claim to unseat Darcy and become the first Swede on the Ryder Cup team with a course-record 62, nine-under-par, in the first found. Lanner's control disappeared almost as fast as it had appeared. He was shoved aside by a second-round 76 that was the second-highest score of the 78 golfers who played all four rounds.

Mark McNulty again was quietly on the prowl. What makes the slight, Zimbabwean so exciting is that you rarely see him coming. He had taken the London Standard Four Stars Pro-Celebrity and the Dunhill British Masters back-to-back some two months earlier, adding them to his South African successes, and now he was hanging just in sight of the lead. His second-round 66 left him 11 under par and two strokes off Dennis Durnian's 129, and his third-round 65 put him at 17-under 196, three behind Antonio Garrido.

McNulty then moved ahead of Garrido with an outward 30 in the fourth round. He stumbled only briefly, a bogey at No. 14 to Garrido's birdie, then charged with two birdies and an eagle over the next three holes to win by three with a European Tour record 259, 25 under par. That beat the 260 set by Kel Nagle in 1961.

Otherwise, the key round was Darcy's 67. It gave him that ninth Order of Merit spot on the Ryder Cup team. He tied for 22nd at 273, just a stroke behind Lanner. Jacklin then made his wild-card selections, and they fit the pre-tournament predictions perfectly — Brown, Olazabal and Lyle.

There was yet another youth who attracted attention, but for a different reason. A new name broke through, and at last Bernhard Langer was no longer the only West German who — as the joke went — could break 80. Golf historians can mark this in their books: Oliver Eckstein, 18 of West Germany, shot 69-65-67-65 for an 18-under par 266 and a share of sixth place. (Langer tied for ninth at 267.) The question came immediately: Would Eckstein be another Langer?

Ebel European Masters-Swiss Open—£338,085
Winner: Anders Forsbrand

Anders Forsbrand, whose only victory in a six-year career was the 1986 Swedish PGA Championship, made the Ebel European Masters-Swiss Open his second in historic fashion, leaving records all over the Crans-sur-Sierre course. Where do you start? Well, he became the first Swede to win a European Tour stroke play event. His closing 62 was a tour record, and so were his 10 under par over the last 12 holes, his 10 birdies and an eagle, and his 192 total (64-66-62) for the last three rounds.

There was one bittersweet note: If the tournament had come one week earlier, the prize would have made him the first Swede in the Ryder Cup. It would have taken the ninth and final place on the Epson Order of Merit. But Forsbrand wasn't complaining. "It's been a great year for us," he said, "with Mats Lanner winning the Epson Grand Prix Match Play title, and he and Ove Sellberg and Magnus Persson getting so close to Ryder Cup selection. There will be plenty more opportunities."

Forsbrand actually came from behind and overran the field in this one. He opened with a one-under-par 71 and was six behind co-leaders John Slaughter and Bill Longmuir, both at 65. Mark Mouland and Ian Mosey shot 66s in the second round and barged into the 36-hole lead at 12-under 132. Forsbrand closed the gap with a 64 for 135, and trailed by three. Then a 66 lifted him to within two strokes after three rounds, a 201 total to Mosey's 199 lead. Then Forsbrand turned unreal. It seems hard to believe, but that closing 62 included two bogeys. He exploded to a three-under-par start with a birdie at No. 1 and an eagle-two at No. 3 on a 50-foot putt. Then he bogeyed two of the next three holes.

His charge into the record book began at No. 7. He drove the 317-yard hole and sank a 25-foot putt for an eagle-two. He birdied No. 8 from eight feet and No. 9 from 12. Over the next six holes, he ran off five more birdies on putts of 15 feet or less, and came home in 30 on a seven-foot birdie putt at No. 18. In all, he needed just 16 putts over that 12-hole stretch. He finished at 25-under-par 263 to win by three over Mouland. The season wasn't over yet, but Forsbrand was right — it had been a great year for the Swedes. And he certainly did his share.

Panasonic European Open—£220,000
Winner: Paul Way

Newspaper writers had to keep their adjectives in check. This was one of the most inspiring stories in years, and even other golfers might be tempted into excess over Paul Way's Panasonic European Open victory at Walton Heath. Michael Williams, golf correspondent for *The Daily Telegraph*, kept it cool and graphic: "Paul Way...came in from not so much out of the cold as out of the deep freeze..."

A quick glance at Way's record tells the story. Way, now only 24, had been a bright light on the European Tour. At 20, he was the youngest member of the 1983 European Ryder Cup team. At 22, he was one of the heroes of the winning 1985 Ryder Cup team. "He can be as good as he wants to be," Tony Jacklin, the European captain, had said. Way won twice, that year — the Whyte & Mackay PGA Championship and the South African Charity Classic. Then the caprices of golf struck so hard he dropped like a stone. He was 125th on the Epson Order of Merit in 1986, and coming into the European Open he not only was 136th on the list, he had missed 13 cuts in 21 events. His 67 in the final round was his first time under 70 this year. Little wonder the crowd was on tip-toes when he came so tentatively to the final green.

Way had gone largely unnoticed early. Jose-Maria Canizares took the first-round lead at five-under-par 67, a stroke ahead of Robert Lee. Six others were bunched at 69, and Way was three off the lead at 70. In the second round, Canizares, who had been advised to give up the game for a few months to allow a rib injury to heal, began to drift with 74. Now it was Bernhard Langer to the front, with a 67—137, moving two strokes ahead of Derrick Cooper and Gordon Brand, Jr. Way was working on a 68, but he three-putted twice on his way to three closing bogeys for a 71. That kept him tantalizingly near, four strokes off the lead at 141. His position wasn't great, but at least he had accomplished something he hadn't done much of lately: He made the cut. In the third round, he posted another 71, and his 212 total lifted him one stroke closer. Langer slipped a bit with 72—210, but stayed a stroke ahead of John Bland and Brand. Langer kept sliding, though. His 75 in the final round set the stage for Way's resurrection.

Way admitted there were times since 1985 that he almost gave up. There was a lesson there. The determination that kept him plugging away pulled him through a tense finish. First, a flash of the old brilliance returned just in time. The putts began to fall. Starting at No. 6 he had five one-putts in a row, and two of them saved par. Then came a burst of three birdies beginning at the ninth. Way came to No. 18 two strokes ahead, but suddenly disaster threatened. His seven-iron approach shot ended up in a grassy swale to the right of the green. He chipped too strong, and the ball ran down the shelf in the green. Was he starting to collapse? It sure looked that way because he left his first putt a full five feet short. Then he pulled himself together. He rammed that putt down, and the crowd erupted. He was in with 67, his lowest score of the season so far, and a nine-under-par 279. Bland, in the final group, was the only threat. He needed a birdie to tie, but made five and settled for second with Brand, two strokes off. Paul Way had come back.

Gordon Brand, Jr., said it best. "Everyone on tour can be proud for what Paul has achieved," he said, "and every young player in the game has a lot to learn from it."

Lancome Trophy—£300,000
Winner: Ian Woosnam

Can you think of any other sport in which the competitors help each other? Golfers do it all the time. Here's another case in point: A frustrated Bernhard Langer suddenly found new life for his game and charged into the first-round lead of the Lancome Trophy. That was right after he received a tip from Ian Woosnam, who then found himself one stroke behind his pupil.

Woosnam went on to win the Lancome, and in turn gave no small thanks to a tip from Greg Norman. You probably could spend all day at this sort of thing and find that every golfer is every other golfer's student and teacher. It still comes down to who can do it in action, and this year, Woosnam was the man.

Woosnam came to the Lancome, at St. Nom la Breteche, near Paris, as the leading money-winner on the European Tour and a three-time winner (four, counting the Hong Kong Open). But he arrived in the depths of a two-month struggle dating back to early July, after he won the Bell's Scottish Open. Then came the tip. Norman advised him to push the hands forward when putting, and also to close the club face slightly. Woosnam also benefited from some self-help. The week before the Lancome, watching himself on television, he noticed that his legs were too stiff. Langer arrived at the Lancome still angry with himself for letting the European Open slip away, and still complaining that he didn't feel comfortable over the ball. Worse, he found himself aiming his shoulders too far left of the target. Woosnam chanced by while he was on the practice tee, and offered that he had the ball too far forward in his stance. Play it back a few inches, Woosnam suggested. The results spoke for themselves.

Langer shot an eight-under-par 64 in the first round to tie Zimbabwe's Tony Johnstone for the lead. Woosnam, working on a 65, got an eye-witness account of his teaching handiwork. He was playing with Langer, and saw that 64 in progress — an eagle-three at No. 4 and six birdies. Then it was the teacher's turn. In the second round, Woosnam went out in 33, and started back with little promise. His drive at No. 10 stayed up in a tree, and he took a five. He got his revenge with six birdies over the final eight holes for a inward 31 and a 64. That gave him a halfway total of 129 and the lead. He might have turned the tournament into a runaway except for Barry Lane, who birdied the last three holes for an inward 31 and a course-record 63. That put Lane at 130, and held Woosnam to just one ahead of the field. Next closest were Johnstone, at 69-133, and Langer, irked by what he termed bad greens and too much grass on the fairways, at 70—134.

Never far from the center of the storm, it seems, is Mark McNulty, winner of the German Open just three weeks earlier. And here he was again. He was four strokes back in the first round at 68, six at the halfway point on 67—135, and four after three rounds on 67—202. Woosnam stood at the head of the class on 69—198 going into the final round, and his battle figured to be with Johnstone, who trailed by one. But it wasn't.

McNulty broke from the pack and kept the heat on Woosnam until an errant tee shot at the par-five 17th cooled him. He had to settle for a 64 and 266 total, second by two. Johnstone finished with 69 and Sandy Lyle 66 to share third at 268, and Langer closed with a fury, tying Lane's course record with a 63 for fifth place at 269. But after McNulty, no one really threatened. Woosnam put the tournament out of reach with three consecutive birdies beginning at No. 15, for a no-bogey 66 and 24-under-par 264, five strokes off the previous tournament record.

Vernons Open—£70,000
Winner: David Llewellyn

Golf fans who kept their eyes glued to the Ryder Cup some 3,500 miles to the west, at Muirfield Village near Columbus, Ohio, missed a heck of a show at Hoylake this week. This was the first Vernons Open, and for three rounds it practically belonged to Rodger Davis. But this was another one that got away, snatched up in the final round by Welshman David Llewellyn, breaking through to his first European victory since joining the tour in 1971. "I had a feeling after the second round that I was in with a chance," said Llewellyn, whose previous successes were two victories on the Safari circuit. He had to fight off the determined Davis down the stretch to take this one.

Llewellyn returned 73-69-72-70 for a four-under-par total of 284 to win by two over Davis' 71-69-74-72—286. Davis shared the first-round lead with Ross Drummond on 71, then made a remarkable move to take the solo lead in the second. Davis, who came into the Vernons standing sixth on the Epson Order of Merit despite not having won, started the second round with a triple-bogey seven at the first hole. "I can't remember the last time I had a triple bogey," he said, shaking his head. "But it just made me concentrate even harder." Indeed. He birdied the next two holes and made the turn in 38, then posted four birdies and an eagle for an inward 31. That put him at 140, two ahead of Llewellyn, whose 69 included what he called "the best back nine I have ever had on a course I have never played before."

Llewellyn caught Davis in the third round, and they went into the fourth tied at two-under-par 214. "All I tried to do was make pars at every hole," Llewellyn said. His conservative play paid a bonus in the form of a two-stroke swing at the par-four fifth, where he holed from 15 feet for a birdie while Davis got a two-putt bogey from seven feet after chipping from the rough. Llewellyn gave up a stroke at No. 10, then got his two-stroke edge back at No. 12 when Davis chipped badly and two-putted for a bogey five. Davis came back with a birdie-two at No. 13, then surrendered the shot with a bogey-six at No. 16. The way Llewellyn was playing, that was fatal. Llewellyn completed the formality with a birdie on the final hole. The 1971 Rookie of the Year had his first victory.

German Masters—£266,890
Winner: Sandy Lyle

The Ryder Cup was a pleasant memory, the Dunhill Cup was in the books. So much for team events and the collective spirit. Now it was back to every man for himself, which did not bode well for Sandy Lyle. He had been in good form for the team play, helping the Europeans to win the Ryder Cup, then helping Scotland to second place in the Dunhill. But as a solitary pursuit, golf had not been rewarding for him for quite some time. His last European win was the 1985 Benson and Hedges International, and his last important win anywhere was the American Tournament Players Championship early in 1987. But otherwise, not much had gone right for him.

So there was no reason to believe that anything would change at the German Masters at the Stuttgarter Golf Club at Stuttgart. Of course, golf being the weird game that it is, this was precisely the time for things to change. And so Lyle, the easy-going Scot, came from nowhere in the final round, caught home favorite Bernhard Langer, the co-promoter of the tournament with IMG, and beat him in a playoff.

Playing superb recovery shots after errant drives, Langer one-putted nine times for 68 and a two-stroke lead over Christy O'Connor, Jr., Tony Charnley, and Jose-Maria Olazabal. Lyle was still his uncertain self — one-over-par 73 and five strokes off the lead — and didn't really surface until the final round. Langer posted 69 in the second round and was tied with O'Connor (67) at 137. Lyle (69) was still five strokes back. Langer led Seve Ballesteros by one through the third round with 71—208, and Lyle was four back at 70—212.

The anticipated shootout between Langer and Ballesteros misfired when Ballesteros crashed with a triple-bogey seven at No. 11. He settled for solo third at 70—279, one stroke out of the picture. The tournament actually was decided by Langer's misplays. Lyle did his part, closing with a seven-birdie 66 for 278, 10 under par. Then he had to wait a half-hour to see whether it was more than just a good round. "I was out of it," Lyle said. "I was three or four behind most of the way."

There was only one way for Lyle to get back in. Langer would have to stumble. And he did. Langer was out in 33 and seemed untouchable at 11 under par. Then came the first of three fatal errors — a bogey at the par-three 15th. He committed the second error at the par-five 18th, a hole he could birdie almost with ease. He put his second shot into a bunker, missed a putt of under five feet, and finished with 70. A surprised Lyle found himself in a playoff.

It was a brief one. They halved the first extra hole in four, and No. 18 was their second, and here Langer self-destructed for the second time in that hour. In regulation play minutes earlier, he had bunkered his approach. This time he hit a three-wood out of bounds, then failed to reach the green after taking his drop. Lyle bunkered his approach, but he made his five. That was good enough. He had his first European win in two years.

Portuguese Open—£100,000
Winner: Robert Lee

When last heard from — or seen, to be more precise — Robert Lee, 26-year-old from London, was bouncing around Muirfield in the British Open, hitting exploding golf balls and wearing a paper bag over his head in practice. It was just a little joke, he said. Muirfield had the last laugh. Lee missed the cut. In the Portuguese Open, the finale of the European Tour's 1987 season, he did nothing to damage his reputation as a fun-lover, the victim of his own accident, but he did much to enhance his reputation as a player. That was a course-record 61 he fired in the first round, and that was the imposing Sam Torrance he held off in the last round.

The season had been marked by odd weather, and it got a fitting farewell at Estoril, near Lisbon. Fierce rains left the short, tree-lined course unplayable on Friday, and forced the tournament to be cut to three rounds. Lee was under heavy attack in the final round, but he goes into the books as a wire-to-wire winner with 61-67-67—195, 12 under par on the 5,697-yard, par-69 course. Two late birdies gave him the one-stroke victory.

Lee, who joined the tour in 1982, had won only twice before — the Cannes Open and the Brazilian Open, both in 1985, but this victory was sweeter. It gave him a sense of vindication. Ryder Cup captain Tony Jacklin had criticized certain young but unnamed European players for being indifferent. Lee, known as something of a clown, felt Jacklin had put him in that group. "I don't drink, except for an occasional glass of wine with dinner," Lee said, "but I still felt Tony's comments were aimed at me. I've proved here that you can stay out late having a good time and still win tournaments."

Lee opened the first round with five birdies in the first six holes en route to an outward 27. That tied his own effort in the 1985 Monte Carlo Open, when he also started with 61. He missed a number of greens in the swirling winds, but he one-putted eight of the first nine holes. A bogey at No. 14 slowed him after birdies at the 11th and 13th, but he dropped a 35-foot putt for a two at No. 16 after a one iron coming in. His crisp iron play cooled off, and he couldn't get close enough for birdies on the last two holes, and stood three shots ahead of Peter Baker and Gordon J. Brand, both with 64s. Torrance was six off the lead at 67.

In the second round Lee shot 67—128 and led by three over Torrance (64) and Bill Longmuir (63), both at 131. Then came the battle royal. It seemed everyone took a shot at Lee in the final round. Christy O'Connor, Jr. went out in 28, but cooled off and settled for 64—198, tied for fifth. Jose Rivero matched Lee's first-round fireworks with an outward 27, then faltered, finishing at 63—199, tied for eighth. Ireland's Philip Walton took the lead on an eagle-eagle-birdie stretch beginning at No. 11. But his attack died in the water at No. 14, and he finished tied for fifth at 64—198. It was up to Torrance to head off Lee. But Lee said no. He holed from 20 feet for a two at No. 16, then drove the 17th and two-putted from eight feet for a birdie. Torrance had to birdie No. 18 to catch him. He gave it a great try, but his five-footer just missed. Then the fun-loving Lee had the time of his life. He was a winner.

12. The African Tours

Fulton Allem, a burly guy with a quick sense of humor, likes to tell of how he gauges his prospects in his running battle with Mark McNulty on the Sunshine Circuit. "If Mark said he was feeling good, then I knew I had a chance," Allem explained with a grin. "But if he said he had a headache or a cold or a sore back or knee or something, then I knew I was in for a hell of a battle." McNulty may or may not have a touch of hypochondria, but that was no imagined illness that hit him at the end of 1987. He was all set to defend his title in the Sun City Million Dollar Challenge, a winner-take-all shootout this time — with the biggest prize in the history of golf, $1 million — and he had to scratch. This time it was pneumonia.

But it was long before the illness hit McNulty that something new and compelling had emerged on the Sunshine Circuit. It should prove instructive some day to look back and see where the 1987 Sunshine Circuit fit in the scheme of golf: Was there an outburst of genuine strength, a sudden upward lurch that signified the tour was growing in power and stature? Was the Sunshine following the European Tour the way the European followed the American in the evolutionary climb? Or was it simply a kind of tremor, a brief and abrupt spasm after which everything calmed back down?

Not that the 1987 Sunshine Circuit was anything like the American or European tours in strength and depth, but within its own context, something definitely seemed different this time. No, the wild-running Mark McNulty had not begun to fade. Instead, it seemed that new and potent forces had emerged. McNulty was still McNulty. He tied for fourth in the first 1987 event, the Palabora Classic, fell silent for a few weeks, then was the King of February with four consecutive victories — the Southern Sun South African Open, the AEIC Charity Classic, the Swazi Sun Pro-Am, and the Trustbank Tournament of Champions. Counting the tailend of 1986, that gave him seven victories in 11 Sunshine tournaments.

But before McNulty bombed February, Allem took two of the first three 1987 events, the Palabora Classic and the Lexington PGA. Allem for years had been McNulty's chief and perhaps only real challenger. And now another force appeared. It was Tony Johnstone, the man who had been rather quiet for some time. He had won three tournaments in 1984, went bone dry for a year, then resurfaced for one victory in 1986. That's good work, but hardly spectacular. In 1987, he was spectacular. He took the ICL International in January, then came back with a vengeance after the summer hiatus to take two events at the end of the year. That's three wins out of 11 events. Counting the Goodyear Classic at the end of 1986, he won four out of 12.

McNulty, by the way, is not a one-dimensional player. After cleaning up on the Sunshine Circuit, he headed again for the European Tour and did all right there, too. In 18 events, he won three times — the London Standard Four Stars Pro-Celebrity and Dunhill British Masters back-to-back, and the Lawrence Batley International. Only Ian Woosnam, with four victories, won more times in Europe than he did. McNulty also had five other top-10 performances. With £189,303 in winnings, he finished a distant second to Woosnam on the Epson Order of Merit, but almost £7,500 ahead of third-place Nick Faldo, the British Open champion.

Now Allem has decided to try his hand overseas. His opportunity came in the form of an invitation to the NEC World Series of Golf, played in August at Firestone South in Akron, Ohio, and he leaped at it. Under American tour rules, a golfer can bypass the grueling qualifying school and win a spot on the tour by finishing in the top 125 on the money list. Allem made it with room to spare by finishing second to Curtis Strange in the World Series, for a payoff of more than $80,000. He added to that figure with a handful of appearances on the American tour late in the season.

While McNulty was busy conquering February on the Sunshine Circuit, the Safari Circuit swung into action elsewhere in Africa. Gordon J. Brand, who won two Safari events in 1986, picked up where he left off by winning the Zimbabwe Open. He had to go to a playoff against Andrew Murray to get it. The Kenya Open the next week also went to a playoff, thanks to a monkey bent on revenge. Brand would have had his second consecutive victory except for the stroke he lost when the angry monkey pelted him with a fig just as he was hitting a drive. Brand missed the ball. The tournament ended in a four-way tie, and Carl Mason went on to beat not only Brand but Roger Chapman and Martin Poxon as well. The Zambia Open completed the picture, with Paul Carrigill beating Mike Miller in a playoff. Brand, by the way, fell off badly on the European Tour in 1987, finishing 33rd on the Epson Order of Merit with £46,717. That was a drop of some £60,000 from his best-ever £106,000 in 1986. Still, 1987 had its rewards. Brand joined Faldo and Howard Clark to help give England its first Dunhill Cup victory.

And the African year could not have climaxed with more drama had it been following a script. This was the Million Dollar Challenge in December, and the star was none other than the man of the year, Ian Woosnam. Woosnam already had a year such as few golfers even dare to fantasize about. He won seven individual titles, including the Suntory World Match Play and the World Cup (and the team title with David Llewellyn), and played a major role in Europe's Ryder Cup victory. He topped the European Order of Merit with £253,717, and had nearly $800,000 in winnings before he arrived at Sun City. He left with the $1 million top prize after locking up a four-stroke victory with an eagle-two at the 71st hole. "I'm not really surprised at my success — I always knew I had the ability," he said. "But I am surprised it has all come together in the same year." It surprised no one that he was named the Ritz Club Golfer of the Year. But he is not yet the man who has everything.

"My ambition now," Woosnam said, "is to win a major championship."

Palabora Classic—R140,000
Winner: Fulton Allem

The expression is "one for the books." And that's precisely what they had at the Palabora Classic. Golf has its perils, but aside from lightning, they rarely are anything more dangerous than rain or sunburn. Not this time.

This one might be unprecedented in golf, as Paul Burley will be telling his grandchildren some day.

Burley, a 25-year-old British golfer, was on the third hole at Hans Marensky Country Club, ready to knock his second shot out of the rough, when suddenly there came a loud crashing from the dense growth behind him. Burley turned, and the sight froze him for an instant. "A hippo came charging out, followed by another," Burley said later. Then it was a question of who could get moving first and fastest. "I threw down my club and ran, with my caddy alongside me," Burley said. "My two playing partners and their caddies were running, too, all dashing for the trees on the far side of the fairway. It was terrifying."

Jimmy Hemphill, executive director of the South African PGA, explained that the hippos made their home in the pools on the 17th hole, and normally came out at night. The hippos, it seems, were interested only in each other and not the least bit in golf. It probably was mating season, Hemphill said. Happily, everything ended well — to a point. The hippos went their way, if loudly, and Burley pulled himself together and returned and parred the hole. But he stumbled to an 80 for the day and missed the halfway cut.

With the hippos out of the way, the stage belonged to Fulton Allem, but only after a tight battle. Chris Williams, a young Johannesburg golfer, was taking a determined grip on the tournament. A pair of 66s for 132 gave him a one-stroke lead after 36 holes. He was now six better than Hugh Baiocchi and eight better than Allem. Williams shot a 72 in the third round and clung to the lead with 204, just one ahead of both Allem (66) and Baiocchi (68).

Allem broke through with a record-tying 65 in the final round for a 271 total, edging Baiocchi (66) by one. Williams finished third with 70—274. The victory ended Allem's frustrating string of three straight runnerup finishes on the 1986 portion of the Sunshine Circuit.

ICL International—R120,000
Winner: Tony Johnstone

The "right" way to play golf means different things to different people, which undoubtedly is a good thing for those people who suffer in sympathy watching Tony Johnstone. For him, the right way is a seemingly endless program of fidgeting before each shot, which has earned him the nickname, "Twitching Tony." But it works for him, as one could see in his breezy six-stroke victory in the ICL International at the Zwartkop Country Club. It was the sixth victory of his career and his second in about a month, the other being the Goodyear Classic in December, 1986.

It took the Zimbabwe-born Johnstone a couple of rounds to take command in the ICL, however. Phil Simmons, the South African left-hander, broke to the front early with a six-under-par 66 for a one-stroke lead in the first round, leaving Johnstone in a small crowd three strokes back, at 69. Simmons stayed firmly on top of things in the second round, shooting a 67 for a 133 total and a three-stroke lead on Johnstone, who moved up to second on a 67 for a 136 total after 36 holes.

The decisive moment came in the third round, at the par-five ninth. Johnstone holed a 25-foot putt for an eagle, and Simmons hit out of bounds and took an eight. Johnstone made up three strokes on Simmons off that five-shot swing. That was pretty much the end of Simmons — he shot a 74 and drifted back into the field — and the beginning of Johnstone. He kept rolling and finished with a 64 and a 200 total that put him five strokes clear.

Johnstone might have been brought down in the final round, but his challengers didn't leap to their opportunities. Their first chance came at the fourth hole, where he hit into a water hazard and double-bogeyed. The door was open, but no one came through. Johnstone's pursuers were busy dropping strokes of their own. Johnstone was so comfortably ahead that even three-putting the 15th and 17th failed to hurt him. He finished with a 71, his only round out of the 60s, and a 17-under-par total of 271. Justin Hobday (72) and Wilhelm Winsnes (65) shared second at 277.

Lexington PGA—R120,000
Winner: Fulton Allem

The Lexington PGA drew a strong field to The Wanderers at Johannesburg, and a heavy challenge was expected at last from a British contingent headed by Mark James. The favorites still were Mark McNulty, who had won three of the six tournaments so far; Tony Johnstone, who had two victories, and Fulton Allem, who had the other and who had finished second twice.

The challenge remained only that — a challenge. This ·was another Zimbabwean/South African show, and this time in the person of Allem, whose worst position in four rounds was a share of the first-round lead with countryman Hugh Baiocchi. Allem was unmolested after that, enjoying no less than a two-stroke lead after each round, including the final, when he won by that over Baiocchi.

Allem and Baiocchi opened with a five-under-par 65. Gordon Manson, age 26, a Scot based at an Austrian resort, was a stroke back, which was the closest a Briton would get. Manson, seeking his first tournament victory, did mount a threat in the second round, catching Allem at the 13th after a burst of four birdies in eight holes. But he bogeyed the 16th when he missed the green and the 18th when he three-putted. Allem, meantime, shook off severe stomach cramps, and with some superb iron play shot a three-under 67 in which he had three birdies and no bogeys. That left him at 132, two ahead of Manson and Baiocchi.

In the third round, only a handful of near-misses kept Allem from turning the PGA into a complete rout. He suffered only two bogeys, one with a bad chip and the other when he rushed a putt. "But I lipped out five times for birdies, and really should have scored several shots better," Allem said. As it was, his two-under 68 gave him a 200 total and a two-stroke lead over Manson (68), Baiocchi (68), and John Bland (67). The final round was almost anti-climactic. Allem held firm, shot a 68 for a 12-under-par 268 total, and beat Baiocchi by two. Manson slipped to a two-over 72 — his only over-par round of the tournament — and finished alone in third place at 274.

Southern Sun South African Open—R100,000
Winner: Mark McNulty

It seemed that Mark McNulty had all but disappeared after winning the first three events on the 1986-87 Sunshine Circuit. He had fallen quiet for four straight. Oh, he played fairly well — tied for seventh in the Goodyear Classic and tied for fourth in the Palabora Classic. But coming from McNulty, this amounted to silence. Now he arrived at Mowbray, Cape Town, for the Southern Sun South African Open, his nemesis. He hadn't won in nine previous tries.

So, given his four-week lapse plus his record in the Open, there was no reason for McNulty or anyone else to suspect his time had finally come. But it had — dramatically, and just in time to catch rival Fulton Allem and beat him in a playoff.

You could measure the drama from the first day. McNulty was so far behind — eight strokes, in fact — that spectators could begin counting him out. It was Wayne Westner, 25-year-old South African, who drew the attention. Westner was playing with a new confidence. "My mind is right now, and the rest of the game just follows," he said, after shooting a six-under-par 66 for a one-stroke lead in the first round. It was a faultless round — six birdies and no bogeys. Allem held second place with a 67, after shaking off waits of as long as 15 minutes at several tees. McNulty was buried deep in the supporting cast with a 74.

Westner's new mental approach continued to pay off in the second round. He carded an eagle and four birdies for a 67—133, stretching his lead to five over Allem, who slumped to a 71—138. McNulty finally surfaced, leaping from the depths to a tie for fourth at 66—140. Westner, hot in pursuit of his first victory since the 1984 ICL Classic in his rookie year, cracked considerably in the third round, but it wasn't enough to knock him out of the lead. He shot a 75 for 208 and a one-stroke lead on the fast-closing Allem (71). McNulty also carded a 71, but it left him at 211, three strokes off the lead. It was an uncomfortable position, but hardly a strange one. Back at the start of the 1986-87 season, in the Helix Wild Coast, he was trailing by four going into the final round. And he made the Helix the first of three straight victories.

Westner would have to wait for another day. He had led the Open for three straight rounds, but the erratic play that shook him in the third round continued. He faded to third place at 73—281 in the burning heat of the final day, while McNulty and Allem were making the Open another of their battle grounds. Allem finished with a 69. McNulty, who increasingly seems able to do what he has to do, produced a 67 that included six birdies, and they were tied at 278. In the playoff, Allem bogeyed the first two holes, No. 16 and No. 17, after hitting bunkers. That left McNulty with his fourth Sunshine victory in eight events, and his first South African Open — "after a 10-year sweat," he said.

AEIC Charity Classic—R100,000
Winner: Mark McNulty

In the United States, the postal service has a motto, something to the effect that rain nor sleet nor dark of night can keep the postman from his appointed rounds. That now seems to be the case with Mark McNulty. Nothing can keep *him* from his appointed rounds, the rounds being practically every golf tournament he enters. McNulty opened the AEIC Charity Classic with the lead, drifted back, then came charging home from four strokes behind to catch Wayne Westner, and then beat him in a playoff. It was merely NcNulty's fifth victory in nine 1986-87 Sunshine Circuit outings, and his second victory of the year.

The first two rounds of the AEIC were played as part of a pro-am, with the golfers playing one round each over the Windsor Park and nearby Randpark courses (both par-71) at Johannesburg, then playing the final 36 holes on Randpark. The feature attraction was the battle between McNulty and Fulton Allem, and more was at stake than a tournament title. The AEIC could go a long way toward deciding who would be No. 1 on the Sunshine Order of Merit, and also reap the additional rewards that would go with it, such as invitations to prestigious events. McNulty staked his claim at the outset, taking the first-round lead with a 65. That put him one ahead of South African rookie Michael Green and four ahead of Allem. But McNulty got his 65 at the Windsor Park course, while Allem got his 69 at Randpark, a longer and tougher layout.

Ian Mosey threatened to crash their party for a while. He shot a 69 at Randpark, needing only 23 putts, one of them a 50-footer for a birdie at No. 6. At Windsor Park in the second round, Mosey was nothing short of remarkable. He hit only four fairways, but his iron play was so spectacular that he was able to carve out seven birdies and an eagle for a six-under-par 65 for 134 and a one-stroke lead at the halfway point.

Westner, whose only victory was the ICL in his rookie year, 1983, made a strong bid for this one with a 67 that gave him a 202 total and a three-stroke lead on Mosey and England's Andrew Chandler, and a four-stroke lead over McNulty. Westner was fresh from a stern lesson. Just a week earlier, he was leading the South African Open by one after three rounds, then faded to a 73 in the final round and settled for third place while McNulty went on to take the title in a playoff with Allem. "I kept my cool today when the birdies were not coming, and did not lose my patience," Westner said. "I will be out to shoot a 65 tomorrow and I don't think anyone will catch me if I can."

Westner was right, to a point. If he had shot 65, no one would have caught him. Even a 67 would have done it. But he dropped strokes over the final few holes and returned a very creditable 68, only to find himself caught. The irrepressible McNulty had roared home with a seven-under-par 64. They were tied at 14-under-par 270, five strokes ahead of the field. McNulty then made short work of the playoff, a birdie on the first hole. McNulty had struck again.

Royal Swazi Sun Pro-Am—R100,000
Winner: Mark McNulty

History may be hard put to decide which was more remarkable in the Royal Swazi Sun Pro-Am — Mark McNulty winning his third title in a row and his sixth of the 1986-87 Sunshine Circuit season, or the incredible assault on par that left the Royal Swazi course at M'Babane in a shambles. This wasn't so much a golf tournament as a candidate for the *Guinness Book of World Records*. Here's a thumbnail study of that attack: Fulton Allem, Hugh Baiocchi, and Tony Johnstone finished at 16 under par, and all that got them was a tie for *fifth* place. And at that, they were three strokes behind the third-place finishers, and *13* behind McNulty's winning 29-under 259.

Here's another example: McNulty came charging home with a 10-under-par 62, and it wasn't even the low round of the tournament. That distinction was taken by Simon Hobday, with an 11-under-par 61 in the second round. It doesn't stand as a record, however, because preferred lies were allowed due to conditions.

McNulty won by six strokes, but the victory wasn't as easy as that margin suggests. He began the tournament in 10th place with 68, four behind the leading 64s by Britain's Andrew Chandler and South Africa's Bobby Lincoln on a day when the temperature reached 100 degrees. Chandler had two bogeys, eight birdies, and an eagle at No. 13, when he holed his second from 88 yards "after having to ask my caddy where the green was." Britain's Malcolm MacKenzie, who was alone in third place with 65, added his contribution to the attack on the course. He made nine birdies, four of them in succession starting from No. 7.

Lincoln fell behind, but Chandler clung to a one-stroke lead through the halfway point with a 67—131, while Hobday leaped from the obscurity of an opening 71 all the way to a tie for second with his 61—132. Hobday, 46-year-old South African veteran, birdied eight of the first nine holes to turn in 28, then picked up three more birdies coming home. McNulty jumped five places, to a tie for fifth, with 65—133.

Then it was into the lead after a third-round 64 put him at 197, one ahead of Hobday. Then came the whirlwind finish for the closing 62. "It was an exciting round," McNulty said, "and I was determined to break 260." McNulty birdied six straight holes, starting at No. 4, and made the turn in 29 en route to his six-stroke victory over Wayne Westner, who matched his career low with a 64 for 265. All told, McNulty had 30 birdies and only one bogey for the tournament, and his 259 bettered his own circuit record by four strokes.

Zimbabwe Open—£50,000
Winner: Gordon J. Brand

Gordon J. Brand was the favorite for the Zimbabwe Open, and for good reason. He was coming off his best year in 1986, when he was runnerup to the British Open and fifth on the Epson European Order of Merit with a personal high of £106,000. Finding Africa to his liking, he also had won both the Ivory Coast and Nigerian Open titles in 1986, and led the Safari

Circuit money list. If those impressive credentials meant anything to Britain's Andrew Murray, it didn't show. Murray forced Brand to work overtime to live up to that advance billing.

Brand's first task in the Zimbabwe Open was to overcome jet lag. He had played in the Austrialian Open the week before, and to get to Royal Harare Golf Club he had to fly overnight Monday from Melbourne, via Singapore and Bahrain, to Heathrow Airport in London. "I just had time to send my laundry home," Brand said. Then he flew overnight Tuesday to Zimbabwe.

Brand entered the final round in second place. He was a stroke behind Zimbabwe's Billy Koen, age 25, who was playing in his first tournament as a professional, and a stroke ahead of Murray, and he played near-flawless golf for a three-under-par 69. But it wasn't enough. While Koen was falling out of the chase, Murray was ringing up five birdies and an eagle en route to a 68. He caught Brand with a four-round total of 277, 11 under par, and off they went into a playoff.

The final round was anything but routine. Koen slipped to 74, but still made a strong pro debut, taking a share of third place. Brand took a bogey-five at the easy eighth, letting Murray move into the lead. Then at the ninth, Brand got a psychological lift that carried him home. He hooked his drive over some trees and into a dense bed of tropical flowers. Local rules permitted him a free drop, rescuing him from a hopeless situation. He went on to birdie four of the next seven holes, and came home in 32 for a 69—277. Murray caught him with a 68, carding an eagle-three at No. 13 to go with five birdies. The playoff ended abruptly. On the first hole, Murray three-putted and Brand made his par four. That gave Brand his fifth career African title.

Trust Bank Tournament of Champions—R150,000
Winner: Mark McNulty

The futility of chasing a hot Mark McNulty was summed up best — but inadvertently — by his nearest rival, Fulton Allem. The final event on the 1986-87 Sunshine Circuit, the Trust Bank Tournament of Champions, at the Kensington course, Johannesburg, had reached the halfway point, and Allem was assessing his chances of winning. "Eight shots is not too much to make up in two rounds," Allem said. "Two 64s and I will win by three shots." *Eight* shots? Not that Allem was being flip. He simply believed he still could win. He also was the only player left with a chance to catch McNulty in the circuit's Order of Merit race. But no one had had a real chance at McNulty since the circuit began late in 1986, and McNulty was still hot. He was not about to open any doors now that the circuit was closing. Besides, Mother Nature perversely had lent him a helping hand.

More than half of the players in the Trust Bank field were stricken by severe stomach upset in the first round, the legacy, many felt, of the water at the Swazi tournament the week before. A doctor spent three hours at Kensington, administering drugs and injections. Many also were left giddy by the heat. Allem, one of the victims, shot a par 72, which left him six strokes off the 66 lead held by South African club pro Steve van Vuuren.

McNulty (68) shared third. He didn't stay there long.

By the halfway point, some observers were already chalking up another McNulty victory, even though his second-round 68 did nothing more than lift him into a share of the lead with South African rookie Peter Van Der Riet on 136. Then McNulty gave himself a dose of reverse inspiration. In the third round, he bogeyed No. 14 after missing a short putt, and he muffed a simple birdie chance at No. 15. "That got me mad," he said. "That really got me fired up for the finish." He tore through the last three holes with birdies for a third straight 68 that carried him four strokes ahead with 204. Gavin Levenson (68) and Tienie Britz (69) shared second on 208.

Except for an early threat by Ian Young, the fourth round was a formality. An eagle and three birdies put Young at five under par after six holes. He cooled down, but he did card the best round, a 65, for his highest finish in five years on the circuit, third place on 278. Levenson took second with 67—275, and McNulty breezed in with a 67 for 271 and a four-stroke victory. That wrapped up an incredible season — four straight closing victories, seven wins in 11 Sunshine events, and a third straight Order of Merit title with R134,690. McNulty, who had won five Sunshine events in 1986, definitely was hot. After a few weeks' break, he would test that heat on the European Tour.

Kenya Open—£60,925
Winner: Carl Mason

The Rules of Golf provide for relief from an "outside agency." But in their wildest moments, the rulesmakers could never have foreseen *this* kind of outside agency, nor what kind of relief to provide. For Gordon J. Brand, seeking his second straight Safari Curcuit title in the 555 Kenya Open, a helmet and a "Mulligan" might have been in order.

This particular outside agency, at Nairobi's Muthaiga Club, was a monkey, and — who knows? — perhaps it cost Brand the title that Britain's Carl Mason took in a four-way playoff. It all began at No. 16 tee during Wednesday's practice round. "A couple of us spotted the monkey in a wild fig tree...and threw a few sticks at it," Brand said. "He must have remembered my face. He seemed very angry." Said tournament administrator Mike Harbage: "...it could only have been a Sykes monkey. They don't take terribly kindly to having things thrown at them."

The monkey refused to leave. Worse, it had a memory like an elephant. When Brand's group came to No. 16 tee in the first round, the monkey bombarded them with figs. "He hit me once and narrowly missed on a couple of other occasions," Brand said. "And I was so unnerved that I missed my drive altogether and dropped a stroke." Brand's 70 left him tied for 13th behind the lead of five-under-par 66 shared by Britain's Richard Fish and Mark Roe. Mason, the 1974 European Rookie of the Year, was in an even deeper hole, at 72.

Roe, age 24, who first joined the tour in 1982, owned the second round. His 67 gave him a halfway total of 133 and a three-stroke lead on Brand (66). Mason, meanwhile, was still to be heard from. His 68 left him seven back, at 140.

Roe weakened in the third round, but his par 71 for 204 still left him in the lead by one over Roger Chapman (67). As for Brand, it wasn't a monkey that hurt him this time. A penalty for moving the ball gave him a 70 and dropped him to a joint third at 206. And finally Mason began to stir, although hardly enough to be considered a threat. He posted his second straight sub-par round, a 67, and stood at 207, just three off the lead. In the final round, Roe fell out of the picture by a stroke with a 72, while Mason birdied the two closing holes for a 68 and was tied at 275 with Brand (69), Chapman (70), and Martin Poxon (66).

Bogeys at the second extra hole knocked Brand and Poxon out of the playoff. Then Mason made short work of Chapman, holing a 25-foot birdie putt at the third to add the Kenya Open to his previous two professional victories, the 1975 Lusaka Open and the 1984 Zambia Open. "I wasn't sure that I was ready for the playoff," Mason said later. "I had lost my game a little bit in the middle. But in such games, you never give up. I kept myself going, and in the end it was good enough."

Zambia Open—£60,000
Winner: Paul Carrigill

Victory can sometimes be more rewarding than most people realize. England's Paul Carrigill, age 28, struggling to make a comeback, put it plaintively after winning the Zambia Open in a playoff over Scotland's Mike Miller. Carrigill won £10,000, Miller £6,660. "The difference between first and second," the relieved Carrigill said, "is more money than I possess."

A 75 put Carrigill four behind Roger Chapman, whose 72—142 gave him a one-stroke lead at the halfway point. (Chapman was to become one of three victims in the tournament.) Miller's 74 put him at 146 and a tie for 12th with Carrigill. In the third round, a 67 hoisted Carrigill into a share of the lead on 213 with Keith Waters (69) and John Fowler (70). The final round was a nail-biter for Carrigill. Miller ran off seven birdies and made only one bogey for a closing 67, and Carrigill had to make three dramatic one-putt pars for a 72 to catch him. Carrigill missed the green at No. 16, but holed from 10 feet for his three; he putted off the green at No. 17, but made a 15-footer coming back, and at No. 18, after hooking his drive into deep rough, he needed a seven-footer for his par. He got it. They tied at seven-under 285.

Carrigill needed one more lifesaver. At the first hole of the playoff, he bunkered his tee shot, overshot the green with his recovery, then left his chip 15 feet short. He holed it for his par. Miller, who had putted six feet past from the fringe, missed on the return.

Minolta Match Play
Winner: Tony Johnstone

The Sunshine Circuit resumed in the second week of November after an eight-month hiatus, and the rampaging Mark McNulty finally met his match (no pun intended) in Tony Johnstone in the Minolta Match Play at

Johannesburg's Crown Mines. McNulty had won the previous four Sunshine events, running through all four weeks of February, then headed for the European Tour, where three titles in 18 appearances helped lift him to second behind Ian Woosnam on the Epson Order of Merit with £189,303. Victory was not as familiar to Johnstone, 31-year-old Zimbabwean, but it was no stranger. He had won the Sunshine Circuit's Goodyear Classic in December, 1986, and followed it up a month later with the ICL International in mid-January. He went winless on the 1987 European Tour, but finished with a personal-high £38,927 (44th on the Order of Merit) in eight seasons on that tour.

The week opened with a field of 96 teeing off in the first round, shooting for the 24 berths in the match play. Among the eight seeds who would get their first action in Thursday's third round were McNulty, Fulton Allem and Gary Player, making one of his rare appearances on the Sunshine Circuit.

The tournament got a neat twist of irony in the first round when Norman Mashaba defeated the man he once caddied for, former Ryder Cup player Michael King. Ian Mosey went through on a hot putter, finishing three-three to edge Zimbabwe rookie Glenn James. "I was lucky I was putting so well" said Mosey, after a one-over-par 73. "I only needed 24 putts all day," Mosey scored another one-stroke victory the next day, dropping a dangerous five-foot downhill putt on the final hole for a par 72 to dismiss Don Robertson of the United States. "It's only willpower and experience that have got me through the past two days," Mosey said. He posted his win just before a storm washed out play and left a number of golfers to complete their matches the next morning. Among them was Denis Durnian, who almost squandered a lead of two he held overnight against former South African amateur champion Etienne Groenewald. Durnian went to four ahead when play resumed in the morning, then let it all slip and needed a par three on No. 18 for a 76 to win by one.

Durnian and Mosey both were dismissed in Thursday's play, which left the tournament an all-South African affair. Roger Wessels, a second-year local pro, beat David Feherty, 74-75, then Durnian, 70-76. Mosey was beaten by Gary Player, who turned 52 the week before. Mosey, a 72-78 victim, could only shrug in admiration. "Gary still doesn't make many mistakes," he said. McNulty edged South Africa's Wilhelm Winsnes, 69-70, and Johnstone had no trouble with Zimbabwe's Teddy Webber, 68-77. On Friday, McNulty beat Wessels in the quarterfinals, 70-76, then met Wayne Bradley in the semifinals. It was no contest. McNulty started with three birdies and an eagle to go six ahead after four holes, and rolled to a 67-73 victory to take his place in the final. Johnstone ousted Schalk van der Merwe in the quarterfinals, 70-72. In the semifinals, Fulton Allem, who had ousted Player, went two up on Johnstone with a trio of birdies starting at the 10th, then slipped back into a tie with a double bogey at No. 15. Johnstone snatched his opportunity with a birdie at No. 16 and went on to take his spot in the final, 73-74.

The final between Johnstone and McNulty was something of a rematch of adversaries dating back to their amateur days. McNulty now was famous for winning from anywhere — leading wire-to-wire, coming from behind in the second or third rounds, and sometimes with just holes to play. So Johnstone faced a formidable task. But he was more than equal to it. Rather then being intimidated, he produced some of his finest golf, a five-under-par 67, to win by two over McNulty. Allem took third with a course-record 64.

Protea Assurance Prosure Challenge—R250,000
Winner: Bobby Lincoln

This was David Feherty's tournament to win, or maybe Fulton Allem's. But while they were battling, Bobby Lincoln, functionally an innocent bystander at the moment, stepped in and picked off the plum. The little-known Lincoln, 34, of Johannesburg, broke through at the last minute for his first Sunshine Circuit victory, the Protea Assurance Prosure Challenge at the par-72 at Germiston Country Club course. But until those dying moments, Lincoln, although playing strong and steady golf, was just in the crowd on the sidelines of the Feherty-Allem duel.

The tournament that ended in a surprise also started with one — Stuart Smith, the young Californian, taking the first-round lead with a six-under-par 66. That put him one ahead of Wilhelm Winsnes, the South African lawyer-turned-golfer. At 68 were Lincoln, Gary Player's son Wayne, and the ever-present Allem, who earlier in the week needed pain-killing injections for strained tendons in both wrists. Feherty, who started from No. 10, made a strong early bid with four consecutive birdies from No. 13, then cooled off in the strong winds. He double-bogeyed his 14th (No. 6), then three-putted his last hole and joined a group at 69, three off the lead.

Feherty got rolling again the next day and surged into the 36-hole lead with a seven-under-par 65 and a 134 total, two ahead of Mark McNulty (70-66—136). Feherty, playing in the morning before the winds came up, bogeyed No. 1 after a bad approach, then holed a bunker shot for an eagle at No. 2. He was really hot coming home, getting three consecutive birdies beginning at No. 11, and adding two more at No. 15 and No. 16 for an inward 31. "I can feel my game coming right," he said. "I tended to be a bit streaky, but my game is getting much steadier now." Smith, the first-round leader, returned a 71 for a 137 total, tied for third with Winsnes (70) and Lincoln (69).

It took a course record to head off Feherty, and that's exactly what the sore-wristed Allem produced in the third round — an eight-under-par 64 for a 202 total, 14 under par. Feherty, his led melting away under Allem's charge, birdied two of the last three holes for a 68 to salvage a share of first at 202. They led by one over McNulty (67) and Lincoln, who posted his third consecutive sub-70 round, a 66.

In the rain-interrupted final round, Feherty's hopes suffered a fatal blow on Saturday when he double-bogeyed No. 4 after hitting into trees, then bogeyed two more on the outward nine. Rain washed out play, leaving 12 players to finish on Sunday morning. As collapses go, Fehrety's wasn't much. But a one-under-par 71, his first round out of the 60s, left him third on 273. Lincoln was the one threatening to fold. He lead Allem by two with two holes to play, then three-putted No. 17 to Allem's birdie. They were even. Now it was Allem's turn to stumble. He three-putted the final hole for a 70, while Lincoln put up a 68 — his fourth round in the 60s — for a 17-under-par 271 total and a one-stroke victory over Allem.

Wild Coast Classic—R150,000
Winner: Tony Johnstone

The Wild Coast Classic, at Casino Beach Country Club, began with two highlights — a bit of inspiration and a weird penalty. The inspiration touched Gordon Manson, Scottish teaching pro based in Austria, who has no desire to play the European Tour. Fired by his famous playing partner, he returned a four-under-par 66 for a share of the first-round lead. "I played with Mark McNulty today, and that helped me," he said. "I picked up the rhythm of his swing and managed to keep it going." (McNulty himself shot a 68, which left him two off the lead, the closest he would get to the hunt.) The weird penalty hit another Scot, Ian Young, and it cost him a share of the lead. At No. 14, his ball rolled off the tee peg just as he started his downswing. He checked his swing, but officials judged that he had intended to hit the ball, so he was penalized one stroke. That gave him a 67, one off the lead. "It was bad luck," Young said. "If it had happened a split second sooner, I would not have started my downswing."

As things turned out, none of it mattered. Tony Johnstone, the Minolta Match Play winner just two weeks earlier, went on a tear for a crushing wire-to-wire victory on 66-64-67-65, a tournament-record total of 262 and a seven-stroke victory over Hugh Baiocchi.

Johnstone opened with 66 to share the first-round lead with Manson and Fulton Allem, and that was as close as anyone would get to him. In the second round, Manson lost the McNulty rhythm and returned a 74 for a 140 total that left him 10 strokes astern through the halfway point. Allem also drifted away. Young was trying to make a move, and was two under through the turn. Then he lost a ball at his tenth hole (No. 1) and couldn't get back on track. He finished the 36 holes at 72—139, nine off the lead. Of the first-round challengers, only Baiocchi could keep pace with the hot Johnstone — more or less. Baiocchi started the second round one behind, returned a powerful 65 for a 132 total, and still lost ground. Johnstone put more air between them with a 64—130.

It was clear now that unless Johnstone ran into some kind of disaster, this was a battle for second place. And the weather didn't help the challengers. The third round was played in a drizzle. Brian Evans, a Portugal-based Briton, charged into the picture with a four-under-par 66, his best of the week. That left him a solid third at 203 — two ahead of Wayne Westner and two behind Baiocchi (69—201), but six off the lead. Johnstone shook off two bogeys, picked up five birdies, and returned a 67 that padded his lead to four over the frustrated Baiocchi, 197-201.

The drizzle turned into a whipping wind and rain in the fourth round. Johnstone said the last three holes were almost unplayable. This left others to wonder what he might have done on a good day. Baiocchi closed with a 68 for 269, a solid second place by four strokes over Evans. Johnstone made do with a five-under-par 65—262 for his second Sunshine victory in three weeks and his third of 1987.

Million Dollar Challenge—US $1,000,000
Winner: Ian Woosnam

Ian Woosnam could have called it a year months ago. He had come to the Million Dollar Challenge in December with a remarkable season already in hand. But when you're hot, you're hot, and not even British Open champion Nick Faldo nor America's leading money-winner Curtis Strange could cool him off. Woosnam made this one almost ceremonial. He was two strokes clear of Faldo with two holes to play when he proceeded to sink a 165-yard seven-iron shot for an eagle-two at the 17th. A par at No. 18 gave him: A four-stroke victory over Faldo, his eighth individual title of the year and golf's first-ever $1 million top prize.

"What a year it's been, and this has just crowned it all," Woosnam said. "Everyone dreams about being a millionaire. If the taxman is not too harsh on me, I might have done it."

The tournament, held at the southern Africa resort of Sun City, in Bophuthatswana, was revamped for the 1987 playing. Except for a $50,000 prize for the low round each day, it was a winner-take-all tournament. Others in the eight-man field were Lanny Wadkins, Jose-Maria Olazabal, Bernhard Langer, and South Africans David Frost and Fulton Allem. Allem himself was having a good year. With a second-place finish in the World Series of Golf, worth $84,000, he won the American tour card he had coveted. He came to Sun City as a replacement for defending champion Mark McNulty, who was suffering from pneumonia. Allem, 31, added a quick $50,000 to his wallet with a 66 that gave him the first-round lead by one over Woosnam. He bogeyed only once, when he missed a short putt after a good chip at No. 8. He followed that with three consecutive birdies, and finished with a six-iron second shot to within three feet at No. 18. Woosnam came home in 32 with some sensational iron play that left him with putts of two feet or less for the four birdies in that stretch.

The second day's $50,000 "lap" money went to Langer for a 68 that left him tied for second with Woosnam (71) at 138. Allem expanded his lead to three strokes with a 69 for a nine-under-par 135, the best two-round total in the six-year-old event. "If anyone's going to catch me, they're going to have to come at me," said Allem, who shook off a double-bogey six at No. 8. Unfortunately for Allem, nobody had to go at him. In the third round, he demolished himself with an eight at No. 9 and came back to the field with a 74, while the relentless Woosnam ground on. He took the lead with a 68—206, one ahead of Faldo (68), two ahead of Frost, and three ahead of Allem. The other four were pretty well out of it by now. Olazabal (70) and Langer (73) shared fifth at 211; Strange was sixth at 72—213, and Wadkins, who was never a factor, was eighth at 72—215.

In the final round, all Woosnam had to do was hold on. But he did better than that — after surviving a scare. A hook suddenly appeared at No. 5. He fought it for three holes, and managed to hold the damage to one bogey — his only bogey of the round — after hitting into a bunker at No. 7. Still, Faldo could not close that one-stroke gap. Then he took himself out at the par-five 14th, where he put his second shot into the greenery and had to chop his way out. A bogey-six left him two behind. If there was still hope for Faldo, Woosnam erased it with that seven-iron eagle at the

17th. "I hit the ball straight at the flag, and I knew it was going to be good," Woosnam said. "But I couldn't see the bottom of the flag, so it was only the wild reaction of the crowd that told me the ball had gone in." So Woosnam came in with a 68 (worth another low-round $50,000) for a 274 total to Faldo's 71—278. No one else was even in the hunt. Frost was third at 72—280, and Olazabal (72), Allem (74), and Strange (70) shared fourth at 283. Langer was sixth at 74—285, and Wadkins last at 75—290.

Safmarine Masters—R170,000
Winner: David Frost

Memory — a painful one, that is — helped spur David Frost to the Safmarine Masters title at Stellenbosch, Cape Town. It hit him in the third round, when South African Ian Palmer was making a charge at him. A leader can get edgy at such times, maybe try something brash. Frost admitted he was tempted, but that's when the memory kicked in — the memory of the British Open in July, when he was tied for second going into the final round, and tried to keep up with the hot start of Paul Azinger, the leader, instead of playing his own game. Frost slipped back to sixth place with a final-round 74, and Nick Faldo took the old cup. Frost learned his lesson. "I played my own game this time," he said. Palmer had started hot in the third round, but Frost stuck to his guns. It paid off.

The Masters opened on a sour note — the condition of the course. Fulton Allem, loudest of the critics, didn't waste time on subtlety. "Something went horribly wrong," he said. "Perhaps their mower broke down. A lot of work needs to be done on this course to make it a fair test of golf. The tees at the World Series (where he was runnerup in August) were four times faster than these greens."

Objections noted, the tournament opened like a land rush, despite a driving rain. Six players tied for the first-round lead at two-under-par 70 — John Bland, Brian Evans, Hugh Baiocchi, Bob Smith, Tony Johnstone (winner of two of the previous three tournaments), and Frost. The unhappy Allem was in a group at par 72. Someone listened to him, though, and the course was in better shape for the second round. Frost found things to his liking and bolted to the front on 67—137 for a one-stroke lead over Palmer, who turned in the day's best round, 65. Frost had only one unsteady moment, a three-putt at No. 3. Baiocchi, Smith, and Johnstone — all eyes were on him — returned 69s and shared third at 139. Then there came a noise from deep in the pack. Denis Durnian, hoping to return to tournament golf after six years as a club pro in Manchester, had opened with a weak 74. Now a 67 carried him to within shouting distance of Frost, at 141, four strokes back.

Then came the crucial third round. Palmer charged early, getting three consecutive birdies starting from No. 3 to go three up on Frost at the 11th. But Palmer's strong iron play didn't entirely compensate for his poor tee shots, and he settled for a 71—209. Frost, meantime, kept his head down and returned a 70 for a 207 total and a two-stroke lead on Palmer. Durnian started with three birdies and an outward 34, but a double bogey at the par-five 12th cooled him down to a 70-211, four behind.

Durian made a great try at overhauling Frost in the final round, with a 65 that included five birdies and an eagle, the best round of the day. But Frost still minded his own business and answered in spades. In an eight-hole stretch, starting at No. 7, he posted four birdies and an eagle of his own on his way to a 66 and a three-stroke victory over Durnian, 273-276.

Goodyear Classic—R150,000
Winner: John Bland

Ireland's David Feherty had one of the steadiest of rounds to close out the Goodyear Classic — 15 pars, two birdies, and only one bogey. The performance had him tied for the lead for a while. But it was a burst at the end that won for 42-year-old John Bland. He birdied four of the last five holes for a 69 and a three-under-par total of 281 on the Humewood Golf Club at Port Elizabeth, wrapping up the Sunshine Circuit for 1987.

It was the South African's 11th victory in a career dating to 1970, but his first on the Sunshine Circuit after three years of frustration. His last previous Sunshine Circuit victory, coincidentally, was the 1984 Goodyear Classic. Not that he had gone empty in the meantime. Bland won the 1986 Suze Open on the European Tour, and that victory may stand as the jewel of his golfing life because he came from behind to beat none other than Seve Ballesteros. "I still find it hard to believe," Bland had said, "that I gave the best player in the world a two-shot start and beat him by four."

The Goodyear Classic was hardly handed to him, however. Among the obstacles were Denis Durnian and Michael King, both of whom opened on 70 against Bland's 71. And it was a dogfight at the end. The hottest hand — for a while — belonged to Scotland's Ian Young, who was out in six-under-par 29. Young birdied the first three holes, then the sixth, seventh, and ninth. He was heading for the very low 60s until he suffered a double-bogey six at No. 13. He recovered for birdies at the 15th and 17th before dropping a stroke at the last for 66. But he was the victim of three earlier rounds in the mid-70s, he finished tied for 13th at 289.

Going into the final round, Bland was at 212 and Feherty at 214. Mark Wiltshire, another South African, authored a crippling 75 in the third round and entered the final round at 217. At one point in the closing holes, Feherty was at level par and tied for the lead. But Bland and Wiltshire broke out of the pack. Wiltshire was the real threat toward the end. He came home in five-under-par 31 for a 66, matching Young for the low round of the week. But the third-round 75 left him too much to do. He finished with a one-under-par 283.

Bland caught fire just in time. A combination of good iron play and sharp putting gave him four consecutive birdies from the 14th, and none of the putts was longer than 12 feet. His 69—281 gave him the victory by two over Wiltshire.

13. The Australasian Tour

One fact of Australian professional golf is that the more the tour struggles, the more controversy it generates, and 1987 was no exception. The major part of the circuit, played in October and November, faces stern competition from Europe and Japan. The time is near when the Australian PGA and the Tournament Players Section will seek to organize their events in January and February. Already foreshadowing that are two half-million dollar tournaments in 1988, at Sanctuary Cove in Queensland and Riverside Oaks, 40 miles west of Sydney.

The playing controversy this year revolved around the astonishing happenings on the scheduled final day of the Australian Open at Royal Melbourne. A stiff northerly wind blew and, although it was otherwise a reasonable day, the round was cancelled because of the pin placement at the third hole. The positioning was so ridiculous that Mark Twain's whimsical observation became reality. "It is good sportsmanship," he once said, "not to pick up golf balls while they are still rolling."

Details of Greg Norman's mixed year have been chronicled elsewhere, but he registered a win in that Australian Open on the fifth day, turning in a magnificent performance to break records for the event and course, previously set by Jack Nicklaus and Gary Player. His rounds of 66 on the second and third days provided spectators with a memorable feast of brilliant golf, but he didn't play in enough events to be eligible for Order of Merit status. Peter Senior won that honor, a welcome bonus for him after the horror of St. Andrews where, at a crucial time in the Dunhill Cup, he hit out of bounds after his opponent, Howard Clark, had done the same.

It was disappointing that more young players did not come through this year, although the same lament was voiced last year. Wayne Riley may well be the best of them but he will need to harness his temperament and learn patience. Certainly the skill is there. Craig Parry and Ian Roberts distinguished themselves by finishing in the top 10 of the European Tour's qualifying school at La Manga in December and they too show much promise for the future. In New Zealand, Greg Turner and Frank Nobilo had disappointing years, but one young player to catch the eye was Grant Waite.

David Graham, in walking away with the Queensland Open, showed again that when he sets his mind to the job and wants to prove a point, he is still a brilliant golfer.

Roger Mackay and Craig Parry won tournaments and both looked good in doing so. Mackay is the more mature of the pair, though Parry aged considerably as the field threatened to swamp him in the New South Wales Open at the Australian Golf Club.

Even when not winning, Norman took most of the publicity, and there was continual speculation about when he would win again. He answered the questions in brilliant fashion and is already committed for major events on the Australian circuit in 1988. That will be marvellous for golf followers but, equally interesting in the future for all players, is whether or not the

PGA's shift of tournament dates will be successful. One area where there is promise of argument over dates is the playing of an Australian Bicentenary event scheduled at the same time as the Air New Zealand Shell Open. New Zealand officials were furious when news came through of Australia's intentions. Those who promote the Australasian golf circuit in years to come may face an interesting challenge.

U-Bix Classic New South Wales PGA—A$100,000
Winner: Peter Senior

There is no more unflappable golfer in Australia than Peter Senior, and this was illustrated in the U-Bix Classic, when Senior played a perfect pressure chip from the edge of the last green to secure a winning birdie.

Senior is a very good golfer, but has sometimes been upstaged by those with prettier swings in his own country. But Senior has a ton of good old-fashioned courage. He was never off the leaderboard in this event played in Canberra, starting strongly and concentrating on the par-fives to set up his birdie opportunities, and winning by one stroke over Gerry Taylor with his 273 total, 19 under par.

An opening-day 67 put Senior in a tie for fourth place behind Peter Jones, who shot 65. Senior shot 65 in the second round, which was by two strokes the low score, and he constantly hammered the flag. He had 72 in the third round and was tied for the lead by Kyi Hla Han, who shot 68, but it was Taylor who challenged strongly on the last day.

When Taylor eagled the 17th, they were tied at 18 under par. Taylor, playing in the next-to-last group, chose to drive down the 10th fairway to open up the green for a six-iron. The idea was right, but his subsequent three putts gave Senior his chance, and Peter made the most of it, finishing with a 69.

Foster's Tattersall Tasmanian Open—A$75,000
Winner: Brian Jones

Fierce winds made it certain that the Foster's Tattersall Tasmanian Open would be won by a player well-versed in handling those conditions. There are few Australians better at playing in the wind than Brian Jones, who kept the ball low while others were being blown out of contention. He shot 283, five under par, and won by a stroke over Mike Colandro.

Jones began with a 69 against a strong northwesterly, then added a 70 when the wind switched to the west and brought the rain in the second round. At that stage, there were many good scores on the board. Colandro was leading with 68-67, and players of the calibre of Roger Mackay, Peter Fowler and Rodger Davis were also ahead of Jones.

At the press conference that evening, Colandro said, "I'm playing so well, it's scary." He was confident indeed, and one of the reasons was that his American training had taught him to punch the ball low and beneath the wind. That was necessary because the course is very testing even in good conditions. On the first two days the average score was 75.

The third day was something else. The fierce winds turned to gale force and the players had enough trouble in keeping their balance when walking between shots, let alone in actually striking the ball. The average score rocketed to 78. There was one incredible round by Peter Jones who had 67 and another almost as good by Ian Baker-Finch, 70.

It was a tight leaderboard at the start of the final round, also played in strong winds. Jones grimly hung on to the lead, calling on the experience of playing the past five years in Japan, where he has won five times. One shot, a deft chip to two feet from an almost impossible position in deep rough near the 15th green, saved par. When Colandro missed on the 18th from nine feet, Jones had registered his first victory in Australia since 1980, when he won the Barclays Australian Classic.

Robert Boyd Transport Australian Match Play Championship—A$100,000
Winner: Ian Baker-Finch

After a close match for 14 holes, Ian Baker-Finch blitzed Ossie Moore, winning 5 and 4 in the final of the Robert Boyd Transport Australian Match Play Championship. Baker-Finch played very well and the secret of his success was the return to his former putting technique. He had studied some old videos of his putting style and found that he had unconsciously changed his stroke.

With a first prize of $20,000, a field of 24 players and the first-round losers receiving $1,000, there was great incentive for all-out attack on players like Greg Norman, David Graham and Rodger Davis. That trio represented Australia in the 1986 Dunhill Nations Cup at St. Andrews and each received a first-round bye at Kingston Heath, a decided advantage on a day where the temperatures soared.

In the early skirmishes, the outstanding match was between Davis and Vaughan Somers, with Davis sinking a 25-foot downhill putt for victory on the 23rd hole. "He never gave up all day," Davis said. Norman, two down after six holes to Mike Clayton, pulled his game together with four birdies and an eagle in five holes to win, 4 and 3, but it took Baker-Finch until the 21st hole to defeat Wayne Smith.

There was great anticipation for the quarter-finals with Norman drawn against Mike Harwood, the young player who stopped his run of victories in 1986 by winning the Australian PGA at Castle Hill. Here at Kingston Heath, Harwood did it again. Harwood, in fact, was stepping forward to congratulate Norman on winning 3 and 2 on the 16th green since Norman, two up at that point, had only a three-foot putt for the match. The ball lipped out, Norman bogeyed the 17th and 18th, smashed his drive into the trees and then put his second shot into the bunker at the 19th. Exit the Great White Shark. Exit Harwood too in the semi-final where, after a splendid fight with Moore, the latter played a nine-iron to within a few inches of the pin on the 18th.

Australian Masters—A$300,000
Winner: Greg Norman

There is a saying in Australian horse racing circles that an astonishingly easy winner has been victorious by "panels of fencing." What better example of that in golf than the performance of Greg Norman in winning the Australian Masters at Huntingdale. He shot 19-under-par 273 and finished nine strokes ahead of Peter Senior. Norman, in the middle of a short Australian visit, was mobbed by teenagers who were enthralled by one of the great sporting performances seen in Australia. He has lifted the game of golf in his home country.

Ominously for the rest of the field, Norman shot 68 in the first round and said later, "Although I scored well I wasn't completely at my best with my putting." The problem seemed to have disappeared on the second day when Greg carded a 67 which included a wonderful series of putts, one for eagle from 22 feet on the seventh hole. He then birdied the eighth, 11th and 12th and, at that stage, was 12 under par. It came as no surprise when he hit two shots to 12 feet on the monster 607-yard par-five 14th. He had to be content with birdie there, and finished with a two-stroke lead over Ian Stanley and a five-shot margin over Senior.

Norman shot 68 in the third round, and his first six holes provided as immaculate golf as you could wish to see. Apart from one hole, his round was virtually error free.

On the last day, other than when his concentration lapsed on the final two holes, Norman continued in similar vein, scoring a 70. He was disappointed for not having broken 70 in all four rounds, but said that overall his play had been something special. "My iron play was probably nine out of 10 over the four days and, in general terms, I played the ball into the greens just as well as I can."

Robert Boyd Transport Victorian Open—A$110,000
Winner: Roger Mackay

At some stage in our golfing careers we have all taken nine strokes on a par-four hole. Okay, if not all, then most of us have. You don't, however, expect Greg Norman to take nine shots and, when eventually he loses the golf tournament, the headline writers have a field day.

It was a moment or, to be more accurate, several moments, of torture. They consisted of: a drive into a low, thick bush; two air shots with a three-iron swung backhand; another three-iron backhand which banged the ball into a second bush; a chip to the fairway; a chip to the green, and three putts.

Roger Mackay, the former Australian Eisenhower Cup player, took advantage of the astonishing sequence of events. After Norman took that 73 in the second round, Mackay could afford a 73 in the third round, then won by matching Norman's 68 in the final round. Mackay had a 277 total, 11 under par, in winning by one stroke.

This was not any ho-hum, run-of-the-mill tournament. On the second day storms and torrential rain hit the course, the greens and just about everything else were flooded and the second round was cancelled. The committee decided to cut the field at 51 after two rounds and play 36 holes on the Sunday.

Each day had its moments. Playing the 14th hole, a 549-yard par five, on the opening day, Mackay hit a good drive to the center of the fairway and then bounced a splendid three-wood 253 yards into the hole for a double eagle. He couldn't see it go in because of the lie of the land, and the cheers of the few around the green merely seemed to go on longer than usual. It lifted him from the pack to the outright lead at seven under par.

Mackay began the last day by hitting an eight-iron into the hole for eagle on the second hole, and finished the round with 73 to Norman's 71. When they came to the 16th hole Mackay, now with a two-shot lead, hit a marvellous drive under great pressure and made par, as did Norman. They parred No. 17 then, on the 18th with the gallery roaring, Mackay hit an eight iron to seven feet, but Norman was inside him. "I knew I had to make par," Mackay said. "He had that birdie look about him and that would have meant a playoff." Mackay made his par and Norman finished things with birdie.

The result was one of the big shocks of the Australian circuit but, with Norman at 10 under par, it was Mackay's own good play which carried him through. And possibly that nine-shot hole which made the "hackers" of the world feel just a little better.

Rich River Classic—A$75,000
Winner: Peter Senior

Peter Senior played up to his reputation as one of the most consistent golfers in Australia over the four days at Echuca to win the Rich River Classic at 15-under-par 273. Although Mike Ferguson finished with a rush, he would have needed a 63 to tie Senior, and that was too much to expect. Ferguson provided the last-day thrills, as he has often done on the Australian circuit. Unlike Senior, his problem has been a lack of consistency.

Fifteen under par was always likely to be difficult to beat on this 6,749-yard course and Senior had another reason to be pleased with his victory. The first-place money took him ahead of Greg Norman in the Australian Order of Merit.

It could not be said that the tournament started in scintillating fashion for Senior. He came to Rich River after missing the cut in the Victorian Open and, seemingly, having blown his chance of leading the Order of Merit. He started the first round with a bogey. There's not much in that to lift your confidence, yet Senior finished with a 62, having covered the back nine in 28, seven under par.

Senior's consistency kept him going even if he did not hit the ball as well as he wanted. It was a case of doing exactly what was required, and the chunky Queenslander clinched his Order of Merit title with a solid par-72 on the last day.

Konica Queensland Open—A$75,000
Winner: David Graham

A two-year drought ended for David Graham when he won the Konica Queensland Open at Coolangatta-Tweed Heads. His last individual first-place check came in the same Queensland event in 1985, but he said before the tournament, "I can still sniff another major. I am very fit, my mind is active and I know I can continue to play well." He proceeded to do just that. Over the final 10 holes, he produced seven birdies with a fine display of precision shotmaking. Runner-up Vaughan Somers said ruefully, "That's what champions do. They let you stay with them for a while, and then they bury you."

Graham's seven-stroke margin, with rounds of 69-71-69-66 for a 275 total, certainly buried his rivals and his performance was watched with great interest.

A most unusual incident involved Bob Shearer. On the third day, Shearer was six under par playing the 18th hole and pulled his drive where spectators were walking towards the tee. When he arrived at the spot, there was no ball. He asked a lady standing nearby if she had seen the ball, and received a stumbling negative. Then, with the allowable five minutes running out, instinct had him chase her 100 yards back down the fairway. "Madam," Shearer said, "I'd like to look in your handbag." "You're being a bit forward," she snapped. Shearer looked at her warily and replied, "Perhaps so, but it's my living and I'll apologize if I'm wrong."

Presto! The ball was wedged between the lipstick and the mascara, and Shearer, avoiding a stroke-and-distance trip back to the tee, made his par after officials allowed him to drop at an agreed-upon spot.

Queensland PGA—A$75,000
Winner: Peter Senior

When Peter Senior won the Queensland PGA, he did it the hard way at the opening playoff hole, and the victim was his friend Jeff Woodland, who had never won a four-round tournament. Senior caught Woodland in the last round with 68 for a 278 total, while Woodland shot a closing 71.

Senior and Woodland started the event in spectacular fashion, shooting course-record 67s in the opening round, with six birdies by Senior and five by Woodland. That however was not as newsworthy as the chain of events which dogged Canadian Eric Kaufmanis on the second day.

Kaufmanis, on the fourth hole, tried to hit his ball at right-angles off a tree stump and on the green. He slightly miscued, the ball rebounded and struck him flush on the forehead. That meant a two-stoke penalty. Dazed, he scored a triple-bogey seven on the hole.

He then discovered he was playing the wrong ball, and had been doing so since the third hole, where he had mistakenly hit Tim Ireland's ball. He was disqualified. But a torrential rain hit the course, the round was cancelled and Kaufmanis was eligible again, with the field scheduled to play 36 holes on the fourth day. He still missed the cut by three shots.

Senior, Woodland and Mike Ferguson distanced themselves from the pack at the half-way stage and, after the first 18 holes on the last day, Woodland had a three-stroke advantage. With 13 holes to play, Senior was four strokes behind. He piled on the pressure with birdies at the sixth and ninth holes, while Woodland had bogeys at the eighth and 10th. Suddenly they were even, but Senior had to salvage par on the 17th with a 10-foot putt. He made it, they tied the last and Senior birdied the first playoff hole to destroy Woodland's hope of a victory.

National Panasonic New South Wales Open—A$150,000
Winner: Craig Parry

"I know now how Lawrence of Arabia must have felt after spending most of his time under the ropes and in the sand." The quip was more in keeping with veteran Lee Trevino's humor. Although Trevino was playing in the New South Wales Open at the Australian Golf Club, the remark actually came from 21-year-old Craig Parry.

Parry had just finished a traumatic last-round 79 where he barely managed to hang on, winning by one stroke over Wayne Riley with a 289 total.

It might have been soul-shattering if the youngster had been beaten after his opening-round 65. The Australian golf course was redesigned several years ago by Jack Nicklaus. It was thought that no one would shoot 65 around there, even on a day when no leaf was ruffled by the breeze. Certainly no one would do it when the wind was blowing, but Parry turned in a remarkable performance.

He showed no signs of cracking on the second day when he fired a 71. Trevino eased into a tie for second place with Riley in the third round, with Parry carding a 74 but still retaining a seven-stroke lead.

It rained so much on the fourth day that the round was postponed until Monday. Parry was left with 24 hours to think about being seven shots ahead, and winning his first four-round event, and it obviously got to him. On the last day, trying to defend his lead, he hit only three greens in regulation on the front nine, only one on the back nine. By the time he came to the 18th, a par five with water protecting the right side of the green, he had to stop and add up how many strokes had been taken.

Ahead of him, as Parry waited, Riley missed a straightforward putt which would have added enormous pressure, but even then Parry still hit his third shot into the water. "At that stage I felt nothing but panic," he said later. "I didn't know what was happening to me." Finally he sank a 15-inch putt for a bogey and the victory. During his career, he may rarely have a putt which seems longer than that one.

E.S.P. Australian PGA Championship—A$170,000
Winner: Roger Mackay

The biggest plus mark about the Australian PGA was that it was played at all. Parts of the Liverpool course were six feet under water. The famous and aptly-named Lakes Golf Club in Sydney, built on sand and scene of some fine tournaments, came to the rescue. It wasn't a cheap change of venue. The sponsors were faced with a bill for another $100,000, the tournament organizers and the media managers were each faced with cuts in fees, and payments still had to be made to both courses.

Roger Mackay had every cause to be very pleased. He won by one stroke with a 284 total following his victory early in the year in the Victorian Open. Mackay, a former Australian Amateur champion, concentrated on geology for some years and then, when the bottom fell out of that market, decided to try his luck as a golfer. He has done well. In two years he has proven to be a tough competitor with a sound swing, and he refuses to be ruffled by pressure.

Mackay was always in contention, starting with 68, two strokes behind leader Ronan Rafferty of Northern Ireland, and held his position on the second and third days. Rafferty provided the disappointment, leading on the opening day and then taking the lead again in the third round with a great par-73 in difficult, blustery conditions. But Rafferty crashed with 78 on the last day.

There was nothing easy about the way Mackay clinched the title. He had to make par-three on the difficult 18th hole and, over the last four holes, he and the others in his group were under threat of receiving two-stroke penalties for slow play. Mackay said, "There was plenty of tension out there with the slow-play warning and the fact that I was having some trouble keeping my concentration." The main challenge came from Mike Colandro, who shot 69, storming home with two eagle-threes and a birdie in the last five holes. He was the leader when Mackay came to the 72nd hole knowing he needed the par to win.

West End South Australian Open—A$100,000
Winner: Ronan Rafferty

Five years is a long time between victories for a 23-year-old golfer, and Northern Ireland's Ronan Rafferty was almost disqualified before he broke that drought in the South Australian Open. Rafferty and Ossie Moore forgot the tournament was starting on Wednesday rather than Thursday, in order to leave Sunday free for the Australian Grand Prix race. Registration had been moved forward a day, and a special committee meeting was necessary for Rafferty and Moore to be allowed to play.

Greg Norman was back to play this event and the Australian Open, and was looking for his second win of the year. He is a magnificent drawing card, and the crowds were some of the biggest ever to attend a golf event in that state.

Rafferty appeared briefly on the leaderboard on the first day, then made a quick surge on the second and third days to be well-positioned going into the last round. Norman was unable to surge past, despite the enormous galleries cheering for him. Instead, Peter Fowler was the one to challenge Rafferty on the final hole with a putt to force a playoff. Rafferty's one-stroke victory came on rounds of 72-68-71-69 for a 280 total.

Rafferty, Fowler and Wayne Grady played together in the final round and they turned on a magnificent exhibition for the biggest one-day crowd in the history of South Australian golf. The Irishman almost threw it away on the par-three 17th, where his tee shot flew to the right and into thick scrub. He decided against taking a penalty, and instead played sideways on to a two-yard wide clear area and, from there, got up and down. Grady wrecked his chances with a double-bogey six on the last hole after hitting into trees off the tee, and it was left to Rafferty and Fowler. After Rafferty made his par, Fowler had a 20-foot putt to force the playoff, which he left agonizingly short.

National Panasonic Western Australian Open—A$80,000
Winner: Gerry Taylor

Robert Trent Jones, Jr., fashioned a beautiful golf course out of two quarries in Perth, Western Australia. He also manufactured one of the most difficult, or so it seemed from the scores, in the Western Australian Open won by Gerry Taylor. The Joondalup course is 20 miles north of Perth and works its way through bushland and the quarries. If the wind blows from the southwest, it can provide problems and so too can the greens which are very large, with enough hillocks to make three-putting a distinct possibility.

Taylor and Brad King, in his first year on the tour, finished tied at 290, two over par, and Taylor won on the second playoff hole. Right from the start the layout seemed to have the upper hand, despite Lyndsay Stephen's course-record 69 on the opening day in calm conditions. Local knowledge counts for a great deal and Stephen, who lives nearby, often plays and practices at the club. But his other rounds were 77, 74 and 76.

David Graham threatened several times but he had one hole, the third along the side of a quarry, which defeated him each day. He blamed no one but himself. "If you can't hit the fairway on this hole then you deserve to make seven two days in a row," he said. "The only way I can get back from here is to shoot 64 or 65," he said after the second round. It didn't work and he had to be satisfied with 73, 72 and the knowledge that his prediction had come true that the winner would have eight three-putt greens over the four days.

King led Taylor by one shot on the 18th tee but both played errant second shots. Taylor hit into the greenside bunker but managed a par-saving putt, while King played his second shot wide of the green into a hollow. "I was undecided on a four or five iron," he said. "I went for the easy four instead of a solid five and pushed it out to the right." The 10-foot putt slid by the cup to force the playoff and then Taylor, with a par at the second extra hole, clinched the title.

National Panasonic Australian Open Championship—A$300,000
Winner: Greg Norman

Greg Norman won the National Panasonic Australian Open by a record 10 shots over Sandy Lyle. Norman was 15 under par with a 273 total, magnificent performance in an event which took five days to finish even though the weather did not cause a postponement.

The scheduled fourth round was a shambles, a fiasco, a shameful day in Australian golf. That round was abandoned at Royal Melbourne after the committee neglected to check the pin placements before the start of play and the third green became unplayable. The golfers refused to continue, the lead having been established by Lyle, who declined to putt out on that green.

Norman, in the final group and leading by seven shots, took 90 minutes from the time he teed off at No. 1 until he walked off the third tee and back to the clubhouse. When he arrived at the third tee, there were five other groups waiting to play. Norman called for officials four times to come to the tee and then, in an unusual reversal of procedure, he walked to the clubhouse to talk to them.

The sequence of events which brought about this unprecedented happening was:

- A 45 mile-an-hour north wind was predicted for Melbourne on the final day. This is a fierce, hot wind which dries out the Royal Melbourne greens and makes putting marginally more hazardous than anywhere else in the world. The Australian Golf Union Championship Committee, despite this forecast, still stuck rigidly to the pin placements announced the day before the start of the tournament. Those placements were marked on each green by a tee peg.
- The Royal Melbourne course superintendent sent out his staff to give the greens their usual shaving and to cut the new holes according to the positions previously marked. The third hole was allegedly cut six feet away from where it should have been, and was positioned on a steep slope. Peter Thomson said that even without the strong winds blowing down the slope the placement would have been "reprehensible."
- No AGU official checked the pin placements, so the error remained undiscovered until the first group arrived at the third green. An early group of players called to the attention of officials that the third green was unputtable. No action was taken until later, when the big-name players protested.
- These protests came in the wake of players infringing the rules when caddies followed the ball after their professional putted and, at what they thought to be the critical moment of the ball stopping, they placed a coin against it, not necessarily behind it. Several times it was open to argument that the coin had been placed there before the ball had stopped rolling. Norman said later. "We were being made a laughing stock. The players were being completely humiliated on that green and the rules were being abused."

One thing that stood out over the five days was the skill of Norman. He loves Royal Melbourne, this was his last chance to win again in 1987 and, with his 10-shot victory, he did it in style. Only Jack Nicklaus 16 years earlier had challenged him statistically with an eight-stroke win over Bruce Crampton in the Open at Royal Hobart.

To beat that margin was Norman's second objective after the winning of the tournament. The third challenge for him was to lower the record for the Royal Melbourne Composite Course, which was held by Gary Player at 278, 10 under par. Norman broke this by five strokes in an awesome display.

The first day belonged not to Norman, nor to Rodger Davis, the defending champion, but to a young Queenslander, Terry Price, who shot 67. Norman shot 70, a solid round. His brilliant 66 on the second day pulled him even with Price, who had 69. Norman said later, "This 66 and my 63 at Turnberry in 1986, are two of the best rounds of golf I have ever played, possibly the best."

When Norman matched that with another 66 on the third day, it was merely a question of by how many strokes he would win. Lyle played superbly in the last two rounds for second place but Price, with an 84, and Jerry Anderson of Canada, 82, faded away. Davis' last-round 66 lifted him above 40 players to fifth place behind club pro Ron Wood and Gordon Brand, Jr.

Air New Zealand Shell Open—NZ$200,000
Winner: Mike Colandro

Mike Colandro felt the world was against him when he arrived for the Air New Zealand Shell Open at the Titirangi course in Auckland. He was suffering with a severe stomach ache and, to make matters worse, the organizers had not mentioned him among the 16 leading players in their publicity hand-outs. "I've been over here many times, never missed the cut, and they don't even have me listed," Colandro complained.

The colorful 34-year-old American, wearing bright knickers and matching pullovers, has been a regular visitor to Australia and New Zealand for seven seasons and his fifth place on the 1987 Order of Merit was his best performance. In contrast to Colandro's arrival, he had a marvellous conclusion to the tournament when he edged out defending champion Rodger Davis by a single shot. With rounds of 70, 65, 68 and 67, for a 10-under-par total of 270, Colandro played superbly and his putting on the final day was magnificent.

The field for the event included overseas players Sandy Lyle, Ronan Rafferty, Sam Torrance, Gordon Brand, Jr., and David Llewellyn, who was the winner of NZ$1,300 in a nine-hole "shoot-out" staged as a preliminary attraction to the main event.

Lyle, after one look at the course, declared he would be putting his driver on "hold" during the tournament and a first-round 68 placed him three shots behind Paul Foley and Wayne Grady, the latter having to contend with a stiff breeze and spiky greens when he played late on the opening day.

A steady drizzle made life uncomfortable for the early players on the second morning but Grady (65-69) still had a share of the lead with Vaughan Somers, who fired another fine 67. Somers' round was the more remarkable because he played in a fierce gale in the afternoon. "The course changed so dramatically in the wind it was hard to make a club selection. Having the honor on the tee was a handicap. You should be able to send the other fellows in to bat," Somers said. Low round of the day, also played in the wind, was American Jim Benepe's 64, which was 10 strokes better than his previous score. One off the pace at 135 were Lyle (68-67), Davis (69-66), Jerry Anderson (69-66), Foley (65-70), and Colandro, who shot a 65.

Lyle, battling the after-effects of a virus as well as the swirling wind, fired 65 on the third day to go into the last round 10 under par and two shots clear of Grady (68), Davis (67) and three ahead of Colandro (68).

The low scoring set up an exciting final day and the galleries were not disappointed when the five leaders were within a shot of each other after nine holes. Colandro had one birdie and eight pars on the front nine, then he birdied the 10th and 12th holes to draw level with Davis and Lyle at 10 under par. Three successive bogeys at Nos. 13, 14 and 15 ended Lyle's run and, for the third time, Grady came unstuck at the difficult par-four 17th, this time with a double bogey. Somers too fell away and it was left to Colandro and Davis to fight it out.

Colandro's putting was the deciding factor. He sank putts of 10 feet at Nos. 14 and 15, for par and birdie respectively, then an eight-footer at the 16th for par and another testing putt of nine feet for par on the 72nd hole. Davis, playing in the final group, three-putted No. 16 and needed a birdie at the last to tie Colandro. His second shot had so much backspin it rolled down off the green and into the hollow. He had to make his chip, but finished just three inches from the hole.

Nissan Mobil New Zealand Open—NZ$150,000
Winner: Ronan Rafferty

The final event on the 1987 Australasian circuit, the Nissan Mobil New Zealand Open, went to extra holes and provided an exciting and extraordinary finish between Larry Nelson and Ronan Rafferty. Nelson's chartered helicopter was circling above as the players were putting out at the fifth playoff hole and Rafferty asked Nelson if he wanted to call it quits. Nelson was scheduled to catch a flight home to the United States and was happy to share the title and prize money, but tournament organizers insisted that the playoff must continue.

So on they went and, at the seventh extra hole, Rafferty made a par, while Nelson could do no better than a bogey after he sliced his tee shot into trees. Nelson raced to the helicopter, but not before he signed an autograph for a young fan and handed him a box of golf balls and tees, a fine gesture from the quiet American. Rafferty and Nelson both shot 71s in the final round for 280 totals, eight under par. It was Rafferty's second victory on the Australasian tour, having earlier won the South Australian Open in Adelaide, and he also had high finishes in the Australian Open at Royal Melbourne and the Air New Zealand Shell Open played at Titirangi the previous week.

Play was suspended for almost an hour on the opening morning when heavy rain caused flooding on some of the greens. David Llewellyn handled the tight Heretaunga course splendidly for a two-under-par 70 and shared the first-round lead with Mike Harwood and 23-year-old New Zealand rookie Grant Waite. Waite had recently completed four years at the University of Oklahoma, and a promising future is predicted for the youngster.

Rafferty considered his opening-round 71 to be boring rather than exciting, but Nelson's 72 was far from that. He was three under after 10 and then three bogeys put him back to even par five holes later. "Putts of around three feet were difficult because of footprints on the green, but otherwise I was happy with the way I played," Nelson said.

A course-record 65 for Nelson in the second round, seven birdies and 11 pars, was two strokes better than the previous record and he led the field by one shot, ahead of Rafferty, 67, and three ahead of Harwood. Nelson's magic was not quite so apparent on the third afternoon but he still shot 71 to be even with Rafferty, 70, at the 54-hole mark. Harwood, 69, remained in third place at 209. Ian Baker-Finch and defending champion Rodger Davis were well in contention, four and five off the pace, respectively. Davis set the course buzzing during the third round with five birdies in the first six holes, but a bogey at the ninth, a double bogey on No. 12 and another bogey on No. 13 undid his fine work on the front nine.

Baker-Finch and Davis both mounted early challenges during the final round but it was Wayne Grady, with a magnificent six-under-par 66, who slipped into outright third place ahead of Harwood and Davis, who shared fourth at 283, five under par.

Rafferty could have made life easier for himself had he not made a double bogey at the 71st hole to drop one shot behind Nelson. However, an immaculate four iron to the green on the 18th and a birdie putt ensured the playoff.

14. The Asia/Japan Tour

America's tattered prestige on the international golf scene got a boost in Asia in 1987. Pros from the United States prevailed on both the year-long Japan Tour and the much-shorter Asia Circuit in unprecedented ways during those seasons and the team representing the U.S. PGA Tour made off with the Kirin Cup in the World Championship of Golf late in the year in Japan.

By far the most impressive American in Asia in 1987 was 32-year-old David Ishii, a native-born Hawaiian who went through the first-class University of Houston collegiate golf program. A virtual unknown before now in international golf circles, Ishii had pretty much limited his play outside of Hawaii to annual trips to Japan, the land of his heritage, and increasingly-extensive campaigning beginning in 1980. His game steadily improved. He won once in 1985, twice in 1986, but few observers, if any, expected what happened in 1987.

Playing a full schedule the first year the Japan PGA included non-resident tour players on its official money list, Ishii outplayed veteran Masashi (Jumbo) Ozaki, one of Japan's all-time golf greats, in the final weeks and seized the No. 1 position in those cash standings for the year, winning ¥86,554,421 (or $618,246 by a conversion average for the year of 140 yen.) He won six times — the Sapporo Tokyu and Mizuno early, the prestigious Japan PGA Championship in July and the Casio World Open and the shared Japan Series in late fall to wrap up the money-winning race. David, who has never held playing privileges on the U.S. tour, would seem to be deserving of a special exemption to get his shot in his home country.

The best-ever performances by Americans as a whole on the Asia Circuit was more of a group display, although Brian Tennyson and Jim Hallet stood out from the rest. Tennyson, one of nine children in an Indiana family, won the Philippine and Indian Opens, the only double winner of the Asia season, while Hallet, a highly-touted New Englander who has yet to achieve full potential, was such a consistent high finisher that he won the overall circuit championship without a victory. Mark Aebli, a double winner in 1985, was the other U.S. victor in 1987, scoring a rare triumph by a non-Taiwanese in the China Open. So well did the American contingent perform that, besides the three victories, U.S. players finished among the top six in all 10 of the Asia Circuit tournaments. Incidentally, Tennyson will be putting his game to the PGA Tour test in 1988, having qualified for playing privileges in late 1987.

Australians Terry Gale (Malaysian Open), Peter Fowler (Singapore Open) and Wayne Smith (Indonesian Open) matched the American victory total, Ian Woosnam launched his remarkable season with a solid victory in the United Airlines Hong Kong Open, Chen Tze Ming nailed the front end of an Asia/Japan double by winning in Thailand, Isao Aoki began his four-victory season with the Dunlop International title and Chen Liang Hsi gave Taiwan two wins and himself a first with his triumph in the Korea Open.

In Japan, the major developments beyond the emergence of David Ishii as a major player involved the continuation of the powerful comeback of Jumbo Ozaki and the surprising comedown of Tsuneyuki (Tommy) Nakajima. Ozaki, 40, who hadn't been a dominant factor in Japan since the late 1970s until he ran off four victories in 1986 and finished second on the money list, maintained that strong pace in 1987 with early-season victories in the rich Chunichi Crowns and Fuji-Sankei back to back and a fall win in the Jun Classic. He led the money race much of the year and could blame a couple of inexplicably-bad finishes for his failure to win the money race for the first time in a decade. Still, he won ¥76,981,199 ($549,866 by our conversion). Nobody else was close to the top.

Even though his three victories pushed his career total to 52, Ozaki yielded the leadership in that department to Isao Aoki, Japan's best-known player because of his international stature. Although Aoki placed fifth on the money list, playing frequently abroad, he hung up four victories, running his career count to 53. Besides the Dunlop, the 45-year-old Aoki won three times in the latter half of the season — the Japan Open, the All Nippon Airways Open and, with David Ishii, the snow-abbreviated Japan Series.

Nakajima played only about half of the Japan Tour season, but still had a poor season by his lofty standards of the earlier 1980s. He won just once — the Tokai Classic — for his 39th title and the 32-year-old international player placed 13th on the final money list, a far cry from his usual position, with just a third of his ¥90,000,000 winnings in 1986. The two places on that money list behind Ishii and Ozaki were claimed by Hajime Meshiai and Masahiro Kuramoto, both with just under ¥50,000,000. While each of them won only once in official events — Meshiai the Hiroshima Open and Kuramoto the Maruman in tour record fashion — they were in the thick of contention time and again all year. The only multiple winner in Japan in 1987 besides Ishii, Ozaki and Aoki was Katsunari Takahashi, who beat Ozaki in the finals of the Japan Match Play Championship after winning the 36-hole Setonaikai and Kuzuha tournaments in succession in the early season.

As usual, foreign visitors fared well in Japan. Besides Ishii, seven other non-Japanese pros scored victories in 1987. The home forces were shut out in the three big-money events in the late season as Graham Marsh scored his 23rd victory in Japan in the Taiheiyo Club Masters and Craig Stadler took the Dunlop Phoenix, the richest of them all, followed by Ishii's win in the Casio. Although Japan evened the ABC Cup — U.S. vs Japan series at eight team victories apiece, Andy Bean spiced his late-season resurgence with an easy capture of the individual title and money. Brian Jones (Mitsubishi Galant) and Ian Baker-Finch (Polaroid Cup Golf Digest) were other Australian winners, ageless Lu Liang Huan took the season-opening Shizuoka Open and Chen Tze Ming completed his aforementioned double by taking the Pepsi-Ube. Six Japanese pros scored their initial wins — Satoshi Higashi (Yomiuri Sapporo Beer), Tadao Nakamura (Niigata), Nobuo Serizawa (Nikkei Cup), Masanobu Kimura (Kansai Open), Noboru Sugai (Suntory Open) and Isamu Sugita (Daikyo Open). Serizawa and Kimura had otherwise strong seasons, too, and should do well in future years.

The leading non-winner of the season had to be Hiroshi Makino, who wound up in three playoffs and was a loser in all of them. His consolation was almost ¥40,000,000 and eighth place on the money list. And, finally, a note for the future. Kazuya Nakajima, 23-year-old brother of Tsuneyuki, led the qualifiers for the 1988 Japan Tour with a solid 289. Have we another dynasty in the fashion of the Ozaki's in the making?

Here, in detail, starting with the 10-event Asia Circuit, is 1987 in the Far East:

San Miguel Philippines Open—US$100,000
Winner: Brian Tennyson

The San Miguel Philippines Open sported a surprise as it returned as the official opener of the 1987 Asia Circuit after a three-year absence because of the country's instability and inability to stage the Far East's oldest national championship properly. Nobody outside of his immediate family would have picked 24-year-old Brian Tennyson to win the venerable event at Wack Wack Golf and Country Club near Manila in late February. Even though the Indiana pro had won at Little Rock, Arkansas, in an event on the TPA Tour, a maverick circuit populated by lesser lights, he had never played in Asia before and had to play in the tournament qualifier just to get into the field.

Nobody was more surprised than Tennyson himself when he wound up the winner that Sunday. He had started the day three strokes off the pace and his one-under-par 71 and even-par 288 did not seem to be the stuff of which undisputed victories are made. However, the top three men after 54 holes failed to exploit their advantages. American Jim Hallet and native son Antolin Fernando faded to 74s and the veteran Chen Tze Ming let victory slip from his grasp on the final hole.

Chen, a six-time winner on the Asia Circuit since 1980, had jumped into the lead Saturday, putting a three-under 69 onto the scoreboard beside earlier rounds of 74 and 71 for 214 and a two-stroke lead over Hallet and Fernando. Tennyson and fellow American Tom Pernice were next at 217. Brian birdied the 17th hole, parred the 18th for his 71 and adjourned to the practice green, figuring his best hope was a playoff out of the last group finishing behind him. Chen needed only a par to win, but hooked his tee shot into an unplayable position in the woods along the 18th fairway. He couldn't reach the green after his drop (one-shot penalty), left his pitch well short of the hole and missed the tying putt. His 75 and 289 still gave him second place, a shot in front of Hallet and Fernando.

Wack Wack exacted its usual toll of high scoring. Only three players were in the 60s in the opening round — Pat Horgan and Pete Izumigawa at 68, Billy Ray Brown at 69 — and nobody bettered 70 Friday when Izumigawa kept his share of the lead with 74 for 142. Chen and Eddie Bagtas, with 69s Saturday, had the last two sub-70 scores of the week.

United Airlines Hong Kong Open—US$150,000
Winner: Ian Woosnam

Great international players such as Peter Thomson and Greg Norman have used victories in the early-year Hong Kong Open as springboards to brilliant seasons, but nothing to compare to what Ian Woosnam brought to pass in 1987 after his four-stroke victory in the United Airlines-sponsored Hong Kong Open on the first of March, a day short of his 29th birthday. The recitation of the other feats during the Welshman's fabulous year can be found elsewhere in this volume, but Woosnam got it all started in solid fashion at the Royal Hong Kong Golf Club, leading a blanket finish of British/Irish pros and becoming Britain's first winner ever in the 30-year-old tournament.

Woosnam positioned himself adequately with a one-under-par 70 in good weather the first day as 19 players broke par, led by New Zealand's Frank Nobilo with 67 and Ireland's David Feherty with 68. Woosnam overtook Feherty to share the lead at 141 Friday when the weather was the big story. Rain and chilling winds drove the scores up, one player off the course and, he admitted later, almost did the same to Feherty. Only Americans Gregg Twiggs and Billy Ray Brown with 70s broke par in the miserable conditions. Nobilo fell three shots behind thanks to a triple-bogey at the par-three fifth hole, where he had to hack three times at a ball plugged in rough.

On Saturday, "the first time I've played in decent weather here," Woosnam led a heavy assault on Royal Hong Kong with a six-under 65 and roared into a three-stroke lead. His was one of 19 sub-par scores on the day of much-improved weather, the 65 highlighted by an eagle chip-in at the par-five ninth and four birdies. Feherty shot 68 and held second place at 209, a shot in front of Scotland's Sam Torrance and Northern Ireland's Ronan Rafferty, who shot his 68 despite a double-bogey start. Woosnam established his strength Sunday with birdies on the first two holes and, although taking four bogeys during the round, promptly closed the door each time with follow-up birdies. With 69, he finished nine under par at 275. Feherty holed a 15-foot par-saver on the final green to salvage a runnerup tie with Torrance, who shot 69 to David's 70. Rafferty took fourth place with 72—282, the $7,500 prize money destined to help with the expenses of his wedding the following Saturday. Said Woosnam afterward: "Hopefully, it will be a big year for me."

Benson & Hedges Malaysian Open—US$150,000
Winner: Terry Gale

Over the years, the Malaysian Open has become the particular province of the Australians. Eight times since 1974, one Aussie or another has walked off with that title on the Asia Circuit. In 1987, with fellow Aussie Stewart Ginn the defending champion, it was Terry Gale winning the Benson & Hedges-sponsored tournament at Subang Golf Club in Kuala Lumpur, his third Malaysian victory in five years and his fifth triumph on that Far East tour. The latest victory was the toughest, as the 40-year-old pro had to go an extra hole before vanquishing American Greg Twiggs, a non-exempt player off the U.S. tour.

Gale jumped off with a share of the first-round led. He made three of his six birdies on the last four holes of the par-72 course where he won the 1983 championship for a 66, joining Canadian Jim Rutledge at the top, two shots in front of 1984 winner Lu Chien Soon of Taiwan. Lu's countryman

Chen Tze Ming took charge Friday with a 66 of his own for 138 and a one-stroke lead over Jeff Maggert and two over Brian Mogg and Steen Tinning of Sweden as Gale stumbled to a 75 and Rutledge to a 78. Gale bounced back in sweltering heat Saturday and matched Chen's 70 to enter the final round tied with Rudy Lavares of the Philippines at 211, three shots behind the Taiwanese leader.

As happened two Sundays earlier in Manila, Chen failed to hold his lead in the final round. He faded to a 73 and missed a tying putt from seven feet on the 18th green. Twiggs, who had earlier rounds of 71, 72 and 70, posted a 67 ahead of the other contenders Sunday and got into the playoff when Gale bogeyed the last hole for a 69 and his 280. However, Terry shook that off quickly and dropped in his three-foot birdie putt on the first extra hole for the $25,000 victory as Twiggs, who had just learned from his caddy that his wallet was missing, missed from similar range. However, the $16,665 second-place money more than made up for the $79 that disappeared with the wallet.

Thai International Thailand Open—US$100,000
Winner: Chen Tze Ming

A sigh of relief had to be one of Chen Tze Ming's reactions after he captured the Thai International Thailand Open in a sudden-death playoff against a relative unknown in international circles at the mid-March fourth stop on the Asia Circuit. Twice in the three previous tournaments, Chen had let victory escape his grasp from positions of third-round leadership and a late run fell short at Hong Kong in the other event. One of the circuit's strongest players, the 32-year-old pro from Taiwan certainly was due.

However, he had to contend with the unexpected challenge of Somsak Sri-sanga, making the strongest bid ever by a native son in the 24-year history of the Thailand Open, coming closer than the country's best-known player, Sukree Onsham, ever came to landing that title. Somsak shot four solid rounds over the Railway Golf Course at Bangkok, a par-71, 6,827-yard layout, had the lead by a stroke after 54 holes, unprecedented for a Thai, and carried Chen three extra holes before succumbing to the Taiwan veteran.

Big John Jacobs, now 47, the American star of the 1984 Asia Circuit, opened the tournament with 66, tying for the lead with another Yank, Tom Pernice, who birdied five of the first eight holes. Chen opened with 70, Somsak with 69. Pernice faded to 75 Friday in the heat of Bangkok, but Jacobs' 68 kept him in front by two over three 66 shooters — Chen, Isamu Sugita and Gregg Twiggs, the playoff loser to Terry Gale the week before in Malaysia. Another 66, this time by Somsak, changed the leadership picture as the Thai pro moved a stroke ahead of Jacobs (72) and Chen (70) with his 205.

Somsak's brilliant showing attracted the tournament's largest crowd ever for the final round and the popular local favorite gave them their money's worth. He matched strokes with his more experienced opponent in their head-to-head duel Sunday, finally shooting 67 to Chen's 66 for the 272s that brought on the playoff. After they matched pars on the 10th and 11th holes, the decision came at the par-five 12th. Somsak's 20-foot putt for a birdie there stopped just short of the cup, then Chen rolled in a 12-footer for his seventh Asia Circuit win to go with four victories in Japan. Jacobs tied for third at 275 with Frankie Minoza.

Charminar Challenge Indian Open—US$100,000
Winner: Brian Tennyson

Brian Tennyson had no desire to join the expansive ranks of golfers who win once and are never really heard from again, at least as a victor. So, he quickly nailed a second victory on the 1987 Asia Circuit, just a month after his triumph in the season-opening Philippines Open, emerging from a group of American and Canadian contenders to score a three-stroke win in the Charminar Challenge Indian Open at Delhi Golf Club in New Delhi, the alternate-year venue of the championship.

Although North Americans had won six times since 1978 — four from the U.S., a Canadian and a Mexican — the tournament had never experienced a finish that had nary an Asian player in the top nine. Five other Yanks, two Canadians and an Australian followed Tennyson in the final standings as the 24-year-old newcomer from Indiana became the only double winner of 1987 on the Asia Circuit. It should be noted, though, that many of the top Asian players passed up India to compete in the non-tour Rolex Masters in Singapore. Chen Tze Ming, coming off his victory in Thailand, made it two in a row in the Rolex Masters, shooting 274 to beat John Jacobs, the third-place finisher in Thailand, by two shots.

Unlike his win at Manila, which was somewhat of a gift because of a last-hole double-bogey by Chen Tze Ming, Brian Tennyson scored a positive victory at New Dehli. After two rounds, he was eight strokes off the pace. U.S. pro Steve Bowman led the first day at 67 with Australian Peter O'Malley and young Indian amateur David D'Souza at 68, then shared the top spot with O'Malley at 139 at the midpoint.

Tennyson jumped into contention Saturday with a stunning 65 as he hit every green and piled up seven birdies. At 212, he was then just two shots off the lead and behind only four countrymen — Mike Cunning, the leader at 210, and Jim Hallet, Greg Bruckner and Bowman at 211. Bowman had shot 72, the others 68. By the turn Sunday, Tennyson had moved into a first-place tie with Hallet and his steady, one-under-par back nine moved him eight under par for the distance and the three-stroke winner over Cunning and Hallett. Bruckner finished at 284 and Bowman, O'Malley, Canadians Jim Rutledge and Rick Gibson and Yankee Jeff Maggert at 286.

Shizuoka Open—¥35,000,000
Winner: Lu Liang Huan

At an age at which his contemporaries in other parts of the world no longer are competitive on the regular tours against the younger stars, 50-year-old Lu Liang Huan, the long-time Taiwanese standout, bowled over a representative field of Japan Tour regulars and captured the season-opening Shizuoka Open at Hamaoka. The popular Mr. Lu fired a six-under-par 66 in the final round to grab the title by two strokes with his final 280. It was his first win in a decade in Japan, the last one, ironically, in the 1977 Shizuoka Open.

After veteran Haruo Yasuda opened the tournament with a 67, then disappeared from contention, Nobumitsu Yuhara and Tomishige Ikeda held sway for two days, first at 142 after rounds of 71-71 and 69-73 respectively and then at 212 after both shot 70s on Saturday. At that point, Toru Nakamura trailed by a stroke after a third-round 68 and Lu shared fourth place at 214 with Brett Ogle, Naomichi Ozaki and Kakuji Matsui. Lu's rounds were 71-74-69. Then came the clincher. The little Taiwanese veteran, an occasional international player in his younger days, produced seven birdies and took a single bogey enroute to the 21st victory of his career and 12th in Japan.

Singapore Open—US$125,000
Winner: Peter Fowler

The second half of the "doubleheader" at Singapore Island Country Club's Bukit course — the Singapore Open — produced final-round excitement that was lacking the week before in the opening, non-tour Rolex Masters when Chen Tze Ming took command early the last day and scored a breezing two-stroke victory. A virtual horde of players battled down the stretch the following Sunday, three wound up in a 72-hole deadlock and Australian Peter Fowler emerged with the title three playoff holes later.

Actually, Fowler was in position Sunday morning for an easy victory. After sharing the first-round lead at 66 with Taiwan's Kuo Chi Hsiung and Hsu Sheng San, two long-time stars of Asia golf, and American Art Russell, Peter seesawed in the next two rounds. Kuo, a nine-time winner on the Asia Circuit whose last victories came in 1980, fired another 66 Friday and took a two-stroke lead over Yank Jim Hallet and three over ultimate playoff participant Jeff Maggert. Back came Fowler Saturday with the week's best round — 65 — and he jumped three shots in front at 201. He had seven birdies and a bogey on the par-71 course. Kuo shot 72 and fell back into a tie for second with Maggert at 204.

When the 27-year-old Fowler faltered in the early going Sunday, four others took up the challenge. With just four holes remaining Kuo, Hsu, Maggert and Ho Ming Chung, another former circuit winner, were all in the fight with Fowler for the title. Ho and Kuo lost ground in the finish, both shooting 71s. Maggert, aided by an early eagle, had 70 for his 274, tying Hsu, who was already in with 68 in his bid for his eighth Asia Circuit victory. Fowler struggled to 73, good enough to qualify for the extra innings, then righted his game in the playoff. However, he needed a little charity at the first extra hole in the form of a missed three-foot birdie putt by Maggert, the little-known American, after Peter had missed from longer range. Nobody had it close at the next hole, the par-three seventh, and all took pars. Then, at the par-four eighth, Fowler hit the green from the trees after hooking his drive and dropped the winning, 15-foot birdie putt. Hsu was then out of it after a bad approach and poor chip and Maggert lipped out his birdie putt. It was Fowler's first Asia Circuit win and the first victory by an Australian at Singapore since Terry Gale's win in 1978.

KSB Setonaikai Open—¥20,600,000
Kuzuha Kokusai—¥18,000,000
Winner: Katsunari Takahashi

Katsunari Takahashi picked off two victories that don't count in the official record book but did in the bank account when he won the 36-hole KSB Setonaikai Open and the Kuzuha Kokusai back to back. In the Setonaikai at Shido Country Club, Takahashi had rounds of 69 and 71, his 140 beating Minoru Nakamura, Mike Harwood of Australia and Yurio Akitomi by two strokes. A week later, Katsunari held off a second-round charge by Australian Brian Jones to win the long-standing Kuzuha Kokusai on the public Kuzuha Golf Course. It was his 11th victory in Japan. He had opened in a four-way tie for the lead at 65 with Noboru Sugai, Futoshi Irino, Shozo Miyamoto and Yoshihiro Funatogawa, then followed with a 66 at the Western Japan city of Hirakata for the winning 131, just enough as Jones charged in with a 63 for 132 to grab second place from five other players. Takahashi won ¥7,600,000 (some $50,000) in the two events.

Indonesian Open—US$100,000
Winner: Wayne Smith

Australians claimed three championships on the Asia Circuit for the first time in 14 years when Wayne Smith followed countryman Peter Fowler's victory at Singapore with his first tour triumph in the Indonesian Open the next Sunday in early April. Terry Gale, one of the most successful of all of the Aussies who have played on the Asia Circuit, won a month before in Malaysia.

Another Australian — 20-year-old Craig Parry — showed the way in the early rounds. He and Thailand youngster Bunchoon Ruangkit opened the tournament with 66s, a shot ahead of Mark Aebli, a two-time winner in Asia in 1985, and Indonesian pro Maan. Then Parry moved a stroke in front with 70 for 136 as Ruangkit had a 71. Roger Mackay, another Aussie, and Malaysia's Marimuthu Ramayah joined him at 137 and Smith was at 138 after rounds of 68 and 70, joined there by Hikaru Emoto and Frankie Minoza.

Smith came to the fore Saturday, shooting a four-under-par 66 over the Rawamangun course of Jakarta Golf Club to vault two strokes in front of Americans Billy Ray Brown and Jim Hallet, who posted 66 and 67, respectively, for their 206s. Parry had a 72 for 208. The big noise of the day was Steve Bowman's hole-in-one at the seventh. He received $11,500 for the ace and promptly gave $2,000 of it to his Indonesian caddy who had convinced him to hit a six iron instead of a five iron on the money shot.

Hallet, the frequent pursuer but non-winner on the 1987 circuit, gave Smith a strong run for his money Sunday. The American had a fine chance to overtake the Western Australian until he bogeyed the 17th and Smith made a spectacular par from the woods on the hole to widen his gap to three strokes. That gave him a comfortable margin going to the final hole, where he bogeyed for 70 and his final 274. Hallet also shot 70 for his 276. Just as the home folks in Thailand a few weeks earlier, the Indonesian fans had one of their own to pull for in the final round. Sukamdi, the youngest of three golfing brothers, had played solidly all week and made a run at the lead Sunday, eventually taking third place at 277 with his closing, 68.

Republic of China Open—US$140,000
Winner: Mark Aebli

It was a typical Republic of China Open — with one notable exception. The course was long, the weather was bad, the scores were high. That's fairly normal for the tournaments on the Asia Circuit in April in Taiwan over the years. Mark Aebli, a 30-year-old Texan from San Antonio, won the 1987 China Open title and that was quite out of the ordinary. Native sons win in Taiwan almost all of the time. In fact, Aebli was just the second American to win that tournament in its 22-year history. He and fellow Yankee John Jacobs have been the only non-Taiwanese winners since 1973.

Aebli, a relative unknown in his own country but the winner of the Philippine and Hong Kong Opens in Asia in 1985, opened the tournament in front, then didn't regain the lead until the final day when his closing 76 in abysmal weather was good enough to give him a two-stroke victory. His total of 294 was just two over par at the Taoyuan Golf and Country Club course, which measures 7,526 yards and is said to be the longest in Asia and one of the biggest in the world. Its opening par-five hole measures 760 yards.

Mark shot 68 — nine birdies — in cloudy, drizzly weather Thursday and few persons then thought that it would turn out to be the only round in the 60s that week-end. He went to the second round with a two-stroke lead over fellow American Mike Cunning, but 48 players were at par or better. When Aebli stumbled to a 78 in gusty winds Friday, Lu Chien Soon of Taiwan and another American, Kevin Cashman, took over first place with five-under-par 143s, a shot in front of Steve Bowman and Hsieh Yu Shu. Bowman and Pat Horgan had 70s, the day's best scores.

The rains continued Saturday and Lu retained a share of the lead with a par-74 round for 217, tied with Bowman of the U.S., who shot 73. Aebli began his move with a 72 that lifted him just a stroke off the lead, where he was deadlocked with Hsieh. Again, 70 was the day's best score, this one by Kuo Chi Hsiung. Conditions went from poor to miserable Sunday with strong winds and heavy rain making play extremely difficult. In such circumstances, Aebli's 76 for the winning 294 was a good score. In fact, nobody even matched par Sunday and the only 75 hoisted yet another American, Mike Standly, into a second-place tie with Hsieh at 296. Aebli actually didn't have the victory secure until he made his only birdie of the terrible day with a 20-foot putt on the 18th green. The 294 winning score was the second highest in tournament history, exceeded only by 295 posted at Linkou International in 1983.

Pocari Sweat Open—¥40,000,000
Winner: Kinpachi Yoshimura

A playoff led Kinpachi Yoshimura to the third victory of his pro career on the Japan Tour. A par on the first extra hole enabled him to defeat Yoshiyuki Isomura, who had held or shared the lead through the first three rounds. Isomura began the tournament at Hiroshima's Hakuryuko Country Club with a 66 and a one-stroke lead over six other players. Yoshiyuki needed only 12 putts to negotiate the last nine holes. He fell into a six-way tie for first place Friday when he shot 70 for 136. Among the other 136 shooters were Yoshimura and 1984 Pocari Sweat winner Tateo Ozaki.

A third-round 67 isolated Isomura in front at 203, 10 under par, and Yoshimura had second place to himself after a 68. Yoshimura's 70 in the final round was enough to forge the tie at 274 with the 30-year-old Isomura, an eight-year veteran seeking his second tour victory. They went to the 18th hole for the playoff and Yoshimura bagged the title with a three-foot par putt as Isomura missed his for par from seven feet.

Maekyung (Korea) Open—US$130,000
Winner: Chen Liang Hsi

One of the lesser lights of the usual strong contingent of Asia Circuit players from Taiwan sparkled in Korea in mid-April. Chen Liang Hsi, a 28-year-old non-winner from the island nation, kept his country's recent hold on the Maekyung (Korea) Open title intact with his three-stroke victory at the Nam Seoul Country Club, following in the recent footsteps of Tsao Chien Teng, another lightly-regarded pro, and Chen Tze Chung, the last two victors in Seoul. It was the eighth Korean victory by a Taiwannese player since 1975.

Until Chen put on his late charge, all indications were that American Brian Tennyson was headed for his third Asia Circuit victory of 1987, a triple that had not been accomplished since Lu Hsi Chuen did it in 1979 and 1980. The first round ended with six players bunched in front with two-under-par 70s, neither Tennyson nor Chen among them. But the American took charge Friday with the week's best round — a 65 — his 137 staking him to a three-stroke lead over fellow Yank Jim Hallet, who shot a pair of 70s. Tennyson slipped to a 74 Saturday, but retained first place by a shot over Chen, Kim Sung Ho of Korea and Frankie Minoza of the Philippines, Kim and Minoza firing 68s and Chen a 70. Tennyson was five under par at 211.

The title battle remained tight on the front nine Sunday. Chen was just one under for the round at the turn after birdies at the first and fourth holes and a bogey at the third. Then, he turned it on with four birdies on the back nine for a 67 and his victorious 279. Tennyson shot a respectable 71 and Kim a 70 to tie for second place at 282. Hallet also had a 70 and tied for fourth with Jeff Hart at 283. The finish virtually clinched the seasonal circuit title for Hallet. Chen collected $21,500 for his victory.

Bridgestone Aso Open—¥35,000,000
Winner: Norio Mikami

Norio Mikami, 40, had won only once in his 16 years on the Japan Tour and that 1979 victory came in a tournament — the Nihon Kokudo Keikaku Summers — that no longer exists. He landed a second title in the Bridgestone Aso Open, never out of the lead after the second round on his way to 280, eight under par, and a four-stroke victory.

Three men who have been around but have never won — Shuichi Sano, 39; Takayoshi Nishikawa, 37, and Hiroshi Haihata — had a moment of glory by sharing the first-round lead with 68s at the Aso Golf Club, a 7,030-yard course. Then, Mikami took over. He shot 67 for 136 and a three-stroke lead over David Ishii, warming up for his big season, and Taisei Inagaki. Makami, who finished a mere 108th on the 1986 money list in Japan, had six birdies and a bogey enroute his 67 while Ishii ran off eight birdies and two bogeys for his 66. Makino stumbled on the front nine Saturday with three bogeys and a double-bogey, blowing his lead, but three birdies on the back nine enabled him to finish the day in a three-way tie at 210 with Ishii (71) and Yoshitaka Yamamoto (73-69-68). Then, Makino got the break he needed to pull away again when he made a hole-in-one at third hole Sunday. He went on to a 70 and the 280, Ishii fading to a 74 and Yamamoto to a 75. Sano, one of the first-round co-leaders, tied Ishii for second at 284 and Yamamoto finished in a tie for fourth with Brian Jones.

Dunlop International Open—¥35,000,000
Winner: Isao Aoki

The regulars who had campaigned through the arduous travel grind of the first nine stops on the Asia Circuit had to step aside for one of Asia's greatest players in late April when the tour reached its final stop in Japan. They became bit players at Ibaraki Golf Club as the talented Isao Aoki reached a landmark in his brilliant career in the Dunlop International Open with his 50th victory.

Besides closing out the Asia Circuit season, the Dunlop is the first important stop on the long and lucrative Japan Tour. Thus, the field is weighted with the best Japanese and other international players of greater repute than most of the Asia Circuit travelers. At Ibaraki Golf Club, players of that stripe took over, led by Aoki, who moved in front the second day, threatened to make it a runaway the third day and barely survived the fourth day.

Isao opened with 69 at Ina, as did 12 other players, all of them trailing only little-known Yoshihisa Kousaka at 66 and Australian Brian Jones at 68. Then, Aoki turned the tables completely. His five-under 67 shot him three strokes in front of Tsuneyuki (Tommy) Nakajima. Another shot back at 140 were David Ishii, Terry Gale and four others. With birdies on the last two holes, Isao widened his lead to five strokes after 65 holes with a 69 for 205. The strong finish distanced him from Yoshitaka Yamamoto, who at one point in the round was just one stroke back. Yamamoto's 70 tied him for second at 210 with Australian Rodger Davis. Nakajima, with 72, slipped to 211 with five others.

Aoki struggled to match par Sunday and eventually made par from the trees on the final hole for that 72, a 277 and a one-stroke victory over Nakajima, who had a fine 67, and Yamamoto, who shot 68 for his 278. Nakajima actually caught Aoki with an eagle at the 14th hole, but lost a stroke coming in.

American Jim Hallet shot 288 and tied for 23rd place, but easily claimed the overall Asia Circuit title over Chen Tze Ming and Brian Tennyson, both 1987 Asia winners, because of his consistently-high finishes.

Chunichi Crowns—¥90,000,000
Winner: Masashi Ozaki

You might say it was a matter of keeping up with the Aoki's for Masashi (Jumbo) Ozaki. One week after Isao Aoki scored his 50th career victory in the Dunlop, Ozaki reached the same lofty total with a resounding win in the Chunichi Crowns, for almost 30 years the kingpin event of the early season on the Japan Tour. Ozaki fired a pair of 66s in the final two rounds of the ¥90,000,000 tournament and ran away to a six-stroke victory at Nagoya Golf Club. He was 12 under par at 268 at the finish in winning the Chunichi Crowns for the first time.

Masaji Kusakabe, another Japanese veteran, drew most of the attention in the early rounds. He opened with 66 and shared the first-round lead with Futoshi Irino and Australian Ian Baker-Finch, then jumped to a three-shot margin with a five-under 65 Friday, picking up four of his five birdies on the back nine. With a 69 Saturday, Masaji retained the lead, but by just two strokes over the charging Ozaki, 200 to 202, with Baker-Finch at 203 and American stars Lanny Wadkins and Scott Simpson with Hajime Meshiai at 204. The winds were up Sunday, but they didn't faze Ozaki, who virtually wrapped up the victory with four birdies on the front nine as Kusakabe faded toward his final 77 and ninth-place finish. Masahiro Kuramoto also shot 66 Sunday to join a four-way tie for second at 274 with Baker-Finch (71), Aoki (68) and Yoshitaka Yamamoto (69).

Fuji-Sankei Classic—¥60,000,000
Winner: Masashi Ozaki

Jumbo Ozaki's resurgence as a dominant player on the Japan Tour began with his first of four 1986 victories in the Fuji-Sankei Classic at the Kawana Hotel's Fuji course at Ito. Upon his return there in 1987, he doubled from two directions — winning the tournament for a second year in a row with his second victory in succession on the 1987 circuit. Again, as in the Chunichi Crowns, Ozaki came from behind to win, this time by two strokes with his nine-under-par 275.

His brother, Tateo (Jet) Ozaki, had a piece of the first-round lead as he and Seiji Ebihara posted strong 65s, heading Toru Nakayama by one and Hajime Meshiai and Ikuo Shirhama by two. Ebihara followed with 69 Friday and at 134 led Toru Nakamura, Tsukasa Watanabe and Meshiai by two shots as Tateo Ozaki shot 72 for 137. Nakamura took over Saturday with a bogey-free 69 for 205 and a one-shot lead over Jumbo Ozaki, who produced a 66 for the second Saturday in a row. Australian veteran Graham Marsh also entered the picture Saturday with 67 for 207 and Ebihara dropped into a fouth-place tie at 208 with Meshiai and Hsieh Min Nan. The battle Sunday developed between Ozaki and Marsh as Nakamura fell back to 75 and a tie for third with Brian Jones. Marsh, mixing four birdies with three bogeys, had the edge on Jumbo until the Japanese star eagled the par-five 16th and followed with a birdie at the 17th for a closing 69 and the two-stroke victory.

Japan Match Play Championship—¥40,000,000
Winner: Katsunari Takahashi

Katsunari Takahashi spoiled Jumbo Ozaki's bid to become the first man to win three consecutive Japan Tour tournaments, but it took 37 holes in the finals of the Japan Match Play Championship to do it. Takahashi, a winner for a third time in 1987, birdied the first extra hole of his finals match against Ozaki to win the prestigious title for the second time in three years. That birdie followed one by Ozaki at the 36th hole to keep the match alive at Mito Golf Club, a par-72 course northeast of Tokyo.

After tight victories over Seiichi Kanai and Masahiro Kuramoto in the first two rounds, Takahashi bulled his way decisively to the finals with a 4-and-3 win over Saburo Fujiki and a 6-and-5 rout of Tadao Nakamura. Ozaki's toughest match came in the semi-finals, in which he outlasted Hsieh Min Nan, the Taiwanese veteran, 1 up. In his earlier matches, Jumbo defeated Taisei Inagaki, 2 and 1; Yasuhiro Funatogawa, 5 and 4, and Yoshitaka Yamamoto, 3 and 2. Hsieh had ousted Isao Aoki, four-time winner of the Match Play, 3 and 2, and Nakamura had eliminated Tsuneyuki Nakajima, the 1983 and 1986 victor, 1 up, in the quarter-finals.

The victory, worth ¥10,000,000, was Takahashi's 12th of his career.

Pepsi-Ube—¥45,000,000
Winner: Chen Tze Ming

Chen Tze Ming, one of the few players who competes regularly on both the Asia and Japan circuits, became the only man to win on both tours in 1987 when he captured the Pepsi-Ube at Ajisu in late May. It was Chen's fifth victory in Japan and his second in three years in the Pepsi-Ube. This time, though, it required a late rally and a playoff birdie to land the title at Ube Country Club.

The fine Taiwanese player, who won the Thailand Open in mid-May and finished second in the overall Asia Circuit standings, did not become a factor in the Pepsi-Ube until the very end. Tsuneyuki Nakajima, winless for the year but still considered Japan's No. 1 player, opened the tournament in front with his five-under-par 67. Jumbo Ozaki was among four men at 68 and Chen among three at 69. Hiroshi Makino edged a stroke in front Friday, his 70-66—136 giving him a shot over Nakajima (70). Tsuneyuki regained a share of first place with Hajime Meshiai and Namio Takasu Saturday.

All were at 208, Takasu after shooting 65. Chen was then three strokes off the pace after rounds of 69-72-70.

None of the leaders could hold on Sunday. Makino inched back into the lead during the round, only to be caught at the end by Chen and his 67, the best round of the day. Makino finished with 69, then lost the playoff when Tze Ming sank a four-foot birdie putt on the first extra hole, winning in overtime just as he had in Thailand.

Mitsubishi Galant—¥56,000,000
Winner: Brian Jones

The Mitsubishi Galant tournament had a carbon-copy tone to it. Australian Brian Jones, a regular in Japan for years, duplicated the feat of Chen Tze Ming the previous week. Just as Chen won the Pepsi-Ube for the second time in three years, so did Jones at Pine Lake Golf Club at Nishiwaki in the Mitsubishi Galant. It was much easier for Brian in 1987 than in 1985 when he had to go four extra holes before prevailing. This time, he broke from a duel with third-round co-leader Koichi Suzuki and registered a three-stroke victory at five-under-par 283.

After little-known Takashi Kubota led the first day with 68, Suzuki surged into first place Friday with a seven-birdie 66 for 138, ahead of Jones by two strokes at that point. After 54 holes, the two men were tied at 211 and at least four strokes ahead of everybody else, setting up the two-man battle Sunday. They matched strokes until Jones birdied the par-four 15th and Suzuki bogeyed it. Suzuki also bogied the last hole for 75, while the Aussie finished with a par 72 after four birdies and four bogeys over the 7,034-yard course. Nobuo Serizawa closed with 71 to tie Suzuki for second place. The win was the fifth for Jones in Japan and his sixth in Asia over the years.

Tohoku Classic—¥42,000,000
Winner: Seiichi Kanai

Seiichi Kanai reestablished the winning touch for the Japanese in the Tohoku Classic after foreigners held sway for two weeks on the Japan Circuit. The veteran Kanai, 46, fired a brilliant 65 in the final round at Nishi Sendai Country Club at Miyagimachi and picked off a two-shot victory with his 13-under-par 275. Although it was his 15th win, his last previous one had been his only one out of the country in the 1986 Hong Kong Open.

It was a good week for the older pros on the Japan Tour. Hiroshi Ishii, also 46, and Kinpachi Yoshimura shot 66s Thursday and shared the first-round lead, a stroke ahead of Tsukasa Watanabe and Tsutomu Irie. Then, Ishii, a nine-title holder from his long career, moved in front alone Friday. His 71 for 137 put him a shot in front of Yoshimura, Irie, Pete Izumikawa and Taiichiro Tanaka. But that was all for Ishii. Hajime Meshiai, who was having a strong year, took over the lead Saturday, scoring eagles on two of the par-five holes enroute to a 67, a 10-under-par 206 and a two-shot advantage over Tanaka and Masaji Kusakabe. Kanai was then at 210 after rounds of 71, 69 and 70. He made up ground in a hurry Sunday, ringing up six birdies on the front nine as he surged in front. He eventually made nine birdies and had a pair of bogeys in shooting the winning 65. Meshiai had a 71 for 277, nipping Teruo Sugihara, the 1986 Tohoku winner, by a stroke for second place.

Sapporo Tokyu Open—¥40,000,000
Winner: David Ishii

David Ishii's splendid season moved into high gear in mid-June when he scored his first of six 1987 victories on the Japan Tour in the Sapporo Tokyu Open. Nothing spectacular or particularly indicative of what was to come. David simply put together four solid, sub-par rounds for 276, 12 under par, and a three-stroke triumph, his fourth in Japan.

The 32-year-old American from Hawaii trailed only the first day when long-time tourist Tadami Ueno opened with 65. Ishii was next at 67 and seized the lead Friday with his 68—135, heading Hideto Shigenobu, the runnerup, by three strokes and third-place Teruo Nakamura by four. Ueno shot 77. Even though his third-round score was a higher 70, Ishii widened his margin to six strokes Saturday as all the early challengers fell back. Masahiro Kurmoto moved into second place at 211 with a 69 and Toru Nakamura into third place with 65 for 212.

Although his final margin dropped to three strokes, Ishii was never really threatened Sunday. Nakamura added a 67 to his third-round 65 to slip second place away from Kuramoto, who shot 69. Ishii posted a one-under-par 71 for the 276 and ¥7,200,000 winner's check.

Yomiuri Sapporo Beer Tournament—¥50,000,000
Winner: Satoshi Higashi

Nobody was more surprised than Satoshi Higashi when he wound up as the winner of the Yomiuri Sapporo Beer tournament. After calculating that he needed a 69 in the final round to carry his four-stroke lead to victory, the 26-year-old non-winner shot 75 and still landed his first-ever title, barely surviving the late charges of Graham Marsh and Hajime Meshiai. He edged them by a stroke with his 280 at the East course of Yomiuri Country Club at Hyogo.

Higashi, the initial first-time winner on the circuit in 1987, lay a shot off the lead after the first 18 holes, his 68 positioning him just behind defending champion Koichi Suzuki, who also scored his first tour victory in the Yomiuri; Tadao Nakamura and Tsutomu Irie at 67. Satoshi went ahead to stay Friday, his 67 for 135 jumping him into a three-shot lead over Marsh and Katsunari Takahashi. Using irons off the tees on a rainy Saturday, Higashi put together a 70 and stretched his lead to four strokes over Takahashi (71), five over Meshiai (70) and seven over Marsh (74). Satoshi's game was far from winning calibre Sunday. He had a double-bogey and five bogeys during the shaky round, but fortunately for him his third-round lead was just big enough as Marsh shot 69 and Meshiai 71 for 281s, one stroke too many.

Mizuno Tournament—¥50,000,000
Winner: David Ishii

David Ishii's second victory of the 1987 Japan Tour season was more admirable than exciting. The Hawaiian pro crafted an eight-stroke triumph, the year's biggest margin, in the Mizuno Tournament at Tokinodai Country Club in late June, two weeks after his initial win at Sapporo.

Ishii had the Mizuno in hand almost from the start. With his opening 67, David trailed only Toru Nakamura, the first-round leader with 66 and his closest pursuer, if that can be said of such a decisive victory. Ishii came back with a six-under 66 of his own Friday and spurted three strokes in front at the halfway point. He chipped in for his seventh birdie of the day on the final green to complete the 66. Nakamura eagled the par-five starting hole, but three subsequent bogeys to go with a pair of birdies left him with a 71 and in a tie for second at 137 with Yoshiyuki Isomura. The veteran Nakamura had another eagle and six birdies Saturday but only got a 68 out of it, gaining just a stroke on Ishii, who had four birdies and a bogey enroute to his 69 and 202. Any potential drama in the final round practically ended on the first hole, where Nakamura double-bogeyed. Ishii breezed from there, his two-under 70 producing the 272 and the eight-stroke final margin over Nakamura, who had a 75 and was overtaken by Chen Tze Ming and his 65, the week's best round and one that boosted him into the runnerup tie from 17th place.

Kanto PGA Championship—¥22,500,000
Winner: Naomichi Ozaki

Tsuneyuki Nakajima had won the Kanto PGA Championship the last two years and, when he opened in front with his four-under-par 68 in the 1987 edition of the long-standing title event in Eastern Japan, all signs pointed to another repeat and Nakajima's long-expected first victory of the 1987 season. The signs were dead wrong, as Tsuneyuki shockingly followed with 78s in the other two rounds of the rain-shortened tournament and left the door open for Naomichi Ozaki to notch his initial win of the year.

Ozaki, the youngest of the three touring brothers at 31, had shared the first-round lead with Nakajima. Then, after heavy storms obliterated the second round and brought the 54-hole decision, Naomichi shot 72 for 140 to remain on top, then tied with Nobumitsu Yuhara, who had 69-71 for his 140. They led Seiji Ebihara and Takashi Murakami by two. Sunday saw a continuation of the Ozaki-Yuhara duel, Ozaki prevailing by a stroke, 212 to 213, taking three bogeys against three birdies for his winning 72 at Shimoakima Golf Club over its soggy 7,127 yards. Yuhara's 73—213 placed him second, two strokes in front of Katsunari Takahashi. Ozaki's victory was his sixth on the Japan Tour. Brother Jumbo won that same title 14 years earlier.

Kansai PGA Championship—¥25,000,000
Winner: Yoshitaka Yamamoto

Meanwhile, in Western Japan, the weather was better and they played all four rounds of the Kansai PGA Championship at Tosa Country Club at Yasu. Yoshitaka Yamamoto roared from three strokes off the pace with a final-round 66 that landed him a five-shot victory, the 14th of his career. He had won just once in the four years since he captured his first Kansai PGA title in 1983.

Although he was always close, Yamamoto didn't take the lead until the final day at the par-72 course. The first round belonged to the veteran Yurio Akitomi, who tied the course record with 66 and led Tadeo Nakamura and Tadami Ueno by a stroke, Hideto Shigenobu, Toshiaki Nakagawa and Yamamoto by two. Shigenobu, the 1982 Kansai PGA winner and holder of five tour titles, took a two-stroke lead Friday with 67 for 135. Nakamura was at 137, Yamamoto (70) and Takeshi Nakaya (71-67) at 138. A 70 was good enough for Shigenobu to add a stroke to his lead Saturday. At 205, he had three strokes on Yamamoto going into the final round. However, he crashed with a 74 Sunday and Yamamoto's 14-under-par 274 was five better than the runnersup — Shigenobu and Nakaya, who finished with a 69 for his 279.

Hiroshima Open—¥40,000,000
Winner: Hajime Meshiai

Hajime Meshiai had been knocking at the door frequently during the previous two months. Second twice, third behind a title playoff, fifth. His quest was answered in mid-July in the Hiroshima Open, in which he seized the lead in the third round and carried it to a two-stroke victory, carding a 13-under-par 275 at Hiroshima Golf Club.

Although he didn't move in front until Saturday, the veteran Meshiai actually set things up with a sizzling 63 in the second round. He had started the tournament with 70, five strokes off the lead of Yoshiyuki Isomura, but was just two back after 36 holes and that only because Isomura followed with 66 for 131. A second 70 was enough to give Meshiai a two-stroke lead Saturday, as Isomura slipped to a 74 and into a runnerup tie with Hiroshi Goda at 205. The victory turned on the 16th hole in the final round. After 15, Meshiai was even for the day and Isomura had caught him. But Yoshiyuki double-bogeyed the 16th and Hajime parred in for the victory, fourth of his career. Lu Liang Huan and Tadao Nakamura shot 68s Sunday and tied Isomura for second place.

Japan PGA Championship—¥60,000,000
Winner: David Ishii

David Ishii joined the distinguished ranks of winners of the venerable Japan PGA Championship the first time he tried, capturing the prized title in late July on the Hamano Golf Course at Ichihara on his 32nd birthday. He closed with a 71 for 280, eight under par, and won by a stroke over Brian Jones and Seiichi Kanai, the PGA champion back in 1972.

Ishii's prospects for his third 1987 victory looked reasonably promising after the first round when he found himself in the fancy company of Isao Aoki and Jumbo Ozaki at 73, three shots behind leader Norio Mikami, a 15-year veteran of the Japan Tour with two wins on his record. Mikami's 70 was a shot better than the rounds of Tadao Nakamura and Ichiro Teramoto, the only other pros to break par on the windy Thursday. Ishii got his putter working on Hamano's fast greens, birdied four of the first five holes, shot 67 and moved into a share of the lead Friday with Jones, who had five birdies and a bogey for 68 and his 140. Mikami skied to 77. Ishii inched a shot in front of Jones Saturday, again going without a bogey in posting his 69 for 209. Jones shot 70 for 210, as Yoshikazu Yokoshima jumped into a tie for third with Kanai by firing the week's best score — 65.

Ishii had a bogey Sunday, but his two birdies for 71 brought him the title in the 61-year-old tournament. Jones hung tough until he bogeyed the 17th. Kanai saved par from a water hazard at the 16th and birdied the 18th for 70 to tie Jones for the runnerup spot.

Niigata Open—¥40,000,000
Winner: Tadao Nakamura

Tadao Nakamura finally became a winner on the Japan Tour after 13 years of trying and did so in quite dramatic fashion. No fewer than eight players had a good chance to win the Niigata Open as it was drawing to a close. Nakamura emerged from that pack with the title when he ran in a 10-foot eagle putt on the final green. It gave him a final 71 and an eight-under-par 276 on the Tsukioka course of Forest Country Club in Niigata.

The lead changed hands constantly during the tournament. Hsieh Min Nan and Taisei Inagaki had it the first day as both shot no-bogey 66s. Tateo Ozaki was the 66 shooter Friday and, with his opening 70, it gave him a one-stroke lead over Takao Kage, Shigeru Kawamata and Hiroshi Ishii. Things bunched up even more Saturday. At the end of that round, Namio Takasu, Nakamura and Ishii were on top with 205s, Takasu and Nakamura after 67s and Ishii after a 68. Hsieh Chin Sheng, with a 65, was among four players just a shot off the lead. Nakamura's final-hole eagle Sunday left Hsieh Chin Sheng, David Ishii, Brian Jones and Kazuo Yoshikawa one stroke short. Ishii was the defending champion.

Nikkei Cup/Nakamura Memorial—¥40,000,000
Winner: Nobuo Serizawa

Nobuo Serizawa didn't have to wait as long as Tadao Nakamura did, but he duplicated Nakamura's achievement of the preceding week by capturing his first Japan Tour tournament in the Nikkei Cup/Nakamura Memorial tournament at Seki. Nubuo gained his initial victory in a different manner, roaring from four strokes off the pace in the final round with a five-under-par 66 to eke out his one-shot win.

Until Serizawa came along in the final round, the tournament seemed to be monopolized by the Ozaki brothers. Tateo Ozaki had an eagle, five birdies and a bogey in shooting 65 in the Thursday round and taking a two-shot lead over Teruo Nakamura and Yoshihisa Iwashita. Then, older brother, Masashi (Jumbo) Ozaki jumped in. The defending champion, with two 1987 wins already to his credit, had opened innocuously with a 72, but rebounded Friday with a bogey-less 64 to tie Nakamura (69) and Masahiro Kuramoto (67) at 136, as Tateo Ozaki shot 73 for 138. Jumbo Ozaki's 71 in the third round put him a stroke in front of the youngest brother, Naomichi (71-68-69), and Yoshinori Mizumaki (72-67-69) and two shots ahead of other brother, Tateo (71), and Kuramoto (73). Serizawa started fast Sunday with birdies on the first two holes. He had five more and a bogey before putting his victory at risk with a second bogey at the last hole. However, Jumbo and Naomichi Ozaki and Masahiro Shiota all fell one stroke short at 278.

Maruman Open—¥60,000,000
Winner: Masahiro Kuramoto

Masahiro Kuramoto ended the frustrations of a winless season by turning the record book of the Japan Tour into a shambles at the Maruman Open. Scoring the first wire-to-wire victory of the 1987 season, Kuramoto set new all-time marks for 36, 54 and 72 holes in a brilliant display of shotmaking at the Higashi Matsuyama Country Club course, a relatively-short, 6,748-yard layout, in the town of the same name. It was the 19th tour victory for the 31-year-old pro.

It went this way: FIRST ROUND — an eagle, six birdies, no bogeys and a 64, one-shot lead over Yoshiyuki Isomura. SECOND ROUND — eleven birdies, a bogey on the 18th hole, first of tournament, and a 62 — 126. The 18-under-par score for 36 holes was a record. Kuramoto's lead was then seven with Naomichi Ozaki the runnerup after 67-66—133. THIRD ROUND — six birdies, a bogey and a 67 — 193. The 23-under-par score for 54 holes set another record. The lead grew to nine strokes, then over Hajime Meshiai, who shot 67 for 202. Jumbo Ozaki was at 203 after a 66. FOURTH ROUND — two birdies, a bogey and a 71 — 264. The 24-under-par total established yet another mark for the circuit, exceeding the old record by a stroke. The 23-under had most recently been shot by Toru Nakamura in the 1984 Japan Series. Ozaki, the defending champion, followed his 66 with a final 65, yet with a 20-under par score of 268 he still lost by four strokes.

KBC Augusta—¥50,000,000
Winner: Saburo Fujiki

Although in quite different fashion, Saburo Fujiki followed Masahiro Kuramoto's lead when the Japan Tour moved to Kyushu Shima Country Club for the KBC Augusta tournament in late August. As Kuramoto was prior to the Maruman Open, Fujiki had experienced a winless 1987; in fact, he had not won on the circuit for three years. He ended the dry spell with a come-from-behind rally and some unintended help from third-round-lead Tateo Ozaki, scoring a two-stroke victory with his 14-under-par 274. It was the seventh win of his career.

Yoshitaka Yamamota took the first-round lead on the strength of a 65-foot eagle putt on the first hole, shooting a 65 to start a stroke in front of leading money-winner David Ishii. Neither player took a bogey. Kuramoto, still riding a hot streak, joined Fujiki in the second-round lead, adding a 67 to his opening 69 for 136. Saburo had the same scores in reverse order. Yamamoto shot 73, slipping into a third-place tie with Ishii, Hajime Meshiai and Tateo Ozaki at 138. Ozaki, another prominent pro seeking his initial win of 1987, climbed a stroke into the lead Saturday when he shot a six-birdie, one-bogey 67 and Fujiki and Kuramoto fired 70s for 206s.

A new Japan Tour record was set, then matched in the final round, but it didn't affect the two men battling for the title. Both Toru Nakamura and Tsuneyuki Nakajima had strings of seven consecutive birdies as they shot 63 and 64, respectively, to join a four-way tie for third place with Meshiai and Yoshima Niizeki. In the title fight, Fujiki shot a solid 68 and got the lead and the victory as Ozaki took three bogeys and scored a 71 for 276.

Kanto Open—¥30,000,000
Winner: Yoshikazu Yokoshima

The Kanto Open suffered the same fate as the Kanto PGA — the loss of a round to weather — but the last one you would expect to complain would be Yoshikazu Yokoshima, who led all the way and won just the two titles in 15 seasons on the Japan Tour. Yokoshima had rounds of 68, 72 and 72 for the four-under-par 212 that gave him a one-stroke victory over consistent 1987 challenger Hajime Meshiai, Katsuji Hasegawa and Nobuo Serizawa, the Nikkei Cup winner three weeks earlier.

The first-round 68 staked Yokoshima to a one-stroke lead at Sobu Country Club at Narita. Shuichi Sano had the runnerup 69 that day. Heavy rains inundated the 7,153 yards of the Sobu course Friday, forcing cancellation of the second round. Yokoshima's 68-72—140 when play resumed Saturday kept him a stroke in front, then over Serizawa, with Tsukasa Watanabe and Hiroshi Makino at 142. The second 72 Sunday gave Yokoshima the victory, but he nearly faced a playoff. Meshiai, the Hiroshima Open winner in July, birdied four back-nine holes to catch Yoshikazu, but bogied the 18th to drop into the runnerup deadlock with Serizawa and Hasegawa at 213.

Kansai Open—¥20,000,000
Winner: Masanobu Kimura

Asahi Kokusai Tojo Country Club's 7,198-yard course exacted a heavy toll on the scoring of the field in the companion regional championship in Western Japan. Only one score in the 60s — a 69 by also-ran Kiyokuni Kimoto in the final round — was posted all week and winner Masanobu Kimura landed his first-ever Japan Tour title with a closing 75 and a four-over-par 292. Toru Nakamura finished second at 294 despite an opening-round 79.

Ichiro Teramoto, one of the oldest players in the field, had the only sub-par round Thursday and the 71 gave him a one-stroke lead over Kimura and Kazuo Yoshikawa. Kimura, in his fifth tour season after a fine collegiate career, shot his only sub-par round Friday — a 71 — and it was erratic with four birdies and three bogeys. Still, it put him three strokes in front as Teramoto took a 77 and Yoshikawa a 74 for his runnerup 146. Kimura absorbed three front-nine bogeys, shot 74 but still led after 54 holes. His 217 gave him a comfortable five-stroke margin over Yoshikawa (76) and Toshiaki Nakagawa (75). In the final round, Kimura was not seriously challenged despite his 75, finishing two ahead of Nakamura and three ahead of Yoshitaka Yamamoto, both of whom shot closing 71s.

Some of the tour players fanned out and competed in one or the other of the four other small-purse regional events the same weekend as the Kanto and Kansai Opens.

The best known of them, Masahiro Kuramoto, returned to where it all began in 1980 and won the *Chu-Shikoku Open* for the sixth time. Just before turning pro in 1980, Kuramoto won the Chu-Shikoku and did so again in each of his first four pro seasons. Eitaro Deguchi landed the *Chubu Open* title for the second year in a row, in 1987 by a seven-stroke margin with his 14-under-par 274. Katsuyoshi Tomori nipped Takamasa Sakai by a stroke with his even-par 288 in the *Kyushu Open*. The scoring was astronomical in the *Hokkaido Open*. Akihiko Kojima, a tournament unknown, defeated Namio Takasu in a playoff after they both posted four-over-par 292s and Katsunari Takahashi, who had won the event the two previous years, finished third with 300, surely the highest score ever to be worth that kind of finish in a pro tournament.

Suntory Open—¥60,000,000
Winner: Noboru Sugai

Another long-time spear-carrier on the Japan Tour finally broke through with his first victory when Noboru Sugai came from behind to win the Suntory Open at Narashino Country Club in Inzaimachi. The 37-year-old Sugai, who was in his 13th season on the circuit, shot a final-round 68 for 278 and a three-stroke victory over Masahiro Kuramoto and American import Larry Nelson, the reigning U.S. PGA champion.

Kuramoto was the major victim. Shooting for his second victory in eight days, Masahiro had taken a two-stroke lead into the final round, but slumped to a 73. Nelson, who started the day even with Sugai, shot 71 and tied Kuramoto for second place at 281. The first-round leader was Yoshimi Niizeki, who parlayed a strong back nine into a 65 and a two-stroke margin over Sugai, Kuramoto and Hajime Meshiai. Kuramoto shook off an early double-bogey, shot 69 and tied Niizeki for the second-round lead when Yoshimi registered a 71 for his 136. They had two strokes on Sugai and Australian Terry Gale with Nelson (139) and Craig Stadler (140) in striking distance.

A par round Saturday established Kuramoto's two-shot lead at 208 Saturday, with Sugai, Niizeki and Nelson at 210, David Ishii and Gale at 211.

All Nippon Airways (ANA) Open—¥50,000,000
Winner: Isao Aoki

It was the week of the veterans in the All Nippon Airways (ANA) Open. Haruo Yasuda, the 44-year-old with 18 victories spread over the Japan Tour since 1968, showed the way at Sapporo Golf Club's Uni course for two days, then Isao Aoki, who was born the same year as Yasuda, took charge and scored his 51st professional victory, heading off a last-ditch run by Tsukasa Watanabe.

Yasuda opened with a five-under-par 67 at Sapporo, establishing a one-stroke lead over Hiroshi Makino and Satoshi Higashi. Five others shot 69. Yasuda, whose last victory had come in 1984, kept the lead Friday, shooting a four-birdie, two-bogey 70 for 137. David Ishii moved into second place with a rather-wild 68 that included seven birdies, a bogey and a double-bogey. Aoki stepped in Saturday as Yasuda headed toward an 11th-place tie. He finished with 75-76. On the other hand, Aoki shot 68 Saturday and climbed from 14th place into a one-stroke lead at 210. In closest pursuit at 211 were Jumbo Ozaki, Hideki Kase and Tademi Ueno. Watanabe hove into view Sunday with five birdies on the front nine, but three bogeys blunted the charge. Aoki had four birdies and four bogeys in a par closing round for 282 and a one-stroke victory over Watanabe. Ozaki and Terry Gale of Australia tied for third at 285.

Jun Classic—¥56,000,000
Winner: Masashi Ozaki

Masashi (Jumbo) Ozaki broke from a three-way tie in the final round and rolled to his third 1987 title the easy way with a five-stroke victory in the Jun Classic at the course of the same name at Ogawa in late September. Rain as well as the pros visited Ogawa during the week, reducing the tournament to 54 holes, but it probably wouldn't have mattered for Ozaki. He was the defending champion and won the tournament for the third time in five years.

Jumbo's younger brother, Tateo, and Akira Ishihara drew the first-day headlines with seven-under-par 65s. Jumbo himself shot 68. Then, the rains came and washed out the second round Friday. The scoring rose on the soggy course Saturday as only five players broke 70. Three of them shared the lead at 137 at day's end. Namio Takasu and Isao Aoki, coming off his ANA win the previous Sunday, shot 68s and Jumbo Ozaki had a 69, thanks to three birdies and an eagle on the back nine after a two-over front side. Aoki had two eagles in his round. Ozaki pulled away quickly in the final round, as birdies escaped Takasu, who shot a par 72, and bogeys came to Aoki, who took a 75. Jumbo carded six birdies and a bogey enroute to 67 and his five-stroke victory at 204. Takasu was second at 209 and Aoki fell into a four-way tie for third at 212.

Tokai Classic—¥60,000,000
Winner: Tsuneyuki Nakajima

Finally. Tsuneyuki Nakajima prevented a personal shutout in 1987 with a come-from-behind victory in the Tokai Classic. Certainly in part because of his frequent forays overseas, the No. 1 player in Japan the last five years had failed to win on his home circuit and it was already October when the Tokai Classic got underway at Miyoshi Country Club at Miyoshicho. The winner of 38 titles, including seven in Japan in 1986, Nakajima put his game in high gear in the final round, produced a 66 and slipped a stroke in front of a faltering Jumbo Ozaki with 282 to take the title.

Nakajima had fallen almost out of sight during the first three rounds, shooting 71, 72 and 73 in succession. Saburo Fujiki was the first-round leader. He shot 67 for a one-stroke edge on Yoshitaka Yamamoto, Satoshi Higashi, Naomichi and Jumbo Ozaki, the previous week's winner at the Jun Classic. However, his brother took the honors Friday, shooting 70 for 138 and a one-stroke lead on Yamamoto. Jumbo had a 74, but returned to the fray in spades Saturday, grabbing the lead with a seven-birdie 67 for 209. Two late bogeys cost Yamamoto at least a share of the lead as he shot 71 for 210. Naomichi soared to 76.

Jumbo Ozaki's round Sunday was as flawed as Nakajima's was flawless. Tsuneyuki made only one birdie on the front nine, but saw his seven-stroke deficit melting as Ozaki double-bogeyed the first, then the eighth and 12th holes, more than counteracting four birdies. Nakajima rattled off five birdies of his own on the back nine for the 66 and the one-stroke victory. Yamamoto plunged to 75 and a three-way tie at 285.

Japan Open Championship—¥60,000,000
Winner: Isao Aoki

The Japan Open Championship wound up in appropriate hands in 1987, just as it had in three of the previous four seasons. The top players in the game are supposed to win the major championships and that's the way it seems to have become in Japan. Isao Aoki, who had won his first Japan Open in 1983, captured the title again in 1987 at Arima Royal Golf Club in Kobe, succeeding Tsuneyuki Nakajima, who had won the Open the two previous seasons and made a good run at a third in a row at Arima Royal.

Graham Marsh, the Australian veteran with 22 Japanese victories on his fine record, jumped off in front Thursday with a seven-under-par 65, the product of eight birdies and a bogey. He was three strokes in front of runnerup Hajime Meshiai at that point, but tied with him at the halfway mark of the championship when Meshiai shot 69 and Marsh 72 for 137s. Aoki and Saburo Fujiki were a stroke back. Fujiki birdied two of the last three holes in Saturday's third round for 69 and took a two-stroke lead over Aoki (71) and three over Meshiai (73).

Isao closed the gap on Fujiki on the front nine and took the lead for good with one of his three birdies at the 12th hole. He went on to a 70 and 279, scoring his third victory of 1987 by a stroke over Nakajima and Nobuo Serizawa. Coming off his Tokai victory the previous Sunday, Nakajima again made a Sunday charge, but this time five birdies on the back nine and 67 weren't quite enough for the defending champion. The year's two money leaders did not fare well, Ozaki withdrawing Friday because of illness and David Ishii ruining his chances with a third-round 77.

Polaroid Cup Golf Digest—¥60,000,000
Winner: Ian Baker-Finch

Another country was heard from in mid-October on the Japan Tour. Ian Baker-Finch, an infrequent visitor to Japan from his native Australia, scored his first victory in that country, taking the Polaroid Cup Golf Digest title with a four-stroke margin. He is the first Australian winner of the Golf Digest, a fixture since 1972 at Tomei Country Club at Susono.

Hideki Kase, 28, a one-time winner on the Japan Tour, launched a bid for another with an opening 66 on a rainy Thursday at Tomei. His closest chasers were Shigenori Mori at 67; Nobuo Serizawa, Kazushige Kohno and veteran Kikuo Arai at 68. Kohno moved in front Friday, putting a 69 with the 68 for 137 and a two-stroke lead over Serizawa, who shot 71 despite a double-bogey on the first hole, and Naomichi Ozaki.

Baker-Finch, who put himself in a hole the first day with a 74, started his comeback Friday with 67 to move within four. Then, on Saturday, with the course being buffeted by the winds of Typhoon Kelly, Ian shot a fine, three-under-par 68 and wound up a stroke in front of the experienced Kohno, who took a 73 for his 210. Tateo Ozaki and Masanobu Kimura were at 211. On the final day, the 26-year-old Baker-Finch displayed near-perfect golf as he shot 66 and widened the gap over Kohno to four strokes with a solid, five-birdie performance. Kohno shot 69 to hold onto second place, two ahead of Ozaki, Kimura and Graham Marsh.

Bridgestone—¥80,000,000
Winner: David Ishii

David Ishii surpassed his career victory record in Japan when he won his fourth 1987 tournament in the Bridgestone at Sodegaura Country Club in Chiba. It took a playoff to achieve that seventh Japanese victory, though. The 32-year-old Hawaiian pro emerged triumphant from the year's first three-way playoff and the first on the regular tour since May. Ishii and the other playoff contenders, Hiroshi Makino and Nobuo Serizawa, got a big lift unintentionally from Jumbo Ozaki, who was headed for a fourth 1987 win himself until he folded in the final round, much as he had done three weeks earlier in the Tokai Classic.

Makino was the first-round leader with a 67 that included an eagle deuce at the 13th hole. He led Hsieh Yu Shu, Yoshitaka Yamamoto, Kinpachi Yoshimura and Takenori Hiraishi by a stroke. Ishii and Serizawa were among seven players at 69. Ozaki and Chen Tze Chung fired 67s Friday and vaulted into first place with 137s, two shots in front of Makino and Yamamoto. Ishii and Serizawa were then at 140. Chen fell away to a 78, but Ozaki advanced to a three-stroke lead when he birdied the last three holes for 70 and 207. Makino, Shigeru Kawamata and Tateo Ozaki, with a 67, followed at 210, Serizawa and Hiraishi at 211, Ishii, Chen Tze Ming and Teruo Sugihara at 212.

Ishii shot 70, Serizawa 71 and Makino 72 to forge the playoff tie at 282 as Ozaki's game inexplicably came apart. His 76 left him a stroke short of the playoff in a fourth-place tie with Tsuneyuki Nakajima and British Open Champion Nick Faldo. Makino exited the playoff on the first extra hole and the other two players halved the next three holes before Ishii birdied the fifth for the victory.

ABC Cup — U.S. vs Japan—¥65,000,000
Winners: Team — Japan; Individual — Andy Bean

Japan evened the record in the ABC Cup team matches with the United States while Andy Bean was launching a late-year rescue of a rather-dismal personal season by running away with the individual title in the international competition at Sports Shinko Country Club at Kawanishi the first of November. In the team competition, in which the best eight of nine scores from each team are counted each day, the United States started in front, was caught Friday, fell well behind Saturday and came up three strokes short, 2,230 to 2,227, at the end. Each national team has won the event eight times with a 17th match ending in a tie.

Bean, winless all year in America, opened with an eight-under-par 64 and finished with a 65 to take the individual title and money with 269. In between those two superlative rounds, Japanese players held the lead. Yoshitaka Yamamoto had a 64 that included an eagle deuce Friday and went two strokes in front of the American. Masahiro Kuramoto came up with the week's third 64 Saturday and his 201 created a three-stroke lead over Bean, six over Gary Hallberg and seven over Yamamoto. Kuramoto's chances fizzled amid an eagle, two birdies, a bogey and two double-bogeys for 73, so it was an eight-stroke swing in Bean's easy victory. Andy had seven birdies in his solid final round.

Kirin Cup World Championship of Golf—¥950,000
Winners: United States

The United States salvaged some international pride when its all-star team took the measure of the squads of the best pros from the European, Australasian and Japan PGA Tours in the Kirin Cup World Championship of Golf at Yomiui Country Club at Tokyo, It was the third year for the team competition, the U.S. having won the first time in Hawaii and Japan in 1986 at Yomiuri. Individual standings were eliminated in 1987.

Each team plays each of the others over the first three days of competition, but it isn't a win/lose situation. The number of individual match victories are accumulated and the two teams with the most points (two per win, one per tie) meet for the championship on the Sunday. As it turned out in 1987, the U.S. team "lost" 7-to-5 matches to Europe and Australasia, but with a 10-2 showing against Japan and a 20-point total gained the championship match against Europe, which compiled 24 points. Given that second shot at Europe, so to speak, the Yanks rolled to a 10-2 victory and the championship, worth $60,000 to each team member. Captain Tom Kite and Payne Stewart led the six-man American team, winning all four of their matches, as did Sandy Lyle for the Europeans. Lanny Wadkins, Curtis Strange and Scott Simpson were the other U.S. winners Sunday as Mark Calcavecchia lost to Lyle, 70-72. The Australia/New Zealand team took third place with a 9-3 victory over Japan Sunday.

Visa Taiheiyo Club Masters—¥90,000,000
Winner: Graham Marsh

The three biggest weeks of the season on the regular Japan Tour — the full complement of top Japanese pros and a sizeable number of leading players from America, Europe and Australia — began with the Visa Taiheiyo Club Masters and the title and its healthy ¥16,200,000 (approximately $120,000) first prize went to one of Japan's distinguished insider/outsiders — Graham Marsh. The veteran Australian, who has played a fairly-heavy schedule in Japan for many years and was in his 13th event of 1987, stormed from behind in the final round on the Taiheiyo Club's Gotemba course and bagged his 23rd win in the country.

It was an exciting finish for Marsh and Tom Watson, neither of whom led during the early rounds. Hiroshi Ishii had that position in the first round with 67. Five men shared second at 69, including Tom Kite, who eagled the final hole. A tremendous jam-up developed Friday as seven players wound up with 137s, among them Craig Stadler, who shot 65, the day's best round. The others were the ever-present-early Hajime Meshiai, Seiichi Kanai, Koichi Suzuki, Yoshiyuki Isomura, Futoshi Irino and Toshimitsu Dai. Marsh (70-69) and Watson (71-68) were among nine at 139.

Suzuki, a two-time winner in his career, edged in front Saturday with four back-nine birdies for a 69 and 206, a stroke ahead of Stadler (70) and Watson (68), two in front of Bernhard Langer (69) and Naomichi Ozaki (68). But, on Sunday, it became pretty much a decision between Marsh and the pursuing Watson. Marsh surged with a 66, with a birdie at the 18th, and posted 276, expecting a playoff. Watson, just two weeks beyond his massive Nabisco victory in Texas, had birdied the 14th and 16th and was expected to do the same at the short, par-five 18th. But Tom caught a bad fairway lie after a lay-up second shot, overshot the green with his pitch and had to settle for par and the runnerup 277, a shot in front of Kikuo Arai, making his only strong showing of the season, two ahead of Langer and three in front of Stadler, who slipped to 73 Sunday. Suzuki finished with a 75.

Dunlop Phoenix—¥140,000,000
Winner: Craig Stadler

Things finally went right in 1987 for Craig Stadler. Beset by two disconcerting rules infractions that had an influence on a winless American season and his absence from the U.S. international teams, Stadler found his troubles continuing in Japan when he put a poor finish on a contending position the last day of the Taiheiyo Club Masters. At last, in the richest tournament in Asia, the able American won a final-round battle against fellow Yank Scott Hoch to take the title in the Dunlop Phoenix tournament in Miyazaki and its ¥25,200,000 (US$180,000) first prize.

The Dunlop Phoenix attracted its usual sterling field, highlighted by the presence of Larry Mize, Scott Simpson and Larry Nelson, the 1987 winners of the three American major championships, and Severiano Ballesteros, but it was little-known Japanese pro Tadami Ueno who took the first-round lead in a tournament that had been won only once since 1974 by a native son. Ueno shot 66 with a bogey at the last hole, taking a one-stroke lead over David Ishii, Koichi Uehara and Kazuo Kanayama. Jumbo Ozaki and Tsuneyuki Nakajima, the 1985 winner, were close at 68.

The 38-year-old Ueno, winner of five small events during his 15-year career, clung to the lead Friday, shooting 68 for 134, 10 under par over the 6,993-yard Phoenix Country Club course. Hiroshi Makino was second at 135, but Stadler made his move with a seven-under 65, jumping from 21st to third place, joining Uehara at 136. Ishii and Jumbo Ozaki, fighting for the money lead on the Japan Tour, were at 137. Stadler birdied the final hole Saturday for a 69 and took a one-stroke lead with his 205. Ueno, who eventually shot 80 on Sunday, was at 206 with Ozaki after a 72. Ozaki shot 69. At that point, Hoch was at 209 (71-71-67).

Stadler maintained his lead on the front nine, although Hoch, winner three times in the rich fall events in Japan in the past, was right on his heels after three early birdies. When Craig ran into trouble on the early holes of the back nine, Hoch overtook him with a birdie at the 13th. While Stadler was parring in, though, Scott was going bogey-birdie-bogey at the 15th, 16th and 17th and parring the 18th for his 278. Stadler's 72 brought the winning 277. Ballesteros tied Hajime Meshiai and Makino for third at 280.

Casio World Open—¥90,000,000
Winner: David Ishii

David Ishii came through the biggest test of his career with flying colors. Facing one of the year's strongest fields with the money-winning title of the Japan Tour on the line, Ishii survived the pressure of a stretch battle to win the Casio World Open at the end of November at Ibusuki Golf Club in Kaimon. The ¥16,200,000 ($115,000) first prize virtually insured the No. 1 position for the 32-year-old Hawaiian.

Although they never outdistanced the rest of the field, Ishii and Scotland's Sam Torrance literally waged a two-man battle for the Casio title from start to finish of the tournament. They began the duel with tournament-leading

67s the first day, as Masashi (Jumbo) Ozaki, David's rival for the money title, opened at 68 with Graham Marsh, the Taiheiyo Masters winner, and American Donnie Hammond. Both Ishii and Torrance birdied the 18th hole for 69s Friday and were joined at their leading 136s by Naomichi Ozaki, who carded a 66. Jumbo Ozaki faded to 75. The Scot edged a stroke in front Saturday despite bogeys on the first two holes. He managed a par 72 for 208 as Ishii took three boeys with his pair of birdies for 73 and 209, tied there with Hammond, who had five back-nine birdies for 70.

Torrance widened his margin to two strokes with a birdie at No. 12 that put him four under for the day and 12 under for the tournament, but suffered a three-stroke swing when he drove out of bounds at No. 14 and took a double-bogey while Ishii was making birdie on the hole off a fine long-iron approach to six feet. David opened the gap to two with a 30-foot birdie putt at the 15th. Sam missed a chance to rebound when he three-putted the 17th green after Ishii took his only bogey. They both birdied the 18th, Ishii after a shaky tee shot and Torrance after two big wood shots and a barely-missed eagle putt. Ishii finished with 67 and 12-under-par 276, Torrance with 70 and 278. Jumbo Ozaki made a strong recovery Sunday, running from four to 10 under par before taking a bogey at No. 17 and three-putting the 18th for par. He tied for third with his 67—279 with Hammond and Masahiro Kuramoto.

Japan Series—¥30,000,000
Co-Winners: David Ishii and Isao Aoki

Winter-like weather put a crimp in the Japan Tour's showcase Japan Series, the season-climaxing tournament limited to the winners of the regular events on the year's circuit. Two separate snow storms reduced the Series to two rounds, the second one coming on the early-December Sunday and leading officials to declare co-leaders David Ishii and Isao Aoki co-winners. It capped the brilliant year of Ishii, playing in the event for the first time, being his sixth victory. It was Aoki's fourth win of 1987 and his fourth Series title.

The unique tournament normally begins on Wednesday at the Yomiuri Country Club in Osaka, but the first snowfall prevented that this time. Play was possible Thursday and Aoki took a one-stroke lead with a 67 on the par-73 course, scoring an eagle at the par-five 10th and four birdies in the solid round. Brian Jones and Jumbo Ozaki shot 68s and Ishii a 69 that day. On the scheduled off day for travel, the scene switched to the Yomiuri club at Tokyo. On the second playing day Saturday, only three pros broke 70, Ishii using his 69 to tie Aoki for the lead at 138. They had a stroke on Yoshitaka Yamamoto, who also shot 69; Jones (71) and Ozaki, who made what turned out to be a quite-costly bogey on the 18th hole of the par-72 course. Snow fell again overnight, making the course unplayable Sunday and ending the tournament.

Daikyo Open—¥70,000,000
Winner: Isamu Sugita

Don't mention playoffs to Hiroshi Makino. For the third time in 1987, Makino found himself in a playoff and for the third time Makino lost, the title of the season-concluding Daikyo Open at Onna in Okinawa going to 29-year-old Isamu Sugita, who had been winless in his nine-year pro career. Sugita birdied the second playoff hole at Daikyo Country Club to defeat Makino and Seiji Ebihara.

Yoshitaka Yamamoto and Masanobu Kimura opened with seven-under-par 64s at Daikyo as Sugita and Taijiro Tanaka had 65s among the 28 players who broke 70. Yamamoto made nine birdies while Kimura closed eagle-birdie for his 64. Kimura had first place to himself Friday after his 70 for 134. He was a stroke in front of Yamamoto (71) and Ebihara (67-68), two ahead of Brian Jones, Tateo Ozaki, Hajime Meshiai and Yoshimi Niizeki. Ebihara shot 69 Saturday to take a two-stroke lead over defending champion Tateo Ozaki and Niizeki, who were at 206. Makino, who has only one 1983 victory on his record, was at 207, Sugita at 208 going into the final round.

Ebihara opened the door for the other two playoff contestants with three back-nine bogeys, establishing the deadlock with the last one at the 18th hole. Sugita had five birdies and three bogeys in his 69 round on the windy Sunday, while Makino started fast with birdies on the first three holes, but played one-over-par golf over the remaining 15 to join the overtime session.

15. The LPGA Tour

Diversity is an enormous virtue on the LPGA Tour. After a season in 1986 when Pat Bradley totally dominated, 1987 was a three-way race for top honors among, in alphabetical order, Jane Geddes, Betsy King and Ayako Okamoto.

Three cheers for Okamoto. The non-American surge that is so obvious on the men's tour was felt in the LPGA, too, as Japan's Okamoto became the first non-American to lead in earnings and become the Player of the Year.

The battle went down to the Japan Classic, the final event of the season. Playing at home, Okamoto finished second to compatriot Yuko Moriguchi, which was enough to pass King for the money title and break a tie with King and Geddes for Player of the Year honors.

Okamoto, with four victories including the Nestle World Championship, finished with earnings of $466,034 to $460,385 for King and $396,818 for Geddes. Besides Player of the Year, she led the Mazda Series and shared first with King for top-10 finishes with 17.

King was not shut out by any means. She, too, won four events, including the Nabisco Dinah Shore. She also had the year's best scoring average of 71.14 to 71.36 for Okamoto and 71.64 for Geddes.

Geddes won the most events, five, including the LPGA Championship. She also was first in sub-par rounds with 51.

And despite their heroics, the Big Three were not the only story in 1987. The international flavor was enhanced even more when England's Laura Davies won the U.S. Women's Open in a Tuesday, 36-hole playoff with Okamoto and JoAnne Carner. The fourth major, the du Maurier Classic, was won by Jody Rosenthal.

Do not forget the joyful walk down the 18th fairway at the Sarasota Classic by Nancy Lopez. The site of her first victory, Sarasota also was where she earned her 35th victory and automatic induction, finally, into the LPGA Hall of Fame. That ceremony, fittingly, took place at Tiffany's in New York.

Finally, looking to the future, Tammie Green was Rookie of the Year, finishing 39th on the money list with earnings of $68,346. Watch for her.

Who can deny that the LPGA Tour is growing. With the ascension of players such as Okamoto and Davies, the tour is spreading from one end of the globe to the other.

Mazda Classic—$200,000
Winner: Kathy Postlewait

Patient and pleasant Kathy Postlewait surprised the LPGA and perhaps even herself by winning the season's first tournament in a one-hole playoff with Betsy King. The triumph was Postlewait's second in 14 pro seasons and her first victory in four playoff attempts. "I was due," Postlewait said. "The law of averages was with me. And this feels better than winning the first time (San Jose Classic in 1983). You can win one time and it can be an accident. When you win twice, you have to think you are doing something right."

The last thing Postlewait did right was sink a six-foot par putt on the first playoff hole, No. 16 at the Stonebridge Country Club in Boca Raton, Florida. King had missed the green with her six-iron approach, resulting in a bogey. The victory was worth $30,000.

Postlewait (73-72-72-69) and King (70-72-71-73) finished the regulation 72 holes at two-under-par 286, one shot ahead of Lauri Peterson, Rosie Jones and Pat Bradley. King began the final round with a one-shot lead but lost it when she hit her drive out of bounds on No. 8 en route to a double bogey. After nine pars, Postlewait charged on the back side with three consecutive birdies on putts of 15, 13 and eight feet. A par and another birdie from five feet put her into the lead, but a bogey on No. 15 dropped her back into a tie with King.

Amy Alcott was the first-round leader with a five-under 67 but finished in a tie for 13th. Cathy Morse shot a career-low, 66, tying the course record, to take a two-shot lead midway in the event but also finished in that unlucky 13th-place tie.

Sarasota Classic—$200,000
Winner: Nancy Lopez

Nancy Lopez won her way into the LPGA Hall of Fame in the Sarasota Classic, the site of her first pro victory nine years before. Lopez became the 11th member of the Hall by coasting to a three-stroke victory on the Bent Tree Country Club course with rounds of 73-66-68-74 for a seven-under-par 281. The triumph earned her berth because it was the 35th victory of her 10-year LPGA career.

The opening round left Lopez six shots behind Chris Johnson, who led with a five-under 67. But it seemed as if Mother Nature wanted Lopez in the Hall as high winds bothered everyone but her for the next two days. Lopez shot 66 in the second round to tie Johnson for the lead, then took a five-shot lead on the field with a brilliant 68 on a day when no other player could break 70.

The final day was for the gallery of about 20,000. Lopez played cautiously and only was challenged once. Baker closed to within one shot with five holes to play but immediately fell back into a tie for second with Anne-Marie Palli at 284. Johnson and Heather Farr tied for fourth at 285.

Tsumura Hawaiian Open—$300,000
Winner: Cindy Rarick

The 1987 LPGA season seemed determined to prove that you can go home again no matter what Thomas Wolfe wrote. Nancy Lopez qualified for the Hall of Fame by winning her 35th tournament in Sarasota, the site of her first pro victory. Then, after one week off for travel time, Cindy Rarick won her first pro event in Hawaii, her "second home" where she played collegiate golf.

Rarick, then Cindy Flom, played from 1978 to 1980 for the University of Hawaii. She used that experience to master the shifting winds at the Turtle Bay Hilton and Country Club course to shoot rounds of 69-71-67 for a nine-under-par 207, two shots better than Jane Geddes.

Alice Ritzman and Chris Johnson shared the first-round lead at 68 each. Then Ritzman and Geddes were tied 139, with Rarick one shot back, going into the final round. With four holes to play, Ritzman, Geddes and Rarick were tied at seven under. But birdie putts of eight and two feet on Nos. 16 and 17 clinched the victory for Rarick. Ritzman bogeyed the last hole to drop into third place at 210.

Besides her Hawaiian connection, Rarick benefited from the calm advice of her husband and caddy, Rick Rarick. "Without all those three putts last year," he said, "Cindy could have won $200,000 instead of $29,000." Her Hawaiian check of $45,000 certainly put her on the right track.

Kemper Open—$300,000
Winner: Jane Geddes

Jane Geddes ruined a honeymoon by taking her first victory of the season at the Kemper Open on the Hawaiian island of Kauai in a playoff with newlywed Cindy Kratzert Gerring. Geddes and Gerring had a standoff in what amounted to 72 holes of match-play competition, each shooting 12-under-par 286, before Geddes won with a bogey on the first playoff hole.

Paired together the first two days, they remained together in the final group for the last two days on the windy (gusts to 53 miles per hour on the final day) Princeville Makai course. "Jane was playing well," Gerring said. "When you play with someone who is playing that well, you tend to do the same." Play well they did. Gerring had the early edge, leading the first three rounds on scores of 66, 68 and 71. Geddes held second with scores of 67-70-69 to be one shot back going into the final round. The only other competitor within shouting distance was Ayako Okamoto, four shots behind Gerring.

Okamoto would hold third place at 280, four shots better than Jan Stephenson. But all the attention was on the top two. Geddes birdied the third hole to tie, then eagled the par-five sixth hole for a one-shot lead. But Gerring stayed right with her, sinking a six-foot par putt on the 72nd hole to force overtime.

The playoff hole was more brutal than artistic. Playing into the heavy winds on the par-four 15th, both put their approach shots in the front left bunker. Geddes came out to the back of the green and two-putted from 20 feet for a bogey. Gerring bladed her ball from the front bunker to the one in the rear, but blasted beautifully to within three feet of the cup — and missed the putt for a losing double bogey.

GNA Classic—$250,000
Winner: Jane Geddes

Jane Geddes obviously believes in striking while her irons are hot. Winner of two consecutive tournaments in 1986, she jumped to the front in 1987 by following her Kemper Open victory with another playoff triumph in the GNA Classic, played at Glendale, California. The year before Geddes won the U.S. Open and Boston Five in successive weeks. She was even stronger in 1987, placing second in the Hawaiian Open before winning the Kemper and GNA, earning $110,000 in three weeks.

Playoffs were part of Geddes' winning personality, too, as three of her first four tour victories were achieved in overtime. In the GNA on the Oakmont course, Geddes rallied from five strokes down in the final round to tie Robin Walton and then defeat her with a birdie on the first extra hole. Both had two-under-par 286 totals on the narrow, difficult course.

After rounds of 74-74-71, Geddes shot a closing course record-tying 67 to catch Walton. Geddes had seven birdies in her first 10 holes and actually took a four-shot lead on Walton before slowing down with a double bogey on No. 15. Walton fought back to tie Geddes in regulation, but could not keep up the pace on the first playoff hole. Walton's bid for a 30-foot birdie brushed the cup but wouldn't fall, allowing Geddes to sink a four-foot birdie putt for the victory.

Betsy King, starting to make her presence felt, too, led after one round with a 67 but was 10 shots worse in the second round. Walton and Colleen Walker shared the second-and third-round lead at two under par after each day. Walker finished third at even-par 288.

Tucson Circle K—$200,000
Winner: Betsy King

Jane Geddes took the week off and Jan Stephenson lost control of her game in the final round, allowing Betsy King to win the Tucson Circle K, and set the foundation for her place among the LPGA's Big Three for 1987.

Stephenson, a self-proclaimed front runner, led for three rounds by shooting 67-70-71 in perfect weather on the Randolph North course in Tucson, Arizona. But cold winds and showers seemed to blow away her game as she closed with a 75 while King came from five shots back with a superb 68 to win by two at seven-under-par 281.

King actually began her charge on the final hole of the third round when she eagled the short par-five. "I obviously think I can win," she said despite still being five shots behind Stephenson after her regressive rounds of 70, 71 and 72.

Stephenson was holding off the field on the final day until the ninth hole. She bogeyed three of four holes, allowing King to close within a shot. Seizing the opportunity, King eagled the par-five 13th with a 205-yard five wood to the green and a 45-foot putt. King held a one shot lead from that point. Playing a group ahead of Stephenson, King played for a safe par on the par-five closing hole, forcing Stephenson to go for a winning eagle or tying birdie. Stephenson's fairway wood found water instead of land, resulting in a bogey and second place at 283. Sandra Palmer shot a closing 70 for third at 284.

Turquoise Classic—$300,000
Winner: Pat Bradley

Astronaut and Admiral Alan Shepard played in the Turquoise Classic pro-am because the tournament had moved to Moon Valley Country Club in Phoenix, Arizona, and he is the only man to hit a golf ball on the moon. But it was Pat Bradley, the LPGA's brightest star in 1986, who was shinning at the end.

Obviously not the dominant force that she was one year before, Bradley caught early leader Penny Pulz and then held off late-moving Chris Johnson for a two-shot victory with a six-under-par 286 total. Bradley's tournament was divided into two distinct halves. She shot 75-74 in the first half and 67-70 in the second. "It's really amazing," Bradley said about winning after such a poor start. "Actually, I should be nowhere to be found, but I bounced back and ended up winning."

Pulz ruled for two days, shooting 69 and 72 despite fierce winds. But Bradley caught her in the third round with her course-record 67 that included eight one-putt greens. The tie going into the last round caused talk about Bradley's collapse at Tucson the year before. She had led Pulz by seven shots going into the last round but shot 76 to a 64 for the victorious Pulz.

Not this time. It was Pulz who unraveled with an 80 to finish tied for 15th at 296, 10 shots back. Johnson, however, kept Bradley honest by shooting 67 on the closing day. Johnson trailed Bradley by just one shot going into the 17th hole, but Bradley clinched the victory with a 16-foot birdie putt. Johnson was second at 288, followed by Lori Garbacz at 290.

Nabisco Dinah Shore Classic—$500,000
Winner: Betsy King

Betsy King discovered something about achieving greatness moments after capturing the Nabisco Dinah Shore Classic in a playoff against Patty Sheehan. King looked within herself in search of elation and discovered exhaustion instead. "My first reaction, funny as it may sound, is how tired I am," she said. "You're under so much pressure in a big event like this. I guess whatever I do the rest of the season, I've already had a great year."

Other fine moments were in store for King, but this was the victory that gave definition to everything else. King already had won eight other titles, including Tucson two weeks earlier, but the Nabisco was her first major championship, a distinction that separates the ladies from the great ladies of the LPGA.

The second and decisive hole of the playoff was almost anticlimatic. King had made a fine up-and-down par on the first playoff hole to stay alive. Then Sheehan three-putted for bogey on the second hole, allowing King to sink a 30-inch putt for the championship. But what a final round had preceded the playoff. The quest for the title involved King, Sheehan and defending champion Pat Bradley, who had won at Phoenix the week before.

King and Bradley were tied for the lead at one-under-par going into the last round. Sheehan, who had shot 77 in the opening round, was three strokes back. King and Sheehan birdied the first three holes, placing King three up on the other two. At the turn King was four under, one ahead of Bradley and two up on Sheehan. King continued to play brilliantly and led for two holes until she bogeyed No. 15. All three were tied at four under.

That was it for Bradley. All she could do was par the last three holes to finish third at four-under 284. "I'm proud of the way I defended my title," she said, "but somebody just played a little better." Two somebodies, actually. On the 16th, Sheehan sank a 15-foot birdie putt. And on the same par-four hole minutes later, King was in the right greenside bunker in two, 45 feet from the cup. She holed out for the tying birdie. Both would par the last two regulation holes for three-under totals of 283.

King had rounds of 68-75-72-68 and the charging Sheehan kept getting better at 77-73-68-65. "After that 77, I cried a little," Sheehan said. "To come back from six over and almost win, well, I'm proud of myself."

Sheehan was not the only golfer to shed tears on the Old Course at Mission Hills Country Club in Rancho Mirage, California. Consider Laura Davies, the reigning British Open champion and British money leader for two years. Davies shot 66 to lead after one round only to suffer through a 17-stroke swing to 83 in winds that gusted to 40 miles per hour on the desert course.

King and Amy Alcott led after the second round despite shooting 75 each for one-under totals. A par 72 on Saturday was enough for King to split the lead with Bradley going into the fateful final round when King discovered just how exhausting greatness can be.

Kyocera Classic—$200,000
Winner: Ayako Okamoto

After eight tour events, Betsy King and Jane Geddes had won two tournaments each. It appeared the LPGA season was going to be match play between a dynamic twosome. That's when Ayako Okamoto stepped forward to make it a threesome at the top.

Winner of 39 previous titles around the world, including seven on the LPGA Tour, Okamoto displayed perfect timing by making the Kyocera (a Japanese manufacturing firm with a plant in San Diego, California) her first title of the LPGA year. The tournament, played opposite the men's Masters, reportedly was in trouble, but a thrilling victory by Okamoto was exactly what was needed to draw a large crowd and please the sponsor. Okamoto had rounds of 66-70-69-70 for 13-under-par 275, good enough to beat King by a shot. Patty Sheehan, who had lost the Nabisco Dinah Shore to King in a playoff the week before, finished a distant third at 282.

Okamoto opened with a tournament record-tying 66 and led the rest of the way into the final round on the Bernardo Heights Country Club course. Then it became match play with King, of whom Okamoto said, "I thought I was playing with a record-breaker."

That's the way it appeared. King birdied six of the first nine holes. Okamoto, who had begun the final round three strokes ahead, found herself two down at the turn. But the tide turned, too, as King bogeyed Nos. 10 and 11. The second bogey was the result of missing a two-foot putt. King bogeyed No. 16, too, and that proved the difference.

Santa Barbara Classic—$300,000
Winner: Jan Stephenson

Some personalities seem destined to lead dramatic lives. Nothing about Jan Stephenson's LPGA career has been bland, including her rush to victory in the Santa Barbara Classic over two of the year's Big Three, Jane Geddes and Ayako Okamoto. Fearing she would miss her tee time for the second round, Stephenson was further detained by a patrolman who ticketed her for speeding to the course. Wiser on the tournament's third and final day, she had her husband drive her to the course so that she could use her driver to fashion her 14th career victory and her first triumph in two years.

Stephenson still had not recovered from losing a six-shot lead to Betsy King with 10 holes to go at Tucson a month earlier. The secret to her success at Santa Barbara was that success caught her by surprise. "I was sure I wouldn't win," she said. "That's why I was real calm."

Not everyone was nearly as calm due to the incredible difference in the tournament's two courses, about 45 miles apart on the California coast. Sandpiper was a seaside course that played easily, while La Purisima was a new, woody island course that took no prisoners.

Missie McGeorge played her first round at Sandpiper and took the lead with a seven-under 66. But she and half the field faced winds of 45 miles per hour on La Purisima in the second round. For McGeorge, it meant an incredible swing of 19 strokes to an 85. Okamoto (72-69) and Stephenson (74-68) benefited by playing La Purisima first when it wasn't as vicious. Geddes (69-79) was not so fortunate. Geddes shot a closing 68 at Sandpiper and did not mind telling anyone who would listen how she felt about La Purisima. "I finished second and feel like I've been punished," she said.

Okamoto entered the final round with a one-shot lead on Stephenson and extended it to three shots on the front. But Okamoto lost her bid for a second consecutive victory on the 175-yard 11th hole when she put a five iron over the green and took a double bogey. Another bogey on No. 13 by Okamoto was all Stephenson needed to surprise herself with victory.

S&H Classic—$225,000
Winner: Cindy Hill

Perhaps the S&H in S&H Classic stood for "Surgery & Hospitalization." That's how this tournament's bizarre week seemed as Cindy Hill came out of a hospital to win, Jan Stephenson went into a hospital to lose a chance for victory, and amazing Myra Blackwelder literally labored through the tournament while seven and one-half months pregnant.

For Hill, the three-shot victory on rounds of 70-66-69-66 was almost a medical miracle. Being treated for severe pancreatic problems, she had not played in eight weeks and had no thoughts of victory before shooting a tournament record 17-under-par 271 on the Pasadena Yacht & Country Club course in St. Petersburg, Florida.

For Stephenson, an excellent chance at a second consecutive victory turned into a medical nightmare. Tied with Hill for the lead after three rounds, Stephenson suffered back, wrist and scalp injuries when her car was struck by another vehicle after leaving the course.

For Blackwelder, the tournament was a relief from the monotony of awaiting the birth of her child. Living near the course, she received her doctor's permission to play. She became a national celebrity when she shared the lead midway in the tournament even though she eventually finished nine shots behind Hill.

Seven players shot 67 each to share the first-round lead. Stephenson and Blackwelder shared the midway lead at 135 with Stephenson finding herself "upstaged" by the "Blackwelder twosome." Hill and Stephenson were tied for first after three rounds at 205. But when Stephenson did not appear for the final round, Hill relaxed and made five birdies in a six-hole stretch on the front nine. That placed her four shots ahead of the field and she coasted home, three shots ahead of Jane Crafter, who had made a mighty rally with rounds of 66 and 64 for the best finish of her career.

United Virginia Bank Classic—$250,000
Winner: Jody Rosenthal

The United Virginia Bank Classic unfolded a scenario that would be rejected by any movie producer as too romantic and implausible to be believed. But Jody Rosenthal discovered that truth often is stranger than fiction. The last round of the tournament was played on Mother's Day, and Rosenthal called her mother, Doreen, to send her love before heading to the first tee. And what did Doreen Rosenthal say: "You know what would make a wonderful Mother's Day present? If you could win, it would be the best present I ever had."

Jody didn't know what to say. She was six shots behind the leader, Cindy Hill, who had won the previous week. Even though Rosenthal had been Rookie of the Year in 1986, she had never finished better than second and didn't see how she could possibly do that well on Mother's Day. Here's how. After rounds of 71 and 72 at the Sleepy Hole Golf Club, Rosenthal shot a career-best 66 for a seven-under-par 209. Meanwhile, Hill and her two nearest competitors at the start of the day — Nancy Lopez and young Sherri Turner — shot 73 each. That left Hill one shot back at 210 with Lopez and Turner tied for third at 211.

Rosenthal played the final round in a threesome nearly one hour ahead of the early leaders. She was paired with Tammie Green, who would finish tied for fifth en route to being named 1987's Rookie of the Year. Rosenthal birdied the last four holes on the front with putts of 20, 15, 25 and 12 feet. She had one more birdie on the 14th that put her in the lead, where she stayed. Forty-five minutes after she finished her round, Rosenthal watched Hill miss a five-foot birdie putt on No. 18 that would have forced a playoff.

Chrysler-Plymouth Classic—$225,000
Winner: Ayako Okamoto

Japan's Ayako Okamoto fashioned back-to-back victories on both sides of the world by winning the Chrysler-Plymouth Classic. On May 1 Okamoto took care of business in Tokyo, her home, by winning $60,000 for first place in the Konica Cup World Ladies Championship. One week later she was in Middletown, New Jersey, collecting $33,750 for her triumph in the Chrysler-Plymouth.

Okamoto had rounds of 70-74-71 for a four-under-par 215 on the difficult Navesink Country Club course. The lowest score of the three-round week was 69, and it was recorded just once by Joan Delk, who had shot 83 the previous day. Tied for second at 217, two shots back, were Colleen Walker and Jane Geddes. The only other player under par was Tammie Green, taking a giant step toward Rookie of the Year honors by finishing fourth at 218.

Okamoto took the first-round lead with her three-under 700, but Walker (72-70) led by two after two rounds. They battled each other in the final round as Geddes never really threatened to win but birdied the final hole to share second. Okamoto took the lead when she birdied the long 15th at about the same time Walker took a bogey on No. 13. A three-putt bogey by Walker on No. 16 gave Okamoto the two-shot cushion she needed to cruise home with her second LPGA victory of the year.

LPGA Championship—$350,000
Winner: Jane Geddes

When the 1987 LPGA Championship ended, more than half of the season remained to be played. But timing aside, the finish was a showcase for the year's Big Three as Jane Geddes won the title with Betsy King finishing second and Ayako Okamoto tied for third.

This one belonged to Geddes, who won the U.S. Open the year before for her first major victory. She proved it was no fluke by conquering the Grizzly Course at the Jack Nicklaus Sports Center on rounds of 72-68-68-67 for a 13-under-par 275, one shot better than King, this year's Nabisco Dinah Shore champion, and three ahead of Okamoto, Rosie Jones and Laurie Rinker. Cathy Morse finished sixth at 279.

Morse was the leader at 10-under 206 going into the final round with Geddes two shots back. But it was King who made the final turn in 32 to go 11 under and take a two-shot lead on Geddes, Okamoto, Morse, Rinker and Lori Garbacz. Birdies by Geddes on Nos. 10 and 14 elevated her into a tie with King at 10 under. But the championship was decided on the watery 16th, a 180-yard par three over a pond. King, playing one group ahead of Geddes, missed the green with a four iron, then knuckled her sand wedge nearly 30 feet past the hole. She two-putted for a bogey.

Geddes, now one up, also used a four iron to land 20 feet from the cup. She drilled the putt directly into the cup as if it had no choice for a birdie and command of her destiny. King never quit. She birdied the final two holes, but Geddes birdied No. 17 and tapped in for par on the final hole to win her second major by a shot.

Corning Classic—$275,000
Winner: Cindy Rarick

If leaders always won, we would have no reason to play or watch tournaments to the end. That's a truism that young Cindy Rarick discovered by winning the Corning Classic after being five shots down with four holes to play.

Let's pick up the tournament right there at the Corning (New York) Country Club. Playing in the next-to-last threesome, Rarick was just playing out the round after a one-under-par effort for 13 holes had dropped her five shots off the lead. Patty Sheehan, however, was five under for the final round and was the leader, one stroke ahead of Betsy King. Rarick didn't think much of it when she made a seven-foot birdie putt and Sheehan parred on No. 15. Now she was four behind with three to play. But everything changed on No. 16. An errant tee shot led to a bogey for Sheehan, while Rarick holed out a 40-foot wedge shot for birdie. Now she was two behind with two to play.

Fate was on her side at No. 17. Sheehan missed a birdie putt that gave Rarick the line to sink a 25-footer for another birdie. One down and one to play. On the final hole, a 377-yard par four, Rarick hit a five-iron approach to within four feet of the cup. Sheehan pushed her eight iron to the right, 40 feet from the cup. That led to a three-putt bogey for Sheehan, followed by an easy birdie for Rarick.

Rarick still had to wait for the final threesome of King, Jane Geddes and Dawn Coe to play the last hole. A birdie for anyone would have meant a playoff, but King and Geddes tied Sheehan for second with pars, and Coe fell into a tie for fifth with a bogey.

Rarick, who won her first title earlier in the year at the Hawaiian Open, shot rounds of 70-69-69-67 for a 13-under 275. She only led the tournament for one hole, but she picked the best one — the last.

Kathryn Young was the first-round leader with a career-best 65. Pat Bradley and Young shared the midway lead at nine-under 135. Coe took the third-round lead on scores of 68-68-67 before shooting 74 on the final day.

McDonald's Championship—$500,000
Winner: Betsy King

Many ways exist to define a champion. Two ways are to examine how a competitor performs when the title is on the line and to examine how he or she survives when their game is not at its best. Betsy King passed both tests when she rallied to capture the lucrative McDonald's Championship.

With four holes to play at the Du Pont Country Club in Wilmington, Delaware, yet another duel was being waged by two of 1987's Big Three. King and Ayako Okamoto were tied for the lead at three under par. But King drained the tournament of its riches and its drama by sinking birdie putts on three of the final four holes to shoot a six-under 278, two shots better than Okamoto, who birdied the final hole to keep second place to herself.

It was King's third victory of the season, and one she did not expect. "I felt like I didn't hit the ball that well," King said. "Experience helps when you are not playing that great. Sometimes you can even win."

An opening round of one-over 72 in the rain placed her six shots behind Cathy Morse, who had shot a career-high 66. Morse shot 70 in the second round to hold her lead by a stroke, while King made up two shots with a 68.

Okamoto made her move in the third round. Her tournament-best effort of six-under 65 was enough to overcome a seven-shot deficit and tie Morse, who shot 72, at five-under 208. King shot an even-par 71 and was content to start the final round three shots back, awaiting the final act before stealing the show and its top prize of $75,000 with her "not so great" 67.

Allison Fenney, 67, and Lisa Young, 68, shared third at 281, one shot behind Okamoto. Morse slipped to 74 on the last day to split fifth place with Val Skinner, 70, at two-under 282.

Mayflower Classic—$350,000
Winner: Colleen Walker

Nobody could blame Colleen Walker for checking her final scorecard four times in the Mayflower Classic to make sure, absolutely sure, she had shot a closing 69 for a 10-under-par 278, good enough for her first victory. Until then, signing incorrect scorecards had been Walker's claim to fame.

Last year she lost $2,000 by signing an incorrect scorecard at the du Maurier Classic. And just three weeks later, she turned herself in for signing another final-round scorecard that was incorrect at the MasterCard International Pro-Am. That one cost her $18,500 because she had finished second.

Not this time. Debra Richard had led the first round with a six-under-par 66 at the Country Club of Indianapolis course. Walker took half of the midway lead, tied at seven-under 37 with Patti Rizzo. But Rizzo shot 70 in the third round to lead Walker by two shots.

Walker, playing a group ahead, birdied the final two holes to give her a week's effort of 67-70-72-69. Rizzo needed a birdie or Bonnie Lauer had to eagle the last hole to force a playoff. Rizzo missed a five-foot birdie effort and Lauer couldn't eagle from 25 feet, so Walker really had earned $53,500 for her first victory. No mistake about it.

Lady Keystone Open—$300,000
Winner: Ayako Okamoto

Instead of quietly asking for permission to enter the LPGA's "Millionaire Club," Ayako Okamoto kicked down the door by rallying for an incredible victory at the Lady Keystone Open at Hershey Country Club in Hershey, Pennsylvania.

After two routine rounds of 70 and 74, Okamoto was in 24th place, eight shots out of the lead, going into the final round of the 54-hole tournament. All she did was shoot an eight-birdie, no-bogey 64 to win by a shot. It was her third victory of the season and the first prize of $45,000 made her the LPGA's 15th career millionaire with earnings of $1,021,300.

Laurie Rinker made a charge of her own with a fine 67 to finish second at 209, while Martha Nause was third at 210. Tied at 211 were Cindy Hill, Cathy Gerring and Ok-Hee Ku. From South Korea, Ku had led the first two rounds with scores of 67 and 69 but faded with a 75 on the final day.

Okamoto began her last-day charge by chipping in for a birdie on the first hole. Then she made four consecutive birdies on Nos. 3 through 6, including a holed sand shot on No. 4. She took the lead for good with a 25-foot birdie putt on No. 14. Rinker challenged with three birdies on Nos. 14, 15 and 16 to climb within a stroke but could do no better than par on the last two holes.

Rochester International—$300,000
Winner: Deb Richard

Often when searching for your first victory, the biggest obstacle can be your own emotions. Deb Richard mastered her anger, then mastered the field to break into the LPGA's victory circle at the Rochester International.

Richard led all four rounds at the Locust Hill Country Club in upper New York on scores of 66-69-73-72 for an eight-under-par 280 and two-shot victory over four competitors. But she thought that 73 in the third round belonged to the officials instead of her.

The second round was delayed four times for a total of five hours because of rain. Officials halted play at 8:52 p.m. — and Richard was one hole short of finishing her round. That meant she had to play that hole at 7:30 Saturday morning, and that meant she had to wait until late Saturday afternoon to play her third round.

"I'm angry," she said after shooting 73. "If there's any consolation to this rotten day, it's that I'm still on top." But a good night's sleep worked wonders for the final round. "I was excited," she said. "I'm a fighter, a perfectionist. I've kicked myself in the pants for 24 years to get where I am."

Not that winning was easy for the University of Florida graduate. She went into the final round one shot ahead of another Florida product, Lori Garbacz, and they were tied with six holes to play. But Garbacz missed par putts of five and seven feet on Nos. 13 and 14 to fall two back, and Richard clinched the victory with a 15-foot birdie on No. 16. Garbacz ended in a second-place tie with Amy Alcott, Shirley Furlong and frustrated Laurie Rinker, who was second for the second consecutive week.

Toledo Classic—$225,000
Winner: Jane Geddes

Should a contender watch the leaderboard or simply "play their own game?" That question led to a strange ending at the Toledo Classic as Jane Geddes literally sneaked by two unobservant rookies to win her fourth title of the season.

Rookies Nancy Taylor and Jill Briles were in the final threesome on the last day at Glengarry Country Club. Both said they never looked at the leaderboards all day. When Taylor sank a par putt on the final hole she thought she had forced a playoff with Briles for the title after shooting a six-under-par 282. Only then did she look up to discover Geddes already had finished at eight-under 280. "I had no clue Geddes was there," Taylor told the press. "It was a mistake. Consider this a learning experience."

Geddes considered it a relatively easy chance for victory. Almost all of the other tour leaders had taken the week off. Taylor had led for three rounds on scores of 68-68-73, three shots better than Geddes going into the last day. "I expected to win," Geddes said. "I thought they would back up to me, but I had to go chase them instead."

Using a brilliant short-iron game, Geddes birdied four holes on the front, all from less than 20 feet. She birdied the par-five 12th on two putts to catch the leaders and passed them with a 12-foot birdie on No. 15. When Geddes finished, both Taylor and Briles were a shot behind with two holes to play — and thought they were tied for the lead. Both bogeyed No. 17, not knowing they had just lost the tournament.

Geddes shot 280 on rounds of 71-73-69-67. After Briles and Taylor, fourth place was shared by Julie Cole and the increasingly frustrated Laurie Rinker, who had placed second the previous two weeks.

du Maurier Classic—$400,000
Winner: Jody Rosenthal

When Jody Rosental came from six shots back to win the United Virginia Bank Classic in early May, it was in answer to a long-distance telephone request from her mother. But when she came from six shots back again to win her first major, the du Maurier Classic, two months later, she did it on her own.

This time she called home after she had won, only to discover her parents were already celebrating. "It's a dream come true," said Rosenthal, the 1986 Rookie of the Year. "My first goal was to win a tournament, and when I did, then I wanted to win a major. Now I want to win another major."

The victim was Ayako Okamoto, who went into the final round of the du Maurier with a six-shot lead on Rosenthal. But a six-under-par 66 by Rosenthal and a fading 74 by Okamoto gave Rosenthal her second victory and prevented Okamoto from capturing her fourth crown of the season.

Rosenthal had rounds of 68-70-68-66 for a stunning 16-under-par 272 on the Islesmere Golf Club course in Laval, Quebec, Canada. Okamoto took second, two shots back, while Canadian Barb Bunkowsky and Shirley Furlong tied for third at 278. Bunkowsky's effort was the best finish by a Canadian in the 14-year history of the tournament.

The first hole of the final round set the tone for the day. Rosenthal sank a 25-foot birdie putt, and Okamoto took a bogey because of a suddenly cold putter. That trend continued until, after 12 holes, Okamoto's six-shot lead had dwindled to one.

Then, as they say in Quebec, the coup de grace. Rosenthal scored four consecutive birdies on putts of 10, eight, 15 and 10 feet to take an amazing four-shot lead with two holes to play. Three putts on No. 17 cost her two shots, but a 20-foot par putt on No. 18 sealed the verdict.

At the beginning it was all Okamoto. She tied the course record with a seven-under 65 in the opening round, making birdies on the first five holes. A 69 in the second round kept Okamoto ahead, then a 66 on Saturday gave her a remarkable 16-under total of 200 after three rounds.

Okamoto did share Saturday's attention with Robin Walton, who shot a tournament-record 64. Walton's round included two eagles as she holed a 118-yard eight iron on No. 6 and a 182-yard three iron on No. 9. Her 64 was a stroke better than the course's 30-year-old competitive record for both men and women.

Boston Five Classic—$300,000
Winner: Jane Geddes

One hot streak scorched another as Jane Geddes defended her title at the Boston Five Classic by holding off the challenge of young Jody Rosenthal, who had won the du Maurier Classic the week before.

After rounds of 73-70 and 67, Geddes birdied the tournament's final hole for another 67 and an 11-under-par total of 277, one shot better than Rosenthal and resurgent Donna White. Rosie Jones and the always-near-by Betsy King finished another shot behind.

The victory was No. 5 of the season for Geddes, who had won seven events in a 12-month period that dated back to winning the Boston Five and the U.S. Open in 1986. Some come to play, but Geddes is infatuated with winning.

"Playing well right now for me is winning," Geddes said. "That's all I come out here for — to win. And now I've won my first title defense."

It wasn't easy. Geddes began the final round at the Tara Ferncroft course near Boston, Massachusetts, three shots behind Becky Pearson, who was nine under for 54 holes. The final threesome consisted of Pearson, Geddes and Rosenthal, but Pearson — coming back from a rib injury that kept her off the tour for nine weeks — could do no better than 16 pars and a pair of bogeys to slip back to seventh.

Geddes held a one-shot lead on Rosenthal with three holes to play, but Rosenthal sank a 15-footer for a birdie on No. 16 to tie. Neither could birdie No. 17 while White, playing ahead, birdied No. 18 to join them at 10 under.

No. 18 was a par five, 485-yard hole that required a 200-yard second shot to carry over a pond fronting the green. A perfect hole for Geddes, one of the tour's longest hitters. Geddes blasted her second wood just over the green, while Rosenthal's second shot barely cleared the pond. Rosenthal chipped to 15 feet and missed — Geddes chipped to six feet and won.

Back in the opening round, Geddes shot 73, placing her six shots behind co-leaders Amy Alcott, Cathy Marino and Sally Quinlan. Rosenthal (69-66) took the midway lead, before Pearson (69-68-70) took brief command going into the final round.

U.S. Open—$367,500
Winner: Laura Davies

Wonderful dreams come true every year on the LPGA Tour but few could ever match Laura Davies' winning of the U.S. Open while still reigning as champion of the British Open she won in the previous season. But like any dream worth having, this one was difficult to achieve.

The U.S. Open began on Thursday and did not end until after an 18-hole international playoff the following Tuesday between Britain's Davies, Japan's Ayako Okamoto and the United States' JoAnne Carner. Davies won with a one-under-par 71 to 73 for Okamoto and 74 for Carner.

The threesome had tied after 72 rain-delayed holes at three-under-par 285 and were the only competitors to finish under par on the difficult Plainfield Country Club course in northern New Jersey. Betsy King and Jody Rosenthal tied for fourth at one-over 289, four shots back.

Okamoto fell back quickly in the playoff with bogeys on Nos. 5 and 6. Davies and Carner, matching booming drives, were tied after 10 holes, but Carner took bogeys on two of the next three holes to drop back.

The victory was something of a redemption for Davies. She had shot an opening 66 in the Dinah Shore only to shoot 83 in the second round and finish 33rd. "That week was a great lesson," she said. "I've learned a lot this year about being a leader."

The entire field learned a lot about nearly impossible conditions. The temperature stayed in the 90s for most of the week even though rainstorms forced the tournament to go an extra day to finish its regulation 72 holes. Lauren Howe passed out on the 13th green in the second round on Friday and was hospitalized for two days. Pat Bradley shot 81-75 to miss two consecutive cuts for the first time in her career. And defending champion Jane Geddes withdrew after three non-contending rounds.

Bonnie Lauer and Dot Germain briefly led by shooting 69 each in the opening round. Davies (72-70) led by a shot at the midway point, then Okamoto (71-72-70) took a one-shot lead on her with Carner three back after 54 holes.

The leaders did not start their final round until Monday. Okamoto took an early three-shot lead with birdies on the second and third holes. But four putts on No. 9 dropped her back into a tie with Davies at three under. Carner rallied to take the lead with a birdie on No. 17 only to drop back into the three-way tie with a bogey on the last hole. Davies was content to par the final hole and wait one more day for her dreams to come true.

A footnote is that Davies almost defended her British Open title on the same week, losing by one stroke at St. Mellion to Alison Nicholas, who shot 296. Davies and Muffin Spencer-Devlin tied for second at 297 when Nicholas prevented a playoff by making birdie on the 72nd hole.

LPGA National Pro-Am—$250,000
Winner: Chris Johnson

Describing herself as "bonkers in the bunkers," Chris Johnson blasted her way to a runaway victory by five strokes over Shirley Furlong in the high altitude LPGA National Pro-Am on two courses in Denver, Colorado.

Johnson led from the start to finish on rounds of 66-71-70-70 for a 11-under-par 277. She started the final round with just a one-shot lead on Sally Quinlan, but Johnson birdied the first two holes and Quinlan bogeyed the first three to cut the suspense short. After 12 holes Johnson led Furlong by four, then made birdie putts of eight feet and five feet after blasting out of the sand, extending her lead to six shots with four holes to play.

The battle for second ended with Furlong finishing a shot ahead of Sara Anne Timms, who was one shot in front of Jan Stephenson and Sherri Turner. Nobody really was complaining as Furlong and Timms collected the largest checks of their careers for second and third.

Henredon Classic—$300,000
Winner: Mary Beth Zimmerman

What keeps golfing tournaments fresh week after week is that the outcome is never guaranteed. Mary Beth Zimmerman cashed in on that truism with a sudden burst to victory in the Henredon Classic near High Point, North Carolina.

With four holes to play in the final round, fans were preparing for a playoff between Nancy Lopez and rebounding Beth Daniel along with a host of others. Five players were tied for the lead, three more were one shot back and nine more were two behind. Anything could happen.

What did happen was that Zimmerman sank a three-foot birdie putt on No. 15, made a two-putt par from 30 feet on No. 16, and then sank two birdie putts of 15 feet each on the final two holes. Meanwhile, that enormous pack just coasted in, allowing her to win by three shots over Lopez, Daniel and Laurie Rinker.

Zimmerman shot rounds of 72-68-66 for a 10-under-par 206 on the Willow Creek Country Club course. The tournament was shortened from 72 to 54 holes after Friday's second round was washed out.

Shelley Hamlin was the first-round leader with 67. After the wet day off, Heather Drew, Colleen Walker, Missie Berteotti and Daniel led at 139 each, with Zimmerman a stroke back. That set the stage for her late heroics as she left the field behind her.

MasterCard International—$225,000
Winner: Val Skinner

Some tournaments are lost instead of won, and Val Skinner felt more like a beneficiary than a winner after her strange battle with Shelley Hamlin in the MasterCard International in Weschester County, north of New York City.

Skinner began the third and final round two shots ahead of Hamlin and at least five ahead of everybody else. And she birdied the first hole to extend her lead by another shot. But her roller coaster headed for the bottom then as she played bogey, double bogey, bogey and bogey on the next four holes, while Hamlin holed a 91-yard wedge shot on No. 9 for an eagle and a four-shot lead.

So much for momentum. Just as Skinner was ready to surrender and Hamlin was thinking about her first victory since the 1978 Patty Berg Classic, the roller coaster shifted again. Hamlin suffered bogeys on Nos. 10 and 11, then had her double bogey on No. 15. They played even after that until Skinner sank a five-foot par putt on the final hole to win.

Skinner had rounds of 67-70-75 for four-under par 212 on two courses, while Hamlin was 69-70-74 for 213. Skinner collected $33,750, but Hamlin was not unhappy with $20,812 after failing to make the tour's top 90 for the past three years.

Ayako Okamoto made a third-round charge with a 69 to finish tied for third at 215 with Sandra Palmer, Dawn Coe, Sherri Turner and Hollis Stacy.

Atlantic City Classic—$225,000
Winner: Betsy King

With seven tournamentts left on the LPGA schedule, Betsy King and Ayako Okamoto began their charge to catch year-long leader Jane Geddes. King made the first move by racing to her fourth victory of the year in the Atlantic City Classic, finishing three shots ahead of Nancy Lopez.

The victory was worth $33,750, pushing King ahead of Geddes in the money race with earnings of $381,775. Okamoto was bidding her time in third place.

King, whose last victory had been 11 tournaments back in the McDonald's Classic, caught the leaders off guard on the final day by making birdies on six of the first nine holes to move from three shots back to four shots ahead of Lopez. King coasted on the backside for a five-under 66, after rounds of 70 and 71, to shoot a six-under 207 on the course at Marriott's Seaview Golf Resort. "I looked at the leaderboard and scared myself," King said of her sudden charge, "but I'm always thinking that I have a chance."

Defending champion Juli Inkster was the first-round leader at 67. Lopez and Beth Daniel then took control at 138 each, three shots ahead of the deceptive King. Lopez held on for a closing 72 to finish second at 210, while Sherri Turner used a course-record 65 for third at 211. Daniel, shooting 74, tied for fourth with Patti Rizzo and Inkster at one-under 212. Okamoto shot a distant 216.

Nestle World Championship—$250,000
Winner: Ayako Okamoto

The outcome of a tournament sometimes rises above logical explanation. The 1987 Nestle World Championship was such a tournament, living up to its name by becoming the last real showdown of the season between the Big Three — Ayako Okamoto, Betsy King and Jane Geddes.

Okamoto won, shooting rounds of 70-68-73-71 for a six-under par 282, one stroke ahead of King and two ahead of Geddes. The victory, Okamoto's fourth of the season, and the first prize of $81,500 would prove to be the winning difference between her and the other two for LPGA annual honors.

It seemed as if the three realized the importance of their battle even though five more official events remained on the schedule. All three admitted to unusual nervousness during the week and even to a lack of confidence in their own ability to win.

Perhaps more pressure was on Okamoto than anyone else. The Japanese press, which followed her every move, was distressed that she had lost the U.S. Women's Open in a playoff to England's Laura Davies and finished second in the du Maurier to Jody Rosenthal. It seemed as if her season would not be considered a success without a major victory such as the World Championship, a battle between the 11 top pros and U.S. Amateur champion Kay Cockerill.

Cockerill caused the early excitement just days after winning her second consecutive U.S. Amateur title. She took the first-round lead with a three-under 69 at the Stouffer PineIsle Resort outside Atlanta, Georgia. Cockerill eventually finished 11 shots out, tied for 10th with defending champion Pat Bradley.

Okamoto moved atop the leaderboard after two rounds of 70 and 68, never to leave it. But Geddes made up six shots in the third round by shooting 67 to tie Okamoto for the lead with King four shots back.

Okamoto and King birdied two of the first four holes in the final round while disaster struck Geddes in the form of a quadruple-bogey nine on the par-five fifth, a result of placing two shots in Lake Lanier. However, Geddes played the next 10 holes in five under, pulling within a stroke of Okamoto.

And bogeys on Nos. 10 and 12 dropped Okamoto into a tie with King, while Geddes slipped back again. But birdies on Nos. 14 and 16 for Okamoto to a sole birdie on No. 16 for King was the difference as both took pars on the final two holes, Okamoto winning with two putts from 12 feet on the final hole.

Rail Classic—$200,000
Winner: Rosie Jones

Role reversal often is a useful tool as Rosie Jones discovered when she switched places with Nancy Lopez to win the Rail Classic, her first victory in six years of trying on the tour.

It was obvious on the final day who was favored by the gallery when Lopez sank a birdie putt on No. 16 to tie Jones for the lead with two holes to play. And after both made pars on the par-five 17th, it came down to one hole for victory.

On the par-four finishing hole, Lopez was seven feet from the cup in two, while Jones had placed her tee shot in the right rough, 132 yards from the green. Jones pulled out her eight iron and later said, "I hit the shot of my life." That shot left her six feet from the pin.

Lopez watched her birdie attempt die to the left. Then Jones made her birdie putt and went into a victory dance. "I remember how it was when I won my first tournament," said Lopez. "Watching Rosie gave me chills."

Lopez, after finishing second in the last three tournaments she had played, was not far from career victory No. 36.

Jones had rounds of 69-69-70 for an eight-under-par 208 at the Rail Golf Club near Springfield, Ohio. Lopez shot 68-71-70 for 209. Betsy King shot a closing 66 to tie Shirley Furlong for third at 210.

Ping Championship—$225,000
Winner: Nancy Lopez

On the rarest of occasions it is easy to predict the winner of a golf tournament before the event begins. Entering the Ping Championship, Nancy Lopez had not won since the second week of the season but had finished second in her last three events. After a champion like Lopez knocks three times, she's bound to kick down the door.

Not that it was easy. She didn't take the lead until she birdied No. 17 on the final day and sank a four-foot par putt on the final hole to avoid a four-player playoff including Jan Stephenson, Muffin Spencer-Devlin and rookie Kelly Leadbetter.

Lopez had rounds of 72-67-71 for a six-under-par 210 at the Columbia-Edgewater Country Club in Portland, Oregon. The other three shot 211 each. Chris Johnson was fifth at 212. Ayako Okamoto, the defending champion, shot a course-record 65 in the closing round to join a four-way tie for sixth.

If nothing else Lopez should have been in a playoff with Leadbetter and would have been except that Leadbetter missed a par putt on the final hole from 18 inches. She was crying when she left the green but would be smiling at the end of the year. Her check for $15,937 would add enough to her earnings to keep her player's card for another season.

Johnson was the first-round leader at 67. Patti Rizzo took the lead (68-69) and Jane Geddes was second (69-69) going into the final round. But Rizzo shot a closing 77 and Geddes had to take an 80. This one seemed ordained for Lopez, but Stephenson's turn was next.

Safeco Classic—$225,000
Winner: Jan Stephenson

Turn-about has always been considered fair play, and Jan Stephenson made up for finishing a stroke behind Nancy Lopez the week before by finishing a stroke ahead to win the Safeco Classic.

"People wonder if it's worth it," Stephenson said about her comeback from an auto accident in May. "When you beat an old rival, there's no feeling like it."

Stephenson won on rounds of 68-70-71-68 for an 11-under-par 277 at the Meridian Valley Country Club near Kent, Washington. Lopez shot 66-67 in her last 36 holes but could do no better than par on the final three holes. Stephenson had gained her winning edge with an eight-foot birdie putt on No. 16.

Rosie Jones fired a 67 to take the first-round lead. Stephenson and Michele Berteotti were the midway leaders at 138 each, before Berteotti and Cindy Hill grabbed the three-quarters lead with 208, a shot ahead of Stephenson. Berteotti shot a closing 72 to finish third at 280, three shots out, and Johnson was fourth at 281.

Lopez, who had four seconds and a first in her last five events, called an end to her season with winnings of $204,823. But Stephenson was far from finished yet.

San Jose Classic—$300,000
Winner: Jan Stephenson

Despite both her skill and beauty, Jan Stephenson may be best remembered as a survivor. She demonstrated that knack once again by winning the San Jose Classic, her second consecutive victory and third of the year.

Stephenson missed six weeks of the season recuperating from four broken ribs because of an auto accident in May. But her game was back in form at the Almaden Golf and Country Club as she broke the course record with rounds of 69-71-65 for an 11-under-par 205. Amy Alcott was second, five strokes back.

Missie Berteotti was the first-round leader with a four-under 68 but would slide to a 78 in the final round. Juli Inkster took control at 138 after two rounds, two shots ahead of Stephenson.

The final round belonged to Jan. She tied for the lead with birdies on the first and third holes, then ran away from the field with four consecutive birdies on Nos. 7 through 10. "This is one of the hottest streaks of my career," she said. "I just hate to see the season end."

Mazda Japan Classic—$350,000
Winner: Yuko Moriguchi

Yes, Yuko Moriguchi won the last event on the 1987 LPGA Tour, but it was compatriot Ayako Okamoto who was carried to the victory ceremony on the shoulders of many of her competitors and friends as Okamoto became the first non-American to become the tour's leading money winner and Player of the Year.

Going into the final event, Okamoto and Betsy King were fighting it out for the money-list title, while Okamoto, King and Jane Geddes were tied for Player of the Year honors.

By finishing second behind Moriguchi, who shot a 10-under-par 206 to win, Okamoto earned $32,375 for her 209 effort. King won $18,375 for finishing fourth at 215. The final totals were $466,034 for Okamoto to $460,385 for King.

Okamoto also took Player of the Year with 68 points to 66 for King and 64 for Geddes, who shot 220 in the final event and finished third on the money list at $396,818 despite a late-season slump.

King did finish the year with the best scoring average at 71.14 to 71.36 for Okamoto.

"Being 36 years old, I am proud of myself for being able to come this far," Okamoto said. "When the U.S. players carried me, I was so happy. I could not have possibly come this far without my friends on the LPGA Tour."

Oh yes, the tournament. Val Skinner shot an opening 67, but it was all Moriguchi after that. She had rounds of 68-66-72 to 68-71-70 for Okamoto. Atsuko Hikage was another five shots back at 214, followed by King.

APPENDIXES

World Money List

This listing of the 200 leading money winners in the world of professional golf in 1987 was compiled from the results of all tournaments carried in the Appendixes of this edition, along with other non-tour and international events for which accurate figures could be obtained and in which the players competed for prize money provided by someone other than the players themselves. Skins games, shootouts and seasonal bonus money are not included. Leader Ian Woosnam's total includes $1,000,000 from winner-takes-all Million Dollar Challenge.

In the 22 years during which World Money Lists have been compiled, the earnings of the player in the 200th position have risen from a total of $3,326 in 1966 to $101,172 in 1987. The top 200 players in 1966 earned a total of $4,680,287. In 1987, the comparable total was $56,654,020.

Because of the fluctuating values of money throughout the world, it was necessary to determine an average value of non-American currency to U.S. money to prepare this listing. The conversion rates used for 1987 were: British pound = US $1.65; 140 Japanese yen = US$1; South African rand = US¢50; Australian/New Zealand dollar = US$.75.

POS.	PLAYER, COUNTRY	TOTAL MONEY
1	Ian Woosnam, Wales	$1,793,268
2	Curtis Strange, U.S.	911,671
3	Paul Azinger, U.S.	844,506
4	Sandy Lyle, Scotland	767,891
5	Greg Norman, Australia	715,838
6	Scott Simpson, U.S.	713,067
7	Miller Barber, U.S.	709,571
8	Payne Stewart, U.S.	704,426
9	Tom Watson, U.S.	694,587
10	Ben Crenshaw, U.S.	671,844
11	Bernhard Langer, West Germany	667,797
12	Severiano Ballesteros, Spain	655,256
13	Bruce Crampton, Australia	645,621
14	Lanny Wadkins, U.S.	643,571
15	David Ishii, U.S.	643,030
16	Chi Chi Rodriguez, U.S.	623,395
17	Masashi Ozaki, Japan	613,867
18	Mark Calcavecchia, U.S.	602,350
19	Larry Mize, U.S.	574,027
20	Tom Kite, U.S.	571,791
21	Bob Charles, New Zealand	571,480
22	Larry Nelson, U.S.	555,190
23	David Frost, South Africa	544,322
24	Nick Faldo, England	541,582
25	Chip Beck, U.S.	525,878
26	Scott Hoch, U.S.	522,442
27	Fred Couples, U.S.	513,766
28	Corey Pavin, U.S.	500,152
29	Isao Aoki, Japan	494,734
30	Craig Stadler, U.S.	491,217
31	Hal Sutton, U.S.	482,771
32	Orville Moody, U.S.	481,881

POS.	PLAYER, COUNTRY	TOTAL MONEY
33	Don Pooley, U.S.	466,130
34	Dan Pohl, U.S.	436,462
35	Gary Player, South Africa	423,372
36	D. A. Weibring, U.S.	420,600
37	Mark O'Meara, U.S.	420,439
38	Mark McCumber, U.S.	413,385
39	Graham Marsh, Australia	412,979
40	Gene Littler U.S.	409,629
41	Mark McNulty, Zimbabwe	408,085
42	Sam Torrance, Scotland	392,291
43	Dale Douglass, U.S.	377,317
44	Hajime Meshiai, Japan	376,101
45	Rodger Davis, Australia	373,827
46	Mike Reid, U.S.	370,671
47	Keith Clearwater, U.S.	353,392
48	Jeff Sluman, U.S.	352,828
49	Masahiro Kuramoto, Japan	352,436
50	Tsuneyuki Nakajima, Japan	351,136
51	Steve Pate, U.S.	350,098
52	Nick Price, Zimbabwe	346,469
53	John Cook, U.S.	339,684
54	Bob Tway, U.S.	337,449
55	Ken Green, U.S.	337,201
56	Howard Clark, England	336,739
57	Brian Jones, Australia	329,559
58	Bobby Wadkins, U.S.	329,087
59	Davis Love III, U.S.	325,253
60	Butch Baird, U.S.	318,714
61	Billy Casper, U.S.	318,643
62	Peter Senior, Australia	317,853
63	Gordon Brand Jr., Scotland	315,104
64	Harold Henning, South Africa	314,253
65	Ken Brown, Scotland	310,877
66	Andy Bean, U.S.	294,423
67	Nobuo Serizawa, Japan	294,414
68	Al Geiberger, U.S.	294,263
69	Chen Tze Chung, Taiwan	291,439
70	Hiroshi Makino, Japan	282,027
71	Jay Haas, U.S.	281,732
72	Yoshitaka Yamamoto, Japan	279,339
73	Chen Tze Ming, Taiwan	278,528
74	Mac O'Grady, U.S.	276,567
75	Joey Sindelar, U.S.	269,951
76	Seiichi Kanai, Japan	267,752
77	Mike Hulbert, U.S.	266,940
78	Ian Baker-Finch, Australia	262,940
79	Fuzzy Zoeller, U.S.	262,351
80	Arnold Palmer, U.S.	259,420
81	Bobby Nichols, U.S.	258,115
82	Naomichi Ozaki, Japan	254,156
83	Dave Hill, U.S.	251,439
84	Gene Sauers, U.S.	251,140
85	Denis Watson, Zimbabwe	250,449
86	Lee Elder, U.S.	246,172
87	J. C. Snead, U.S.	240,999
88	Gary Hallberg, U.S.	239,072
89	Katsunari Takahashi, Japan	236,228
90	Peter Thomson, Australia	234,004
91	Kenny Knox, U.S.	233,433
92	Toru Nakamura, Japan	233,383

POS.	PLAYER, COUNTRY	TOTAL MONEY
93	Dave Barr, Canada	231,261
94	Steve Jones, U.S.	228,855
95	Ronan Rafferty, Northern Ireland	227,082
96	George Burns, U.S.	226,721
97	Robert Wrenn, U.S.	224,724
98	John Mahaffey, U.S.	220,038
99	Jose Rivero, Spain	218,787
100	Curt Byrum, U.S.	216,905
101	Jodie Mudd, U.S.	211,423
102	Tadao Nakamura, Japan	210,713
103	Wayne Levi, U.S.	209,072
104	Chris Perry, U.S.	204,602
105	Donnie Hammond, U.S.	204,380
106	Gordon J. Brand, England	202,066
107	Sam Randolph, U.S.	200,947
108	Larry Mowry, U.S.	200,151
109	Water Zembriski, U.S.	200,036
110	Jose-Maria Olazabal, Spain	194,331
111	Doug Tewell, U.S.	189,923
112	Hale Irwin, U.S.	189,648
113	Clarence Rose, U.S.	187,420
114	Don January, U.S.	186,919
115	Anders Forsbrand, Sweden	184,235
116	Tim Simpson, U.S.	181,861
117	Howard Twitty, U.S.	177,912
118	Eamonn Darcy, Ireland	177,457
119	Tateo Ozaki, Japan	176,717
120	Morris Hatalsky, U.S.	176,304
121	Buddy Gardner, U.S.	176,297
122	Mike Donald, U.S.	173,984
123	Wayne Grady, Australia	169,849
124	Ronnie Black, U.S.	169,658
125	David Llewellyn, Wales	167,832
126	Roger Maltbie, U.S.	166,882
127	Saburo Fujiki, Japan	166,273
128	Bruce Lietzke, U.S.	166,258
129	Bill Glasson, U.S.	164,951
130	Koichi Suzuki, Japan	163,198
131	Dan Forsman, U.S.	161,723
132	Noboru Sugai, Japan	161,712
133	Dave Rummells, U.S.	161,220
134	Tsukasa Watanabe, Japan	160,088
135	Danny Edwards, U.S.	159,998
136	Ben Smith, U.S.	159,293
137	Gay Brewer, U.S.	157,259
138	Fulton Allem, South Africa	157,256
139	Johnny Miller, U.S.	156,444
140	Yoshikazu Yokoshima, Japan	156,185
141	Lennie Clements, U.S.	154,614
142	John Inman, U.S.	154,386
143	Terry Gale, Australia	152,472
144	Mark Wiebe, U.S.	151,567
145	Bobby Clampett, U.S.	151,182
146	Bob Brue, U.S.	150,685
147	Russ Cochran, U.S.	150,460
148	Bob Gilder, U.S.	150,275
149	David Edwards, U.S.	148,217
150	Raymond Floyd, U.S.	147,944
151	Tom Purtzer, U.S.	147,237
152	Tom Byrum, U.S.	146,384

POS.	PLAYER, COUNTRY	TOTAL MONEY
153	Doug Sanders, U.S.	144,145
154	Ove Sellberg, Sweden	144,007
155	Hugh Baiocchi, South Africa	143,836
156	Kinpachi Yoshimura, Japan	141,687
157	Mats Lanner, Sweden	141,257
158	Masanobu Kimura, Japan	139,803
159	Mark Mouland, Wales	138,928
160	Seiji Ebihara, Japan	138,419
161	Gil Morgan, U.S.	137,980
162	Isamu Sugita, Japn	137,554
163	Willie Wood, U.S.	137,495
164	Bob Lohr, U.S.	137,108
165	Charles Owens, U.S.	136,480
166	Peter Jacobsen, U.S.	136,341
167	Peter Fowler, Australia	136,153
168	Richard Zokol, Canada	135,331
169	Nobumitsu Yuhara, Japan	131,568
170	Hsieh Min Nan, Taiwan	129,886
171	Lu Liang Huan, Taiwan	129,813
172	Roberto de Vicenzo, Argentina	128,687
173	Rick Fehr, U.S.	127,675
174	Blaine McCallister, U.S.	124,170
175	Jim Ferree, U.S.	123,383
176	Jim King, U.S.	122,197
177	Brad Faxon, U.S.	120,604
178	John Bland, South Africa	119,693
179	John Brodie, U.S.	119,006
180	Bob Eastwood, U.S.	118,827
181	Jose-Maria Canizares, Spain	116,455
182	Teruo Nakamura, Japan	115,457
183	Rocco Mediate, U.S.	115,264
184	David Feherty, Northern Ireland	112,747
185	Tommy Aaron, U.S.	112,516
186	Namio Takasu, Japan	111,877
187	Kikuo Arai, Japan	111,312
188	Tony Johnstone, Zimbabwe	110,634
189	Ed Fiori, U.S.	110,532
190	Yoshiyuki Isomura, Japan	109,873
191	Don Massengale, U.S.	109,666
192	Kenny Perry, U.S.	108,814
193	Tony Sills, U.S.	107,508
194	Andrew Magee, U.S.	106,598
195	Dick Mast, U.S.	104,768
196	Des Smyth, Ireland	104,237
197	Ken Still, U.S.	103,813
198	Christy O'Connor Jr., Ireland	103,529
199	Antonio Garrido, Spain	101,287
200	Carl Mason, England	101,172

The Sony Ranking

The Sony Ranking is based on a rolling three-year total. There are four grades of tournaments: Grade 1 (major championships), Grade 2 (leading tournaments and championships), Grade 3 (intermediate tournaments and major invitational events), and Grade 4 (other tournaments and invitational events). Current-year points are multiplied by four; previous-year points, by two; and third-year points, by one, to provide more emphasis on current ability.

POS.	PLAYER, COUNTRY	POINTS	POS.	PLAYER, COUNTRY	POINTS
1	Greg Norman, Australia	1231	46	Fred Couples, U.S.	341
2	Seve Ballesteros, Spain	1169	47	Nick Price, Zimbabwe	339
3	Bernhard Langer, W. Germany	1112	48	Mac O'Grady, U.S.	318
4	Sandy Lyle, Scotland	879	49	Jose-Maria Olazabal, Spain	307
5	Curtis Strange, U.S.	873	50	Calvin Peete, U.S.	304
6	Ian Woosnam, Wales	830	51	Mike Reid, U.S.	287
7	Payne Stewart, U.S.	717	52	Chen Tze Chung, Taiwan	282
8	Lanny Wadkins, U.S.	697	53	John Mahaffey, U.S.	277
9	Mark McNulty, Zimbabwe	673	54	John Cook, U.S.	272
10	Ben Crenshaw, U.S.	668		Mark McCumber, U.S.	272
11	Paul Azinger, U.S.	649	56	Jay Haas, U.S.	265
12	Larry Mize, U.S.	645	57	Ken Green, U.S.	264
13	Rodger Davis, Australia	626	58	Jodie Mudd, U.S.	262
14	Nick Faldo, England	623		Ronan Rafferty, N. Ireland	262
15	Tsuneyuki Nakajima, Japan	617	60	Davis Love III, U.S.	248
16	Tom Watson, U.S.	616		Doug Tewell, U.S.	248
17	Scott Simpson, U.S.	592	62	Ken Brown, Scotland	240
18	Masashi Ozaki, Japan	591		Jose Rivero, Spain	240
19	Isao Aoki, Japan	580	64	Hugh Baiocchi, S. Africa	237
20	Hal Sutton, U.S.	579	65	Jack Nicklaus, U.S.	236
21	Tom Kite, U.S.	563		Brian Jones, Australia	236
22	David Frost, S. Africa	556	67	Joey Sindelar, U.S.	233
23	Larry Nelson, U.S.	551	68	Gordon J. Brand, England	232
24	Corey Pavin, U.S.	528	69	Fulton Allem, S. Africa	228
25	David Ishii, U.S.	515		Roger Maltbie, U.S.	228
26	Mark O'Meara, U.S.	503	71	Donnie Hammond, U.S.	227
27	Scott Hoch, U.S.	499	72	Naomichi Ozaki, Japan	224
28	Craig Stadler, U.S.	493	73	Jeff Sluman, U.S.	216
29	Dan Pohl, U.S.	491	74	Steve Pate, U.S.	212
	Bob Tway, U.S.	491	75	Tateo Ozaki, Japan	211
31	Mark Calcavecchia, U.S.	454	76	Mike Hulbert, U.S.	204
32	Don Pooley, U.S.	432	77	J.C. Snead, U.S.	202
33	Gordon Brand, Jr., Scotland	425	78	George Burns, U.S.	201
34	Andy Bean, U.S.	423	79	Anders Forsbrand, Sweden	200
35	Graham Marsh, Australia	420	80	Toru Nakamura, Japan	198
36	Chip Beck, U.S.	406	81	Jim Thorpe, U.S.	192
37	Raymond Floyd, U.S.	392	82	Gene Sauers, U.S.	188
38	Peter Senior, Australia	380	83	Wayne Levi, U.S.	187
39	Fuzzy Zoeller, U.S.	372		Chen Tze Ming, Taiwan	187
40	Ian Baker-Finch, Australia	365		David Graham, Australia	187
41	Howard Clark, England	361	86	Denis Watson, Zimbabwe	182
42	Bobby Wadkins, U.S.	357	87	Hajime Meshiai, Japan	180
43	D.A. Weibring, U.S.	356	88	Wayne Grady, Australia	179
44	Sam Torrance, Scotland	349	89	Johnny Miller, U.S.	177
45	Masahiro Kuramoto, Japan	347	90	Curt Byrum, U.S.	175

POS.	PLAYER, COUNTRY	POINTS	POS.	PLAYER, COUNTRY	POINTS
91	Dave Barr, Canada	174	147	Willie Wood, U.S.	95
	Seiichi Kanai, Japan	174	148	Lennie Clements, U.S.	94
93	Mark Wiebe, U.S.	173		Kikuo Arai, Japan	94
94	Jose-Maria Canizares, Spain	171	150	Bob Lohr, U.S.	92
	John Bland, S. Africa	171		Tom Purtzer, U.S.	92
96	Clarence Rose, U.S.	170		Nobumitsu Yuhara, Japan	92
97	Danny Edwards, U.S.	168	153	Andy North, U.S.	91
	Keith Clearwater, U.S.	168	154	Tom Byrum, U.S.	90
99	Kenny Knox, U.S.	167	155	Bobby Clampett, U.S.	89
100	Lee Trevino, U.S.	163	156	Ossie Moore, Australia	88
	Katsunari Takahashi, Japan	163	157	Bob Murphy, U.S.	87
102	Dan Forsman, U.S.	157		Sam Randolph, U.S.	87
103	Yoshitaka Yamamoto, Japan	156	159	Carl Mason, England	86
104	Gary Hallberg, U.S.	155		Noel Ratcliffe, Australia	86
105	Bruce Lietzke, U.S.	148	161	Steve Jones, U.S.	84
	Tim Simpson, U.S.	148	162	Saburo Fujiki, Japan	82
	David Feherty, Ireland	148	163	Ian Mosey, England	80
108	Mark James, England	146	164	David Llewellyn, Wales	79
109	Tony Johnstone, Zimbabwe	142	165	Ed Fiori, U.S.	76
110	Hubert Green, U.S.	140		Bob Shearer, Australia	76
	Paul Way, England	140		David A. Russell, England	76
112	Nobou Serizawa, Japan	139	168	Ronnie Black, U.S.	74
113	Peter Fowler, Australia	137	169	Noboru Sugai, Japan	73
114	Ove Sellberg, Sweden	136	170	Russ Cochran, U.S.	72
	Hiroshi Makino, Japan	136	171	Tsukasa Watanabe, Japan	68
116	Peter Jacobsen, U.S.	133		Jeff Hawkes, S. Africa	68
117	Buddy Gardner, U.S.	132	173	David Ogrin, U.S.	67
	Terry Gale, Australia	132		Kinpachi Yoshimura, Japan	67
119	Koichi Suzuki, Japan	131	175	Bob Eastwood, U.S.	66
120	Rick Fehr, U.S.	130		Gerry Taylor, Australia	66
121	Christy O'Connor, Jr., Ireland	127	177	Vicente Fernandez, Argentina	65
122	Gary Koch, U.S.	125	178	Akiyoshi Omashi, Japan	64
123	Howard Twitty, U.S.	124		Yoshikazu Yokoshima, Japan	64
124	Eamonn Darcy, Ireland	122		Philip Walton, Ireland	64
125	Mark Mouland, Wales	120	181	Roger Chapman, England	63
126	Robert Wrenn, U.S.	119	182	Brad Faxon, U.S.	62
127	Gil Morgan, U.S.	117		Lyndsay Stephen, Australia	62
128	Manuel Pinero, Spain	115	184	Hale Irwin, U.S.	61
129	David Edwards, U.S.	114		Scott Verplank, U.S.	61
130	Tony Sills, U.S.	113		Hsieh Min Nan, Taiwan	61
131	Morris Hatalsky, U.S.	112		Mike Harwood, Australia	61
	Des Smyth, Ireland	112	188	Dave Rummells, U.S.	60
133	Bill Glasson, U.S.	111	189	Larry Rinker, U.S.	59
134	Roger Mackay, Australia	110		Brian Marchbank, Scotland	59
135	Phil Blackmar, U.S.	109		Tadao Nakamura, Japan	59
136	Antonio Garrido, Spain	108	192	Dan Halldorson, Canada	58
137	Greg Turner, New Zealand	103		Blaine McCallister, U.S.	58
138	Magnus Persson, Sweden	102	194	Rick Hartmann, U.S.	56
139	Mike Donald, U.S.	101		Bobby Cole, S. Africa	56
	Teruo Sugihara, Japan	101	196	Jack Renner, U.S.	55
141	Mats Lanner, Sweden	100	197	Mike Sullivan, U.S.	54
142	Robert Lee, England	99	198	Bill Sander, U.S.	52
	Vaughan Somers, Australia	99		Seiji Ebihara, Japan	52
144	Pat McGowan, U.S.	98		Wayne Smith, Australia	52
145	Mike Colandro, U.S.	96		Brian Tennyson, U.S.	52
	Chris Perry, U.S.	96			

World's Winners of 1987

Spalding Invitational	Ken Green
Fila International	Hale Irwin
MONY Tournament of Champions	Mac O'Grady
Bob Hope Chrysler Classic	Corey Pavin
Phoenix Open	Paul Azinger
AT&T Pebble Beach National Pro-Am	Johnny Miller
Hawaiian Open	Corey Pavin
Shearson Lehman Bros. Andy Williams	George Burns
Los Angeles Open	T.C. Chen
Doral Ryder Open	Lanny Wadkins
Honda Classic	Mark Calcavecchia
Hertz Bay Hill Classic	Payne Stewart
USF&G Classic	Ben Crenshaw
Tournament Players Championship	Sandy Lyle
Greater Greensboro Open	Scott Simpson
Masters Tournament	Larry Mize
Deposit Guaranty Classic	David Ogrin
MCI Heritage Classic	Davis Love III
Big 'I' Houston Open	Jay Haas
Panasonic Las Vegas Invitational	Paul Azinger
Byron Nelson Golf Classic	Fred Couples
Colonial National Invitation	Keith Clearwater
Georgia-Pacific Atlanta Golf Classic	Dave Barr
Memorial Tournament	Don Pooley
Kemper Open	Tom Kite
Manufacturers Hanover Westchester Classic	J.C. Snead
U.S. Open Championship	Scott Simpson
Canon Sammy Davis Jr.-Greater Hartford	Paul Azinger
Canadian Open	Curtis Strange
Anheuser-Busch Golf Classic	Mark McCumber
Hardee's Golf Classic	Kenny Knox
Buick Open	Robert Wrenn
Federal Express St. Jude Classic	Curtis Strange
PGA Championship	Larry Nelson
The International	John Cook
Fred Meyer Challenge	Payne Stewart/Isao Aoki
Beatrice Western Open	D.A. Weibring
NEC World Series of Golf	Curtis Strange
Provident Classic	John Inman
B.C. Open	Joey Sindelar
Bank of Boston Classic	Sam Randolph
Canadian PGA	Jerry Anderson
Greater Milwaukee Open	Gary Hallberg
Ryder Cup	Europe
Southwest Golf Classic	Steve Pate
Southern Open	Ken Brown
Pensacola Open	Doug Tewell
Walt Disney World/Oldsmobile Golf Classic	Larry Nelson
Seiko Tucson Open	Mike Reid
Nabisco Championship	Tom Watson
Centel Classic	Keith Clearwater
Isuzu Kapalua International	Andy Bean
World Cup	Wales/Ian Woosnam
J.C. Penney Classic	Steve Jones/Jane Crafter
Chrysler Team Championship	Mike Hulbert/Bob Tway

EUROPEAN TOUR

Moroccan Open	Howard Clark
Jersey Open	Ian Woosnam
Suze Cannes Open	Seve Ballesteros
Cepsa Madrid Open	Ian Woosnam
Italian Open	Sam Torrance
Epson Grand Prix of Europe	Mats Lanner
Peugeot Spanish Open	Nick Faldo
Whyte & Mackay PGA Championship	Bernhard Langer
London Standard Four Stars Pro-Celebrity	Mark McNulty
Dunhill British Masters	Mark McNulty
Peugeot French Open	Jose Rivero
Volvo Belgian Open	Eamonn Darcy
Johnnie Walker Monte Carlo Open	Peter Senior
Carrolls Irish Open	Bernhard Langer
Bell's Scottish Open	Ian Woosnam
British Open Championship	Nick Faldo
KLM Dutch Open	Gordon Brand Jr.
Scandinavian Enterprise Open	Gordon Brand Jr.
PLM Open	Howard Clark
Benson & Hedges International	Noel Ratcliffe
Lawrence Batley International	Mark O'Meara
German Open	Mark McNulty
Ebel European Masters/Swiss Open	Anders Forsbrand
Panasonic European Open	Paul Way
Lancome Trophy	Ian Woosnam
Vernons Open	David Llewellyn
Dunhill Cup	England
German Masters	Sandy Lyle
Suntory World Match Play Championship	Ian Woosnam
Portuguese Open	Robert Lee

AFRICAN TOURS

Palabora Classic	Fulton Allem
ICL International	Tony Johnstone
Lexington PGA	Fulton Allem
Southern Sun South African Open	Mark McNulty
AECI Charity Classic	Mark McNulty
Royal Swazi Sun Pro-Am	Mark McNulty
Trust Bank Tournament of Champions	Mark McNulty
Zimbabwe Open	Gordon J. Brand
Kenya Open	Carl Mason
Zambia Open	Paul Carrigill
Minolta Match Play Championship	Tony Johnstone
Protea Assurance	Bobby Lincoln
Wild Coast Classic	Tony Johnstone
Million Dollar Challenge	Ian Woosnam
Safmarine South African Masters	David Frost
Goodyear Classic	John Bland

AUSTRALIAN TOUR

U-Bix New South Wales PGA	Peter Senior
Foster's Tattersall Tasmanian Open	Brian Jones
Robert Boyd Transport Australian Match Play	Ian Baker-Finch
Australian Masters	Greg Norman
Robert Boyd Transport Victorian Open	Roger Mackay
Rich River Classic	Peter Senior
Konica Queensland Open	David Graham
Queensland PGA	Peter Senior

National Panasonic New South Wales Open	Chris Parry
E.S.P. Australian PGA	Roger Mackay
West End South Australian Open	Ronan Rafferty
National Panasonic Western Australia Open	Gerry Tayor
National Panasonic Australian Open	Greg Norman
Air New Zealand Open	Mike Colandro
New Zealand Open	Ronan Rafferty

ASIA/JAPAN TOUR

San Miguel Philippines Open	Brian Tennyson
United Airlines Hong Kong Open	Ian Woosnam
Benson & Hedges Malaysian Open	Terry Gale
Thai International Thailand Open	T.M. Chen
Shizuoka Open	Lu Liang Huan
Charminar Challenge Indian Open	Brian Tennyson
Rolex Masters	T.M. Chen
Singapore Open	Peter Fowler
Indonesian Open	Wayne Smith
Pocari Sweat Open	Kinpachi Yoshimura
Republic of China Open	Mark Aebli
Bridgestone ASO Open	Norio Mikami
Maekyung Korea Open	Chen Liang Hsi
Dunlop Japan International Open	Isao Aoki
Chunichi Crowns	Jumbo Ozaki
Fuji Sankei Classic	Jumbo Ozaki
Japan PGA Match Play	Katsunari Takahashi
Pepsi Ube	T.M. Chen
Mitsubishi Galant	Brian Jones
Tohoku Classic	Seiichi Kanai
Sapporo Tokyu Open	David Ishii
Yomiuri Sapporo Open	Saporu Higashi
Mizuno Open Tournament	David Ishii
Kanto PGA Championship	Naomichi Ozaki
Kansai PGA Championship	Yoshitaka Yamamoto
Hiroshima Open	Hajime Meshiai
Japan PGA Championship	David Ishii
Niigata Open	Tadao Nakamura
Nikkei Cup/Nakamura Memorial Tournament	Noboru Serizawa
Maruman Nihonkai Open	Masahiro Kuramoto
KBC Augusta	Saburo Fujiki
Chu-Shikoku Open	Masahiro Kuramoto
Kansai Open	Masanobu Kimura
Kanto Open	Yoshikazu Yokoshima
Chibu Open	Eitaro Deguchi
Kyushu Open	Katsuyoshi Tomuri
Hokkaido Open	Akihiko Kojima
Suntory Open	Noboru Sugai
ANA Sapporo Open	Isao Aoki
Jun Classic	Jumbo Ozaki
Tokai Classic	Tommy Nakajima
Japan Open	Isao Aoki
Golf Digest	Ian Baker-Finch
Bridgestone Tournament	David Ishii
ABC Cup, Japan vs. USA	Andy Bean/Japan
Kirin Cup	United States
Visa Taiheiyo Club Masters	Graham Marsh
Dunlop Phoenix	Craig Stadler
Casio World Open	David Ishii
Japan Series	David Ishii/Isao Aoki
Daikyo Open	Isamu Sugita

SENIOR TOUR

MONY Senior Tournament of Champions	Don January
Seniors Classic	Harold Henning
General Foods PGA Senior Championship	Chi Chi Rodriguez
World Seniors Match Play Championship	Bruce Crampton
Del E. Webb Arizona Classic	Billy Casper
Vintage Chrysler Invitational	Bob Charles
GTE Senior Classic	Bob Charles
Chrysler Cup	International Team
Doug Sanders Kingwood Celebrity Classic	Bruce Crampton
Coca Cola Grand Slam Championship	Gene Littler
Liberty Mutual Legends of Golf	Orville Moody
	Bruce Crampton
Sunwest Bank-Charley Pride Classic	Bob Charles
Vantage at the Dominion	Chi Chi Rodriguez
United Hospitals Championship	Chi Chi Rodriguez
Silver Pages Classic	Chi Chi Rodriguez
Denver Champions of Golf	Bruce Crampton
Senior Players Reunion Pro-Am	Chi Chi Rodriguez
Mazda Senior Tournament Players Championship	Gary Player
Northville Invitational	Gary Player
Greater Grand Rapids Open	Billy Casper
Greenbriar/American Express Championship	Bruce Crampton
USGA Senior Open	Gary Player
MONY Syracuse Classic	Bruce Crampton
British Seniors Open	Neil Coles
NYNEX/Golf Digest Commemorative	Gene Littler
Digital Classic	Chi Chi Rodriguez
Rancho Murieta Gold Rush	Orville Moody
GTE Northwest Classic	Chi Chi Rodriguez
Showdown Classic	Miller Barber
Vantage Bank One Classic	Bruce Crampton
PaineWebber World Seniors Invitational	Gary Player
Crestar Classic	Larry Mowry
Newport Cup	Miller Barber
Vantage Championship	Al Geiberger
Pepsi Challenge	Larry Mowry
Hilton Head International	Al Geiberger
Las Vegas Classic	Al Geiberger
Fairfield Barnett Classic	Dave Hill
Gus Machado Classic	Gene Littler
Mauna Lani Challenge	Bob Charles
GTE Kaanapali Classic	Orville Moody
Mazda Champions	Miller Barber/Nancy Lopez

LPGA TOUR

Mazda Classic	Kathy Postlewait
Sarasota Classic	Nancy Lopez
Tsumura Hawaiian Ladies Open	Cindy Rarick
Women's Kemper Open	Jane Geddes
GNA/Glendale Federal Classic	Jane Geddes
Circle K Tucson Open	Betsy King
Standard Register Turquoise Classic	Pat Bradley
Nabisco Dinah Shore	Betsy King
Kyocera Inamori Classic	Ayako Okamoto
Santa Barbara Open	Jan Stephenson
S&H Golf Classic	Cindy Hill
United Virginia Bank Golf Classic	Jody Rosenthal
Chrysler-Plymouth Classic	Ayako Okamoto
Mazda LPGA Championship	Jane Geddes
LPGA Corning Classic	Cindy Rarick

McDonald's Championship	Betsy King
Mayflower Classic	Colleen Walker
Lady Keystone Open	Ayako Okamoto
Rochester International	Deb Richard
Jamie Farr Toledo Classic	Jane Geddes
du Maurier Classic	Jody Rosenthal
Boston Five Classic	Jane Geddes
U.S. Women's Open	Laura Davies
Columbia Savings LPGA National Pro-Am	Chris Johnson
Henredon Classic	Mary Beth Zimmerman
MasterCard International Pro-Am	Val Skinner
Atlantic City LPGA Classic	Betsy King
Nestle World Championship	Ayako Okamoto
Rail Charity Classic	Rosie Jones
Cellular One-Ping Golf Championship	Nancy Lopez
Safeco Classic	Jan Stephenson
Konica San Jose Classic	Jan Stephenson
Mazda Japan Classic	Yuko Moriguchi
Nichirei Cup	United States/Fukumi Tani

Multiple Winners of 1987

PLAYER	WINS	PLAYER	WINS
Ian Woosnam	8	Fulton Allem	2
Bruce Crampton	7	Ian Baker-Finch	2
Mark McNulty	7	Andy Bean	2
Chi Chi Rodriguez	7	Gordon Brand, Jr.	2
David Ishii	6	Billy Casper	2
Jane Geddes	5	Howard Clark	2
Isao Aoki	4	Keith Clearwater	2
Bob Charles	4	Nick Faldo	2
Betsy King	4	Brian Jones	2
Ayako Okamoto	4	Masahiro Kuramoto	2
Gary Player	4	Bernhard Langer	2
Peter Senior	4	Sandy Lyle	2
Paul Azinger	3	Roger Mackay	2
Miller Barber	3	Larry Mowry	2
Chen Tze Ming	3	Larry Nelson	2
Al Geiberger	3	Greg Norman	2
Tony Johnstone	3	Corey Pavin	2
Gene Littler	3	Ronan Rafferty	2
Nancy Lopez	3	Cindy Rarick	2
Orville Moody	3	Jody Rosenthal	2
Masashi Ozaki	3	Scott Simpson	2
Jan Stephenson	3	Brian Tennyson	2
Curtis Strange	3		

Career World Money List

The following is a listing of the 50 leading money-winners for their careers through the 1987 season. It includes active and inactive players. The World Money List from this and the 21 previous editions of this annual and a table prepared for a companion book, THE WONDERFUL WORLD OF PROFESSIONAL GOLF (Atheneum, 1973), form the basis for this compilation. Additional figures were taken from official records of major golf associations, although the shortcomings in records-keeping in professional golf outside the United States in the 1950s and 1960s and exclusions from U.S. records in a few cases during those years prevent these figures from being completely accurate and complete. Conversions of foreign currency figures to U.S. dollars are based on average values during the particular year involved.

POS.	PLAYER, COUNTRY	TOTAL MONEY
1	Jack Nicklaus, U.S.	$6,028,010
2	Tom Watson, U.S.	5,605,220
3	Severiano Ballesteros, Spain	4,771,378
4	Lee Trevino, U.S.	4,721,939
5	Raymond Floyd, U.S.	4,479,802
6	Isao Aoki, Japan	4,361,464
7	Lanny Wadkins, U.S.	4,304,666
8	Miller Barber, U.S.	4,192,056
9	Greg Norman, Australia	4,066,730
10	Gary Player, South Africa	4,050,622
11	Tom Kite, U.S.	4,046,215
12	Curtis Strange, U.S.	3,748,890
13	Gene Littler, U.S.	3,678,274
14	Ben Crenshaw, U.S.	3,615,136
15	Billy Casper, U.S.	3,611,669
16	Johnny Miller, U.S.	3,597,995
17	Hale Irwin, U.S.	3,580,838
18	Don January, U.S.	3,528,370
19	Arnold Palmer, U.S.	3,479,109
20	Bernhard Langer, West Germany	3,420,191
21	Andy Bean, U.S.	3,275,624
22	David Graham, Australia	3,235,675
23	Craig Stadler, U.S.	3,202,085
24	Tsuneyuki Nakajima, Japan	3,197,143
25	Graham Marsh, Australia	3,192,721
26	Masashi Ozaki, Japan	2,788,576
27	Hubert Green, U.S.	2,764,971
28	John Mahaffey, U.S.	2,734,756
29	Ian Woosnam, Wales	2,695,389
30	Bruce Crampton, Australia	2,692,660
31	Sandy Lyle, Scotland	2,664,960
32	Tom Weiskopf, U.S.	2,630,667
33	Larry Nelson, U.S.	2,614,501
34	Fuzzy Zoeller, U.S.	2,595,365
35	Bob Charles, New Zealand	2,500,431
36	Bruce Lietzke, U.S.	2,484,483
37	Lee Elder, U.S.	2,423,130
38	Nick Faldo, England	2,384,853
39	Calvin Peete, U.S.	2,380,237
40	Hal Sutton, U.S.	2,366,805

POS.	PLAYER, COUNTRY	TOTAL MONEY
41	Chi Chi Rodriguez, U.S.	2,296,722
42	Payne Stewart, U.S.	2,282,335
43	Mark O'Meara, U.S.	2,265,048
44	Scott Simpson, U.S.	2,235,494
45	Gil Morgan, U.S.	2,222,619
46	Gay Brewer, U.S.	2,052,109
47	J. C. Snead, U.S.	2,036,609
48	Scott Hoch, U.S.	2,028,856
49	George Archer, U.S.	2,012,422
50	Jerry Pate, U.S.	1,919,369

LPGA Money List

POS.	PLAYER	MONEY
1	Betsy King	$504,535.00
2	Ayako Okamoto	478,034.00
3	Nancy Lopez	454,823.00
4	Jane Geddes	409,241.00
5	Jan Stephenson	262,278.00
6	Patty Sheehan	246,507.00
7	Jody Rosenthal	238,041.50
8	Cindy Rarick	235,198.00
9	Chris Johnson	226,305.00
10	Rosie Jones	219,500.00
11	Colleen Walker	209,065.00
12	Juli Inkster	175,272.50
13	Val Skinner	174,414.00
14	Laurie Rinker	174,199.00
15	Kathy Postlewait	171,797.00
16	Pat Bradley	141,707.00
17	Shirley Furlong	141,557.00
18	Sherri Turner	131,708.00
19	Cindy Hill	131,430.00
20	Amy Alcott	125,531.00
21	Jane Crafter	124,876.00
22	Cathy Gerring	115,539.00
23	Muffin Spencer-Devlin	114,842.00
24	Patti Rizzo	98,455.00
	Sally Quinlan	98,455.00
26	Sandra Palmer	96,539.00
27	Debbie Massey	96,502.00
28	Hollis Stacy	88,121.00
29	Beth Daniel	87,683.00
30	Lori Garbacz	87,619.00
31	Penny Hammel	85,737.00
32	Debra A. Richard	84,890.00
33	Mary Beth Zimmerman	84,009.00
34	Dawn Coe	81,545.00
35	Cathy Morse	78,049.00
36	Tammie Green	76,308.00
37	Martha Nause	75,162.00
38	Marta Figueras-Dotti	73,866.00
39	Lisa Young	73,794.00
40	Lauri Peterson	71,454.00
41	Ku Ok Hee	70,996.00

POS.	PLAYER	MONEY
42	Allison Finney	68,802.00
43	JoAnne Carner	66,601.00
44	Barb Bunkowsky	66,327.00
45	Robin Walton	65,054.00
46	Michele M. Berteotti	63,977.00
47	Alice Ritzman	63,842.00
48	Missie McGeorge	63,259.00
49	Bonnie Lauer	62,034.00
50	Donna White	60,686.00

Above list includes LPGA official money, J. C. Penney, Nekkei Cup, Mazda Championship, Spalding and several other non-tour US events.

The U.S. Tour

Spalding Invitational

Pebble Beach Golf Links, Pebble Beach, California
Par 36-36 — 72; 6,799 yards

December 31-January 3
purse, $250,000

PLAYER	SCORES				TOTAL	MONEY
Ken Green	67	70	66	71	274	$50,000
Willie Wood	67	73	71	64	275	25,750
Don Pooley	74	71	64	66	275	25,750
Jan Stephenson	69	72	66	69	276	10,625
Lennie Clements	67	69	72	68	276	10,625
Patty Sheehan	69	70	69	68	276	10,625
George Archer	72	68	67	69	276	10,625
Mark Calcavecchia	67	67	73	70	277	5,500
Al Geiberger	65	69	71	73	278	3,425
Dave Stockton	68	70	71	69	278	3,425
Barry Jaeckel	72	69	67	70	278	3,425
Lon Hinkle	73	68	72	65	278	3,425
Ron Stelten	66	68	73	72	279	2,800
Bob Eastwood	76	65	67	72	280	2,400
Peter Oosterhuis	69	72	69	70	280	2,400
Mark Lye	67	70	72	71	280	2,400
Gary McCord	65	76	69	71	281	1,800
Danny Edwards	65	71	76	69	281	1,800
Dan Halldorson	70	69	72	70	281	1,800
Bob Gilder	69	73	70	69	281	1,800
Greg Norman	69	71	73	68	281	1,800
Roger Maltbie	71	73	70	68	282	1,450
Juli Inkster	72	71	67	72	282	1,450
Rob Boldt	70	71	72	70	283	1,300
Johnny Miller	72	69	72	71	284	1,200
Rick Fehr	71	73	71	69	824	1,200
Duffy Waldorf	65	70	72	77	284	1,200
Sam Randolph	70	69	75	71	285	1,032
Laurie Rinker	73	72	69	71	285	1,032
Ray Arinno	71	70	71	73	285	1,032
Andy North	72	73	67	73	285	1,032
Mark Wiebe	69	71	73	73	286	950
Larry Ziegler	72	73	67	74	286	950

	SCORES				TOTAL	MONEY
Charlie Gibson	72	70	70	75	287	870
Greg Chapman	74	70	69	74	287	870
Tim Norris	72	74	71	70	287	870
Jay Overton	70	72	75	70	287	870
Chuck Milne	74	76	67	70	287	870
Steve Pate	75	69	72	71	287	870
Jane Geddes	70	73	76	75	288	797
Roy Vucinich	75	71	71	71	288	797
Bob Boldt	70	75	72	72	289	785
Bob Irving	71	74	73	71	289	785
Nathaniel Crosby	73	74	72	70	289	785
Ed Luethke	74	71	72	73	290	775
Mike Reid	78	74	68	71	291	767
Bob Ford	75	72	72	72	291	767
Bobby Clampett	72	76	71	73	292	755
John Buczek	73	73	72	74	292	755
David Glenz	76	71	72	73	292	755

FILA Invitational

Fiddlesticks Country Club, Fort Myers, Florida
Par 36-36 — 72; 7,162 yards

January 1-3
purse, $250,000

	SCORES			TOTAL	MONEY
Hale Irwin	69	68	70	207	$75,000
Calvin Peete	72	71	69	212	31,250
Scott Verplank	66	71	75	212	31,250
Bernhard Langer	69	71	74	214	17,250
Mark O'Meara	74	73	68	215	13,875
Davis Love III	69	71	75	215	13,875
Curtis Strange	73	70	73	216	12,500
Joey Sindelar	71	75	71	217	11,500
Corey Pavin	74	70	73	217	11,500
Andy Bean	74	70	73	217	11,500
Ben Crenshaw	71	73	75	219	10,500
Jim Thorpe	78	79	72	229	10,000

MONY Tournament of Champions

LaCosta Country Club, Carlsbad, California
Par 36-36 — 72; 7,022 yards

January 7-10
purse, $500,000

	SCORES				TOTAL	MONEY
Mac O'Grady	65	72	70	71	278	$90,000
Rick Fehr	68	67	73	71	279	55,000
Mark Calcavecchia	65	75	70	70	280	29,800
Greg Norman	69	70	70	71	280	29,800
Ben Crenshaw	72	70	71	68	281	20,000
Hal Sutton	72	69	69	71	281	20,000
Ray Floyd	70	68	74	70	282	17,500
Donnie Hammond	70	71	71	71	283	15,566.67
Sandy Lyle	72	72	71	68	283	15,566.67
Doug Tewell	70	70	72	71	283	15,566.66
John Mahaffey	70	68	71	75	284	14,000.00

	SCORES				TOTAL	MONEY
Corey Pavin	68	73	74	70	285	12,950.00
Calvin Peete	76	72	69	68	285	12,950.00
Gene Sauers	72	72	71	71	286	11,900.00
Dan Forsman	76	72	66	73	287	10,666.67
Tom Kite	76	70	67	74	287	10,666.67
Bob Tway	71	68	78	70	287	10,666.66
Dan Pohl	70	73	75	70	288	10,000
Curtis Strange	73	72	71	73	289	9,700
Mark Wiebe	70	72	75	72	289	9,700
Mike Hulbert	74	75	72	70	291	9,400
Fuzzy Zoeller	75	72	70	75	292	9,200
Jim Thorpe	72	71	75	75	293	9,000
Ernie Gonzalez	74	71	74	75	294	8,525
Ken Green	71	74	74	75	294	8,525
Kenny Knox	74	74	71	75	294	8,525
Bob Murphy	74	76	71	73	294	8,525
Andy Bean	82	71	69	73	295	8,200
Fred Wadsworth	72	84	73	73	302	8,100

Bob Hope Chrysler Classic

PGA West Country Club, LaQuinta, California
Par 36-36 — 72; 7,000 yards

January 14-18
purse, $900,000

Bermuda Dunes Country Club, Bermuda Dunes, California
Par 36-36 — 72; 6,837 yards

Indian Wells Country Club, Palm Desert, California
Par 36-36 — 72; 6,478 yards

Tamarisk Country Club, Palm Springs, California
Par 36-36 — 72; 6,819 yards

	SCORES					TOTAL	MONEY
Corey Pavin	72	71	65	66	67	341	$162,000
Bernhard Langer	68	66	68	70	70	342	97,200
Mark Calcavecchia	69	67	71	66	72	345	61,200
Andy Bean	63	68	75	72	70	348	39,600
David Frost	68	71	72	69	68	348	39,600
Jeff Sluman	68	71	68	67	76	350	29,137.50
Blaine McCallister	70	69	71	69	71	350	29,137.50
Chen Tze Chung	70	73	67	72	68	350	29,137.50
Ed Fiori	67	68	72	72	71	350	29,137.50
Larry Rinker	68	70	72	70	71	361	22,500
Bob Tway	67	69	70	74	71	351	22,500
Charles Bolling	70	67	70	71	73	351	22,500
Hal Sutton	71	71	75	67	68	352	17,400
Fred Couples	69	69	71	75	68	352	17,400
Dan Forsman	65	74	72	71	70	352	17,400
Jay Delsing	68	72	73	68	72	353	14,400
Danny Edwards	69	69	76	67	72	353	14,400
David Edwards	61	74	72	69	77	353	14,400
Willie Wood	66	69	75	66	78	354	11,295
Joey Sindelar	72	69	70	69	74	354	11,295
Curtis Strange	70	74	69	70	71	354	11,295
Ray Floyd	69	68	68	74	75	354	11,295
Davis Love III	74	73	71	67	70	355	8,640

	SCORES					TOTAL	MONEY
Bobby Cole	70	75	69	71	70	355	8,640
Al Geiberger	67	69	74	70	75	355	8,640
Mark O'Meara	69	73	72	72	70	356	6,795
John Mahaffey	72	73	73	66	72	356	6,795
Scott Simpson	73	72	72	67	72	356	6,795
Johnny Miller	72	67	69	71	77	356	6,795
Payne Stewart	68	71	74	70	74	357	5,467.67
Howard Twitty	69	72	69	72	75	357	5,467.67
Tom Watson	70	74	68	74	71	357	5,467.67
Don Pooley	73	72	73	68	71	357	5,467.67
Ken Green	76	70	70	68	73	357	5,467.66
Mark Hayes	67	76	71	71	72	357	5,467.66
D.A. Weibring	71	74	70	71	72	358	3,874.89
Kenny Knox	69	71	73	72	73	358	3,874.89
Dave Rummells	74	67	71	73	73	358	3,874.89
Ken Brown	68	70	75	70	75	358	3,874.89
Bobby Clampett	73	69	70	73	73	358	3,874.89
Mike Donald	72	71	69	72	74	358	3,874.89
Jim Gallagher, Jr.	69	71	68	77	73	358	3,874.89
Jay Haas	70	71	72	70	75	358	3,874.89
Mike Hulbert	71	74	72	66	75	358	3,874.88
Steve Pate	72	67	72	73	75	359	2,438
Mike Sullivan	74	72	70	68	75	359	2,438
Lennie Clements	71	70	72	73	73	359	2,438
Jack Renner	72	70	72	68	77	359	2,438
Mike Reid	70	70	73	70	76	359	2,438
J.C. Snead	71	68	74	71	75	359	2,438
Dan Halldorson	66	77	70	69	77	359	2,438
Craig Stadler	75	72	69	70	73	359	2,438
Peter Jacobsen	70	71	70	72	76	359	2,438

Phoenix Open

TPC of Scottsdale, Scottsdale, Arizona
Par 35-36 — 71; 6,992 yards

January 22-25
purse, $600,000

	SCORES				TOTAL	MONEY
Paul Azinger	67	69	65	67	268	$108,000
Hal Sutton	67	71	67	64	269	64,800
Fuzzy Zoeller	67	69	66	70	272	31,200
Bob Tway	71	69	63	69	272	31,200
Mark Calcavecchia	68	66	70	68	272	31,200
Mark O'Meara	63	71	70	69	273	20,100
Corey Pavin	65	69	66	73	273	20,100
Bobby Clampett	64	73	69	66	273	20,100
Andy North	70	70	65	69	274	15,000
Payne Stewart	69	71	70	64	274	15,000
Don Pooley	70	68	67	69	274	15,000
Gene Sauers	68	67	71	68	274	15,000
Calvin Peete	69	69	69	67	274	15,000
Doug Tewell	72	68	62	73	275	11,400
Howard Twitty	68	65	74	69	276	9,600
Bobby Wadkins	69	68	67	72	276	9,600
Chen Tze Chung	72	67	67	70	276	9,600
George Burns	72	64	68	72	276	9,600
Bruce Lietzke	68	69	68	71	276	9,600
Ron Streck	69	68	69	71	277	6,744

	SCORES				TOTAL	MONEY
Bob Gilder	70	71	67	69	277	6,744
Roger Maltbie	71	69	68	69	277	6,744
Ronnie Black	69	72	67	69	277	6,744
Ernie Gonzalez	63	72	72	70	277	6,744
Tom Purtzer	69	67	72	70	278	4,482.86
Larry Rinker	68	69	72	69	278	4,482.86
Wayne Levi	70	69	70	69	278	4,482.86
Tom Kite	68	69	68	73	278	4,482.86
John Mahaffey	69	71	69	69	278	4,482.86
Sandy Lyle	71	71	68	68	278	4,482.85
Rocco Mediate	66	70	70	72	278	4,482.85
Curtis Strange	71	65	71	72	279	3,396
Fred Couples	68	72	69	70	279	3,396
Davis Love III	71	69	66	73	279	3,396
David Frost	70	71	69	69	279	3,396
Jay Haas	68	66	68	77	279	3,396
Mike Reid	71	70	70	69	280	2,520
Mark Wiebe	69	71	68	72	280	2,520
Mark Lye	71	69	68	72	280	2,520
Mike Morley	71	71	71	67	280	2,520
Buddy Gardner	70	71	68	71	280	2,520
Peter Jacobsen	71	68	69	72	280	2,520
Russ Cochran	70	68	72	70	280	2,520
Bobby Cole	69	70	72	69	280	2,520
Joey Sindelar	72	69	71	69	281	1,756.80
Ken Brown	68	68	73	72	281	1,756.80
Rick Fehr	70	71	73	67	281	1,756.80
Dave Barr	70	72	70	69	281	1,756.80
Dan Forsman	72	70	70	69	281	1,756.80
Mike Sullivan	74	68	72	68	282	1,401.60
Donnie Hammond	71	69	73	69	282	1,401.60
Brad Faxon	64	74	73	71	282	1,401.60
Dan Pohl	71	69	69	73	282	1,401.60
Ken Green	72	67	71	72	282	1,401.60
Bill Glasson	70	71	70	71	282	1,401.60
Keith Fergus	71	71	70	70	282	1,401.60
Mark Hayes	69	70	71	72	282	1,401.60
Dave Eichelberger	69	72	71	70	282	1,401.60
Steve Jones	65	68	74	75	282	1,401.60

AT&T Pebble Beach National Pro-Am

Pebble Beach Golf Links
Par 36-36 — 72; 6,799 yards

Cypress Point Club
Par 36-36 — 72; 6,506 yards

Spyglass Hill Golf Links
Par 36-36 — 72; 6,810 yards

Pebble Beach, California

January 29-February 1
purse, $600,000

	SCORES				TOTAL	MONEY
Johnny Miller	72	72	68	66	278	$108,000
Payne Stewart	69	69	69	72	279	64,800
Lanny Wadkins	68	69	72	71	280	34,800

	SCORES				TOTAL	MONEY
Bernhard Langer	72	69	68	71	280	34,800
Fred Couples	70	70	72	69	281	24,000
Larry Mize	71	71	71	69	282	19,425
Danny Edwards	70	69	72	71	282	19,425
Bob Tway	72	71	72	67	282	19,425
Dan Pohl	69	75	71	67	282	19,425
Mark Wiebe	71	72	73	67	283	15,000
Rick Fehr	71	74	73	65	283	15,000
Ken Brown	73	70	71	69	283	15,000
Sandy Lyle	68	71	70	75	284	12,000
Isao Aoki	69	70	74	71	284	12,000
Fuzzy Zoeller	73	70	71	71	285	8,715
Leonard Thompson	70	73	71	71	285	8,715
Jack Nicklaus	72	72	70	71	285	8,715
Keith Clearwater	74	72	70	69	285	8,715
Tom Byrum	68	74	71	72	285	8,715
Andy Bean	73	73	72	67	285	8,715
Lennie Clements	72	70	69	74	285	8,715
Ben Crenshaw	75	71	71	68	285	8,715
Richard Zokol	69	75	73	69	286	5,190
Mark O'Meara	70	71	72	73	286	5,190
Curtis Strange	72	75	71	68	286	5,190
Kenny Knox	71	71	73	71	286	5,190
Rex Caldwell	67	78	67	74	286	5,190
George Burns	72	72	72	70	286	5,190
Tom Kite	74	70	74	69	287	3,990
Corey Pavin	74	71	71	71	287	3,990
John Mahaffey	69	75	71	72	287	3,990
Peter Jacobsen	74	72	70	71	287	3,990
Roger Maltbie	69	72	74	73	288	3,037.50
Ken Green	69	77	71	71	288	3,037.50
Larry Rinker	71	77	70	70	288	3,037.50
Mike Hulbert	73	73	72	70	288	3,037.50
Gene Sauers	72	72	70	74	288	3,037.50
Jay Haas	71	75	73	69	288	3,037.50
Mike Donald	72	69	69	78	288	3,037.50
John Cook	70	71	74	73	288	3,037.50
Pat McGowan	78	72	69	70	289	2,340
Willie Wood	69	75	71	74	289	2,340
Sam Randolph	74	73	72	70	289	2,340
Chris Perry	76	72	71	71	290	1,864.80
Andrew Magee	73	73	70	74	290	1,864.80
Bill Glasson	72	73	73	72	290	1,864.80
Andy Dillard	71	75	72	72	290	1,864.80
Bobby Clampett	75	75	69	71	290	1,864.80
Tom Watson	69	74	74	74	291	1,480.80
Mark Lye	74	68	74	75	291	1,480.80
Bobby Wadkins	69	71	76	75	291	1,480.80
Brad Fabel	72	73	73	73	291	1,480.80
Bobby Cole	72	68	79	72	291	1,480.80

Curtis Strange's second-half surge included wins at the Canadian, Memphis and World Series events. He set a U.S. money record and was chosen Player of the Year by several magazines.

Paul Azinger was U.S. PGA Player of the Year and won at Phoenix, Las Vegas and Hartford.

U.S. Tour

Lanny Wadkins had a victory at Doral.

Tom Kite won for the seventh straight year.

Tom Watson broke a slump in the Nabisco event.

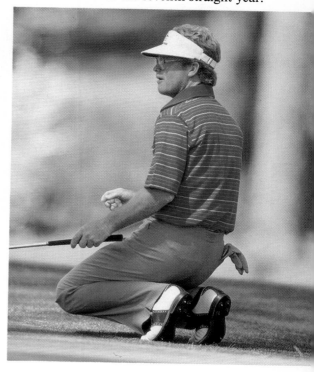

Corey Pavin had a hot early season.

Payne Stewart's victory dance at Bay Hill.

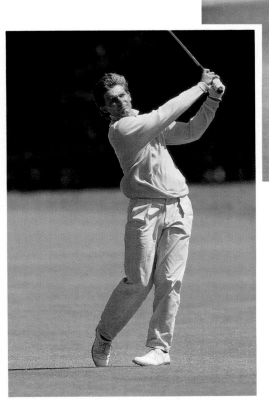

Rookie Keith Clearwater won twice.

U.S. Tour

Taiwan's T.C. Chen was successful at Los Angeles.

Britain's Sandy Lyle had a tough TPC victory.

South African David Frost had a superb year.

Neil Coles won the first Senior British Open at Turnberry.

Chi Chi Rodriguez dominated the U.S. senior circuit.

Senior Tour

Another major title for Gary Player in the
USGA Senior Open.

Player's Internationals won the Chrysler Cup over Arnold
Palmer's squad.

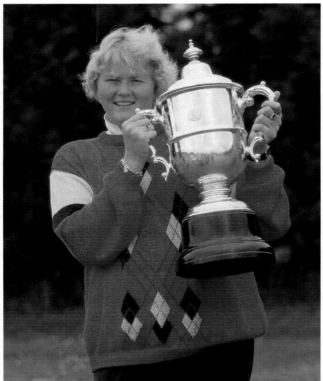

Britain's Laura Davies took home the U.S. Open trophy.

Betsy King added the Nabisco Dinah Shore to her record.

LPGA Tour

Ayako Okamoto won the LPGA's richest prize in the Nestle World Championship.

The LPGA title went to Jane Geddes.

Jody Rosenthal won the duMaurier Classic.

Ian Woosnam scored eight worldwide victories and set a money record.

European Tour

Mark McNulty's seven wins included three in Europe.

Australian Peter Senior won one in Europe.

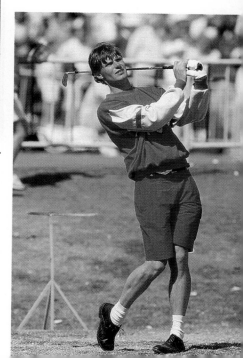

Anders Forsbrand led the Swedish advance.

Most impressive was Bernhard Langer in the Whyte & Mackay PGA and
Carrolls Irish Open.

European Tour

Gordon Brand, Jr. won the Dutch
and Scandinavian titles.

Howard Clark's two wins were
the Moroccan and PLM events.

Sam Torrance took the Italian
title.

Hawaii-born David Ishii was a star in Japan, leading the money list.

Jumbo Ozaki battled Ishii for the money title.

Asia/Japan Tour

Isao Aoki's victories included the Japan Open.

Tommy Nakajima finally won in October.

Massy Kuramoto had another fine year.

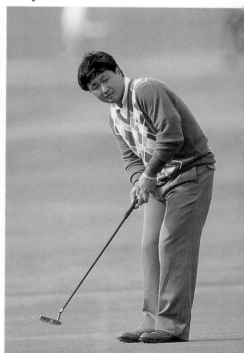

Race driver Nigel Mansell and Greg Norman: two guys for whom just a good year isn't enough.

In 1986, Norman crossed the $1 million mark in the Dunhill Cup; this time, his Australian team lost in the semifinals.

Hawaiian Open

Waialae Country Club, Honolulu, Hawaii
Par 36-36 — 72; 6,975 yards

February 5-8
purse, $600,000

	SCORES				TOTAL	MONEY
Corey Pavin	65	75	66	64	270	$108,000
Craig Stadler	70	68	62	70	270	64,800
(Pavin defeated Stadler on second hole of sudden-death playoff)						
Paul Azinger	70	66	65	70	271	40,800
Larry Mize	69	66	70	67	272	26,400
Lanny Wadkins	69	68	67	68	272	26,400
Jodie Mudd	69	72	67	65	273	17,528.58
Curtis Strange	69	71	64	69	273	17,528.57
John Cook	69	71	64	69	273	17,528.57
Fred Couples	69	65	68	71	273	17,528.57
Curt Byrum	69	68	69	67	273	17,528.57
Ben Crenshaw	75	66	66	66	273	17,528.57
Steve Jones	70	67	68	68	273	17,528.57
Scott Simpson	69	68	68	69	274	10,920
Bobby Wadkins	71	68	66	69	274	10,920
Gene Sauers	72	67	69	66	274	10,920
Brad Fabel	70	72	64	68	274	10,920
John Mahaffey	71	69	68	66	274	10,920
Lon Hinkle	70	70	67	68	275	8,400
Larry Nelson	73	66	70	66	275	8,400
Mike Donald	75	68	64	68	275	8,400
Dave Rummells	71	71	65	69	276	6,720
Bernhard Langer	70	64	71	71	276	6,720
Mark Lye	72	67	66	71	276	6,720
Brett Upper	69	69	68	71	277	4,860
Jack Renner	66	71	74	66	277	4,860
Tom Watson	67	71	71	68	277	4,860
J.C. Snead	70	69	67	71	277	4,860
Mac O'Grady	66	72	67	72	277	4,860
Jay Don Blake	71	73	66	67	277	4,860
Jeff Sluman	73	67	70	68	278	3,900
Barry Jaeckel	70	70	69	69	278	3,900
Calvin Peete	72	68	68	70	278	3,900
George Burns	69	70	71	69	279	3,465
John Inman	70	74	66	69	279	3,465
Richard Zokol	68	72	72	68	280	2,771.25
Clarence Rose	73	70	68	69	280	2,771.25
Bob Eastwood	71	69	67	73	280	2,771.25
Wayne Levi	72	68	73	67	280	2,771.25
David Canipe	71	70	68	71	280	2,771.25
Danny Edwards	71	71	70	68	280	2,771.25
Isao Aoki	68	72	71	69	280	2,771.25
Ronnie Black	73	68	70	69	280	2,771.25
Denis Watson	71	73	70	67	281	1,872
Scott Hoch	72	68	74	67	281	1,872
Charles Bolling	71	71	72	67	281	1,872
Andy North	69	69	74	69	281	1,872
Philip Jonas	71	71	68	71	281	1,872
Rick Dalpos	74	69	70	68	281	1,872
Rocco Mediate	70	70	73	68	281	1,872
Howard Twitty	69	72	74	67	282	1,461
Rex Caldwell	70	69	74	69	282	1,461
Loren Roberts	71	72	69	70	282	1,461
Tom Purtzer	70	73	69	70	282	1,461

Shearson Lehman Brothers Andy Williams Open

Torrey Pines Golf Course, LaJolla, California
South Course: Par 36-36 — 72; 7,021 yards
North Course: Par 36-36 — 72; 6,659 yards

February 12-15
purse, $500,000

	SCORES				TOTAL	MONEY
George Burns	63	68	70	65	266	$90,000
J.C. Snead	64	69	66	71	270	44,000
Bobby Wadkins	68	66	67	69	270	44,000
Pat McGowan	66	69	69	68	272	22,000
Buddy Gardner	69	68	65	70	272	22,000
Peter Jacobsen	67	70	67	69	273	14,607.15
Ray Floyd	65	68	66	74	273	14,607.15
Scott Simpson	69	66	71	67	273	14,607.14
Bill Sander	70	68	69	66	273	14,607.14
David Frost	67	71	65	70	273	14,607.14
David Edwards	70	66	65	72	273	14,607.14
Curt Byrum	69	65	70	69	273	14,607.14
Bruce Lietzke	71	66	68	69	274	9,374
Hal Sutton	69	67	66	72	274	9,375
Tom Watson	68	69	66	71	274	9,375
Lennie Clements	70	65	66	73	274	9,375
Gene Sauers	71	66	69	69	275	7,250
Andy Dillard	68	71	70	66	275	7,250
Fred Couples	70	67	69	69	275	7,250
Brad Faxon	67	68	70	70	275	7,250
D.A. Weibring	68	72	67	69	276	5,800
Lon Hinkle	64	68	69	75	276	5,800
Bobby Cole	65	72	70	70	277	3,671.24
Dave Rummells	68	67	68	74	277	3,671.23
Don Pooley	70	68	72	67	277	3,671.23
Mike Sullivan	67	72	69	69	277	3,671.23
Steve Elkington	69	69	69	70	277	3,671.23
Brad Greer	71	69	67	70	277	3,671.23
Ray Barr, Jr.	68	66	71	72	277	3,671.23
John Adams	69	68	68	72	277	3,671.23
Andy Bean	70	62	71	74	277	3,671.23
Chip Beck	69	64	70	74	277	3,671.23
Seve Ballesteros	69	69	69	70	277	3,671.23
Ronnie Black	70	70	65	72	277	3,671.23
Dan Halldorson	68	65	72	72	277	3,671.23
Blaine McCallister	71	69	67	71	278	2,253.43
Tim Simpson	67	66	74	71	278	2,253.43
Howard Twitty	68	68	69	73	278	2,253.43
Mark McCumber	66	69	67	76	278	2,253.43
Johnny Miller	71	66	66	75	278	2,253.43
Jay Don Blake	65	72	70	71	278	2,253.43
Steve Pate	69	70	67	72	278	2,253.42
Duffy Waldorf	69	67	72	71	279	1,700
Mark O'Meara	73	67	70	69	279	1,700
Bob Lohr	66	69	66	78	279	1,700
Bob Eastwood	66	69	70	74	279	1,700
Bobby Clampett	70	68	73	69	280	1,301.67
Gary Koch	67	72	69	72	280	1,301.67
David Hobby	70	69	71	70	280	1,301.67
Mike Hulbert	69	68	72	71	280	1,301.67
Willie Wood	69	70	66	75	280	1,301.66
Richard Zokol	67	69	70	74	280	1,301.66

Los Angeles Open ✓

Riviera Country Club, Pacific Palisades, California
Par 35-36 — 71; 7,029 yards

February 19-22
purse, $600,000

	SCORES				TOTAL	MONEY
Chen Tze Chung	70	67	67	71	275	$108,000
Ben Crenshaw	71	69	66	69	275	64,800
(Chen defeated Crenshaw on first hole of playoff)						
Danny Edwards	73	64	68	71	276	40,800
Bobby Wadkins	66	72	68	71	277	23,625
Lanny Wadkins	73	65	73	66	277	23,625
Don Pooley	70	69	69	69	277	23,625
Steve Pate	71	71	68	67	277	23,625
Donnie Hammond	70	72	67	69	278	18,600
Seve Ballesteros	69	70	69	71	279	17,400
Bob Tway	75	70	66	69	280	12,857.15
Pat McGowan	71	72	65	72	280	12,857.15
Bill Sander	70	66	79	65	280	12,857.14
Mark O'Meara	73	71	66	70	280	12,857.14
Rick Dalpos	70	72	67	71	280	12,857.14
Scott Hoch	69	69	72	70	280	12,857.14
Nick Price	72	67	75	66	280	12,857.14
Sam Randolph	73	66	70	72	281	7,590
Craig Stadler	72	66	73	70	281	7,590
Mike Reid	74	68	68	71	281	7,590
Jay Delsing	72	69	72	68	281	7,590
Rick Fehr	68	69	70	74	281	7,590
Calvin Peete	70	71	67	73	281	7,590
Mark Brooks	71	71	71	68	281	7,590
Fred Couples	73	69	69	70	281	7,590
Masashi Ozaki	69	75	67	71	282	4,680
Dan Pohl	73	70	69	70	282	4,680
Roger Maltbie	74	68	71	69	282	4,680
Jeff Sluman	70	74	70	68	282	4,680
Bobby Cole	69	71	71	71	282	4,680
Mike Donald	70	72	68	73	283	3,645
Joey Sindelar	69	74	67	73	283	3,645
Jack Renner	69	73	72	69	283	3,645
Peter Jacobsen	69	74	69	71	283	3,645
Tom Purtzer	70	70	71	72	283	3,645
Ronnie Black	71	72	71	69	283	3,645
Loren Roberts	72	72	70	70	284	2,704.29
Steve Elkington	74	71	71	68	284	2,704.29
Davis Love III	76	69	68	71	284	2,704.29
Mike Bender	70	75	70	69	284	2,704.29
Mark McCumber	70	72	73	69	284	2,704.28
Bruce Lietzke	70	70	74	70	284	2,704.28
Chip Beck	70	72	71	71	284	2,704.28
Dave Eichelberger	72	73	71	69	285	2,160
Phil Blackmar	71	69	72	73	285	2,160
Dick Mast	71	69	75	71	286	1,602
Scott Simpson	70	71	74	71	286	1,602
Tim Simpson	72	73	73	68	286	1,602
Duffy Waldorf	68	71	71	76	286	1,602
Mark Pfeil	73	72	71	70	286	1,602
Mac O'Grady	70	74	73	69	286	1,602
Fred Wadsworth	75	70	69	72	286	1,602
Jodie Mudd	78	67	69	72	286	1,602
Keith Clearwater	69	73	72	72	286	1,602
Kikuo Arai	71	71	73	71	286	1,602

Doral Ryder Open

Doral Country Club, Blue Course, Miami, Florida
Par 36-36 — 72; 6,939 yards

February 26-March 1
purse, $1,000,000

	SCORES				TOTAL	MONEY
Lanny Wadkins	75	66	66	70	277	$180,000
Don Pooley	70	69	71	70	280	74,666.67
Tom Kite	67	76	69	68	280	74,666.67
Seve Ballesteros	71	66	74	69	280	74,666.66
David Edwards	73	70	71	67	281	40,000
J.C. Snead	71	73	68	70	282	33,500
Fred Couples	73	64	74	71	282	33,500
Bruce Lietzke	70	71	72	69	282	33,500
Mike Sullivan	73	68	76	66	283	24,000
Scott Simpson	71	69	72	71	283	24,000
Dave Rummells	74	71	70	68	283	24,000
Ed Fiori	72	71	71	69	283	24,000
Lennie Clements	69	68	74	72	283	24,000
Ken Brown	68	72	69	74	283	24,000
Tom Watson	70	72	71	71	284	16,500
Brad Faxon	76	67	70	71	284	16,500
Andy Dillard	72	70	71	71	284	16,500
Chen Tze Chung	70	72	72	70	284	16,500
Gene Sauers	73	67	74	71	285	13,000
David Graham	72	72	72	69	285	13,000
Phil Blackmar	67	73	74	71	285	13,000
Craig Stadler	71	70	75	70	286	8,775
Willie Wood	72	73	71	70	286	8,775
Tony Sills	70	69	77	70	286	8,775
Bob Murphy	72	70	71	73	286	8,775
Paul Azinger	73	72	72	69	286	8,775
Ronnie Black	74	70	69	73	286	8,775
Jack Nicklaus	69	74	73	70	286	8,775
Bernhard Langer	65	72	76	73	286	8,775
Fuzzy Zoeller	73	69	73	72	287	6,210.40
Mike Reid	71	72	71	73	287	6,210.40
Mark McCumber	70	72	75	70	287	6,210.40
David Frost	71	73	74	69	287	6,210.40
Wayne Levi	69	72	74	72	287	6,210.40
Isao Aoki	73	71	70	74	388	4,824.67
John Mahaffey	73	68	73	74	288	4,824.67
Donnie Hammond	73	71	73	71	288	4,824.67
George Burns	71	71	73	73	288	4,824.67
Corey Pavin	70	72	73	73	288	4,824.66
Mark Calcavecchia	69	70	73	76	288	4,824.66
Joey Sindelar	73	70	74	72	289	3,700
Bobby Wadkins	71	71	74	73	289	3,700
John Adams	72	70	75	72	289	3,700
Buddy Gardner	69	71	79	70	289	3,700
Bob Eastwood	71	74	75	69	289	3,700
Ben Crenshaw	75	69	72	74	290	2,913.34
Tim Simpson	73	71	74	72	290	2,913.33
Bill Rogers	71	67	77	75	290	2,913.33
Calvin Peete	72	70	78	71	291	2,405
Tom Sieckmann	68	71	81	71	291	2,405
Scott Hoch	71	72	76	72	291	2,405
Bob Gilder	70	75	75	71	291	2,405
Bill Kratzert	73	70	75	73	291	2,405
Dick Mast	73	70	77	71	291	2,405

	SCORES				TOTAL	MONEY
Bruce Fleisher	74	70	77	70	291	2,405
Ernie Gonzalez	70	74	75	72	291	2,405

Honda Classic

TPC at Eagle Trace, Coral Springs, Florida
Par 36-36 — 72; 7,037 yards

March 5-8
purse, $600,000

	SCORES				TOTAL	MONEY
Mark Calcavecchia	69	72	68	70	279	$108,000
Payne Stewart	75	68	68	71	282	52,800
Bernhard Langer	70	67	70	75	282	52,800
Bruce Lietzke	69	70	70	75	284	28,800
Clarence Rose	72	79	65	69	285	21,900
Greg Norman	77	72	67	69	285	21,900
Isao Aoki	74	76	67	68	285	21,900
John Mahaffey	78	70	71	67	286	17,400
Steve Elkington	73	73	68	72	286	17,400
Brad Fabel	74	75	68	69	286	17,400
Tim Simpson	74	71	73	69	287	13,200
George Burns	71	74	69	73	287	13,200
Ken Green	73	72	69	73	287	13,200
Chen Tze Chung	73	69	72	73	287	13,200
Mark McCumber	70	72	70	76	288	10,200
Dan Halldorson	74	73	71	70	288	10,200
Bob Gilder	77	70	72	69	288	10,200
Dick Mast	73	76	70	70	289	8,100
Mike Sullivan	65	77	72	75	289	8,100
Bob Eastwood	75	76	70	68	289	8,100
Lou Graham	72	74	70	73	289	8,100
Willie Wood	75	70	73	72	290	6,240
Tsuneyuki Nakajima	78	67	71	74	290	6,240
Brad Faxon	69	75	71	75	290	6,240
Mike Donald	75	76	70	70	291	4,900
Lon Hinkle	73	74	71	73	291	4,900
Jay Don Blake	74	75	68	74	291	4,900
Jeff Sluman	72	74	72	74	292	3,660
Jim Thorpe	77	72	71	72	292	3,660
Tom Purtzer	75	73	72	72	292	3,660
Hale Irwin	75	73	71	73	292	3,660
Morris Hatalsky	76	71	71	74	292	3,660
Trevor Dodds	77	72	68	75	292	3,660
Mike Bender	73	71	73	75	292	3,660
Ray Floyd	75	75	72	70	292	3,660
Charles Bolling	70	74	74	74	292	3,660
Rocco Mediate	76	75	69	72	292	3,660
Mark Wiebe	75	75	76	67	293	2,700
Scott Simpson	73	76	75	69	293	2,700
Kenny Knox	70	76	75	72	293	2,700
Barry Jaeckel	76	75	72	71	294	1,899.28
Andy Bean	77	73	75	69	294	1,899.28
Bill Britton	74	75	73	72	294	1,899.28
Mark O'Meara	75	74	73	72	294	1,899.27
Jim Wilson	75	73	73	73	294	1,899.27
David Peoples	73	75	76	70	294	1,899.27
Ron Streck	77	70	73	74	294	1,899.27
Buddy Gardner	80	71	68	75	294	1,899.27

	SCORES				TOTAL	MONEY
Bobby Cole	72	75	73	74	294	1,899.27
Andy Dillard	72	79	73	70	294	1,899.27
Pat McGowan	76	71	73	74	294	1,899.27

Hertz Bay Hill Classic

Bay Hill Club and Lodge, Orlando, Florida
Par 36-35 — 71; 7,103 yards

March 12-15
purse, $600,000

	SCORES				TOTAL	MONEY
Payne Stewart	69	67	63	65	264	$108,000
David Frost	67	68	65	67	267	64,800
Dan Pohl	70	70	65	70	275	40,800
Larry Mize	69	69	72	66	276	28,800
Ben Crenshaw	75	67	71	64	277	24,000
Bernhard Langer	69	70	69	70	278	20,850
Tsuneyuki Nakajima	70	70	68	70	278	20,850
Scott Simpson	71	69	70	69	279	18,000
Chip Beck	72	66	72	69	279	18,000
Davis Love III	74	73	66	67	280	14,400
Tom Kite	68	72	71	69	280	14,400
Curtis Strange	71	66	68	75	280	14,400
Curt Byrum	70	71	72	67	280	14,400
Hal Sutton	72	71	68	70	281	9,900
Mike Nicolette	74	67	70	70	281	9,900
Tom Purtzer	73	70	71	67	281	9,900
Dave Rummells	70	69	72	70	281	9,900
Ray Floyd	69	68	71	73	281	9,900
Isao Aoki	69	70	72	70	281	9,900
Denis Watson	71	69	68	74	282	7,240
Tim Simpson	68	68	76	70	282	7,240
Keith Clearwater	75	71	70	66	282	7,240
Howard Twitty	71	71	69	72	283	5,190
Dan Halldorson	74	70	68	71	283	5,190
Greg Norman	74	70	71	68	283	5,190
Fuzzy Zoeller	73	70	71	69	283	5,190
Mark McCumber	74	66	70	73	283	5,190
Phil Blackmar	71	72	71	69	283	5,190
Donnie Hammond	73	71	73	67	284	3,815
Don Pooley	73	71	73	67	284	3,815
Rocco Mediate	71	72	69	72	284	3,815
Steve Pate	67	74	73	70	284	3,815
Paul Azinger	72	70	72	70	284	3,815
Ken Brown	73	69	70	72	284	3,815
Clarence Rose	69	76	71	69	285	3,022.50
Tom Watson	71	70	69	75	285	3,022.50
Sandy Lyle	71	71	69	74	285	3,022.50
Brad Bryant	68	73	72	72	285	3,022.50
Mark Lye	70	71	74	71	286	2,220
Bob Tway	71	76	69	70	286	2,220
Leonard Thompson	73	74	68	71	286	2,220
Bobby Cole	71	70	74	71	286	2,220
Andy Bean	69	70	75	72	286	2,220
Buddy Gardner	70	75	72	69	286	2,220
Brad Faxon	66	76	72	72	286	2,220
Antonio Cerda	71	71	71	73	286	2,220
Mike Donald	76	67	71	72	286	2,220

	SCORES				TOTAL	MONEY
Andy North	74	70	73	70	287	1,602
Chen Tze Chung	71	74	71	71	287	1,602

USF&G Classic

Lakewood Country Club, New Orleans, Louisiana
Par 36-36 — 72; 7,080 yards

March 19-22
purse, $500,000

	SCORES				TOTAL	MONEY
Ben Crenshaw	66	68	67	67	268	$90,000
Curtis Strange	67	71	66	67	271	54,000
Ronnie Black	67	67	69	70	273	34,000
Dick Mast	64	68	73	70	275	20,666.67
Keith Clearwater	69	70	65	71	275	20,666.67
Sam Randolph	67	71	70	67	275	20,666.66
Tom Watson	69	69	66	72	276	14,041.67
John Mahaffey	71	68	68	69	276	14,041.67
Ken Brown	71	70	68	67	276	14,041.67
Jay Delsing	69	72	65	70	276	14,041.67
Brett Upper	67	69	69	71	276	14,041.66
Jay Haas	67	71	66	72	276	14,041.66
Jim Thorpe	71	63	72	71	277	9,375
Mike Sullivan	69	66	71	71	277	9,375
Pat McGowan	70	68	67	72	277	9,375
Steve Elkington	68	69	70	70	277	9,375
Nick Price	67	70	72	69	278	6,542.86
Duffy Waldorf	71	68	69	70	278	6,542.86
Hal Sutton	70	65	73	70	278	6,542.86
Mark Lye	73	69	69	67	278	6,542.86
John Inman	69	70	69	70	278	6,542.86
Brian Claar	66	70	70	72	278	6,542.85
Nick Faldo	70	67	68	73	278	6,542.85
David Peoples	69	70	67	73	279	3,783.34
Peter Jacobsen	69	70	72	68	279	3,783.34
Bob Gilder	65	68	72	74	279	3,783.34
Phil Blackmar	67	70	70	72	279	3,783.33
Bill Glasson	69	68	69	73	279	3,783.33
Morris Hatalsky	70	70	69	70	279	3,783.33
Jim Colbert	70	70	69	70	279	3,783.33
Kenny Perry	71	70	71	67	279	3,783.33
David Graham	71	68	69	71	279	3,783.33
Robert Wrenn	69	73	70	68	280	2,585.72
Tim Simpson	69	69	72	70	280	2,585.72
Jodie Mudd	69	73	70	68	280	2,585.72
Gary Hallberg	72	67	72	69	280	2,585.71
Ed Fiori	68	70	72	70	280	2,585.71
Roy Biancalana	70	70	70	70	280	2,585.71
Bobby Clampett	73	68	68	71	280	2,585.71
Jay Don Blake	68	70	71	72	281	1,800
Dave Rummells	70	69	72	70	281	1,800
Mike McCullough	75	67	70	69	281	1,800
Jack Renner	71	69	70	71	281	1,800
Antonio Cerda	69	71	71	70	281	1,800
Mike Hulbert	70	68	69	74	281	1,800
Steve Pate	67	75	70	69	281	1,800
Tim Norris	70	68	69	74	281	1,800
Scott Verplank	71	68	71	72	282	1,290

	SCORES				TOTAL	MONEY
Calvin Peete	74	68	71	69	282	1,290
Fred Couples	69	73	66	74	282	1,290
John Cook	71	69	73	69	282	1,290

Tournament Players Championship

Tournament Players Club, Ponte Vedra, Florida   March 26-29
Par 36-36 — 72; 6,857 yards   purse, $1,000,000

	SCORES				TOTAL	MONEY
Sandy Lyle	67	71	66	70	274	$180,000
Jeff Sluman	70	66	69	69	274	108,000
(Lyle defeated Sluman on third hole of playoff)						
Mark O'Meara	68	65	69	73	275	68,000
Scott Simpson	69	65	68	74	276	44,000
Greg Norman	67	68	71	70	276	44,000
Paul Azinger	68	70	68	71	277	36,000
Dan Pohl	68	66	75	69	278	32,250
Bill Glasson	69	69	68	72	278	32,250
Tom Purtzer	69	67	72	71	279	27,000
Tom Kite	72	70	67	70	279	27,000
Ben Crenshaw	70	68	66	75	279	27,000
Larry Mize	70	70	69	71	280	21,000
Mark McCumber	69	71	69	71	280	21,000
Brad Fabel	67	68	75	70	280	21,000
Mike Reid	72	69	69	71	281	16,000
Tsuneyuki Nakajima	69	70	70	72	281	16,000
Hubert Green	69	71	72	69	281	16,000
David Frost	70	69	71	71	281	16,000
Steve Jones	66	67	76	72	281	16,000
Mark Wiebe	70	69	71	72	282	11,650
Chris Perry	68	71	70	73	282	11,650
Morris Hatalsky	73	69	70	70	282	11,650
Keith Clearwater	73	70	71	68	282	11,650
Nick Price	71	68	68	76	283	7,737.50
Hal Sutton	68	74	71	70	283	7,737.50
Hale Irwin	68	68	74	73	283	7,737.50
Isao Aoki	68	73	72	70	283	7,737.50
Mike Hulbert	71	71	71	70	283	7,737.50
Buddy Gardner	69	69	75	70	283	7,737.50
Ken Green	71	72	69	71	283	7,737.50
Bernhard Langer	72	71	71	69	283	7,737.50
Gene Sauers	68	72	72	72	284	5,414.29
Curt Byrum	69	68	73	74	284	5,414.29
David Edwards	70	70	70	74	284	5,414.29
John Mahaffey	70	72	69	73	284	5,414.29
Dave Rummells	68	71	73	72	284	5,414.28
Jack Renner	70	73	69	72	284	5,414.28
Bob Gilder	73	68	72	71	284	5,414.28
Clarence Rose	73	69	70	73	285	4,400
Scott Hoch	76	65	70	74	285	4,400
Don Pooley	74	68	73	71	286	3,900
Mike Nicolette	73	69	70	74	286	3,900
Bobby Cole	70	70	71	75	286	3,900
Chen Tze Chung	71	69	73	74	287	3,023.34
Chip Beck	71	71	76	69	287	3,023.34
Bill Rogers	69	73	69	76	287	3,023.33

	SCORES				TOTAL	MONEY
Bob Murphy	73	70	69	75	287	3,023.33
John Inman	73	70	72	72	287	3,023.33
Lennie Clements	74	67	72	74	287	3,023.33
Jay Haas	70	73	74	71	288	2,435
Mark Calcavecchia	73	69	73	73	288	2,435
Corey Pavin	75	68	70	75	288	2,435
Rocco Mediate	71	72	76	69	288	2,435

Greater Greensboro Open

Forest Oaks Country Club, Greensboro, North Carolina   April 2-5
Par 36-36 — 72; 6,954 yards   purse, $600,000

	SCORES				TOTAL	MONEY
Scott Simpson	70	73	69	79	282	$108,000
Clarence Rose	72	68	75	69	284	64,800
Payne Stewart	74	71	70	70	285	31,200
Tom Byrum	71	70	72	72	285	31,200
Kenny Knox	75	72	71	67	285	31,200
John Cook	72	73	72	69	286	21,600
Bill Sander	70	72	75	70	287	18,075
Mark O'Meara	74	69	74	70	287	18,075
Howard Twitty	73	68	75	71	287	18,075
Chip Beck	73	71	73	70	287	18,075
Brian Claar	73	72	70	73	288	15,000
Gene Sauers	71	74	70	74	289	13,200
Tom Purtzer	74	72	75	68	289	13,200
Chris Perry	74	75	73	68	290	11,100
Vance Heafner	73	72	74	71	290	11,100
Robert Thompson	75	70	75	71	291	9,300
Hal Sutton	75	73	72	71	291	9,300
Rex Caldwell	77	70	71	73	291	9,300
Lennie Clements	71	74	74	72	291	9,300
Dan Pohl	74	69	78	71	292	5,712
Joey Sindelar	75	70	73	74	292	5,712
Scott Verplank	72	73	73	74	292	5,712
Andy North	71	72	75	74	292	5,712
Danny Edwards	70	69	76	77	292	5,712
Gibby Gilbert	70	70	78	74	292	5,712
Donnie Hammond	70	74	76	72	292	5,712
Hale Irwin	74	73	76	69	292	5,712
Bob Lohr	72	74	71	75	292	5,712
Andrew Magee	73	73	73	73	292	5,712
Dave Rummells	70	73	77	73	293	3,487.50
Duffy Waldorf	73	74	72	74	293	3,487.50
Jeff Sluman	72	72	73	76	293	3,487.50
Keith Clearwater	73	72	73	75	293	3,487.50
Bill Glasson	74	75	74	70	293	3,487.50
Gary Hallberg	71	72	76	74	293	3,487.50
Barry Jaeckel	73	71	75	74	293	3,487.50
Larry Nelson	77	71	71	74	293	3,487.50
Dave Stockton	72	73	77	72	294	2,520
Don Shirey, Jr.	75	70	80	69	294	2,520
John Adams	74	70	78	72	294	2,520
Tim Norris	75	73	73	73	294	2,520
Charles Bolling	72	73	75	74	294	2,520
Bobby Cole	72	70	77	75	294	2,520

	SCORES				TOTAL	MONEY
Leonard Thompson	72	75	78	70	295	1,864.80
Mark Brooks	72	72	75	76	295	1,864.80
Brad Faxon	76	72	75	72	295	1,864.80
Joe Inman	73	72	76	74	295	1,864.80
John McComish	75	71	78	71	295	1,864.80
Bill Britton	71	76	76	73	296	1,480.80
Chen Tze Chung	68	76	77	75	296	1,480.80
Dan Forsman	72	75	73	76	296	1,480.80
Jack Renner	75	74	77	70	296	1,480.80
Dick Mast	76	73	74	73	296	1,480.80

Deposit Guaranty Classic

Hattiesburg Country Club, Hattiesburg, Mississippi
Par 35-35 — 70; 6,594 yards

April 9-12
purse, $200,000

	SCORES				TOTAL	MONEY
David Ogrin	66	68	69	64	267	$36,000
Nick Faldo	67	67	67	67	268	21,600
Richard Zokol	69	67	65	68	269	10,400
Jeff Grygiel	67	69	64	69	269	10,400
Bill Glasson	65	69	67	68	269	10,400
John Inman	64	71	70	65	270	6,700
Ed Dougherty	66	68	66	70	270	6,700
Tom Pernice Jr.	66	68	67	69	270	6,700
Duffy Waldorf	66	67	69	69	271	4,800
Robert Wrenn	69	62	68	72	271	4,800
John McComish	68	66	68	69	271	4,800
Rex Caldwell	69	68	70	64	271	4,800
Aki Ohmachi	68	71	66	66	271	4,800
Steve Elkington	72	63	67	69	271	4,800
Rick Dalpos	68	70	66	68	272	3,100
Tony Sills	64	71	65	72	272	3,100
Mike Smith	70	67	66	69	272	3,100
Brad Bryant	66	67	68	71	272	3,100
Dave Eichelberger	67	71	67	67	272	3,100
Billy Pierot	70	70	63	69	272	3,100
Ray Barr, Jr.	69	67	68	69	273	2,240
Mike West	62	71	67	73	273	2,240
Jim Gallagher, Jr.	67	72	70	64	273	2,240
Vance Heafner	70	69	67	68	274	1,547.50
Rocco Mediate	67	71	67	69	274	1,547.50
Kermit Zarley	72	68	68	66	274	1,547.50
John Adams	71	64	71	68	274	1,547.50
Dewey Arnette	70	70	64	70	274	1,547.50
Ray Stewart	71	68	68	67	274	1,547.50
Phil Hancock	70	66	69	69	274	1,547.50
Victor Regalado	70	67	69	68	274	1,547.50
Rod Curl	69	69	69	68	275	1,157.50
Bob Lunn	64	71	67	72	275	1,157.50
Andrew Magee	69	67	69	70	275	1,157.50
Mike Nicolette	71	66	71	67	275	1,157.50
Mike Donald	69	71	67	69	276	901.43
Steve Jones	67	68	71	70	276	901.43
Robert Thompson	67	70	68	71	276	901.43
Denny Hepler	68	73	68	67	276	901.43
Frank Conner	68	71	66	71	276	901.43

	SCORES				TOTAL	MONEY
Bill Sander	65	72	71	68	276	901.43
Bruce Soulsby	72	68	65	71	276	901.42
Davis Love III	68	70	72	67	277	680
Dennis Trixler	71	69	66	71	277	680
Philip Jonas	69	69	69	70	277	680
Bill Israelson	68	69	66	74	277	680
Tony Grimes	68	71	71	68	278	549.34
Brian Claar	69	67	70	72	278	549.33
Gibby Gilbert	67	75	67	69	278	549.33
Bill Britton	69	70	71	69	279	498
David Allen	68	71	69	71	279	498

Masters Tournament

Augusta National Golf Club, Augusta, Georgia
Par 36-36 — 72; 6,905 yards

April 9-12
purse, $867,100

	SCORES				TOTAL	MONEY
Larry Mize	70	72	72	71	285	$162,000
Severiano Ballesteros	73	71	70	71	285	79,200
Greg Norman	73	74	66	72	285	79,200
(Mize won playoff, defeating Ballesteros on first hole and Norman on second hole)						
Ben Crenshaw	75	70	67	74	286	37,200
Roger Maltbie	76	66	70	74	286	37,200
Jodie Mudd	74	72	71	69	286	37,200
Jay Haas	72	72	72	73	289	26,200
Bernhard Langer	71	72	70	76	289	26,200
Jack Nicklaus	74	72	73	70	289	26,200
Tom Watson	71	72	74	72	289	26,200
D. A. Weibring	72	75	71	71	289	26,200
Chip Beck	75	72	70	73	290	17,640
Chen Tze Chung	74	69	71	76	290	17,640
Mark McCumber	75	71	69	75	290	17,640
Curtis Strange	71	70	73	76	290	17,640
Lanny Wadkins	73	72	70	75	290	17,640
Paul Azinger	77	73	69	72	291	13,050
Mark Calcavecchia	73	72	78	68	291	13,050
Sandy Lyle	77	74	68	72	291	13,050
Craig Stadler	74	74	72	71	291	13,050
Bobby Wadkins	76	69	73	74	292	10,800
Gary Koch	76	75	72	70	293	9,750
Nick Price	73	73	71	76	293	9,750
John Cook	69	73	74	78	294	7,900
Tom Kite	73	74	74	73	294	7,900
Mark O'Meara	75	74	71	74	294	7,900
David Graham	73	77	72	73	295	6,267
Donnie Hammond	73	75	74	73	295	6,267
Corey Pavin	71	71	81	72	295	6,267
Scott Simpson	72	75	72	76	295	6,267
Denis Watson	76	74	73	72	295	6,267
Fuzzy Zoeller	76	71	76	72	295	6,267
Calvin Peete	71	77	75	73	296	5,200
Gene Sauers	75	73	74	74	296	5,200
Andy Bean	75	69	78	75	297	4,257
Howard Clark	74	71	77	75	297	4,257
Hubert Green	80	71	74	72	297	4,257
John Mahaffey	73	75	76	73	297	4,257

	SCORES				TOTAL	MONEY
Gary Player	75	75	71	76	297	4,257
Joey Sindelar	74	70	81	72	297	4,257
Mark Wiebe	73	74	71	79	297	4,257
Johnny Miller	75	75	71	77	298	3,333
Payne Stewart	71	75	74	78	298	3,333
Jim Thorpe	77	74	76	71	298	3,333
David Frost	75	70	77	78	300	2,800
Kenny Knox	75	75	75	75	300	2,800
Don Pooley	76	75	76	73	300	2,800
Mike Hulbert	76	75	71	79	301	2,400
Bruce Lietzke	75	74	77	76	302	2,300
Tommy Aaron	72	76	76	81	305	2,200
Dave Barr	79	68	79	79	305	2,200
Billy Casper	77	74	75	79	305	2,200
Mac O'Grady	72	79	79	75	305	2,200
*Robert Lewis Jr.	74	77	79	79	309	

Out of Final 36 Holes

			TOTAL	
*Stewart Alexander	76	76	152	
*Billy Andrade	74	78	152	
George Burns	78	74	152	
Ray Floyd	75	77	152	
Dan Pohl	81	71	152	
Scott Verplank	76	76	152	
Rick Fehr	78	75	153	
Andy North	79	74	153	
Hal Sutton	77	76	153	
Bob Tway	78	75	153	
Tsuneyuki Nakajima	73	81	154	
Larry Nelson	75	79	154	
Jose-Maria Olazabal	79	75	154	
Charles Coody	75	80	155	
Ken Green	78	77	155	
Bob Murphy	82	73	155	
Masashi Ozaki	73	82	155	
*David Curry	78	78	156	
*Chris Kite	80	76	156	
*Garth McGimpsey	79	77	156	
Lee Trevino	80	76	156	
Fred Wadsworth	74	82	156	
Ernie Gonzalez	77	80	157	
Isao Aoki	81	77	158	
Doug Ford	79	81	160	
Arnold Palmer	83	77	160	
*Jay Sigel	77	83	160	
Gay Brewer	80	81	161	
*Brian Montgomery	77	84	161	
Doug Tewell	85	76	161	
Art Wall	85	76	161	

(Professionals who did not complete 72 holes received $1,500)

MCI Heritage Classic

Harbour Town Golf Links, Hilton Head Island, South Carolina
Par 36-35 — 71; 6,657 yards

April 16-19
purse, $650,000

	SCORES				TOTAL	MONEY
Davis Love III	70	67	67	67	271	$117,000
Steve Jones	67	66	67	72	272	70,200
Gene Sauers	69	67	64	73	273	37,700
Mark Wiebe	69	67	70	67	273	37,700
Bob Murphy	69	70	66	69	274	23,725
Howard Twitty	66	69	72	67	274	23,725
Mark Calcavecchia	66	73	67	68	274	23,725
Mark Hayes	64	68	70	73	275	17,550
Larry Nelson	69	70	66	70	275	17,550
Tom Kite	71	72	67	65	275	17,550
Jay Haas	71	70	65	69	275	17,550
David Frost	67	71	71	66	275	17,550
Hale Irwin	74	66	65	71	276	12,187.50
Scott Hoch	66	69	67	74	276	12,187.50
D.A. Weibring	70	69	69	68	276	12,187.50
Ray Floyd	69	68	69	70	276	12,187.50
Blaine McCallister	71	68	70	68	277	9,100
Lanny Wadkins	69	70	69	69	277	9,100
Greg Norman	72	70	69	66	277	9,100
Mac O'Grady	70	68	68	71	277	9,100
John Cook	66	71	71	69	277	9,100
Tom Purtzer	73	71	67	67	278	7,280
Tim Norris	74	69	68	69	280	6,240
Barry Jaeckel	69	73	69	69	280	6,240
Bobby Wadkins	70	70	68	72	280	6,240
David Ogrin	68	74	72	67	281	4,332.30
Joe Inman	68	71	67	75	281	4,332.30
Denis Watson	73	67	69	72	281	4,332.30
Johnny Miller	69	69	71	72	281	4,332.30
Fuzzy Zoeller	68	71	68	74	281	4,332.30
Brett Upper	68	72	68	73	281	4,332.30
Corey Pavin	69	72	68	72	281	4,332.30
Ken Green	70	72	71	68	281	4,332.30
Chip Beck	75	68	67	71	281	4,332.30
Paul Azinger	70	71	71	69	281	4,332.30
John Inman	72	68	71	71	282	3,128
Sam Randolph	72	71	73	66	282	3,128
Bill Rogers	71	69	69	73	282	3,128
Curtis Strange	74	70	71	67	282	3,128
Gary Koch	69	74	66	74	283	2,405
Bernhard Langer	66	71	72	74	283	2,405
Larry Rinker	72	70	69	72	823	2,405
Wayne Levi	72	70	70	71	823	2,405
Dan Forsman	72	70	70	71	283	2,405
Buddy Gardner	70	71	71	71	283	2,405
Nick Faldo	70	67	71	75	283	2,405
Curt Byrum	71	70	69	74	284	1,669.58
Doug Tewell	71	74	69	70	284	1,669.57
Rick Fehr	73	68	71	72	284	1,669.57
Danny Edwards	72	71	70	71	284	1,669.57
Bob Eastwood	73	69	71	71	284	1,669.57
Ronnie Black	75	70	67	72	284	1,669.57
Jim Colbert	70	71	70	73	284	1,669.57

Big 'I' Houston Open

TPC at The Woodlands, The Woodlands, Texas
Par 36-36 — 72; 7,042 yards

April 23-26
purse, $600,000

	SCORES				TOTAL	MONEY
Jay Haas	69	69	71	67	276	$108,000
Buddy Gardner	69	70	67	70	276	64,800
(Haas defeated Gardner on first hole of playoff.)						
Payne Stewart	70	68	72	67	277	40,800
Nick Price	71	69	68	71	279	26,400
Wayne Levi	70	67	71	71	279	26,400
Aki Ohmachi	69	69	71	71	280	20,100
George Burns	73	70	68	69	280	20,100
Gary Hallberg	70	72	69	69	280	20,100
Steve Pate	74	69	68	70	281	15,600
Russ Cochran	69	70	74	68	281	15,600
Andrew Magee	70	72	70	69	281	15,600
Ken Brown	71	71	69	70	281	15,600
Curtis Stange	70	73	71	68	282	11,250
Howard Twitty	68	71	71	72	282	11,250
Dan Forsman	69	69	68	76	282	11,250
Frank Conner	74	71	69	68	282	11,250
Jack Renner	69	69	71	74	283	8,400
Mike McCullough	73	66	70	74	283	8,400
Curt Byrum	71	70	72	70	283	8,400
Danny Edwards	73	66	72	72	283	8,400
Mark O'Meara	72	70	71	70	283	8,400
Loren Roberts	70	74	69	71	284	5,570
Chris Perry	73	72	71	68	284	5,570
Rocco Mediate	72	73	71	68	284	5,570
Larry Mize	70	69	76	69	284	5,570
Greg Norman	73	72	74	65	284	5,570
Lennie Clements	72	69	70	73	284	5,570
Rick Fehr	74	71	70	70	285	4,260
Dave Barr	66	72	71	76	285	4,260
Steve Elkington	71	73	68	73	285	4,260
Clarence Rose	70	72	70	74	286	3,558
Dave Rummells	73	72	72	69	286	3,558
Leonard Thompson	70	71	70	75	286	3,558
Davis Love III	70	73	69	74	286	3,558
Barry Jaeckel	72	70	69	75	286	3,558
Bill Rogers	69	74	72	72	287	2,826
Ray Barr, Jr.	72	71	71	73	287	2,826
Mike Nicolette	73	71	71	72	287	2,826
Ed Fiori	66	74	71	76	287	2,826
Mike Reid	74	69	70	74	287	2,826
Jeff Lewis	69	74	69	76	288	2,280
Dewey Arnette	71	69	73	75	288	2,280
Larry Rinker	69	75	69	75	288	2,280
Ronnie Black	74	71	71	72	288	2,280
Mike Smith	70	73	74	72	289	1,716
Antonio Cerda	73	70	73	73	289	1,716
Keith Fergus	74	70	73	72	289	1,716
Steve Jones	69	73	70	77	289	1,716
John Inman	73	70	74	72	289	1,716
Jay Don Blake	73	72	71	73	289	1,716

Panasonic Las Vegas Invitational

Las Vegas, Nevada

April 29-May 3
purse, $1,250,000

Las Vegas Country Club
Par 36-36 — 72; 7,162 yards

Desert Inn Country Club
Par 36-36 — 72; 7,111 yards

Spanish Trail Country Club
Par 36-36 — 72; 7,088 yards

	SCORES				TOTAL	MONEY
Paul Azinger	68	72	67	64	271	$225,000
Hal Sutton	67	66	72	67	272	135,000
Curtis Strange	70	69	67	67	273	85,000
Kenny Perry	68	67	70	69	274	55,000
Ken Brown	64	71	70	69	274	55,000
Payne Stewart	67	71	69	68	275	43,437.50
David Frost	70	69	67	69	275	43,437.50
Denis Watson	65	72	71	68	276	36,250
Donnie Hammond	69	70	70	67	276	36,250
Fred Couples	66	73	68	69	276	36,250
Dan Pohl	68	72	65	72	277	27,500
Blaine McCallister	67	74	68	68	277	27,500
Nick Price	69	70	72	66	277	27,500
Craig Stadler	69	70	71	67	277	27,500
Davis Love III	68	73	72	65	278	21,875
Jodie Mudd	67	72	70	69	278	21,875
Greg Norman	71	71	67	70	279	14,750
Fuzzy Zoeller	72	72	68	67	279	14,750
Mark Wiebe	70	71	69	69	279	14,750
Andrew Magee	69	68	69	73	279	14,750
Dave Rummells	70	73	70	66	279	14,750
Bruce Soulsby	68	71	68	72	279	14,750
Sam Randolph	67	72	72	68	279	14,750
Ray Barr, Jr.	69	71	69	70	279	14,750
Phil Blackmar	67	75	69	68	279	14,750
Bob Eastwood	74	68	71	66	279	14,750
Bob Tway	66	73	73	68	280	9,437.50
Ken Green	67	75	70	68	280	9,437.50
John Mahaffey	69	69	72	71	281	7,609.38
Tom Putzer	70	71	68	72	281	7,609.38
Hale Irwin	67	74	69	71	281	7,609.38
Danny Edwards	70	71	71	69	281	7,609.38
Roger Maltbie	68	76	67	70	281	7,609.37
David Peoples	69	76	66	70	281	7,609.37
Mark O'Meara	68	73	72	68	281	7,609.37
Chris Perry	69	75	67	70	281	7,609.37
Scott Verplank	69	71	70	72	282	5,250
Ben Crenshaw	71	71	68	72	282	5,250
Ed Fiori	69	71	71	71	282	5,250
Dave Barr	67	73	73	69	282	5,250
Ronnie Black	67	71	73	71	282	5,250
Bobby Clampett	69	67	73	73	282	5,250
Lennie Clements	67	71	70	74	282	5,250
Jim Colbert	68	74	70	70	282	5,250
Tim Simpson	67	75	70	71	283	3,440.63
Gene Sauers	68	71	73	71	283	3,440.63

	SCORES				TOTAL	MONEY
Jay Don Blake	70	76	66	71	283	3,440.63
David Graham	72	67	71	73	283	3,440.63
Jay Haas	69	73	71	70	283	3,440.62
Tom Byrum	66	72	74	71	283	3,440.62
Andy Dillard	69	72	72	70	283	3,440.62
David Edwards	67	76	69	71	283	3,400.62

Byron Nelson Classic

Las Colinas Sports Club, Irving, Texas
Par 35-35 — 70; 6,767 yards

May 7-10
purse, $600,000

	SCORES				TOTAL	MONEY
Fred Couples	65	67	64	70	266	$108,000
Mark Calcavecchia	73	66	63	64	266	64,800
(Couples defeated Calcavecchia on third hole of playoff.)						
Bob Lohr	69	62	67	69	267	40,800
Craig Stadler	69	67	67	65	268	26,400
Donnie Hammond	68	63	68	69	268	26,400
Greg Norman	64	68	67	70	269	19,425
Tom Kite	70	65	68	66	269	19,425
Ben Crenshaw	66	65	67	71	269	19,425
Tom Byrum	66	65	69	69	269	19,425
David Frost	67	70	66	67	270	15,600
Ray Barr, Jr.	69	66	67	68	270	15,600
Mike Reid	68	66	70	67	271	12,600
Gary Hallberg	65	72	64	70	271	12,600
Brad Faxon	69	65	71	66	271	12,600
Tim Norris	68	67	70	67	272	9,900
Jay Don Blake	68	67	67	70	272	9,900
Rick Dalpos	69	68	65	70	272	9,900
David Edwards	69	68	71	64	272	9,900
Mark O'Meara	72	64	64	73	273	6,313.34
Kenny Knox	69	68	69	67	273	6,313.34
Dick Mast	67	72	67	67	273	6,313.34
Chris Perry	70	69	67	67	273	6,313.33
Howard Twitty	68	69	69	67	273	6,313.33
Bobby Wadkins	70	68	66	69	273	6,313.33
Payne Stewart	64	71	66	72	273	6,313.33
Bill Rogers	71	68	63	71	273	6,313.33
Mike McCullough	69	68	68	68	273	6,313.33
Steve Jones	68	69	68	69	274	3,904.29
John Adams	68	68	71	67	274	3,904.29
Charles Bolling	67	72	68	67	274	3,904.29
Steve Elkington	66	71	65	72	274	3,904.29
Jeff Sluman	69	66	68	71	274	3,904.28
Lanny Wadkins	71	68	69	66	274	3,904.28
Bill Britton	67	67	68	72	274	3,904.28
D.A. Weibring	66	69	70	70	275	2,895
Mark Wiebe	66	70	67	72	275	2,895
Keith Clearwater	67	68	70	70	275	2,895
David Canipe	69	68	70	68	275	2,895
Tony Grimes	68	71	66	70	275	2,895
Jim Carter	68	69	71	67	275	2,895
Dennis Trixler	68	69	73	66	276	1,989.34
Dewey Arnette	71	67	69	69	276	1,989.34
Danny Briggs	69	64	70	73	276	1,989.34

	SCORES				TOTAL	MONEY
Duffy Waldorf	66	71	67	72	276	1,989.33
Harry Taylor	69	67	67	73	276	1,989.33
Bobby Clampett	68	68	71	69	276	1,989.33
Gary Krueger	65	70	68	73	276	1,989.33
Paul Azinger	69	69	69	69	276	1,989.33
Dave Barr	69	68	71	68	276	1,989.33
Dave Stockton	72	66	71	68	277	1,447.20
Ron Streck	67	71	67	72	277	1,447.20
Brett Upper	70	68	70	69	277	1,447.20
Ed Dougherty	69	69	71	68	277	1,447.20
Antonio Cerda	69	70	70	68	277	1,447.20

Colonial National Invitation

Colonial Country Club, Fort Worth, Texas
Par 35-35 — 70; 7,116 yards

May 14-17
purse, $600,000

	SCORES				TOTAL	MONEY
Keith Clearwater	67	71	64	64	266	$108,000
Davis Love III	69	69	65	66	269	64,800
Dan Pohl	69	67	66	68	270	40,800
Scott Simpson	67	66	70	69	272	26,400
Curtis Strange	68	66	70	68	272	26,400
Jeff Sluman	68	69	68	68	273	20,100
Larry Mize	68	69	69	67	273	20,100
Ben Crenshaw	67	69	65	72	273	20,100
Doug Tewell	68	66	68	72	274	16,200
Scott Hoch	68	68	71	67	274	16,200
Tom Byrum	67	69	67	71	274	16,200
Bob Tway	68	70	70	67	275	11,400
Bobby Wadkins	67	69	73	66	275	11,400
Bruce Lietzke	69	67	69	70	275	11,400
Dave Barr	68	70	70	67	275	11,400
Mark Lye	69	66	68	72	275	11,400
Chip Beck	66	67	71	71	275	11,400
Fred Wadsworth	69	69	70	68	276	8,400
Gary Hallberg	70	68	67	71	276	8,400
Nick Price	70	68	71	67	276	8,400
Lon Hinkle	68	68	70	71	277	6,480
Tom Kite	69	69	69	70	277	6,480
Steve Elkington	70	63	71	73	277	6,480
Barry Jaeckel	70	67	71	69	277	6,480
Howard Twitty	69	69	69	71	278	4,680
Jack Renner	70	68	70	70	278	4,680
Paul Azinger	70	66	70	72	278	4,680
David Frost	69	69	69	71	278	4,680
Corey Pavin	70	70	68	70	278	4,680
Jim Colbert	69	70	69	71	279	3,565.72
Mike Hulbert	72	67	69	71	279	3,565.72
John Mahaffey	69	68	72	70	279	3,565.72
Mike Reid	68	71	68	72	279	3,565.71
Bill Rogers	65	69	75	70	279	3,565.71
Brad Fabel	74	64	69	72	279	3,565.71
Bill Glasson	69	69	70	71	279	3,565.71
Ed Fiori	69	68	71	72	280	2,760
Steve Pate	71	69	71	69	280	2,760
Bill Sander	66	72	70	72	280	2,760

	SCORES				TOTAL	MONEY
Gene Sauers	69	68	72	71	280	2,760
Dan Forsman	67	72	69	73	281	2,220
Mark Brooks	67	71	72	71	281	2,220
Hale Irwin	70	70	72	69	281	2,220
Peter Jacobsen	68	68	74	71	281	2,220
Mark Hayes	68	70	72	71	281	2,220
D.A. Weibring	70	69	71	72	282	1,701
Bob Gilder	68	68	73	73	282	1,701
Tony Sills	68	70	77	67	282	1,701
Joey Sindelar	70	70	69	73	282	1,701
*Tray Tyner	69	70	74	69	282	

Georgia-Pacific Atlanta Classic

Atlanta Country Club, Marietta, Georgia
Par 36-36 — 72; 7,007 yards

May 21-24
purse, $600,000

	SCORES				TOTAL	MONEY
Dave Barr	66	68	66	65	265	$108,000
Larry Mize	71	64	69	65	269	64,800
Lanny Wadkins	66	68	70	66	270	34,800
Chip Beck	67	68	68	67	270	34,800
Steve Pate	67	66	67	71	271	22,800
Gary Hallberg	70	69	66	66	271	22,800
Bobby Wadkins	66	68	65	73	272	20,100
Bob Tway	71	69	67	66	273	18,600
Don Pooley	70	68	69	67	274	16,200
Dan Pohl	68	67	70	69	274	16,200
Bill Sander	69	69	68	68	274	16,200
Greg Twiggs	70	69	70	66	275	11,760
Davis Love III	65	65	72	73	275	11,760
Hal Sutton	70	71	67	67	275	11,760
Jodie Mudd	70	66	70	69	275	11,760
George Burns	64	69	71	71	275	11,760
Bob Lohr	67	68	71	70	276	9,000
Willie Wood	71	68	68	69	276	9,000
Tom Kite	70	67	68	71	276	9,000
Jack Renner	67	66	73	71	277	7,240
Gary Koch	67	66	76	68	277	7,240
Antonio Cerda	69	67	71	70	277	7,240
Leonard Thompson	66	72	70	70	278	5,760
Richard Zokol	72	63	72	71	278	5,760
Jay Don Blake	69	67	71	71	278	5,760
Dick Mast	69	70	68	72	279	4,170
Scott Hoch	72	69	65	73	279	4,170
Corey Pavin	67	69	72	71	279	4,170
Rocco Mediate	68	69	72	70	279	4,170
Clarence Rose	69	72	67	71	279	4,170
Harry Taylor	70	67	72	70	279	4,170
Fuzzy Zoeller	68	68	68	75	279	4,170
Jim Carter	69	70	66	74	279	4,170
Ray Stewart	68	68	71	73	280	3,240
Russ Cochran	66	70	71	73	280	3,240
Ken Green	73	64	72	71	280	3,240
Bob Murphy	70	70	69	72	281	2,580
Rick Pearson	71	68	70	72	281	2,580
Fred Wadsworth	70	70	71	70	281	2,580

	SCORES				TOTAL	MONEY
Duffy Waldorf	73	66	71	71	281	2,580
D.A. Weibring	69	71	69	72	281	2,580
Jay Haas	69	70	71	71	281	2,580
Dewey Arnette	68	69	75	69	281	2,580
Tom Sieckmann	67	68	75	72	282	1,672.80
Ron Streck	71	70	73	68	282	1,672.80
Mike Nicolette	67	71	72	72	282	1,672.80
Scott Verplank	68	70	71	73	282	1,672.80
Buddy Gardner	69	67	71	75	282	1,672.80
Jim Colbert	68	72	67	75	282	1,672.80
Tom Garner	69	65	77	71	282	1,672.80
Peter Jacobsen	70	69	71	72	282	1,672.80
Frank Conner	71	69	68	74	282	1,672.80
Keith Clearwater	73	67	74	68	282	1,672.80

Memorial Tournament

Muirfield Village Golf Club, Dublin, Ohio
Par 36-36 — 72; 7,104 yards

May 28-31
purse, $849,290

	SCORES				TOTAL	MONEY
Don Pooley	70	67	65	70	272	$140,000
Curt Byrum	64	71	69	71	275	84,000
Denis Watson	75	66	65	70	276	40,443.34
Chip Beck	70	69	69	68	276	40,443.33
Scott Hoch	67	64	67	78	276	40,443.33
Sandy Lyle	69	70	69	69	277	26,038.34
David Frost	68	70	70	69	277	26,038.33
Larry Nelson	69	69	70	69	277	26,038.33
John Cook	69	69	72	68	278	19,480
Scott Simpson	68	68	72	70	278	19,480
Hal Sutton	74	64	68	72	278	19,480
John Mahaffey	69	71	65	73	278	19,480
Craig Stadler	71	67	71	69	278	19,480
Tom Watson	67	69	71	72	279	14,950
Ken Green	69	74	68	68	279	14,950
Larry Mize	68	72	69	70	279	14,950
D.A. Weibring	71	69	73	67	280	12,222.50
Dave Rummells	70	70	69	71	280	12,222.50
Dan Pohl	71	71	68	70	280	12,222.50
Dave Barr	70	70	69	71	280	12,222.50
Mac O'Grady	70	70	70	71	281	9,660
Tim Simpson	71	73	69	68	281	9,660
Joey Sindelar	66	76	70	69	281	9,660
Fred Couples	71	72	75	64	282	7,793.34
Fred Wadsworth	68	68	71	75	282	7,793.33
Bruce Lietzke	72	71	72	67	282	7,793.33
Hale Irwin	74	72	69	68	283	6,700
Buddy Gardner	69	70	71	73	283	6,700
Greg Norman	70	72	69	72	283	6,700
Keith Clearwater	72	72	72	68	284	5,769
Donnie Hammond	73	72	67	72	284	5,769
Payne Stewart	74	69	70	71	284	5,769
Willie Wood	73	67	69	75	284	5,769
Mark Hayes	69	75	69	71	284	5,769
Lanny Wadkins	70	70	69	76	285	4,863.75
Johnny Miller	73	70	71	71	285	4,863.75

	SCORES				TOTAL	MONEY
Ben Crenshaw	71	73	70	71	285	4,863.75
Curtis Strange	70	69	72	74	285	4,863.75
Wayne Levi	72	73	72	69	286	3,980
Ian Woosnam	71	69	73	73	286	3,980
Jay Haas	71	74	70	71	286	3,980
Gene Sauers	69	72	73	72	286	3,980
Sam Randolph	71	71	70	74	286	3,980
Mark McCumber	71	73	70	72	286	3,980
Bobby Wadkins	70	73	72	71	286	3,980
Tom Kite	69	70	73	75	287	3,021.43
David Graham	68	73	74	72	287	3,021.43
Jim Thorpe	70	68	72	77	287	3,021.43
Calvin Peete	71	71	71	74	287	3,021.43
Clarence Rose	75	71	72	69	287	3,021.43
Jose-Maria Olazabal	72	74	74	67	287	3,021.43
Jodie Mudd	69	74	73	71	287	3,021.42

Kemper Open

TPC at Avenel, Potomac, Maryland
Par 36-35 — 71; 6,864 yards

June 4-7
purse, $700,000

	SCORES				TOTAL	MONEY
Tom Kite	64	69	68	69	270	$126,000
Howard Twitty	66	67	73	71	277	61,600
Chris Perry	66	66	70	75	277	61,600
Greg Norman	64	73	68	73	278	28,933.34
Mike Reid	69	69	69	71	278	28,933.33
Scott Simpson	70	67	70	71	278	28,933.33
Roger Maltbie	74	67	69	69	279	22,575
Ken Green	72	71	68	68	279	22,575
Larry Mize	67	67	72	74	280	18,900
George Burns	69	67	68	76	280	18,900
Scott Hoch	65	68	72	75	280	18,900
Ed Dougherty	70	69	69	73	281	16,100
Ray Floyd	68	70	71	73	282	13,533.34
Dave Barr	70	70	66	76	282	13,533.33
Keith Clearwater	68	66	73	75	282	13,533.33
Fred Wadsworth	71	71	71	70	283	10,500
Bill Britton	72	68	72	71	283	10,500
David Frost	71	72	70	70	283	10,500
Jay Haas	67	70	76	70	283	10,500
Hale Irwin	70	73	71	69	283	10,500
Payne Stewart	66	75	73	70	284	7,280
Fred Couples	69	73	68	74	284	7,280
John Mahaffey	72	72	68	72	284	7,280
Denny Hepler	67	70	75	72	284	7,280
Mike Hulbert	68	70	70	76	284	7,280
Nick Price	73	71	68	73	285	4,970
J.C. Snead	71	69	72	73	285	4,970
Doug Tewell	69	68	75	73	285	4,970
Lee Trevino	71	70	70	74	285	4,970
Buddy Gardner	75	69	69	72	285	4,970
Peter Jacobsen	72	71	67	75	285	4,970
Sandy Lyle	67	69	74	75	285	4,970
Jack Renner	74	69	72	71	286	4,043
Russ Cochran	70	70	73	73	286	4,043

	SCORES				TOTAL	MONEY
Tony Sills	72	70	70	75	287	3,233
Brian Tennyson	71	72	70	74	287	3,233
John Adams	73	69	72	73	287	3,233
Chip Beck	71	71	71	74	287	3,233
Bob Eastwood	68	75	73	71	287	3,233
Kenny Perry	69	71	72	75	287	3,233
Steve Elkington	69	73	71	74	287	3,233
Sam Randolph	69	70	75	73	287	3,233
Tom Sieckmann	70	71	74	73	288	2,310
Leonard Thompson	72	71	72	73	288	2,310
Mark McCumber	66	72	75	75	288	2,310
Mike McCullough	70	71	73	74	288	2,310
Kenny Knox	71	73	71	73	288	2,310
Charles Bolling	66	76	70	77	289	1,759.34
Loren Roberts	73	68	71	77	289	1,759.34
Dave Rummells	71	70	73	75	289	1,759.33
Mike Sullivan	70	73	69	77	289	1,759.33
Denis Watson	70	64	74	81	289	1,759.33
Rocco Mediate	71	72	70	76	289	1,759.33

Manufacturers Hanover Westchester Classic

Westchester Country Club, Harrison, New York
Par 36-35 — 71; 6,723 yards

June 11-14
purse, $600,000

	SCORES				TOTAL	MONEY
J. C. Snead	71	70	65	70	276	$108,000
Severiano Ballesteros	66	67	71	72	276	64,800
(Snead defeated Ballesteros on first hole of playoff.)						
Roger Maltbie	71	67	68	71	277	40,800
Morris Hatalsky	71	68	72	67	278	24,800
Mike Donald	69	70	72	67	278	24,800
Mike Reid	68	66	69	75	278	24,800
Fred Couples	70	69	73	67	279	19,350
Sandy Lyle	65	72	71	71	279	19,350
Oki Ohmachi	72	72	68	68	280	16,800
Chris Perry	69	69	67	75	280	16,800
Ken Green	75	70	65	71	281	13,800
Harry Taylor	71	71	69	70	281	13,800
Doug Tewell	68	68	73	72	281	13,800
Rocco Mediate	71	74	70	67	282	10,800
David Edwards	74	68	68	72	282	10,800
Bruce Soulsby	72	71	70	69	282	10,800
Russ Cochran	74	69	70	70	283	8,700
Chip Beck	72	69	70	72	283	8,700
Wayne Levi	73	68	71	71	283	8,700
Loren Roberts	66	71	71	75	283	8,700
Keith Clearwater	74	72	67	71	284	5,802.86
Gil Morgan	74	72	65	73	284	5,802.86
John Inman	70	75	68	71	284	5,802.86
Ed Dougherty	71	70	71	72	284	5,802.86
Kenny Perry	73	72	71	68	284	5,802.86
Curt Byrum	69	69	74	72	284	5,802.85
Dick Mast	70	72	71	71	284	5,802.85
Jay Delsing	71	72	72	70	285	3,904.29
Lennie Clements	73	69	72	71	285	3,904.29
Rick Dalpos	74	70	71	70	285	3,904.29

	SCORES				TOTAL	MONEY
Jay Haas	68	69	75	73	285	3,904.29
Steve Jones	71	74	67	73	285	3,904.28
Mike Sullivan	71	71	71	72	285	3,904.28
Tom Pernice, Jr.	74	68	69	74	285	3,904.28
Frank Conner	72	72	71	71	286	2,832.86
Andy Dillard	73	72	69	72	286	2,832.86
Kenny Knox	71	74	69	72	286	2,832.86
Leonard Thompson	74	69	74	69	286	2,832.86
Scott Simpson	71	74	68	73	286	2,832.86
John Adams	69	72	70	75	286	2,832.85
Don Pooley	73	69	73	71	286	2,832.85
Vance Heafner	70	70	73	74	287	2,160
Greg Ladehoff	76	69	70	72	287	2,160
Bill Kratzerf	73	69	71	74	287	2,160
Mark Wiebe	68	70	73	76	287	2,160
Bob Lohr	73	70	69	76	288	1,800
Mark Hayes	69	74	73	72	288	1,800
Dave Eichelberger	69	72	73	75	289	1,548
Dan Halldorson	71	74	71	73	289	1,548
Robert Wrenn	75	69	71	74	289	1,548
Greg Twiggs	74	69	72	74	289	1,548

U.S. Open Championship

Olympic Club, Lakeside Course, San Francisco, California
Par 35-35 — 70; 6,727 yards

June 18-21
purse, $825,000

	SCORES				TOTAL	MONEY
Scott Simpson	71	68	70	68	277	$150,000
Tom Watson	72	65	71	70	278	75,000
Seve Ballesteros	68	75	68	71	282	46,240
Bernhard Langer	69	69	73	72	283	24,542.80
Ben Crenshaw	67	72	72	72	283	24,542.80
Curtis Strange	71	72	69	71	283	24,542.80
Larry Mize	71	68	72	72	283	24,542.80
Bobby Wadkins	71	71	70	71	283	24,542.80
Jim Thorpe	70	68	73	73	284	15,004.20
Dan Pohl	75	71	69	69	284	15,004.20
Tommy Nakajima	68	70	74	72	284	15,004.20
Lennie Clements	70	70	70	74	284	15,004.20
Mac O'Grady	71	69	72	72	284	15,004.20
Bob Eastwood	73	66	75	71	285	12,065.34
Isao Aoki	71	73	70	71	285	12,065.33
Tim Simpson	76	66	70	73	285	12,065.33
David Frost	70	72	71	73	286	9,747.29
Mark Calcavecchia	73	68	73	72	286	9,747.29
Nick Price	69	74	69	74	286	9,747.29
Jim Woodward	71	74	72	69	286	9,747.29
Jumbo Ozaki	71	69	72	74	286	9,747.28
Kenny Knox	72	71	69	74	286	9,747.28
Jodie Mudd	72	75	71	68	286	9,747.28
Steve Pate	71	72	72	72	287	7,719.72
Peter Jacobsen	72	71	71	73	287	7,719.72
Don Pooley	74	72	72	69	287	7,719.72
Danny Edwards	72	70	72	73	287	7,719.71
Jay Don Blake	70	75	71	71	287	7,719.71
Craig Stadler	72	68	74	73	287	7,719.71

	SCORES				TOTAL	MONEY
John Mahaffey	72	72	67	76	287	7,719.71
Ken Green	71	74	75	68	288	6,554.60
Hal Sutton	74	70	70	74	288	6,554.60
Keith Clearwater	74	71	64	79	288	6,554.60
Tony Sills	71	70	75	72	288	6,554.60
Dale Douglass	70	73	69	76	288	6,554.60
Denis Watson	69	74	72	74	289	5,626
Sandy Lyle	70	74	72	73	289	5,626
John Cook	70	68	76	75	289	5,626
Barry Jaeckel	73	70	72	74	289	5,626
Lanny Wadkins	73	71	72	73	289	5,626
Rodger Davis	75	68	72	74	289	5,626
Scott Hoch	72	70	77	70	289	5,626
Wayne Grady	73	70	74	73	290	4,856.67
Ray Floyd	68	73	76	73	290	4,856.67
Sam Randolph	71	71	76	72	290	4,856.66
Tom Kite	76	69	70	76	291	4,240
Jack Nicklaus	70	68	76	77	291	4,240
Ralph Landrum	72	71	74	74	291	4,240
Fred Couples	72	71	73	75	291	4,240
Roger Maltbie	73	73	75	70	291	4,240
David Graham	71	76	72	73	292	3,462.15
Ed Dougherty	73	67	78	74	292	3,462.15
Joey Sindelar	75	71	75	71	292	3,462.14
David Hobby	77	70	73	72	292	3,462.14
Greg Norman	72	69	74	77	292	3,462.14
Mark McCumber	72	72	69	79	292	3,462.14
Gil Morgan	72	71	76	73	292	3,462.14
Eddie Kirby	73	69	75	76	293	3,178.24
Jack Renner	73	73	71	76	293	3,178.24
Bob Lohr	76	67	79	71	293	3,178.24
Gene Sauers	72	69	73	79	293	3,178.23
Duffy Waldorf	74	69	75	75	293	3,178.23
Bob Gilder	72	72	70	79	293	3,178.23
Mark Wiebe	70	67	77	79	293	3,178.23
Mike Smith	73	71	74	75	293	3,178.23
Mark McNulty	73	72	73	76	294	3,165
Russ Cochran	71	69	81	73	294	3,165
Jose-Maria Olazabal	76	69	76	74	295	3,165
Tom Purtzer	74	73	77	71	295	3,165
Bob Tway	70	71	79	75	295	3,165
Jim Carter	75	72	75	74	296	3,165
Donnie Hammond	75	71	76	74	296	3,165
Gary Hallberg	71	72	69	85	297	3,165
David Ogrin	74	72	74	78	298	3,165
Dave Eichelberger	72	75	77	76	300	3,165
Fred Wadsworth	75	71	77	77	300	3,165
Dave Rummells	74	73	76	78	301	3,165

Out of Final 36 Holes

Paul Azinger	76	72			148	
John Morse	74	74			148	
Ernie Gonzalez	72	76			148	
Doug Tewell	75	73			148	
Robert Wrenn	74	74			148	
Joey Rassett	75	73			148	
Kevin Klier	76	72			148	
Payne Stewart	74	74			148	
Mark Lye	78	70			148	

	SCORES		TOTAL	MONEY
Gary Krueger	74	74	148	
Scott Hazledine	77	71	148	
Mike Nicolette	76	72	148	
Johnny Miller	71	77	148	
Mike Donald	76	72	148	
Jim White	76	72	148	
Andy North	74	74	148	
Steve Gotsche	72	76	148	
Calvin Peete	73	75	148	
Don Bies	76	73	149	
Mike Hulbert	73	76	149	
Brian Tennyson	75	74	149	
Jim Colbert	76	73	149	
Tom Lehman	77	72	149	
Fred Funk	74	75	149	
Chen Tze Chung	75	74	149	
Patrick Horgan	76	73	149	
Kirk Triplett	75	74	149	
Bart Bryant	75	75	150	
John Grund	76	74	150	
Bill Buttner	72	78	150	
Darrell Kestner	73	77	150	
Hale Irwin	79	71	150	
Brandel Chamblee	73	77	150	
Chip Beck	77	74	151	
Mike Reid	74	77	151	
Larry Nelson	76	75	151	
Lee Trevino	73	78	151	
Bill Britton	77	74	151	
Scott Verplank	78	73	151	
Mark Aebli	75	76	151	
Bill Glasson	77	75	152	
Fuzzy Zoeller	78	74	152	
Bob Lunn	75	77	152	
Ivan Smith	74	78	152	
Jim Booros	76	76	152	
Gary Pinns	74	78	152	
Gary Koch	77	75	152	
Hubert Green	77	75	152	
Jay Overton	78	74	152	
Greg Parker	77	76	153	
Greg Powers	76	77	153	
Robert Boyd	83	70	153	
*Buddy Alexander	76	77	153	
Roy Biancalana	78	76	154	
David Canipe	79	75	154	
D.A. Weibring	77	77	154	
Andy Bean	74	80	154	
Scott Steger	77	77	154	
Steve Brady	77	77	154	
Bill Bergin	73	81	154	
Frank Conner	79	75	154	
Mark Brooks	79	75	154	
Alan Tapie	78	77	155	
Griffin Rudolph	77	78	155	
Mike Miles	79	76	155	
Jerry Haas	75	80	155	
Mark O'Meara	76	79	155	
John Kudysch	84	72	156	
Larry Emery	79	77	156	

	SCORES				TOTAL	MONEY
Jeff Maggert	79	78			157	
Brian Fogt	77	80			157	
Loren Roberts	79	78			157	
Joey Edwards	81	78			159	
Charles Bolling	81	79			160	
Norm Becker	83	77			160	
Adam Adams	77	84			161	
Robert Gadna	86	76			162	
Dave Barr	72	WD				
Corey Pavin	WD					

(All professionals who started but did not complete 72 holes received $600.)

Canon Sammy Davis Jr. Greater Hartford Open

TPC of Connecticut, Cromwell, Connecticut
Par 36-35 — 71; 6,786 yards

June 25-28
purse, $700,000

	SCORES				TOTAL	MONEY
Paul Azinger	69	65	63	72	269	$126,000
Wayne Levi	64	68	68	70	270	61,600
Dan Forsman	65	69	69	67	270	61,600
Lee Trevino	67	69	70	66	272	30,800
*Gene Sauers	66	68	68	70	272	30,800
John Inman	70	66	67	70	273	24,325
Doug Tewell	68	68	68	69	273	24,325
Bernhard Langer	65	65	72	72	274	20,300
Bob Lohr	68	68	67	71	274	20,300
Denis Watson	65	72	69	68	274	20,300
Gil Morgan	70	67	67	71	275	15,400
Fuzzy Zoeller	67	73	67	68	275	15,400
Tom Watson	67	68	70	70	275	15,400
Dave Rummells	72	67	68	68	275	15,400
Russ Cochran	69	71	65	71	276	11,200
Chip Beck	69	68	69	70	276	11,200
Tony Sills	71	68	67	70	276	11,200
Dan Pohl	69	68	70	69	276	11,200
Clarence Rose	68	68	70	70	276	11,200
Mark McCumber	71	68	69	69	277	8,155
Davis Love III	71	67	69	70	277	8,155
Jay Haas	69	71	70	67	277	8,155
Tom Sieckmann	71	70	67	69	277	8,155
David Canipe	70	69	68	71	278	5,810
Jim Carter	71	70	64	73	278	5,810
Vance Heafner	68	67	71	72	278	5,810
Jim Thorpe	65	70	73	70	278	5,810
Tim Simpson	68	69	67	74	278	5,810
George Burns	72	67	69	71	279	4,550
Hale Irwin	72	68	70	69	279	4,550
Ed Fiori	72	68	69	70	279	4,550
Ron Streck	68	72	70	69	279	4,550
J.C. Snead	68	70	70	71	279	4,550
Peter Jacobsen	70	71	70	69	280	3,692.50
Mike Hulbert	68	70	70	72	280	3,692.50
Howard Twitty	68	72	68	72	280	3,692.50
Steve Pate	67	71	70	72	280	3,692.50
Willie Wood	73	68	70	70	281	3,010

	SCORES				TOTAL	MONEY
Robert Wrenn	71	70	70	70	281	3,010
Mike Smith	71	70	69	71	281	3,010
Mike Sullivan	68	72	73	68	281	3,010
Mark O'Meara	70	70	73	68	281	3,010
Andy Dillard	70	70	69	73	282	2,184
Ronnie Black	69	67	73	73	282	2,184
Bill Britton	71	71	70	70	282	2,184
Brad Faxon	70	72	69	71	282	2,184
Bob Gilder	70	72	66	74	282	2,184
Mike Donald	70	72	72	68	282	2,184
Duffy Waldorf	70	71	69	72	282	2,184
Bobby Cole	71	71	70	71	283	1,653.75
Brian Claar	69	69	69	76	283	1,653.75
Lennie Clements	69	71	72	71	283	1,653.75
Roger Maltbie	71	71	68	73	283	1,653.75
Scott Hoch	72	69	69	73	283	1,653.75
Richard Zokol	72	69	71	71	283	1,653.75
Harry Taylor	68	67	73	75	283	1,653.75
Robert Thompson	71	71	69	72	283	1,653.75

Canadian Open

Glen Abbey Golf Club, Oakville, Ontario, Canada
Par 35-37 — 72; 7,102 yards

July 2-5
purse, $600,000

	SCORES				TOTAL	MONEY
Curtis Strange	71	70	66	69	276	$108,000
Jodie Mudd	73	69	69	68	279	44,800
David Frost	71	67	72	69	279	44,800
Nick Price	72	67	70	70	279	44,800
Mike McCullough	72	67	68	74	281	22,800
Mark McCumber	72	70	72	67	281	22,800
John Cook	75	71	66	70	282	16,850
Pat McGowan	71	69	72	70	282	16,850
Brad Faxon	72	69	72	69	282	16,850
Richard Zokol	70	68	69	75	282	16,850
Craig Stadler	75	67	68	72	282	16,850
Joey Sindelar	68	74	69	71	282	16,850
Mac O'Grady	71	72	72	68	283	12,000
Steve Jones	72	69	72	70	283	12,000
Paul Azinger	73	70	70	71	284	10,500
Lon Hinkle	76	67	70	71	284	10,500
Dan Pohl	71	71	71	72	285	9,600
Ed Dougherty	72	71	69	74	286	7,560
Dave Eichelberger	73	72	70	71	286	7,560
Bobby Clampett	72	71	69	74	286	7,560
Mike Donald	75	72	70	69	286	7,560
Jim Nelford	72	72	69	73	286	7,560
Sam Randolph	74	69	70	73	286	7,560
Brad Fabel	75	71	69	72	287	4,860
Isao Aoki	75	69	74	69	287	4,860
Rocco Mediate	77	66	70	74	287	4,860
Jack Nicklaus	72	70	72	73	287	4,860
Ernie Gonzalez	70	73	67	77	287	4,860
David Graham	72	71	73	71	287	4,860
Steve Pate	70	72	75	71	288	3,990
Mike Smith	72	72	71	73	288	3,990

	SCORES				TOTAL	MONEY
Dave Barr	78	67	67	77	289	2,983.64
Curt Byrum	77	70	72	70	289	2,983.64
David Ogrin	74	73	73	69	289	2,983.64
Bob Gilder	72	72	69	76	289	2,983.64
Fred Wadsworth	72	70	75	72	289	2,983.64
Mark Wiebe	74	72	71	72	289	2,983.64
Tom Purtzer	69	71	76	73	289	2,983.64
Danny Edwards	71	76	69	73	289	2,983.63
Dan Halldorson	73	74	71	71	289	2,983.63
Robert Thompson	72	74	73	70	289	2,983.63
Mike Reid	74	73	70	72	289	2,983.63
Davis Love III	78	68	69	75	290	1,924
Bob Lohr	72	72	75	71	290	1,924
Dick Mast	74	68	70	78	290	1,924
Brett Upper	72	74	69	75	290	1,924
Ron Streck	75	72	74	69	290	1,924
Clarence Rose	73	71	72	74	290	1,924
Jim Carter	71	76	71	73	291	1,516
Morris Hatalsky	71	72	72	76	291	1,516
Tom Sieckmann	72	72	75	72	291	1,516

Anheuser-Busch Classic

Kingsmill Golf Club, Williamsburg, Virginia
Par 36-35 — 71; 6,746 yards

July 9-12
purse, $612,000

	SCORES				TOTAL	MONEY
Mark McCumber	65	69	67	66	267	$110,160
Bobby Clampett	69	66	65	68	268	66,096
Scott Hoch	67	66	68	69	270	41,616
John Cook	66	67	66	72	271	29,376
Chris Perry	69	69	68	66	272	23,256
Denis Watson	68	69	69	66	272	23,256
Tim Simpson	67	65	69	73	274	19,737
D.A. Weibring	68	71	66	69	274	19,737
Tom Sieckmann	65	68	69	73	275	17,136
Vance Heafner	71	65	66	73	275	17,136
Richard Zokol	68	71	68	69	276	14,076
Bob Gilder	71	68	69	68	276	14,076
Rocco Mediate	72	69	70	65	276	14,076
Sam Randolph	68	70	71	68	277	11,322
Steve Pate	68	66	72	71	277	11,322
Jay Don Blake	67	69	71	71	278	10,098
Jeff Lewis	68	71	68	71	278	10,098
Bobby Wadkins	72	68	69	70	279	7,448.92
Joey Sindelar	70	69	68	72	279	7,448.92
Tony Sills	68	72	69	70	279	7,448.92
Hal Sutton	70	72	68	69	279	7,448.91
Fred Wadsworth	66	71	70	72	279	7,448.91
John Mahaffey	67	70	70	72	279	7,448.91
Tim Norris	69	70	73	67	279	7,448.91
Mike Smith	69	71	68	72	280	4,572.52
Scott Verplank	69	73	74	64	280	4,572.52
Bill Britton	70	68	71	71	280	4,572.52
Ron Streck	66	69	74	71	280	4,572.51
Harry Taylor	69	70	73	68	280	4,572.51
Dave Eichelberger	66	68	74	72	280	4,572.51

	SCORES				TOTAL	MONEY
Gibby Gilbert	67	72	72	69	280	4,572.51
Clarence Rose	72	70	70	69	281	3,542.25
Jim Gallagher, Jr.	70	66	75	70	281	3,542.25
Hubert Green	71	68	69	73	281	3,542.25
David Canipe	70	71	72	68	281	3,542.25
Mike Sullivan	69	66	75	72	282	2,696.48
Scott Simpson	71	71	71	69	282	2,696.48
John Inman	70	70	69	73	282	2,696.48
Kenny Perry	67	72	68	75	282	2,696.48
Jeff Sluman	71	70	71	70	282	2,696.47
Kermit Zarley	71	71	73	67	282	2,696.47
Curtis Strange	70	72	65	75	282	2,696.47
Russ Cochran	72	68	72	70	282	2,696.47
John Adams	70	68	77	68	283	1,706.26
Tom Byrum	71	71	73	68	283	1,706.26
Bill Kratzert	74	68	69	72	283	1,706.26
Bill Glasson	71	71	68	73	283	1,706.26
David Ogrin	69	73	72	69	283	1,706.26
Mark Brooks	70	71	71	71	283	1,706.26
Billy Pierot	70	69	71	73	283	1,706.25
Ernie Gonzalez	72	69	70	72	283	1,706.25
Blaine McCallister	72	69	71	71	283	1,706.25
Bob Eastwood	72	70	74	67	283	1,706.25

Hardee's Classic

Oakwood Country Club, Coal Valley, Illinois
Par 35-35 — 70; 6,606 yards

July 16-19
purse, $500,000

	SCORES				TOTAL	MONEY
Kenny Knox	67	66	66	66	265	$90,000
Gil Morgan	66	69	63	68	266	54,000
Mark McCumber	64	67	69	67	267	34,000
Scott Hoch	68	68	65	67	268	24,000
Brad Fabel	64	65	71	69	269	20,000
Jack Renner	69	69	69	63	270	17,375
Perry Arthur	67	67	69	67	270	17,375
Tom Shaw	68	67	68	68	271	13,000
Fred Wadsworth	65	67	68	71	271	13,000
Chris Perry	71	66	69	65	271	13,000
Jeff Sluman	65	72	67	67	271	13,000
Jim Gallagher, Jr.	69	63	71	68	271	13,000
Bob Eastwood	71	66	66	68	271	13,000
Dave Rummells	63	71	69	69	272	9,000
Dan Pohl	69	66	73	64	272	9,000
Tom Purtzer	67	64	72	69	272	9,000
Andrew Magee	74	65	66	68	273	7,250
Ron Streck	66	67	70	70	273	7,250
Bob Lohr	66	68	68	71	273	7,250
Morris Hatalsky	66	69	71	67	273	7,250
Mike Smith	71	61	74	68	274	5,200
Mike Nicolette	72	63	68	71	274	5,200
Mike Sullivan	66	66	70	72	274	5,200
Billy Pierot	69	65	72	68	274	5,200
Bill Glasson	68	71	67	68	274	5,200
Willie Wood	67	69	70	69	275	3,775
John McComish	67	70	70	68	275	3,775

	SCORES				TOTAL	MONEY
Mike Morley	68	66	72	69	275	3,775
Russ Cochran	68	68	68	71	275	3,775
D.A. Weibring	65	74	68	69	276	3,175
John Mahaffey	68	68	66	74	276	3,175
Trevor Dodds	69	69	69	69	276	3,175
Charles Bolling	67	65	73	71	276	3,175
Ray Stewart	65	68	72	72	277	2,366.67
Leonard Thompson	69	70	68	70	277	2,366.67
Bobby Clampett	66	68	71	72	277	2,366.67
Mike Bender	70	66	71	70	277	2,366.67
Ed Dougherty	71	68	67	71	277	2,366.67
Curt Byrum	69	69	73	66	277	2,366.67
Bruce Soulsby	66	72	72	67	277	2,366.66
Joey Sindelar	69	68	71	69	277	2,366.66
Dan Forsman	68	68	68	73	277	2,366.66
Brian Tennyson	69	69	71	69	278	1,461
Tim Simpson	67	72	71	68	278	1,461
Harry Taylor	71	68	68	71	278	1,461
Kermit Zarley	70	68	70	70	278	1,461
Mike McCullough	66	68	75	69	278	1,461
Jay Don Blake	72	66	71	69	278	1,461
Mark Brooks	67	69	72	70	278	1,461
Phil Hancock	70	68	72	68	278	1,461
George Archer	67	70	70	71	278	1,461
Dan Halldorson	67	69	70	72	278	1,461

Buick Open

Warwick Hills Country Club, Grand Blanc, Michigan
Par 36-36 — 72; 7,014 yards

July 23-26
purse, $600,000

	SCORES				TOTAL	MONEY
Robert Wrenn	65	63	67	67	262	$108,000
Dan Pohl	69	68	67	65	269	64,800
Scott Hoch	67	68	69	66	270	40,800
Ken Green	66	66	69	70	271	28,800
Jodie Mudd	67	67	69	69	272	21,900
Gil Morgan	67	69	68	68	272	21,900
Don Pooley	68	66	69	69	272	21,900
Tom Kite	72	67	69	65	273	17,400
Trevor Dodds	70	69	63	71	273	17,400
Brad Faxon	70	68	67	68	273	17,400
Kenny Perry	73	65	69	67	274	11,914.29
Dave Rummells	71	68	67	68	274	11,914.29
Buddy Gardner	70	69	68	67	274	11,914.29
Jay Haas	65	71	66	72	274	11,914.29
Mike Reid	70	66	71	67	274	11,914.28
Jack Renner	68	69	67	70	274	11,914.28
David Graham	72	67	68	67	274	11,914.28
Payne Stewart	66	72	68	69	275	8,100
Chris Perry	67	73	68	67	275	8,100
Ray Floyd	69	69	69	68	275	8,100
John Adams	67	68	70	70	275	8,100
Ted Schulz	68	70	67	72	277	6,240
Tom Byrum	67	73	68	69	277	6,240
Dick Mast	70	69	69	69	277	6,240
Lanny Wadkins	70	70	66	72	278	4,900

	SCORES				TOTAL	MONEY
Mark Calcavecchia	70	70	69	69	278	4,900
Jim Carter	70	69	71	68	278	4,900
J.C. Snead	66	71	73	69	279	3,740
Scott Verplank	70	71	67	71	279	3,740
Bob Gilder	72	65	72	70	279	3,740
Curt Byrum	67	68	71	73	279	3,740
Mark Brooks	70	71	68	70	279	3,740
Keith Clearwater	71	67	69	72	279	3,740
Ed Dougherty	64	70	72	73	279	3,740
Davis Love III	71	66	69	73	279	3,740
Russ Cochran	68	69	70	72	279	3,740
Sam Randolph	67	72	69	72	280	2,400
Denis Watson	72	69	72	67	280	2,400
Ron Streck	68	69	72	71	280	2,400
Leonard Thompson	67	70	70	73	280	2,400
Mac O'Grady	71	70	70	69	280	2,400
George Archer	69	70	69	72	280	2,400
Andrew Magee	66	73	73	68	280	2,400
Gary Krueger	70	66	74	70	280	2,400
Dan Halldorson	70	69	69	72	280	2,400
Bob Eastwood	70	69	72	69	280	2,400
Bobby Wadkins	74	67	68	72	281	1,522.50
D.A. Weibring	69	69	71	72	281	1,522.50
Ed Fiori	73	67	73	68	281	1,522.50
John Inman	70	70	70	71	281	1,522.50
Dewey Arnette	65	73	72	71	281	1,522.50
Dave Barr	69	69	71	72	281	1,522.50
Jay Don Blake	67	74	71	69	281	1,522.50
Ben Crenshaw	68	69	70	74	281	1,522.50

Federal Express St. Jude Classic

Colonial Country Club, Cordova, Tennessee
Par 36-36 — 72; 7,282 yards

July 30-August 2
purse, $724,043

	SCORES				TOTAL	MONEY
Curtis Strange	70	68	68	69	275	$130,328
Denis Watson	74	65	71	66	276	47,787
Russ Cochran	66	73	68	69	276	47,787
Mike Donald	72	67	68	69	276	47,787
Tom Kite	72	70	67	67	276	47,787
Fuzzy Zoeller	71	66	70	70	277	26,066
Bob Tway	70	70	69	69	278	24,255
Willie Wood	71	72	70	66	279	20,273
Ronnie Black	68	72	72	67	279	20,273
Curt Byrum	72	70	70	67	279	20,273
Gil Morgan	69	70	74	66	279	20,273
Loren Roberts	71	70	71	68	280	15,205
Chip Beck	69	72	68	71	280	15,205
Andy Dillard	67	69	70	74	280	15,205
Harry Taylor	72	70	69	70	281	10,185.12
Tim Simpson	70	69	71	71	281	10,185.11
Payne Stewart	68	73	72	68	281	10,185.11
Jay Don Blake	68	70	69	74	281	10,185.11
Antonio Cerda	67	74	72	68	281	10,185.11
Hubert Green	69	73	65	74	281	10,185.11
Scott Hoch	71	69	69	72	281	10,185.11

	SCORES				TOTAL	MONEY
Hale Irwin	69	73	69	70	281	10,185.11
Tsuneyuki Nakajima	70	70	70	71	281	10,185.11
Hal Sutton	71	68	74	69	282	6,009.60
Bobby Wadkins	72	70	76	64	282	6,009.60
Jeff Sluman	68	73	75	66	282	6,009.60
Jodie Mudd	72	69	72	69	282	6,009.60
Brad Faxon	72	68	72	70	282	6,009.60
Scott Verplank	72	70	71	70	283	4,706.20
Larry Nelson	70	71	70	72	283	4,706.20
Kenny Perry	71	71	72	69	283	4,706.20
Steve Pate	69	74	73	67	283	4,706.20
Kenny Knox	72	72	74	65	283	4,706.20
Dave Rummells	73	70	71	70	284	3,352.40
Tom Sieckmann	72	71	70	71	284	3,352.40
Perry Arthur	70	70	73	71	284	3,352.40
Bill Britton	70	73	71	70	284	3,352.40
Jim Carter	73	70	70	71	284	3,352.40
John Riegger	73	68	71	72	284	3,352.40
Larry Rinker	71	71	72	70	284	3,352.40
Trevor Dodds	68	67	74	75	284	3,352.40
David Peoples	75	67	73	69	284	3,352.40
Larry Mize	68	72	73	71	284	3,352.40
Howard Twitty	73	69	70	73	285	2,250.40
Brian Claar	74	69	73	69	285	2,250.40
Rick Dalpos	69	74	71	71	285	2,250.40
Ernie Gonzalez	73	68	75	69	285	2,250.40
Andrew Magee	73	71	71	70	285	2,250.40
Mike Sullivan	68	73	75	70	286	1,829.67
Don Pooley	69	68	76	73	286	1,829.67
Griffin Rudolph	70	70	75	71	286	1,829.66

PGA Championship

PGA National Golf Club, Champions Course,
Palm Beach Gardens, Florida
Par 36-36 — 72; 7,002 yards

August 6-9
purse, $900,000

	SCORES				TOTAL	MONEY
Larry Nelson	70	72	73	72	287	$150,000
Lanny Wadkins	70	70	74	73	287	90,000
(Nelson defeated Wadkins on first hole of playoff.)						
Scott Hoch	74	74	71	69	288	58,750
D.A. Weibring	73	72	67	76	288	58,750
Mark McCumber	74	69	69	77	289	37,500
Don Pooley	73	71	73	72	289	37,500
Ben Crenshaw	72	70	74	74	290	27,500
Bobby Wadkins	68	74	71	77	290	27,500
Curtis Strange	70	76	71	74	291	22,500
Seve Ballesteros	72	70	72	78	292	17,000
Tom Kite	72	77	71	72	292	17,000
David Frost	75	70	71	76	292	17,000
Nick Price	76	71	70	75	292	17,000
Curt Byrum	74	75	68	76	293	10,750
Ray Floyd	70	70	73	80	293	10,750
David Edwards	69	75	77	72	293	10,750
Tom Watson	70	79	73	71	293	10,750

			SCORES		TOTAL	MONEY
Jeff Sluman	72	69	78	74	293	10,750
Dan Pohl	71	78	75	69	293	10,750
Peter Jacobsen	73	75	73	73	294	8,500
Gil Morgan	75	74	70	76	295	7,500
Bernhard Langer	70	78	77	70	295	7,500
James Hallet	73	78	73	71	295	7,500
Ken Brown	73	74	73	76	296	5,975
Payne Stewart	72	75	75	74	296	5,975
Gene Sauers	76	74	68	78	296	5,975
Jack Nicklaus	76	73	74	73	296	5,975
Ronnie Black	76	70	76	75	297	4,383.34
Russ Cochran	73	76	69	79	297	4,383.34
Nick Faldo	73	73	77	74	297	4,383.34
Chris Perry	75	75	74	73	297	4,383.34
Bobby Clampett	71	72	77	77	297	4,383.33
John Cook	76	70	72	79	297	4,383.33
Roger Maltbie	74	72	75	76	297	4,383.33
Bruce Lietzke	75	76	74	72	297	4,383.33
Jay Haas	74	70	76	77	297	4,383.33
Brad Fabel	73	73	77	74	297	4,383.33
Hal Sutton	73	74	74	76	297	4,383.33
Craig Stadler	75	72	75	75	297	4,383.33
Phil Blackmar	74	72	80	72	298	3,400
Denis Watson	76	75	72	75	298	3,400
Robert Wrenn	75	72	76	75	298	3,400
Bobby Cole	71	74	75	79	299	3,050
Buddy Gardner	75	74	79	71	299	3,050
Tim Simpson	71	70	81	77	299	3,050
Mac O'Grady	78	70	71	80	299	3,050
Bob Betley	72	79	77	72	300	2,400
Tom Byrum	79	72	76	73	300	2,400
Chen Tze Chung	76	75	76	73	300	2,400
Donnie Hammond	76	74	79	71	300	2,400
Fred Funk	69	79	79	73	300	2,400
Bob Tway	78	71	76	75	300	2,400
Scott Simpson	78	73	76	73	300	2,400
Tom Purtzer	75	73	81	71	300	2,400
Mike Reid	71	79	74	76	300	2,400
Chip Beck	75	74	72	80	301	1,856
Morris Hatalsky	76	75	75	75	301	1,856
Hubert Green	74	73	80	74	301	1,856
Mike Sullivan	73	72	74	82	301	1,856
Lonnie Nielsen	78	73	74	76	301	1,856
Steve Jones	72	75	74	81	302	1,740
Jim Woodward	79	72	69	82	302	1,740
Steve Pate	76	73	76	77	302	1,740
Fuzzy Zoeller	76	71	76	80	303	1,700
Andy Bean	73	78	76	79	306	1,650
John Mahaffey	77	72	77	80	306	1,650
Mark Wiebe	78	73	75	80	306	1,650
Arnold Palmer	76	75	79	76	306	1,650
Ray Freeman	71	77	74	85	307	1,600.04
Greg Norman	73	78	79	79	309	1,600.03
Lindy Miller	73	78	82	78	311	1,600.02
John Jackson	77	74	84	78	313	1,600.01
Lon Hinkle	74	76	79	89	318	1,600
Mark McNulty	73	73	75	WD		

Out of Final 36 Holes	SCORES		TOTAL	MONEY
Tsuneyuki Nakajima	78	74	152	
J.C. Snead	73	79	152	
Brad Faxon	77	76	153	
Danny Edwards	77	76	153	
Ernie Gonzalez	77	76	153	
Jack Seltzer	78	75	153	
Andy North	75	78	153	
Fred Couples	80	74	154	
Blaine McCallister	74	80	154	
David Graham	79	75	154	
Tom Brannen	76	78	154	
Gibby Gilbert	75	79	154	
Fred Wadsworth	78	76	154	
Jim Thorpe	75	79	154	
Jim Kallam	79	76	155	
Steve Heckel	76	79	155	
Ken Green	75	80	155	
Larry Gilbert	74	81	155	
Mark O'Meara	77	78	155	
Larry Mize	75	81	156	
Mark Hayes	75	81	156	
Rodger Davis	79	77	156	
George Burns	73	83	156	
Steve Veriato	76	80	156	
Howard Twitty	79	77	156	
Tony Sills	81	75	156	
Jose-Maria Olazabal	79	77	156	
Davis Love III	74	83	157	
Mike Hulbert	73	84	157	
David Glenz	77	80	157	
Doug Tewell	77	80	157	
Wheeler Stewart	80	77	157	
Corey Pavin	78	79	157	
Wayne Levi	76	82	158	
Kenny Knox	80	78	158	
Pat McGowan	78	80	158	
Dan Forsman	78	80	158	
Tom Wargo	84	74	158	
Dana Quigley	79	79	158	
Peter Oakley	83	75	158	
Paul Azinger	82	77	159	
Mark Calcavecchia	79	80	159	
Dave Stockton	79	80	159	
Joey Sindelar	80	79	159	
Isao Aoki	82	78	160	
Rick Fehr	82	78	160	
Keith Clearwater	85	75	160	
Gary Hallberg	74	86	160	
Jodie Mudd	85	76	161	
Ian Woosnam	86	75	161	
Don Padgett	81	80	161	
Mike San Filippo	80	81	161	
Clarence Rose	81	80	161	
Dwight Nevil	85	77	162	
Ted Goin	82	80	162	
Lennie Clements	86	76	162	
Bob Lendzion	78	84	162	
Rick Acton	79	85	164	

	SCORES		TOTAL	MONEY
Bob Groff	83	81	164	
Bob Lohr	75	89	164	
Tom Tatum	83	81	164	
Jay Overton	81	83	164	
Scott Oulds	79	85	164	
David Gosiewski	88	77	165	
Bruce Lehnhard	84	82	166	
Mike Schuchart	82	84	166	
Jeff Bailey	84	84	168	
Paul Ryiz	84	84	168	
Tony Milam	83	87	170	
Jim Petralia	91	80	171	
Jack Kiefer	84	88	172	
Jack McKelvey	83	90	173	
Dick Goetz	86	87	173	
Calvin Peete	75	WD		
Johnny Miller	76	WD		
James Blair	DQ			
Lee Trevino	WD			

(All players who started and failed to complete 72 holes received $1,000.)

The International

Castle Pines Golf Club, Castle Rock, Colorado   August 12-16
Par 36-36 — 72; 7,503 yards   purse, $1,115,280

FIRST ROUND

WEDNESDAY

13   Chip Beck, $10,000.
12   Richard Mast, Jack Nicklaus, $6,250 each.
11   Tim Simpson, $2,500.
10   Steve Elkington.
9   Fred Couples, Bob Gilder, Mark Lye, Steve Jones.
8   Nick Price, Rocco Mediate.
7   Tom Watson, Craig Stadler, Scott Simpson, Greg Norman, Dave Rummells, Chris Perry, Ed Fiori, Gary Hallberg, Ray Barr, Jr., Ronnie Black, Bob Eastwood, Peter Jacobsen.
6   Billy Ray Brown, Mark Calcavecchia, David Frost, Barry Jaeckel, Mark McCumber, Tim Norris, Ron Streck, Richard Zokol.
5   Tom Byrum, John Cook, Ken Green, David Hobby, John Inman, Harry Taylor, Mark Wiebe.
4   Mark O'Meara.

THURSDAY

14   Bruce Lietzke, $10,000.
10   Dan Forsman, $7,500.
9   Bob Tway, Joey Sindelar, Dan Pohl, Denis Watson, $1,875 each.
7   Tony Sills, Fuzzy Zoeller, Mike Hulbert, Bill Britton.
6   Kenny Perry, Jim Nelford, Steve Pate, David Graham, Larry Rinker, Gene Sauers.
5   Andrew Magee, Mark Pfeil, Wayne Levi, Jim Blair, Philip Jonas.
4   Morris Hatalsky, John Adams, Curt Byrum, Howard Twitty, Sam Randolph, Ben Crenshaw, David Edwards, Billy Andrade, Rodger Davis, Ray Stewart.
3   Brad Faxon, Antonio Cerda, D.A. Weibring, Corey Pavin, Mark Brooks, Duffy Waldorf.
2   Rick Dalpos, Ken Brown.

SECOND ROUND

13 Steve Jones, $10,000.
10 John Inman, $7,500.
9 Brad Faxon, Curt Byrum, $3,750 each.
6 Ken Brown, David Frost, Joey Sindelar.
5 Mark Lye.
4 Ronnie Black, David Edwards, Craig Stadler, Corey Pavin, Ken Green, Fuzzy Zoeller, Fred Couples.
3 Howard Twitty, Rocco Mediate, Richard Zokol, Nick Price, David Rummells.
2 Mike Hulbert, Ed Fiori, Tim Simpson, Bob Tway, Dick Mast, Ken Perry, Andrew Magee, John Adams, Mark O'Meara, Ben Crenshaw, Billy Ray Brown, Bob Eastwood.
1 Denis Watson, Scott Simpson, Bruce Lietzke, Peter Jacobsen, Tim Norris, Rodger Davis, Jim Blair.
0 Mark McCumber, Gene Sauers, John Cook, Gary Hallberg, D.A. Weibring, Tom Watson, Steve Pate.
-1 David Graham, Bob Gilder, Chip Beck, Chris Perry.
-2 Ron Streck, Morris Hatalsky, Tony Sills, Harry Taylor.

FAILED TO QUALIFY

-2 Rick Dalpos, $2,300.
-3 Billy Andrade, Steve Elkington, Wayne Levi, Sam Randolph, $2,250 each.
-4 Mark Wiebe, Ray Barr, Jack Nicklaus, $2,180 each.
-5 Dan Forsman, Antonio Cerda, Ray Stewart, Dan Pohl, Tom Byrum, Greg Norman, $2,090 each.
-6 Mark Calcavecchia, Duffy Waldorf, Jim Nelford, Bill Britton, Mark Pfeil, $1,980 each.
-7 Larry Rinker, Barry Jaeckel, David Hobby, Philip Jonas, Mark Brooks, $1,840 each.

THIRD ROUND

13 Chip Beck, $10,000.
10 Ken Green, Andrew Magee, $6,250 each.
7 D.A. Weibring, Bruce Lietzke, $1,250 each.
6 Morris Hatalsky, Corey Pavin, Richard Zokol, Ken Brown, Ben Crenshaw, Tom Watson.
5 Joey Sindelar.
4 Steve Pate, Mike Hulbert, Nick Price, Fuzzy Zoeller, John Cook, Scott Simpson.

FAILED TO QUALIFY

4 Denis Watson, $14,000.
3 Rodger Davis, Ed Fiori, David Frost, Tim Norris, Brad Faxon, Mark McCumber, Dick Mast, Gene Sauers, Ronnie Black, $9,788 each.
2 Chris Perry, Peter Jacobsen, $6,950 each.
1 Mark Lye, Bob Gilder, John Adams, Rocco Mediate, Tim Simpson, Bob Tway, $5,430 each.
0 Ron Streck, Howard Twitty, Curt Byrum, Bob Eastwood, Harry Taylor, Steve Jones, $3,800 each.
-1 Billy Ray Brown, Ken Perry, $3,000 each.
-2 Mark O'Meara, David Graham, $2,670 each.
-3 John Inman, David Edwards, Fred Couples, $2,460 each.
-4 Jim Blair, Tony Sills, $2,340 each.

FOURTH ROUND

11	John Cook, $180,000.
9	Ken Green, $108,000.
6	Scott Simpson, Mike Hulbert, Ben Crenshaw, Chip Beck, $48,000 each.
5	D.A. Weibring, Fuzzy Zoeller, $32,250 each.
4	Tom Watson, Corey Pavin, $28,000 each.
2	Nick Price, $25,000.
1	Morris Hatalsky, Steve Pate, $22,000.
–1	Ken Brown, Joey Sindelar, $18,500 each.
–3	Richard Zokol, $17,000.
–4	Bruce Lietzke, $16,000.
–5	Andrew Magee, $15,000.

Fred Meyer Challenge

Portland Golf Club, Portland, Oregon
Par 36-36 — 72; 6,544 yards

August 17-18
purse, $500,000

	SCORES		TOTAL	MONEY (Each)
Payne Stewart/Isao Aoki	66	61	127	$50,000
Peter Jacobsen/Curtis Strange	62	67	129	40,000
Chi Chi Rodriguez/Fuzzy Zoeller	68	62	130	32,500
Lee Trevino/Fred Couples	67	63	130	32,500
Bob Gilder/Bob Tway	69	63	132	27,500
Gary Player/Wayne Player	67	66	133	25,000
Arnold Palmer/Greg Norman	68	67	135	22,500
Jack Nicklaus/Jack Nicklaus II	65	71	136	20,000

Beatrice Western Open

Butler National Golf Club (9 Holes)
Oak Brook Golf Club (9 Holes)
Oakbrook, Illinois

August 22-23
purse, $800,000

Par 36-36 — 72; 6,752 yards

(Shortened to 54 holes, 36 on Sunday — flood conditions.)

	SCORES			TOTAL	MONEY
D.A. Weibring	70	69	68	207	$144,000
Larry Nelson	72	67	69	208	70,400
Greg Norman	69	70	69	208	70,400
Lennie Clements	70	69	70	209	31,500
David Frost	70	71	68	209	31,500
Mike Reid	71	69	69	209	31,500
Greg Powers	71	70	68	209	31,500
Davis Love III	70	70	70	210	21,600
Mark Hayes	72	68	70	210	21,600
Brian Fogt	71	67	72	210	21,600
Bob Tway	69	71	70	210	21,600
Bobby Wadkins	69	72	69	210	21,600
Dave Eichelberger	72	67	72	211	14,133.34
Hal Sutton	70	69	72	211	14,133.34

	SCORES			TOTAL	MONEY
Bruce Lietzke	72	67	72	211	14,133.33
Mike Donald	69	70	72	211	14,133.33
Richard Zokol	70	73	68	211	14,133.33
Payne Stewart	72	68	71	211	14,133.33
Dave Barr	70	68	74	212	9,360
Gary Krueger	71	71	70	212	9,360
Brad Greer	70	72	70	212	9,360
Joey Sindelar	70	71	71	212	9,360
Kenny Perry	71	69	72	212	9,360
Tom Purtzer	72	69	71	212	9,360
Jim Carter	72	72	69	213	6,106.67
Roy Biancalana	70	71	72	213	6,106.67
Tom Kite	70	71	72	213	6,106.67
Mark Lye	72	71	70	213	6,106.67
Bob Gilder	70	69	74	213	6,106.66
Tony Sills	72	72	69	213	6,106.66
Andy Dillard	69	73	72	214	4,960
Mike Hulbert	72	72	70	214	4,960
Ron Streck	71	73	70	214	4,960
Charles Bolling	70	72	73	215	3,540
George Burns	72	72	71	215	3,540
Steve Pate	72	73	70	215	3,540
David Ogrin	71	75	69	215	3,540
John McComish	72	71	72	215	3,540
Mark McCumber	72	72	71	215	3,540
Scott Hoch	72	74	69	215	3,540
David Edwards	70	75	70	215	3,540
Ed Dougherty	69	73	73	215	3,540
Wayne Grady	72	71	72	215	3,540
Scott Simpson	71	72	72	215	3,540
Robert Thompson	71	72	72	215	3,540
Bobby Clampett	71	73	72	216	2,176
Antonio Cerda	71	75	70	216	2,176
Ernie Gonzalez	71	71	74	216	2,176
Danny Edwards	72	73	71	216	2,176
Willie Wood	69	70	77	216	2,176
Howard Twitty	70	76	70	216	2,176

NEC World Series of Golf

Firestone Country Club, South Course, Akron, Ohio
Par 35-35 — 70; 7,173 yards

August 27-30
purse, $800,000

	SCORES				TOTAL	MONEY
Curtis Strange	70	66	68	71	275	$144,000
Fulton Allem	71	70	67	70	278	86,400
Mac O'Grady	69	72	69	69	279	54,400
Fred Couples	70	71	69	70	280	33,066.67
Bobby Wadkins	64	74	70	72	280	33,066.67
Larry Nelson	69	73	70	68	280	33,066.66
Paul Azinger	69	69	74	69	281	25,800
Mike Hulbert	68	74	68	71	281	25,800
Tom Kite	70	73	65	74	282	23,200 .
Rick Fehr	72	69	69	73	283	20,033.34
Ben Crenshaw	73	72	71	67	283	20,033.33
Greg Norman	70	69	71	73	283	20,033.33
Rodger Davis	70	74	71	69	284	14,500

	SCORES				TOTAL	MONEY
Ray Floyd	72	71	70	71	284	14,500
Scott Hoch	70	71	70	73	284	14,500
Larry Mize	67	74	70	73	284	14,500
Dan Pohl	72	67	71	74	284	14,500
Scott Simpson	71	70	71	72	284	14,500
Payne Stewart	72	71	71	70	284	14,500
Keith Clearwater	70	74	71	70	285	10,000
Jay Haas	73	66	80	66	285	10,000
D.A. Weibring	68	76	68	73	285	10,000
Kenny Knox	67	73	71	75	286	8,666.67
Mark McCumber	70	74	68	74	286	8,666.67
Davis Love III	68	72	66	80	286	8,666.66
Dave Barr	73	70	70	74	287	7,900
Mark Calcavecchia	70	74	70	73	287	7,900
Johnny Miller	70	75	70	72	287	7,900
Robert Wrenn	75	72	70	70	287	7,900
Masashi Ozaki	71	74	72	71	288	7,300
J.C. Snead	70	75	73	70	288	7,300
Mike Harwood	71	71	76	71	289	6,950
Gene Sauers	71	74	74	70	289	6,950
Jim Thorpe	73	70	75	72	290	6,800
George Burns	71	73	74	73	291	6,700
Corey Pavin	71	73	74	74	292	6,500
Lanny Wadkins	76	70	71	75	292	6,500
Fred Wadsworth	71	67	72	82	292	6,500
Isao Aoki	72	74	75	73	294	6,250
Ernie Gonzalez	73	70	71	80	294	6,250
John Cook	72	69	79	75	295	6,100
Bob Lendzion	76	76	70	73	305	6,000

Provident Classic

Valleybrook Golf and Country Club, Hixson, Tennessee
Par 35-35 — 70; 6,641 yards

August 27-30
purse, $450,000

	SCORES				TOTAL	MONEY
John Inman	65	67	67	66	265	$81,000
Bill Glasson	65	69	66	66	266	39,600
Rocco Mediate	66	63	69	68	266	39,600
Tim Simpson	64	71	66	66	267	21,600
Blaine McCallister	67	67	65	69	268	17,100
Robert Thompson	67	69	62	70	268	17,100
Morris Hatalsky	64	67	74	64	269	14,025
Richard Zokol	69	67	66	67	269	14,025
Joey Sindelar	62	68	70	69	269	14,025
Jay Don Blake	69	68	66	67	270	10,350
Andrew Magee	65	67	72	66	270	10,350
Jim Carter	68	65	68	69	270	10,350
Ray Stewart	67	66	69	68	270	10,350
Greg Powers	66	66	69	69	270	10,350
Phil Blackmar	68	67	67	69	271	7,425
Gary Koch	66	67	71	67	271	7,425
Leonard Thompson	69	64	67	71	271	7,425
Tim Norris	67	67	68	69	271	7,425
Steve Elkington	67	67	69	69	272	5,647.50
Jay Delsing	68	70	64	70	272	5,647.50
Willie Wood	67	66	69	70	272	5,647.50

	SCORES				TOTAL	MONEY
Tom Sieckmann	67	69	65	71	272	5,647.50
Dewey Arnette	69	67	69	68	273	3,792.86
Vance Heafner	69	70	68	66	273	3,792.86
Bob Wolcott	70	68	68	67	273	3,792.86
Don Shirey, Jr.	69	67	68	69	273	3,792.86
Harry Taylor	69	70	63	71	273	3,792.86
Brad Faxon	67	67	71	68	273	3,792.85
Ed Dougherty	70	69	66	68	273	3,792.85
Pat McGowan	69	69	66	70	274	2,857.50
Steve Lowery	69	68	68	69	274	2,857.50
Gary Hallberg	69	67	66	72	274	2,857.50
Rocky Thompson	73	68	65	68	274	2,857.50
Dan Forsman	69	69	68	69	275	2,373.75
Russ Cochran	68	72	68	67	275	2,373.75
Antonio Cerda	67	67	66	75	275	2,373.75
Scott Verplank	70	66	67	72	275	2,373.75
Dan Halldorson	69	67	70	70	276	2,070
Loren Roberts	69	67	72	68	276	2,070
Bob Lunn	70	66	71	70	277	1,620
Bill Kratzert	72	66	70	69	277	1,620
Phil Hancock	67	69	71	70	277	1,620
Duffy Waldorf	67	72	68	70	277	1,620
Billy Pierot	73	68	66	70	277	1,620
Dave Rummells	67	68	71	71	277	1,620
Clarence Rose	69	72	69	67	277	1,620
Mike Nicolette	70	70	68	69	277	1,620
John Horne	69	69	71	69	278	1,118.58
Danny Briggs	67	69	70	72	278	1,118.57
Mike Donald	67	72	67	72	278	1,118.57
Dennis Trixler	73	68	68	69	278	1,118.57
Bill Sander	64	71	71	72	278	1,118.57
David Peoples	70	65	67	76	278	1,118.57
Jim Nelford	67	68	67	76	278	1,118.57

B. C. Open

En-Joie Golf Club, Endicott, New York
Par 37-34 — 71; 6,966 yards

September 3-6
purse, $400,000

	SCORES				TOTAL	MONEY
Joey Sindelar	65	63	69	69	266	$72,000
Jeff Sluman	69	68	68	65	270	43,200
Tony Sills	69	68	69	69	275	23,200
Mike McCullough	69	71	69	66	275	23,200
Wayne Levi	71	67	69	69	276	14,050
Ken Green	69	72	66	69	276	14,050
Tim Simpson	69	70	67	70	276	14,050
Mike Nicolette	72	69	67	68	276	14,050
Paul Azinger	69	70	69	69	277	11,200
Craig Stadler	68	69	72	68	277	11,200
Antonio Cerda	67	71	70	70	278	8,800
Mike Bender	71	72	69	66	278	8,800
John McComish	69	71	70	68	278	8,800
Roger Maltbie	70	66	71	71	278	8,800
Blaine McCallister	71	67	72	69	279	6,800
Trevor Dodds	71	69	69	70	279	6,800
Chris Perry	70	68	70	71	279	6,800

	SCORES			TOTAL	MONEY
Jay Don Blake	71	69	69	71	280	5,216
Rex Caldwell	69	69	71	71	280	5,216
Jim Carter	74	70	70	66	280	5,216
Steve Jones	70	69	72	69	280	5,216
Payne Stewart	69	73	69	69	280	5,216
Peter Jacobsen	69	66	76	70	281	3,560
Brad Faxon	73	71	69	68	281	3,560
Bob Tway	73	71	72	65	281	3,560
Billy Pierot	69	72	67	73	281	3,560
Jack Renner	69	72	71	69	281	3,560
Jeff Lewis	69	73	70	70	282	2,547.50
Mark Lye	68	74	71	69	282	2,547.50
Gary McCord	70	69	71	72	282	2,547.50
Dan Halldorson	72	72	69	69	282	2,547.50
Vance Heafner	73	66	72	71	282	2,547.50
Bill Glasson	72	70	72	68	282	2,547.50
Howard Twitty	71	73	67	71	282	2,547.50
Ted Schulz	73	71	68	70	282	2,547.50
Bobby Cole	73	70	71	69	283	1,802.86
Andrew Magee	70	73	70	70	283	1,802.86
Dan Forsman	73	71	73	66	283	1,802.86
Denis Watson	69	69	73	72	283	1,802.86
Kenny Perry	68	71	74	70	283	1,802.86
Jay Haas	68	71	75	69	283	1,802.85
Mark Wiebe	72	68	74	69	283	1,802.85
Kenny Knox	70	71	74	69	284	1,400
Jim Gallagher, Jr.	72	70	73	69	284	1,400
Ed Dougherty	68	74	71	71	284	1,400
Rocco Mediate	71	67	74	73	285	1,108.80
Bill Kratzert	72	72	71	70	285	1,108.80
Jay Delsing	66	74	76	69	285	1,108.80
Greg Twiggs	75	67	72	71	285	1,108.80
Mike Sullivan	73	70	70	72	285	1,108.80

Bank of Boston Classic

Pleasant Valley Country Club, Sutton, Massachusetts
Par 36-35 — 71; 7,110 yards

September 10-13
purse, $500,000

	SCORES			TOTAL	MONEY
Sam Randolph	67	68	64	199	$90,000
Wayne Grady	67	68	68	203	37,333.34
Ray Stewart	65	73	65	203	37,333.33
Gene Sauers	68	67	68	203	37,333.33
John Mahaffey	65	71	68	204	17,562.50
Curtis Strange	65	69	70	204	17,562.50
Clarence Rose	68	67	69	204	17,562.50
Steve Pate	69	66	69	204	17,562.50
Tom Byrum	68	69	68	205	13,000
Gary Hallberg	71	68	66	205	13,000
Lee Trevino	66	67	72	205	13,000
Larry Rinker	69	66	70	205	13,000
Brad Bryant	70	70	66	206	10,000
Tim Simpson	70	69	67	206	10,000
Frank Conner	73	68	66	207	7,262.50
Paul Azinger	67	69	71	207	7,262.50
George Burns	67	72	68	207	7,262.50

	SCORES			TOTAL	MONEY
Blaine McCallister	71	66	70	207	7,262.50
Jeff Lewis	71	70	66	207	7,262.50
Denis Watson	69	71	67	207	7,262.50
Mike Reid	68	70	69	207	7,262.50
Billy Pierot	71	69	67	207	7,262.50
Bill Britton	72	67	69	208	4,600
Mark Hayes	71	68	69	208	4,600
Robert Wrenn	70	70	68	208	4,600
Bruce Soulsby	69	69	70	208	4,600
Mark Brooks	69	71	69	209	3,122.73
Mark O'Meara	72	69	68	209	3,122.73
Bob Murphy	69	68	72	209	3,122.73
Jay Haas	67	68	74	209	3,122.73
Peter Jacobsen	70	70	69	209	3,122.73
Buddy Gardner	70	66	73	209	3,122.73
Dave Eichelberger	70	66	73	209	3,122.73
Tony Sills	70	68	71	209	3,122.73
Kenny Knox	69	72	68	209	3,122.73
Ed Fiori	68	73	68	209	3,122.72
Nick Price	69	72	68	209	3,122.72
Lennie Clements	69	68	73	210	1,805.84
David Canipe	69	72	69	210	1,805.84
Ernie Gonzalez	70	67	73	210	1,805.84
Dave Rummells	71	67	72	210	1,805.84
Jay Don Blake	69	69	72	210	1,805.83
Jodie Mudd	70	69	71	210	1,805.83
Roger Maltbie	69	70	71	210	1,805.83
Mike McCullough	70	69	71	210	1,805.83
Tsuneyuki Nakajima	74	67	69	210	1,805.83
Wayne Levi	70	69	71	210	1,805.83
David Frost	69	71	70	210	1,805.83
Bill Sander	71	68	71	210	1,805.83
Chris Perry	73	68	70	211	1,206
David Peoples	69	71	71	211	1,206
Steve Jones	77	64	70	211	1,206
Jim Gallagher, Jr.	69	72	70	211	1,206
Dennis Trixler	67	72	72	211	1,206

Greater Milwaukee Open

Tuckaway Country Club, Franklin, Wisconsin
Par 36-36 — 72; 7,030 yards

September 17-20
purse, $500,000

	SCORES				TOTAL	MONEY
Gary Hallberg	70	66	67	66	269	$108,000
Wayne Levi	68	68	68	67	271	52,800
Robert Wrenn	65	68	70	68	271	52,800
Larry Ziegler	64	68	72	68	272	26,400
Dan Pohl	67	67	72	66	272	26,400
Tom Byrum	72	67	68	67	274	20,100
Bill Kratzert	68	71	67	68	274	20,100
Nick Price	67	65	74	68	274	20,100
Fred Couples	71	69	65	70	275	17,400
Mark Calcavecchia	68	68	70	71	277	14,400
Corey Pavin	69	67	71	70	277	14,400
Wayne Grady	71	70	66	70	277	14,400
Gene Sauers	71	70	67	69	277	14,400

		SCORES			TOTAL	MONEY
Charles Bolling	71	70	69	68	278	10,200
Steve Pate	73	68	68	69	278	10,200
Andy North	66	71	71	70	278	10,200
Barry Jaeckel	71	71	69	67	278	10,200
Richard Zokol	69	68	71	70	278	10,200
Tsuneyuki Nakajima	62	76	72	69	279	7,530
David Frost	70	71	71	67	279	7,530
Ron Streck	70	71	66	72	279	7,530
Tom Purtzer	72	68	69	70	279	7,530
Ronnie Black	70	71	69	70	280	5,190
Phil Blackmar	69	72	67	72	280	5,190
Bill Britton	70	69	72	69	280	5,190
Jodie Mudd	72	68	70	70	280	5,190
Buddy Gardner	72	69	71	68	280	5,190
Mike Reid	71	71	70	68	280	5,190
Jay Delsing	70	72	71	68	281	3,900
David Ogrin	69	72	67	73	281	3,900
Aki Ohmachi	71	70	69	71	281	3,900
Lanny Wadkins	71	69	71	70	281	3,900
Don Shirey, Jr.	72	68	68	73	281	3,900
Chris Perry	72	69	70	71	282	2,965.72
Mark Hayes	69	73	70	70	282	2,965.72
Loren Roberts	70	69	70	73	282	2,865.72
Brian Claar	71	69	70	72	282	2,965.71
Curt Byrum	71	70	69	72	282	2,965.71
Greg Ladehoff	70	69	71	72	282	2,965.71
Larry Rinker	72	69	71	70	282	2,965.71
Perry Arthur	70	70	73	70	283	2,160
Dave Barr	68	71	73	71	283	2,160
Rex Caldwell	68	70	74	71	283	2,160
Bill Glasson	68	71	72	72	283	2,160
Ernie Gonzalez	69	73	72	69	283	2,160
Ray Stewart	71	69	73	70	283	2,160
Jim Carter	70	72	73	69	284	1,692
Vance Heafner	68	70	74	72	284	1,692
Mike Bender	72	70	75	68	285	1,424.40
Mark O'Meara	71	71	71	72	285	1,424.40
Gary Pinns	69	70	75	71	285	1,424.40
Kenny Perry	70	72	69	74	285	1,424.40
Bob Lohr	74	65	74	72	285	1,424.40
Dan Forsman	72	69	71	73	285	1,424.40
Ray Gallagher, Jr.	68	74	72	71	285	1,424.40
Howard Twitty	70	71	72	72	285	1,424.40
Duffy Waldorf	70	70	73	72	285	1,424.40
Tim Simpson	70	71	72	72	285	1,424.40

Ryder Cup Matches

Muirfield Village Golf Club, Dublin, Ohio   September 25-27
Par 36-36 — 72; 7,114 yards

FINAL SCORE: Europe 15, United States 13

FRIDAY

Foursomes
Curtis Strange and Tom Kite (US) defeated Sam Torrance and Howard Clark, 4 and 2.
Hal Sutton and Dan Pohl (US) defeated Ken Brown and Bernhard Langer, 2 and 1.

Nick Faldo and Ian Woosnam (E) defeated Lanny Wadkins and Larry Mize, 2 up.
Severiano Ballesteros and Jose-Maria Olazabal (E) defeated Larry Nelson and Payne
  Stewart, 1 up.

Fourball
Gordon Brand Jr. and Jose Rivero (E) defeated Ben Crenshaw and Scott Simpson, 3
  and 2.
Sandy Lyle and Langer (E) defeated Andy Bean and Mark Calcavecchia, 1 up.
Faldo and Woosnam (E) defeated Sutton and Pohl, 2 and 1.
Ballesteros and Olazabal (E) defeated Strange and Kite, 2 and 1.
EUROPE LEADS, 6-2.

SATURDAY

Foursomes
Strange and Kite (US) defeated Rivero and Brand, 3 and 1.
Faldo and Woosnam halved with Sutton and Mize.
Lyle and Langer (E) defeated Wadkins and Nelson, 2 and 1.
Ballesteros and Olazabal (E) defeated Crenshaw and Stewart, 1 up.

Fourball
Woosnam and Faldo (E) defeated Strange and Kite, 5 and 4.
Bean and Stewart (US) defeated Eamonn Darcy and Brand, 3 and 2.
Sutton and Mize (US) defeated Ballesteros and Olazabal, 2 and 1.
Lyle and Langer (E) defeated Wadkins and Nelson, 1 up.
EUROPE LEADS, 10½-5½.

SUNDAY

Singles
Bean (US) defeated Woosnam, 1 up.
Clark (E) defeated Pohl, 1 up.
Torrance halved with Mize.
Calcavecchia (US) defeated Faldo, 1 up.
Stewart (US) defeated Olazabal, 2 up.
Simpson (US) defeated Rivero, 2 and 1.
Kite (US) defeated Lyle, 3 and 2.
Darcy (E) defeated Crenshaw, 1 up.
Langer halved with Nelson.
Ballesteros (E) defeated Strange, 2 and 1.
Wadkins (US) defeated Brown, 3 and 2.
Brand halved with Sutton.

Southwest Classic

Fairway Oaks Golf and Racquet Club, Abilene, Texas   September 24-27
Par 36-36 — 72; 7,189 yards   purse, $400,000

	SCORES				TOTAL	MONEY
Steve Pate	67	71	68	67	273	$72,000
Dan Halldorson	66	66	72	70	274	26,400
Bob Eastwood	65	69	69	71	274	26,400
David Edwards	70	67	65	72	274	26,400
Mark O'Meara	68	70	67	69	274	26,400
Paul Azinger	69	67	72	69	277	13,900
Tony Sills	71	67	71	68	277	13,900
Ronnie Black	67	71	69	71	278	12,000

	SCORES				TOTAL	MONEY
Vance Heafner	69	68	70	71	278	12,000
Mike Hulbert	73	67	72	67	279	10,000
Hale Irwin	70	68	65	76	279	10,000
Russ Cochran	70	70	69	70	279	10,000
Mark Brooks	70	69	71	70	280	6,857.15
Don Shirey, Jr.	69	67	75	69	280	6,857.15
Steve Bowman	70	70	70	70	280	6,857.14
Bill Kratzert	68	68	72	72	280	6,857.14
Ed Fiori	69	69	71	71	280	6,857.14
Duffy Waldorf	70	68	71	71	280	6,857.14
Corey Pavin	67	73	69	71	280	6,857.14
Hubert Green	70	71	70	70	281	4,496
Bob Gilder	68	72	73	68	281	4,496
Frank Conner	66	68	78	69	281	4,496
Tsuneyuki Nakajima	70	69	73	69	281	4,496
Aki Ohmachi	69	73	72	67	281	4,496
Gil Morgan	68	68	71	75	282	2,988.58
Curt Byrum	71	71	67	73	282	2,988.57
Bob Lohr	66	72	74	70	282	2,988.57
Lon Hinkle	72	67	68	75	282	2,988.57
Dan Forsman	66	70	73	73	282	2,988.57
Philip Parkin	70	73	69	70	282	2,988.57
David Peoples	71	67	73	71	282	2,988.57
David Graham	71	70	75	67	283	2,315
Jeff Sluman	70	70	72	71	283	2,315
Jim Simons	68	75	72	68	283	2,315
Joey Rassett	68	72	72	71	283	2,315
Jeff Grygiel	69	70	74	71	284	1,722.23
Ed Dougherty	68	72	72	72	284	1,722.23
Curt Byrum	71	69	73	71	284	1,722.22
Davis Love III	70	69	73	72	284	1,722.22
Mike McCullough	73	68	70	73	284	1,722.22
Mark Lye	72	67	72	73	284	1,722.22
Andrew Magee	72	70	73	69	284	1,722.22
Willie Wood	68	75	70	71	284	1,722.22
Jim Nelford	70	68	76	70	284	1,722.22
Danny Briggs	76	67	73	69	285	1,171.20
Bobby Cole	68	72	74	71	285	1,171.20
Ron Streck	72	70	72	71	285	1,171.20
D.A. Weibring	69	72	72	72	285	1,171.20
Craig Stadler	72	69	73	71	285	1,171.20
Jim Carter	73	70	72	71	286	957.34
Doug Johnson	70	70	74	72	286	957.34
Brian Claar	71	70	72	73	286	957.33
Antonio Cerda	71	69	74	72	286	957.33
Trey Tyner	72	71	69	74	286	957.33
Greg Twiggs	69	73	74	70	286	957.33

Southern Open

Green Island Country Club, Columbus, Georgia
Par 35-35 — 70; 6,791 yards

October 1-4
purse, $400,000

	SCORES				TOTAL	MONEY
Ken Brown	65	64	69	68	266	$72,000.00
Mike Hulbert	65	66	72	70	273	29,866.67
David Frost	63	71	73	66	273	29,866.67

	SCORES				TOTAL	MONEY
Larry Mize	70	65	70	68	273	29,866.66
Rex Caldwell	69	67	70	68	274	16,000
Mark Lye	70	68	68	69	275	14,400
Hale Irwin	66	68	69	73	276	13,400
Larry Nelson	71	66	72	68	277	12,000
Wayne Levi	70	69	69	69	277	12,000
Vance Heafner	65	69	77	67	278	10,800
Dan Forsman	67	70	72	70	279	9,600
J.C. Snead	68	72	71	68	279	9,600
Frank Conner	71	67	71	71	280	7,733.34
Robert Wrenn	71	67	71	71	280	7,733.33
Tony Sills	71	67	73	69	280	7,733.33
Keith Clearwater	67	69	75	70	281	5,800
Phil Blackmar	69	68	74	70	281	5,800
Mark McCumber	69	67	71	74	281	5,800
Gibby Gilbert	67	69	74	71	281	5,800
Willie Wood	71	69	73	68	281	5,800
Billy Pierot	69	65	77	70	281	5,800
Philip Parkin	69	68	76	69	282	4,320
Jay Haas	69	70	69	74	282	4,320
John Cook	69	72	72	70	283	3,240
Russ Cochran	71	71	75	66	283	3,240
Jeff Sluman	72	69	72	70	283	3,240
Ted Schulz	72	71	73	67	283	3,240
Dave Rummells	70	73	73	67	283	3,240
Jack Renner	68	70	73	72	283	3,240
Roger Maltbie	69	70	74	71	284	2,377.15
Barry Jaeckel	70	70	74	70	284	2,377.15
Andy Bean	71	70	71	72	284	2,377.14
Chris Perry	71	71	71	71	284	2,377.14
Ray Stewart	69	69	72	74	284	2,377.14
Payne Stewart	74	68	72	70	284	2,377.14
Don Pooley	69	72	73	70	284	2,377.14
Brian Claar	72	70	73	70	285	1,720
David Canipe	70	72	72	71	285	1,720
Mac O'Grady	69	73	71	72	285	1,720
Scott Hoch	70	69	76	70	285	1,720
Bill Kratzert	71	71	76	67	285	1,720
Donnie Hammond	74	67	74	70	285	1,720
Denis Watson	70	72	75	68	285	1,720
Mike Donald	70	71	73	72	286	1,243.20
David Ogrin	75	68	72	71	286	1,243.20
Kenny Knox	71	70	76	69	286	1,243.20
Don Shirey, Jr.	69	72	71	74	286	1,243.20
Tim Simpson	72	69	74	71	286	1,243.20
Philip Jonas	74	69	70	74	287	969.15
Harry Taylor	72	69	73	73	287	969.15
Calvin Peete	71	70	76	70	287	969.14
Peter Oosterhuis	71	71	74	71	287	969.14
John Horne	72	69	73	73	287	969.14
Jim Gallagher, Jr.	70	72	73	72	287	969.14
Hal Sutton	70	71	76	70	287	969.14

Pensacola Open

Perdido Bay Resort, Pensacola, Florida
Par 35-36 — 71; 7,093 yards

October 8-11
purse, $300,000

	SCORES				TOTAL	MONEY
Doug Tewell	69	66	66	68	269	$54,000
Phil Blackmar	67	69	66	70	272	26,400
Danny Edwards	67	67	68	70	272	26,400
Mark McCumber	72	68	68	67	275	13,200
David Ogrin	72	71	66	66	275	13,200
Jeff Sluman	67	71	69	69	276	10,425
Clarence Rose	71	70	70	65	276	10,425
David Canipe	75	67	69	66	277	9,000
John Mahaffey	66	69	73	69	277	9,000
Mike Hulbert	70	70	66	72	278	7,800
Mike Reid	69	69	69	71	278	7,800
Tom Byrum	71	68	66	74	279	6,300
Bruce Lietzke	68	70	68	73	279	6,300
Steve Jones	69	73	69	68	279	6,300
John Adams	70	69	70	71	280	4,650
Kenny Knox	70	68	69	73	280	4,650
Dick Mast	68	75	67	70	280	4,650
Dan Forsman	73	68	72	67	280	4,650
Keith Clearwater	71	72	70	67	280	4,650
Bruce Soulsby	70	70	70	70	280	4,650
Chip Beck	71	68	71	71	281	3,120
John Cook	70	69	70	72	281	3,120
Trevor Dodds	67	67	71	76	281	3,120
Bob Tway	75	68	68	70	281	3,120
Steve Pate	70	72	72	67	281	3,120
Dan Halldorson	68	74	68	72	282	2,175
Brad Greer	74	65	74	69	282	2,175
Robert Wrenn	71	68	72	71	282	2,175
Tony Sills	70	70	74	68	282	2,175
Joey Sindelar	68	74	71	69	282	2,175
Greg Twiggs	69	72	69	72	282	2,175
Jim Carter	68	71	70	74	283	1,736.25
Frank Conner	72	71	69	71	283	1,736.25
Jim Nelford	73	70	72	68	283	1,736.25
Aki Ohmachi	71	69	69	74	283	1,736.25
John McComish	70	72	69	73	284	1,321.88
Nolan Henke	71	70	72	71	284	1,321.88
Jim Dent	73	71	71	69	284	1,321.88
Bill Sander	73	71	68	72	284	1,321.88
Mark Wiebe	71	71	70	72	284	1,321.87
Nick Price	70	74	72	68	284	1,321.87
Mac O'Grady	71	72	67	74	284	1,321.87
Pat McGowan	73	70	70	71	284	1,321.87
Brian Claar	72	72	71	70	285	867
Scott Hoch	70	71	72	72	285	867
Ed Dougherty	74	69	71	71	285	867
Steve Elkington	72	71	70	72	285	867
Willie Wood	72	72	69	72	285	867
Leonard Thompson	73	70	73	69	285	867
Griffin Rudolph	71	69	73	72	285	867
Tim Norris	73	71	72	69	285	867

Walt Disney World/Oldsmobile Classic

Walt Disney World, Lake Buena Vista, Florida
Magnolia Course: Par 36-36 — 72; 7,190 yards
Palm Course: Par 36-36 — 72; 6,967 yards
Lake Buena Vista Course: Par 36-36 — 72; 6,706 yards

October 15-18
purse, $600,000

	SCORES				TOTAL	MONEY
Larry Nelson	68	69	68	63	268	$100,000
Morris Hatalsky	68	67	67	67	269	52,800
Mark O'Meara	63	68	69	69	269	52,800
Steve Pate	66	68	65	71	270	28,800
David Frost	69	65	68	69	271	21,900
Mike Reid	69	67	68	67	271	21,900
Mac O'Grady	68	68	67	68	271	21,900
Nick Price	68	68	68	68	272	18,600
Donnie Hammond	71	65	71	66	273	15,600
Fuzzy Zoeller	69	69	71	64	273	15,600
Don Shirey, Jr.	70	70	70	63	723	15,600
Tom Kite	69	65	71	68	273	15,600
Paul Azinger	69	71	69	65	274	11,600
Loren Roberts	70	66	67	71	274	11,600
Jodie Mudd	69	68	69	68	274	11,600
Brad Greer	68	70	68	69	275	9,600
Mike Hulbert	72	69	66	68	275	9,600
Clarence Rose	68	69	69	69	275	9,600
Bob Eastwood	72	68	70	66	276	6,525
Bobby Wadkins	66	71	69	70	276	6,525
Don Pooley	69	65	71	71	276	6,525
Mark McCumber	68	67	68	73	276	6,525
Aki Ohmachi	72	67	69	68	276	6,525
Andrew Magee	66	67	69	74	276	6,525
John Mahaffey	70	69	70	67	276	6,525
Dick Mast	70	69	66	71	276	6,525
Russ Cohran	69	70	70	68	277	3,993.75
Ed Dougherty	69	67	73	68	277	3,993.75
Perry Arthur	72	70	68	67	277	3,993.75
Curtis Strange	71	66	69	71	277	3,993.75
Dan Pohl	68	73	67	69	277	3,992.75
Dave Rummells	70	70	70	67	277	3,993.75
Joey Sindelar	71	69	65	72	277	3,993.75
Bruce Leitzke	69	69	70	69	277	3,993.75
Bob Gilder	67	65	73	73	278	3,022.50
Doug Tewell	72	68	70	68	278	3,022.50
Jeff Sluman	69	69	71	69	278	3,022.50
Rocco Mediate	71	66	68	73	278	3,022.50
Dan Halldorson	69	67	73	70	279	2,107.64
Tom Byrum	69	70	71	69	279	2,107.64
Jay Don Blake	70	70	70	69	279	2,107.64
Curt Byrum	70	67	70	72	279	2,107.64
Tim Simpson	71	66	68	74	279	2,107.64
Larry Rinker	72	67	70	70	279	2,107.64
Bruce Soulsby	68	67	70	74	279	2,107.64
Dave Barr	73	69	70	67	279	2,107.63
Fred Wadsworth	72	67	71	69	279	2,107.63
Gene Sauers	70	74	66	69	279	2,107.63
Steve Jones	71	69	68	71	279	2,107.63
Jay Haas	70	71	66	73	280	1,417.50
Steve Elkington	70	69	71	70	280	1,417.50
Lanny Wadkins	70	69	73	68	280	1,417.50
Robert Wrenn	70	71	69	70	280	1,417.50

	SCORES				TOTAL	MONEY
Craig Stadler	70	71	68	71	280	1,417.50
David Ogrin	70	69	73	68	280	1,417.50
Gil Morgan	68	69	73	70	280	1,417.50
Tim Norris	73	68	69	70	280	1,417.50

Seiko Tucson Open

TPC at Starpass, Tucson, Arizona
Par 36-36 — 72; 7,010 yards

October 22-25
purse, $600,000

	SCORES				TOTAL	MONEY
Mike Reid	64	69	68	67	268	$108,000
Mark Calcavecchia	67	71	65	69	272	39,600
Chip Beck	69	65	67	71	272	39,600
Fuzzy Zoeller	67	66	64	75	272	39,600
Hal Sutton	69	62	68	73	272	39,600
Jay Haas	68	68	65	72	273	20,100
Corey Pavin	70	66	73	64	273	20,100
Dan Pohl	71	64	70	68	273	20,100
*Mike Springer	70	67	69	68	274	
Fred Couples	68	66	71	70	275	16,200
Robert Thompson	71	66	70	68	275	16,200
Craig Stadler	69	67	67	72	275	16,200
Ed Dougherty	70	69	68	69	276	11,400
Larry Mize	67	72	65	72	276	11,400
Jeff Sluman	70	69	70	67	276	11,400
Tim Simpson	70	68	69	69	276	11,400
Steve Pate	69	68	69	70	276	11,400
Bill Sander	68	64	70	74	276	11,400
Dave Barr	68	67	68	74	277	7,302.86
Tom Watson	72	69	69	67	277	7,302.86
Bob Tway	73	65	71	68	277	7,302.86
Duffy Waldorf	68	73	68	68	277	7,302.86
Payne Stewart	70	63	72	72	277	7,302.86
George Burns	67	70	70	70	277	7,302.85
Wayne Grady	71	69	70	67	277	7,302.85
Ronnie Black	69	67	72	70	278	4,293.34
Leonard Thompson	70	72	69	67	278	4,293.34
Don Pooley	70	73	67	68	278	4,293.34
Trevor Dodds	71	69	66	72	278	4,293.33
Danny Edwards	68	72	69	69	278	4,293.33
Hale Irwin	68	71	72	67	278	4,293.33
Buddy Gardner	68	72	69	69	278	4,293.33
Willie Wood	69	69	70	70	278	4,293.33
Clarence Rose	70	70	70	68	278	4,293.33
David Frost	68	67	68	76	279	3,315
Mike Smith	69	70	69	71	279	3,315
Bob Eastwood	68	69	74	69	280	2,583.34
Ron Streck	71	70	68	71	280	2,583.34
J.C. Snead	69	71	68	72	280	2,583.34
Mark Brooks	69	70	71	70	280	2,583.33
Jodie Mudd	74	68	70	68	280	2,583.33
Mark O'Meara	71	70	67	72	280	2,583.33
Blaine McCallister	66	73	69	72	280	2,583.33
Tony Grimes	68	71	72	69	280	2,583.33
Don Shirey, Jr.	70	69	69	72	280	2,583.33
Paul Azinger	71	63	70	77	281	1,756.80
Jim Carter	71	68	70	72	281	1,756.80

	SCORES				TOTAL	MONEY
John McComish	66	72	72	71	281	1,756.80
Peter Jacobsen	70	67	69	75	281	1,756.80
Jack Renner	70	70	73	68	281	1,756.80
*Bill Mayfair	73	67	73	68	281	

Centel Classic

Killearn Golf and Country Club, Tallahassee, Florida
Par 36-36 — 72; 7,124 yards

October 29-November 1
purse, $500,000

	SCORES				TOTAL	MONEY
Keith Clearwater	71	68	68	71	278	$90,000
Joey Sindelar	71	69	67	72	279	33,000
Bill Kratzert	69	67	72	71	279	33,000
Bill Glasson	70	71	69	69	279	33,000
Bob Lohr	70	72	67	70	279	33,000
Greg Powers	69	72	71	68	280	15,125
Mike Hulbert	69	72	70	69	280	15,125
Buddy Gardner	69	68	72	71	280	15,125
Bob Gilder	71	70	71	68	280	15,125
John Mahaffey	71	71	72	66	280	15,125
Hubert Green	69	71	68	72	280	15,125
Ronnie Black	72	67	70	72	281	11,000
Russ Cochran	71	72	67	71	281	11,000
Tom Sieckmann	66	70	71	75	282	9,250
Frank Conner	69	70	72	71	282	9,250
David Peoples	74	71	70	68	283	7,750
Mike Sullivan	71	69	73	70	283	7,750
Donnie Hammond	71	69	74	69	283	7,750
Nolan Henke	72	72	70	69	283	7,750
Ed Fiori	72	72	69	71	284	6,033.34
Bob Eastwood	69	73	69	73	284	6,033.33
Dave Eichelberger	74	68	68	74	284	6,033.33
Jay Overton	69	69	72	75	285	3,925
Tim Norris	72	68	70	75	285	3,925
David Ogrin	72	73	73	67	285	3,925
Bill Sander	71	68	69	77	285	3,925
Bob Murphy	70	71	71	73	285	3,925
Jim Nelford	75	70	69	71	285	3,925
Kenny Knox	72	73	69	71	285	3,925
Dave Barr	68	73	69	75	285	3,925
Steve Elkington	73	70	70	72	285	3,925
David Edwards	73	71	71	70	285	3,925
Bruce Soulsby	72	69	74	71	286	2,585.72
Loren Roberts	70	73	69	74	286	2,585.72
Mark Lye	72	70	71	73	286	2,585.72
Ron Streck	72	70	70	74	286	2,585.71
Billy Pierot	72	72	70	72	286	2,585.71
George Burns	72	69	72	73	286	2,585.71
Dan Forsman	68	72	72	74	286	2,585.71
Don Shirey, Jr.	73	72	71	71	287	2,000
Dick Mast	72	72	68	75	287	2,000
Perry Arthur	71	69	74	73	287	2,000
Phil Blackmar	77	68	69	73	287	2,000
Keith Kulzer	72	71	74	71	288	1,600
Aki Ohmachi	73	72	67	76	288	1,600
Andrew Magee	72	73	72	71	288	1,600

	SCORES				TOTAL	MONEY
Ray Barr, Jr.	73	70	74	71	288	1,600
Ray Stewart	70	72	73	74	289	1,256.67
Jim Simons	73	69	72	75	289	1,256.67
Mike McCullough	73	71	72	73	289	1,256.67
Vance Heafner	71	73	71	74	289	1,256.67
David Jackson	72	73	70	74	289	1,256.66
Mark Brooks	72	73	72	72	289	1,256.66

Nabisco Championship of Golf

Oak Hills Country Club, San Antonio, Texas
Par 35-35 — 70; 6,576 yards

October 29-November 1
purse, $2,000,000

	SCORES				TOTAL	MONEY
Tom Watson	65	66	69	68	268	$360,000
Chip Beck	71	67	68	64	270	216,000
Greg Norman	67	70	68	66	271	138,000
Paul Azinger	73	66	67	67	273	96,000
Hal Sutton	71	69	67	67	274	68,800
Mark Calcavecchia	67	68	69	70	274	68,800
Ben Crenshaw	68	67	75	64	274	68,800
Nick Price	67	71	69	67	274	68,800
Corey Pavin	73	65	68	68	274	68,800
Don Pooley	71	68	68	68	275	55,400
Mark O'Meara	69	69	66	71	275	55,400
Fred Couples	73	67	67	69	276	48,800
Scott Hoch	72	66	71	67	276	48,800
Larry Mize	66	73	67	70	276	48,800
Scott Simpson	73	71	69	65	278	44,000
Mike Reid	69	66	74	70	279	42,400
Mac O'Grady	70	70	75	65	280	39,600
David Frost	66	71	73	70	280	39,600
Tom Kite	75	70	70	65	280	39,600
Bernhard Langer	68	69	69	74	280	39,600
Larry Nelson	76	68	68	69	281	36,800
Payne Stewart	72	69	68	72	281	36,800
Steve Pate	69	68	74	70	281	36,800
D.A. Weibring	68	71	73	71	283	34,800
Bobby Wadkins	73	73	70	67	283	34,800
Mark McCumber	74	66	70	74	284	33,600
Jeff Sluman	74	71	70	70	285	33,000
Dan Pohl	73	68	69	75	285	33,000
Lanny Wadkins	71	72	74	69	286	32,400
Curtis Strange	73	74	73	73	293	32,000

Isuzu Kapalua International

Kapalua Golf Club, Bay Course, Kapalua, Maui, Hawaii
Par 36-36 — 72; 6,879 yards

November 11-14
purse, $600,000

	SCORES				TOTAL	MONEY
Andy Bean	66	65	69	67	267	$150,000
Lanny Wadkins	67	67	69	67	270	84,000
Sandy Lyle	65	69	67	71	272	53,000
Ben Crenshaw	72	66	69	66	273	38,000
Ian Woosnam	68	70	70	68	276	30,000
Nick Faldo	67	73	70	67	277	20,500
Chip Beck	71	70	68	68	277	20,500
Scott Hoch	69	70	69	70	278	13,666.67
Jose-Maria Olazabal	70	69	67	72	278	13,666.67
Bobby Clampett	70	71	67	70	278	13,666.66
Don Pooley	70	69	73	67	279	9,375
Mark O'Meara	72	68	73	66	279	9,375
Joey Sindelar	72	68	69	70	279	9,375
Bruce Lietzke	68	71	70	70	279	9,375
Hale Irwin	72	71	69	68	280	7,750
John Mahaffey	71	68	70	71	280	7,750
Jeff Sluman	72	72	71	66	281	6,750
Payne Stewart	67	69	77	68	281	6,750
Fred Couples	70	69	72	70	281	6,750
David Ishii	71	70	71	71	283	6,250
Dave Barr	71	73	72	68	284	5,750
Peter Jacobsen	71	74	70	69	284	5,750
David Frost	74	68	73	69	284	5,750
Scott Simpson	75	69	73	68	285	5,000
Corey Pavin	73	70	73	69	285	5,000
George Burns	73	70	70	72	285	5,000
Keith Clearwater	73	75	73	65	286	4,250
Gene Sauers	72	75	70	69	286	4,250
Mac O'Grady	75	71	68	72	286	4,250
Jay Haas	74	70	73	70	287	3,750
Bobby Wadkins	75	71	73	69	288	3,000
Howard Clark	71	70	76	71	288	3,000
Rodger Davis	73	75	70	70	288	3,000
Ken Green	77	68	71	72	288	3,000
Mark Calcavecchia	73	68	73	74	288	3,000
Denis Watson	72	69	71	77	289	2,375
Jack Nicklaus	73	70	75	71	289	2,375
Lee Trevino	73	69	70	78	290	2,300
Warren Chancellor	73	71	74	74	292	2,250
Davis Love III	78	70	73	72	293	2,200
Casey Nakama	72	76	77	73	298	2,150
Jack Nicklaus II	74	76	76	78	304	2,075
Mark Rolfing	85	76	78	71	310	2,025

World Cup

Kapalua Golf Club, Bay Course, Kapalua, Maui, Hawaii
Par 36-36 — 72; 6,879 yards

November 18-21
purse, $750,000

	INDIVIDUAL SCORES				TOTAL
WALES (574) — $100,000 each					
Ian Woosnam	67	70	65	72	274
David Llewellyn	76	75	73	76	300
SCOTLAND (574) — $55,000 each					
Sandy Lyle	68	69	71	71	279
Sam Torrance	75	71	71	78	295

(Wales defeated Scotland on second hole of playoff, 10-11.)

UNITED STATES (576) — $40,000 each					
Ben Crenshaw	70	73	69	74	286
Payne Stewart	70	73	73	74	290
IRELAND (580) — $26,500 each					
Ronan Rafferty	70	71	69	77	287
Eamonn Darcy	71	76	73	73	293
AUSTRALIA (580) — $26,500 each					
Rodger Davis	73	71	72	73	289
Ossie Moore	70	73	70	78	291
ARGENTINA (582) — $15,000 each					
Armando Saavedra	70	75	67	74	286
Eduardo Romero	73	71	73	79	296
SWEDEN (583) — $10,000 each					
Ove Sellberg	71	73	70	74	288
Mats Lanner	72	71	73	79	295
TAIWAN (584) — $6,500 each					
Hsieh Yu-shu	75	70	74	69	288
Lin Chia	75	72	73	76	296
CANADA (584) — $6,500 each					
Dave Barr	71	72	72	75	290
Jerry Anderson	73	73	74	74	294
ENGLAND (588) — $4,000 each					
Howard Clark	68	77	73	71	289
Mark James	74	76	72	77	299
JAPAN (592) — $2,500 each					
Koichi Suzuki	69	70	72	72	283
Katsurari Takahashi	74	76	77	82	309
DENMARK (595) — $2,500 each					
Anders Sorenson	74	75	73	73	295
Steen Tinning	72	78	74	76	300
NEW ZEALAND (595) — $2,500 each					
Frank Nobilo	75	73	71	78	297
Greg Turner	72	76	74	76	298
SPAIN (600) — $2,500 each					
Jose Rivero	71	74	71	80	296
Jose-Maria Canizares	78	79	74	73	304

WEST GERMANY (600) — $2,500 each

Oliver Ekstein	75	74	71	76	296
Torsten Giedeon	74	81	73	76	304

ITALY (602) — $2,500 each

Giuseppi Cali	74	78	70	78	300
Silvio Grappasonni	71	75	78	78	302

MEXICO (606) — $2,500 each

Feliciano Esparza	76	74	77	70	297
Ernesto Perez Acosta	77	81	72	79	309

FRANCE (607) — $2,500 each

Marc Antoine Farry	72	77	70	75	294
Emmanuel Dussart	81	77	75	80	313

COLOMBIA (610) — $2,500 each

Rigoberto Velasquez	75	73	74	78	300
Eduardo Martinez	74	81	77	78	310

PHILIPPINES (610) — $2,500 each

Mario Siodina	72	78	74	77	301
Eduardo Bagtas	74	82	75	78	309

BRAZIL (612) — $2,500 each

Priscillo Diniz	71	76	79	76	302
Rafael Navarro	73	83	75	79	310

VENEZUELA (612) — $2,500 each

Ramon Munoz	75	76	74	77	302
Julian Santana	77	80	75	78	310

AUSTRIA (615) — $2,500 each

Oswald Gartenmaier	77	76	77	76	306
Franz Laimer	78	79	76	76	309

SOUTH KOREA (623) — $2,500 each

Sung Ho Kim	78	80	75	73	306
Yoon Soo Choi	81	79	76	81	317

MALAYSIA (633) — $2,500 each

Marimuthu Ramayah	76	79	81	78	314
Nazamuddin Yusuf	82	80	75	82	319

SWITZERLAND (633) — $2,500 each

Carlos Duran	75	79	76	84	314
Alain Jeanquartier	75	85	79	80	319

PORTUGAL (634) — $2,500 each

Carlos Aleixo	76	77	76	83	312
Rogerio Valente	76	84	78	84	322

HONG KONG (637) — $2,500 each

Yau Sui Ming	77	80	77	81	315
Alex Tang	79	79	80	84	322

BERMUDA (638) — $2,500 each

Dwayne Pearman	76	79	81	77	313
Keith Smith	82	82	75	86	325

FIJI (642) — $2,500 each

Arun Kumar	75	80	75	80	310
Bose Lutunatabua	86	84	81	81	332

BELGIUM (645) — $2,500 each

Philippe Toussaint	76	79	81	83	319
Vincent Duysters	75	80	86	85	326

SINGAPORE (651) — $2,500 each

M. Murugiah	79	88	75	83	325
Lim Kian Kee	83	82	80	81	326

INTERNATIONAL TROPHY

WINNER — Woosnam - 274 - $50,000. ORDER OF FINISH: Lyle - 279; Suzuki - 283; Saavedra, Crenshaw - 286; Rafferty - 287; Hsieh, Sellberg - 288; Clark, Davis - 289; Barr, Stewart - 290; Moore - 291; Darcy - 293; Farry, Anderson - 294; Sorenson, Lanner, Torrance - 295; Rivero, Ekstein, Lin, Romero - 296; Nobilo, Esparza - 297; Turner - 298; James - 299; Llewellyn, Tinning, Velasquez, Cali - 300; Siodina - 301; Grappasonni, Diniz, Munoz - 302; Canizares, Giedeon - 304; Gartenmaier, Sung - 306; Takahashi, Acosta, Bagtas, Laimer - 309; Martinez, Navarro, Santana, Kumar - 310; Aleixo - 312; Dussart, Pearman - 313; Ramayah, Duran - 314; Yau Sui Ming - 315; Yoon - 317; Yusuf, Jeanquartier, Toussaint - 319; Valente, Tang - 322; Smith, Murugiah - 325; Duysters, Lim Kian Kee - 326; Lutunatabua - 332.

J. C. Penney Classic

Bardmoor Country Club, Largo, Florida
Par 36-36 — 72; 6,464 yards

December 3-6
purse, $650,000

	SCORES				TOTAL	MONEY (Each)
Jane Crafter/Steve Jones	65	69	66	68	268	$65,000
Debbie Massey/Mark McCumber	66	68	65	71	270	38,000
Donna White/Morris Hatalsky	65	70	69	67	271	21,650
Betsy King/Doug Tewell	67	69	67	68	271	21,650
Muffin Spencer-Devlin/Denis Watson	68	70	70	64	272	13,000
Cathy Gerring/Bill Kratzert	69	71	65	67	272	13,000
Dawn Coe/Ronnie Black	66	66	72	69	273	9,500
Rosie Jones/Robert Wrenn	67	67	69	70	273	9,500
Patty Sheehan/Fred Couples	70	69	69	66	274	7,750
Juli Inkster/Tom Purtzer	66	70	70	68	274	7,750
Cathy Morse/Jeff Sluman	69	68	68	69	274	7,750
Colleen Walker/Mike Donald	69	70	67	68	274	7,750
Martha Nause/Larry Mize	67	71	69	68	275	5,750
Sally Quinlan/Bill Glasson	66	71	67	71	275	5,750
Robin Walton/Rick Fehr	68	67	68	72	275	5,750
Dale Eggeling/Wayne Levi	70	66	66	73	275	5,750
Beth Daniel/Chip Beck	71	70	67	68	276	4,375
Kathy Whitworth/Richard Zokol	70	69	69	68	276	4,375
Val Skinner/Mike Hulbert	65	74	70	67	276	4,375
Laura Davies/Willie Wood	69	71	66	70	276	4,375
Chris Johnson/John Mahaffey	67	69	72	69	277	3,250
Jill Briles/Buddy Gardner	67	71	70	69	277	3,250
Laurie Rinker/Larry Rinker	67	72	72	66	277	3,250
Marta Figgueras-Dotti/Brad Fabel	71	71	69	66	277	3,250
Alice Miller/Dan Forsman	69	71	69	68	277	3,250
Myra Blackwelder/Russ Cochran	66	71	72	69	278	2,350
Jan Stephenson/Paul Azinger	65	70	73	70	278	2,350
Lori Garbacz/Gary Koch	72	65	69	72	278	2,350

	SCORES				TOTAL	MONEY
Kathy Postlewait/J.C. Snead	71	71	69	68	279	2,125
Cindy Rarick/Keith Clearwater	67	68	71	73	279	2,125

Chrysler Team Championship

Palm Beach Polo Club
Par 36-36 — 72; 7,050 yards

December 10-13
purse, $452,000

Wellington Club
Par 36-36 — 72; 6,935

Greenview Cove Country Club
Par 36-36 — 72; 6,986 yards

West Palm Beach, Florida

	SCORES				TOTAL	MONEY (Team)
Mike Hulbert/Bob Tway	61	59	64	66	250	$100,000
Fred Couples/Mike Donald	62	63	64	62	251	57,000
Gary Hallberg/Scott Hoch	61	66	62	63	252	35,000
Jeff Sluman/Robert Wrenn	62	63	66	63	254	21,333.34
Peter Jacobsen/Johnny Miller	65	63	62	64	254	21,333.33
Keith Clearwater/Rick Fehr	66	63	62	63	254	21,333.33
Clarence Rose/Tim Simpson	62	67	63	64	256	17,200
Dewey Arnette/Jodie Mudd	63	65	63	66	257	15,000
Barney Thompson/Tom Valentine	66	64	63	64	257	15,000
Bobby Clampett/Bill Glasson	64	63	66	64	257	15,000
Greg Ladehoff/Dave Rummells	64	65	65	64	258	13,000
Payne Stewart/Mark Wiebe	64	64	66	65	259	11,000
John Mahaffey/Leonard Thompson	65	68	61	65	259	11,000
Mark Hayes/Tom Pernice	64	63	64	68	259	11,000
Jay Delsing/Steve Pate	66	65	65	64	260	8,000
Rick Cramer/Steve Jones	67	66	63	64	260	8,000
Mark Calcavecchia/Ken Green	66	63	65	66	260	8,000
Dick Mast/David Peoples	63	66	66	65	260	8,000
Larry Rinker/Brett Upper	64	67	65	64	260	8,000
John Adams/Bill Sander	67	66	63	64	260	8,000
Lennie Clements/Kenny Knox	64	66	62	68	260	8,000
Barry Jaeckel/Gary McCord	66	66	64	65	261	5,000
Tom Pruitt/Fred Wadsworth	63	65	67	66	261	5,000
Gary Koch/Tom Purtzer	64	63	67	67	261	5,000
Rex Caldwell/Gregg Twiggs	68	64	63	66	261	5,000
Charlie Epps/Blaine McCallister	65	63	64	69	261	5,000
Ray Barr/John Horne	64	66	65	67	262	3,600
Jim Colbert/Jim Simons	64	67	65	67	263	3,100
Jim Nelford/Richard Zokol	64	62	69	68	263	3,100
Doug Tewell/Tom Woodward	65	65	66	68	264	2,800
Brad Faxon/Willie Wood	67	65	64	69	265	2,600

The U.S. Senior Tour

MONY Senior Tournament of Champions

LaCosta Country Club, Carlsbad, California
Par 36-36 — 72; 6,813 yards

January 7-10
purse, $100,000

	SCORES				TOTAL	MONEY
Don January	67	72	73	75	287	$30,000
Butch Baird	70	68	72	77	287	18,000
(January defeated Baird on fourth hole of playoff.)						
Chi Chi Rodriguez	71	74	71	73	289	12,500
Dale Douglass	74	71	75	70	290	9,000
Gene Littler	70	72	75	73	290	9,000
Bruce Crampton	72	75	74	71	292	6,000
Charles Owens	73	74	76	73	296	5,000
Lee Elder	72	75	77	73	297	4,000
Miller Barber	71	75	77	75	298	3,500
Jim Ferree	77	73	77	74	301	3,000

Seniors Classic

Gary Player Country Club, Sun City, Bophuthatswana
Par 36-36 — 72

January 30-February 1
purse, US$300,000

	SCORES			TOTAL	MONEY
Harold Henning	75	69	70	214	US$90,000
Billy Casper	72	72	70	214	47,000
(Henning defeated Casper on first hole of playoff.)					
Peter Thomson	77	74	67	218	30,000
Orville Moody	70	75	75	220	25,000
Gay Brewer	72	75	74	221	22,000
Doug Sanders	70	78	74	222	19,000
Denis Hutchinson	72	75	75	222	19,000
Roberto de Vicenzo	75	76	74	225	17,000
Christy O'Connor	81	73	78	232	16,000
Al Balding	81	78	79	238	15,000

General Foods PGA Senior Championship

PGA National Golf Club, Palm Beach Gardens, Florida
Par 36-36 — 72; 6,520 yards

February 11-15
purse, $260,000

	SCORES				TOTAL	MONEY
Chi Chi Rodriguez	70	69	76	67	282	$47,000
Dale Douglass	74	66	69	74	283	29,500
Bobby Nichols	74	72	68	72	286	16,250
Bob Charles	72	73	70	71	286	16,250
Harold Henning	74	73	67	75	289	10,608.34
Lee Elder	73	73	70	73	289	10,608.33
Jack Fleck	71	73	73	72	289	10,608.33
Gary Player	74	73	68	75	290	8,500
Butch Baird	73	71	72	75	291	7,025

	SCORES				TOTAL	MONEY
Orville Moody	74	75	68	74	291	7,025
Doug Sanders	74	71	74	73	292	5,800
Billy Casper	75	73	73	71	292	5,800
Charles Owens	73	73	74	73	293	4,550
Joe Jimenez	71	70	76	76	293	4,550
Jim King	78	73	67	75	293	4,550
Arnold Palmer	75	72	72	75	294	3,650
Bob Toski	73	75	72	74	294	3,650
Al Chandler	79	74	70	71	294	3,650
Bob Bruno	76	72	72	75	295	3,250
Bruce Crampton	74	71	74	77	296	3,050
Bob Duden	75	76	73	74	298	2,850
Gene Borek	79	72	69	79	299	2,350
Adolph Popp	77	78	72	72	299	2,350
Jim Ferree	74	76	73	76	299	2,350
George Lanning	72	78	74	75	299	2,350
Bill Collins	75	74	79	72	300	1,950
Charles Sifford	77	76	72	76	301	1,750
Casmere Jawor	73	78	74	76	301	1,750
Howie Johnson	76	73	76	76	301	1,750
Gardner Dickinson	81	73	74	74	302	1,466.67
Bill Johnston	78	78	73	73	302	1,466.67
Jerry Barber	75	77	74	76	302	1,466.66
Ed Rubis	78	78	73	74	303	1,300
John Frillman	74	80	71	78	303	1,300
Richard Rhyan	74	79	74	76	303	1,300
Ray Montgomery	73	76	80	75	304	1,150
Gay Brewer	73	77	73	81	304	1,150
Tom Nieporte	73	78	77	76	304	1,150
Billy Maxwell	76	75	74	80	305	975
Joe Campbell	77	73	75	80	305	975
Jim Cochran	78	75	74	78	305	975
Bob Ross	78	77	79	71	305	975
Art Wall	80	77	73	76	306	813.75
Ralph Terry	79	78	77	72	306	813.75
Ralph Montoya	81	73	74	78	306	813.75
Dick Howell	79	77	77	73	306	813.75
Bob McCallister	79	74	74	80	307	740
Billy Farrell	80	75	77	75	307	740
Dow Finsterwald	78	76	78	75	307	740
Ken Still	78	76	72	81	307	740
J.C. Goosie	79	77	74	77	307	740
Pete Hessemer	79	75	76	77	307	740
Earl Puckett	81	75	75	76	307	740

World Seniors' Match Play Championship

Coolangatta-Tweed Heads Golf Club, Coolangatta, Queensland February 27-March 1
Par 36-36 — 72; 6,725 yards purse, A$165,000

FIRST ROUND

Bruce Crampton defeated Christy O'Connor, 3 and 2
Bob Charles defeated Bob Rosburg, 2 up
Arnold Palmer defeated Bobby Nichols, 2 and 1
Miller Barber defeated Doug Sanders, 6 and 5

SEMI-FINALS

Bruce Crampton defeated Bob Charles, 1 up
Miller Barber defeated Arnold Palmer, 2 and 1

THIRD-FOURTH PLACE PLAYOFF

Bob Charles defeated Arnold Palmer, 2 and 1

FINAL

Bruce Crampton defeated Miller Barber, 1 up

PRIZE MONEY: Crampton A$60,000, Barber $30,000, Charles $20,000, Palmer $15,000, O'Connor, Rosburg, Nichols, Sanders $10,000 each.

Del E. Webb Arizona Classic

Hillcrest Golf Club, Sun City West, Arizona
Par 36-36 — 72; 6,672 yards

March 12-15
purse, $200,000

	SCORES			TOTAL	MONEY
Billy Casper	68	65	68	201	$30,000
Dale Douglass	69	67	70	206	15,500
Bob Charles	64	70	72	206	15,500
Miller Barber	65	68	74	207	11,700
Chi Chi Rodriguez	65	70	73	208	8,250
Charles Owens	69	69	70	208	8,250
John Brodie	69	68	73	210	6,100
Ben Smith	68	69	73	210	6,100
Gary Player	71	71	68	210	6,100
Paul Harney	67	70	74	211	4,875
Ken Still	70	69	72	211	4,875
Bob Erickson	69	67	76	212	3,931.25
Gene Borek	72	66	74	212	3,931.25
Jim Feree	69	72	71	212	3,931.25
Tommy Jacobs	71	73	68	212	3,931.25
Bobby Nichols	68	74	71	213	3,100
Lee Elder	70	67	76	213	3,100
Orville Moody	71	71	71	213	3,100
Bruce Crampton	71	71	71	213	3,100
Gene Littler	71	67	76	214	2,350
Walter Zembriski	70	70	74	214	2,350
Gay Brewer	67	71	76	214	2,350
Dean Sheetz	70	70	74	214	2,350
Harold Henning	71	69	74	214	2,350
George Lanning	67	74	73	214	2,350
Jim King	72	69	74	215	1,950
Mike Fetchick	73	72	70	215	1,950
Billy Maxwell	72	73	71	216	1,542.86
Denny Felton	69	71	76	216	1,542.86
Tommy Aaron	69	71	76	216	1,542.86
George Bayer	72	71	73	216	1,542.86
Al Chandler	74	71	71	216	1,542.86
Bill Johnston	73	71	72	216	1,542.85
Bob Brue	65	72	79	216	1,542.85
Charles Sifford	69	74	74	217	1,225
Bob Rosburg	69	73	75	217	1,225
Joe Jimenez	70	71	76	217	1,225
Art Wall	70	75	72	217	1,225
Gordon Jones	71	66	81	218	1,050

	SCORES			TOTAL	MONEY
Fred Hawkins	73	72	74	219	950
Bill Collins	69	74	76	219	950
El Collins	73	72	74	219	950

Vintage Chrysler Invitational

The Vintage Club, Indian Wells, California
Mountain Course: Par 36-36 — 72; 6,907 yards
Desert Course: Par 35-36 — 71; 6,213 yards

March 19-22

purse, $270,000

	SCORES				TOTAL	MONEY
Bob Charles	72	70	73	70	285	$40,500
Bobby Nichols	72	70	76	71	289	15,750
Bruce Crampton	73	72	73	71	289	15,750
Butch Baird	80	66	72	71	289	15,750
Gary Player	72	75	73	69	289	15,750
Howie Johnson	70	75	71	73	289	15,750
Dale Douglass	75	67	75	72	289	15,750
Chi Chi Rodriguez	74	74	72	69	289	15,750
Walter Zembriski	76	68	74	73	291	8,775
George Lanning	77	72	74	69	292	7,447.50
Orville Moody	75	71	75	71	292	7,447.50
Don January	79	73	72	68	292	7,447.50
Billy Casper	78	71	77	67	293	6,277.50
Arnold Palmer	76	71	73	74	294	5,490
Jim Ferree	78	73	75	68	294	5,490
Miller Barber	71	77	75	71	294	5,490
Paul Harney	77	75	72	71	295	4,725
Bob Toski	74	71	75	75	295	4,725
Tommy Aaron	78	72	72	75	297	4,185
Charles Sifford	78	73	76	70	297	4,185
Bill Collins	82	69	74	72	297	4,185
Gay Brewer	79	72	71	76	298	3,645
John Brodie	73	75	75	75	298	3,645
Bob Brue	73	76	80	70	299	3,307.50
Ben Smith	81	70	74	74	299	3,307.50
George Bayer	73	71	79	76	299	3,307.50
Don Fairfield	76	78	76	70	300	2,921.25
Peter Thomson	77	75	74	74	300	2,921.25
Bill Johnston	77	72	77	74	300	2,921.25
Lee Elder	76	73	79	72	300	2,921.25
Doug Sanders	76	76	80	69	301	2,590
Gene Littler	78	79	72	74	303	2,455
Doug Ford	81	75	75	73	304	2,134.38
Art Wall	81	76	76	71	304	2,134.38
Harold Henning	76	75	81	72	304	2,134.37
Charles Owens	77	78	79	70	304	2,134.37
Mike Souchak	79	79	72	75	305	1,881.25
Roberto de Vicenzo	78	77	78	72	305	1,881.25
Jerry Barber	77	75	76	77	305	1,881.25
Buck Adams	80	77	74	75	306	1,780
Kyle Burton	83	73	79	72	307	1,712.50
Gordon Jones	77	73	83	74	307	1,712.50
Ken Still	82	73	77	76	308	1,645
Bob Erickson	81	76	77	75	309	1,577.50
Joe Jimenez	85	74	78	73	310	1,510
J.C. Goosie	82	73	84	74	313	1,510

GTE Senior Classic

Wood Ranch Golf Club, Simi Valley, California
Par 36-36 — 72; 6,727 yards

March 26-29
purse, $275,000

	SCORES			TOTAL	MONEY
Bob Charles	67	67	74	208	$41,250
Bruce Crampton	70	71	71	212	24,250
Harold Henning	72	69	74	215	19,950
Chi Chi Rodriguez	75	71	71	217	16,700
Charles Owens	73	77	69	219	13,300
Billy Casper	74	75	71	220	8,680
Roberto de Vicenzo	72	72	76	220	8,680
Howie Johnson	74	71	75	220	8,680
Walter Zembriski	72	74	74	220	8,680
Bobby Nichols	72	72	76	220	8,680
Arnold Palmer	71	74	75	220	8,680
Butch Baird	72	74	75	221	5,987.50
Tommy Aaron	69	74	78	221	5,987.50
Gary Player	75	69	77	221	5,987.50
Dale Douglass	72	73	76	221	5,987.50
Miller Barber	72	81	69	222	4,975
Gene Borek	74	73	75	222	4,975
Bob Brue	76	71	76	223	4,525
Art Wall	78	72	73	223	4,525
Tommy Jacobs	73	75	76	224	4,112.50
George Lanning	72	78	74	224	4,112.50
Doug Sanders	75	76	74	225	3,625
Gordon Jones	78	74	73	225	3,625
Dick King	77	73	77	227	2,971.43
Robert Rawlins	77	76	74	227	2,971.43
John Brodie	74	75	78	227	2,971.43
Al Balding	77	73	77	227	2,971.43
Bill Johnston	76	78	73	227	2,971.43
Orville Moody	76	77	74	227	2,971.43
Gene Littler	81	72	74	227	2,971.42
Ken Still	81	74	73	228	2,262.50
Gay Brewer	72	82	74	228	2,262.50
Paul Harney	75	77	76	228	2,262.50
Jim Ferree	76	78	74	228	2,262.50
Jim Cochran	79	77	73	229	1,925
Bob Rosburg	71	77	81	229	1,925
Ben Smith	77	73	79	229	1,925
Peter Thomson	79	74	76	229	1,925
Bill Collins	75	74	81	230	1,662.50
Art Silvestrone	76	73	81	230	1,662.50
Dan Sikes	79	77	74	230	1,662.50
Jim King	77	75	78	230	1,662.50

Chrysler Cup

Tournament Players Club at Prestancia, Sarasota, Florida
Par 36-36 — 72; 6,763 yards

April 2-5
purse, $600,000

FINAL RESULT: International, 59.5; United States, 40.7.

FIRST ROUND
Better Ball Match

Bruce Crampton-Harold Henning (Int.) defeated Miller Barber-Don January, 6 and 5.
Arnold Palmer-Chi Chi Rodriguez (U.S.) defeated Peter Butler-Christy O'Connor, 5 and 4.
Dale Douglass-Gene Littler (U.S.) halved with Bob Charles-Gary Player (Int.)
Roberto de Vicenzo-Peter Thomson (Int.) defeated Billy Casper-Lee Elder, 1 up.
STANDINGS: International 10, U.S. 6

SECOND ROUND
Singles Stroke Match

Crampton (Int.) defeated Rodriguez, 69-70.
Elder (U.S.) defeated de Vicenzo, 72-74.
Henning (Int.) defeated Palmer, 72-73.
Douglass (U.S.) defeated Thomson, 68-74.
Littler (U.S.) defeated Butler, 75-76.
Player (Int.) defeated Barber, 69-78.
Charles (Int.) defeated January, 69-73.
O'Connor (Int.) defeated Casper, 69-72.
STANDINGS: International 20, U.S. 12.

THIRD ROUND
Better-Ball Stroke

	SCORES			POINTS
Player-Charles (Int.)	32	34	66	9
Crampton-Henning (Int.)	32	34	66	9
Thomson-de Vicenzo (Int.)	34	34	68	5
Rodriguez-Barber (U.S.)	34	34	68	5
O'Connor-Butler (Int.)	34	36	70	3
Douglass-Littler (U.S.)	36	35	71	1
Palmer-January (U.S.)	36	35	71	1
Casper-Elder (U.S.)	35	36	71	1

STANDINGS: International 46, U.S. 20.

FOURTH ROUND
Individual Stroke Play

	SCORES			POINTS
Rodriguez (U.S.)	33	35	68	10
Douglass (U.S.)	34	35	69	8
Charles (Int.)	34	36	70	2.7
de Vicenzo (Int.)	35	35	70	2.7
O'Connor (Int.)	37	33	70	2.7
Casper (U.S.)	35	35	70	2.7
Player (Int.)	34	36	70	2.7
Henning (Int.)	37	33	70	2.7
January (U.S.)	36	36	72	
Thomson (Int.)	36	36	72	
Butler (Int.)	37	36	73	
Barber (U.S.)	35	39	74	
Crampton (Int.)	35	39	74	
Palmer (U.S.)	38	36	74	

	SCORES		POINTS
Elder (U.S.)	37	37	74
Littler (U.S.)	40	35	75

Each member of International team received $50,000; each member of the U.S. team received $25,000.

Doug Sanders Kingwood Celebrity Classic

Deerwood Golf Club, Houston, Texas
Par 36-36 — 72; 6,564 yards

April 17-19
purse, $198,296

	SCORES			TOTAL	MONEY
Bruce Crampton	72	69	72	211	$30,000
Charlie Owens	69	72	70	211	22,000
(Crampton defeated Owens on first hole of playoff.)					
Butch Baird	71	70	72	213	18,000
Art Wall	75	68	72	215	15,000
Bobby Nichols	66	74	77	217	12,000
Bob Toski	75	72	71	218	9,000
Walter Zembriski	73	70	76	219	6,833
Dale Douglass	72	71	76	219	6,833
Roberto de Vicenzo	71	77	71	219	6,833
Billy Maxwell	74	73	73	220	5,066
Gardner Dickinson	75	71	74	220	5,066
Jack Fleck	71	81	68	220	5,066
George Bayer	69	75	77	221	4,066
Ben Smith	76	72	73	221	4,066
Howie Johnson	72	72	77	221	4,066
Charlie Sifford	72	72	78	222	3,500
Gay Brewer	73	75	74	222	3,500
Doug Sanders	77	75	71	223	3,200
Bill Collins	76	74	74	224	3,000
Jimmy Powell	75	75	75	225	2,700
John Brodie	79	75	71	225	2,700
Doug Ford	73	74	79	226	2,450
Bob Goalby	76	77	73	226	2,450
Dow Finsterwald	80	77	70	227	2,300
Fred Hawkins	75	73	80	228	2,200
Christy O'Connor	80	76	73	229	2,050
Jim Ferree	71	76	82	229	2,050
Bob Erickson	75	78	77	230	1,850
Mike Souchak	76	78	76	230	1,850
Mike Fetchick	83	73	75	231	1,650
Bob Rosburg	74	80	77	231	1,650
Bill Johnston	77	78	77	232	1,375
Al Besselink	75	80	77	232	1,375
Julius Boros	81	80	72	233	1,300
Lionel Hebert	79	79	78	236	1,250

Coca-Cola Grand Slam Championship

Oak Hills Country Club, Tokyo, Japan
Par 36-36 — 72; 6,660 yards

April 17-19
purse, $300,000

	SCORES			TOTAL	MONEY
Gene Littler	68	67	69	204	$60,000
Miller Barber	68	67	71	206	41,000
Lee Elder	69	73	66	208	28,000
Don January	70	69	70	209	18,400
Bob Charles	70	67	72	209	18,400
Chi Chi Rodriguez	72	68	70	210	12,000
Bob Brue	67	73	71	211	10,000
Tadashi Kitsuda	68	68	76	212	8,500
Shigeru Uchida	71	73	69	213	6,250
Joe Jimenez	71	72	70	213	6,250
Hsieh Yung Yo	73	70	70	213	6,250
Lu Liang Huan	73	70	70	213	6,250
Hideo Jibiki	73	72	69	214	4,775
George Lanning	73	70	71	214	4,775
Peter Thomson	71	70	73	214	4,775
Harold Henning	67	67	80	214	4,775
Ichio Satou	75	69	71	215	3,820
Masao Hara	74	70	71	215	3,820
Billy Casper	70	73	72	215	3,820
Ichirou Togawa	72	71	72	215	3,820
Orville moody	66	71	78	215	3,820
Tommy Aaron	72	74	71	217	3,300
Kanehiko Uchida	75	71	71	217	3,300
Arnold Palmer	70	74	73	217	3,300
Osamu Kimura	75	71	72	218	3,100
Hiroshi Gunji	77	75	67	219	2,950
Chen Sei Ha	76	72	71	219	2,950
Tomoo Ishii	73	78	70	221	2,750
Ben Arda	75	72	74	221	2,750
Chen Chien Chung	71	76	75	222	2,600
Al Chandler	75	75	74	224	2,500
Torakichi Nakamura	80	73	72	225	2,400
Sadao Ogawa	73	74	79	226	2,300
Tsugio Gotou	77	74	76	227	2,200
Shinzu Arai	80	70	78	228	2,100
Masatoyo Kuroda	81	75	81	237	2,000

Liberty Mutual Legends of Golf

Onion Creek Country Club, Austin, Texas
Par 35-35 — 70; 6,584 yards

April 23-26
purse, $600,000

	SCORES				TOTAL	MONEY (Team)
Orville Moody/Bruce Crampton	63	65	59	64	251	$120,000
Bobby Nichols/Butch Baird	61	67	65	62	255	65,000
Peter Thomson/Ben Smith	64	67	61	64	256	44,000
Miller Barber/Bob Charles	61	62	65	68	256	44,000
Billy Capser/Gay Brewer	65	66	63	63	257	29,000
Don January/Gene Littler	67	61	65	65	258	25,000
Lee Elder/Chi Chi Rodriguez	68	67	64	61	260	19,000
Roberto de Vicenzo/Ken Still	65	66	65	64	260	19,000

	SCORES				TOTAL	MONEY
Jim Ferree/Charles Sifford	63	68	67	63	261	14,000
Gardner Dickinson/Don Massengale	66	65	64	66	261	14,000
Dow Finsterwald/Dale Douglass	62	67	68	64	261	14,000
Paul Harney/Jackie Burke	65	64	66	68	263	12,000
Tommy Aaron/Bob Goalby	67	65	69	67	268	11,000
Doug Sanders/Billy Maxwell	64	67	70	69	270	10,000
Bob Toski/Mike Fetchick	66	68	69	68	271	10,000
Charles Owens/Mike Souchak	67	65	70	70	272	10,000
Jay Hebert/Lionel Hebert	69	72	65	66	272	10,000
Bill Collins/Dan Sikes	68	66	68	70	272	10,000
Al Balding/Art Wall Jr.	69	68	65	70	272	10,000
Johnny Pott/Tommy Jacobs	68	70	72	68	278	10,000

SUPER SENIORS

	SCORES				TOTAL	MONEY
Jerry Barber/Doug Ford	66	61	66	67	260	$20,000
Fred Haas/Fred Hawkins	67	67	69	64	267	15,000
George Bayer/Bill Johnston	67	69	66	67	269	12,000
Howie Johnson/Jack Fleck	65	67	68	70	270	10,999.50
Julius Boros/Kel Nagle	66	67	68	69	270	10,999.50
Sam Snead/Tommy Bolt	69	71	67	67	274	10,998
Chick Harbert/Ted Kroll	68	68	72	69	277	10,000
Bob Hamilton/Paul Runyan	76	78	74	76	304	9,999

Sunwest Bank-Charley Pride Classic

Four Hills Country Club, Albuquerque, New Mexico
Par 36-36 — 72; 6,722 yards

May 1-3
purse, $250,000

	SCORES			TOTAL	MONEY
Bob Charles	70	70	68	208	$37,500
Dale Douglass	71	68	70	209	22,000
Bobby Nichols	71	68	71	210	18,200
Bruce Crampton	68	74	69	211	13,687.50
Jimmy Powell	71	68	72	211	13,687.50
Billy Casper	72	72	68	212	8,925
Orville Moody	69	74	69	212	8,925
Lee Elder	68	73	72	213	7,283.34
El Collins	70	72	71	213	7,283.33
Gene Littler	69	74	70	213	7,283.33
Jim Ferree	71	70	73	214	5,875
Larry Mowry	71	81	62	214	5,875
Miller Barber	73	73	69	215	4,806.25
Al Chandler	71	72	72	215	4,806.25
Bob Erickson	71	75	69	215	4,806.25
Ken Still	73	70	72	215	4,806.25
Bill Collins	71	75	70	216	3,900
Don Massengale	75	72	69	216	3,900
Ralph Terry	73	67	76	216	3,900
Paul Harney	74	72	71	217	3,090
Harold Henning	70	75	72	217	3,090
Chi Chi Rodriguez	70	71	76	217	3,090
Bob Stone	72	75	70	217	3,090
Peter Thomson	73	74	70	217	3,090
Gene Borek	71	72	76	219	2,637.50
Bob Brue	73	73	73	219	2,637.50
Dan Morgan	74	75	71	220	2,450
Rafe Botts	72	74	75	221	2,200

	SCORES			TOTAL	MONEY
Joe Jimenez	74	73	74	221	2,200
Howie Johnson	74	75	72	221	2,200
Tom Nielsen	71	72	78	221	2,200
Charles Owens	71	76	74	221	2,200

Vantage At The Dominion

The Dominion Country Club, San Antonio, Texas   May 8-10
Par 36-36 — 72; 6,814 yards   purse, $250,000

	SCORES			TOTAL	MONEY
Chi Chi Rodriguez	67	67	69	203	$37,500
Butch Baird	70	69	67	206	22,000
J.C. Goosie	64	71	73	208	15,191.67
Miller Barber	71	69	68	208	15,191.67
Charles Owens	73	65	70	208	15,191.66
Don January	70	69	70	209	8,925
Billy Casper	69	67	73	209	8,925
Harold Henning	71	72	67	210	6,987.50
Bob Charles	67	73	70	210	6,987.50
Bobby Nichols	69	72	69	210	6,987.50
Gene Littler	69	69	72	210	6,987.50
Bruce Crampton	71	71	69	211	5,650
Bob Goalby	75	69	68	212	5,087.50
Lee Elder	70	71	71	212	5,087.50
Ben Smith	71	68	74	213	4,400
El Collins	72	71	70	213	4,400
Jim King	70	72	71	213	4,400
Mike Fetchick	67	73	73	213	4,400
Jack Fleck	71	72	71	214	3,537.50
Al Kelley	70	72	72	214	3,537.50
Walter Zembriski	73	69	72	214	3,537.50
Kel Nagle	68	73	73	214	3,537.50
Rafe Botts	74	69	71	214	3,537.50
Bob Erickson	73	71	71	215	2,762.50
Peter Thomson	72	74	69	215	2,762.50
Billy Maxwell	69	71	75	215	2,762.50
Dale Douglass	74	71	70	215	2,762.50
Fred Hawkins	69	72	74	215	2,762.50
Gay Brewer	73	69	73	215	2,762.50
Bob Brue	73	69	73	215	2,762.50
Howie Johnson	73	74	69	216	2,029.17
Bill Collins	73	74	69	216	2,029.17
Gordon Jones	70	72	74	216	2,029.17
Doug Ford	73	71	72	216	2,029.17
Art Wall	73	70	73	216	2,029.17
Larry Mowry	70	74	72	216	2,029.17
Al Chandler	72	70	74	216	2,029.16
John Brodie	70	76	70	216	2,029.16

United Hospitals Championship

Chester Valley Golf Club, Malvern, Pennsylvania
Par 35-35 — 70; 6,406 yards

May 15-17
purse, $225,000

	SCORES			TOTAL	MONEY
Chi Chi Rodriguez	70	69	63	202	$33,750
Lee Elder	67	66	70	203	19,250
Gary Player	67	71	67	205	15,850
Miller Barber	67	72	67	206	13,250
Dale Douglass	64	73	72	209	10,650
Jim King	70	72	68	210	7,762.50
Paul Harney	73	66	71	210	7,762.50
Tommy Aaron	67	72	72	211	6,612.50
Bob Charles	74	72	65	211	6,612.50
Billy Casper	71	75	66	212	5,800
Dick King	70	71	72	213	4,900
Bob Brue	70	74	69	213	4,900
Joe Jimenez	68	73	72	213	4,900
Gene Littler	69	73	72	214	4,187.50
Bruce Crampton	69	75	70	214	4,187.50
Orville Moody	73	71	71	215	3,625
Bobby Nichols	70	73	72	215	3,625
Jim Ferree	71	75	69	215	3,625
Gay Brewer	73	76	68	217	2,707.15
Walter Zembriski	70	73	74	217	2,707.15
Art Silvestrone	72	72	73	217	2,707.14
Bob Erickson	71	71	75	217	2,707.14
Jerry Barber	71	75	71	217	2,707.14
Butch Baird	71	72	74	217	2,707.14
Gene Borek	72	74	71	217	2,707.14
Gardner Dickinson	76	72	70	218	2,200
Bob Goalby	71	75	72	218	2,200
Ken Still	74	72	73	219	1,760.72
Buck Adams	73	71	75	219	1,760.72
J.C. Goosie	72	74	73	219	1,760.72
Arnold Palmer	75	72	72	219	1,760.71
Jay Hyon	75	71	73	219	1,760.71
Mike Souchak	73	73	73	219	1,760.71
Billy Maxwell	71	73	75	219	1,760.71

Silver Pages Classic

Quail Creek Golf and Country Club, Oklahoma City, Oklahoma
Par 36-36 — 72; 6,708 yards

May 22-24
purse, $250,000

	SCORES			TOTAL	MONEY
Chi Chi Rodriguez	66	65	69	200	$37,500
Bruce Crampton	67	68	68	203	21,500
Miller Barber	66	71	69	206	14,833.34
Bob Charles	69	67	70	206	14,833.33
Ken Still	69	68	69	206	14,833.33
Joe Jimenez	70	69	68	207	8,750
Harold Henning	66	69	72	207	8,750
Peter Thomson	70	68	71	209	7,083.34
Bobby Nichols	70	69	70	209	7,083.33
Tommy Aaron	73	69	67	209	7,083.33
Don Massengale	66	71	73	210	5,875

	SCORES			TOTAL	MONEY
Jerry Barber	72	68	71	211	4,956.25
James Barber	68	68	75	211	4,956.25
Mike Souchak	75	67	69	211	4,956.25
Walter Zembriski	70	68	73	211	4,956.25
Gene Littler	70	70	72	212	4,050
Gay Brewer	70	73	69	212	4,050
Bob Brue	69	74	69	212	4,050
Dale Douglass	73	70	70	213	2,855
Butch Baird	70	71	72	213	2,855
Paul Harney	71	68	74	213	2,855
George Lanning	70	74	69	213	2,855
Orville Moody	70	74	69	213	2,855
Tommy Jacobs	71	70	72	213	2,855
Dick King	71	70	72	213	2,855
Larry Mowry	72	69	72	213	2,855
Jim King	66	70	77	213	2,855
Bill Johnston	70	73	70	213	2,855
Charles Owens	70	71	73	214	1,887.50
Dave Hill	71	71	72	214	1,887.50
Gardner Dickinson	71	71	72	214	1,887.50
Fred Hawkins	73	72	69	214	1,887.50
Fred Haas	72	70	72	214	1,887.50
John Brodie	72	70	72	214	1,887.50

Denver Champions of Golf

TPC at Plum Creek, Castle Rock, Colorado
Par 36-36 — 72; 6,700 yards

May 29-31
purse, $250,000

	SCORES			TOTAL	MONEY
Bruce Crampton	73	64	67	204	$37,500
Walter Zembriski	69	68	68	205	21,500
Dale Douglass	70	69	67	206	17,800
John Brodie	68	72	67	207	13,350
Bob Charles	70	68	69	207	13,350
Miller Barber	72	70	68	210	9,100
Gene Littler	71	71	70	212	7,412.50
Peter Thomson	74	71	67	212	7,412.50
Gary Player	72	68	72	212	7,412.50
Lee Elder	71	71	70	212	7,412.50
Gay Brewer	69	72	72	213	5,650
Bob Stone	75	66	72	213	5,650
El Collins	72	71	72	215	4,925
Dave Hill	72	74	69	215	4,925
Bobby Nichols	70	72	74	216	4,500
Ralph Terry	75	72	70	217	3,800
Ken Still	69	74	74	217	3,800
Jim Cochran	75	72	70	217	3,800
George Lanning	70	71	76	217	3,800
Bob Goalby	73	73	71	217	3,800
Roland Stafford	74	71	73	218	2,962.50
Charles Owens	74	68	76	218	2,962.50
Tommy Jacobs	72	76	70	218	2,962.50
Tommy Aaron	75	72	71	218	2,962.50
Rafe Botts	76	74	69	219	2,525
Charles Sifford	75	75	69	219	2,525
Howie Johnson	75	69	75	219	2,525

	SCORES			TOTAL	MONEY
Peter Carriell	75	74	71	220	2,212.50
Al Chandler	71	73	76	220	2,212.50
Ben Smith	67	80	74	221	1,795.84
Gordon Waldespuhl	77	74	70	221	1,795.84
Ralph Haddad	74	76	71	221	1,795.83
Dan Morgan	75	72	74	221	1,795.83
Bob Brue	68	77	76	221	1,795.83
Larry Mowry	72	74	75	221	1,795.83

Senior Players Reunion Pro-Am

Bent Tree Country Club, Dallas, Texas
Par 36-36 — 72; 6,804 yards

June 5-7
purse, $200,000

	SCORES			TOTAL	MONEY
Chi Chi Rodriguez	67	69	65	201	$30,093
Bruce Crampton	64	69	69	202	17,057
Gary Player	71	67	65	203	14,057
Harold Henning	68	70	67	205	11,757
Dave Hill	69	69	68	206	9,457
Bobby Nichols	69	69	70	208	7,157
Bob Charles	69	71	69	209	6,657
Don Massengale	71	70	69	210	5,657
Orville Moody	69	68	73	210	5,657
Peter Thomson	70	70	70	210	5,657
Butch Baird	71	72	68	211	4,232
Mike Fetchick	71	69	71	211	4,232
Charles Sifford	76	68	67	211	4,232
Walter Zembriski	72	71	68	211	4,232
Miller Barber	70	72	70	212	3,657
Tommy Aaron	74	69	70	213	3,257
Rafe Botts	68	72	73	213	3,257
Gene Littler	74	70	69	213	3,257
George Lanning	70	74	70	214	2,757
Arnold Palmer	75	68	71	214	2,757
Jack Fleck	71	72	72	215	2,457
Al Kelley	72	72	71	215	2,457
Charles Owens	72	71	72	215	2,457
Roland Stafford	72	71	73	216	2,257
Tommy Bolt	75	70	72	217	1,857
Gay Brewer	71	73	73	217	1,857
J.C. Goosie	75	72	70	217	1,857
Dick King	75	72	70	217	1,857
Ray Montgomery	72	71	74	217	1,857
Dan Morgan	71	73	73	217	1,857
Jimmy Powell	71	72	74	217	1,857

Mazda Senior Tournament Players Championship

Sawgrass Country Club, Jacksonville, Florida
Par 36-36 — 72; 6,636 yards

June 11-14
purse, $400,000

	SCORES				TOTAL	MONEY
Gary Player	69	73	69	69	280	$60,000
Bruce Crampton	70	70	71	70	281	32,000

	SCORES				TOTAL	MONEY
Chi Chi Rodriguez	65	72	74	70	281	32,000
Billy Casper	70	68	72	73	283	24,200
Charles Owens	67	73	71	73	284	15,900
Arnold Palmer	69	72	72	71	284	15,900
Doug Sanders	73	71	72	68	284	15,900
Miller Barber	68	75	71	71	285	12,000
Walter Zembriski	72	70	71	72	285	12,000
Don Massengale	75	72	68	71	286	9,633.34
Butch Baird	71	69	74	72	286	9,633.33
Bob Charles	70	75	74	67	286	9,633.33
Gay Brewer	68	74	71	74	287	8,200
Bob Brue	72	72	70	74	288	7,400
Roberto de Vicenzo	73	78	65	72	288	7,400
Roland Stafford	71	71	74	72	288	7,400
Lee Elder	71	74	74	70	289	6,200
Gene Littler	72	76	69	72	289	6,200
Bobby Nichols	72	70	73	74	289	6,200
Al Kelley	75	74	70	71	290	5,400
Bill Johnston	71	75	73	72	291	5,100
J.C. Goosie	71	75	73	73	292	4,800
Peter Thomson	72	76	71	73	292	4,800
Al Chandler	74	75	71	74	294	4,100
Dale Douglass	70	76	74	74	294	4,100
Dick King	69	73	75	77	294	4,100
Orville Moody	76	74	76	68	294	4,100
Charles Sifford	72	78	71	73	294	4,100
Jim King	75	72	76	72	295	3,300
Dan Morgan	74	73	74	74	295	3,300
Jimmy Powell	77	76	72	70	295	3,300
Don January	73	76	76	71	296	2,975
James Barber	72	76	72	77	297	2,625
Gardner Dickinson	80	74	72	71	297	2,625
Harold Henning	73	70	79	75	297	2,625
Billy Maxwell	66	75	79	77	297	2,625
Ben Smith	74	75	74	74	297	2,625
Ken Still	76	74	74	73	297	2,625
Bob Toski	73	75	73	77	298	2,225
Art Wall	79	75	72	72	298	2,225
Jerry Barber	72	75	75	77	299	1,925
Gene Borek	74	77	74	74	299	1,925
John Brodie	74	74	79	72	299	1,925
Jim Ferree	73	74	78	74	299	1,925
Tommy Aaron	77	74	76	73	300	1,625
Doug Ford	75	77	75	73	300	1,625
Jim Cochran	74	76	76	75	301	1,375
El Collins	74	75	77	75	301	1,375
Mike Fetchick	74	79	77	71	301	1,375
Bill Collins	72	76	75	79	302	825
Howie Johnson	77	78	74	73	302	825
George Lanning	78	77	76	71	302	825
Larry Mowry	70	78	77	77	302	825
Ralph Terry	79	76	72	75	302	825
Gordon Waldesphul	74	79	73	76	302	825

Northville Invitational

Meadow Brook Club, Jericho, New York
Par 36-36 — 72; 6,475 yards

June 18-21
purse, $300,000

	SCORES				TOTAL	MONEY
Gary Player	67	70	68	73	278	$100,000
Bruce Crampton	70	71	67	70	278	40,000
(Player defeated Crampton on second hole of playoff.)						
Ben Smith	73	70	69	68	280	25,000
Chi Chi Rodriguez	70	72	67	73	282	13,250
Dave Hill	73	68	69	72	282	13,250
Orville Moody	72	66	73	72	283	7,450
John Brodie	72	68	72	71	283	7,450
Charles Owens	68	72	74	70	284	6,450
Gay Brewer	73	67	70	74	284	6,450
Jim King	71	71	69	74	285	5,425
Billy Casper	68	72	72	73	285	5,425
Gene Littler	68	73	73	72	286	4,600
Roberto de Vincenzo	70	69	73	74	286	4,600
Butch Baird	73	74	68	73	288	4,150
Walter Zembriski	72	72	70	76	290	3,800
Bob Bruno	72	73	70	75	290	3,800
Bob Erickson	73	72	72	74	291	3,500
Harold Henning	72	73	71	76	292	3,300
Gene Borek	75	76	67	75	293	3,100
Doug Sanders	75	78	73	70	296	2,900
Charlie Sifford	69	75	76	77	297	2,675
Bob Toski	73	75	72	78	298	2,475
George Lanning	77	76	71	74	298	2,475
Jim Ferree	78	72	71	77	298	2,475
Ralph Terry	75	78	73	73	299	2,225
Art Silvestrone	74	73	77	75	299	2,225
Chuck Workman	76	76	71	78	301	2,075
Bob Stone	77	79	70	77	303	1,975
Mike Fetchick	76	76	76	77	305	1,875
Harold Kolb	78	74	74	80	306	1,775
Al Chandler	73	75	78	80	306	1,775

Greater Grand Rapids Open

Elks Country Club, Grand Rapids, Michigan
Par 36-35 — 71; 6,453 yards

June 26-28
purse, $250,000

	SCORES			TOTAL	MONEY
Bill Casper	68	68	64	200	$37,500
Miller Barber	70	70	63	203	21,500
Jim King	70	69	67	206	17,800
Dave Hill	69	69	69	207	14,800
Walter Zembriski	69	71	68	208	11,900
Tommy Aaron	65	73	71	209	9,100
Orville Moody	68	71	71	210	7,105
Harold Henning	72	69	69	210	7,105
J.C. Goosie	70	69	71	210	7,105
Quinton Gray	72	68	70	210	7,105
Howie Johnson	74	68	68	210	7,105
Gene Littler	70	72	69	211	4,567.86
Charles Owens	72	71	68	211	4,567.86

	SCORES			TOTAL	MONEY
Lee Elder	72	71	68	211	4,567.86
Bob Brue	71	71	69	211	4,567.86
Dale Douglass	73	71	67	211	4,567.86
Roland Stafford	72	71	68	211	4,567.85
Bruce Crampton	71	72	68	211	4,567.85
Bobby Nichols	71	68	73	212	3,550
Bob Charles	68	74	71	213	3,158.34
Gary Player	69	74	70	213	3,158.33
Joe Jimenez	70	75	68	213	3,158.33
Art Wall	72	73	69	214	2,775
Mike Fetchick	73	70	71	214	2,775
Roberto de Vicenzo	70	73	71	214	2,775
Dick King	73	73	69	215	2,400
James Barber	73	76	66	215	2,400
Jerry Barber	71	74	70	215	2,400
Ben Smith	75	68	73	216	1,846.43
Gordon Waldespuh	71	71	74	216	1,846.43
Doug Sanders	72	74	70	216	1,846.43
Larry Mowry	73	70	73	216	1,846.43
Al Chandler	72	73	71	216	1,846.43
Jack Fleck	74	73	69	216	1,846.43
Billy Maxwell	74	71	71	216	1,846.42

Greenbrier/American Express Championship

Greenbrier Country Club, White Sulphur Springs, West Virginia   July 3-5
Par 36-36 — 72; 6,709 yards   purse, $225,000

	SCORES			TOTAL	MONEY
Bruce Crampton	63	70	67	200	$34,000
Orville Moody	67	71	68	206	19,200
Don January	70	68	71	209	13,250
Bobby Nichols	68	70	71	209	13,250
Lee Elder	72	68	69	209	13,250
Billy Maxwell	67	72	71	210	7,187.50
Gary Player	71	74	65	210	7,187.50
Kel Nagle	71	67	72	210	7,187.50
Gardner Dickinson	71	69	70	210	7,187.50
Harold Henning	71	72	68	211	5,316.67
Billy Casper	71	69	71	211	5,316.67
Dale Douglass	73	72	66	211	5,316.66
Don Massengale	70	70	73	213	4,308.34
Charles Sifford	76	70	67	213	4,308.33
Joe Jimenez	72	73	68	213	4,308.33
Peter Thomson	74	71	69	214	3,737.50
George Lanning	72	68	74	214	3,737.50
Gordon Waldespuhl	71	74	70	215	3,081.25
Art Wall	75	69	71	215	3,081.25
Jim King	74	75	66	215	3,081.25
Butch Baird	70	72	73	215	3,081.25
Ben Smith	71	74	71	216	2,335.72
Bob Brue	76	69	71	216	2,335.72
Al Chandler	74	73	69	216	2,335.72
Del Snyder	71	73	72	216	2,335.71
Ray Montgomery	70	76	70	216	2,335.71
Tommy Aaron	76	68	72	216	2,335.71
Gay Brewer	73	72	71	216	2,335.71

	SCORES			TOTAL	MONEY
Dave Hill	73	72	72	217	1,825
J.C. Goosie	73	74	70	217	1,825
Mike Fetchick	76	70	71	217	1,825

USGA Senior Open

Brooklawn Country Club, Fairfield, Connecticut   July 9-12
Par 36-35 — 71; 6,599 yards   purse, $300,000

	SCORES				TOTAL	MONEY
Gary Player	69	68	67	66	270	$47,000
Doug Sanders	68	71	72	65	276	24,000
Chi Chi Rodriguez	68	68	70	71	277	17,164
Orville Moody	72	72	66	69	279	12,525
Don Massengale	69	70	70	71	280	9,855
Bob Brue	70	70	70	71	281	8,097.50
Dale Douglass	71	71	68	71	281	8,097.50
Gene Borek	68	76	67	71	282	6,660.50
Harold Henning	72	69	70	71	282	6,660.50
Larry Mowry	68	72	72	71	283	5,524.34
Peter Thomson	66	73	72	72	283	5,524.33
Walter Zembriski	70	70	71	72	283	5,524.33
Miller Barber	70	73	68	73	284	4,927
Arnold Palmer	69	69	74	73	285	4,376
John Brodie	67	70	74	74	285	4,376
Bob Charles	73	68	68	76	285	4,376
Gordon Jones	66	75	73	71	285	4,376
Fred Hawkins	70	71	75	72	286	3,896
Tommy Aaron	71	73	74	69	287	3,531.25
Butch Baird	70	73	72	72	287	3,531.25
John Frillman	71	75	73	68	287	3,531.25
Bobby Nichols	69	70	74	74	287	3,531.25
Bob Duden	74	74	71	69	288	3,182.50
Charles Jones	69	72	74	73	288	3,182.50
Bob Bruno	75	70	73	71	289	2,865
J.C. Goosie	72	71	74	72	289	2,865
Dick Hendrickson	71	73	74	71	289	2,865
Dave Hill	71	74	71	73	289	2,865
Billy Maxwell	76	71	71	71	289	2,865
Gay Brewer	72	72	76	70	290	2,491
Joe Campbell	70	76	70	74	290	2,491
Jack Fleck	77	68	73	72	290	2,491
Robert Rawlins	74	67	75	74	290	2,491
Ken Towns	74	74	70	72	290	2,491
Jerry Barber	69	77	74	71	291	2,145.58
Billy Casper	75	72	70	74	291	2,145.57
Bruce Crampton	70	73	76	72	291	2,145.57
Walker Inman Jr.	69	73	73	76	291	2,145.57
Jim King	74	72	72	73	291	2,145.57
George Lanning	72	71	75	73	291	2,145.57
Ken Still	74	74	67	76	291	2,145.57
*Dennis Iden	73	75	75	69	292	
Bob Toski	70	79	71	72	292	1,917
Joe Lopez	73	74	69	77	293	1,860
Al Chandler	74	73	72	75	294	1,774.50
Casmere Jawor	72	75	74	73	294	1,774.50
*Luther Godwin	73	73	77	72	295	

	SCORES			TOTAL	MONEY
Joe Jimenez	76	73	70	76	295	1,689
Don Hoenig	72	76	74	74	296	1,632
*Robert Moyers	77	72	75	72	296	

MONY Syracuse Classic

Lafayette Country Club, Syracuse, New York   July 16-19
Par 36-36 — 72; 6,540 yards   purse, $250,000

	SCORES			TOTAL	MONEY
Bruce Crampton	65	67	65	197	$37,500
Chi Chi Rodriguez	68	67	68	203	21,500
Peter Thomson	68	68	69	205	17,800
Walter Zembriski	72	67	67	206	14,800
Dave Hill	70	72	66	208	10,500
Joe Jimenez	72	70	66	208	10,500
Larry Mowry	68	73	68	209	8,400
Jim King	70	69	71	210	6,781.25
Lee Elder	69	73	68	210	6,781.25
James Barber	67	71	72	210	6,781.25
Orville Moody	66	75	69	210	6,781.25
Jack Fleck	73	69	69	211	4,956.25
Gene Littler	68	70	73	211	4,956.25
Ralph Terry	70	70	71	211	4,956.25
Miller Barber	67	70	74	211	4,956.25
Bobby Nichols	71	69	72	212	4,050
Jim Ferree	73	70	69	212	4,050
Quinton Gray	67	73	72	212	4,050
Bob Erickson	72	73	68	213	3,425
Ben Smith	73	69	71	213	3,425
Howie Johnson	70	73	71	214	2,962.50
Charles Owens	70	71	73	214	2,962.50
Gordon Waldespuhl	72	73	69	214	2,962.50
Bob Brue	69	72	73	214	2,962.50
Rafe Botts	70	75	70	215	2,525
Art Wall	73	72	70	215	2,525
Charles Sifford	67	75	73	215	2,525
J.C. Goosie	68	72	76	216	2,212.50
Dick Howell	71	72	73	216	2,212.50
Denny Felton	70	71	76	217	1,916.67
Robert Rawlins	70	73	74	217	1,916.67
Charles Coody	69	76	72	217	1,916.66

British Seniors Open

Turnberry Golf Club, Ailsa Course, Turnberry, Scotland   July 23-26
Par 35-35 — 70; 6,486 yards   purse, £147,000

	SCORES				TOTAL	MONEY
Neil Coles	66	73	67	73	279	£25,000
Bob Charles	67	74	72	67	280	16,400
Arnold Palmer	68	73	70	74	285	9,150
Peter Butler	73	72	68	73	286	7,350
Harold Henning	68	73	78	70	289	6,150
Ross Whitehead	70	78	69	74	291	4,720

	SCORES				TOTAL	MONEY
Gary Player	69	75	72	75	291	4,720
Rafe Botts	72	73	76	77	298	3,610
Peter Thomson	77	73	70	79	299	3,235
Brian Huggett	74	72	75	79	300	2,880
Mohamed Moussa	72	79	71	79	301	2,710
Denis Hutchinson	72	73	78	79	302	2,560
Norman Drew	73	75	77	78	303	2,257.50
Jack Wilkshire	75	76	74	78	303	2,257.50
Michael Skerritt	75	74	75	79	303	2,257.50
Denis Scanlon	73	73	78	79	303	2,257.50
Austin Skerritt	77	75	74	78	304	1,910
Paddy Skerritt	70	76	78	80	304	1,910
David Snell	75	73	75	81	304	1,910
Joseph Hardwick	72	73	82	78	305	1,703.33
Keith MacDonald	77	77	74	77	305	1,703.33
Joseph Hunter	72	80	75	78	305	1,703.33
Michael Murphy	76	78	80	73	307	1,600
Frederick Boobyer	74	81	75	77	307	1,600
Ernie Jones	76	82	76	74	308	1,520
John Panton	78	76	72	82	308	1,520
David Mercer	77	78	75	79	309	1,380
John Goodwin	75	79	76	79	309	1,380
Hugh Boyle	79	78	73	79	309	1,380
Alexander King	71	76	81	81	309	1,380
Christy O'Connor	77	74	74	84	309	1,380
David Talbot	81	79	73	77	310	1,260
George Lanning	77	81	75	78	311	1,200
Kel Nagle	76	76	77	82	311	1,200
Derek Strachan	79	74	79	80	312	1,120
Peter Gill	82	79	71	80	312	1,120
Gordon Cunningham	76	79	80	78	313	1,040
Richard King	79	75	78	81	313	1,040
Bryon Hutchinson	79	71	77	77	314	980
Lionel Platts	83	76	79	78	316	922.50
John Thorne	75	80	79	82	316	922.50
Ian Smith	78	83	76	80	317	840
El Collins	73	79	82	83	317	840
David Melville	76	79	76	86	317	840
Thomas Jefferson	76	82	79	81	318	750
Pat Leslie	79	77	78	84	318	750
Ian Alexander	76	80	76	86	318	750
Michael Plumbridge	77	78	77	86	318	750
John Nicol	73	80	82	84	319	690
Freddie Sunderland	80	82	73	84	319	690

Nynex/Golf Digest Commemorative

Sleepy Hollow Country Club, Scarborough, New York
Par 35-35 — 70; 6,545 yards

July 31-August 2
purse, $250,000

	SCORES			TOTAL	MONEY
Gene Littler	67	68	65	200	$37,500
Dale Douglass	67	67	67	201	21,500
Miller Barber	67	68	67	202	17,800
Roland Stafford	69	65	70	204	14,800
Jim Ferree	68	68	69	205	11,900
Orville Moody	71	68	67	206	9,100

	SCORES			TOTAL	MONEY
Butch Baird	68	71	69	208	6,571.43
Gardner Dickinson	70	68	70	208	6,571.43
George Lanning	70	71	67	208	6,571.43
Larry Mowry	66	73	69	208	6,571.43
Doug Sanders	70	67	71	208	6,571.43
Peter Thomson	73	67	68	208	6,571.43
Bob Brue	70	69	69	208	6,571.42
John Brodie	67	74	68	209	4,675
Lee Elder	71	70	68	209	4,675
Doug Dalziel	68	71	71	210	3,509.38
Roberto de Vicenzo	70	70	70	210	3,509.38
Don Massengale	67	74	69	210	3,509.38
Charles Sifford	68	73	69	210	3,509.38
Rafe Botts	69	70	71	210	3,509.37
Al Chandler	68	71	71	210	3,509.37
Dick Howell	74	69	67	210	3,509.37
Chi Chi Rodriguez	73	68	69	210	3,509.37
Jerry Barber	72	67	72	211	2,337.50
Bob Bruno	68	75	68	211	2,337.50
Bill Collins	67	71	73	211	2,337.50
Bob Erickson	71	68	72	211	2,337.50
Howie Johnson	73	69	69	211	2,337.50
Ben Smith	71	69	71	211	2,337.50
Mike Souchak	70	66	75	211	2,337.50
Bob Toski	69	73	69	211	2,337.50

Digital Classic

Nashawtuc Country Club, Concord, Massachusetts
Par 36-36 — 72; 6,649 yards

August 6-9
purse, $250,000

	SCORES			TOTAL	MONEY
Chi Chi Rodriguez	65	66	67	198	$37,500
Orville Moody	67	69	70	206	21,500
Harold Henning	65	70	73	208	17,800
Larry Mowry	71	69	69	209	13,350
Peter Thomson	70	68	71	209	13,350
Bob Brue	71	70	69	210	8,750
Dale Douglass	68	73	69	210	8,750
Tommy Aaron	70	70	71	211	7,400
Gardner Dickinson	71	73	67	211	7,400
Bill Collins	74	69	69	212	5,916.67
Lee Elder	70	70	72	212	5,916.67
Miller Barber	69	76	67	212	5,916.66
Gay Brewer	70	73	70	213	4,925
Ben Smith	69	75	69	213	4,925
Rafe Botts	72	72	70	214	4,300
Bob Charles	70	70	74	214	4,300
Roberto de Vicenzo	73	69	72	214	4,300
Dan Morgan	71	75	69	215	3,550
Doug Sanders	74	70	71	215	3,550
Walter Zembriski	72	69	74	215	3,550
Butch Baird	72	71	73	216	2,900
Charles Coody	71	73	72	216	2,900
Jim King	68	73	75	216	2,900
Don Massengale	69	71	76	216	2,900
Ralph Terry	71	74	71	216	2,900

	SCORES			TOTAL	MONEY
Howard Pierson	70	71	76	217	2,400
Jimmy Powell	67	75	75	217	2,400
Ken Still	69	73	75	217	2,400
Bob Goalby	75	73	70	218	2,025
George Lanning	76	71	71	218	2,025
Gordon Waldespuhl	73	73	72	218	2,025

Rancho Murieta Gold Rush

Rancho Murieta Country Club, North Course,
Rancho Murieta, California
Par 36-36 — 72; 6,657 yards

August 14-16
purse, $300,000

	SCORES			TOTAL	MONEY
Orville Moody	69	67	69	205	$45,000
Butch Baird	72	66	69	207	26,000
Lee Elder	70	71	68	209	21,500
Harold Henning	72	73	66	210	18,000
Dale Douglass	68	72	71	211	12,800
Bob Brue	68	72	71	211	12,800
Chi Chi Rodriguez	70	71	71	212	9,625
Gene Littler	73	69	70	212	9,625
Arnold Palmer	74	69	71	214	8,162.50
Tommy Aaron	72	71	71	214	8,162.50
Fred Hawkins	73	71	71	215	6,633.34
Roberto de Vicenzo	69	74	72	215	6,633.33
Billy Casper	74	70	71	215	6,633.33
Ken Towns	72	69	75	216	5,650
Don Massengale	73	72	71	216	5,650
Charles Sifford	73	76	68	217	5,200
Walter Zembriski	73	74	71	218	4,450
Bill Collins	67	79	72	218	4,450
Gay Brewer	75	71	72	218	4,450
Bob Charles	73	74	71	218	4,450
Bob Erickson	73	73	73	219	3,650
Don January	72	74	73	219	3,650
J.C. Goosie	75	71	73	219	3,650
Charles Coody	71	73	76	220	3,200
Bruce Crampton	72	76	72	220	3,200
Jim Ferree	73	74	73	220	3,200
Doug Sanders	74	75	72	221	2,750
Jim King	75	76	70	221	2,750
Miller Barber	74	74	73	221	2,750
Bobby Nichols	74	74	74	222	2,412.50
John Brodie	74	75	73	222	2,412.50
Art Wall	75	74	74	223	1,987.50
Ken Still	69	73	81	223	1,987.50
Larry Mowry	72	80	71	223	1,987.50
Tommy Jacobs	79	71	73	223	1,987.50
Doug Ford	76	71	76	223	1,987.50
Al Chandler	72	76	75	223	1,987.50
Peter Thomson	72	75	77	224	1,700
Mike Souchak	78	72	75	225	1,550
George Lanning	78	76	71	225	1,550
Rafe Botts	75	70	80	225	1,550

GTE Northwest Classic

Inglewood Country Club, Kenmore, Washington
Par 37-35 — 72; 6,501 yards

August 21-23
purse, $300,000

	SCORES			TOTAL	MONEY
Chi Chi Rodriguez	70	68	68	206	$45,000
Butch Baird	70	68	69	207	26,000
Arnold Palmer	71	72	66	209	19,750
Miller Barber	68	69	72	209	19,750
Larry Mowry	69	71	70	210	14,500
Ben Smith	70	69	72	211	11,100
Jimmy Powell	72	72	68	212	9,625
Orville Moody	71	67	74	212	9,625
Dale Douglass	71	71	71	213	8,525
Gordon Jones	69	72	73	214	6,925
Jack Fleck	69	73	72	214	6,925
Bruce Crampton	72	73	69	214	6,925
Bob Charles	72	69	73	214	6,925
Gene Littler	74	69	72	215	5,500
J.C. Goosie	73	72	70	215	5,500
Bill Collins	72	71	72	215	5,500
Gary Player	74	73	69	216	4,750
Bob Erickson	77	69	70	216	4,750
Charles Sifford	74	72	71	217	4,033.34
Ken Still	77	71	69	217	4,033.33
Bob Brue	69	77	71	217	4,033.33
Harold Henning	75	70	73	218	3,650
Walter Zembriski	72	73	74	219	3,125
Robert Rawlins	73	77	69	219	3,125
Jim King	70	74	75	219	3,125
Kel Nagle	76	70	73	219	3,125
Doug Dalziel	75	72	72	219	3,125
Jim Cochran	73	73	73	219	3,125
Bill Johnston	74	73	73	220	2,600
Billy Maxwell	72	74	75	221	2,412.50
John Brodie	71	76	74	221	2,412.50
James Barber	77	76	69	222	2,125
Rafe Botts	73	77	72	222	2,125
Denny Felton	74	73	75	222	2,125
Art Silvestrone	73	76	74	223	1,850
George Lanning	72	76	75	223	1,850
Quinton Gray	72	79	72	223	1,850
Roland Stafford	79	75	70	224	1,512.50
Art Wall	75	75	74	224	1,512.50
Al Mengert	79	72	73	224	1,512.50
Charles Coody	76	73	75	224	1,512.50
Al Chandler	74	73	77	224	1,512.50
Doug Ford	75	79	70	224	1,512.50

Showdown Classic

Jeremy Ranch, Park City, Utah
Par 36-36 — 72; 7,103 yards

August 28-30
purse, $325,000

	SCORES			TOTAL	MONEY
Miller Barber	71	67	72	210	$45,000
Bruce Crampton	69	73	69	211	26,000

	SCORES			TOTAL	MONEY
Chi Chi Rodriguez	75	70	70	215	15,020
Gary Player	71	73	71	215	15,020
Bobby Nichols	76	65	74	215	15,020
Orville Moody	72	72	71	215	15,020
Charles Coody	69	77	69	215	15,020
Walter Zembriski	76	70	70	216	8,525
Don Massengale	70	71	75	216	8,525
John Brodie	79	66	71	216	8,525
J.C. Goosie	74	71	72	217	7,100
Ralph Terry	72	78	68	218	6,025
Ken Still	78	68	72	218	6,025
Butch Baird	72	70	76	218	6,025
Bob Brue	73	72	73	218	6,025
Dale Douglass	73	71	75	219	5,200
Robert Rawlins	71	75	74	220	4,750
Billy Casper	73	70	77	220	4,750
Roland Stafford	71	75	75	221	4,033.34
Ben Smith	72	72	77	221	4,033.33
Jim Cochran	72	73	76	221	4,033.33
Billy Maxwell	73	76	73	222	3,500
Mike Fetchick	72	76	74	222	3,500
Bob Goalby	74	73	75	222	3,500
Jimmy Powell	77	72	74	223	3,125
Jerry Barber	76	71	76	223	3,125
Al Kelley	75	74	76	225	2,825
Rafe Botts	75	77	73	225	2,825
Dean Sheetz	76	78	72	226	2,475
Jim King	76	76	74	226	2,475
Hap Rose	73	80	73	226	2,475
Don Johnson	82	73	72	227	2,030
Gordon Jones	71	77	79	227	2,030
Doug Dalziel	72	77	78	227	2,030
Al Chandler	70	77	80	227	2,030
Doug Ford	77	77	73	227	2,030
Howie Johnson	75	76	77	228	1,662.50
Bill Johnston	74	77	77	228	1,662.50
Joe Jimenez	72	78	78	228	1,662.50
Quinton Gray	71	78	79	228	1,662.50

Vantage Bank One Classic

Griffin Gate Golf Club, Lexington, Kentucky
Par 36-35 — 71; 6,640 yards

September 4-6
purse, $225,000

	SCORES			TOTAL	MONEY
Bruce Crampton	63	64	70	197	$33,750
Joe Jimenez	69	67	67	203	16,116.67
Bob Charles	72	65	66	203	16,116.67
Miller Barber	67	67	69	203	16,116.66
Ben Smith	69	66	69	204	9,350
Gene Littler	69	67	68	204	9,350
Al Geiberger	69	68	68	205	6,900
Lee Elder	73	65	67	205	6,900
Harold Henning	68	67	70	205	6,900
Walter Zembriski	70	70	66	206	5,316.67
Doug Sanders	65	71	70	206	5,316.67
Orville Moody	68	71	67	206	5,316.66

	SCORES			TOTAL	MONEY
Pat Schwab	69	71	67	207	4,308.34
Dale Douglass	69	66	72	207	4,308.33
Billy Casper	69	67	71	207	4,308.33
Bobby Nichols	67	72	69	208	3,625
Tommy Aaron	67	71	70	208	3,625
Gay Brewer	69	69	70	208	3,625
Dave Hill	67	72	70	209	3,175.00
Jim King	63	74	73	210	2,743.75
Dick Howell	71	71	68	210	2,743.75
Gardner Dickinson	73	65	72	210	2,743.75
Jim Cochran	69	71	70	210	2,743.75
Art Wall	75	69	68	212	2,100
Art Silvestrone	70	72	70	212	2,100
Gordon Waldespuhl	67	71	74	212	2,100
Charles Owens	76	68	68	212	2,100
Howie Johnson	72	70	70	212	2,100
J.C. Goosie	72	71	69	212	2,100
Joe Campbell	69	72	71	212	2,100
Bob Erickson	71	69	72	212	2,100
Bob Goalby	75	67	71	213	1,446.43
James Barber	73	67	73	213	1,446.43
Jerry Barber	74	69	70	213	1,446.43
Mike Fetchick	74	71	68	213	1,446.43
Pete Brown	74	66	73	213	1,446.43
Bob Brue	76	67	70	213	1,446.43
Paul Thomas	71	72	70	213	1,446.42
Charles Sifford	72	72	70	214	1,125
Dean Refram	70	71	73	214	1,125
Kel Nagle	72	73	69	214	1,125
Al Kelley	74	71	69	214	1,125
El Collins	70	71	73	214	1,125

PaineWebber World Invitational

Quail Hollow Country Club, Charlotte, North Carolina
Par 36-36 — 72; 6,819 yards

September 9-12
purse, $250,000

(Shortened to 54 holes because of rain.)

	SCORES			TOTAL	MONEY
Gary Player	68	67	72	207	$37,500
Bob Charles	70	67	70	207	22,500
(Player defeated Charles on first hole of playoff.)					
Dave Hill	70	69	69	208	18,750
Butch Baird	73	68	70	211	15,625
Chi Chi Rodriguez	67	71	75	213	9,250
Jim King	72	73	68	213	9,250
Larry Mowry	71	75	67	213	9,250
Arnold Palmer	73	72	68	213	9,250
Jim Ferree	72	72	69	213	9,250
Charles Coody	72	71	71	214	6,875
Orville Moody	70	71	74	215	5,656.25
Jerry Barber	72	71	72	215	5,656.25
Miller Barber	71	72	72	215	5,656.25
Bob Brue	73	71	71	215	5,656.25
Bob Toski	76	68	72	216	4,375
Don Massengale	70	74	72	216	4,375

	SCORES			TOTAL	MONEY
Al Geiberger	71	75	70	216	4,375
Bruce Crampton	74	71	71	216	4,375
Ken Still	69	71	77	217	3,500
George Lanning	75	72	70	217	3,500
Buck Adams	72	72	73	217	3,500
Walter Zembriski	71	76	71	218	3,000
Tommy Aaron	73	75	70	218	3,000
J.C. Goosie	73	71	74	218	3,000
Gene Littler	75	72	72	219	2,633.34
Charles Owens	70	77	72	219	2,633.33
Charles Sifford	73	72	74	219	2,633.33
Howie Johnson	75	70	76	221	2,337.50
Bob Erickson	79	70	72	221	2,337.50
Ralph Terry	76	73	73	222	1,978.13
Doug Sanders	72	74	76	222	1,978.13
Joe Jimenez	74	75	73	222	1,978.12
Gordon Jones	76	76	70	222	1,978.12
Gay Brewer	75	72	76	223	1,712.50
Fred Hawkins	76	73	74	223	1,712.50
Jimmy Powell	75	72	76	223	1,712.50
Roland Stafford	72	76	76	224	1,525
Billy Maxwell	76	72	76	224	1,525
Rafe Botts	74	78	72	224	1,525
Peter Thomson	72	77	76	225	1,400

Crestar Classic

Hermitage Country Club, Manakin-Sabot, Virginia
Par 36-36 — 72; 6,644 yards

September 18-20
purse, $325,000

	SCORES			TOTAL	MONEY
Larry Mowry	67	69	67	203	$48,750
Gary Player	66	71	67	204	25,800
Bob Charles	68	66	70	204	25,800
Dale Douglass	68	68	69	205	19,550
Chi Chi Rodriguez	68	68	70	206	15,750
Gene Littler	67	70	70	207	10,562.50
Al Geiberger	71	68	68	207	10,562.50
Butch Baird	68	71	68	207	10,562.50
Miller Barber	70	69	68	207	10,562.50
Orville Moody	66	72	71	209	8,150
Arnold Palmer	73	69	67	209	8,150
John Brodie	69	71	71	211	7,050
Bob Brue	70	71	70	211	7,050
Joe Jimenez	72	71	69	212	5,975
Dave Hill	69	75	68	212	5,975
Billy Casper	72	70	70	212	5,975
Walter Zembriski	72	72	69	213	4,837
George Lanning	70	73	70	213	4,837
Bruce Crampton	72	69	72	213	4,837
Jim Cochran	72	73	68	213	4,837
Ken Still	74	69	71	214	4,150
Don Massengale	70	75	70	215	3,610
Billy Maxwell	71	72	72	215	3,610
Jim King	73	71	71	215	3,610
Gordon Jones	70	72	73	215	3,610
Bill Collins	73	70	72	215	3,610

	SCORES			TOTAL	MONEY
Gay Brewer	72	70	74	216	3,000
Jim Ferree	74	70	72	216	3,000
Mike Fetchick	71	73	72	216	3,000
Fred Hawkins	71	71	75	217	2,625
Al Chandler	70	74	73	217	2,625
Boots Widener	71	74	73	218	2,100
Al Kelley	72	73	73	218	2,100
Charles Mehok	72	74	72	218	2,100
Quinton Gray	72	72	74	218	2,100
Charles Coody	76	68	74	218	2,100
Rafe Botts	71	77	70	218	2,100
Roberto de Vicenzo	70	75	73	218	2,100
Peter Thomson	74	73	72	219	1,537.50
Charles Sifford	72	75	72	219	1,537.50
Bobby Nichols	76	71	72	219	1,537.50
Bob Goalby	74	71	74	219	1,537.50
Jack Fleck	72	71	76	219	1,537.50
Doug Dalziel	73	71	75	219	1,537.50

Newport Cup

Newport Country Club, Newport, Rhode Island
Par 36-36 — 72; 6,566 yards

September 26-28
purse, $200,000

	SCORES			TOTAL	MONEY
Miller Barber	67	70	65	202	$30,000
Bruce Crampton	68	70	67	205	18,000
Bob Charles	71	72	64	207	14,000
Gary Player	71	72	65	208	12,000
Joe Jimenez	72	68	70	210	9,000
Jim Ferree	70	71	69	210	9,000
George Lanning	72	70	70	212	7,250
Lee Elder	72	74	66	212	7,250
Charles Sifford	77	71	65	213	6,500
Bob Brue	70	71	73	214	5,500
Dale Douglass	73	73	68	214	5,500
Dave Hill	71	75	68	214	5,500
Bobby Nichols	73	71	71	215	4,700
Gardner Dickinson	72	73	70	215	4,700
Chi Chi Rodriguez	73	72	71	216	4,200
Butch Baird	74	76	66	216	4,200
Howie Johnson	73	76	67	216	4,200
Jerry Barber	75	75	67	217	3,800
Billy Maxwell	76	71	71	218	3,500
Jim King	74	74	70	218	3,500
Peter Thomson	76	74	69	219	2,975
Gay Brewer	76	74	69	219	2,975
Bill Collins	71	75	73	219	2,975
Roberto de Vicenzo	71	78	70	219	2,975
Tommy Aaron	74	75	71	220	2,600
Billy Casper	70	75	75	220	2,600
Doug Ford	73	76	71	220	2,600
Doug Sanders	73	74	74	221	2,400
Mike Fetchick	71	78	73	222	2,300
Walter Zembriski	80	74	69	223	2,200
Al Balding	74	75	77	226	2,100
Bob Goalby	75	77	75	227	2,000

	SCORES			TOTAL	MONEY
Al Chandler	77	75	78	230	1,850
Fred Hawkins	81	75	74	230	1,850
Julius Boros	78	77	77	232	1,700
Mike Souchak	81	78	78	237	1,600

Vantage Championship

Tanglewood Golf Club, Clemmons, North Carolina
Par 35-35 — 70; 6,606 yards

October 2-4
purse, $900,000

	SCORES			TOTAL	MONEY
Al Geiberger	72	67	67	206	$135,000
Dave Hill	67	76	65	208	81,000
Gene Littler	70	67	72	209	67,300
Orville Moody	66	74	70	210	56,050
Don January	68	71	72	211	39,175
Gay Brewer	67	71	73	211	39,175
Butch Baird	74	70	68	212	30,175
Miller Barber	70	72	70	212	30,175
Gary Player	75	71	67	213	26,800
Walt Zembriski	73	71	70	214	20,350
Peter Thomson	72	70	72	214	20,350
Billy Casper	69	76	69	214	20,350
Bruce Crampton	71	71	72	214	20,350
Jim Cochran	69	71	74	214	20,350
Dale Douglass	69	71	74	214	20,350
Ben Smith	73	71	71	215	14,200
Arnold Palmer	73	69	73	215	14,200
Gordon Jones	71	72	72	215	14,200
Bobby Nichols	69	78	68	215	14,200
Chi Chi Rodriguez	72	73	70	215	14,200
Don Massengale	73	71	72	216	10,825
Charles Coody	68	76	72	216	10,825
Ken Still	69	71	76	216	10,825
Jim Ferree	69	75	72	216	10,825
Bob Erickson	73	70	74	217	9,475
Doug Sanders	72	78	67	217	9,475
Bob Goalby	73	72	73	218	8,350
John Brodie	71	73	74	218	8,350
Jimmy Powell	72	67	79	218	8,350
El Collins	73	71	75	219	6,685
Bob Brue	77	66	76	219	6,685
Howie Johnson	74	74	71	219	6,685
Larry Mowry	69	78	72	219	6,685
Billy Maxwell	74	74	71	219	6,685
Al Kelley	71	76	73	220	5,762.50
James Barber	75	68	77	220	5,762.50
Rafe Botts	70	74	77	221	5,312.50
Jim King	74	74	73	221	5,312.50
Lee Elder	73	77	72	222	4,525
George Lanning	74	74	74	222	4,525
Tommy Aaron	73	73	76	222	4,525
Mike Fetchick	71	71	80	222	4,525
Jack Fleck	77	73	72	222	4,525

Pepsi Challenge

Horseshoe Bend Country Club, Atlanta, Georgia
Par 36-36 — 72; 6,960 yards

October 9-11
purse, $250,000

	SCORES			TOTAL	MONEY
Larry Mowry	70	67	66	203	$37,500
Gene Littler	71	68	66	205	21,500
Bob Charles	74	68	67	209	16,300
Bruce Crampton	72	68	69	209	16,300
Arnold Palmer	66	67	77	210	10,500
Miller Barber	68	71	71	210	10,500
Bill Collins	70	71	70	211	8,400
Butch Baird	71	69	72	212	7,083.34
Gary Player	72	65	75	212	7,083.33
Dave Hill	67	71	74	212	7,083.33
Don Massengale	73	70	70	213	5,650
Gay Brewer	73	72	68	213	5,650
Dale Douglass	72	74	68	214	4,800
Bob Brue	72	72	70	214	4,800
Billy Casper	71	71	72	214	4,800
Dick Howell	73	72	70	215	4,175
Lee Elder	73	70	72	215	4,175
Walter Zembriski	72	71	73	216	3,800
Al Geiberger	74	70	73	217	3,333.34
Art Wall	72	74	71	217	3,333.33
Charles Sifford	71	73	73	217	3,333.33
Roland Stafford	74	71	73	218	2,837.50
Bob Toski	72	74	72	218	2,837.50
Bob Erickson	74	74	70	218	2,837.50
Mike Fetchick	72	72	74	218	2,837.50
Dan Morgan	73	72	74	219	2,157.15
Bobby Nichols	75	70	74	219	2,157.15
Ken Still	78	74	67	219	2,157.14
Jim King	75	70	74	219	2,157.14
Fred Hawkins	73	73	73	219	2,157.14
Joe Jimenez	72	73	74	219	2,157.14
Bill Byars	74	74	71	219	2,157.14
Peter Thomson	73	76	71	220	1,637.50
Orville Moody	74	74	72	220	1,637.50
George Lanning	72	71	77	220	1,637.50
James Barber	74	72	74	220	1,637.50
Gordon Jones	76	71	74	221	1,330
Dow Finsterwald	74	76	71	221	1,330
Doug Ford	74	73	74	221	1,330
Buck Adams	67	77	77	221	1,330
Howard Brown	78	73	70	221	1,330

Hilton Head International

Harbour Town Golf Links, Hilton Head Island, South Carolina
Par 36-35 — 71; 6,435 yards

October 16-18
purse, $250,000

	SCORES			TOTAL	MONEY
Al Geiberger	70	68	71	209	$37,500
Jim Ferree	73	68	68	209	21,500
(Geiberger defeated Ferree on first hole of playoff.)					
Bruce Crampton	67	74	69	210	16,300

	SCORES			TOTAL	MONEY
Charles Coody	70	69	71	210	16,300
Bruce Devlin	71	73	67	211	10,500
Butch Baird	69	72	70	211	10,500
Gary Player	72	71	69	212	8,400
Dave Hill	72	71	70	213	7,083.34
Walter Zembriski	70	71	72	213	7,083.33
Orville Moody	69	73	71	213	7,083.33
Billy Casper	69	72	73	214	5,875
Dick King	74	70	71	215	5,425
Dale Douglass	73	69	74	216	5,050
Ben Smith	76	69	72	217	4,550
Gene Littler	72	72	73	217	4,550
Don Massengale	72	73	72	217	4,550
Doug Dalziel	76	70	72	218	4,050
Doug Sanders	77	71	71	219	3,675
Jim King	77	69	73	219	3,675
Ken Still	72	72	76	220	3,093.75
Chi Chi Rodriguez	75	74	71	220	3,093.75
Denny Felton	72	76	72	220	3,093.75
Miller Barber	74	69	77	220	3,093.75
Charles Owens	71	76	74	221	2,712.50
Tommy Aaron	71	78	72	221	2,712.50
Dan Morgan	76	72	74	222	2,525
Charles Sifford	78	73	72	223	2,212.50
Joe Jimenez	72	78	73	223	2,212.50
Al Kelley	75	78	70	223	2,212.50
Harold Henning	72	74	77	223	2,212.50
Ray Montgomery	74	78	72	224	1,787.50
Mike Fetchick	72	76	76	224	1,787.50
George Lanning	81	73	70	224	1,787.50
Gene Borek	77	71	76	224	1,787.50
Bob Erickson	79	76	70	225	1,525
Gordon Jones	77	76	72	225	1,525
Jim Cochran	73	77	75	225	1,525
Art Silvestrone	74	76	76	226	1,250
Quinton Gray	73	74	79	226	1,250
Fred Hawkins	73	74	79	226	1,250
Jimmy Powell	76	74	76	226	1,250
Larry Mowry	72	81	73	226	1,250
J.C. Goosie	76	73	77	226	1,250

Las Vegas Classic

Desert Inn and Country Club, Las Vegas, Nevada
Par 36-36 — 72; 6,824 yards

November 6-8
purse, $250,000

	SCORES			TOTAL	MONEY
Al Geiberger	68	73	62	203	$37,500
Chi Chi Rodriguez	71	70	66	207	22,500
Bob Charles	67	69	72	208	17,187.50
Charles Coody	71	68	69	208	17,187.50
Arnold Palmer	69	71	69	209	12,500
Bobby Nichols	69	71	70	210	9,062.50
Miller Barber	71	71	68	210	9,062.50
Orville Moody	69	75	67	211	7,812.50
Bruce Crampton	72	72	67	211	7,812.50
Lee Elder	72	72	68	212	6,875

	SCORES			TOTAL	MONEY
Don January	71	71	71	213	6,062.50
Bob Erickson	70	72	71	213	6,062.50
Dale Douglass	77	68	70	215	5,083.34
Gary Player	70	73	72	215	5,083.33
Gordon Jones	72	71	72	215	5,083.33
Bob Toski	73	73	70	216	3,767.86
Walter Zembriski	76	72	68	216	3,767.86
Bob Brue	70	72	74	216	3,767.86
Billy Casper	71	74	71	216	3,767.86
J.C. Goosie	74	72	70	216	3,767.86
Ben Smith	71	75	70	216	3,767.85
Gene Littler	73	73	70	216	3,767.85
Don Massengale	72	72	73	217	2,937.50
Bruce Devlin	72	74	71	217	2,937.50
Ken Still	70	74	74	218	2,687.50
Harold Henning	74	73	71	218	2,687.50
Jimmy Powell	72	71	76	219	2,437.50
Joe Jimenez	72	74	73	219	2,437.50
Doug Sanders	71	78	71	220	2,125
Tommy Aaron	72	77	71	220	2,125
Howie Johnson	74	76	70	220	2,125
Charles Owens	74	76	71	221	1,875
Bob Stone	74	77	71	222	1,731.25
Jim Ferree	73	76	73	222	1,731.25
Fred Hawkins	74	78	71	223	1,606.25
Rafe Botts	70	78	75	223	1,606.25
Butch Baird	75	77	72	224	1,387.50
Dow Finsterwald	74	75	75	224	1,387.50
Mike Fetchick	78	73	73	224	1,387.50
Doug Ford	72	78	74	224	1,387.50
Dave Hill	72	79	73	224	1,387.50

Fairfield Barnett Classic

Suntree Country Club, Melbourne, Florida
Par 36-36 — 72; 6,590 yards

November 13-15
purse, $200,000

	SCORES			TOTAL	MONEY
Dave Hill	68	66	68	202	$30,000
Al Geiberger	72	67	68	207	15,500
Lee Elder	68	71	68	207	15,500
Larry Mowry	69	68	71	208	10,550
Bruce Crampton	71	66	71	208	10,550
Gene Littler	72	66	71	209	7,100
Art Wall	72	69	69	210	5,850
Walter Zembriski	70	71	69	210	5,850
Doug Sanders	68	73	69	210	5,850
Bob Charles	72	70	68	210	5,850
Doug Dalziel	70	72	69	211	4,175
Dale Douglass	68	71	72	211	4,175
J.C. Goosie	68	73	70	211	4,175
Buck Adams	75	69	67	211	4,175
Chi Chi Rodriguez	70	68	74	212	3,300
Bobby Nichols	67	69	76	212	3,300
Jim Ferree	71	71	70	212	3,300
John Brodie	73	70	69	212	3,300
Jim King	73	71	69	213	2,633.34

	SCORES			TOTAL	MONEY
Bruce Devlin	68	73	72	213	2,633.33
Miller Barber	73	69	71	213	2,633.33
Joe Jimenez	70	70	74	214	2,400
Howie Johnson	70	73	72	215	2,200
Al Kelley	72	68	75	215	2,200
Gordon Jones	69	71	75	215	2,200
Arnold Palmer	71	71	74	216	1,950
Bob Brue	69	74	73	216	1,950
Jimmy Powell	71	74	72	217	1,650
Bill Johnston	69	71	77	217	1,650
George Lanning	73	69	75	217	1,650
Charles Coody	69	74	74	217	1,650
Charles Owens	73	69	76	218	1,375
Charles Sifford	71	72	75	218	1,375
Roland Stafford	77	71	70	218	1,375
Don Massengale	74	71	73	218	1,375
Ken Still	74	71	74	219	1,200
Ralph Terry	70	77	72	219	1,200
Charles Mehok	74	71	74	219	1,200
Ben Smith	72	76	72	220	1,000
Mike Souchak	77	71	72	220	1,000
Fred Hawkins	73	72	75	220	1,000
Mike Fetchick	74	71	75	220	1,000
Butch Baird	73	72	75	220	1,000

Gus Machado Classic

Key Biscayne Golf Club, Key Biscayne, Florida
Par 35-36 — 71; 6,715 yards

November 20-22
purse, $300,000

	SCORES			TOTAL	MONEY
Gene Littler	71	67	69	207	$45,000
Orville Moody	69	70	71	210	26,000
Bob Toski	71	70	70	211	18,000
Larry Mowry	70	70	71	211	18,000
Bob Charles	69	70	72	211	18,000
Roland Stafford	72	70	70	212	10,550
Dale Douglass	74	69	69	212	10,550
Chi Chi Rodriguez	74	70	70	214	9,250
Lee Elder	69	72	74	215	8,525
Walter Zembriski	70	77	69	216	7,450
Bob Brue	69	74	73	216	7,450
Charles Owens	70	75	72	217	5,233.34
Bob Erickson	72	73	72	217	5,233.34
Billy Casper	73	73	71	217	5,233.34
Doug Sanders	73	71	73	217	5,233.33
Al Kelley	74	73	70	217	5,233.33
Don Massengale	74	72	71	217	5,233.33
Al Geiberger	74	75	68	217	5,233.33
Tommy Aaron	71	71	75	217	5,233.33
Miller Barber	72	71	74	217	5,233.33
Harold Henning	73	70	75	218	3,500
Dave Hill	73	72	73	218	3,500
Butch Baird	72	71	75	218	3,500
James Barber	74	70	74	218	3,500
John Brodie	72	70	76	218	3,500
Pat Schwab	69	73	77	219	2,975

	SCORES			TOTAL	MONEY
Gordon Jones	71	75	73	219	2,975
Bruce Crampton	72	71	77	220	2,608.34
Ken Still	74	72	74	220	2,608.33
Charles Coody	74	71	75	220	2,608.33
Bobby Nichols	74	74	73	221	2,287.50
Jim Ferree	73	75	73	221	2,287.50
Dick Peacock	73	78	71	222	1,900
Bob Goalby	78	68	76	222	1,900
Howie Johnson	77	73	72	222	1,900
Fred Hawkins	73	77	72	222	1,900
Bruce Devlin	70	80	72	222	1,900
Gay Brewer	80	70	72	222	1,900
Ben Smith	74	71	79	224	1,512.50
Charles Sifford	74	75	75	224	1,512.50
Doug Dalziel	75	75	74	224	1,512.50
Julius Boros	76	73	75	224	1,512.50

Mauna Lani Challenge

Mauna Lani Bay Resort, Hawaii, Hawaii
Par 36-36 — 72

December 4-6
purse, $300,000

	SCORES			TOTAL	MONEY
Bob Charles	68	70	69	207	$45,000
Dale Douglass	77	65	67	209	22,500
Ben Smith	74	71	67	212	15,000
Chi Chi Rodriguez	72	70	70	212	15,000
Al Geiberger	71	72	70	213	9,000
Bruce Devlin	74	63	76	213	9,000
Dave Hill	71	70	73	214	6,000
Bob Erickson	71	71	73	215	5,400
Jim King	72	71	73	216	4,500
Bobby Nichols	70	73	73	216	4,500
Bruce Crampton	72	70	75	217	3,318
Orville Moody	69	70	78	217	3,318
Harold Henning	72	75	70	217	3,318
Peter Thomson	74	73	70	217	3,318
Tommy Aaron	70	74	74	218	2,925
John Kalinka	73	75	70	218	2,925
Mike Fetchick	73	74	71	218	2,925
Bob Brue	75	71	73	219	2,700
Don Massengale	77	71	72	220	2,475
Gordon Jones	74	72	74	220	2,475

GTE Kaanapali Classic

Royal Kaanapali Golf Club, North Course, Kaanapali, Maui
Par 36-36 — 72; 6,750 yards

December 11-13
purse, $300,000

	SCORES		TOTAL	MONEY
Orville Moody	65	67	132	$45,000
John Brodie	68	67	135	26,000
Dave Hill	68	68	136	21,500
Bob Charles	70	67	137	18,000
Bobby Nichols	67	71	138	12,800

	SCORES		TOTAL	MONEY
Bruce Devlin	75	63	138	12,800
Al Geiberger	70	69	139	8,893.75
Tommy Aaron	69	70	139	8,893.75
Charles Coody	67	72	139	8,893.75
Doug Dalziel	68	71	139	8,893.75
Harold Henning	72	68	140	7,100
Jim King	70	71	141	6,400
Dale Douglass	68	73	141	6,400
Bob Erickson	73	69	142	5,200
Don January	70	72	142	5,200
Jack Fleck	69	73	142	5,200
Bruce Crampton	70	72	142	5,200
Gene Borek	72	70	142	5,200
Chi Chi Rodriguez	71	72	143	4,150
Peter Thomson	71	72	143	4,150
Ben Smith	72	72	144	3,127.50
Ralph Terry	71	73	144	3,127.50
Bob Toski	72	72	144	3,127.50
Al Kelley	73	71	144	3,127.50
Gene Littler	69	75	144	3,127.50
El Collins	73	71	144	3,127.50
Bob Brue	71	73	144	3,127.50
Kyle Burton	72	72	144	3,127.50
Billy Casper	73	71	144	3,127.50
Jim Cochran	71	73	144	3,127.50
Ray Beallo	73	72	145	2,287.50
Dow Finsterwald	71	74	145	2,287.50
Bob Stone	71	75	146	1,821.88
Don Massengale	71	75	146	1,821.88
Howie Johnson	73	73	146	1,821.88
Miller Barber	73	73	146	1,821.88
Don Schuppert	72	74	146	1,821.87
Ken Still	72	74	146	1,821.87
John Kalinka	73	73	146	1,821.87
George Bayer	74	72	146	1,821.87

Mazda Champions

Tryall Golf and Beach Club, Sandy Bay, Jamaica
Par 34-37 — 71; 6,324 yards

December 18-20
purse, $850,000

	SCORES			TOTAL	MONEY (Each)
Miller Barber/Nancy Lopez	65	63	63	191	$250,000
Arnold Palmer/Colleen Walker	65	62	67	194	50,000
Orville Moody/Jan Stephenson	68	64	64	196	22,500
Bruce Crampton/Betsy King	68	63	65	196	22,500
Gene Littler/Jody Rosenthal	69	63	65	197	14,333.50
Don January/Juli Inkster	66	65	66	197	14,333.50
Butch Baird/Chris Johnson	64	65	68	197	14,333
Dale Douglass/Rosie Jones	67	66	65	198	9,000
Billy Casper/Patty Sheehan	67	64	67	198	9,000
Chi Chi Rodriguez/Ayako Okamoto	68	65	67	200	7,000
Bob Charles/Jane Geddes	70	63	68	201	6,250
Bobby Nichols/Kathy Postlewait	67	68	69	204	5,750

The European Tour

Moroccan Open

Royal Golf Dar Es Salaam, Rabat, Morocco
Par 36-37 — 73; 7,362 yards

March 19-22
purse, £165,000

	SCORES				TOTAL	MONEY
Howard Clark	73	73	66	72	284	£27,500
Mark James	71	70	72	74	287	18,320
Peter Baker	71	72	77	68	288	10,330
Sam Torrance	75	73	71	70	289	8,220
Ron Commans	74	72	71	73	290	5,950
Manuel Pinero	75	73	70	72	290	5,950
Ian Woosnam	72	71	73	74	290	5,950
Jose-Maria Olazabal	71	75	72	73	291	3,915
Ian Young	75	71	69	76	291	3,915
Jimmy Heggarty	70	78	69	75	292	3,175
Wayne Riley	75	76	70	71	292	3,175
Eamonn Darcy	67	75	76	75	293	2,665
Mark Mouland	71	75	75	72	293	2,665
Ronan Rafferty	73	71	72	77	293	2,665
Andrew Stubbs	70	72	76	75	293	2,665
Gordon Brand Jr.	71	77	73	73	294	2,290
Ignacio De Leon	70	72	73	79	294	2,290
Christy O'Connor Jr.	70	75	75	74	294	2,290
Jose-Maria Canizares	73	73	76	73	295	1,891.43
Roger Chapman	73	72	74	76	295	1,891.43
Mark Davis	72	73	74	76	295	1,891.43
David Feherty	77	71	72	75	295	1,891.43
Anders Forsbrand	71	77	71	76	295	1,891.43
Miguel Martin	72	75	75	73	295	1,891.43
Paul Thomas	76	73	75	71	295	1,891.43
Gordon J. Brand	75	74	73	74	296	1,580
Tony Charnley	73	72	76	75	296	1,580
Barry Lane	75	74	75	72	296	1,580
Andrew Oldcorn	73	74	72	77	296	1,580
Martin Poxon	69	75	74	78	296	1,580
David Llewellyn	68	78	75	76	297	1,362.50
David J. Russell	73	75	74	75	297	1,362.50
Andrew Sherborne	75	72	73	77	297	1,362.50
David Williams	76	74	72	75	297	1,362.50
Dana Banke	73	72	78	75	298	1,100
Richard Boxall	77	73	77	71	298	1,100
Denis Durnian	75	76	73	74	298	1,100
Richard Fish	75	74	72	77	298	1,100
Rick Hartmann	75	74	73	76	298	1,100
Jose Rivero	77	73	74	74	298	1,100
Ove Sellberg	73	73	75	77	298	1,100
Sandy Stephen	71	74	81	72	298	1,100
Steen Tinning	74	74	77	73	298	1,100
David Gilford	71	74	75	79	299	830
Yvon Houssin	72	72	76	79	299	830
Magnus Persson	78	72	75	74	299	830
David Ray	75	74	73	77	299	830
Des Smyth	75	75	72	77	299	830
Ronald Stelten	72	77	76	74	299	830
Glyn Davies	74	73	77	76	300	750

Jersey Open

La Moye Golf Club, St. Brelade, Jersey
Par 36-36 — 72; 6,759 yards

April 9-12
purse, £97,000

	SCORES				TOTAL	MONEY
Ian Woosnam	68	67	72	72	279	£16,160
Bill Malley	69	72	69	70	280	10,760
Jose-Maria Canizares	68	74	67	72	281	5,460
David A. Russell	69	67	71	74	281	5,460
Bernard Gallacher	71	67	73	71	282	3,750
Sam Torrance	70	72	71	69	282	3,750
Anders Forsbrand	72	70	73	68	283	2,496.67
Andrew Murray	70	69	73	71	283	2,496.67
David J. Russell	68	71	72	72	283	2,496.66
Denis Durnian	71	68	70	75	284	1,860
Christy O'Connor Jr.	70	68	76	70	284	1,860
Lee Jones	70	69	75	71	285	1,504
Mark Mouland	69	71	67	78	285	1,504
John O'Leary	70	71	72	72	285	1,504
Martin Poxon	71	69	74	71	285	1,504
Ronan Rafferty	68	69	73	75	285	1,504
Michael Allen	71	69	75	71	286	1,214
Roger Chapman	74	71	71	70	286	1,214
Michael McLean	67	70	73	76	286	1,214
Philip Walton	70	69	76	71	286	1,214
Peter Mitchell	73	67	72	74	286	1,214
Peter Baker	71	73	73	70	287	1,050
Stephen Bennett	73	70	71	73	287	1,050
Richard Boxall	75	70	71	71	287	1,050
David Llewellyn	70	75	71	71	287	1,050
Gerry Taylor	70	73	74	70	287	1,050
Warren Humphreys	72	68	75	74	288	874.29
Michael King	65	76	73	74	288	874.29
Brian Marchbank	73	72	73	70	288	874.29
Miguel Martin	70	72	72	74	288	874.29
Magnus Persson	69	71	76	72	288	874.29
Glenn Ralph	72	68	75	73	288	874.29
Des Smyth	69	68	77	74	288	874.29
Justin Hobday	68	73	73	75	289	730
Bill Longmuir	71	70	73	75	289	730
John Morgan	70	72	71	76	289	730
Frank Nobilo	68	73	76	72	289	730
Mark Roe	73	70	74	72	289	730
Paul Way	71	70	74	74	289	730
Eamonn Darcy	70	72	77	71	290	620
David Jones	75	70	78	67	290	620
Carl Mason	74	70	72	74	290	620
Bill McColl	74	71	72	73	290	620
Wayne Smith	70	72	77	71	290	620
Gordon J. Brand	73	70	78	70	291	480
Gordon Brand Jr.	72	69	79	71	291	480
Neil Hansen	74	70	74	73	291	480
Rick Hartmann	73	72	74	72	291	480
Jimmy Heggarty	73	72	73	73	291	480
David Ray	72	70	77	72	291	480
Andrew Sherborne	71	69	76	75	291	480
Grant Turner	69	73	75	74	291	480
Keith Waters	66	72	75	78	291	480

Suze (Cannes) Open

Cannes Mougins Golf Club, Cannes, France
Par 36-36 — 72; 6,786 yards

April 16-19
purse, £152,905

	SCORES				TOTAL	MONEY
Severiano Ballesteros	69	70	68	68	275	£25,484.20
Ian Woosnam	73	64	68	70	275	16,992.86
(Ballesteros defeated Woosnam on first hole of playoff.)						
Mark McNulty	68	74	70	71	283	9,561.67
Philip Walton	72	69	69	75	285	7,645.26
Gordon Brand Jr.	69	74	72	71	286	6,483.18
Mitch Adcock	73	68	73	73	287	4,969.42
Miguel Martin	70	73	73	71	287	4,969.42
Gordon J. Brand	74	72	70	72	288	3,057.25
David Jones	71	70	76	71	288	3,057.25
Chris Moody	73	68	76	71	288	3,057.25
Magnus Persson	71	72	72	73	288	3,057.25
Glenn Ralph	73	70	77	68	288	3,057.25
Sam Torrance	72	70	72	74	288	3,057.25
Richard Boxall	72	75	72	70	289	2,349.64
Howard Clark	75	71	69	74	289	2,349.64
Des Smyth	73	71	73	73	290	2,130.48
Greg Turner	74	73	75	68	290	2,130.48
Paul Curry	70	70	75	76	291	1,916.41
Neil Hansen	75	72	73	71	291	1,916.41
Gavin Levenson	73	71	72	75	291	1,916.41
Anders Forsbrand	74	72	70	76	292	1,653.07
Warren Humphreys	78	72	70	72	292	1,653.07
Bill McColl	73	71	72	76	292	1,653.07
Mark Roe	77	71	74	70	292	1,653.07
John Slaughter	72	71	71	78	282	1,653.07
David Williams	76	68	72	76	292	1,653.07
John Morgan	73	74	74	72	293	1,447.50
Manuel Pinero	73	76	71	73	293	1,447.50
Dillard Pruitt	74	75	72	72	293	1,447.50
Peter Senior	71	71	74	77	293	1,447.50
Emmanuel Dussart	72	76	73	73	294	1,243.63
Jeff Hawkes	72	71	75	76	294	1,243.63
Michael King	75	71	74	74	294	1,243.63
Frank Nobilo	75	75	73	71	294	1,243.63
Ove Sellberg	73	74	73	74	294	1,243.63
Wayne Smith	73	72	74	75	294	1,243.63
John Bland	75	71	74	75	295	983.69
Giuseppe Cali	73	74	74	74	295	983.69
Jimmy Heggarty	73	71	73	78	295	983.69
Mats Lanner	73	71	75	76	295	983.69
Bill Longmuir	72	75	70	78	295	983.69
Brian Marchbank	75	74	70	76	295	983.69
Paul Thomas	73	73	74	75	295	983.69
Simon Bishop	71	72	76	77	296	818.89
Malcolm Mackenzie	72	72	76	76	296	818.89
John O'Leary	74	73	74	75	296	818.89
John Clifford	78	72	71	76	297	754.33
Antonio Garrido	74	71	80	72	297	754.33
Frederic Regard	78	70	74	75	297	754.33
Roger Chapman	75	70	76	77	298	693.17
Tony Charnley	73	73	77	75	298	693.17
Jacques France	75	74	75	74	298	693.17

Cepsa Madrid Open

Puerta de Hierro Golf Club, Madrid, Spain   April 22-25
Par 36-36 — 72; 6,941 yards   purse, £165,000

	SCORES				TOTAL	MONEY
Ian Woosnam	67	67	69	66	269	£27,500
Wayne Grady	67	73	68	64	272	18,320
Severiano Ballesteros	69	67	71	66	273	10,330
Nick Faldo	70	71	69	64	274	8,220
Jose Rivero	69	70	72	66	277	7,000
Howard Clark	72	68	71	68	279	5,850
Ove Sellberg	71	72	69	69	281	5,000
John Bland	68	74	69	71	282	3,710
Mark Mouland	73	70	70	69	282	3,710
Roman Rafferty	70	74	69	69	282	3,710
Tony Charnley	72	74	68	69	283	3,050
Denis Durnian	69	69	73	73	284	2,790
Ian Mosey	69	70	73	72	284	2,790
Gordon J. Brand	68	68	76	73	285	2,390
Jose-Maria Canizares	72	69	75	69	285	2,390
John Clifford	72	75	69	69	285	2,390
Manuel Pinero	69	74	70	72	285	2,390
Mark Roe	74	70	72	69	285	2,390
Paul Curry	70	71	73	72	286	1,918.33
Mats Lanner	69	76	69	72	286	1,918.33
Jose-Maria Olazabal	70	69	75	72	286	1,918.33
Martin Poxon	71	76	74	65	286	1,918.33
Sam Torrance	71	72	72	71	286	1,918.33
Grant Turner	71	73	70	72	286	1,918.33
Eamonn Darcy	69	77	70	71	287	1,655
Jeff Hawkes	72	71	71	73	287	1,655
Miguel Martin	72	73	71	71	287	1,655
Wayne Smith	74	73	72	68	287	1,655
Des Smyth	68	76	73	71	288	1,530
Michael Allen	70	71	73	75	289	1,455
Bill Longmuir	75	71	68	75	289	1,455
Andrew Chandler	71	75	70	74	290	1,240
Jose Davila	71	77	73	69	290	1,240
Vicente Fernandez	74	74	71	71	290	1,240
Bernard Gallacher	71	74	73	72	290	1,240
Warren Humphreys	70	77	72	71	290	1,240
Glenn Ralph	71	74	71	74	290	1,240
David J. Russell	71	70	74	75	290	1,240
Bob E. Smith	74	74	73	69	290	1,240
Ron Commans	72	73	72	74	291	1,040
Carl Mason	71	75	73	72	291	1,040
Neil Hansen	67	76	73	76	292	960
Grant Turner	68	75	74	75	292	960
Antonio Garrido	73	74	73	73	293	842
Philip Harrison	74	73	75	71	293	842
Mark James	72	74	74	73	293	842
Brian Marchbank	69	75	77	72	293	842
Ronald Stelten	71	76	70	76	293	842
Manuel Calero	71	75	76	72	294	740
Mark McNulty	74	72	73	75	294	740
Christy O'Connor Jr.	74	73	74	73	294	740
Philip Walton	69	79	71	75	294	740

Italian Open

Monticello Golf Club, Milan, Italy
Par 36-36 — 72; 7,054 yards

April 30-May 3
purse, £141,045

	SCORES				TOTAL	MONEY
Sam Torrance	64	68	71	68	271	£23,507.28
Jose Rivero	68	69	68	66	271	15,655.85
(Torrance defeated Rivero on sixth hole of playoff.)						
Nick Faldo	70	67	69	66	272	8,819.93
Peter Senior	70	67	68	70	275	7,052.19
David Feherty	71	68	69	68	276	5,458.39
Ronan Rafferty	70	71	68	67	276	5,458.39
Miguel Martin	69	71	67	71	278	3,878.70
David J. Russell	71	69	68	70	278	3,878.70
Barry Lake	70	69	73	67	279	2,858.48
Robert Lee	70	70	70	59	279	2,858.48
Malcolm Mackenzie	70	67	73	69	279	2,858.48
Hugh Baiocchi	72	70	71	67	280	2,232.02
Eamonn Darcy	73	67	67	73	280	2,232.02
Denis Durnian	70	69	70	71	280	2,232.02
Bill Longmuir	73	71	69	67	280	2,232.02
Gordon Brand Jr.	75	66	69	71	281	1,865.30
John O'Leary	71	73	71	66	281	1,865.30
Ove Sellberg	72	69	72	68	281	1,865.30
Andrew Stubbs	73	67	72	69	281	1,865.30
Michael Allen	70	72	70	70	282	1,607.90
Neil Hansen	72	70	70	70	282	1,607.90
Bob E. Smith	70	68	71	73	282	1,607.90
Grant Turner	73	70	69	70	282	1,607.90
Bruce Zabriski	73	71	68	70	282	1,607.90
Mitch Adcock	71	70	70	72	283	1,417.49
Jose-Maria Canizares	72	71	72	68	283	1,417.49
Vicente Fernandez	71	72	69	71	283	1,417.49
Andrew Murray	72	71	68	72	283	1,417.49
Stephen Bennett	73	71	69	71	284	1,181.24
Giuseppe Cali	75	67	74	68	284	1,181.24
Mike Clayton	70	71	70	73	284	1,181.24
Derrick Cooper	74	70	67	73	284	1,181.24
David Gilford	73	71	69	71	284	1,181.24
Magnus Persson	72	68	71	73	284	1,181.24
Manuel Pinero	68	72	72	72	284	1,181.24
Edward Webber	71	72	73	68	284	1,181.24
Emmanuel Dussart	74	69	72	70	285	1,001.41
Andrew Sherborne	71	72	69	73	285	1,001.41
Magnus Sunesson	72	71	72	70	285	1,001.41
Steen Tinning	71	70	73	71	285	1,001.41
Tony Charnley	73	71	70	72	286	846.26
Sandy Lyle	74	69	72	71	286	846.26
David Ray	71	71	70	74	286	846.26
Costantino Rocca	73	71	69	73	286	846.26
Mark Roe	73	71	73	69	286	846.26
John Slaughter	73	70	73	70	286	846.26
Alessandro Rogato	71	72	69	74	286	846.26
Baldovino Dassu	71	72	68	76	287	662.91
Rick Hartmann	71	73	71	72	287	662.91
Armando Saavedra	70	73	71	73	287	662.91
Sandy Stephen	71	69	73	74	287	662.91
David Williams	70	72	75	70	287	662.91
Alberto Croce	70	73	74	70	287	662.91

Epson Grand Prix of Europe Match Play Championship

St. Pierre Golf and Country Club, Chepstow, England
Par 35-36 — 71; 6,700 yards

May 7-10
purse, £250,000

FIRST ROUND

Brian Marchbank defeated Jose-Maria Canizares, 2 up.
Philip Walton defeated Philip Parkin, 3 and 1.
John O'Leary defeated Andrew Chandler, 2 and 1.
Miguel Martin defeated Bernard Gallacher, 4 and 2.
Manuel Pinero defeated Stephen Bennett, 4 and 3.
Antonio Garrido defeated Roger Chapman, 1 up, 22 holes.
Sam Torrance defeated Carl Mason, 3 and 2.
John Morgan defeated Mark James, 1 up.
Mark Roe defeated Tony Johnstone, 2 and 1.
Tommy Armour III defeated John Bland, 3 and 2.
Ove Sellberg defeated Eamonn Darcy, 2 and 1.
Jeff Hawkes defeated David Feherty, 1 up.
Vaughan Somers defeated Nick Faldo, 4 and 2.
Robert Lee defeated Paul Thomas, 5 and 4.
Greg Turner defeated Ross Drummond, 2 and 1.
Gordon Brand Jr. defeated Vicente Fernandez, 1 up.
Des Smyth defeated Christy O'Connor Jr., 3 and 2.
Mats Lanner defeated Ian Baker-Finch, 5 and 3.
Neil Hansen defeated Peter Fowler, 3 and 1.
Ian Mosey defeated Rick Hartmann, 3 and 2.
Hugh Biaocchi defeated Michael McLean, 3 and 1.
Jose Rivero defeated Ronan Rafferty, 3 and 2.
Mark Mouland defeated Mike Clayton, 4 and 2.
Peter Senior defeated Anders Forsbrand, 2 and 1.
(All first-round losers received £1,500)

SECOND ROUND

Severiano Ballesteros defeated Marchbank, 3 and 2.
Walton defeated O'Leary, 1 up.
Pinero defeated Martin, 1 up.
Garrido defeated Rodger Davis, 1 up.
Torrance defeated Ian Woosnam, 3 and 2.
Morgan defeated Roe, 4 and 3.
Armour defeated Sellberg, 1 up, 20 holes.
Hawkes defeated Howard Clark, 3 and 2.
Jose-Maria Olazabal defeated Somers, 1 up.
Turner defeated Lee, 1 up, 23 holes.
Smyth defeated Brand Jr., 1 up.
Lanner defeated Gordon J. Brand, 4 and 2.
Mark McNulty defeated Hansen, 4 and 3.
Baiocchi defeated Mosey, 3 and 2.
Rivero defeated Mouland, 2 and 1.
Senior defeated Bernhard Langer, 1 up.
(All second-round losers received £3,000)

THIRD ROUND

Ballesteros defeated Walton, 3 and 2.
Pinero defeated Garrido, 2 up.
Torrance defeated Morgan, 1 up.
Hawkes defeated Armour, 3 and 1.
Turner defeated Olazabal, 1 up.
Lanner defeated Smyth, 1 up, 19 holes.
Baiocchi defeated McNulty, 1 up.

Senior defeated Rivero, 2 and 1.
(All third-round losers received £4,500)

QUARTER-FINALS

Ballesteros defeated Pinero, 3 and 1.
Hawkes defeated Torrance, 1 up.
Lanner defeated Turner, 3 and 2.
Senior defeated Baiocchi, 1 up.
(All quarter-final losers received £7,500)

SEMI-FINALS

Hawkes defeated Ballesteros, 4 and 3.
Lanner defeated Senior, 1 up.

PLAYOFF FOR THIRD-FOURTH PLACE

Ballesteros defeated Senior, 1 up, 19 holes.
(Ballesteros received £15,000, Senior £10,000)

FINAL

Lanner defeated Hawkes, 1 up.
(Lanner received £50,000, Hawkes £25,000)

Peugeot Spanish Open

Las Brisas Golf Club, Malaga, Spain
Par 37-35 — 72; 6,817 yards

May 14-17
purse, £175,000

	SCORES				TOTAL	MONEY
Nick Faldo	72	72	71	72	286	£29,160
Hugh Baiocchi	73	69	72	74	288	15,195
Severiano Ballesteros	70	72	74	72	288	15,195
Jerry Anderson	75	72	72	72	291	8,750
Mark James	77	72	72	71	292	7,400
Mark McNulty	77	70	74	72	293	5,675
Ronan Rafferty	72	72	76	73	293	5,675
Rodger Davis	71	78	73	72	294	3,853.33
Sandy Lyle	74	70	75	75	294	3,853.33
Lyndsay Stephen	73	71	77	73	294	3,853.33
Eamonn Darcy	74	74	70	77	295	3,260
Vicente Fernandez	74	75	75	72	296	2,980
Christy O'Connor Jr.	69	76	73	78	296	2,980
Denis Durnian	71	69	81	76	297	2,511.67
Wayne Grady	74	73	75	75	297	2,511.67
Mike Harwood	79	72	76	70	297	2,511.67
Philip Parkin	74	71	77	75	297	2,511.67
Jose Rivero	77	70	78	72	297	2,511.67
Ian Woosnam	71	74	75	77	297	2,511.67
John Bland	74	78	72	74	298	1,955
Peter Fowler	75	74	75	74	298	1,955
Bernard Gallacher	75	73	74	76	298	1,955
Jeff Hawkes	71	81	73	73	298	1,955
Mats Lanner	69	75	74	80	298	1,955
Andrew Murray	74	74	74	76	298	1,955
Dillard Pruitt	77	72	72	77	298	1,955
Steen Tinning	75	77	73	73	298	1,955
Richard Boxall	73	79	70	77	299	1,577.50
Bill Malley	74	74	74	77	299	1,577.50

	SCORES				TOTAL	MONEY
Frederic Regard	74	74	76	75	299	1,577.50
Aughan Somers	76	75	71	77	299	1,577.50
Juan Anglada	73	77	75	75	300	1,420
Bill Longmuir	78	73	71	78	300	1,420
Malcolm Mackenzie	76	74	77	73	300	1,420
Manuel Calero	80	73	73	75	301	1,240
Lee Jones	76	75	75	75	301	1,240
Barry Lane	75	77	74	75	301	1,240
Carl Mason	77	72	76	76	301	1,240
David Williams	75	77	73	76	301	1,240
Manuel Montes	73	73	79	76	301	1,240
Howard Clark	74	76	78	74	302	1,020
Frank Nobilo	72	80	75	75	302	1,020
Sam Torrance	75	76	70	81	302	1,020
Grant Turner	78	73	76	75	302	1,020
Manuel Sanchez	76	75	79	72	302	1,020
David Jones	76	77	75	75	303	885
Santiago Luna	70	74	82	77	303	885
Mariano Aparicio	74	76	80	74	304	782
Martin Poxon	74	75	81	74	304	782
Peter Senior	77	76	74	77	304	782
Des Smyth	75	74	79	76	304	782
Keith Waters	75	77	79	73	304	782

Whyte & Mackay PGA Championship

Wentworth Club, West Course, Virginia Water, England
Par 35-37 — 72; 6,945 yards

May 22-25
purse, £220,000

	SCORES				TOTAL	MONEY
Bernhard Langer	66	69	68	67	270	£36,660
Severiano Ballesteros	70	67	68	69	274	24,440
Jose-Maria Canizares	68	69	72	69	278	12,380
Peter Senior	70	71	71	66	278	12,380
Ian Baker-Finch	71	68	71	70	280	7,280
Ken Brown	71	71	69	69	280	7,280
Wayne Grady	75	71	66	68	280	7,280
Rick Hartmann	68	69	73	70	280	7,280
Ian Mosey	72	72	68	69	281	4,920
Lyndsay Stephen	72	71	72	67	282	4,400
Peter Fowler	71	75	73	64	283	3,920
Sandy Lyle	76	70	68	69	283	3,920
Rodger Davis	75	73	71	65	284	3,480
Bernard Gallacher	74	71	69	70	284	3,480
John Bland	72	72	71	70	285	3,030
Philip Parkin	74	70	70	71	285	3,030
Ove Sellberg	72	72	70	71	285	3,030
Ian Woosnam	69	78	70	68	285	3,030
Gordon Brand Jr.	74	71	71	70	286	2,683.33
Jose-Maria Olazabal	71	75	70	70	286	2,683.33
Jose Rivero	73	74	73	66	286	2,683.33
Howard Clark	78	69	73	67	287	2,400
Mike Clayton	74	74	70	69	287	2,400
Eamonn Darcy	71	71	76	69	287	2,400
Anders Forsbrand	73	71	71	72	287	2,400
Stephen McAllister	71	71	75	70	287	2,400
Denis Durnian	69	74	74	71	288	2,015

	SCORES				TOTAL	MONEY
Antonio Garrido	74	73	68	73	288	2,015
Mark Mouland	71	74	71	72	288	2,015
Ronan Rafferty	74	73	75	66	288	2,015
David A Russell	74	72	72	70	288	2,015
David J. Russell	71	76	68	73	288	2,015
Hugh Baiocchi	73	70	76	70	289	1,650
Ross Drummond	70	74	75	70	289	1,650
Vicente Fernandez	72	73	73	71	289	1,650
Neil Hansen	73	71	74	71	289	1,650
Christy O'Connor Jr.	72	73	70	74	289	1,650
David Williams	72	72	72	73	289	1,650
Nick Faldo	70	77	72	71	290	1,440
David Jones	77	71	71	71	290	1,440
Sam Torrance	76	67	75	72	290	1,440
Keith Waters	71	75	71	73	290	1,440
Bill McColl	74	73	71	73	291	1,340
Tony Charnley	74	74	72	72	292	1,240
Robert Lee	70	77	73	72	292	1,240
Gavin Levenson	74	74	75	69	292	1,240
Des Smyth	75	71	69	77	292	1,240
Roger Chapman	72	76	72	73	293	1,080
Miguel Martin	69	71	71	82	293	1,080
Eddie Polland	75	73	75	70	293	1,080
Vaughan Somers	74	72	73	74	293	1,080
Manuel Calero	74	74	72	74	294	940
Mike Harwood	71	74	76	73	294	940
Andrew Oldcorn	71	77	71	75	294	940
Ron Commans	73	72	75	75	295	782

London Standard Four Stars National Pro-Celebrity

Moor Park Golf Club, Rickmansworth, England
Par 37-35 — 72; 6,817 yards

May 28-31
purse, £138,500

	SCORES				TOTAL	MONEY
Mark McNulty	70	67	69	67	273	£21,660
Sam Torrance	67	69	72	65	273	14,440
(McNulty defeated Torrance on second hole of playoff.)						
Tony Charnley	68	69	72	67	276	8,140
Peter Senior	69	68	70	70	277	6,005
Des Smyth	69	70	70	68	277	6,005
Roger Chapman	70	69	71	68	278	4,225
Jim Rutledge	70	70	70	68	278	4,225
Derrick Cooper	69	66	69	75	279	2,918.33
Brian Marchbank	69	68	75	67	279	2,918.33
Lyndsay Stephen	70	70	68	71	279	2,918.33
Robert Lee	69	70	72	69	280	2,330
Carl Mason	69	69	69	73	280	2,330
Jose-Maria Canizares	67	70	74	70	281	2,030
Neil Coles	68	71	71	71	281	2,030
Ron Commans	70	68	73	70	281	2,030
Hugh Baiocchi	68	69	71	74	282	1,688
Ross Drummond	70	70	72	70	282	1,688
Gavin Levenson	68	72	69	73	282	1,688
Frank Nobilo	67	71	74	70	282	1,688
Philip Walton	70	68	73	71	282	1,688
Gordon Brand Jr.	71	69	72	71	283	1,460

	SCORES				TOTAL	MONEY
Denis Durnian	67	71	71	74	283	1,460
Ronald Stelten	70	71	72	70	283	1,460
David Williams	69	74	73	67	283	1,460
Clive Tucker	74	67	69	73	283	1,460
Manuel Calero	73	68	71	72	284	1,300
Wayne Grady	70	71	74	69	284	1,300
David J. Russell	70	73	72	69	284	1,300
Nathaniel Crosby	72	69	73	71	285	1,081.25
Eamonn Darcy	71	72	72	70	285	1,081.25
Neil Hansen	71	72	72	70	285	1,081.25
Rick Hartmann	72	73	71	69	285	1,081.25
Tommy Horton	72	72	72	69	285	1,081.25
Tony Johnstone	72	69	72	72	285	1,081.25
John O'Leary	69	73	73	70	285	1,081.25
Paul Thomas	71	72	72	70	285	1,081.25
Tommy Armour III	74	68	73	71	286	835
Richard Boxall	69	70	75	72	286	835
Antonio Garrido	72	74	69	71	286	835
Warren Humphreys	70	71	74	71	286	835
Barry Lane	73	69	76	68	286	835
Andrew Oldcorn	73	68	72	73	286	835
Peter Teravainen	69	72	74	71	286	835
Andrew Chandler	74	71	76	66	287	670
Vicente Fernandez	71	74	69	73	287	670
Peter Fowler	69	71	74	73	287	670
Bill Longmuir	70	76	71	70	287	670
Chris Moody	75	70	74	68	287	670
Christy O'Connor Jr.	73	69	74	71	287	670
Emilio Rodriguez	70	69	74	74	287	670
Keith Waters	73	70	72	72	287	670

Dunhill British Masters

Woburn Golf and Country Club, Bucks, England
Par 34-38 — 72; 6,913 yards

June 4-7
purse, £200,000

	SCORES				TOTAL	MONEY
Mark McNulty	71	65	71	67	274	£33,333
Ian Woosnam	67	68	72	68	275	21,117
Hugh Baiocchi	67	70	72	69	278	10,690
Christy O'Connor Jr.	71	66	71	70	278	10,690
Jose Rivero	74	67	71	68	280	8,070
Mike Clayton	72	69	71	69	281	6,180
Rodger Davis	72	72	68	69	281	6,180
Ken Brown	71	69	71	71	282	4,275
Eamonn Darcy	70	66	77	69	282	4,275
Brian Marchbank	70	73	71	68	282	4,275
Nick Faldo	71	69	72	71	283	3,326.67
Tony Johnstone	70	70	73	70	283	3,326.67
Mats Lanner	68	70	71	74	283	3,326.67
Carl Mason	68	70	74	72	284	2,855
Mark Roe	73	69	69	73	284	2,855
Sam Torrance	71	68	75	70	284	2,855
John Bland	71	74	69	71	285	2,542.50
Ron Commans	72	69	70	74	285	2,542.50
Ian Baker-Finch	72	70	73	72	287	2,283.33
Bernhard Langer	70	69	75	73	287	2,283.33

	SCORES				TOTAL	MONEY
Manuel Pinero	71	72	72	72	287	2,283.33
Tommy Armour III	69	71	77	71	288	2,070
David Feherty	72	73	74	69	288	2,070
Ove Sellberg	70	69	78	71	288	2,070
Gordon Brand Jr.	70	71	74	74	289	1,870
Roger Chapman	73	72	73	71	289	1,870
Antonio Garrido	68	70	75	76	289	1,870
Rick Hartmann	71	71	75	72	289	1,870
Mark James	72	65	81	71	289	1,870
Ross Drummond	74	72	73	71	290	1,695
Michael King	71	69	72	78	290	1,695
Bill Longmuir	73	73	74	71	291	1,545
Wayne Riley	75	71	73	72	291	1,545
David A. Russell	72	73	70	76	291	1,545
Peter Senior	70	72	73	76	291	1,545
Neil Coles	75	70	76	71	292	1,272.14
Vicente Fernandez	70	72	76	74	292	1,272.14
Anders Forsbrand	75	70	72	75	292	1,272.14
Wayne Grady	74	71	74	73	292	1,272.14
Robert Lee	74	69	75	74	292	1,272.14
Chris Moody	74	72	73	73	292	1,272.14
John Morgan	72	72	74	74	292	1,272.14
David Jones	71	75	74	73	293	1,005
Barry Lane	74	69	78	72	293	1,005
Miguel Martin	75	71	73	74	293	1,005
Andrew Oldcorn	74	72	78	69	293	1,005
Vaughan Somers	73	68	75	77	293	1,005
Brian Waites	76	70	74	73	293	1,005
Jose-Maria Canizares	71	72	75	76	294	835
Tony Charnley	71	71	79	73	294	835
Derrick Cooper	73	68	78	75	294	835
Peter Fowler	74	71	74	75	294	835
Neil Hansen	72	74	72	76	294	835
Jeff Hawkes	70	73	78	73	294	835
Ronan Rafferty	74	70	79	71	294	835

Peugeot French Open

St. Cloud Golf Club, Paris, France
Par 35-37 — 72; 6,733 yards

June 10-13
purse, £250,320

	SCORES				TOTAL	MONEY
Jose Rivero	68	67	71	63	269	£41,879.87
Howard Clark	64	68	69	69	270	27,896.46
Hugh Baiocchi	68	66	66	71	271	14,149.28
Sam Torrance	66	67	64	72	272	14,149.28
Nick Faldo	70	66	64	72	272	7,321.77
David Feherty	68	70	68	66	272	7,321.77
Jose-Maria Olazabal	73	68	66	65	272	7,321.77
Ove Sellberg	68	68	69	67	272	7,321.77
Peter Senior	69	69	67	67	272	7,321.77
Joey Sindelar	70	64	66	72	272	7,321.77
Gordon Brand Jr.	67	68	65	73	273	4,473.48
Manuel Calero	69	69	65	70	273	4,473.48
Eamonn Darcy	67	69	71	67	274	3,940.69
Philip Walton	74	68	66	66	274	3,940.69
Richard Boxall	71	70	67	67	275	3,468.21

	SCORES				TOTAL	MONEY
Bill Longmuir	67	70	68	70	275	3,468.21
Mark McNulty	70	67	68	70	275	3,468.21
Ian Woosnam	73	66	67	69	275	3,468.21
Mike Clayton	72	66	66	72	276	3,116.36
Denis Durnian	70	73	67	67	277	2,978.14
Ronald Stelten	75	65	68	69	277	2,978.14
Tommy Armour III	77	65	68	68	278	2,525.76
Peter Baker	71	71	66	70	278	2,525.76
Roger Chapman	71	68	72	67	278	2,525.76
Rick Hartmann	73	68	70	67	278	2,525.76
Jeff Hawkes	69	71	71	67	278	2,525.76
Robert Lee	72	67	71	68	278	2,525.76
Carl Mason	68	73	68	69	278	2,525.76
Mark Mouland	70	71	68	69	278	2,525.76
Craig Stadler	75	68	69	66	278	2,525.76
Lyndsay Stephen	72	70	69	67	278	2,525.76
Ken Brown	73	69	68	69	279	1,935.16
Derrick Cooper	71	68	68	72	279	1,935.16
Barry Lane	69	66	73	71	279	1,935.16
Brian Marchbank	70	68	68	73	279	1,935.16
Andrew Oldcorn	68	73	69	69	279	1,935.16
Dan Pohl	68	69	70	72	279	1,935.16
David J. Russell	69	69	71	70	279	1,935.16
David A. Russell	69	70	71	69	279	1,935.16
Michael Allen	72	67	72	69	280	1,583.31
Peter Fowler	74	69	67	70	280	1,583.31
Mike Harwood	70	71	70	69	280	1,583.31
Michael King	69	70	69	72	280	1,583.31
Gavin Levenson	69	70	69	72	280	1,583.31
Michael McLean	71	69	71	69	280	1,583.31
Ross Drummond	69	71	72	69	281	1,306.86
Anders Forsbrand	73	70	67	71	281	1,306.86
Neil Hansen	69	71	72	69	281	1,306.86
Christy O'Connor Jr.	73	70	67	71	281	1,306.86
Manuel Pinero	71	70	70	70	281	1,306.86

Volvo Belgian Open

Royal Waterloo Golf Club, Brussels, Belgium
Par 36-35 — 71; 6,683 yards

June 17-20
purse, £150,000

(Fourth round rained out; event shortened to 54 holes.)

	SCORES			TOTAL	MONEY
Eamonn Darcy	69	67	64	200	£25,000
Nick Faldo	69	67	65	201	11,183.33
Ronan Rafferty	72	65	64	201	11,183.33
Ian Woosnam	66	66	69	201	11,183.33
Peter Fowler	71	66	68	205	5,805
Barry Lane	73	64	68	205	5,805
Gavin Levenson	71	68	67	206	4,125
Wayne Westner	71	68	67	206	4,125
Michael Allen	73	68	66	207	2,693.57
Andrew Oldcorn	69	69	69	207	2,693.57
David J. Russell	72	67	68	207	2,693.57
Ove Sellberg	69	73	65	207	2,693.57
Michel Tapia	72	69	66	207	2,693.57

	SCORES			TOTAL	MONEY
Greg Turner	70	67	70	207	2,693.57
Billy Andrade	67	70	70	207	2,693.57
Neil Hansen	70	69	69	208	2,140
Jeff Hall	72	69	68	209	1,920
Mark Mouland	72	67	70	209	1,920
Glenn Ralph	69	70	70	209	1,920
Ian Young	74	68	67	209	1,920
Peter Baker	71	70	69	210	1,541
Richard Boxall	73	70	67	210	1,541
Manuel Calero	72	68	70	210	1,541
Tony Charnley	71	71	68	210	1,541
Howard Clark	71	66	73	210	1,541
Mike Clayton	72	66	72	210	1,541
Mark Davis	69	70	71	210	1,541
John Morgan	70	69	71	210	1,541
Dillard Pruitt	69	68	73	210	1,541
Emilio Rodriguez	73	70	67	210	1,541
Ian Baker-Finch	72	70	69	211	1,220
Simon Bishop	71	73	67	211	1,220
Giuseppe Cali	74	69	68	211	1,220
Paul Curry	72	72	67	211	1,220
David Gilford	71	69	71	211	1,220
Ian Mosey	71	71	69	211	1,220
Stephen Bennett	71	70	71	212	931.67
Kelly Clair	75	68	69	212	931.67
Tony Johnstone	72	69	71	212	931.67
Carl Mason	73	71	68	212	931.67
Wayne Riley	71	69	72	212	931.67
John Slaughter	70	71	71	212	931.67
Andrew Stubbs	70	70	72	212	931.67
Johan Rystroem	74	69	69	212	931.67
Carl Magnus Stroemberg	72	72	68	212	931.67
Ross Drummond	75	69	69	213	720
Emmanuel Dussart	70	72	71	213	720
Philip Harrison	76	66	71	213	720
Lee Jones	70	72	71	213	720
Robert Lee	70	72	71	213	720
Ross McFarlane	73	68	72	213	720
Costantino Rocca	74	70	69	213	720

Johnnie Walker Monte Carlo Open

Mont Agel Golf Club, La Turbie, France

June 24-27
purse, £204,400

First/Fourth rounds: Par 34-35 — 69; 6,198 yards
Second/Third rounds: Par 34-34 — 68; 5,882 yard

	SCORES				TOTAL	MONEY
Peter Senior	66	63	65	66	260	£34,062.34
Rodger Davis	71	63	65	62	261	22,687.79
Philip Walton	66	65	73	62	266	12,795.09
Severiano Ballesteros	68	66	68	65	267	9,437.92
Paul Curry	67	69	63	68	267	9,437.92
Ian Baker-Finch	69	62	69	69	269	5,743.48
Gordon J. Brand	70	66	68	65	269	5,743.48
Gavin Levenson	69	65	65	70	269	5,743.48
Brian Marchbank	63	70	65	71	269	5,743.48

	SCORES				TOTAL	MONEY
Fulton Allem	68	70	68	64	270	3,924.38
Silvio Grappasonni	67	68	69	66	270	3,924.38
Robert Lee	69	68	67	67	271	3,164.03
Michael McLean	68	65	70	68	271	3,164.03
Jose Rivero	70	68	69	64	271	3,164.03
Greg Turner	66	67	71	67	271	3,164.03
Curtis Strange	65	68	67	71	271	3,164.03
Neal Briggs	72	64	70	66	272	2,698.01
Roger Chapman	66	70	67	69	272	2,698.01
Ron Commans	69	69	69	66	273	2,459.55
John Slaughter	66	71	69	67	273	2,459.55
Ronald Stelten	71	69	67	66	273	2,459.55
Juan Anglada	67	66	67	74	274	2,238.12
John Bland	67	66	67	74	274	2,238.12
Justin Hobday	68	68	65	73	274	2,238.12
John O'Leary	71	68	68	67	274	2,238.12
Hugh Baiocchi	71	64	70	70	275	1,900.87
Giuseppe Cali	69	65	77	64	272	1,900.87
Peter Fowler	72	67	67	69	275	1,900.87
Antonio Garrido	69	69	70	67	275	1,900.87
Philip Parkin	73	65	68	69	275	1,900.87
Art Russell	67	68	67	73	275	1,900.87
Wayne Smith	70	67	67	71	275	1,900.87
Grant Turner	70	67	68	71	276	1,676.03
Lee Fickling	65	71	69	72	277	1,573.84
Jaime Gonzalez	67	70	69	71	277	1,573.84
John Morgan	68	65	72	72	277	1,573.84
Emilio Rodriguez	70	68	67	72	277	1,573.84
Peter Allan	71	66	72	69	278	1,349
Tommy Armour III	70	68	69	71	278	1,349
Gordon Brand Jr.	73	66	69	70	278	1,349
Santiago Luna	71	68	69	70	278	1,349
Frederic Regard	70	65	72	71	278	1,349
Peter Teravainen	70	69	68	71	278	1,349
Ian Young	68	69	71	70	278	1,349
Stephen Bennett	70	69	71	69	279	1,042.41
Tony Johnstone	69	69	71	70	279	1,042.41
Chris Moody	66	69	73	71	279	1,042.41
Mark Mouland	72	67	72	68	279	1,042.41
Andrew Murray	72	68	70	69	279	1,042.41
David Ray	74	66	71	68	279	1,042.41
David A. Russell	68	70	66	75	279	1,042.41
Ove Sellberg	69	71	70	69	279	1,042.41

Carrolls Irish Open

Portmarnock Golf Club, Dublin, Ireland
Par 36-36 — 72; 7,102 yards

July 2-5
purse, £215,032

	SCORES				TOTAL	MONEY
Bernhard Langer	67	68	66	68	269	£35,838.75
Sandy Lyle	70	70	71	68	279	23,892.50
Rodger Davis	69	72	69	72	282	12,099.17
Ian Woosnam	72	74	69	67	282	12,099.17
Howard Clark	71	71	73	68	283	9,079.15
John Bland	70	75	70	69	284	7,502.25
David Jones	73	72	75	65	285	6,403.19

	SCORES				TOTAL	MONEY
Gordon Brand Jr.	73	70	73	71	287	5,351.92
Roger Chapman	72	73	71	73	289	4,176.41
Mark O'Meara	74	71	74	70	289	4,176.41
David A. Russell	72	75	74	68	289	4,176.41
Bob E. Smith	72	71	75	71	289	4,176.41
Ian Baker-Finch	72	69	77	72	290	3,262.76
Jaime Gonzalez	70	70	76	74	290	3,262.76
Mark McNulty	71	72	70	77	290	3,262.76
Peter Senior	74	75	72	69	290	3,262.76
Sam Torrance	69	72	74	75	290	3,262.76
Mitch Adcock	72	72	74	73	291	2,612.25
Ken Brown	68	77	79	67	291	2,612.25
Nick Faldo	78	70	76	67	291	2,612.25
Mark Mouland	73	73	69	76	291	2,612.25
David Ray	77	70	72	72	291	2,612.25
Wayne Westner	75	72	73	71	291	2,612.25
Anders Forsbrand	72	74	73	73	292	2,258.64
Tony Johnstone	72	74	74	72	292	2,258.64
John Morgan	75	72	70	75	292	2,258.64
Tommy Armour III	75	74	74	70	293	1,887.51
Gordon J. Brand	67	74	74	78	293	1,887.51
Bernard Gallacher	76	69	75	73	293	1,887.51
Gavin Levenson	74	73	72	74	293	1,887.51
Graham Marsh	73	77	72	71	293	1,887.51
Andrew Murray	74	73	73	73	293	1,887.51
John O'Leary	74	72	73	74	293	1,887.51
Philip Walton	75	71	74	73	293	1,887.51
Stephen Bennett	72	70	78	74	294	1,490.89
Eamonn Darcy	77	71	72	74	294	1,490.89
Christy O'Connor Jr.	74	74	73	73	294	1,490.89
Dillard Pruitt	74	76	75	69	294	1,490.89
Glenn Ralph	78	71	70	75	294	1,490.89
Mark Roe	77	71	70	76	294	1,490.89
Ian Young	77	73	70	74	294	1,490.89
Derrick Cooper	75	73	75	72	295	1,165.95
Lee Fickling	72	72	80	71	295	1,165.95
Michael King	74	76	73	72	295	1,165.95
Barry Lane	75	72	75	73	295	1,165.95
Mats Lanner	70	73	75	77	295	1,165.95
Noel Ratcliffe	78	71	72	74	295	1,165.95
Bob Shearer	68	81	79	67	295	1,165.95
Andrew Sherborne	74	75	75	71	295	1,165.95
Des Smyth	70	72	76	77	295	1,165.95
Sandy Stephen	71	76	77	71	295	1,165.95

Bell's Scottish Open

Gleneagles Hotel, King's Course, Gleneagles, Scotland   July 8-11
Par 35-36 — 71; 6,744 yards   purse, £200,000

	SCORES				TOTAL	MONEY
Ian Woosnam	65	65	66	68	264	£33,330
Peter Senior	68	66	65	72	271	22,200
Rodger Davis	68	67	69	68	272	11,260
Anders Forsbrand	68	68	67	69	272	11,260
Jose-Maria Olazabal	74	62	71	66	273	8,470
Severiano Ballesteros	68	65	72	70	275	6,500

	SCORES				TOTAL	MONEY
Roger Chapman	68	64	71	72	275	6,500
Fred Couples	70	70	65	71	276	5,000
Eamonn Darcy	73	69	69	66	277	4,053.33
Ross Drummond	69	70	68	70	277	4,053.33
Mark James	70	72	68	67	277	4,053.33
Tony Charnley	71	67	69	71	278	3,240
Howard Clark	72	69	67	70	278	3,240
Brian Marchbank	66	72	70	70	278	3,240
Gordon Brand Jr.	71	68	69	71	279	2,653.33
Tom Kite	71	65	69	71	279	2,653.33
Mark McNulty	74	67	70	68	279	2,653.33
Ronan Rafferty	70	68	68	73	279	2,653.33
Sam Torrance	70	64	69	76	279	2,653.33
Russell Weir	70	70	73	66	279	2,653.33
Jerry Anderson	70	67	69	74	280	2,280
Nick Faldo	71	69	71	69	280	2,280
Ossie Moore	70	69	67	74	280	2,280
John O'Leary	71	71	69	70	281	2,130
Noel Ratcliffe	68	69	72	72	281	2,130
Wayne Grady	71	72	72	67	282	1,980
Graham Marsh	68	72	69	73	282	1,980
Bob Shearer	73	68	70	71	282	1,980
Peter Fowler	72	71	71	69	283	1,653.33
Bernard Gallacher	69	67	74	73	283	1,653.33
Jimmy Heggarty	73	69	72	69	283	1,653.33
Tommy Horton	70	72	69	72	283	1,653.33
Michael King	71	68	72	72	283	1,653.33
David Llewellyn	72	68	69	74	283	1,653.33
Miguel Martin	76	68	71	68	283	1,653.33
John Slaughter	76	63	70	74	283	1,653.33
Gerry Taylor	72	69	74	68	283	1,653.33
*Colin Montgomerie	73	67	72	71	283	
Ken Brown	68	71	70	75	284	1,380
Emmanuel Dussart	73	67	71	73	284	1,380
Andrew Oldcorn	69	75	71	69	284	1,380
Jose Rivero	74	68	72	70	284	1,380
Derrick Cooper	74	69	68	74	285	1,260
Ove Sellberg	75	69	72	69	285	1,260
Mike Clayton	72	72	69	73	286	1,080
Neil Coles	73	67	74	72	286	1,080
Sandy Lyle	73	71	72	70	286	1,080
Bill Malley	69	72	71	74	286	1,080
Dillard Pruitt	68	71	70	77	286	1,080
Grant Turner	68	73	71	74	286	1,080
Greg J. Turner	73	69	68	76	286	1,080

British Open Championship

Honourable Company of Edinburgh Golfers, Muirfield, Scotland   July 16-19
Par 36-35 — 71; 6,963 yards (6,781 - 3rd rd)   purse, £651,850

	SCORES				TOTAL	MONEY
Nick Faldo	68	69	71	71	279	£75,000
Paul Azinger	68	68	71	73	280	49,500
Rodger Davis	64	73	74	69	280	49,500
Ben Crenshaw	73	68	72	68	281	31,000
Payne Stewart	71	66	72	72	281	31,000

	SCORES				TOTAL	MONEY
David Frost	70	68	70	74	282	26,000
Tom Watson	69	69	71	74	283	23,000
Nick Price	68	71	72	73	284	18,666.67
Craig Stadler	69	69	71	75	284	18,666.67
Ian Woosnam	71	69	72	72	284	18,666.67
Mark Calcavecchia	69	70	72	74	285	13,500
Graham Marsh	69	70	72	74	285	13,500
Mark McNulty	71	69	75	70	285	13,500
Jose-Maria Olazabal	70	73	70	72	285	13,500
Masashi Ozaki	69	72	71	73	285	13,500
Hal Sutton	71	70	73	71	285	13,500
Ken Brown	69	73	70	74	286	7,450
Eamonn Darcy	74	69	72	71	286	7,450
Raymond Floyd	72	68	70	76	286	7,450
Wayne Grady	70	71	76	69	286	7,450
Bernhard Langer	69	69	76	72	286	7,450
Sandy Lyle	76	69	71	70	286	7,450
Mark Roe	74	68	72	72	286	7,450
Lee Trevino	67	74	73	72	286	7,450
Gerry Taylor	69	68	75	75	287	5,300
Gordon Brand Jr.	73	70	75	70	288	4,833.33
David Feherty	74	70	77	67	288	4,833.33
Larry Mize	68	71	76	73	288	4,833.33
Danny Edwards	71	73	72	73	289	4,200
Anders Forsbrand	73	69	73	74	289	4,200
Ken Green	67	76	74	72	289	4,200
Lanny Wadkins	72	71	75	71	289	4,200
Fuzzy Zoeller	71	70	76	72	289	4,200
David Graham	69	73	78	70	290	3,900
Manuel Calero	71	74	75	71	291	3,500
Ross Drummond	79	66	77	69	291	3,500
Jay Haas	69	74	76	72	291	3,500
Greg Norman	71	71	74	75	291	3,500
Bob Tway	67	72	75	77	291	3,500
Andy Bean	70	73	75	74	292	3,025
Gordon J. Brand	72	72	74	74	292	3,025
Derrick Cooper	74	72	78	68	292	3,025
Fred Couples	70	74	78	70	292	3,025
Fulton Allem	74	69	77	73	293	2,825
Brian Marchbank	72	72	76	73	293	2,825
Carl Mason	70	69	78	76	293	2,825
Ossie Moore	71	72	76	74	293	2,825
Larry Nelson	70	75	76	73	294	2,675
John Slaughter	72	71	76	75	294	2,675
Severiano Ballesteros	73	70	77	75	295	2,525
Mats Lanner	71	74	79	71	295	2,525
Sam Torrance	76	69	77	73	295	2,525
Philip Walton	72	73	75	75	295	2,525
Billy Andrade	74	69	78	75	296	2,350
Roger Chapman	70	73	79	74	296	2,350
John O'Leary	71	73	79	73	296	2,350
Ove Sellberg	71	72	78	76	297	2,250
*Paul Mayo	72	70	75	80	297	
Brian Jones	73	72	80	73	298	2,150
Bill McColl	71	75	77	75	298	2,150
Tommy Nakajima	73	72	77	76	298	2,150
Howard Clark	72	73	78	76	299	1,975
Neil Hansen	75	69	80	75	299	1,975
Miguel Martin	74	71	77	77	299	1,975
Scott Simpson	75	71	82	71	299	1,975

	SCORES				TOTAL	MONEY
Hugh Baiocchi	72	73	78	77	300	1,750
Brandel Chamblee	73	72	77	78	300	1,750
Mark O'Meara	73	72	82	73	300	1,750
Tateo Ozaki	72	73	78	77	300	1,750
Gary Player	72	74	79	75	300	1,750
Wayne Westner	71	75	84	71	301	1,600
Tom Kite	73	72	81	76	302	1,600
Jack Nicklaus	74	71	81	76	302	1,600
Jeff Hawkes	71	74	80	78	303	1,600
*Ricky Willison	75	71	83	76	305	
Chris Moody	76	70	81	79	306	1,600
David Jones	72	74	83	78	307	1,600
Anthony Stevens	71	75	82	84	312	1,600

Out of Final 36 Holes

	SCORES		TOTAL
David Gilford	70	77	147
Masahiro Kuramoto	74	73	147
Barry Lane	76	71	147
Gavin Levenson	75	72	147
Malcolm Mackenzie	76	71	147
Christy O'Connor Jr.	74	73	147
Andrew Sherborne	72	75	147
Des Smyth	72	75	147
Jim Thorpe	74	73	147
Mitch Adcock	77	71	148
Bernard Gallacher	75	73	148
Peter Harrison	73	75	148
Mark James	75	73	148
Michael King	75	73	148
Philip Parkin	77	71	148
Manuel Pinero	75	73	148
Vaughan Somers	76	72	148
Paul Thomas	75	73	148
Russell Weir	72	76	148
*Roger Winchester	73	75	148
Tony Charnley	75	74	149
Vicente Fernandez	78	71	149
Davis Love III	72	77	149
Ian Mosey	77	72	149
Andrew Oldcorn	75	74	149
Magnus Persson	72	77	149
Anders Sorensen	74	75	149
Paul Way	75	74	149
Teddy Webber	77	72	149
Ian Young	74	75	149
Ian Baker-Finch	74	76	150
Stephen Bennett	71	79	150
Adam Hunter	77	73	150
Bill Longmuir	79	71	150
Stephen McCallister	75	75	150
Corey Pavin	73	77	150
Jose Rivero	76	74	150
Johan Rystroem	73	77	150
Tze Ming Chen	78	73	151
T.C. Chen	78	73	151
Denis Durnian	72	79	151
Paul Kent	73	78	151
Robert Lee	74	77	151
*David Curry	80	71	151

	SCORES	TOTAL	MONEY
Andrew Brooks	78 74	152	
Jose-Maria Canizares	72 80	152	
Paul Carrigill	78 74	152	
Jim Hallet	75 77	152	
Mike Harwood	76 76	152	
David Llewellyn	77 75	152	
Bill Malley	78 74	152	
Peter Senior	74 78	152	
John Bland	79 74	153	
Steve Cipa	75 78	153	
Arnold Palmer	75 78	153	
Martin Poxon	77 76	153	
Ronan Rafferty	76 77	153	
David Ray	78 75	153	
*Christian Hardin	73 80	153	
Jerry Anderson	77 77	154	
*Steven Bottomley	81 73	154	
Keith Hird	75 79	154	
*Eoghan O'Connell	77 77	154	
Mark Wiltshire	78 77	155	
*John Ambridge	75 80	155	
*Freddy George	74 81	155	
*Jeremy Robinson	77 78	155	
John Clifford	82 74	156	
Martin Gray	80 77	157	
Per-Arne Brostedt	74 84	158	
*D. Jones	80 78	158	
*Stephen Hamer	81 78	159	
Geoff Tickell	78 82	160	
Craig Parry	81 81	162	
Peter Jacobsen	81 WD		

(All professionals who did not complete 72 holes received £400.)

KLM Dutch Open

Hilversum Golf Club, Hilversum, Holland
Par 36-36 — 72; 6,673 yards

July 23-26
purse, £180,000

	SCORES				TOTAL	MONEY
Gordon Brand Jr.	69	67	67	69	272	£30,000
David A. Russell	66	68	73	66	273	20,000
Magnus Persson	70	68	68	68	274	11,300
Antonio Garrido	70	69	67	69	275	8,300
Jose-Maria Olazabal	69	69	68	69	275	8,300
Eamonn Darcy	69	67	71	69	276	5,400
Manuel Pinero	68	70	74	64	276	5,400
Mark Roe	68	66	72	70	276	5,400
Severiano Ballesteros	67	72	68	70	277	3,553.33
David Feherty	65	72	70	70	277	3,553.33
Bill Malley	66	73	72	66	277	3,553.33
Tony Johnstone	66	68	75	69	278	3,100
Christy O'Connor Jr.	69	69	72	69	279	2,800
Jose Rivero	72	69	67	71	279	2,800
Bob E. Smith	69	72	65	73	279	2,800
Roger Chapman	72	68	70	70	280	2,560
David Williams	70	71	72	67	280	2,560
Rodger Davis	71	73	71	66	281	2,440

	SCORES				TOTAL	MONEY
Jerry Anderson	69	63	75	75	282	2,320
Philip Walton	67	71	73	71	282	2,320
Tony Charnley	72	72	71	68	283	2,040
Miguel Martin	70	71	71	71	283	2,040
Ronan Rafferty	68	68	70	77	283	2,040
Keith Waters	69	68	73	73	283	2,040
Roger Mackay	68	71	73	71	283	2,040
Gordon J. Brand	71	72	73	68	284	1,733.33
Michael King	68	70	74	72	284	1,733.33
Carl Mason	70	70	73	71	284	1,733.33
Jose Davila	70	69	72	74	285	1,580
Ross Drummond	72	69	71	73	285	1,580
Rick Hartmann	69	70	73	73	285	1,580
Jimmy Heggarty	70	71	71	73	285	1,580
Peter Baker	67	72	72	75	286	1,420
Jose-Maria Canizares	66	70	76	74	286	1,420
Chris Moody	70	68	74	74	286	1,420
Ian Young	70	67	72	77	286	1,420
Kelly Clair	70	73	70	74	287	1,220
Emmanuel Dussart	73	71	71	72	287	1,220
David Gilford	71	72	73	71	287	1,220
Vaughan Somers	69	73	71	74	287	1,220
Ronald Stelten	71	70	74	72	287	1,220
Grant Turner	69	69	72	77	287	1,220
David Llewellyn	70	69	74	75	288	1,060
Des Smyth	74	66	73	75	288	1,060
Tommy Armour III	72	69	74	74	289	940
Mark Mouland	72	73	70	74	289	940
Frank Nobilo	72	70	74	73	289	940
Chen Tze Chung	71	73	72	73	289	940
Hugh Baiocchi	74	69	71	76	290	785
Mark James	74	71	69	76	290	785
Juan Pinero	74	70	75	71	290	785
Paul Way	72	72	74	72	290	785

Scandinavian Enterprise Open

Ullna Golf Club, Stockholm, Sweden
Par 36-36 — 72; 6,724 yards

July 30-August 2
purse, £193,236

	SCORES				TOTAL	MONEY
Gordon Brand Jr.	64	71	71	71	277	£32,202.90
Magnus Persson	72	68	69	68	277	21,440.28
(Brand defeated Persson on first hole of playoff.)						
David Llewellyn	68	67	72	71	278	12,096.62
Carl Mason	72	68	67	72	279	8,922.71
Ronan Rafferty	68	65	69	77	279	8,922.71
Bob Shearer	70	71	69	70	280	6,763.29
David Williams	74	69	68	70	281	5,314.01
Ian Woosnam	66	74	70	71	281	5,314.01
Jeff Hall	71	69	72	70	282	3,636.71
Rick Hartmann	68	66	72	76	282	3,636.71
Mikael Hoeberg	74	67	66	75	282	3,636.71
Des Smyth	65	66	72	79	282	3,636.71
Magnus Sunesson	70	68	70	74	282	3,636.71
Graham Marsh	68	69	73	73	283	2,782.61
Christy O'Connor Jr.	68	75	68	72	283	2,782.61

	SCORES				TOTAL	MONEY
John O'Leary	70	68	70	75	283	2,782.61
Emilio Rodriguez	71	66	73	73	283	2,782.61
Mark Mouland	69	71	72	72	284	2,402.51
Dillard Pruitt	68	72	72	72	284	2,402.51
Ove Sellberg	66	76	72	70	284	2,402.51
Per-Arne Brostedt	69	71	71	74	285	2,173.91
Bill Longmuir	73	69	73	70	285	2,173.91
David J. Russell	70	71	70	74	285	2,173.91
Johan Rystroem	70	71	72	72	285	2,173.91
Manuel Calero	68	71	70	77	286	1,913.04
Denis Durnian	71	70	72	73	286	1,913.04
Bryan Norton	69	72	74	71	286	1,913.04
John Slaughter	70	72	74	70	286	1,913.04
Craig Stadler	68	70	72	76	286	1,913.04
Brian Marchbank	71	70	71	75	287	1,657
Chris Moody	67	72	74	74	287	1,657
John Morgan	71	72	69	75	287	1,657
Bruce Zabriski	69	72	71	75	287	1,657
Ian Baker-Finch	72	68	73	75	288	1,391.30
Richard Boxall	74	69	71	74	288	1,391.30
Andrew Chandler	70	70	77	71	288	1,391.30
Steve Cipa	71	71	74	72	288	1,391.30
Derrick Cooper	69	74	73	72	288	1,391.30
Jose Davila	72	70	75	71	288	1,391.30
Malcolm Mackenzie	69	69	70	80	288	1,391.30
Andrew Sherborne	71	70	79	68	288	1,391.30
Teddy Webber	69	72	69	78	288	1,391.30
Kelly Clair	68	72	73	76	289	1,140.10
Vaughan Somers	70	71	74	74	289	1,140.10
Ulf Rohden	72	69	77	71	289	1,140.10
Daniel Westermark	68	74	73	74	289	1,140.10
Peter Baker	71	70	74	75	290	1,004.83
Mark Davis	71	68	75	76	290	1,004.83
Mats Hallberg	69	70	76	75	290	1,004.83
*Christian Hardin	73	69	73	75	290	
Howard Clark	69	70	82	70	291	830.92
Emmanuel Dussart	73	68	74	76	291	830.92
Robert Lee	68	67	79	77	291	830.92
Frank Nobilo	71	70	74	76	291	830.92
Anders Sorensen	71	72	74	74	291	830.92
Michel Tapia	71	71	73	76	291	830.92

PLM Open

Ljunghusens Golf Club, Malmo, Sweden
Par 35-37 — 72; 6,687 yards

August 6-9
purse, £145,210

	SCORES				TOTAL	MONEY
Howard Clark	68	73	67	63	271	£24,201.36
Ossie Moore	73	63	69	68	273	16,137.46
Peter Senior	67	69	67	71	274	9,080.35
Gordon J. Brand	70	68	70	68	276	6,708.62
Vicente Fernandez	72	68	70	66	276	6,708.62
Ronan Rafferty	68	71	69	69	277	5,082.28
Chris Moody	71	68	67	72	278	4,356.24
Anders Forsbrand	70	72	69	68	279	3,120.76
Barry Lane	70	70	71	68	279	3,120.76

	SCORES				TOTAL	MONEY
Magnus Persson	70	70	67	72	279	3,120.76
Des Smyth	68	72	70	69	279	3,120.76
Andrew Chandler	72	67	68	73	280	2,407.23
Rick Hartmann	69	72	71	68	280	2,407.23
Bill Malley	71	69	72	68	280	2,407.23
Brian Marchbank	72	70	70	69	281	2,074.86
Bryan Norton	74	71	65	71	281	2,074.86
Bob E. Smith	72	70	72	67	281	2,074.86
Simon Bishop	70	68	69	75	282	1,675.94
Per-Arne Brostedt	68	69	71	74	282	1,675.94
Manuel Calero	73	70	68	71	282	1,675.94
David Feherty	67	70	71	74	282	1,675.94
Robert Lee	69	70	75	68	282	1,675.94
John O'Leary	71	68	73	70	282	1,675.94
Jim Rutledge	69	72	68	73	282	1,675.94
Vaughan Somers	73	68	70	71	282	1,675.94
Bill Longmuir	73	70	69	71	283	1,394
Wayne Riley	69	72	71	71	283	1,394
David J. Russell	65	72	72	74	283	1,394
John Slaughter	71	74	68	70	283	1,394
Bruce Zabriski	73	72	66	72	283	1,394
Ian Baker-Finch	71	71	68	74	284	1,219.75
Mats Hallberg	71	70	69	74	284	1,219.75
Neil Hansen	69	73	71	71	284	1,219.75
John Morgan	72	67	70	75	284	1,219.75
Jeremy Bennett	69	74	72	70	285	1,007.47
Richard Boxall	75	68	70	72	285	1,007.47
Mats Lanner	72	73	69	71	285	1,007.47
Ulf Nilsson	74	70	68	73	285	1,007.47
Dillard Pruitt	74	69	71	71	285	1,007.47
Anthony Stevens	74	69	69	73	285	1,007.47
Murray Supple	71	73	71	70	285	1,007.47
Peter Fowler	72	72	73	69	286	805.42
Tommy Horton	70	73	69	74	286	805.42
Emilio Rodriguez	72	72	69	73	286	805.42
Johan Rystroem	72	73	73	68	286	805.42
Heinz P. Thuel	72	73	74	67	286	805.42
Malcolm Mackenzie	72	70	71	74	287	716.36
Robin Mann	73	69	73	72	287	716.36
Frank Nobilo	72	70	72	73	287	716.36
Tony Charnley	72	71	73	72	288	648.60
Denis Durnian	70	75	71	72	288	648.60
Steen Tining	71	73	70	74	288	648.60
David Williams	71	74	70	73	288	648.60

Benson & Hedges International Open

Fulford Golf Club, York, England
Par 36-36 — 72; 6,809 yards

August 13-16
purse, £200,000

	SCORES				TOTAL	MONEY
Noel Ratcliff	69	70	70	66	275	£33,330
Ove Sellberg	70	69	69	69	277	22,200
Nick Faldo	74	68	66	70	278	11,260
Jose-Maria Olazabal	69	71	71	67	278	11,260
Ross McFarlane	69	72	68	70	279	8,470
Ian Baker-Finch	70	69	71	70	280	4,602.50

	SCORES				TOTAL	MONEY
Jose-Maria Canizares	68	73	70	69	280	4,602.50
Antonio Garrido	69	68	72	71	280	4,602.50
Michael King	71	67	71	71	280	4,602.50
Bernhard Langer	69	67	71	73	280	4,602.50
Mark Mouland	70	68	71	71	280	4,602.50
Dillard Pruitt	69	72	71	68	280	4,602.50
Bruce Zabriski	76	66	70	68	280	4,602.50
Gordon J. Brand	68	71	72	70	281	2,820
Jeff Hawkes	72	70	69	70	281	2,820
Sam Torrance	65	70	77	69	281	2,820
David Williams	69	74	70	68	281	2,820
Ian Woosnam	71	71	68	71	281	2,820
Rick Hartmann	70	73	70	69	282	2,313.33
Barry Lane	69	67	72	74	282	2,313.33
Sandy Lyle	72	71	71	68	282	2,313.33
John Morgan	70	71	69	72	282	2,313.33
John O'Leary	71	68	72	71	282	2,313.33
David A. Russell	70	67	71	74	282	2,313.33
Peter Baker	74	65	74	70	283	1,920
Derrick Cooper	70	72	72	69	283	1,920
Anders Forsbrand	68	72	72	71	283	1,920
Bill Malley	68	75	66	74	283	1,920
Brian Marchbank	71	71	66	75	283	1,920
Andrew Oldcorn	72	66	74	71	283	1,920
Jose Rivero	70	71	70	72	283	1,920
Neal Briggs	69	75	70	70	284	1,640
David Jones	68	72	71	73	284	1,640
Chris Moody	69	75	70	70	284	1,640
Simon Bishop	75	68	71	71	285	1,360
Peter Fowler	68	71	77	69	285	1,360
Bernard Gallacher	69	69	73	74	285	1,360
David Llewellyn	72	71	70	72	285	1,360
Miguel Martin	71	72	72	70	285	1,360
Peter Mitchell	66	73	72	74	285	1,360
Ian Mosey	72	72	70	71	285	1,360
Christy O'Connor Jr.	72	72	71	70	285	1,360
Peter Senior	66	71	69	79	285	1,360
Vaughan Somers	71	70	69	75	285	1,360
James Spence	69	70	72	74	285	1,360
Andrew Chandler	75	68	71	72	286	1,060
Bill Longmuir	66	69	76	75	286	1,060
Mark Roe	72	71	74	69	286	1,060
Paul Way	71	70	72	73	286	1,060
Mitch Adcock	73	70	70	74	287	840
Tommy Armour III	69	72	72	74	287	840
Richard Boxall	71	73	71	72	287	840
Neil Coles	70	71	76	70	287	840
John Slaughter	68	73	70	76	287	840
Sandy Stephen	67	74	73	73	287	840
Grant Turner	72	71	71	73	287	840

Lawrence Batley International

Royal Birkdale Golf Club, Southport, England
Par 35-37 — 72; 7,022 yards

August 20-23
purse, £140,000

	SCORES				TOTAL	MONEY
Mark O'Meara	71	64	70	66	271	£23,330
Carl Mason	74	67	65	68	274	15,550
Andrew Oldcorn	68	68	71	68	275	8,760
Nick Faldo	72	65	70	69	276	6,470
Sam Torrance	67	72	70	67	276	6,470
Howard Clark	72	65	72	68	277	4,900
Tony Johnstone	75	66	68	69	278	3,850
David Llewellyn	69	69	69	71	278	3,850
Ian Baker-Finch	73	66	69	71	279	2,383.33
Simon Bishop	70	69	73	67	279	2,383.33
John Bland	73	71	67	68	279	2,383.33
Neil Hansen	68	72	73	66	279	2,383.33
Michael King	74	66	67	72	279	2,383.33
Barry Lane	70	71	69	69	279	2,383.33
Christy O'Connor Jr.	74	68	70	67	279	2,383.33
Mark Roe	73	70	68	68	279	2,383.33
Des Smyth	70	71	70	68	279	2,383.33
Peter Baker	71	70	67	72	280	1,704
Roger Chapman	70	74	66	70	280	1,704
Denis Durnian	74	68	71	67	280	1,704
Jose Rivero	70	70	70	70	280	1,704
Ian Woosnam	70	70	70	70	280	1,704
Peter Carsbo	70	70	70	71	281	1,460
Eamonn Darcy	75	68	66	72	281	1,460
Jeff Hawkes	71	74	70	66	281	1,460
Roger Maltbie	72	73	66	70	281	1,460
Greg J. Turner	70	73	70	68	281	1,460
David Feherty	67	69	70	76	282	1,280
Bill Longmuir	72	71	70	69	282	1,280
Bill Malley	72	70	69	71	282	1,280
Philip Walton	74	68	71	69	282	1,280
Hugh Baiocchi	74	68	70	71	283	1,052.50
Gordon J. Brand	69	70	73	71	283	1,052.50
Vicente Fernandez	74	70	71	68	283	1,052.50
Miquel Martin	73	72	69	69	283	1,052.50
Peter Senior	73	69	71	70	283	1,052.50
Bob Shearer	71	72	71	69	283	1,052.50
Bob E. Smith	67	70	72	74	283	1,052.50
Michel Tapia	75	69	69	70	283	1,052.50
Tommy Armour III	71	71	71	72	285	865
Jeremy Bennett	72	69	70	74	285	865
Emmanuel Dussart	73	72	71	69	285	865
Dillard Pruitt	73	70	71	71	285	865
Teddy Webber	75	67	72	72	286	775
Ian Young	72	72	71	71	286	775
Stephenn Bennett	72	68	76	71	287	710
Tom Lamore	72	69	7	75	287	710
Ove Sellberg	73	69	73	72	287	710
Brian Waites	72	73	72	70	287	710
Brian Marchbank	73	72	68	75	288	640
Martin Poxon	71	74	71	72	288	640
Keith Waters	75	68	68	77	288	640

German Open

Frankfurter Golf Club, Frankfurt, Germany
Par 35-36 — 71; 6,726 yards

August 28-31
purse, £271,185

	SCORES				TOTAL	MONEY
Mark McNulty	65	66	65	63	259	£45,196.61
Antonio Garrido	64	66	63	69	262	30,101.69
Denis Durnian	64	65	69	65	263	14,005.65
Peter Fowler	67	65	67	64	263	14,005.65
Barry Lane	67	64	66	66	263	14,005.65
Oliver Eckstein	69	65	67	65	266	8,135.59
Dillard Pruitt	69	64	68	65	266	8,135.59
Des Smyth	70	64	67	65	266	8,135.59
Gordon Brand Jr.	68	69	68	62	267	5,496.05
Jose-Maria Canizares	68	68	66	65	267	5,496.05
Bernhard Langer	68	67	67	65	267	5,496.05
Christy O'Connor Jr.	72	67	66	63	268	4,664.41
Ronan Rafferty	69	70	65	65	269	4,366.10
Jeff Hawkes	68	69	66	67	270	4,149.15
Brian Marchbank	67	65	66	73	271	3,823.73
Peter Senior	68	69	68	66	271	3,823.73
Sam Torrance	69	69	63	70	271	3,823.73
Neil Hansen	71	69	67	65	272	3,322.04
Mats Lanner	62	76	66	68	272	3,322.04
Bill Longmuir	73	68	63	68	272	3,322.04
Miquel Martin	69	67	66	70	272	3,322.04
Severiano Ballesteros	66	69	67	71	273	2,847.46
Eamonn Darcy	68	69	69	67	273	2,847.46
David Feherty	70	67	69	67	273	2,847.46
Rick Hartmann	69	66	69	69	273	2,847.46
Robert Lee	67	67	71	68	273	2,847.46
Wayne Westner	67	66	70	70	273	2,847.46
David Williams	70	70	66	67	273	2,847.46
Ian Baker-Finch	67	72	66	69	274	2,332.20
Gordon J. Brand	68	68	67	71	274	2,332.20
Paul Curry	70	69	68	67	274	2,332.20
John Morgan	71	67	67	69	274	2,332.20
Andrew Murray	69	67	69	69	274	2,332.20
Manuel Pinero	66	68	68	72	274	2,332.20
Manuel Calero	72	69	65	69	275	1,979.66
Ron Commans	68	71	67	69	275	1,979.66
Carl Mason	68	71	68	68	275	1,979.66
Mark Mouland	67	71	68	69	275	1,979.66
Vaughan Somers	69	68	72	66	275	1,979.66
Ian Young	69	68	69	69	275	1,979.66
Michael Allen	71	67	70	68	276	1,627.12
Billy Andrade	71	69	70	66	276	1,627.12
Ross Drummond	71	69	67	69	276	1,627.12
Anders Forsbrand	68	69	73	66	276	1,627.12
Ian Mosey	67	67	72	70	276	1,627.12
Glenn Ralph	70	71	70	65	276	1,627.12
Art Russell	69	71	67	69	276	1,627.12
Stephen Bennett	69	69	68	71	277	1,301.69
Ossie Moore	74	63	71	69	277	1,301.69
Frank Nobilo	68	70	69	70	277	1,301.69
Jose-Maria Olazabal	71	69	67	70	277	1,301.69
Simon Owen	70	71	67	69	277	1,301.69

Ebel European Masters—Swiss Open

Crans-Sur-Sierre Golf Club, Switzerland
Par 36-36 — 72; 6,811 yards

September 3-6
purse, £338,085

		SCORES			TOTAL	MONEY
Anders Forsbrand	71	64	66	62	263	£56,346.23
Mark Mouland	66	66	69	65	266	37,527.49
Glenn Ralph	68	66	67	66	267	21,164.97
Jose Rivero	70	65	68	65	268	16,904.28
Ian Mosey	66	66	67	70	269	14,317.72
Sandy Lyle	71	65	66	68	270	10,987.18
Philip Walton	68	66	69	67	270	10,987.18
Jose-Maria Canizares	68	67	65	71	271	6,710.79
Nick Faldo	71	67	67	66	271	6,710.79
Mike Harwood	70	69	66	66	271	6,710.79
Bill Longmuir	65	68	67	71	271	6,710.79
Mark McNulty	69	67	69	66	271	6,710.79
Des Smyth	66	71	65	69	271	6,710.79
Santiago Luna	68	68	71	65	272	5,072.30
Scott Simpson	67	67	69	69	272	5,072.30
Michael Allen	67	72	67	67	273	4,389.41
Roger Chapman	66	69	65	73	273	4,389.41
Tony Charnley	67	66	72	68	273	4,389.41
Robert Lee	69	67	69	68	273	4,389.41
Gavin Levenson	68	68	67	70	273	4,389.41
Tommy Armour III	68	72	66	68	274	3,653.77
Ian Baker-Finch	71	68	70	65	274	3,653.77
Eamonn Darcy	66	68	71	69	274	3,653.77
Bill Malley	71	69	63	71	274	3,653.77
Chris Moody	74	66	67	67	274	3,653.77
Manuel Pinero	69	71	65	69	274	3,653.77
Donnie Hammond	72	68	66	68	274	3,653.77
Andrew Chandler	67	69	70	69	275	3,093.69
Christy O'Connor Jr.	67	70	68	70	275	3,093.69
Sam Torrance	67	71	68	69	275	3,093.69
Gordon Brand Jr.	72	65	70	69	276	2,565.51
Peter Fowler	67	69	69	71	276	2,565.51
David Llewellyn	69	71	69	67	276	2,565.51
John Morgan	68	70	68	70	276	2,565.51
Frank Nobilo	70	70	69	67	276	2,565.51
Magnus Persson	68	67	71	70	276	2,565.51
Martin Poxon	71	69	67	69	276	2,565.51
Ove Sellberg	69	68	71	68	276	2,565.51
Peter Senior	69	71	65	71	276	2,565.51
Juan Anglada	68	68	67	74	277	1,925.66
Richard Boxall	70	70	71	66	277	1,925.66
Gordon J. Brand	69	69	69	70	277	1,925.66
Bernard Gallacher	69	68	71	69	277	1,925.66
Barry Lane	68	70	68	71	277	1,925.66
Mats Lanner	67	69	71	70	277	1,925.66
Brian Marchbank	70	68	70	69	277	1,925.66
Peter Teravainen	69	70	68	70	277	1,925.66
Mark Calcavecchia	69	71	70	67	277	1,925.66
Larry Mize	67	70	70	70	277	1,925.66

Panasonic European Open

Walton Heath Golf Club, Surrey, England
Par 36-36 — 72; 7,108 yards

September 10-13
purse, £220,000

	SCORES				TOTAL	MONEY
Paul Way	70	71	71	67	279	£36,660
John Bland	69	72	70	70	281	19,100
Gordon Brand Jr.	70	69	72	70	281	19,100
Christy O'Connor Jr.	70	70	72	70	282	11,000
Ian Woosnam	73	71	74	65	283	9,320
Neil Coles	71	70	75	68	284	6,180
Mark Mouland	71	72	72	69	284	6,180
Greg Norman	71	72	69	72	284	6,180
Ronan Rafferty	74	70	69	71	284	6,180
Jose-Maria Canizares	67	74	78	66	285	3,738.33
Rodger Davis	69	71	72	73	285	3,738.33
Nick Faldo	73	73	70	69	285	3,738.33
Bernhard Langer	70	67	73	75	285	3,738.33
Robert Lee	68	72	76	69	285	3,738.33
Wayne Westner	72	73	73	67	285	3,738.33
Severiano Ballesteros	70	71	75	70	286	2,866
Gordon J. Brand	71	75	72	68	286	2,866
Howard Clark	70	74	72	70	286	2,866
Brian Marchbank	75	71	73	67	286	2,866
Des Smyth	69	75	73	69	286	2,866
Bill Longmuir	73	70	75	69	287	2,540
Mark McNulty	75	70	71	71	287	2,540
David Ray	73	74	69	71	287	2,540
Roger Chapman	71	70	78	68	288	2,365
John Slaughter	70	75	72	71	288	2,365
Tony Charnley	76	72	73	69	290	2,050
Derrick Cooper	69	70	75	76	290	2,050
Bernard Gallacher	75	67	77	71	290	2,050
Mark James	73	71	74	72	290	2,050
Frank Nobilo	73	72	75	70	290	2,050
Sam Torrance	76	71	71	72	290	2,050
Brian Waites	73	72	76	69	290	2,050
Peter Senior	71	70	80	70	291	1,750
Vaughan Somers	71	74	76	70	291	1,750
Eamonn Darcy	74	73	72	73	292	1,580
Vicente Fernandez	75	73	71	73	292	1,580
Tommy Horton	74	71	74	73	292	1,580
Bob E. Smith	71	72	77	72	292	1,580
Magnus Sunesson	74	70	75	73	292	1,580
Mark Davis	73	70	79	71	293	1,400
Denis Durnian	73	73	74	73	293	1,400
Mark Roe	73	69	76	75	293	1,400
Andrew Sherborne	73	75	70	75	293	1,400
Ian Baker-Finch	73	73	75	73	294	1,220
David Llewellyn	74	71	75	74	294	1,220
Barry Lane	75	70	76	73	294	1,220
Emilio Rodriguez	72	76	71	75	294	1,220
Clive Tucker	71	70	77	76	294	1,220
Rick Hartmann	72	74	75	74	295	1,000
Jeff Hawkes	70	71	77	77	295	1,000
Sandy Lyle	75	73	76	71	295	1,000
Michael McLean	75	71	74	75	295	1,000
Ove Sellberg	69	77	77	72	295	1,000
David Williams	69	74	76	76	295	1,000

Lancome Trophy

St. Nom-la-Breteche Golf Club, Paris, France
Par 36-36 — 72; 6,713 yards

September 17-20
purse, £300,000

	SCORES				TOTAL	MONEY
Ian Woosnam	65	64	69	66	264	£50,000
Mark McNulty	68	67	67	64	266	33,300
Tony Johnstone	64	69	66	69	268	16,890
Sandy Lyle	67	69	66	66	268	16,890
Bernhard Langer	64	70	72	63	269	12,700
Ronan Rafferty	69	67	67	68	271	10,500
David Feherty	67	69	68	68	272	7,740
Mark James	66	71	70	65	272	7,740
Raymod Floyd	69	69	65	69	272	7,740
Tony Charnley	71	67	70	66	274	5,760
Barry Lane	67	63	73	71	274	5,760
Jose-Maria Canizares	73	67	68	67	275	5,160
Gordon Brand Jr.	68	70	68	70	276	4,515
Rodger Davis	70	67	70	69	276	4,515
David Llewellyn	74	68	68	66	276	4,515
Manuel Pinero	68	71	69	68	276	4,515
Severiano Ballesteros	72	67	71	67	277	3,960
Des Smyth	66	70	70	71	277	3,960
Anders Forsbrand	70	67	72	69	278	3,660
Robert Lee	72	68	69	69	278	3,660
Howard Clark	68	70	72	69	279	3,510
John Bland	68	72	71	69	280	3,240
Mats Lanner	72	70	71	67	280	3,240
Mark Mouland	68	72	73	67	280	3,240
Ove Sellberg	69	71	73	67	280	3,240
Kenny Knox	70	74	68	68	280	3,240
Neil Coles	67	70	72	72	281	2,790
Nick Faldo	73	70	70	68	281	2,790
Peter Fowler	72	72	70	67	281	2,790
Rick Hartmann	71	71	71	68	281	2,790
Jose Rivero	72	71	67	71	281	2,790
Hugh Baiocchi	72	69	69	72	282	2,460
Gavin Levenson	71	69	68	74	282	2,460
Paul Way	73	66	68	75	282	2,460
Ian Baker-Finch	72	70	71	70	283	2,250
Emmanuel Dussart	72	72	72	67	283	2,250
Antonio Garrido	70	69	72	72	283	2,250
Sam Torrance	71	73	72	67	283	2,250
Eamonn Darcy	73	69	69	73	284	1,980
Jeff Hawkes	68	76	71	69	284	1,980
Brian Marchbank	74	68	72	70	284	1,980
John O'Leary	71	72	68	73	284	1,980
Mark Roe	70	67	73	74	284	1,980
Roger Chapman	66	76	72	71	285	1,650
Bill Longmuir	72	70	70	73	285	1,650
Jose-Maria Olazabal	69	75	72	69	285	1,650
Glenn Ralph	70	71	76	68	285	1,650
David A. Russell	70	70	74	71	285	1,650
Bobby Clampett	69	75	72	69	285	1,650
Vicente Fernandez	71	72	70	73	286	1,350
Miquel Martin	72	71	72	71	286	1,350
Christy O'Connor Jr.	72	70	73	71	286	1,350
Philip Walton	71	74	74	67	286	1,350

Vernons Open

Royal Liverpool Golf Club, Hoylake, England
Par 36-36 — 72; 7,050 yards

September 24-27
purse, £70,000

	SCORES				TOTAL	MONEY
David Llewellyn	73	69	72	70	284	£10,500
Rodger Davis	71	69	74	72	286	7,105
Philip Walton	74	70	72	71	287	5,180
Andrew Oldcorn	75	76	70	67	288	4,200
Paul Way	74	74	72	69	289	3,360
John Morgan	74	77	70	69	290	2,835
Bill Longmuir	74	78	71	68	291	2,088.33
Mark Davis	73	72	74	72	291	2,088.33
Peter Cowen	74	74	71	72	291	2,088.33
Neal Briggs	78	72	73	69	292	1,505.00
Ian Mosey	77	71	71	73	292	1,505.00
David Ray	75	73	73	72	293	1,264.66
David Jones	77	73	70	73	293	1,264.66
Richard Boxall	77	75	68	73	293	1,264.66
Michael King	78	72	71	74	295	1,137.50
Ross Drummond	71	72	76	76	295	1,137.50
Brian Waites	78	76	71	71	296	1,067.50
Hugh Baiocchi	75	73	76	72	296	1,067.50
Russell Weir	75	74	73	75	297	1,000.50
Mark Johnson	72	78	70	77	297	1,000.50
Kevin Jones	75	80	72	71	298	875
Phil Weaver	79	72	75	72	298	875
Paul Thomas	74	75	75	74	298	875
David Gilford	78	72	73	75	298	875
Hendrick Buhrman	78	73	69	78	298	875
Chris Gray	75	78	77	69	299	735
Lee Jones	75	77	75	72	299	735
John Harrison	73	75	77	74	299	735
Andrew Murray	79	73	75	73	300	632.33
David J. Russell	76	71	79	74	300	632.33
Jimmy Heggarty	75	73	76	76	300	632.33

Dunhill Cup

Old Course, St. Andrews, Scotland
Par 36-36 — 72; 6,933 yards

October 1-4
purse, US$1,000,000

FIRST ROUND

CANADA DEFEATED NEW ZEALAND, 2½-½
Dave Barr (C) defeated Bruce Soulsby, 71-74; Dan Halldorson (C) halved with Greg Turner, 74-74; Richard Zokol (C) defeated Frank Nobilo, 72-74.

JAPAN DEFEATED MALAYSIA, 2-1
Marimuthu Ramayah (M) defeated Koichi Suzuki, 74-75; Nobuo Serizawa (J) defeated Sahabudin Yusof, 70-76; Nobumitsu Yuhara (J) defeated Zainal Abidin Yusof, 75-80.

UNITED STATES DEFEATED ITALY, 3-0
Curtis Strange (US) defeated Costantino Rocca, 71-72; D. A. Weibring (US) defeated Silvio Grappasonni, 69-77; Mark O'Meara (US) defeated Giuseppe Cali, 70-75.

SPAIN DEFEATED THE PHILIPPINES, 3-0
Jose Rivero (S) defeated Frankie Minoza, 68-75; Jose-Maria Olazabal (S) defeated Rudy Lavares, 71-80; Jose-Maria Canizares (S) defeated Eddie Bagtas, 72-77.

IRELAND DEFEATED FRANCE, 3-0
Ronan Rafferty (I) defeated Michel Tapia, 71-76; Eamonn Darcy (I) defeated Gery Watine, 72-76; Des Smyth (I) defeated Emmanuel Dussart, 74-76.

SCOTLAND DEFEATED ZIMBABWE, 3-0
Sandy Lyle (S) defeated Tim Price, 71-73; Gordon Brand Jr. (S) defeated Anthony Edwards, 70-72; Sam Torrance (S) defeated William Koen, 72-73.

ENGLAND DEFEATED MEXICO, 2½-½
Howard Clark (E) halved with Ernesto Perez Acosta, 71-71; Nick Faldo (E) defeated Carlos Espinoza, 70-75; Gordon J. Brand (E) defeated Feliciano Esparza, 74-81.

AUSTRALIA DEFEATED SWEDEN, 2-1
Ove Sellberg (S) defeated Rodger Davis, 69-75; Greg Norman (A) defeated Mats Lanner, 70-71; Peter Senior (A) defeated Anders Forsbrand, 67-70.

(First round losers received US $7,500 each.)

SECOND ROUND

UNITED STATES DEFEATED JAPAN, 2-1
Strange (US) defeated Suzuki, 68-70; Yuhara (J) defeated Weibring, 69-75; O'Meara (US) defeated Serizawa, 70-70, third extra hole.

AUSTRALIA DEFEATED CANADA, 2-1
Barr (C) defeated Senior, 73-73, first extra hole; Norman (A) defeated Zokol, 71-71, fifth extra hole; Davis (A) defeated Halldorson, 63-73.

SCOTLAND DEFEATED IRELAND, 2-1
Torrance (S) defeated Rafferty, 69-74; Lyle (S) defeated Darcy, 67-72; Smyth (I) defeated Brand Jr., 67-73.

ENGLAND DEFEATED SPAIN, 2-1
Rivero (S) defeated Clark, 72-77; Faldo (E) defeated Olazabal, 71-77; Brand (E) defeated Canizares, 71-74.

(Second round losers received US $15,000 each.)

SEMI-FINALS

SCOTLAND DEFEATED UNITED STATES, 3-0
Torrance (S) defeated Strange, 69-73; Lyle (S) defeated O'Meara, 70-71; Brand Jr. (S) defeated Weibring, 73-74.

ENGLAND DEFEATED AUSTRALIA, 2-1
Clark (E) defeated Senior, 73-74; Norman (A) defeated Brand, 68-69; Faldo (E) defeated Davis, 71-72.

PLAYOFF—THIRD-FOURTH PLACES

UNITED STATES DEFEATED AUSTRALIA, 2-1
O'Meara (US) defeated Senior, 71-72; Davis (A) defeated Weibring, 70-71; Strange (US) defeated Norman, 62-70.

(Each U.S. player received US $36,666; each Australian player received US $26,666.)

FINALS

ENGLAND DEFEATED SCOTLAND, 2-1
Faldo (E) defeated Lyle, 66-69; Brand (E) defeated Torrance, 64-69; Brand Jr. (S) defeated Clark, 68-73.

(Each English player received US$100,000; each Scottish player received US$50,000.)

German Masters

Stuttgarter Golf Club, Stuttgart, West Germany
Par 36-36 — 72; 6,809 yards

October 8-11
purse, £266,890

	SCORES				TOTAL	MONEY
Sandy Lyle	73	69	70	66	278	£44,480.40
Bernhard Langer	68	69	71	70	278	29,624.69
(Lyle defeated Langer on second hole of playoff.)						
Severiano Ballesteros	72	70	67	70	279	16,703.92
Gordon Brand Jr.	74	71	67	69	281	13,344.45
Jose-Maria Olazabal	70	74	67	71	282	9,550.18
Ian Woosnam	79	68	69	66	282	9,550.18
Greg Norman	77	68	69	68	282	9,550.18
Michael Allen	75	68	71	69	283	5,996.11
Tony Charnley	70	71	71	71	283	5,996.11
Peter Fowler	73	71	70	69	283	5,996.11
Manuel Pinero	72	69	70	73	284	4,599.39
Jose Rivero	71	71	70	72	284	4,599.39
Ove Sellberg	73	72	70	69	284	4,599.39
Tommy Armour III	66	72	72	75	285	4,003.34
Jim Rutledge	72	72	73	68	285	4,003.34
Rick Hartmann	77	65	72	72	286	3,603.00
Barry Lane	72	73	72	69	286	3,603.00
Christy O'Connor Jr.	70	67	73	76	286	3,603.00
Jose-Maria Canizares	72	71	74	70	287	3,211.56
Eamonn Darcy	78	69	71	69	287	3,211.56
Emilio Rodriguez	76	70	75	66	287	3,211.56
Anders Forsbrand	74	72	72	70	288	3,002.51
John O'Leary	76	72	68	72	288	3,002.51
Gordon J. Brand	71	73	71	74	289	2,762.30
Emmanuel Dussart	71	74	72	72	289	2,762.30
Mark McNulty	74	75	68	72	289	2,762.30
Andrew Murray	73	74	74	68	289	2,762.30
Bernard Gallacher	75	73	72	70	290	2,482.07
Andrew Oldcorn	74	70	76	70	290	2,482.07
Philip Walton	72	73	74	71	290	2,482.07
Hugh Baiocchi	73	71	73	74	291	2,166.25
Ian Mosey	75	72	73	71	291	2,166.25
David A. Russell	73	70	74	74	291	2,166.25
David J. Russell	73	69	76	73	291	2,166.25
Armando Saavedra	73	76	69	73	291	2,166.25
Peter Teravainen	77	72	68	74	291	2,166.25
Ron Commans	76	73	73	70	292	1,921.60
Ronan Rafferty	75	73	72	72	292	1,921.60
Teddy Webber	79	67	74	72	292	1,921.60
Antonio Garrido	75	73	73	72	293	1,708.09
Tony Johnstone	73	73	77	70	293	1,708.09
Carl Mason	76	70	71	76	293	1,708.09
John Morgan	73	74	75	71	293	1,708.09
John Slaughter	78	72	71	72	293	1,708.09

	SCORES				TOTAL	MONEY
Manuel Calero	74	74	71	75	294	1,361.14
Roger Chapman	75	74	74	71	294	1,361.14
Vicente Fernandez	78	72	71	73	294	1,361.14
Colin Montegomerie	72	71	77	74	294	1,361.14
Frank Nobilo	76	70	73	75	294	1,361.14
Mark Roe	77	73	77	67	294	1,361.14
Andrew Stubbs	73	77	72	72	294	1,361.14
Paul Thomas	77	71	72	74	294	1,361.14

Suntory World Match Play Championship

Wentworth Club,
West Course, Virginia Water, Surrey, England
Par 434 534 444 — 35; 345 434 455 — 37 — 72;
6,945 yards

October 15-19
purse, £265,000

FIRST ROUND

Mark McNulty defeated Howard Clark, 2 and 1

McNulty	545	433	545	38	343	443	346	34	72
Clark	434	644	443	36	244	434	455	35	71
Clark leads, 1 up									
McNulty	334	434	454	34	335	534	44		
Clark	445	544	444	38	244	534	44		

Sandy Lyle defeated David Ishii at 39th hole

Lyle	535	534	443	36	245	543	455	37	73
Ishii	435	444	434	35	334	434	454	34	69
Ishii leads, 4 up									
Lyle	425	435	343	38	344	534	455	37	70
Ishii	535	524	554	38	344	525	365	37	75
Match all-square									
Lyle	434								
Ishii	435								

Seve Ballesteros defeated Katsunari Takahashi, 4 and 2

Ballesteros	525	423	543	33	244	534	445	35	68
Takahashi	424	424	434	31	345	434	555	38	69
Ballesteros leads, 1 up									
Ballesteros	334	434	444	33	444	334	3		
Takahashi	434	434	444	34	354	C34	4		

Ian Woosnam defeated Sam Randolph, 4 and 3

Woosnam	534	444	344	35	345	434	444	35	70
Randolph	434	534	434	34	344	434	454	35	69
Randolph leads, 1 up									
Woosnam	334	523	444	32	344	434			
Randolph	436	535	444	38	444	434			

SECOND ROUND

Mark McNulty defeated Greg Norman, 1 hole

Norman	534	C34	443	X	244	434	453	33	X
McNulty	445	W24	344	X	334	434	444	33	X
McNulty leads, 1 up									
Norman	444	434	444	35	344	335	345	34	69
McNulty	425	434	434	33	344	434	445	35	68

Sandy Lyle defeated Larry Mize, 7 and 6

Mize	535	644	444	39	345	335	455	37	76
Lyle	534	433	443	33	345	333	445	34	67

Lyle leads, 7 up

Mize	444	533	434	34	244	
Lyle	534	433	344	33	344	

Seve Ballesteros defeated Scott Simpson, 5 and 4

Ballesteros	444	424	434	33	234	524	45W	X	X
Simpson	535	434	343	34	344	435	456	38	72

Ballesteros leads, 5 up

Ballesteros	436	434	445	37	344	43
Simpson	544	534	433	35	344	43

Ian Woosnam defeated Nick Faldo, 1 hole

Woosnam	434	434	445	35	344	334	345	33	68
Faldo	525	424	343	32	344	334	454	34	66

Faldo leads, 1 up

Woosnam	425	434	434	33	344	423	454	33	66
Faldo	534	434	344	34	334	434	435	33	67

SEMI-FINALS

Sandy Lyle defeated Mark McNulty at 39th hole

McNulty	435	434	445	36	435	533	455	37	73
Lyle	435	544	444	37	344	445	465	39	76

McNulty leads, 2 up

McNulty	445	534	336	37	244	435	455	36	73
Lyle	434	535	544	37	434	534	345	35	72

Match all-square

McNulty	435
Lyle	434

Ian Woosnam defeated Seve Ballesteros, 1 hole

Ballesteros	434	433	545	35	344	434	454	35	70
Woosnam	534	434	444	35	344	334	455	35	70

Match all-square

Ballesteros	44C	434	444	X	24C	334	345	X	X
Woosnam	424	434	344	32	344	434	454	35	67

FINAL

Ian Woosnam defeated Sandy Lyle, 1 hole

Lyle	434	444	543	35	344	444	343	33	68
Woosnam	435	434	334	33	335	435	354	35	68

Lyle leads, 1 up

Lyle	434	434	444	34	344	435	345	35	69
Woosnam	434	534	434	34	244	434	444	33	67

THIRD PLACE

Seve Ballesteros defeated Mark McNulty at 20th hole

McNulty	436	434	344	35	233	435	455	34	69
Ballesteros	43W	434	454	X	344	333	444	32	X

Match all-square

McNulty	44
Ballesteros	43

PRIZE MONEY: Woosnam £75,000; Lyle £40,000; Ballesteros £30,000; McNulty £20,000; Faldo, Mize, Norman, Simpson £15,000 each; Clark, Ishii, Randolph, Takahashi £10,000 each.

LEGEND: C—conceded hole to opponent; W—won hole by concession without holing out; X-no total score.

Portuguese Open

Estoril Golf Club, Estoril, Lisbon, Portugal   October 29-November 1
Par 33-36 — 69; 5,697 yards   purse, £100,000

(Tournament reduced to 54 holes; Friday round cancelled, rain.)

	SCORES			TOTAL	MONEY
Robert Lee	61	67	67	195	£16,660
Sam Torrance	67	64	65	196	11,100
Ove Sellberg	69	65	63	197	5,630
Andrew Sherborne	65	67	65	197	5,630
Christy O'Connor Jr.	69	65	64	198	3,580
Philip Walton	71	63	64	198	3,580
Ian Young	69	66	63	198	3,580
Peter Baker	64	69	66	199	2,370
Jose Rivero	70	66	63	199	2,370
John O'Leary	66	66	68	200	2,000
Ross Drummond	66	67	68	201	1,780
Carl Mason	68	65	68	201	1,780
Billy Andrade	69	66	67	202	1,474
Oliver Eckstein	69	67	66	202	1,474
David Llewellyn	67	67	68	202	1,474
Bill Longmuir	68	63	71	202	1,474
David Williams	74	63	65	202	1,474
Roger Chapman	68	67	68	203	1,225
Neil Hansen	70	68	65	203	1,225
Manuel Pinero	70	66	67	203	1,225
Des Smyth	71	64	68	203	1,225
Gordon J. Brand	64	74	66	204	1,050
Brian Marchbank	67	71	66	204	1,050
John Morgan	71	67	66	204	1,050
Andrew Murray	70	65	69	204	1,050
Magnus Persson	69	68	67	204	1,050
Costantino Rocca	67	70	67	204	1,050
Grant Turner	66	72	66	204	1,050
Neal Briggs	69	69	67	205	848.57
Per-Arne Brostedt	70	66	69	205	848.57
Andrea Canessa	71	68	66	205	848.57
Jose Davila	70	66	69	205	848.57
Miguel Martin	67	69	69	205	848.57
Armando Saavedra	71	68	66	205	848.57
Keith Waters	69	69	67	205	848.57
Jose-Maria Canizares	67	70	69	206	740
Santiago Luna	68	68	70	206	740
David Ray	74	67	65	206	740
Peter Carsbo	69	69	69	207	670
Anders Forsbrand	69	69	69	207	670
Jeff Hall	70	65	72	207	670
Mark James	67	74	66	207	670
Joe Higgins	71	69	68	208	590
Colin Montgomerie	75	66	67	208	590

	SCORES			TOTAL	MONEY
Martin Poxon	72	69	67	208	590
Steen Tinning	68	70	70	208	590
Mats Lanner	70	69	70	209	490
Nicholas Mitchell	68	68	73	209	490
Juan Quiros	71	69	69	209	490
Anthony Stevens	71	69	69	209	490
Andrew Stubbs	67	72	70	209	490
Magnus Sunesson	66	71	72	209	490

The African Tours

Palabora Classic

Hans Merensky Golf Club, Phalaborwa
Par 36-36 — 72; 6,727 yards

January 7-11
purse, R140,000

	SCORES				TOTAL	MONEY
Fulton Allem	67	73	66	65	271	R22,400
Hugh Baiocchi	69	69	68	66	272	16,100
Chris Williams	66	66	72	70	274	9,800
Jeff Hawkes	68	72	67	68	275	5,973.33
Hendrik Buhrmann	72	67	68	68	275	5,973.33
Mark McNulty	71	67	68	69	275	5,973.33
Phil Jonas	67	69	72	69	277	3,850
John Fourie	67	66	69	75	277	3,850
Mark James	69	69	73	67	278	2,695
Gavin Levenson	67	76	68	67	278	2,695
Jon Mannie	67	75	68	68	278	2,695
Trevor Dodds	66	70	71	71	278	2,695
Rick Hartman	68	69	75	67	279	2,240
Teddy Webber	71	68	73	68	280	1,995
Bobby Lincoln	74	71	67	68	280	1,995
Justin Hobday	71	72	69	68	280	1,995
Tony Johnstone	71	71	69	69	280	1,995
Robbie Stewart	67	70	72	72	281	1,785
Ian Palmer	71	67	70	73	281	1,785
Robert Richardson	73	69	73	67	282	1,478.40
John Bland	72	73	70	67	282	1,478.40
Stuart Smith	69	71	74	68	282	1,478.40
Bob E. Smith	71	72	71	68	282	1,478.40
Wayne Westner	75	69	69	69	282	1,478.40
Garth Pearson	71	69	72	70	282	1,478.40
Warren Humphreys	71	70	70	71	282	1,478.40
Brian Evans	70	70	69	73	282	1,478.40
Malcolm McKenzie	70	67	71	74	282	1,478.40
Steve Van Vuuren	65	71	68	78	282	1,478.40
Michael Archer	71	74	69	69	283	1,225
Mike White	70	71	71	71	283	1,225

ICL International

Zwartkop Country Club, Pretoria
Par 36-36 — 72; 7,125 yards

January 14-17
purse, R120,000

	SCORES				TOTAL	MONEY
Tony Johnstone	69	67	64	71	271	R19,200
Wilhelm Winsnes	69	72	71	65	277	11,100
Justin Hobday	71	67	67	72	277	11,100
John Bland	69	70	71	69	279	5,520
Hugh Baiocchi	69	70	71	69	279	5,520
Ian Palmer	68	72	70	70	280	3,640
Phil Simmons	66	67	74	73	280	3,640
Bobby Lincoln	70	70	69	71	280	3,640
Chris Williams	70	70	74	67	281	2,310
Simon Bishop	72	68	71	70	281	2,310
Malcolm McKenzie	70	69	70	72	281	2,310
Gordon Manson	69	68	70	74	281	2,310
Mark James	70	75	68	69	282	1,860
Fulton Allem	71	69	69	73	282	1,860
Warren Humphreys	71	72	68	72	283	1,680
Phil Jonas	70	69	72	72	283	1,680
Gavin Levenson	67	72	67	77	283	1,680
Simon Hobday	73	72	69	70	284	1,473
Robert Richardson	69	71	72	72	284	1,473
Trevor Dodds	72	72	68	72	284	1,473
Andre Cruse	73	70	67	74	284	1,473
Ian Young	74	71	71	69	285	1,284
Wayne Westner	74	69	72	70	285	1,284
Bob E. Smith	73	67	75	70	285	1,284
Mark Wiltshire	72	70	71	72	285	1,284
Mark McNulty	70	68	73	74	285	1,284
Teddy Webber	71	70	75	70	286	1,140
Denis Durnian	73	67	73	73	286	1,140
Alan Henning	69	68	75	74	286	1,140
Rick Hartman	74	68	74	71	287	961.33
Richard Kaplan	69	78	70	70	287	961.33
Mark Hartness	73	71	72	71	287	961.33
Chris Moody	70	70	75	72	287	961.33
Jeff Hawkes	71	72	72	72	287	961.33
Mark Bright	74	68	72	73	287	961.33
Paul Van Zyl	70	76	69	72	287	961.33
Bobby Verwey	71	73	69	74	287	961.33
Joe Dlamini	71	71	70	75	287	961.33

Lexington PGA Championship

Wanderers Golf Club, Johannesburg
Par 35-35 — 70; 6,960 yards

January 21-24
purse, R120,000

	SCORES				TOTAL	MONEY
Fulton Allem	65	67	68	68	268	R19,200
Hugh Baiocchi	65	69	68	68	270	13,800
Gordon Manson	66	68	68	72	274	8,400
Ian Palmer	66	71	71	69	277	5,120
Chris Williams	71	68	65	73	277	5,120
John Bland	68	67	67	75	277	5,120
Denis Durnian	68	72	71	68	279	2,910

	SCORES				TOTAL	MONEY
Simon Bishop	69	69	72	69	279	2,910
Malcolm McKenzie	71	71	68	69	279	2,910
Robbie Stewart	71	68	67	73	279	2,910
Trevor Dodds	70	72	69	69	280	1,932
Jeff Hawkes	73	68	69	70	280	1,932
Phil Jonas	74	68	67	71	280	1,932
Jon Mannie	71	69	69	71	280	1,932
Ian Mosey	67	70	70	73	280	1,932
Bobby Verwey	68	70	69	74	281	1,532
Phil Simmons	73	68	73	67	281	1,532
Andre Cruse	71	72	70	68	281	1,532
Mark McNulty	68	72	70	71	281	1,532
Brian Evans	69	70	71	71	281	1,532
Robert Richardson	71	68	69	73	281	1,532
Vin Baker	69	71	74	69	283	1,284
Garth Pearson	68	72	72	71	283	1,284
Warren Humphreys	69	71	72	71	283	1,284
Ian Young	69	73	70	71	283	1,284
Roger Wessels	71	71	69	72	283	1,284
Michael Green	73	67	73	71	284	1,158
Ron McCann	70	72	70	72	284	1,158
Rick Hartman	75	70	69	71	285	1,053
Chris Moody	72	69	71	73	285	1,053
Teddy Webber	70	70	72	73	285	1,053
Stuart Smith	71	68	70	76	285	1,053

Southern Sun South African Open Championship

Mowbray Golf Club, Cape Town
Par 36-36 — 72; 6,664 yards

February 4-7
purse, R100,000

	SCORES				TOTAL	MONEY
Mark McNulty	74	66	71	67	278	R16,221
Fulton Allem	67	71	71	69	278	11,659
(McNulty defeated Allem on second hole of playoff.)						
Wayne Westner	66	67	75	73	281	7,097
Hendrik Buhrmann	76	68	71	67	282	5,069
Phil Harrison	72	73	74	66	285	2,957.33
Ian Palmer	72	70	76	67	285	2,957.33
Chris Williams	76	69	72	68	285	2,957.33
Bobby Verwey	73	74	68	70	285	2,957.33
John Bland	70	72	72	71	285	2,957.33
Teddy Webber	70	72	71	72	285	2,957.33
Andre Cruse	73	69	78	66	286	1,825
Gordon Manson	76	70	74	67	287	1,584.25
Wilhelm Winsnes	75	70	74	68	287	1,584.25
Simon Bishop	70	74	74	69	287	1,584.25
Ian Young	70	69	76	72	287	1,584.25
Simon Hobday	70	76	69	73	288	1,420
Hugh Baiocchi	78	71	69	71	289	1,343.50
Tony Johnstone	70	72	72	75	289	1,343.50
Bob E. Smith	74	73	75	68	290	1,201.75
Peter Evans	70	74	77	69	290	1,201.75
Jeff Hawkes	73	72	73	72	290	1,201.75
Ian Mosey	72	69	75	74	290	1,201.75
Peter Van Der Riet	77	70	74	70	291	1,100.50
Frank Edmonds	74	71	74	72	291	1,100.50

	SCORES				TOTAL	MONEY
Michaeil Bullock	72	70	80	70	292	1,009
Warren Humphreys	73	73	74	72	292	1,009
David Russell	74	72	73	73	292	1,009
Jimmy Johnson	72	75	70	75	292	1,009
Robert Lendzion	73	75	74	71	293	824.60
Mervyn Galant	71	71	79	72	293	824.60
Rick Hartman	73	71	77	72	293	824.60
Mark Bright	75	72	74	72	293	824.60
Brian Evans	77	70	74	72	293	824.60
Chris Moody	76	71	74	72	293	824.60
Joe Dlamini	69	75	74	75	293	824.60
Ron McCann	72	74	72	75	293	824.60
Alan Henning	74	75	68	76	293	824.60
David O'Kelly	72	73	71	77	293	824.60

AECI Charity Classic

Rand Park Golf Club, Johannesburg
Par 36-35 — 71; 7,320 yards

February 11-14
purse, R100,000

	SCORES				TOTAL	MONEY
Mark McNulty	65	70	71	64	270	R16,000
Wayne Westner	72	63	67	68	270	11,500
(McNulty defeated Westner on first hole of playoff.)						
Ian Palmer	68	69	70	68	275	6,000
Ian Mosey	69	65	71	70	275	6,000
Andrew Chandler	68	69	68	71	276	4,200
Gavin Levenson	67	69	72	69	277	3,300
Phil Simmons	72	68	67	70	277	3,300
Joe Dlamini	72	66	71	70	279	2,500
Phil Harrison	73	72	69	66	280	2,100
Don Robertson	70	71	69	70	280	2,100
Fulton Allem	69	70	70	72	281	1,700
Tony Johnstone	71	69	68	73	281	1,700
Mike White	67	68	71	75	281	1,700
Bobby Verwey, Jr.	72	69	73	68	282	1,475
Bob E. Smith	72	71	70	69	282	1,475
Gert Von Biljon	70	74	70	69	283	1,375
Chris Williams	68	73	70	72	283	1,375
John Fourie	73	68	72	71	284	1,250
Hendrik Buhrmann	73	69	71	71	284	1,250
Malcolm McKenzie	72	67	70	75	284	1,250
Stuart Smith	75	67	74	69	285	1,085
Warren Humphreys	69	75	71	70	285	1,085
Bobby Lincoln	74	69	70	72	285	1,085
Teddy Webber	68	68	74	75	285	1,085
Wilhelm Winsnes	71	72	68	74	285	1,085
Michael Green	66	71	69	79	285	1,085
Robert Richardson	72	71	74	69	286	920
Simon Bishop	71	70	75	70	286	920
Hugh Baiocchi	72	73	72	69	286	920
Mark James	71	68	74	73	286	920
Jimmy Johnson	71	69	71	75	286	920

Royal Swazi Sun Pro-Am

Royal Swazi Sun Country Club, Mbabane, Swaziland
Par 36-36 — 72; 6,708 yards

February 19-22
purse, R100,000

	SCORES				TOTAL	MONEY
Mark McNulty	68	65	64	62	259	R16,000
Wayne Westner	67	65	69	64	265	11,500
John Bland	67	69	65	68	269	6,000
Simon Hobday	71	61	66	71	269	6,000
Fulton Allem	66	68	68	70	272	3,600
Hugh Baiocchi	70	63	68	71	272	3,600
Tony Johnstone	66	67	67	72	272	3,600
Ian Palmer	66	73	70	64	273	2,233.33
Teddy Webber	68	68	70	67	273	2,233.33
Malcolm McKenzie	65	67	71	70	273	2,233.33
Chris Moody	67	68	68	71	274	1,750
Vin Baker	67	67	70	70	274	1,750
Bob E. Smith	73	68	70	64	275	1,487.50
Joe Dlamini	68	71	66	70	275	1,487.50
Ian Mosey	68	72	66	69	275	1,487.50
Andrew Chandler	64	67	70	74	275	1,487.50
Frank Edmonds	68	68	70	70	276	1,300
Jeff Hawkes	71	67	68	70	276	1,300
Mike White	68	70	64	74	276	1,300
Richard Kaplan	69	69	72	67	277	1,147.50
Tienie Britz	71	67	72	67	277	1,147.50
Allan Henning	70	68	72	67	277	1,147.50
Justin Hobday	68	67	74	68	277	1,147.50
Jon Mannie	68	71	72	67	278	1,040
Robert Richardson	70	70	70	68	278	1,040
Phil Simmons	74	68	68	68	278	1,040
Jimmy Johnson	70	71	72	66	279	920
Brian Evans	66	71	73	69	279	920
Phil Harrison	70	68	71	70	279	920
Denis Durnian	71	69	69	70	279	920
Bobby Verwey	72	66	68	73	279	920

Zimbabwe Open

Royal Harare Golf Club, Harare, Zimbabwe
Par 36-36 — 72; 7,082 yards

February 19-22
purse, £50,200

	SCORES				TOTAL	MONEY
Gordon J. Brand	74	65	69	69	277	£8,365.46
Andrew Murray	68	69	72	68	277	5,574.30
(Brand defeated Murray on first hole of playoff.)						
John Morgan	73	69	68	71	281	2,827.30
Billy Koen	70	65	72	74	281	2,827.30
Mark Johnson	68	72	72	71	283	2,126.51
Andrew Stubbs	67	76	70	71	284	1,757.03
Lee Jones	71	71	71	72	285	1,506.02
Andrea Canessa	74	73	73	66	286	1,188.75
Mark Mouland	74	69	74	69	286	1,188.75
Rui Da Costa	76	71	74	66	287	933.07
David Williams	72	75	71	69	287	933.07
Richard Fish	70	70	70	77	287	933.07
Tim Price	72	72	75	69	288	761.55

	SCORES				TOTAL	MONEY
Mike Miller	77	74	68	69	288	761.55
Stephen Bennett	78	71	69	70	288	761.55
Peter Baker	74	69	74	71	288	761.55
Neil Burke	73	75	72	69	289	650.60
John Fowler	70	74	74	71	289	650.60
Joe Higgins	69	72	69	79	289	650.60
Roger Chapman	73	73	72	72	290	598.39
Dana Banke	74	71	72	73	290	598.39
David Llewellyn	76	72	68	74	290	598.39
Carl Mason	74	71	73	73	291	542.17
Keith Waters	74	72	72	73	291	542.17
Grant Turner	74	71	71	75	291	542.17
David Jones	76	72	68	75	291	542.17
Magnus Sunesson	71	76	75	70	292	493.98
Glyn Davis	71	71	75	75	292	493.98
Peter Harrison	72	75	75	71	293	421.69
Murray Supple	74	74	74	71	293	421.69
Glenn Ralph	69	76	74	74	293	421.69
Tony Charnley	70	76	72	75	293	421.69
Mats Hallberg	73	73	72	75	293	421.69
Peter Cowen	74	71	72	76	293	421.69
Peter Barber	74	72	71	76	293	421.69

Trust Bank Tournament of Champions

Kensington Golf Club, Johannesburg
Par 35-37 — 72; 6,716 yards

February 25-28
purse, R150,000

	SCORES				TOTAL	MONEY
Mark McNulty	68	68	68	67	271	R25,000
Gavin Levenson	69	71	68	67	275	17,135
Ian Young	72	71	70	65	278	10,430
Tienie Britz	70	69	69	72	280	7,450
Bob E. Smith	71	72	70	68	281	4,954.25
Robert Richardson	72	72	67	70	281	4,954.25
John Bland	71	71	67	72	281	4,954.25
Denis Durnian	72	68	69	72	281	4,954.25
Wayne Westner	71	70	74	67	282	2,980
Fulton Allem	72	72	70	68	282	2,980
Justin Hobday	72	74	67	69	282	2,980
Mark Hartness	71	71	75	66	283	2,279.70
Bobby Lincoln	73	74	68	68	283	2,279.70
Phil Harrison	72	69	73	69	283	2,279.70
Simon Hobday	70	70	70	73	283	2,279.70
Hendrik Buhrmann	70	69	72	72	283	2,279.70
Frank Edmonds	73	70	69	72	284	2,011.50
Tertius Claassens	71	72	73	69	285	1,799.92
Tony Johnstone	73	74	69	69	285	1,799.92
Jannie Le Grange	74	73	68	70	285	1,799.92
Ian Mosey	72	75	68	70	285	1,799.92
Hugh Baiocchi	71	70	73	71	285	1,799.92
Wayne Bradley	74	70	73	69	286	1,594.30
Ian Palmer	70	75	68	73	286	1,594.30
Teddy Webber	69	70	72	75	286	1,594.30
Mike White	72	71	74	70	287	1,415.50
Warren Humphreys	74	73	68	72	287	1,415.50
Peter Evans	70	69	74	74	287	1,415.50

	SCORES				TOTAL	MONEY
Mervyn Galant	69	72	71	75	287	1,415.50
Mark Wiltshire	69	68	72	78	287	1,415.50

Kenya Open

Muthaiga Golf Club, Nairobi, Kenya
Par 36-35 — 71; 6,765 yards

February 26-March 1
purse, £60,925

	SCORES				TOTAL	MONEY
Carl Mason	72	68	67	68	275	£9,868.16
Roger Chapman	70	68	67	70	275	4,454.65
Gordon J. Brand	70	66	70	69	275	4,454.65
Martin Poxon	69	69	71	66	275	4,454.65

(Mason won playoff, defeating Brand and Poxon on second hole, Chapman on third hole.)

	SCORES				TOTAL	MONEY
Mark Roe	66	67	71	72	276	2,437.08
David Williams	68	69	71	69	277	1,751.26
Joe Higgins	70	69	67	71	277	1,751.26
David Llewellyn	67	71	68	71	277	1,751.26
David Jagger	76	70	67	66	279	1,217.86
Mats Lanner	75	66	71	67	279	1,217.86
Andrew Murray	70	67	69	73	279	1,217.86
Mark Mouland	71	68	73	68	280	948.46
Andrea Canessa	68	71	71	70	280	948.46
Peter Carsbo	68	73	67	72	280	948.46
Stephen Bennett	67	70	70	73	280	948.46
Malcolm Gregson	68	73	68	71	280	948.46
Glenn Ralph	73	70	70	68	281	799.04
Keith Waters	74	71	67	69	281	799.04
Paul Kent	71	68	71	71	281	799.04
Tony Charnley	74	70	71	67	282	727.13
Anthony Edwards	73	72	70	67	282	727.13
Bill Longmuir	69	73	69	71	282	727.13
Wraith Grant	71	71	71	70	283	659.21
Bill McColl	71	67	74	71	283	659.21
Richard Fish	66	71	75	71	283	659.21
John Fowler	74	73	69	68	284	599.92
Brian Marchbank	74	72	69	69	284	599.92
Mats Hallberg	71	68	73	72	284	599.92
John Morgan	74	72	71	68	285	545.98
Dana Banke	73	66	72	74	285	545.98
David Jones	72	72	67	74	285	545.98
*David Farrar	71	71	72	71	285	

Zambian Open

Lusaka Golf Club, Lusaka, Zambia
Par 35-38 — 73; 7,259 yards

March 5-8
purse, £60,000

	SCORES				TOTAL	MONEY
Paul Carrigill	71	75	67	72	285	£10,000
Mike Miller	72	74	72	67	285	6,660

(Carrigill defeated Miller on first hole of playoff.)

	SCORES				TOTAL	MONEY
Keith Waters	75	69	69	73	286	3,100
Mark Mouland	71	74	70	71	286	3,100

	SCORES				TOTAL	MONEY
David Llewellyn	72	75	72	67	286	3,100
Grant Turner	74	76	67	70	287	1,950
John Morgan	74	73	72	68	287	1,950
Tony Charnley	72	76	71	69	288	1,346.66
Mark Roe	73	73	74	68	288	1,346.66
John Fowler	73	70	70	75	288	1,346.66
Jeffrey Pinsent	70	74	73	72	289	1,070
Bill McColl	75	69	73	72	289	1,070
Peter Carsbo	70	76	69	75	290	930
David Williams	72	74	74	70	290	930
Gordon J. Brand	74	72	75	69	290	930
David Ray	69	77	74	72	292	820
Andrew Stubbs	73	74	71	74	292	820
Andrew Murray	72	75	79	67	293	780
Emmanuel Dussart	71	74	75	74	294	760
Mark Johnson	77	74	70	74	295	740
Glenn Ralph	72	77	73	74	296	700
Joe Higgins	78	73	73	72	296	700
Paul Kent	74	78	76	68	296	700
David Jones	73	71	77	76	297	640
Bill Longmuir	78	73	72	74	297	640
Stephen Bennett	73	76	77	71	297	640
Lee Jones	72	73	75	78	298	560
Mats Hallberg	71	75	76	76	298	560
Glyn Davies	72	77	78	71	298	560
Gary Smith	72	73	77	76	298	560
Tim Price	76	71	81	70	298	560

Protea Assurance Prosure Challenge

Germiston Golf Club, Germiston
Par 36-35 — 71; 7,127 yards

November 18-21
purse, R250,000

	SCORES				TOTAL	MONEY
Bobby Lincoln	68	69	66	68	271	R40,000
Fulton Allem	68	70	64	70	272	28,750
David Feherty	69	65	68	71	273	17,500
Mark McNulty	70	66	67	71	274	12,500
Stuart Smith	66	71	70	70	277	10,500
Roger Wessels	70	73	68	67	278	8,250
Hugh Baiocchi	72	69	68	69	278	8,250
Desmond Terblanche	70	76	67	66	279	6,250
Gert V. Biljon	71	70	69	71	281	5,000
Gavin Levinson	69	72	69	71	281	5,000
Wayne Westner	71	69	70	71	281	5,000
Simon Hobday	71	75	70	67	283	3,906.25
John Bland	72	73	70	68	283	3,906.25
Ian Young	74	66	69	74	283	3,906.25
Wilhelm Winsnes	67	70	71	75	283	3,906.25
Michael King	75	71	71	67	284	3,375
Chris Williams	70	76	66	72	284	3,375
Schalk V.D. Merwe	75	68	69	72	284	3,375
Denis Durnian	75	72	71	67	285	2,962.50
Wayne Bradley	71	72	71	71	285	2,962.50
Phil Simmons	70	74	69	72	285	2,962.50
Robbie Stewart	72	67	70	76	285	2,962.50
Allan Henning	73	72	69	72	286	2,712.50

	SCORES				TOTAL	MONEY
Ross Palmer	71	71	71	73	286	2,712.50
Brian Evans	77	70	71	70	288	2,340.63
Wayne Player	68	78	72	70	288	2,340.63
Jon Mannie	74	73	71	70	288	2,340.63
Ian Palmer	69	72	75	72	288	2,340.63
Mark Wiltshire	72	73	71	72	288	2,340.63
Tony Johnstone	75	71	70	72	288	2,340.63
Hendrik Buhrmann	71	74	70	73	288	2,340.63
Jannie Le Grange	71	70	72	75	288	2,340.63

Wild Coast Classic

Casino Beach Country Club, Casino Beach
Par 35-35 — 70; 6,452 yards

November 24-27
purse, R150,000

	SCORES				TOTAL	MONEY
Tony Johnstone	66	64	67	65	262	R24,000
Hugh Baiocchi	67	65	69	68	269	17,250
Brian Evans	68	69	66	70	273	10,500
Bob E. Smith	69	68	69	68	274	7,500
Wayne Westner	68	68	69	70	275	5,850
John Bland	68	71	67	69	275	5,850
Mark McNulty	68	71	69	68	276	4,500
Teddy Webber	73	68	70	68	279	3,525
David Feherty	72	68	70	69	279	3,525
Tertius Claassens	72	68	70	70	280	2,662.50
Ian Palmer	68	72	70	70	280	2,662.50
Roger Wessels	71	70	68	71	280	2,662.50
Michael King	75	66	68	71	280	2,662.50
Fulton Allem	66	74	75	66	281	2,062.50
Peter Mkata	70	69	70	72	281	2,062.50
Mark Wiltshire	72	70	68	71	281	2,062.50
Jannie Le Grange	71	72	66	72	281	2,062.50
Wilhelm Winsnes	70	69	69	73	281	2,062.50
Gordon Manson	66	74	66	75	281	2,062.50
Denis Durnian	73	71	67	71	282	1,800
Phil Harrison	69	72	70	72	283	1,717.50
Ian Mosey	69	72	68	74	283	1,717.50
Ian Young	67	72	74	71	284	1,560
Mark Hartness	70	73	70	71	284	1,560
Don Robertson	72	71	70	71	284	1,560
Simon Hobday	67	71	74	72	284	1,560
Kevin Stone	71	77	65	71	284	1,560
Len O'Kennedy	70	72	76	67	285	1,357.50
Bobby Verwey	73	67	75	70	285	1,357.50
Gavin Levinson	71	73	70	71	285	1,357.50
Hendrik Buhrmann	73	67	71	74	285	1,357.50

Million Dollar Challenge

Gary Player Country Club, Sun City, Bophuthatswana
Par 36-36 — 72; 7,665 yards

December 3-6
purse, US $1,000,000

	SCORES				TOTAL	MONEY
Ian Woosnam	67	71	68	68	274	$1,000,000
Nick Faldo	68	71	68	71	278	
David Frost	70	70	68	72	280	
Fulton Allem	66	69	74	74	283	
Jose-Maria Olazabal	68	73	72	70	283	
Curtis Strange	72	69	72	70	283	
Bernhard Langer	70	68	73	74	285	
Lanny Wadkins	71	72	72	75	290	

Safmarine Masters

Stellenbosch Golf Club, Cape Town
Par 37-35 — 72; 7,036 yards

December 9-12
purse, R170,000

	SCORES				TOTAL	MONEY
David Frost	70	67	70	66	273	R27,200
Denis Durnian	74	67	70	65	276	19,550
Ian Palmer	73	65	71	71	280	11,900
John Bland	70	71	73	67	281	8,500
Ian Mosey	73	70	72	68	283	6,120
Fulton Allem	72	69	73	69	283	6,120
Tony Johnstone	70	69	74	70	283	6,120
Gavin Levenson	73	70	72	70	285	4,250
Teddy Webber	73	70	73	70	286	3,400
Peter Oosterhuis	73	73	68	72	286	3,400
Hugh Baiocchi	70	69	73	74	286	3,400
Steve V. Vuuren	77	68	74	68	287	2,601
Douglas Wherry	71	73	74	69	287	2,601
Andrew Chandler	74	73	70	70	287	2,601
Robbie Stewart	77	66	72	72	287	2,601
Mark Hartness	73	69	71	74	287	2,601
Ashley Roestoff	74	75	69	70	288	2,210
Tertius Claassens	75	74	68	71	288	2,210
Desmond Terblanche	71	72	70	75	288	2,210
Wayne Westner	71	75	74	69	289	1,950.75
Mark Wiltshire	76	71	71	71	289	1,950.75
Brian Evans	70	75	72	72	289	1,950.75
Bob E. Smith	70	69	75	75	289	1,950.75
Simon Bishop	78	69	71	72	290	1,793.50
David Feherty	76	66	73	75	290	1,793.50
Ian Young	72	70	78	71	291	1,691.50
Phil Jonas	72	71	76	72	291	1,691.50
Don Robertson	75	73	75	69	292	1,516.40
Gordon Manson	73	76	74	69	292	1,516.40
Chris Williams	76	72	73	71	292	1,516.40
Steven Jacobs	75	73	73	71	292	1,516.40
Dean V. Staden	74	73	69	76	292	1,516.40

Goodyear Classic

Humewood Golf Club, Port Elizabeth
Par 35-35 — 70; 6,454 yards

December 17-20
purse, R150,000

	SCORES				TOTAL	MONEY
John Bland	71	69	72	69	281	R24,000
Mark Wiltshire	71	71	75	66	283	17,250
David Feherty	74	72	68	70	284	8,100
Roger Wessels	67	76	70	71	284	8,100
Craigen Pappas	70	70	72	72	284	8,100
Bobby Verwey	67	71	75	72	285	5,400
Derek James	70	75	70	72	287	4,500
Greg McDonald	74	73	73	68	288	3,060
Denis Durnian	70	75	73	70	288	3,060
Phil Simmons	72	71	75	70	288	3,060
Richard Kaplan	69	75	70	74	288	3,060
Wayne Westner	71	72	69	76	288	3,060
Ian Young	74	74	75	66	289	2,190
Hugh Baiocchi	72	70	77	70	289	2,190
Chris Williams	72	67	77	73	278	2,190
John Fourie	74	70	72	73	289	2,190
Fulton Allem	72	74	67	76	289	2,190
Wayne Bradley	72	74	76	68	290	1,734.38
Mark Hartness	73	75	73	69	290	1,734.38
Andrew Chandler	74	76	70	70	290	1,734.38
Robbie Stewart	72	74	73	71	290	1,734.38
Wilhelm Winsnes	75	73	70	72	290	1,734.38
Tom Nosewicz	72	74	71	73	290	1,734.38
Michael King	70	74	74	72	290	1,734.38
Tony Johnstone	72	72	71	75	290	1,734.38
Gavin Levenson	76	73	74	68	291	1,447.50
Rick Hartman	75	75	73	68	291	1,447.50
Bobby Lincoln	73	73	74	71	291	1,447.50
Malcolm McKenzie	72	69	78	72	291	1,447.50
Jeff Hawkes	74	76	71	71	292	1,295
Gordon Manson	74	74	72	72	292	1,295
Steven Burnett	68	76	71	77	292	1,295

The Australasian Tour

U-Bix Classic New South Wales PGA

Federal Golf Club, Canberra, A.C.T.
Par 36-37 — 73; 6,853 yards

January 23-26
purse, A$100,000

	SCORES				TOTAL	MONEY
Peter Senior	67	65	72	69	273	A$18,000
Gerry Taylor	69	68	71	66	274	10,800
Gordon Brand Jr.	70	71	67	69	277	5,940
Vaughan Somers	69	68	70	70	277	5,940
Stewart Ginn	72	71	66	69	278	3,595
Lyndsay Stephen	69	69	71	69	278	3,595

	SCORES				TOTAL	MONEY
Peter Jones	65	71	69	73	278	3,595
Bob Shearer	66	70	72	70	278	3,595
Dan Talbot	72	69	69	69	279	2,700
Wayne Grady	68	71	71	70	280	1,960
Brett Officer	68	69	71	72	280	1,960
Brett Ogle	67	69	75	69	280	1,960
Roger Mackay	69	67	74	70	280	1,960
Anthony Gilligan	73	69	68	71	281	1,400
Mats Lanner	73	69	68	71	281	1,400
Russell Swanson	69	69	74	69	281	1,400
Mike Colandro	75	70	69	68	282	1,152
Jeff Senior	68	74	71	69	282	1,152
Brian Jones	71	69	74	68	282	1,152
Rodger Davis	69	69	74	70	282	1,152
Kyi Hla Han	66	70	68	78	282	1,152
Shizuo Mori	72	70	70	71	283	960
Glenn Vines	68	74	70	71	283	960
Chris Tickner	69	71	72	71	283	960
Peter McWhinney	71	67	72	73	283	960
Tony Maloney	74	71	67	72	284	820
Greg Hohnen	75	70	66	73	284	820
Terry Gale	70	70	74	70	284	820
Leigh Hunter	70	74	70	71	285	684
David Armstrong	70	73	68	74	285	684
Craig Parry	74	68	72	71	285	684
Ian Baker-Finch	72	69	72	72	285	684
Stephen Jackson	72	69	72	72	285	684

Foster's Tattersall Tasmanian Open

Tasmania Golf Club, Hobart, Tasmania
Par 37-35 — 72; 6,794 yards

January 28-February 1
purse, A$75,000

	SCORES				TOTAL	MONEY
Brian Jones	69	70	74	70	283	A$13,500
Mike Colandro	68	67	77	72	284	8,100
Peter Senior	71	70	75	69	285	4,010
Roger Mackay	68	69	75	73	285	4,010
Ian Baker-Finch	73	69	70	73	285	4,010
Gordon Brand Jr.	72	68	77	69	286	2,865
Peter Jones	72	75	67	73	287	2,565
George Serhan	74	70	77	67	288	2,130
Rodger Davis	67	71	81	69	288	2,130
Frank Nobilo	74	74	72	69	289	1,470
Wayne Riley	73	67	79	70	289	1,470
Peter McWhinney	71	69	76	73	289	1,470
Peter O'Malley	67	71	78	73	289	1,470
David Smith	71	74	75	70	290	1,080
Ken Trimble	75	70	73	72	290	1,080
Tony Maloney	71	72	79	69	291	945
Gerry Taylor	72	72	78	69	291	945
Greg Hohnen	71	70	76	74	291	945
Brett Ogle	73	72	75	72	292	825
Bob Shearer	68	71	78	75	292	825
Peter Fowler	66	71	80	75	292	825
Ken Dukes	74	74	75	70	293	690
Stephen Jackson	75	72	76	70	293	690

	SCORES				TOTAL	MONEY
Wayne Grady	70	74	77	72	293	690
Stewart Ginn	71	73	76	73	293	690
Mike Harwood	70	71	77	75	293	690
Ian Stanley	73	71	72	77	293	690
*Jon Evans	73	78	73	70	294	
Craig Warren	74	74	73	73	294	534
Steen Tinning	70	72	80	72	294	534
Craig Parry	73	73	76	72	294	534
Russell Swanson	72	76	73	73	294	534
Peter Croker	74	74	73	73	294	534

Robert Boyd Transport Australian Match Play Championship

Kingston Heath Golf Club, Melbourne, Victoria
Par 36-36 — 72; 6,814 yards

February 6-8
purse, A$100,000

FIRST ROUND

Wayne Smith defeated Brian Jones, 3 and 2
Peter Fowler defeated Greg Turner, 5 and 3
Lyndsay Stephen defeated Stewart Ginn, 3 and 2
Vaughan Sommers defeated Jack Nicklaus Jr., 2 and 1
Brett Ogle defeated Magnus Persson, 1 up
Peter Senior defeated Jeff Senior, 1 up, 19 holes
*David Ecob defeated Anders Forsbrand, 7 and 6
Mike Clayton defeated Wayne Riley, 1 up
(Each losing player received A$1,000.)

SECOND ROUND

Greg Norman defeated Clayton, 4 and 3
Mike Harwood defeated Ecob, 1 up
Ossie Moore defeated Senior, 1 up
Bob Shearer defeated Ogle, 1 up, 20 holes
Stephen defeated Ian Stanley, 1 up, 19 holes
David Graham defeated Fowler, 2 and 1
Ian Baker-Finch defeated Smith, 1 up, 21 holes
Rodger Davis defeated Somers, 1 up, 23 holes
(Each losing player received A$2,857.)

QUARTER-FINALS

Harwood defeated Norman, 1 up, 19 holes
Moore defeated Shearer, 5 and 4
Stephen defeated Rodger Davis, 5 and 4
Baker-Finch defeated Graham, 7 and 5
(Each losing player received A$3,500.)

SEMI-FINALS

Moore defeated Harwood, 1 up
Baker-Finch defeated Stephen, 2 and 1

THIRD-FOURTH PLACE PLAYOFF

Harwood defeated Stephen, 2 up

FINAL

Baker-Finch defeated Moore, 5 and 4
(Baker-Finch received A$20,000, Moore A$15,000, Harwood A$10,000,
  Stephen A$8,000.)

Australian Masters

Huntingdale Golf Club, Melbourne, Victoria
Par 37-36 — 73; 6,955 yards

February 12-15
purse, A$300,000

	SCORES				TOTAL	MONEY
Greg Norman	68	67	68	70	273	A$54,000
Peter Senior	72	68	71	71	282	32,400
Vaughan Somers	73	68	69	73	283	20,700
Scott Hoch	72	73	69	70	284	14,940
Graham Marsh	72	73	68	72	285	11,970
David Feherty	71	70	71	73	285	11,970
Frank Nobilo	75	71	69	71	286	9,100
Wayne Grady	68	73	72	73	286	9,100
Roger Mackay	70	72	69	75	286	9,100
Ian Woosnam	75	68	72	72	287	7,080
Ian Baker-Finch	69	73	73	73	288	6,120
Peter O'Malley	73	73	72	71	289	5,400
*David Ecob	75	68	74	73	290	
Chris Tickner	73	74	70	73	290	4,680
Lu Chien Soon	69	71	76	74	290	4,680
Lyndsay Stephen	72	74	74	71	291	3,980
David Graham	72	71	73	75	291	3,980
Ian Stanley	72	65	74	80	291	3,980
Jeff Senior	77	72	69	74	292	3,440
Ronan Rafferty	73	73	71	75	292	3,440
Gordon J. Brand	72	69	74	77	292	3,440
Bernhard Langer	74	74	74	71	293	2,940
*Stephen Taylor	72	72	79	70	293	
George Serhan	75	73	73	72	293	2,940
Terry Gale	77	72	76	68	293	2,940
Peter Fowler	76	71	72	74	293	2,940
Sam Torrance	75	66	76	76	293	2,940
Mike Clayton	71	74	80	69	294	2,205
Noel Ratcliffe	74	71	76	73	294	2,205
Rob McNaughton	73	72	76	73	294	2,205
Peter Jones	72	75	74	73	294	2,205
John Clifford	73	74	73	74	294	2,205
Stewart Ginn	72	72	75	75	294	2,205
Peter McWhinney	68	76	74	76	294	2,205
Brett Ogle	73	72	71	78	294	2,205
Brett Officer	76	74	71	74	295	1,800
Hsieh Yu Shu	74	75	75	71	295	1,800
Mats Lanner	72	74	73	76	295	1,800
Larry Canning	71	72	77	76	296	1,620
Ho Ming Chung	74	74	75	73	296	1,620
Steen Tinning	73	72	79	72	296	1,620
Brian Jones	77	73	72	75	297	1,380
Mike Cahill	73	76	75	73	297	1,380
Ossie Moore	72	73	79	73	297	1,380
Tony Maloney	77	70	77	73	297	1,380
Mike Colandro	75	73	73	76	297	1,380
Bob Shearer	75	73	75	75	298	1,110
Robert Lee	71	76	75	76	298	1,110
Gordon Brand Jr.	72	77	78	71	298	1,110
Ken Dukes	72	78	76	72	298	1,110

Robert Boyd Transport Victorian Open

Kingston Heath Golf Club, Melbourne, Victoria
Par 36-36 — 72; 6,814 yards

February 19-22
purse, A$110,000

	SCORES				TOTAL	MONEY
Roger Mackay	66	70	73	68	277	A$19,800
Greg Norman	66	73	71	68	278	11,880
Sam Torrance	70	66	71	74	281	7,590
Ronan Rafferty	72	72	74	65	282	5,027
Rodger Davis	69	73	71	69	282	5,027
Ian Baker-Finch	70	70	73	71	284	4,202
David Feherty	69	73	69	74	285	3,762
Ian Woosnam	76	68	71	71	286	3,278
Paul Foley	70	72	74	71	287	2,783
Terry Gale	70	69	72	76	287	2,783
Nick Faldo	76	70	72	70	288	2,112
Ian Stanley	70	71	74	73	288	2,112
Stewart Ginn	73	72	73	71	289	1,804
Ian Roberts	72	74	72	72	290	1,540
Greg Turner	76	71	77	66	290	1,540
Mike Clayton	72	70	74	74	290	1,540
*David Ecob	71	72	71	77	291	
Mike Cahill	76	71	73	71	291	1,353
Wayne Grady	72	72	76	71	291	1,353
*Paul Moloney	71	74	72	75	292	
Peter O'Malley	75	70	75	72	292	1,166
Steve Bann	73	71	72	76	292	1,166
Brett Ogle	72	70	76	74	292	1,166
Jeff Senior	74	74	72	72	292	1,166
Peter Jones	72	69	76	75	292	1,166
*Jon Evans	75	70	74	74	293	
George Serhan	69	76	73	75	293	946
Mike Ferguson	75	69	76	73	293	946
David Graham	77	66	76	74	293	946
Mike Colandro	72	70	80	71	293	946
Simon Owen	71	67	74	81	293	946

Rich River Classic

Rich River Golf Club, Echuca, Victoria
Par 37-35 — 72; 6,749 yards

February 26-March 1
purse, A$75,000

	SCORES				TOTAL	MONEY
Peter Senior	62	68	71	72	273	A$13,500
Mike Ferguson	72	69	69	65	275	8,100
Peter Jones	72	68	70	66	276	4,455
Peter Fowler	71	63	70	72	276	4,455
Mike Harwood	67	70	72	69	278	3,120
Wayne Riley	66	72	69	72	279	2,865
Mike Colandro	70	69	67	74	281	2,565
Mike Clayton	73	69	71	69	282	2,010
John Clifford	72	69	74	67	282	2,010
David Smith	67	71	71	73	282	2,010
Paul Foley	69	70	73	71	283	1,530
Ossie Moore	71	69	72	72	284	1,350
Jeff Senior	74	70	71	69	285	1,095
Larry Canning	71	70	74	70	285	1,095

	SCORES				TOTAL	MONEY
Eric Couper	71	68	73	73	285	1,095
Roger Stephens	69	70	74	72	285	1,095
Steve Bann	71	72	70	73	286	881.25
Tim Elliott	70	72	70	74	286	881.25
Rob McNaughton	70	72	72	72	286	881.25
Rodger Davis	71	69	73	73	286	881.25
Terry Hulls	69	75	70	73	287	780
Peter O'Malley	70	74	71	72	287	780
Robert Stephens	71	75	71	71	288	660
Roger Mackay	75	69	73	71	288	660
Bob Shearer	71	71	73	73	288	660
George Sherhan	73	69	72	74	288	660
Anthony Gilligan	74	68	75	71	288	660
Ken Dukes	72	69	74	73	288	660
Mark A. Nash	73	70	74	72	289	530
Vic Bennetts	69	73	72	75	289	530
David Armstrong	68	73	70	78	289	530

Konica Queensland Open

Coolangatta-Tweed Heads Golf Club, Coolangatta, Queensland October 8-11
Par 36-36 — 72; 6,745 yards purse, A$75,000

	SCORES				TOTAL	MONEY
David Graham	69	71	69	66	275	A$13,500
Vaughan Somers	69	72	69	72	282	8,100
David Smith	68	72	74	69	283	5,175
Brett Officer	72	71	74	68	285	3,427.50
Mike Colandro	68	69	71	77	285	3,427.50
Peter McWhinney	70	71	73	72	286	2,715
Wayne Riley	68	76	72	70	286	2,715
Peter O'Malley	70	74	73	70	287	1,690
Ian Roberts	72	76	71	68	287	1,690
Jerry Anderson	71	73	75	68	287	1,690
Lucien Tinkler	70	71	73	73	287	1,690
Mark Officer	72	74	72	69	287	1,690
Mike Harwood	68	71	77	71	287	1,690
Jeff Woodland	72	73	74	69	288	1,080
Ken Trimble	73	70	71	74	288	1,080
Mike Clayton	71	73	73	72	289	990
Jeff Senior	70	73	73	74	290	847.50
Steve Bann	69	72	74	75	290	847.50
Bob Shearer	69	75	66	80	290	847.50
Peter Jones	69	76	68	77	290	847.50
Mike Cahill	73	74	75	68	290	847.50
Jim Benepe	73	68	76	73	290	847.50
Kyi Hla Han	72	77	72	70	291	705
Stewart Ginn	76	73	71	71	291	705
Ossie Moore	69	74	76	72	291	705
David Armstrong	68	71	78	75	292	600
Roger Mackay	71	68	79	74	292	600
Rodger Davis	71	76	71	74	292	600
Jon Evans	71	70	75	76	292	600
Wayne Case	75	71	74	73	293	510

Queensland PGA

Pacific Golf Club, Brisbane, Queensland
Par 36-36 — 72; 6,820 yards

October 15-18
purse, A$75,000

	SCORES				TOTAL	MONEY
Peter Senior	67	72	71	68	278	A$13,500
Jeff Woodland	67	73	67	71	278	8,100
(Senior defeated Woodland on the first hole of playoff.)						
Peter McWhinney	69	73	70	72	284	5,175
Mike Harwood	72	71	70	72	285	3,735
Jim Benepe	68	73	75	71	287	3,120
Mike Ferguson	68	71	76	74	289	2,555
Ossie Moore	70	74	72	73	289	2,555
Wayne Riley	73	72	69	75	289	2,555
Mike Clayton	70	72	74	74	290	1,897.50
Roger Mackay	68	73	73	76	290	1,897.50
Anders Sorensen	75	73	73	70	291	1,254
Brad Andrews	69	77	72	73	291	1,254
Gerry Taylor	73	74	72	72	291	1,254
Kirk Triplett	72	76	71	72	291	1,254
Mike Cahill	74	71	73	73	291	1,254
Brad King	73	74	75	70	292	945
Brett Officer	74	75	71	72	292	945
Hank Baran	73	76	71	72	292	945
Craig Parry	72	74	73	74	293	810
David Smith	77	70	74	72	293	810
Lyndsay Stephen	75	73	74	71	293	810
Rick Gibson	72	74	73	74	293	810
Trevor McDonald	71	75	73	75	294	735
Garry Merrick	70	77	75	73	295	675
John Victorsen	73	75	73	74	295	675
Jon Evans	75	73	72	75	295	675
Jason Deep	74	72	75	75	296	600
Wayne Smith	75	74	73	74	296	600
Andrew LaBrooy	71	72	74	80	297	521.25
Macon Moye	71	76	73	77	297	521.25

National Panasonic New South Wales Open

Australian Golf Club, Sydney, New South Wales
Par 36-36 — 72; 7,026 yards

October 22-26
purse, A$150,000

	SCORES				TOTAL	MONEY
Craig Parry	65	71	74	79	289	A$27,000
Wayne Riley	70	75	72	73	290	16,200
Ian Baker-Finch	73	73	73	72	291	8,910
Rodger Davis	72	72	74	73	291	8,910
Jeff Woodland	74	73	73	72	292	5,700
Mike Colandro	73	75	71	73	292	5,700
Simon Owen	72	71	79	70	292	5,700
Jim Benepe	74	71	75	73	293	4,470
Jerry Anderson	72	76	71	75	294	3,337.50
Lee Trevino	73	72	72	77	294	3,337.50
Mike Harwood	76	72	71	75	294	3,337.50
Terry Gale	71	73	75	75	294	3,337.50
Lyndsay Stephen	73	71	77	74	295	2,340
Peter Fowler	74	69	77	75	295	2,340

	SCORES				TOTAL	MONEY
*Lester Peterson	76	71	74	75	296	
Roger Mackay	74	69	75	78	296	2,100
Garry Merrick	71	76	75	75	297	1,890
Jeff Senior	79	70	73	75	297	1,890
Peter Senior	72	76	77	72	297	1,890
Brad King	74	72	76	76	298	1,560
Kyi Hla Han	77	70	75	76	298	1,560
Matt Cole	71	75	75	77	298	1,560
Peter Jones	73	73	76	76	298	1,560
Vic Bennetts	74	75	74	75	298	1,560
Paul Foley	73	72	73	80	298	1,560
Bob Shearer	73	75	78	73	299	1,230
Craig Warren	73	73	75	78	299	1,230
Kirk Triplett	72	77	72	78	299	1,230
Rick Gibson	72	73	74	80	299	1,230
Vaughan Somers	76	75	73	75	299	1,230

E.S.P. Australian PGA Championship

The Lakes Golf Club, Sydney, New South Wales
Par 36-37 — 73; 6,832 yards

October 29-November 1
purse, A$170,000

	SCORES				TOTAL	MONEY
Roger Mackay	68	72	74	70	284	A$30,600
Mike Colandro	70	72	74	69	285	18,360
Mike Clayton	71	74	72	70	287	10,098
Stewart Ginn	74	67	73	73	287	10,098
Wayne Riley	73	70	74	71	288	6,783
Bob Shearer	71	67	81	69	288	6,783
George Serhan	68	77	74	70	289	5,440
Vaughan Sommers	71	69	74	75	289	5,440
Brad King	72	72	75	71	290	3,782.50
Graham Marsh	70	74	74	72	290	3,782.50
Ray Picker	73	72	75	70	290	3,782.50
Ronan Rafferty	66	73	73	78	290	3,782.50
Peter McWhinney	73	70	78	70	291	2,652
Steve Bann	72	74	73	72	291	2,652
Peter Senior	71	74	70	77	292	2,255.33
Jon Evans	70	76	71	75	292	2,255.33
Frank Nobilo	71	72	74	75	292	2,255.33
Edward Harper	70	74	76	73	293	1,841.66
Charles Raulerson	74	72	75	72	293	1,841.66
John Clifford	71	74	77	71	293	1,841.66
Peter Fowler	74	73	75	71	293	1,841.66
Rick Gibson	71	71	75	76	293	1,841.66
Anthony Gilligan	71	70	72	80	293	1,841.66
Brett Ogle	71	76	72	75	294	1,564
Brian Jones	68	73	78	75	294	1,564
Ken Trimble	75	72	72	76	295	1,394
Mike Ferguson	75	73	74	73	295	1,394
Paul Foley	73	73	74	75	295	1,394
Ian Stanley	68	74	79	75	296	1,201.33
Robert Stephens	72	74	73	77	296	1,201.33

West End South Australian Open

Grange Golf Club Composite Course, Adelaide, South Australia
Par 37-35 — 72; 6,748 yards

November 11-14
purse, A$100,000

	SCORES				TOTAL	MONEY
Ronan Rafferty	72	68	71	69	280	A$18,000
Peter Fowler	71	71	68	71	281	10,800
Wayne Grady	71	72	66	73	282	6,900
Peter O'Malley	73	71	72	67	283	4,980
Ian Roberts	73	66	74	71	284	3,990
Mike Harwood	70	71	71	72	284	3,990
Brett Ogle	72	72	68	73	285	3,033.33
Greg Norman	72	69	73	71	285	3,033.33
Ossie Moore	74	73	68	70	285	3,033.33
Anders Sorensen	75	65	75	72	287	2,360
Wayne Smith	75	73	71	70	289	1,672
David Merriman	74	71	71	73	289	1,672
Kyi Hla Han	75	72	71	71	289	1,672
Greg Alexander	75	72	72	70	289	1,672
Roger Mackay	71	67	70	81	289	1,672
*Cameron Howell	72	75	72	71	290	
Craig Parry	72	73	77	68	290	1,204
David Graham	73	69	72	76	290	1,204
Bob Shearer	68	70	76	76	290	1,204
Lucien Tinkler	79	67	71	73	290	1,204
Matt Cole	72	74	71	73	290	1,204
George Daves	77	72	69	73	291	1,020
Jon Evans	72	72	74	73	291	1,020
Ken Trimble	76	72	72	71	291	1,020
John Erickson	74	72	69	77	292	940
Bob Lendzion	77	70	71	75	293	800
David Smith	75	70	71	77	293	800
Lyndsay Stephen	71	74	72	76	293	800
Mike Colandro	76	73	72	72	293	800
Vaughan Somers	73	74	73	73	293	800

National Panasonic Western Australian Open

Joondalup Country Club, Perth, Western Australia
Par 36-36 — 72; 6,919 yards

November 19-22
purse, A$80,000

	SCORES				TOTAL	MONEY
Gerry Taylor	72	70	73	75	290	A$14,400
Brad King	70	75	72	73	290	8,640
(Taylor defeated King on second hole of playoff.)						
Craig Parry	71	71	74	75	291	5,520
Bob Lendzion	74	72	75	71	292	3,984
Charles Raulerson	76	73	73	72	294	3,040
Roger Stephens	72	74	74	74	294	3,040
Peter O'Malley	78	75	72	69	294	3,040
Anders Forsbrand	77	72	75	71	295	2,384
Lyndsay Stephen	69	77	74	76	296	2,024
Wayne Smith	73	72	79	72	296	2,024
David Graham	74	78	73	72	297	1,392
Peter Jones	70	76	77	74	297	1,392
George Serhan	74	75	69	79	297	1,392
Vaughan Somers	72	71	76	78	297	1,392

	SCORES				TOTAL	MONEY
Jim Benepe	73	74	73	78	298	1,088
Rick Gibson	74	80	74	70	298	1,088
John Erickson	77	74	76	72	299	921.60
Russell Swanson	77	74	75	73	299	921.60
Kris Moe	78	75	78	68	299	921.60
Patrick Burke	73	76	74	76	299	921.60
Peter McWhinney	72	82	70	75	299	921.60
Anthony Painter	70	74	79	77	300	752
David Armstrong	77	75	70	78	300	752
Gordon Brand Jr.	76	74	72	78	300	752
Ken Trimble	78	73	74	75	300	752
Ray Picker	73	79	76	72	300	752
David Merriman	74	75	74	78	301	595.20
Garry Merrick	75	77	73	76	301	595.20
Jason Deep	72	75	81	73	301	595.20
Roger Mackay	77	76	74	74	301	595.20

National Panasonic Australian Open Championship

Royal Melbourne Composite Course, Melbourne, Victoria   November 26-30
Par 36-37 — 72; 6,979 yards   purse, A$300,000

	SCORES				TOTAL	MONEY
Greg Norman	70	66	66	71	273	A$54,000
Sandy Lyle	69	75	69	70	283	32,400
Gordon Brand Jr.	71	72	70	73	286	17,820
Ron Wood	70	72	67	77	286	17,820
Rodger Davis	69	79	73	66	287	12,480
Jim Benepe	77	70	70	71	288	9,690
Larry Nelson	75	71	69	73	288	9,690
Ronan Rafferty	69	74	71	74	288	9,690
Wayne Smith	69	68	77	74	288	9,690
Anders Forsbrand	75	72	73	69	289	6,200
Ian Roberts	74	72	71	72	289	6,200
Greg Turner	69	74	71	75	289	6,200
Charles Raulerson	71	72	76	71	290	4,380
David Merriman	71	70	77	72	290	4,380
Mike Colandro	70	74	72	74	290	4,380
Wayne Grady	73	73	73	71	290	4,380
Jason Deep	73	73	72	73	291	3,525
Vaughan Somers	72	73	73	73	291	3,525
Ken Trimble	73	70	73	75	291	3,525
Peter O'Malley	70	69	73	79	291	3,525
Jerry Anderson	71	68	71	82	292	3,180
Brett Ogle	73	68	75	77	293	2,880
Gerry Taylor	70	76	76	71	293	2,880
Tim Elliott	71	72	78	72	293	2,880
Rob McNaughton	72	72	75	74	293	2,880
Craig Parry	73	73	75	73	294	2,205
Ossie Moore	71	72	75	76	294	2,205
Ken Dukes	71	72	74	77	294	2,205
Russell Swanson	72	74	72	76	294	2,205
Kris Moe	75	73	72	74	294	2,205
Terry Gale	74	72	74	74	294	2,205
Mike Clayton	74	73	74	73	294	2,205
Terry Price	67	69	74	84	294	2,205
Brad King	69	71	75	80	295	1,650

	SCORES				TOTAL	MONEY
Edward Harper	72	73	75	75	295	1,650
Jon Evans	72	76	71	76	295	1,650
Peter Fowler	72	71	75	77	295	1,650
Mark A. Nash	73	70	78	74	295	1,650
Anthony Painter	73	76	72	74	295	1,650
Peter Jones	74	74	72	75	295	1,650
Peter Senior	75	73	71	76	295	1,650
Bob Shearer	73	74	73	76	296	1,230
*Bradley Hughes	75	71	73	77	296	
George Serhan	70	70	75	81	296	1,230
Jeff Senior	74	72	75	75	296	1,230
John Erickson	74	74	74	74	296	1,230
John Clifford	71	74	67	84	296	1,230
Patrick Burke	75	74	70	77	296	1,230
Anthony Gilligan	73	73	72	79	297	810
Jeff Woodland	70	77	72	78	297	810
Brett Officer	76	73	73	75	297	810

Air New Zealand Shell Open

Titirangi Golf Club, Auckland
Par 35-35 — 70; 6,286 yards

December 3-6
purse, NZ$200,000

	SCORES				TOTAL	MONEY
Mike Colandro	70	65	68	67	270	NZ$36,000
Rodger Davis	69	66	67	69	271	21,600
Sandy Lyle	68	67	65	73	273	13,800
Wayne Grady	65	69	68	72	274	9,140
Vaughan Somers	67	67	71	69	274	9,140
Peter Fowler	68	71	70	66	275	7,240
Paul Foley	65	70	69	71	275	7,240
Ronan Rafferty	69	70	68	69	276	5,960
Jim Benepe	74	64	71	70	279	5,400
David Smith	67	72	72	69	280	4,720
Jerry Anderson	69	66	72	74	281	3,840
Craig Warren	70	70	70	71	281	3,840
Mike Harwood	71	71	68	72	282	3,280
Gordon Brand Jr.	74	68	71	71	284	2,960
Ken Trimble	73	70	73	69	285	2,653.33
Barry Vivian	72	71	69	73	285	2,653.33
Stewart Ginn	69	73	69	74	285	2,653.33
Tony Maloney	69	77	71	69	286	2,166.66
Mike Ferguson	69	75	70	72	286	2,166.66
George Daves	68	71	74	73	286	2,166.66
Wayne Riley	67	73	73	73	286	2,166.66
Bob Shearer	70	71	70	75	286	2,166.66
Jon Evans	67	73	71	75	286	2,166.66
Grant Kenny	75	71	69	72	287	1,605
Stuart Reese	73	72	70	72	287	1,605
Gerry Taylor	69	71	75	72	287	1,605
Robin Smalley	70	72	72	73	287	1,605
Glen Joyner	71	71	71	74	287	1,605
Macon Moye	69	73	70	75	287	1,605
David Llewellyn	68	72	73	74	287	1,605
Randy Erskine	69	71	71	76	287	1,605

Nissan Mobil New Zealand Open

Wellington Golf Club, Heretaunga
Par 36-36 — 72; 6,771 yards

December 10-13
purse, NZ$150,000

	SCORES				TOTAL	MONEY
Ronan Rafferty	71	67	70	71	279	NZ$27,000
Larry Nelson	72	65	71	71	279	16,200
(Rafferty defeated Nelson on the seventh playoff hole.)						
Wayne Grady	72	74	69	66	281	10,350
Mike Harwood	70	70	69	74	283	6,855
Rodger Davis	72	71	70	70	283	6,855
Mike Ferguson	72	71	71	70	284	5,730
Ossie Moore	75	73	67	70	285	5,130
David Llewellyn	70	72	76	68	286	4,260
Ian Baker-Finch	72	70	70	74	286	4,260
Tim Elliott	72	75	68	72	287	3,540
Ken Trimble	73	71	72	72	288	3,060
Anders Forsbrand	72	73	70	74	289	2,700
Bob Shearer	73	75	75	67	290	2,075
Mike Colandro	73	75	71	71	290	2,075
Stewart Ginn	74	72	73	71	290	2,075
Richard Gilkey	76	69	73	72	290	2,075
Paul Foley	71	71	73	75	290	2,075
Wayne Smith	76	67	71	76	290	2,075
Simon Owen	75	73	71	73	292	1,680
Terry Gale	75	73	71	73	292	1,680
Craig Warren	73	75	74	71	293	1,530
Eric Kaufmanis	73	75	72	73	293	1,530
Wayne Case	72	74	71	76	293	1,530
Peter Fowler	74	71	76	73	294	1,260
Paul Minifie	75	72	73	74	294	1,260
Andrew LaBrooy	72	75	74	73	294	1,260
Anthony Painter	71	72	76	75	294	1,260
Grant Waite	70	75	74	75	294	1,260
Tony Maloney	73	73	70	78	294	1,260
Anthony Gilligan	79	73	72	71	295	1,050

The Asia/Japan Tour

San Miguel Philippines Open

Wack Wack Golf and Country Club, East Course, Manila
Par 36-36 — 72; 7,089 yards

February 19-22
purse, US$100,000

	SCORES				TOTAL	MONEY
Brian Tennyson	73	71	73	71	288	US$16,660
Chen Tze Ming	74	71	69	75	289	11,110
Antolin Fernando	72	73	71	74	290	5,630
Jim Hallet	75	70	71	74	290	5,630

	SCORES				TOTAL	MONEY
Billy Ray Brown	69	76	73	73	291	4,240
Ho Ming Chung	74	75	71	72	292	3,250
Greg Twiggs	71	73	77	71	292	3,250
Tom Pernice	70	74	73	76	293	2,500
Rudy Lavares	72	77	73	72	294	2,033.33
David Peege	72	74	75	73	294	2,033.33
Dave Tentis	72	75	72	75	294	2,033.33
Kyi Hla Han	75	76	72	72	295	1,700
Marimuthu Ramayah	74	76	71	74	295	1,700
Roger Antonio	72	77	74	74	297	1,416
Danny Briggs	72	73	75	77	297	1,416
Kuo Chi Hsiung	78	74	73	72	297	1,416
Lu Hsi Chuen	75	76	74	72	297	1,416
Alan Pate	71	76	74	76	297	1,416
Tommy Armour III	72	74	74	78	298	1,172
Eddie Bagtas	73	77	69	79	298	1,172
Lai Chung Jen	74	75	71	78	298	1,172
Lin Chia	74	76	76	72	298	1,172
Art Russell	75	74	73	76	298	1,172
Paterno Braza	71	78	76	74	299	1,030
Chung Chun Hsing	71	77	76	75	299	1,030
Hsu Chi San	77	71	76	75	299	1,030
Eleuterio Nival	74	74	76	75	299	1,030
Mike Standly	73	74	79	73	299	1,030
Vic Arda	76	75	78	71	300	799.09
Steve Chapman	78	72	75	75	300	799.09
Ignacio de Leon	77	73	76	74	300	799.09
Pat Horgan	68	77	79	76	300	799.09
Pete Izumigawa	68	74	80	78	300	799.09
Li Wen Sheng	70	77	76	77	300	799.09
Lu Chien Soon	76	76	77	71	300	799.09
Jeff Maggert	70	74	76	80	300	799.09
Mario Manubay	74	74	79	73	300	799.09
Tracy Nakazaki	78	74	79	69	300	799.09
Victor Regalado	76	75	77	72	300	799.09

United Airlines Hong Kong Open

Royal Hong Kong Golf Club, Composite Course, Kowloon
Par 36-35 — 71; 6,724 yards

February 26-March 1
purse, US$150,000

	SCORES				TOTAL	MONEY
Ian Woosnam	70	71	65	69	275	US$25,000
Sam Torrance	71	71	68	69	279	13,025
David Feherty	68	73	68	70	279	13,025
Ronan Rafferty	69	73	68	72	282	7,500
Brian Tennyson	72	72	70	69	283	5,805
Chen Tze Ming	72	73	69	69	283	5,805
Graham Marsh	71	72	68	73	284	4,125
Greg Twiggs	75	70	71	68	284	4,125
Mike Morley	77	71	68	69	285	3,050
Dave Tentis	71	72	70	72	285	3,050
Lee Kang Sun	69	73	74	69	285	3,050
Anders Forsbrand	72	73	69	72	286	2,198
Terry Gale	73	73	72	68	286	2,198
Wayne Smith	70	73	72	71	286	2,197
Ian Baker-Finch	76	72	72	66	286	2,198

	SCORES				TOTAL	MONEY
Shigenori Mori	71	72	69	74	286	2,197
Jim Rutledge	72	75	72	67	286	2,198
Hung Wen Neng	71	77	70	68	286	2,197
Jeff Maggert	73	72	70	71	286	2,197
John McGough	70	76	71	70	287	1,732
Frankie Minoza	73	71	73	70	287	1,732
Stewart Ginn	70	76	71	70	287	1,733
Hsu Sheng San	73	73	73	68	287	1,733
John Benda	74	75	73	66	288	1,610
Jim Hallet	69	78	72	69	288	1,610
Frank Nobilo	67	77	72	73	289	1,370
Kuo Chi Hsiung	71	74	74	70	289	1,370
Chung Chun Hsing	69	77	70	73	289	1,370
Shen Chung Shyan	73	73	73	70	289	1,370
Brett Ogle	69	77	72	71	289	1,370
Hsieh Yu Shu	71	73	72	73	289	1,370
Rick Gibson	76	73	73	67	289	1,370
Bill Israelson	73	72	70	74	289	1,370
Steve Bowman	73	74	71	71	289	1,370

Benson & Hedges Malaysian Open

Subang Golf Club, Kuala Lumpur, Malaysia
Par 36-36 — 72; 7,067 yards

March 5-8
purse, US$150,000

	SCORES				TOTAL	MONEY
Terry Gale	66	75	70	69	280	US$25,000
Greg Twiggs	71	72	70	67	280	16,665
(Gale defeated Twiggs on first hole of playoff.)						
Chen Tze Ming	72	66	70	73	281	9,390
Rudy Lavares	71	71	69	72	283	7,500
Tom Pernice	72	73	71	68	284	4,965
Brian Mogg	69	71	75	69	284	4,965
Alan Pate	72	70	72	70	284	4,965
Shen Chung Shyan	72	70	71	71	284	4,965
Jim Hallet	73	73	67	72	285	3,360
Hsien Chin Sheng	72	71	70	73	286	3,000
Wayne Smith	75	72	71	69	287	2,700
Tommy Armour III	71	73	72	71	287	2,700
Mark Aebli	72	72	70	74	288	2,295
Jim Rutledge	66	78	68	75	288	2,295
Steen Tinning	71	69	73	75	288	2,295
Jeff Maggert	72	67	73	76	288	2,295
Billy Ray Brown	72	71	77	69	289	1,794
Mike Cunning	73	74	72	70	289	1,794
Steve Chapman	77	68	72	72	289	1,794
Kyi Hla Han	71	74	72	72	289	1,794
Hsieh Yu Shu	70	75	72	72	289	1,794
Peter Fowler	69	73	75	72	289	1,794
Brett Ogle	69	76	70	74	289	1,794
Choi Youn Soo	70	73	72	74	289	1,795
Yau Sui Ming	71	70	77	72	290	1,477
Marimuthu Ramayah	73	71	74	72	290	1,477
Frankie Minoza	74	72	71	73	290	1,477
Lee Kang Sun	73	72	71	74	290	1,477
Victor Regalado	71	71	73	57	290	1,477
Mike Allen	71	72	71	76	290	1,477

Thai International Thailand Open

Railway Golf Course, Bangkok, Thailand
Par 36-35 — 71; 6,827 yards

March 19-22
purse, US$100,000

	SCORES				TOTAL	MONEY
Chen Tze Ming	70	66	70	66	272	US$16,660
Somsak Sri-Sanga	69	70	66	67	272	11,110
(Chen defeated Somsak on third hole of playoff.)						
Frankie Minoza	69	68	72	66	275	5,630
John Jacobs	66	68	72	69	275	5,630
Isamu Sugita	70	66	72	68	276	4,240
Lu Hsi Chuen	67	72	68	70	277	3,500
Dave Tentis	74	70	67	68	279	2,750
Greg Twiggs	70	66	73	70	279	2,750
Carolos Espinosa	74	72	64	70	280	2,240
Peter Fowler	70	69	70	72	281	1,866.67
Tsao Chien Teng	68	74	72	67	281	1,866.67
Mike Cunning	71	71	67	72	281	1,866.67
Kyi Hla Han	74	65	72	71	282	1,615
Jeff Maggert	69	70	70	73	282	1,615
Victory Regalado	68	71	70	74	283	1,350
Mario Siodina	68	72	73	70	283	1,350
Chung Chun Hsing	71	71	71	70	283	1,350
Hsu Sheng San	71	72	67	73	283	1,350
Prasarn Rueyruen	69	72	72	70	283	1,350
Brett Ogle	74	72	69	69	284	1,071
Craig Parry	74	69	70	71	284	1,071
Jim Rutledge	68	73	73	70	284	1,071
Hsien Chin Sheng	73	69	74	68	284	1,071
Kuo Chi Hsiung	73	70	68	73	284	1,071
Liao Kuo Chih	68	71	72	73	284	1,071
Tommy Armour III	69	73	71	71	284	1,071
Danny Briggs	69	74	69	72	284	1,071
Jim Hallet	73	68	71	72	284	1,071
Don Klenk	71	71	70	72	284	1,071
Stewart Ginn	71	72	72	70	285	856
Lin Chie Hsiang	72	71	69	73	285	856
Mike Allen	69	71	71	74	285	856
Billy Ray Brown	70	71	71	73	285	856
Art Russell	69	68	76	72	285	856

Charminar Challenge Indian Open

Delhi Golf Club, New Delhi, India
Par 36-36 — 72; 6,869 yards

March 19-22
purse, US$100,000

	SCORES				TOTAL	MONEY
Brian Tennyson	74	73	65	68	280	US$16,660
Mike Cunning	71	71	68	73	283	8,685
Jim Hallet	72	71	68	72	283	8,685
Greg Bruckner	73	70	68	73	284	5,000
Steve Bowman	67	72	72	75	286	3,096
Peter O'Malley	68	71	79	68	286	3,096
Jim Rutledge	72	72	72	70	286	3,096
Rick Gibson	70	75	70	71	286	3,096
Jeff Maggert	71	74	71	70	286	3,096

	SCORES				TOTAL	MONEY
Peter Fowler	73	74	67	74	288	2,000
John McGough	72	72	74	71	289	1,753
Casey Nakama	70	74	75	70	289	1,753
Peter Jones	71	74	71	73	289	1,753
Chini	73	73	68	76	290	1,530
Lu Hsi Chuen	76	70	72	72	290	1,530
Carlos Espinosa	72	71	76	72	291	1,315
Tony Maloney	74	69	74	74	291	1,315
Lin Chie Hsiang	71	75	71	74	291	1,315
Lu Ho Tsai	73	73	73	72	291	1,315
Greg Conley	72	69	77	74	292	1,185
Li Wen Sheng	71	75	75	71	292	1,185
Tsao Chien Teng	75	71	74	73	293	1,086
Craig McClellan	75	72	74	72	293	1,086
Dave Tentis	74	74	75	70	293	1,086
Hsieh Yu Shu	79	71	70	73	293	1,086
Mike Morley	77	74	67	75	293	1,086
Brian Mogg	69	75	76	74	294	942
Scott Spence	73	73	75	73	294	942
Fred Dupre	71	77	74	72	294	942
Jorge Coghlan	75	75	72	72	294	942
George Serhan	75	75	70	74	294	942

Shizuoka Open

Shizuoka Country Club, Hamaoka Course, Shizuoka
Par 72; 6,919 yards

March 19-22
purse, ¥35,000,000

	SCORES				TOTAL	MONEY
Lu Liang Huan	71	74	69	66	280	¥6,300,000
Nobumitsu Yuhara	71	71	70	70	282	3,500,000
Naomichi Ozaki	72	73	69	70	284	2,030,000
Toru Nakamura	70	75	68	71	284	2,030,000
Tsutomu Irie	71	73	72	69	285	1,260,000
Koichi Uehara	70	77	71	67	285	1,260,000
Seiji Ebihara	69	74	74	68	285	1,260,000
Tomishige Ikeda	69	73	70	74	286	962,500
Kakuji Matsui	70	74	70	72	286	962,500
Yutaka Suzuki	69	75	73	70	287	805,000
Hisashi Suzumura	73	74	71	70	288	672,000
Teruo Nakamura	72	76	72	68	288	672,000
Brett Ogle	74	71	69	75	289	567,000
Kinpachi Yoshimura	70	78	71	70	289	567,000
Yoshimi Nizeki	75	73	67	75	290	444,500
Katsuji Hasegawa	72	76	70	72	290	444,500
Koichi Moriguchi	74	73	72	71	290	444,500
Yoshitaka Yamamoto	75	76	69	70	290	444,500
Masashi Ozaki	73	76	70	72	291	357,000
Eitaro Deguchi	71	76	72	72	291	357,000
Aki Ohmachi	74	76	74	68	292	316,750
Taichiro Kanatani	74	77	68	73	292	316,750
Katsunari Takahashi	73	75	69	75	292	316,750
Tsukasa Watanabe	74	75	71	72	292	316,750
Kikuo Arai	75	72	69	77	293	280,000
Seichi Kanai	78	73	71	71	293	280,000
Minoru Kawakami	76	75	69	73	293	280,000
Teruo Suzumura	74	75	73	71	293	280,000

	SCORES				TOTAL	MONEY
Osamu Watanabe	70	76	75	72	293	280,000
Hiroshi Oku	73	73	75	73	294	242,900
Hideto Shigenobu	73	77	72	72	294	242,900
Norio Suzuki	72	78	74	70	294	242,900
Nobuo Serizawa	72	78	73	71	294	242,900
Yasuhiro Miyamoto	73	74	71	76	294	242,900
Akihito Yokoyama	75	76	70	73	294	242,900

Singapore Open

Royal Singapore Golf Club, Bukit Course, Singapore   March 26-29
Par 35-36 — 71; 6,674 yards   purse, US$125,000

	SCORES				TOTAL	MONEY
Peter Fowler	66	70	65	73	274	US$20,825
Jeff Maggert	68	67	69	70	274	13,888
Hsu Sheng San	66	70	70	68	274	13,888
(Fowler defeated Maggert and Hsu on third hole of playoff.)						
Kuo Chi Hsiung	66	66	72	71	275	6,250
Ho Ming Chung	70	67	70	71	278	5,300
Jim Rutledge	70	69	70	70	279	4,375
Jim Hallet	68	66	73	72	279	4,375
Chen Tze Ming	72	71	69	68	280	3,125
Art Russell	66	73	71	70	280	3,125
Casey Nakama	68	70	74	69	281	2,500
Isamu Sugita	73	70	68	70	281	2,500
Hsieh Yu Shu	72	71	71	68	282	2,175
Roger Mackay	72	70	71	69	282	2,175
Mario Siodina	73	69	72	69	283	1,963
Scott Spence	71	72	73	67	283	1,963
Chung Chun Hsing	72	71	72	69	284	1,750
John Jacobs	68	76	70	70	284	1,750
Lu Chien Soon	70	74	70	70	284	1,750
Craig McClellan	69	73	71	71	284	1,750
Chen Liang Hsi	70	68	74	72	284	1,750
Peter McWhinney	68	69	73	74	284	1,750
Carlos Espinosa	70	72	71	72	285	1,425
Shimon Takamatsu	71	68	73	73	285	1,425
Jeff Hart	74	69	73	69	285	1,425
Per Arne Brostedt	72	70	74	69	285	1,425
Lin Chie Hsiang	73	71	73	68	285	1,425
Dave Tentis	70	73	70	72	285	1,425
Don McMillian	70	69	73	74	286	1,213
Anthony Gilligan	72	72	71	71	286	1,213
Wayne Smith	70	68	74	74	286	1,213
Kyi Hla Han	69	73	74	70	286	1,213
Eleuterio Nival	73	69	73	71	286	1,213
Lin Chia	73	71	74	68	286	1,213
Lu Hsi Chuen	71	73	70	72	286	1,213
Greg Conley	70	73	75	68	286	1,213
Mike Standly	71	71	72	72	286	1,213

KSB Setonaikai Open

Shido Country Club   March 28-29
Par 72; 6,339 yards   purse, ¥20,600,000

	SCORES		TOTAL	MONEY
Katsunari Takahashi	69	71	140	¥4,000,000
Minoru Nakamura	71	71	142	1,250,000
Michael Harwood	71	71	142	1,250,000
Yurio Akitomi	69	73	142	1,250,000
Kikuo Arai	74	69	143	496,700
Yoshimi Nizeki	70	73	143	496,700
Satsuki Takahashi	69	74	143	496,700
Teruo Sugihara	69	74	143	496,700
Brett Ogle	69	74	143	496,700
Tsutomu Irie	68	75	143	496,700
Hiroshi Gouda	72	72	144	360,000
Kazuo Kanayama	73	71	144	360,000
Seiichi Koizumi	70	74	144	360,000
Hideto Shigenobu	70	74	144	360,000
Toshimitsu Kai	68	76	144	360,000
Yoshinori Mizumaki	73	72	145	266,700
Joji Furuki	72	73	145	266,700
Yasuhiro Miyamoto	72	73	145	266,700
Masami Itoh	73	72	145	266,700
Futoshi Irino	71	74	145	266,700
Keiichi Kobayashi	70	75	145	266,700
Taichiro Kanatani	73	73	146	220,000
Taijiro Tanaka	74	72	146	220,000
Kenji Sogame	69	77	146	220,000
Mike Forgan	73	74	147	177,500
Hisashi Terada	72	75	147	177,500
Akimitsu Tokita	73	74	147	177,500
Masaru Amano	73	74	147	177,500
Satoshi Higashi	73	74	147	177,500
Akihito Yokoyama	73	77	147	177,500

Kuzuha Kokusai

Kuzuha Public Golf Course, Kuzuha   April 4-5
Par 70; 6,238 yards   purse, ¥18,000,000

	SCORES		TOTAL	MONEY
Katsunari Takahashi	65	66	131	¥3,600,000
Brian Jones	69	63	132	1,800,000
Seiji Ebihara	68	66	134	806,400
Brett Ogle	69	65	134	806,400
Keiichi Kobayashi	67	67	134	806,400
Saburo Fujiki	66	68	134	806,400
David Ishii	67	67	134	806,400
Lu Liang Huan	69	66	135	522,000
Hajime Meshiai	69	67	136	416,667
Yoshitaka Yamamoto	69	67	136	416,667
Noboru Sugai	65	71	136	416,666
Yoshimi Nizeki	71	66	137	234,667
Kazushige Kohno	70	67	137	234,667
Seiichi Kanai	68	69	137	234,667
Koichi Suzuki	68	69	137	234,667

	SCORES			TOTAL	MONEY
Motomasa Aoki	68	69		137	234,667
Tsukasa Watanabe	68	69		137	234,667
Norio Suzuki	68	69		137	234,666
Futoshi Irino	65	72		137	234,666
Shozo Miyamoto	65	72		137	234,666
Hiroshi Ishii	70	68		138	160,100
Eitaro Deguchi	70	68		138	160,100
Masaji Kusakabe	70	68		138	160,100
Yoshiyuki Isomura	70	68		138	160,100
Tadami Ueno	69	69		138	160,100
Koichi Inoue	69	69		138	160,100
Michael Harwood	68	70		138	160,100
Koichi Uehara	68	70		138	160,100
Toru Nakamura	66	72		138	160,100
Yoshihiro Funatogawa	65	73		138	160,100

Indonesian Open

Jakarta Golf Club, Rawamangun Course, Jakarta, Indonesia

Par 35-35 — 70; 6,466 yards

April 2-5

purse, US$100,000

	SCORES				TOTAL	MONEY
Wayne Smith	68	70	66	70	274	US$16,600
Jim Hallet	70	69	67	70	276	11,110
*Sukamdi	70	71	68	68	277	
Yuan Chin Chi	71	69	70	68	278	5,630
Craig Parry	66	70	72	70	278	5,630
Marimuthu Ramayah	70	67	72	70	279	3,580
Lu Hsi Chuen	69	70	71	69	279	3,580
Brian Mogg	72	71	69	67	279	3,580
Bunchoo Ruangkit	66	71	70	73	280	2,068
Hiraku Emoto	69	69	73	69	280	2,068
Billy Ray Brown	69	71	66	74	280	2,068
Jim Rutledge	73	68	70	69	280	2,068
Peter O'Malley	71	71	67	71	280	2,068
Roger Mackay	68	69	74	70	281	1,573
Frankie Minoza	70	68	69	74	281	1,573
Jeff Maggert	74	70	68	69	281	1,573
Chip Drury	73	68	72	69	282	1,400
Steve Bowman	70	69	70	74	283	1,310
Eleuterio Nival	69	73	73	68	283	1,310
Rick Gibson	68	72	68	76	284	1,187
Mark Aebli	67	73	72	72	284	1,187
Greg Bruckner	68	73	67	76	284	1,187
Mike Standly	71	71	69	73	284	1,187
*Wiratchant	74	69	71	70	284	
Kasyadi	71	69	70	75	285	1,072
Chen Liang Hsi	71	72	68	74	285	1,072
Lu Ho Tsai	73	71	69	72	285	1,072
Casey Nakama	76	69	69	71	285	1,072
Kris Moe	72	68	77	69	286	913
Peter Jones	68	72	73	73	286	913
Katsuyoshi Tomori	71	70	71	74	286	913
Steve Chapman	72	71	73	70	286	913
Greg Conley	71	72	70	73	286	913
Hsu Chi San	71	72	72	71	286	913
Anthony Gilligan	72	73	68	73	286	913

Republic of China Open

Taoyuan Golf and Country Club, Taipei, Taiwan
Par 37-37 — 74; 7,526 yards

April 9-12
purse, US$140,000

	SCORES				TOTAL	MONEY
Mark Aebli	68	78	72	76	294	US$22,857
Mike Standly	73	75	73	75	296	11,907
Hsieh Yu Shu	71	73	74	78	296	11,907
Lu Chien Soon	71	72	74	80	297	6,857
Hsu Huang Lung	72	73	74	79	298	5,307
Steve Bowman	72	72	73	81	298	5,307
Lee Wen Sheng	74	73	74	78	299	4,114
Marimuthu Ramayah	75	73	73	79	300	3,250
Yu Chin Han	74	73	72	81	300	3,250
Chen Chien Chin	74	74	74	79	301	2,560
Hsieh Min Nan	73	73	76	79	301	2,560
Lu Hsi Chuen	76	74	71	80	301	2,560
Jim Hallet	72	78	76	76	302	2,099
Frankie Minoza	74	73	78	77	302	2,099
Lai Chung Jen	75	71	76	80	302	2,099
Steve Chapman	75	75	73	79	302	2,099
Ho Ming Chung	76	75	74	78	303	1,735
Hikaru Emoto	73	73	74	83	303	1,735
Lu Liang Huan	71	75	74	83	303	1,735
Kuo Chi Hsiung	73	77	70	83	303	1,735
George Serhan	75	73	79	77	304	1,489
Brian Mogg	76	75	75	78	304	1,489
Tony Maloney	76	75	74	79	304	1,489
Roger Mackay	74	76	76	78	304	1,489
Masaru Amano	71	74	78	81	304	1,489
Lin Chia	72	76	74	82	304	1,489
Hsieh Chin Sheng	73	76	73	82	304	1,489
Chen Tze Ming	77	73	77	78	305	1,290
Chen Liang Hsi	74	73	78	80	305	1,290
Craig Parry	75	76	73	81	305	1,290

Pocari Sweat Open

Hakuryuko County Club, Diawacho, Hiroshima
Par 72; 6,780 yards

April 9-12
purse, ¥40,000,000

	SCORES				TOTAL	MONEY
Kinpachi Yoshimura	68	68	68	70	274	¥7,200,000
Yoshiyuki Isomura	66	70	67	71	274	4,000,000
(Yoshimura defeated Isomura on first hole of playoff.)						
Pete Izumikawa	70	68	70	68	276	2,320,000
Graham Marsh	70	68	70	68	276	2,320,000
Seiji Ebihara	71	68	70	68	277	1,600,000
Seiichi Kanai	68	68	73	69	278	1,440,000
Hiroshi Makino	68	70	72	69	279	1,220,000
Tateo Ozaki	68	68	74	69	279	1,220,000
Masanobu Kimura	72	68	72	68	280	1,040,000
Haruo Yasuda	67	69	71	74	281	920,000
Kazushige Kohno	70	70	70	72	282	800,000
Koichi Uehara	69	70	73	71	283	602,000
Teruo Nakamura	69	70	75	69	283	602,000
Noboru Sugai	72	70	70	71	283	602,000

	SCORES				TOTAL	MONEY
Taijiro Tanaka	69	72	70	72	283	602,000
Saburo Fujiki	71	68	71	73	283	602,000
David Ishii	68	69	75	71	283	602,000
Yoshitaka Yamamoto	70	71	70	74	285	375,000
Kikuo Arai	73	71	70	71	285	375,000
Nobuo Serizawa	72	71	69	73	285	375,000
Ikuo Shirahama	73	69	74	69	285	375,000
Hitoshi Kato	75	70	67	73	285	375,000
Shuichi Sano	71	67	74	73	285	375,000
Takao Kage	67	74	73	71	285	375,000
Hisashi Terada	69	70	76	70	285	375,000
Hiroshi Takenaka	69	72	72	72	285	375,000
Tsutomu Irie	70	70	71	75	286	296,000
Yoshimi Niizeki	74	70	71	71	286	296,000
Tsukasa Watanabe	68	70	70	78	286	296,000
Mike Ferguson	70	71	72	73	286	296,000
Brian Jones	69	70	74	73	286	296,000
Taisei Inagaki	67	73	74	72	286	296,000
Masaji Kusakabe	70	73	73	70	286	296,000

Maekyung (Korea) Open

Nam Seoul Country Club, Seoul, Korea
Par 36-36 — 72; 6,861 yards

April 16-19
purse, US$130,000

	SCORES				TOTAL	MONEY
Chen Liang Hsi	74	68	70	67	279	US$21,500
Brian Tennyson	72	65	74	71	282	11,250
Kim Sung Ho	71	73	68	70	282	11,250
Jim Hallet	70	70	73	70	283	6,000
Jeff Hart	73	70	70	70	283	6,000
Peter Fowler	72	69	72	72	285	4,500
Koichi Suzuki	70	72	73	72	287	3,150
Frankie Minoza	73	71	68	75	287	3,150
Chen Tze Ming	72	72	71	72	287	3,150
Kuo Chi Hsiung	70	76	69	72	287	3,150
Park Nam Sin	72	73	73	70	288	2,400
Satsuki Takahashi	71	73	73	72	289	2,050
Craig McClellan	74	70	72	73	289	2,050
Cho Ho Sang	73	70	75	71	289	2,050
Choi Yoon Soo	75	70	69	75	289	2,050
Ossie Moore	74	70	71	75	290	1,730
Lin Chia	75	69	75	71	290	1,730
Kwak Yu Hyun	74	70	74	72	290	1,730
Rodger Davis	75	73	72	71	291	1,522
Hsieh Chin Sheng	70	73	73	75	291	1,522
Cho Chul Sang	70	75	74	72	291	1,522
Ahn Kwang Nung	73	73	70	75	291	1,522
Choi Sang Ho	75	73	72	71	291	1,522
Shizuo Mori	72	72	73	75	292	1,277
Chung Cun Hsing	73	71	74	74	292	1,277
Hsieh Yu Shu	75	72	73	72	292	1,277
John Jacobs	72	75	70	75	292	1,277
Jeff Maggert	74	73	72	73	292	1,277
Han Jang Sang	74	73	70	75	292	1,277
Hong Young Pyo	71	72	71	78	292	1,277
Kim Hak Seh	70	71	74	77	292	1,277

Bridgestone Aso Open

Aso Golf Club, Aso, Kumamoto
Par 72; 7,030 yards

April 16-19
purse, ¥35,000,000

	SCORES				TOTAL	MONEY
Norio Mikami	69	67	74	70	280	¥6,300,000
David Ishii	73	66	71	74	284	2,940,000
Shuichi Sano	68	72	74	70	284	2,940,000
Yoshitaka Yamamoto	73	69	68	75	285	1,540,000
Brian Jones	74	72	71	68	285	1,540,000
Toru Nakamura	73	70	71	72	286	1,190,000
Tadao Nakamura	70	72	72	72	286	1,190,000
Katsunari Takahashi	72	72	74	69	287	1,015,000
Seiji Ebihara	72	71	73	72	288	644,875
Graham Marsh	71	72	71	74	288	644,875
Masanobu Kimura	70	78	72	68	288	644,875
Noboru Sugai	74	70	71	73	288	644,875
Tsukasa Watanabe	74	72	71	71	288	644,875
Ikuo Shirahama	73	72	72	71	288	644,875
Masaji Kusakabe	72	68	73	75	288	644,875
Futoshi Irino	71	70	72	75	288	644,875
Yoshikazu Yokoshima	71	73	72	73	289	420,000
Taichiro Kanatani	70	75	67	78	290	360,500
Ryoichi Takamoto	72	72	73	73	290	360,500
Hajime Meshiai	71	70	74	75	290	360,500
Norio Inoue	73	70	75	72	290	360,500
Haruhito Yamamoto	71	72	70	78	291	315,000
Kiyoshi Maita	74	73	73	71	291	315,000
Yoshiyuki Isomura	74	72	74	72	292	273,000
Seiichi Kanai	73	71	71	77	292	273,000
Hiroshi Makino	74	71	73	74	292	273,000
Yutaka Suzuki	74	74	75	69	292	273,000
Nobuo Serizawa	73	68	74	77	292	273,000
Takao Kage	70	74	71	77	292	273,000
Namio Takasu	73	71	74	74	292	273,000
Hiromichi Namiki	69	72	74	77	292	273,000
Taiichi Nakagawa	73	75	74	70	292	273,000

Dunlop International Open

Ibaraki Golf Club, Ina, Japan
Par 36-36 — 72; 7,163 yards

April 23-26
purse, US$350,000

	SCORES				TOTAL	MONEY
Isao Aoki	69	67	69	72	277	US$64,000.00
Yoshitaka Yamamoto	69	71	70	68	278	29,866.66
Tsuneyuki Nakajima	71	68	72	67	278	29,866.66
Seiichi Kanai	69	72	70	68	279	15,644.44
Rodger Davis	70	72	68	69	279	15,644.44
David Ishii	71	69	71	69	280	12,088.88
Chen Tze Chung	72	70	69	69	280	12,088.88
Tsukasa Watanabe	71	74	68	69	282	10,311.11
Chen Liang Hsi	73	73	68	69	283	7,409.77
Graham Marsh	72	73	71	67	283	7,409.77
Pat Horgan	73	74	71	65	283	7,409.77
Toru Nakamura	71	73	70	69	283	7,409.77
Koichi Suzuki	70	70	71	72	283	7,409.77

	SCORES				TOTAL	MONEY
Hiroshi Makino	73	69	70	73	285	5,333.33
Isamu Sugita	69	71	72	73	285	5,333.33
Tsutomu Irie	69	71	72	74	286	4,039.11
Ian Baker-Finch	69	73	70	74	286	4,039.11
Teruo Nakamura	69	73	69	75	286	4,039.11
Peter Fowler	73	71	73	69	286	4,039.11
John Jacobs	70	72	71	73	286	4,039.11
Nobumitsu Yuhara	76	71	73	67	287	3,342.22
Terry Gale	71	69	73	74	287	3,342.22
Jim Hallet	72	71	72	73	288	2,986.66
Namio Takasu	72	74	70	72	288	2,986.66
Hideto Shigenobu	72	71	72	73	288	2,986.66
Masahiro Kuramoto	75	68	72	73	288	2,986.66
Seiji Ebihara	69	75	72	72	288	2,986.66
Masaji Kusakabe	72	72	73	72	289	2,702.22
Yasushi Katayama	70	75	70	74	289	2,702.22
Brian Jones	68	74	74	73	289	2,702.22

Chunichi Crowns

Nagoya Golf Club, Wago Course, Nagoya
Par 35-35 — 70; 6,491 yards

April 30-May 3
purse, ¥90,000,000

	SCORES				TOTAL	MONEY
Masashi Ozaki	69	67	66	66	268	¥16,200,000
Ian Baker-Finch	66	68	69	71	274	5,760,000
Masahiro Kuramoto	69	69	70	66	274	5,760,000
Isao Aoki	69	69	68	68	274	5,760,000
Yoshitaka Yamamoto	70	70	65	69	274	5,760,000
Brian Jones	70	70	69	66	275	3,060,000
Scott Simpson	68	70	66	71	275	3,060,000
Kioichi Uehara	71	70	69	66	276	2,610,000
Masaji Kusakabe	66	65	69	77	277	1,966,500
Futoshi Irino	66	72	71	68	277	1,966,500
Hajime Meshiai	73	65	66	73	277	1,966,500
David Ishii	68	70	69	70	277	1,966,500
Terry Gale	68	70	70	70	278	1,248,000
Bobby Wadkins	73	66	69	70	278	1,248,000
Hsieh Min Nan	71	72	67	68	278	1,248,000
Lanny Wadkins	71	67	66	74	278	1,248,000
Seiichi Kanai	68	71	69	70	278	1,248,000
Graham Marsh	71	74	64	69	278	1,248,000
Haruo Yasuda	75	69	68	67	279	882,000
Lu Liang Huan	70	71	66	72	279	882,000
Shigeru Uchida	73	70	67	69	279	882,000
Chen Tze Chung	68	72	68	71	279	882,000
Lu Hsi Chuen	71	68	71	71	281	747,000
Keiichi Kobayashi	74	70	68	69	281	747,000
Kenny Knox	67	69	74	71	281	747,000
Teruo Sugihara	72	72	70	67	281	747,000
Katsunari Takahashi	69	71	69	72	281	747,000
Naomichi Ozaki	72	73	67	69	281	747,000
Hideto Shigenobu	71	71	72	68	282	648,720
Seiji Ebihara	73	65	76	68	282	648,720
Kinpachi Yoshimura	72	68	69	73	282	648,720
Doug Tewell	71	72	73	66	282	648,720
Hubert Green	73	69	72	68	282	648,720

Fuji Sankei Classic

Kawana Hotel, Fuji Course, Ito
Par 71; 6,694 yards

May 7-10
purse, ¥60,000,000

	SCORES				TOTAL	MONEY
Masashi Ozaki	68	72	66	69	275	¥10,800,000
Graham Marsh	73	67	67	70	277	6,000,000
Brian Jones	69	71	70	70	280	3,480,000
Toru Nakamura	68	68	69	75	280	3,480,000
David Ishii	71	72	69	70	282	1,956,000
Masahiro Kuramoto	71	71	69	71	282	1,956,000
Seiji Ebihara	65	69	74	74	282	1,956,000
Hajime Meshiai	67	69	72	74	282	1,956,000
Hsieh Min Nam	68	71	69	74	282	1,956,000
Isao Aoki	71	69	71	72	283	1,125,600
Yoshitaka Yamamoto	70	75	69	69	283	1,125,600
Lu Lian Huan	75	70	66	72	283	1,125,600
Tsuneyuki Nakajima	68	73	72	70	283	1,125,600
Tateo Ozaki	65	72	77	69	283	1,125,600
Hideto Shigenobu	75	71	67	71	284	864,000
Seichi Kanai	71	72	72	70	285	681,600
Naomichi Ozaki	74	72	70	69	285	681,600
Terry Gale	70	68	75	72	285	681,600
Chen Tze Ming	72	72	71	70	285	681,600
Toru Nakayama	66	72	72	75	285	681,600
Noboru Sugai	68	75	74	69	286	535,200
Namio Takasu	68	72	74	72	286	535,200
Shigeru Uchida	72	71	71	72	286	535,200
Hiromichi Namiki	73	73	68	72	286	535,200
Mike Hulbert	72	72	69	73	286	535,200
Koichi Uehara	72	69	76	70	287	462,000
Katsunari Takahashi	74	72	72	69	287	462,000
Ikuo Shirahama	67	72	79	69	287	462,000
Saburo Fujiki	71	73	72	71	287	462,000
Taijiro Tanaka	71	72	71	73	287	462,000
Kiyoshi Maita	69	71	72	75	287	462,000

Japan Match Play Championship

Mito Golf Club, Mito, Ibaraki
Par 36-36 — 72; 6,728 yards

May 14-17
purse, ¥40,000,000

FIRST ROUND

Tsuneyuki Nakajima defeated Masanobu Kimura, 3 and 2.
Hajime Meshiai defeated Yoshihisa Iwashita, 4 and 3.
Koichi Suzuki defeated Tsukasa Watanabe, 1 up.
Tadao Nakamura defeated Eitaro Deguchi, 3 and 2.
Masahiro Kuramoto defeated Masaji Kusakabe, 2 and 1.
Kutsunari Takahashi defeated Seiichi Kanai, 1 up.
Kinpachi Yoshimura defeated Tateo Ozaki, 6 and 5.
Saburo Fujiki defeated Hiroshi Ishii, 2 up.
Masashi Ozaki defeated Taisei Inaguki, 2 and 1.
Yasuhiro Funatogawa defeated Hideto Shigenobu, 1 up.
Yoshitaka Yamamoto defeated Toru Nakamura, 5 and 4.
Nobumitsu Yuhara defeated Haruo Yasuda, 1 up.
Isao Aoki defeated Futoshi Irino, 5 and 4.

Shinsaku Maeda defeated Yoshimi Niizeki, 6 and 4.
Hsieh Min Nan defeated Naomichi Ozaki, 2 and 1.
Hiroshi Makino defeated Kikuo Arai, 1 up.
(Each losing player received ¥200,000.)

SECOND ROUND

Nakajima defeated Meshiai, 4 and 3.
Tadeo Nakamura defeated Suzuki, 2 and 1.
Takahashi defeated Kuramoto, 1 up, 19 holes.
Fujiki defeated Yoshimura, 4 and 3.
Masashi Ozaki defeated Funatogawa, 5 and 4.
Yamamoto defeated Yuhara, 1 up.
Aoki defeated Maeda, 2 and 1.
Hsieh defeated Makino, 1 up, 20 holes.
(Each losing player received ¥400,000.)

QUARTER-FINALS

Nakamura defeated Nakajima, 1 up.
Takahashi defeated Fujiki, 4 and 3.
Ozaki defeated Yamamoto, 3 and 2.
Hsieh defeated Aoki, 3 and 2.
(Each losing player received ¥800,000.)

SEMI-FINALS

Takahashi defeated Nakamura, 6 and 5.
Ozaki defeated Hsieh, 1 up.

THIRD-FOURTH PLACE PLAYOFF

Nakamura defeated Hsieh.
(Nakamura received ¥3,000,000, Hsieh ¥2,000,000.)

FINAL

Takahashi defeated Ozaki, 1 up, 37 holes.
(Takahashi received ¥10,000,000, Ozaki ¥5,000,000.)

Pepsi Ube

Ube Country Club, Mannenike-Kita Course, Ajisu
Par 36-36 — 72; 7,059 yards

May 21-24
purse, ¥45,000,000

	SCORES				TOTAL	MONEY
Chen Tze Ming	69	72	70	67	278	¥8,100,000
Hiroshi Makino	70	66	73	69	278	4,500,000
(Chen defeated Makino on first hole of playoff.)						
Hajime Meshiai	73	66	69	73	281	3,060,000
Seiichi Kanai	71	71	68	72	282	1,860,000
Tsuneyuki Nakajima	67	70	71	74	282	1,860,000
Noboru Sugai	70	72	68	72	282	1,860,000
Takeshi Shibata	69	70	74	70	283	1,440,000
Namio Takasu	70	73	65	76	284	1,170,000
Hiroshi Ishii	69	75	68	72	284	1,170,000
Ikuo Shirahama	71	73	69	71	284	1,170,000
Koichi Suzuki	68	72	73	72	285	828,000
Yoshihisa Iwashita	68	72	71	74	285	828,000
Akihito Yokoyama	71	75	70	69	285	828,000
Tohru Nakamura	71	73	71	71	286	597,600
Masaji Kusakabe	71	70	72	73	286	597,600

	SCORES				TOTAL	MONEY
Hsieh Min Nan	71	73	68	74	286	597,600
Noboru Sugai	70	71	71	74	286	597,600
Shotaro Watanabe	78	67	69	72	286	597,600
Shigeru Kawamata	74	72	70	71	287	432,000
Joji Furuki	75	70	69	73	287	432,000
Kinya Aoyagi	68	77	71	71	287	432,000
Shuji Sano	73	72	70	72	287	432,000
David Ishii	70	74	68	75	287	432,000
Kazuo Kanayama	72	71	71	74	288	378,000
Hiromichi Namiki	71	74	69	74	288	378,000
Katsuyoshi Tomori	74	71	72	71	288	378,000
Naomichi Ozaki	71	74	71	73	289	355,500
Noboru Inoue	71	72	70	76	289	355,500
Pete Izumikawa	70	75	73	72	290	320,400
Katsuji Hasegawa	73	74	73	70	290	320,400
Yoshikazu Yokoshima	75	71	73	71	290	320,400
Tadami Ueno	70	73	77	70	290	320,400
Takenori Hiraishi	75	71	72	72	290	320,400
Hsieh Chin-Seng	79	67	72	72	290	320,400

Mitsubishi Galant

Pine Lake Golf Club, Nishiwaki, Hyogo
Par 36-36 — 72; 7,034 yards

May 28-31
purse, ¥56,000,000

	SCORES				TOTAL	MONEY
Brian Jones	70	70	71	72	283	¥10,080,000
Koichi Suzuki	72	66	73	75	286	4,704,000
Nobuo Serizawa	69	74	72	71	286	4,704,000
Graham Marsh	74	74	70	71	289	2,314,666
Seiichi Kanai	78	69	73	69	289	2,314,666
Taiichiro Tanaka	74	74	71	70	289	2,314,666
Masaji Kusakabe	74	73	72	71	290	1,708,000
Yasuhiro Funatogawa	73	74	71	72	290	1,708,000
Shigeru Kawamata	74	74	68	75	291	1,372,000
Haruo Yasuda	72	75	73	71	291	1,372,000
Hiroshi Ishii	78	70	71	73	292	1,030,133
Tsutomu Horiuchi	76	70	72	74	292	1,030,133
Yoshihisa Iwashita	72	71	72	77	292	1,030,133
Kikuo Arai	73	75	73	72	293	743,680
Yoshikazu Yokoshima	73	75	75	70	293	743,680
David Ishii	73	76	71	73	293	743,680
Akihito Yokoyama	73	76	73	71	293	743,680
Yoshitaka Yamamoto	72	76	73	72	293	743,680
Seiichi Koizumi	72	74	75	73	294	560,000
Seiji Ebihara	76	70	75	73	294	560,000
Chen Tze Ming	77	72	71	74	294	560,000
Tsukasa Watanabe	75	74	73	73	295	504,000
Katsuyoshi Tomori	74	75	76	70	295	504,000
Tadao Nakamura	73	76	76	71	296	464,800
Kinpachi Yoshimura	74	76	71	75	296	464,800
Lu Hsi Chuen	71	77	74	74	296	464,800
Norio Suzuki	71	74	77	74	296	464,800
Masahiro Kuramoto	77	70	74	76	297	414,400
Takashi Kubota	68	76	77	76	297	414,400
Koichi Uehara	71	79	72	75	297	414,400
Hiromichi Namiki	72	76	73	76	297	414,400
Koji Nishiwaki	79	70	71	77	297	414,400

Tohoku Classic

Nishi Sendai Country Club, Miyagimachi, Miyagi
Par 36-36 — 72; 7,009 yards

June 4-7
purse, ¥42,000,000

	SCORES				TOTAL	MONEY
Seiichi Kanai	71	69	70	65	275	¥7,500,000
Hajime Meshiai	69	70	67	71	277	4,200,000
Teruo Sugihara	70	73	68	67	278	2,900,000
Terry Gale	71	68	70	71	280	2,000,000
Hiroshi Makino	71	68	70	72	281	1,425,000
Norio Mikami	73	71	68	69	281	1,425,000
Taiichiro Tanaka	68	70	70	73	281	1,425,000
Tsukasa Watanabe	67	73	72	69	281	1,425,000
Kinpachi Yoshimura	66	72	72	72	282	927,500
Saburo Fujiki	77	67	69	69	282	927,500
David Ishii	73	70	71	68	282	927,500
Katsunari Takahashi	74	72	71	65	282	927,500
Chen Tze Chung	74	69	70	70	283	606,000
Tadao Nakamura	70	71	71	71	283	606,000
Masaji Kusakabe	69	70	69	75	283	606,000
Tadami Ueno	70	72	72	69	283	606,000
Yoshihisa Iwashita	73	70	70	70	283	606,000
Satsuki Takahashi	71	70	70	73	284	414,833
Hiromichi Namiki	70	70	73	71	284	414,833
Shigeru Kawamata	70	73	70	71	284	414,833
Lu Liang Huang	68	73	72	71	284	414,833
Koichi Suzuki	70	75	68	71	284	414,833
Graham Marsh	70	73	73	68	284	414,833
Kikuo Arai	71	72	73	69	285	340,166
Tsutomu Irie	67	71	71	76	285	340,166
Namio Takasu	68	73	71	73	285	340,166
Kazushige Kohno	73	71	69	72	285	340,166
Noboru Sugai	70	72	70	73	285	340,166
Yoshitaka Yamamoto	72	69	70	74	285	340,166
Nobuo Serizawa	71	69	73	73	286	302,333
Yutaka Hagawa	74	72	71	69	286	302,333
Hideki Kase	72	70	73	71	286	302,333

Sapporo Tokyu Open

Sapporo Kokusai Country Club, Hokkaido
Par 36-36 — 72; 6,949 yards

June 11-14
purse, ¥40,000,000

	SCORES				TOTAL	MONEY
David Ishii	67	68	70	71	276	¥7,200,000
Toru Nakamura	73	74	65	67	279	4,000,000
Masahiro Kuramoto	71	71	69	69	280	2,720,000
Chen Tze Ming	71	72	73	68	284	1,920,000
Noboru Sugai	72	71	70	72	285	1,370,000
Tsukasa Watanabe	75	69	70	71	285	1,370,000
Hiromichi Namiki	68	72	73	72	285	1,370,000
Katasunari Takahashi	72	70	75	68	285	1,370,000
Nobuo Serizawa	73	67	72	74	286	874,000
Taiichiro Kanaya	74	72	72	68	286	874,000
Isao Aoki	71	73	72	70	286	874,000
Brian Jones	70	73	70	73	286	874,000
Teruo Nakamura	71	68	75	73	287	624,000

	SCORES				TOTAL	MONEY
Teruo Sugihara	73	73	71	70	287	624,000
Nobumitsu Yuhara	72	70	72	73	287	624,000
Seiji Ebihara	72	74	69	73	288	468,000
Masaji Kusakabe	73	74	68	73	288	468,000
Ichiro Ino	73	73	68	74	288	468,000
Hajime Meshiai	73	73	71	71	288	468,000
Kazuo Yoshikawa	71	71	76	71	289	369,600
Shoichi Sato	69	74	73	73	289	369,600
Shigeru Kawamata	69	75	74	71	289	369,600
Ryoichi Takamoto	72	72	71	74	289	369,600
Hideto Shigenobu	69	69	78	73	289	369,600
Norio Mikami	72	73	76	69	290	316,000
Tadao Nakamura	73	70	76	71	290	316,000
Ikuo Shirahama	69	71	74	76	290	316,000
Tadami Ueno	65	77	75	73	290	316,000
Kikuo Arai	75	73	71	71	290	316,000
Seiichi Kanai	71	76	75	68	290	316,000

Yomiuri Sapporo Beer Tournament

Yomiuri Country Club, East Course, Nishinomiya, Hyogo
Par 36-36 — 72; 7,023 yards

June 18-21
purse, ¥50,000,000

	SCORES				TOTAL	MONEY
Satoshi Higashi	68	67	70	75	280	¥9,000,000
Graham Marsh	70	68	74	69	281	4,200,000
Hajime Meshiai	69	71	70	71	281	4,200,000
Katsunari Takahashi	69	69	71	73	282	2,200,000
Koichi Suzuki	67	73	71	71	282	2,200,000
Katsuyoshi Tomori	74	70	68	71	283	1,700,000
Masaji Kusakabe	68	74	73	68	283	1,700,000
Naomichi Ozaki	73	69	73	69	284	1,300,000
Shigeru Kawamata	74	71	72	67	284	1,300,000
Terry Gale	69	71	73	71	284	1,300,000
Nobumitsu Yuhara	69	72	75	69	285	960,000
Lu Liang Huan	71	70	72	72	285	960,000
Chen Tze Ming	71	70	72	73	286	810,000
Teruo Nakamura	68	75	72	71	286	810,000
Yoshihisa Iwashita	70	70	75	72	287	612,000
Joji Furuki	68	73	71	75	287	612,000
Misao Yamamoto	70	69	75	73	287	612,000
David Ishii	68	75	74	70	287	612,000
Pete Izumikawa	73	71	76	67	287	612,000
Noboru Sugai	75	69	73	71	288	490,000
Yoshitaka Yamamoto	72	72	74	70	288	490,000
Takao Kage	71	69	76	73	289	416,250
Hideto Shigenobu	71	73	75	70	289	416,250
Tomohiro Maruyama	69	73	74	73	289	416,250
Kazuo Kanayama	70	73	73	73	289	416,250
Hiroshi Makino	69	72	75	73	289	416,250
Yoshikazu Yokoshima	70	72	74	73	289	416,250
Tateo Ozaki	72	70	70	77	289	416,250
Katsuji Hasegawa	71	74	72	72	289	416,250

Mizuno Tournament

Tokinodai Country Club, Bijodai Course, Hakui, Ishikawa
Par 36-36 — 72; 6,804 yards

June 25-28
purse, ¥50,000,000

	SCORES				TOTAL	MONEY
David Ishii	67	66	69	70	272	¥9,000,000
Chen Tze Ming	73	70	72	65	280	4,200,000
Toru Nakamura	66	71	68	75	280	4,200,000
Masashi Ozaki	69	70	71	71	281	2,400,000
Noboru Sugai	70	74	73	66	283	1,630,000
Shigeru Kawamata	74	70	69	70	283	1,630,000
Masahiro Kuramoto	73	68	70	72	283	1,630,000
Yoshitaka Yamamoto	70	70	72	71	283	1,630,000
Yoshiyuki Isomura	69	68	74	72	283	1,630,000
Naomichi Ozaki	75	72	71	66	284	1,075,000
Hsieh Min Nan	71	73	68	72	284	1,075,000
Frankie Minoza	72	75	69	69	285	920,000
Yoshiharu Harato	72	74	71	69	286	693,333
Saburo Fujiki	70	74	72	70	286	693,333
Hajime Meshiai	70	71	73	72	286	693,333
Masaji Kusakabe	71	70	73	72	286	693,333
Norio Mikami	74	73	68	71	286	693,333
Lu Lian Huan	72	68	75	71	286	693,333
Noriichi Kawakami	69	76	71	71	287	480,000
Namio Takasu	69	73	75	70	287	480,000
Eitaro Deguchi	75	68	69	75	287	480,000
Shinsaku Maeda	69	76	71	71	287	480,000
Takenori Hiraishi	69	71	71	76	287	480,000
Yasuhiro Funatogawa	72	74	69	73	288	415,000
Seiichi Kanai	76	68	74	70	288	415,000
Taruo Nakamura	72	70	72	74	288	415,000
Yoshio Ichikawa	69	73	73	73	288	415,000
Yoichi Yamamoto	71	71	75	72	289	370,000
Brett Ogle	71	73	72	73	289	370,000
Hiroshi Ishii	71	72	76	70	289	370,000
Koichi Suzuki	74	72	73	70	289	370,000
Nobuo Serizawa	73	73	71	72	289	370,000

Kanto PGA Championship

Shimoakima Golf Club, Annaka, Gumma
Par 36-36 — 72; 7,127 yards

July 2-5
purse, ¥22,500,000

(Tournament shortened to 54 holes because of rain.)

	SCORES			TOTAL	MONEY
Naomichi Ozaki	68	72	72	212	¥4,050,000
Nobumitsu Yuhara	69	71	73	213	2,250,000
Katsunari Takahashi	72	71	72	215	1,530,000
Taiichiro Tanaka	71	74	74	219	1,080,000
Nobuo Serizawa	74	73	73	220	810,000
Fujio Kobayashi	75	73	72	220	810,000
Fumio Tanaka	70	76	74	220	810,000
Seiji Ebihara	69	73	79	221	523,800
Kohichi Suzuki	70	78	73	221	523,800
Kazushige Kohno	77	70	74	221	523,800
Motomasa Aoki	72	73	76	221	523,800

	SCORES			TOTAL	MONEY
Harumitsu Hamano	72	75	74	221	523,800
Seiichi Kanai	74	75	73	222	364,500
Yoshikazu Yokoshima	77	75	70	222	364,500
Noboru Sugai	71	74	78	223	259,714
Joji Furuki	75	72	76	223	259,714
Ryoichi Tomomitsu	72	77	74	223	259,714
Katsuji Hasegawa	76	74	73	223	259,714
Yoshihisa Iwashita	75	76	72	223	259,714
Takashi Murakami	69	73	81	223	259,714
Ryoichi Takamoto	75	75	73	223	259,714
Tsuneyuki Nakajima	68	78	78	224	199,500
Kikuo Arai	73	77	74	224	199,500
Hsieh Min Nan	73	77	74	224	199,500
Aki Ohmachi	74	72	79	225	184,500
Ikuo Shirahama	76	74	75	225	184,500
Satoshi Higashi	76	75	74	225	184,500
Tohru Kurihara	74	77	75	226	166,500
Namio Takasu	76	74	76	226	166,500
Yasuhiro Funatogawa	72	76	78	226	166,500
Shuichi Sano	72	75	79	226	166,500
Noboru Ishii	73	77	76	226	166,500

Kansai PGA Championship

Tosa Country Club, Yasu, Kochi   July 2-5
Par 36-36 — 72; 6,718 yards   purse, ¥25,000,000

	SCORES				TOTAL	MONEY
Yoshitaka Yamamoto	68	70	70	66	274	¥4,500,000
Hideto Shigenobu	68	67	70	74	279	2,100,000
Takeshi Nakaya	71	67	72	69	279	2,100,000
Mitsuhiro Kitta	69	72	70	71	282	1,200,000
Tadami Ueno	67	72	73	71	283	815,000
Tatsuya Shiraishi	70	72	71	70	283	815,000
Yurio Akitomi	66	75	73	69	283	815,000
Nobuhiro Yoshino	73	72	70	68	283	815,000
Tadao Nakamura	67	70	74	72	283	815,000
Teruo Sugihara	72	68	71	73	284	575,000
Shinsaku Maeda	71	71	72	72	286	442,000
Teruo Nakamura	72	72	72	70	286	442,500
Akio Tomita	70	74	73	69	286	442,500
Tsutomu Horiuchi	72	71	70	73	286	442,500
Tsutomu Irie	72	70	71	74	287	360,000
Tohru Nakamura	71	73	72	72	288	315,000
Teruo Suzuki	73	73	71	71	288	315,000
Toyotake Nakao	70	74	72	73	289	252,000
Koichi Inoue	72	71	74	72	289	252,000
Toshiaki Nakagawa	68	72	75	74	289	252,000
Hiroshi Oku	75	72	73	69	289	252,000
Akimitsu Tokita	74	70	71	74	289	252,000
Shigeru Uchida	72	69	74	75	290	217,500
Yoshinori Ohnishi	76	70	75	69	290	217,500
Masahiro Kuramoto	72	74	69	76	291	202,500
Yasuo Sone	71	72	73	75	291	202,500
Takenori Hiraishi	73	71	72	75	291	202,500
Masahiro Shiota	71	71	75	74	291	202,500
Hiromichi Takezaki	72	74	74	72	292	182,500

	SCORES				TOTAL	MONEY
Masato Okamura	73	73	71	75	292	182,500
Tomio Araki	72	72	71	77	292	182,500
Kazuo Kanayama	70	73	72	77	292	182,500

Hiroshima Open

Hiroshima Golf Club, Higachi-Hiroshima
Par 36-36 — 72; 6,865 yards

July 9-12
purse, ¥40,000,000

	SCORES				TOTAL	MONEY
Hajime Meshiai	70	63	70	72	275	¥7,200,000
Lu Liang Huan	72	69	68	68	277	2,880,000
Yoshiyuki Isomura	65	66	74	72	277	2,880,000
Tadao Nakamura	70	66	73	68	277	2,880,000
Hideto Shigenobu	68	67	72	71	278	1,520,000
Katsuyoshi Tomori	72	69	72	65	278	1,520,000
Hiroshi Goda	68	69	68	74	279	1,100,000
Joji Furuki	71	68	70	70	279	1,100,000
Katsuji Hasegawa	72	68	72	67	279	1,100,000
Seiichi Kanai	66	70	72	71	279	1,100,000
Hiromichi Namiki	71	70	70	69	280	768,000
Naomichi Ozaki	69	68	74	69	280	768,000
Kinpachi Yoshimura	74	70	72	65	281	672,000
Tomohiro Maruyama	74	70	70	68	282	576,000
Yoshihisa Takasaka	71	68	73	70	282	576,000
Yoshitaka Yamamoto	73	69	69	71	282	576,000
Haruo Yasuda	72	68	69	74	283	436,000
Teruo Nakamura	76	68	73	66	283	436,000
Nobuo Serizawa	71	67	73	72	283	436,000
Nobumitsu Yuhara	68	68	73	74	283	436,000
Noburu Sugai	69	72	71	72	284	362,000
Ikuo Shirahama	70	70	71	73	284	362,000
Yoshimi Niizeki	72	69	73	70	284	362,000
Tadami Ueno	73	70	69	72	284	362,000
Nobuhiro Yoshino	75	67	70	73	285	324,000
Satoshi Higashi	73	69	70	73	285	324,000
Kazushige Kohno	71	72	69	73	285	324,000
Yoshihisa Iwasahita	71	68	75	71	285	324,000
Isao Isozaki	67	73	72	74	286	288,320
Takao Kage	71	72	71	72	286	288,320
Tomishige Ikeda	69	72	73	72	286	288,320
Kazuo Yoshikawa	72	68	72	74	286	288,320
Saburo Fujiki	68	73	75	70	286	288,320

Japan PGA Championship

Hamano Golf Club, Inchihara, Chiba
Par 36-36 — 72; 7,217 yards

July 23-26
purse, ¥60,000,000

	SCORES				TOTAL	MONEY
David Ishii	73	67	69	71	280	¥10,800,000
Seiichi Kanai	72	70	69	70	281	5,040,000
Brian Jones	72	68	70	71	281	5,040,000
Isao Aoki	73	71	71	67	282	2,880,000

	SCORES				TOTAL	MONEY
Yoshikazu Yokoshima	72	74	65	72	283	2,400,000
Tadao Nakamura	71	73	68	73	285	2,160,000
Kinpachi Yoshimura	75	74	68	69	286	1,920,000
Norio Mikami	70	77	68	72	287	1,560,000
Katsunari Takahashi	76	72	70	69	287	1,560,000
Chen Tze Ming	72	69	72	74	287	1,560,000
Hsieh Min Nan	73	72	72	71	288	1,104,000
Hideto Shigenobu	75	74	68	71	288	1,104,000
Kazushige Kohno	75	72	70	71	288	1,104,000
Saburo Fujiki	74	73	74	68	289	900,000
Yurio Akitomi	76	73	70	70	289	900,000
Tomohiro Maruyama	75	72	73	70	290	648,000
Teruo Nakamura	75	71	71	73	290	648,000
Hisashi Suzumura	75	74	70	71	290	648,000
Yoshihisa Iwashita	72	69	72	77	290	648,000
Yoshimi Niizeki	72	72	73	73	290	648,000
Nobumitsu Yuhara	79	72	70	69	290	648,000
Hiroshi Oku	77	72	66	75	290	648,000
Kazuo Kanayama	76	76	70	69	291	486,000
Shinsaku Maeda	79	73	66	73	291	486,000
Seiji Ebihara	73	72	71	75	291	486,000
Noriji Asai	79	69	75	68	291	486,000
Tohru Nakamura	73	76	70	72	291	486,000
Joji Furuki	78	72	68	73	291	486,000
Katsuji Hasegawa	73	70	73	75	291	486,000
Hiromichi Namiki	77	71	72	71	291	486,000
Yoshitaka Yamamoto	76	73	69	74	292	415,800
Hajime Meshiai	76	71	72	73	292	415,800
Masahiro Shiota	75	74	73	70	292	415,800
Masaji Kusakabe	74	76	70	72	292	415,800
Noboru Fujiike	76	76	70	71	293	381,600
Masahiro Kuramoto	76	74	72	71	293	381,600
Satoshi Higashi	80	69	72	72	293	381,600
Ikuo Shirahama	74	71	76	73	294	338,400
Hisao Inoue	73	74	71	76	294	338,400
Noboru Sugai	76	76	71	71	294	338,400
Masashi Ozaki	73	78	70	73	294	338,400
Tadami Ueno	78	74	69	73	294	338,400
Taichiro Kanaya	78	72	74	70	294	338,400
Toshiaki Namiki	77	73	73	72	295	283,200
Shigeru Kawamata	75	76	71	73	295	283,200
Taiichiro Tanaka	77	75	74	69	295	283,200
Kenji Sogame	77	75	68	75	295	283,200
Tsutomu Irie	76	76	72	71	295	283,200
Shozo Miyamoto	75	76	70	74	295	283,200

Niigata Open

Forest Country Club, Tsukioka Course, Niigata
Par 35-36 — 71; 7,025 yards

July 30-August 2
purse, ¥40,000,000

	SCORES				TOTAL	MONEY
Tadao Nakamura	67	71	67	71	276	¥7,200,000
Hsieh Chin Sheng	70	72	65	70	277	2,560,000
Brian Jones	73	67	68	69	277	2,560,000
David Ishii	72	69	67	69	277	2,560,000
Kazuo Yoshikawa	70	72	67	68	277	2,560,000

	SCORES				TOTAL	MONEY
Nobuo Serizawa	71	70	68	69	278	1,293,333
Namio Takasu	70	68	67	73	278	1,293,333
Hsieh Min Nan	66	73	72	67	278	1,293,333
Toshimitsu Kai	73	66	71	69	279	874,000
Tateo Ozaki	70	66	71	72	279	874,000
Hideto Shigenobu	67	72	68	72	279	874,000
Takao Kage	71	66	70	72	279	874,000
Taruo Nakamura	70	73	68	69	280	576,000
Shigeru Kawamata	67	70	71	72	280	576,000
Katsunari Takahashi	70	69	68	73	280	576,000
Ichiro Teramoto	72	70	69	69	280	576,000
Namiki Hiromichi	71	70	72	67	280	576,000
Hiroshi Ishii	67	70	68	76	281	412,000
Akihito Yokoyama	71	69	71	70	281	412,000
Noboru Sugai	67	72	74	68	281	412,000
Koji Nakajima	69	70	68	74	281	412,000
Saburo Fujiki	74	72	68	68	282	360,000
Kikuo Arai	69	72	71	70	282	360,000
Gregory Meyer	68	73	71	71	283	344,000
Kazuo Kanayama	73	71	68	72	284	336,000
Taiichiro Tanaka	75	70	67	73	285	312,000
Chen Tze Ming	74	72	71	68	285	312,000
Seiichi Koizumi	68	73	72	72	285	312,000
Taisei Inagaki	66	73	69	77	285	312,000
Kenji Tokuyama	72	69	75	69	285	312,000

Nikkei Cup/Nakamura Memorial Tournament

Gifuseki Country Club, Seki, Gifu
Par 35-36 — 71; 6,926 yards

August 13-16
purse, ¥40,000,000

	SCORES				TOTAL	MONEY
Nobuo Serizawa	70	70	71	66	277	¥7,200,000
Naomichi Ozaki	71	68	69	70	278	2,880,000
Masahiro Shiota	72	68	70	68	278	2,880,000
Masashi Ozaki	72	64	71	71	278	2,880,000
Yoshinori Mizumaki	72	67	69	71	279	1,600,000
Fujio Kobayashi	69	74	70	67	280	1,360,000
Teruo Nakamura	67	69	74	70	280	1,360,000
Nobumitsu Yuhara	71	68	73	69	281	1,160,000
Katsunari Takahashi	71	70	70	71	282	920,000
Masahiro Kuramoto	69	67	73	73	282	920,000
Seiichi Kanai	72	73	67	70	282	920,000
Yoshihisa Iwashita	67	70	73	73	283	736,000
Masaru Amano	71	71	71	71	284	672,000
Yasuhiro Funatogawa	68	74	74	69	285	552,000
Hajime Meshiai	69	73	72	71	285	552,000
Koichi Suzuki	71	71	71	72	285	552,000
David Ishii	73	71	71	70	285	552,000
Keiiji Tejima	71	72	74	69	286	421,333
Isao Sugita	69	73	74	70	286	421,333
Tateo Ozaki	65	73	71	77	286	421,333
Hikaru Emoto	74	71	70	72	287	347,428
Hideto Shigenobu	72	71	74	70	287	347,428
Shuichi Sano	72	72	72	71	287	347,428
Ryoichi Takamoto	71	72	73	71	287	347,428
Tohru Nakamura	70	71	74	72	287	347,428

	SCORES				TOTAL	MONEY
Eitaro Deguchi	69	74	76	68	287	347,428
Noboru Sugai	69	72	70	76	287	347,428
Akira Yabe	71	73	69	75	288	304,000
Katsuyoshi Tomori	72	67	76	73	288	304,000
Atsushi Ikehara	72	71	75	70	288	304,000

Maruman Open

Higashi Matsuyama Country Club, Higashi Matsuyama   August 20-23
Par 36-36 — 72; 6,748 yards   purse, ¥60,000,000

	SCORES				TOTAL	MONEY
Masahiro Kuramoto	64	62	67	71	264	¥10,800,000
Masashi Ozaki	70	67	66	65	268	6,000,000
Hajime Meshiai	66	69	67	69	271	4,080,000
Yoshiyuki Isomura	65	73	69	66	273	2,640,000
Naomichi Ozaki	67	66	72	68	273	2,640,000
Tadao Nakamura	67	71	67	69	274	2,040,000
Nobuo Serizawa	69	69	66	70	274	2,040,000
Terry Gale	70	68	69	69	276	1,560,000
David Ishii	68	69	67	72	276	1,560,000
Katsunari Takahashi	70	70	70	66	276	1,560,000
Taisei Inagaki	70	67	70	70	277	1,200,000
Hiroshi Makino	66	73	70	69	278	1,016,000
Takenori Hiraishi	71	66	69	72	278	1,016,000
Seiki Okuda	68	69	71	70	278	1,016,000
Hisao Inoue	74	68	68	69	279	692,571
Joji Furuki	69	69	70	71	279	692,571
Teruo Nakamura	68	67	71	73	279	692,571
Futoshi Irino	68	71	71	69	279	692,571
Chen Tze Ming	69	68	73	69	279	692,571
Katsuyoshi Tomori	73	68	69	69	279	692,571
Shoichi Sato	67	74	70	68	279	692,571
Masaji Kusakabe	70	71	69	70	280	532,000
Isao Isozaki	69	72	71	68	280	532,000
Brian Jones	71	69	71	69	280	532,000
Akio Toyoda	68	68	73	72	281	498,000
Saburo Fujiki	71	71	73	66	281	498,000
Katsuji Hasegawa	72	71	72	67	282	468,000
Hsieh Min Nan	69	74	69	70	282	468,000
Yoshiyuki Omori	73	69	71	69	282	468,000
Hiroshi Ishii	71	71	70	71	283	426,600
Yasuhiro Funatogawa	71	69	73	70	283	426,600
Ikuo Shirahama	68	70	71	74	283	426,600

KBC Augusta

Kyushu Shima Country Club, Shima   August 27-30
Par 36-36 — 72; 7,130 yards   purse, ¥50,000,000

	SCORES				TOTAL	MONEY
Saburo Fujiki	67	69	70	68	274	¥9,000,000
Tateo Ozaki	69	69	67	71	276	5,000,000
Tsuneyuki Nakajima	72	72	70	64	278	2,400,000

	SCORES				TOTAL	MONEY
Toru Nakamura	72	71	72	63	278	2,400,000
Hajime Meshiai	71	67	69	71	278	2,400,000
Yoshimi Niizeki	71	70	69	68	278	2,400,000
Yoshitaka Yamamoto	65	73	72	71	281	1,600,000
Chen Tze Ming	70	71	70	71	282	1,300,000
Koichi Suzuki	67	74	70	71	282	1,300,000
Keiji Tejima	72	67	70	73	282	1,300,000
David Ishii	66	72	72	73	283	920,000
Masahiro Kuramoto	69	67	70	77	283	920,000
Jeff Sluman	71	70	69	73	283	920,000
Nobumitsu Yuhara	70	69	70	75	284	750,000
Isamu Sugita	71	74	68	71	284	750,000
Joji Furuki	72	71	73	69	285	660,000
Seiichi Kanai	72	73	70	71	286	532,000
Katsunari Takahashi	70	72	72	72	286	532,000
Hisao Inoue	68	74	72	72	286	532,000
Ikuo Shirahama	73	73	68	72	286	532,000
Shigeru Uchida	74	70	72	70	286	532,000
Lu Liang Huan	69	73	73	72	287	460,000
Fujio Kobayashi	72	73	75	68	288	440,000
Eitaro Deguchi	72	71	71	75	289	405,000
Isao Isozaki	72	71	72	74	289	405,000
Kinpachi Yoshimura	71	75	69	74	289	405,000
Naomichi Ozaki	67	74	72	76	289	405,000
Kazuo Kanayama	70	73	73	73	289	405,000
Katsuyoshi Tomori	71	72	76	70	289	405,000
Yoshiyuki Isomura	71	76	73	70	290	360,000
Teruo Sugihara	72	73	69	76	290	360,000
Hiroshi Makino	73	74	72	71	290	360,000

Kanto Open

Sobu Country Club, Narita
Par 35-37 — 72; 7,153 yards

September 3-6
purse, ¥30,000,000

(Second round rained out; shortened to 54 holes)

	SCORES			TOTAL	MONEY
Yoshikazu Yokoshima	66	72	72	212	¥4,500,000
Hajime Meshiai	71	72	70	213	1,500,000
Katsuji Hasegawa	74	70	69	213	1,500,000
Nobuo Serizawa	71	70	72	213	1,500,000
Masaji Kusakabe	74	69	71	214	675,000
Yoshinori Mizumaki	73	74	67	214	675,000
Tomohiro Maruyama	70	75	69	214	675,000
Noboru Sugai	70	73	72	215	506,250
Masaru Amano	75	71	69	215	506,250
Tsukasa Watanabe	73	69	73	215	506,250
Hiroshi Makino	73	69	73	215	506,250
Nobumitsu Yuhara	73	72	71	216	393,750
Tsuneyuki Nakajima	75	70	71	216	393,750
Kazushige Kawano	70	73	73	216	393,750
Futoshi Irino	72	71	73	216	393,750
Naomichi Ozaki	73	75	69	217	303,750
Hsieh Min Nan	74	70	73	217	303,750
Seiji Ebihara	74	72	71	217	303,750
Seiichi Kanai	71	73	73	217	303,750

	SCORES			TOTAL	MONEY
Yasuhiro Funatogawa	74	71	72	217	303,750
Koichi Suzuki	73	70	74	217	303,750
Takashi Kubota	71	74	73	218	258,750
Saburo Fujiki	77	71	70	218	258,750
Shuichi Sano	69	77	72	218	258,750
Susumu Murai	74	74	70	218	258,750
Masami Aihara	73	75	71	219	221,250
Akira Yabe	76	70	73	219	221,250
Hiromi Ogino	78	70	71	219	221,250
Taisei Inaba	75	76	68	219	221,250
Hideki Kase	73	73	73	219	221,250
Koichi Hirabayashi	75	73	71	219	221,250

Kansai Open

Asahi Kokusai Tojo Country Club, Tojo
Par 36-36 — 72; 7,198 yards

September 3-6
purse, ¥20,000,000

	SCORES				TOTAL	MONEY
Masanobu Kimura	72	71	74	75	292	¥5,000,000
Toru Nakamura	79	72	72	71	294	2,500,000
Yoshitaka Yamamoto	75	74	75	71	295	1,300,000
Kazuo Yoshikawa	72	74	76	74	296	1,000,000
Toshiaki Nakagawa	76	71	75	74	296	1,000,000
Ichiro Teramoto	71	77	77	73	298	800,000
Kazuo Kanayama	75	75	73	76	299	616,666
Hisao Inoue	76	75	72	76	299	616,666
Tsutomu Irie	75	74	76	74	299	616,666
Tetsuro Nishida	74	75	76	75	300	500,000
Hajime Matsui	76	76	76	73	301	400,000
Yoshinori Ichioka	76	73	74	78	301	400,000
Osamu Watanabe	77	75	78	71	301	400,000
Toshimitsu Kai	79	76	71	76	302	275,000
Yoshiharu Harato	77	75	76	74	302	275,000
Kiyokuni Kimoto	78	77	79	69	303	200,000
Yasuo Sone	75	76	74	78	303	200,000
Tsutomu Horiuchi	76	76	76	76	304	200,000
Kenji Tokuyama	76	76	71	81	304	200,000
Hiromichi Takezaki	78	73	76	77	304	200,000
Yoshio Ichikawa	75	75	80	75	305	160,000
Koji Kobayashi	74	78	71	82	305	160,000
Yoshiyuki Isomura	77	75	75	79	306	160,000
Matsuo Kimura	77	78	73	78	306	160,000
Shozo Miyamoto	78	76	75	77	306	160,000
Keiichi Kobayashi	79	76	76	76	307	130,000
Teruo Sugihara	74	78	79	76	307	130,000
Yoichi Yamamoto	77	77	76	77	307	130,000
Kenji Kataoka	78	74	80	75	307	130,000
Kunihiko Kimoto	74	79	77	77	307	130,000

Chubu Open

Egi Country Club,
Par 36-36 — 72; 7,182 yards

September 3-6
purse, ¥15,000,000

	SCORES				TOTAL	MONEY
Eitaro Deguchi	71	67	66	70	274	¥4,000,000
Masami Ito	70	72	69	70	281	1,350,000
Hiroshi Ishii	69	71	69	72	281	1,350,000
Masahiro Shioda	74	70	70	67	281	1,350,000
Akimitsu Tokita	75	67	69	73	284	600,000
Tadao Nakamura	70	72	69	73	284	600,000
Shigeru Uchida	73	71	72	71	287	326,666
Shunji Kanazawa	70	72	71	74	287	326,666
Yoshihisa Kosaka	67	74	71	75	287	326,666
Tomio Araki	73	68	71	75	287	326,666
Kazutomo Niwa	76	70	70	71	287	326,666
Shoichi Yamamoto	70	74	71	72	287	326,666
Muneyoshi Nakagawa	73	69	72	74	288	180,000
Akio Toyoda	70	74	70	74	288	180,000
Katsuhiko Urata	73	70	72	73	288	180,000
Koichi Inoue	70	71	73	75	289	150,000
Yuzo Noda	72	74	71	72	289	150,000
Hiroaki Uenishi	71	73	73	72	289	150,000
Norihiko Matsumoto	71	72	74	73	290	117,500
Teruo Suzumura	71	71	71	77	290	117,500
Tsuguhiko Bando	72	69	76	73	290	117,500
Seiji Terashima	75	71	72	72	290	117,500

Kyushu Open

Aso Izuka Golf Club,
Par 36-36 — 72; 6,952 yards

September 3-6
purse, ¥15,000,000

	SCORES				TOTAL	MONEY
Katsuyoshi Tomori	70	73	75	70	288	¥4,000,000
Takamasa Sakai	72	75	69	73	289	2,000,000
Reiji Bando	74	69	77	74	294	750,000
Masahiro Nakajima	74	74	71	75	294	750,000
Toshiya Shibutani	74	74	72	75	295	550,000
Keiji Tejima	75	78	75	69	297	425,000
Tatsuya Shiraishi	77	74	71	75	297	425,000
Kinpachi Yoshimura	72	74	78	74	298	325,000
Noboru Shibata	74	74	75	75	298	325,000
Noriichi Kawakami	74	79	72	75	300	193,333
Yurio Akitomi	73	75	76	76	300	193,333
Norio Suzuki	76	70	77	77	300	193,333
Shigemi Nakazono	78	71	74	78	301	145,000
Isamu Sugita	77	78	72	74	301	145,000
Noboru Fujiiki	75	76	74	76	301	145,000
Yoshihiro Hori	78	72	73	78	301	145,000
Kunio Koike	78	75	76	72	301	145,000

Hokkaido Open

Otaru Country Club,
Par 36-36 — 72; 7,106 yards

September 4-6
purse, ¥10,000,000

	SCORES				TOTAL	MONEY
Akihiko Kojima	71	76	72	73	292	¥3,000,000
Namio Takasu	73	74	76	69	292	1,500,000
(Kojima defeated Takasu in playoff.)						
Katsunari Takahashi	78	73	73	76	300	1,000,000
Shoichi Sato	74	76	76	76	302	525,000
Koichi Uehara	74	78	78	72	302	525,000
Mitsuyoshi Goto	75	77	76	75	303	325,000
Satoshi Sudo	74	69	77	83	303	325,000
Yoshiyuki Omori	75	77	75	77	304	210,000
Mamoru Takahashi	76	77	78	73	304	210,000
Yoshiharu Takai	75	78	77	75	305	180,000
Ryoichi Takamoto	73	76	74	83	306	130,000
Susumu Mori	80	78	72	76	306	130,000
Yasuo Kuninaka	76	80	76	76	308	130,000
Masaaki Shiraishi	76	78	81	73	308	130,000
Toshinori Horiki	77	77	75	80	309	115,000
Hiroshi Todate	75	78	76	80	309	115,000
Kesahiko Uchida	82	77	78	75	312	100,000
Toshiaki Nakamura	79	78	80	76	313	100,000
Kanae Nobechi	81	77	80	77	315	100,000
Kenji Takeda	81	78	81	76	316	100,000

Suntory Open

Narashino Country Club, Inzaimachi
Par 36-36 — 72; 7,100 yards

September 10-13
purse, ¥60,000,000

	SCORES				TOTAL	MONEY
Noboru Sugai	67	71	72	68	278	¥10,800,000
Larry Nelson	70	69	71	71	281	5,040,000
Masahiro Kuramoto	67	69	72	73	281	5,040,000
Yoshimi Niizeki	65	71	74	73	283	2,640,000
Terry Gale	69	69	73	72	283	2,640,000
Hiroshi Makino	70	73	70	71	284	1,940,000
David Ishii	71	73	67	73	284	1,940,000
Toshimitsu Kai	70	74	74	66	284	1,940,000
Seiichi Kanai	73	70	71	71	285	1,470,000
Masashi Ozaki	71	71	73	70	285	1,470,000
Hajime Meshiai	67	75	72	72	286	1,152,000
Graham Marsh	75	69	70	72	286	1,152,000
Shigeru Kawamata	72	72	73	70	287	900,000
Kazushige Kawano	72	72	74	69	287	900,000
Yoshikazu Yokoshima	69	74	72	72	287	900,000
Craig Stadler	72	68	77	70	287	900,000
Namio Takasu	70	71	74	73	288	638,400
Haruo Yasuda	68	71	77	72	288	638,400
Chen Tze Ming	70	71	73	74	288	638,400
Satoshi Higashi	69	72	75	72	288	638,400
Isao Isozaki	71	72	72	73	288	638,400
Katsuji Hasegawa	70	72	75	72	289	512,000
Shoichi Sato	69	73	74	73	289	512,000
Katsunari Takahashi	73	73	70	73	289	512,000

	SCORES				TOTAL	MONEY
Tadao Nakamura	72	71	76	70	289	512,000
Toru Nakamura	68	75	75	71	289	512,000
Seiki Okuda	70	71	75	73	289	512,000
Kazuo Yoshikawa	71	70	76	73	290	450,000
Tadami Ueno	72	74	72	72	290	450,000
Brian Jones	73	71	74	72	290	450,000
Hsien Min Nan	70	73	74	73	290	450,000

All Nippon Airways (ANA) Open

Sapporo Golf Club, Uni course, Unicho　　　　　September 17-20
Par 36-36 — 72; 7,031 yards　　　　　　　　purse, ¥50,000,000

	SCORES				TOTAL	MONEY
Isao Aoki	72	70	68	72	282	¥9,000,000
Tsukasa Watanabe	71	68	75	69	283	5,000,000
Masashi Ozaki	70	70	71	74	285	2,900,000
Terry Gale	71	72	73	69	285	2,900,000
Chen Tze Ming	72	70	71	73	286	1,800,000
Hsieh Min Nan	72	71	74	69	286	1,800,000
Chen Tze Chung	75	69	70	72	286	1,800,000
Hideki Kase	69	73	69	76	287	1,300,000
Tadami Ueno	73	70	68	76	287	1,300,000
Brian Jones	74	73	68	72	287	1,300,000
Haruo Yasuda	67	70	75	76	288	960,000
Yoshitaka Yamamoto	73	72	70	73	288	960,000
Kikuo Arai	73	70	75	71	289	810,000
Shoichi Sato	69	71	74	75	289	810,000
Taisei Inagaki	73	68	74	75	290	635,000
David Ishii	70	68	74	78	290	635,000
Namio Takasu	69	72	73	76	290	635,000
Hajime Meshiai	73	72	72	73	290	635,000
Yoshikazu Yokoshima	73	71	75	72	291	500,000
Masanobu Kimura	72	74	72	73	291	500,000
Isamu Sugita	70	72	75	74	291	500,000
Tsutomu Irie	70	71	76	75	292	432,000
Katsuyoshi Tomori	69	74	74	75	292	432,000
Naomichi Ozaki	70	72	71	79	292	432,000
Katsunari Takahashi	70	72	77	73	292	432,000
Katsuji Hasegawa	72	74	71	75	292	432,000
Hideto Shigenobu	72	71	70	80	293	380,000
Yutaka Hagawa	75	71	74	73	293	380,000
Hiroshi Makino	68	77	70	78	293	380,000
Yoshihiko Nakada	71	72	77	73	293	380,000
Masaji Kusakabe	73	74	70	76	293	380,000

Jun Classic

Jun Classic Country Club, Ogawa
Par 36-36 — 72; 7,097 yards

September 24-27
purse, ¥56,000,000

(Second round rained out; shortened to 54 holes)

	SCORES			TOTAL	MONEY
Masashi Ozaki	68	69	67	204	¥7,560,000
Namio Takasu	69	68	72	209	4,200,000
Yoshinori Kaneko	71	71	70	212	2,016,000
Isao Aoki	69	68	75	212	2,016,000
Koichi Suzuki	71	69	72	212	2,016,000
Yoshikazu Yokoshima	70	69	73	212	2,016,000
John Mahaffey	72	71	70	213	1,344,000
Yoshitaka Yamamoto	71	71	72	214	1,092,000
Tsutomu Irie	72	72	70	214	1,092,000
Tadao Nakamura	66	75	73	214	1,092,000
Shuichi Sano	70	74	71	215	772,600
Hiroshi Makino	70	70	75	215	772,600
David Ishii	70	75	70	215	772,600
Hideki Kase	72	73	71	216	537,600
Masahiro Kuramoto	68	75	73	216	537,600
Tateo Ozaki	65	78	73	216	537,600
Brian Jones	71	74	71	216	537,600
Hsieh Min Nan	72	70	74	216	537,600
Shigaru Kawamata	70	76	70	216	537,600
Katsuyoshi Tomori	74	72	71	217	388,080
Chen Tze Chung	71	73	73	217	388,080
Seiichi Kanai	73	73	71	217	388,080
Seiji Ebihara	70	75	72	217	388,080
Chen Tze Ming	68	77	72	217	388,080
Hajime Meshiai	71	70	77	218	336,000
Nobuo Serizawa	74	73	71	218	336,000
Nobumitsu Yuhara	72	76	70	218	336,000
Kikuo Arai	74	74	70	218	336,000
Ichiro Inou	69	74	75	218	336,000
Yurio Akitomi	69	74	76	219	295,000
Hiroshi Ishii	73	71	75	219	295,000
Saburo Fujiki	75	72	72	219	295,000
Hideto Shigenobu	75	72	72	219	295,000
Motomasa Aoki	68	76	75	219	295,000

Tokai Classic

Miyoshi Country Club, Miyoshicho
Par 36-36 — 72; 7,110 yards

October 1-4
purse, ¥60,000,000

	SCORES				TOTAL	MONEY
Tsuneyuki Nakajima	71	72	73	66	282	¥10,800,000
Masashi Ozaki	68	74	67	74	283	6,000,000
Brian Jones	69	74	73	69	285	3,120,000
Teruo Nakamura	75	71	72	67	285	3,120,000
Yoshitaka Yamamoto	68	71	71	75	285	3,120,000
Futoshi Irino	72	68	71	75	286	2,040,000
Graham Marsh	71	72	72	71	286	2,040,000
Namio Takasu	74	73	67	73	287	1,650,000
Naomichi Ozaki	68	70	76	73	287	1,650,000

	SCORES				TOTAL	MONEY
Katsuji Hasegawa	74	71	71	72	288	1,380,000
Isamu Sugita	69	74	75	71	289	1,104,000
Bob Tway	75	74	66	74	289	1,104,000
Katsunari Takahashi	74	68	71	76	289	1,104,000
Toshiki Matsui	74	73	67	76	290	936,000
Hiroshi Makino	70	72	78	71	291	734,400
Corey Pavin	74	75	71	71	291	734,400
Tadami Ueno	72	73	73	73	291	734,400
Tsutomu Irie	72	73	74	72	291	734,400
Teruo Sugihara	70	76	75	70	291	734,400
Lu Liang Huan	73	72	72	75	292	564,000
Seiichi Kanai	73	71	76	72	292	564,000
Yoshimi Niizeki	75	67	78	72	292	564,000
Saburo Fujiki	67	76	74	75	292	564,000
Yoshikazu Yokoshima	71	71	77	74	293	486,000
Chen Tze Ming	71	74	75	73	293	486,000
Noboru Sugai	70	74	76	73	293	486,000
Tsukasa Watanabe	73	72	76	72	293	486,000
Kikuo Arai	73	73	74	73	293	486,000
Tadao Nakamura	72	74	75	72	293	486,000
Joji Furuki	72	71	73	78	294	426,600
Seiji Kusakabe	74	74	75	71	294	426,600
Brett Ogle	76	73	73	72	294	426,600

Japan Open Championship

Arima Royal Golf Club, Kobe
Par 36-36 — 72; 7,034 yards

October 8-11
purse, ¥60,000,000

	SCORES				TOTAL	MONEY
Isao Aoki	70	68	71	70	279	¥10,000,000
Tsuneyuki Nakajima	71	74	68	67	280	5,000,000
Nobuo Serizawa	70	72	69	69	280	5,000,000
Saburo Fujiki	70	68	69	74	281	3,000,000
Naomichi Ozaki	70	70	72	70	282	2,500,000
Tsutomu Irie	73	70	70	71	284	2,200,000
Graham Marsh	65	72	75	73	285	1,900,000
Futoshi Irino	69	73	73	70	285	1,900,000
Hajime Meshiai	68	69	73	76	286	1,600,000
Seiichi Kanai	76	69	71	71	287	1,400,000
David Ishii	71	73	77	66	287	1,400,000
Masanobu Kimura	70	74	72	71	287	1,400,000
Shinsaku Maeda	72	72	71	73	288	1,050,000
Teruo Sugihara	73	71	71	73	288	1,050,000
Hideki Kase	71	71	70	76	288	1,050,000
Ichiro Teramoto	72	71	71	74	288	1,050,000
Taisei Inagaki	75	66	73	75	289	666,000
Toru Nakamura	74	73	70	72	289	666,000
Kazuo Kanayama	76	71	69	73	289	666,000
Haruo Yasuda	71	73	73	72	289	666,000
Tadami Ueno	73	73	72	71	289	666,000
Pete Izumikawa	75	70	74	71	290	522,000
Tadao Nakamura	71	74	73	72	290	522,000
Yoshimi Watanabe	70	75	73	72	290	522,000
Wayne Smith	72	73	71	74	290	522,000
Katsunari Takahashi	70	71	75	74	290	522,000
Tateo Ozaki	70	73	74	75	292	450,000

	SCORES				TOTAL	MONEY
Noboru Sugai	71	74	72	75	292	450,000
Terry Gale	76	69	73	74	292	450,000
Yoshikazu Yokoshima	73	70	78	71	292	450,000
Yoshio Fumiyama	74	73	69	76	292	450,000
Kenji Mori	72	72	73	75	292	450,000
Akihito Yokoyama	74	69	74	75	292	450,000
Brian Jones	72	73	75	73	293	395,000
Isao Isozaki	76	69	73	75	293	395,000
Hiroshi Makino	73	75	73	72	293	395,000
Yoshitaka Yamamoto	73	73	75	72	293	395,000
Teruo Nakamura	76	72	71	75	294	355,000
Tsukasa Watanabe	72	76	75	71	294	355,000
Koichi Suzuki	69	77	76	72	294	355,000
Tomohiro Maruyama	70	75	71	78	294	355,000
Hisashi Terada	71	75	75	74	295	320,000
Seiji Ebihara	74	73	72	76	295	320,000
Ian Stanley	72	73	74	76	295	320,000
Brian Tennyson	76	71	72	77	296	290,000
Hsieh Min Nan	75	73	75	73	296	290,000
Satsuki Takahashi	71	76	74	75	296	290,000
Harumitsu Hamano	74	72	77	74	297	275,000
Masaji Kusakabe	73	73	74	78	298	265,000
Toshimitsu Kai	73	74	73	78	298	265,000
Yoshihisa Iwashita	75	72	74	77	298	265,000

Polaroid Cup Golf Digest

Tomei Country Club, Susono
Par 35-36 — 71; 6,770 yards

October 15-18
purse, ¥60,000,000

	SCORES				TOTAL	MONEY
Ian Baker-Finch	74	67	68	66	275	¥10,800,000
Kazushige Kohno	68	69	73	69	279	6,000,000
Tateo Ozaki	71	70	70	70	281	3,120,000
Masanobu Kimura	74	69	68	70	281	3,120,000
Graham Marsh	70	71	73	67	281	3,120,000
Chen Tze Ming	74	68	72	68	282	2,040,000
Naomichi Ozaki	69	70	73	70	282	2,040,000
Hiroshi Ishii	70	73	72	68	283	1,560,000
Chen Tze Chung	73	71	75	64	283	1,560,000
Taisei Inagaki	77	67	74	65	283	1,560,000
D. A. Weibring	74	75	67	68	284	1,200,000
Yoshimi Nizeki	72	71	72	70	285	904,000
Hajime Meshiai	74	69	72	70	285	904,000
Teruo Sugihara	70	70	75	70	285	904,000
Yoshikazu Yokoshima	74	69	70	72	285	904,000
Saburo Fujiki	72	72	73	68	285	904,000
Hiroshi Makino	75	69	72	69	285	904,000
Katsuji Hasegawa	70	72	75	69	286	632,000
Yutaka Hagawa	70	73	74	69	286	632,000
Masahiro Kuramoto	73	76	71	66	286	632,000
Tadao Nakamura	72	71	74	70	287	552,000
Isao Aoki	74	72	73	68	287	552,000
Kikuo Arai	68	72	75	72	287	552,000
Toshimitsu Kai	73	70	76	69	288	480,000
Masaru Amano	70	73	73	72	288	480,000
Futoshi Irino	74	73	71	70	288	480,000
Toru Nakamura	71	74	72	71	288	480,000

	SCORES				TOTAL	MONEY
Nobuo Serizawa	68	71	73	76	288	480,000
Isamu Sugita	71	69	79	69	288	480,000
Teruo Nakamura	73	72	73	70	288	480,000

Bridgestone

Sodegaura Country Club, Chiba
Par 36-36 — 72; 7,120 yards

October 22-25
purse, ¥80,000,000

	SCORES				TOTAL	MONEY
David Ishii	69	71	72	70	282	¥14,400,000
Hiroshi Makino	67	72	71	72	282	6,720,000
Nobuo Serizawa	69	71	71	71	282	6,720,000
(Ishii won playoff, defeating Makino on first and Serizawa on fourth extra hole.)						
Nick Faldo	71	71	72	69	283	3,306,666
Tsuneyuki Nakajima	73	71	70	69	283	3,306,666
Masashi Ozaki	70	67	70	76	283	3,306,666
Shigeru Kawamata	69	73	68	74	284	2,560,000
Tateo Ozaki	72	71	67	75	285	2,080,000
Katsuji Hasegawa	69	72	75	69	285	2,080,000
Toru Nakamura	69	73	74	69	285	2,080,000
Chen Tze Ming	71	69	72	74	286	1,472,000
Naomichi Ozaki	70	76	71	69	286	1,472,000
Takenori Hiraishi	68	72	71	75	286	1,472,000
Shigeru Kubota	72	74	73	68	287	1,104,000
Haruo Yasuda	74	70	71	72	287	1,104,000
Katsunari Takahashi	69	72	72	74	287	1,104,000
Seiji Ebihara	73	70	73	71	287	1,104,000
Ryoichi Takamoto	72	72	71	73	288	824,000
Yoshitaka Yamamoto	68	71	77	72	288	824,000
Katsuyoshi Tomori	75	68	70	75	288	824,000
Joji Furuki	75	70	72	71	288	824,000
Masahiro Kuramoto	71	71	73	74	289	700,000
Chen Tze Chung	70	67	78	74	289	700,000
Seiichi Kanai	70	71	75	73	289	700,000
Yoshimi Watanabe	73	70	73	73	289	700,000
Kenji Mori	69	71	76	74	290	624,000
Teruo Sugihara	71	70	71	78	290	624,000
Yoshinori Kaneko	72	74	76	68	290	624,000
Yoshio Fumiyama	70	74	74	72	290	624,000
Hsieh Min Nan	70	75	74	71	290	624,000

ABC Cup — U.S. vs Japan

Sports Shinko Country Club, Kawanishi
Par 36-36 — 72; 6,850 yards

October 29-November 1
purse, ¥43,750,000

	SCORES				TOTAL	MONEY
Andy Bean	64	72	68	65	269	¥6,500,000
Masahiro Kuramoto	66	71	64	73	274	3,250,000
Yoshitaka Yamamoto	70	64	74	69	277	1,475,000
Katsunari Takahashi	70	71	70	66	277	1,475,000
Naomichi Ozaki	70	68	73	68	279	950,000
Willie Wood	69	73	70	67	279	950,000

	SCORES				TOTAL	MONEY
Gary Hallberg	65	74	68	72	279	950,000
Hale Irwin	70	69	71	70	280	850,000
Johnny Miller	67	69	74	71	281	725,000
Bill Rogers	66	72	76	67	281	725,000
Nobumitsu Yuhara	67	75	67	72	281	725,000
Chris Perry	66	71	73	71	281	725,000
Toru Nakamura	69	69	73	72	283	575,000
Hajime Meshiai	69	71	70	73	283	575,000
Seiichi Kanai	71	71	71	72	285	500,000
Tateo Ozaki	76	72	71	67	286	425,000
Sam Randolph	72	71	76	67	286	425,000
Bruce Lietzke	75	73	73	70	291	350,000

TEAM RESULTS

Japan 2,227; United States 2,230. Best eight scores counted for each team each day. Each Japanese player received ¥1,600,000, each U.S. player ¥800,000 in team competition.

Kirin Cup World Championship of Golf

Yomiuri Country Club, Tokyo, Japan
Par 36-36 — 72; 7,017 yards

November 5-8
purse, $950,000

THURSDAY

EUROPE defeated UNITED STATES, 7—5.
Payne Stewart (U.S.) defeated Ian Woosnam, 68—71.
Sandy Lyle (Europe) defeated Lanny Wadkins, 68—72.
Bernhard Langer (Europe) and Mark Calcavecchia (U.S.) tied, 67—67.
Jose-Maria Olazabal (Europe) defeated Scott Simpson, 68—69.
Tom Kite (U.S.) defeated Ken Brown, 68—71.
Nick Faldo (Europe) defeated Curtis Strange, 70—73.

AUSTRALIA/NEW ZEALAND tied with JAPAN, 6—6.
Tateo Ozaki (Japan) defeated Ian Baker-Finch, 71—73.
Brian Jones (A/NZ) and Hajime Meshiai (Japan) tied, 68—68.
Peter Senior (A/NZ) defeated Isao Aoki, 70—72.
Masashi Ozaki (Japan) defeated Graham Marsh, 69—74.
Rodger Davis (A/NZ) and Tsuneyuki Nakajima (Japan) tied, 72—72.
Greg Norman (A/NZ) defeated Toru Nakamura, 67—74.

FRIDAY

EUROPE defeated JAPAN, 10—2.
Lyle (Europe) defeated Nakamura, 69—72.
Woosnam (Europe) defeated Meshiai, 68—69.
Faldo (Europe) defeated Tateo Ozaki, 68—71.
Langer (Europe) defeated Nakajima, 68—72.
Masashi Ozaki (Japan) defeated Brown, 65—69.
Olazabal (Europe) defeated Aoki, 68—72.

AUSTRALIA/NEW ZEALAND defeated UNITED STATES, 7—5.
Stewart (U.S.) defeated Jones, 70—72.
Wadkins (U.S.) and Marsh (A/NZ) tied, 73—73.
Davis (A/NZ) defeated Simpson, 70—72.
Norman (A/NZ) defeated Strange, 68—70.
Kite (U.S.) defeated Senior, 69-72.
Baker-Finch (A/NZ) defeated Calcavecchia, 68—73.

SATURDAY

EUROPE defeated AUSTRALIA/NEW ZEALAND, 7—5.
Lyle (Europe) defeated Marsh, 67—71.
Woosnam (Europe) defeated Davis, 67—68.
Brown (Europe) defeated Jones, 70—73.
Baker-Finch (A/NZ) defeated Faldo, 66—69.
Norman (A/NZ) defeated Olazabal, 69—73.
Langer (Europe) and Senior (A/NZ) tied, 70—70.

UNITED STATES defeated JAPAN, 10—2.
Stewart (U.S.) defeated Tateo Ozaki, 65—70.
Calcavecchia (U.S.) defeated Nakamura, 68—70.
Wadkins (U.S.) defeated Meshiai, 72—73.
Simpson (U.S.) defeated Aoki, 70—72.
Nakajima (Japan) defeated Strange, 68—70.
Kite (U.S.) defeated Ozaki, 66—68.

THREE-ROUND RESULTS: Europe 24, United States 20, Australia/New Zealand 18, Japan 10.

SUNDAY

PLAYOFF FOR THIRD-FOURTH PLACE

AUSTRALIA/NEW ZEALAND defeated JAPAN, 9—3.
Marsh (A/NZ) defeated Aoki, 71—72.
Senior (A/NZ) defeated Tateo Ozaki, 74—75.
Davis (A/NZ) and Nakamura (Japan) tied, 69—69.
Jones (A/NZ) defeated Masashi Ozaki, 71—77.
Baker-Finch (A/NZ) defeated Meshiai, 73—75.
Nakajima (Japan) defeated Norman, 67—71.

FINALS

UNITED STATES defeated EUROPE, 10—2.
Stewart (U.S.) defeated Woosnam, 70—72.
Lyle (Europe) defeated Calcavecchia, 70—72.
Wadkins (U.S.) defeated Langer, 70—71.
Simpson (U.S.) defeated Faldo, 68—72.
Strange (U.S.) defeated Brown, 70—71.
Kite (U.S.) defeated Olazabal, 69—71.

PRIZE MONEY: Each U.S. player received $60,000, European $35,000, Austrialian/New Zealander $25,000, Japanese $20,000.

VISA Taiheiyo Club Masters

Taiheiyo Club, Gotemba Course, Gotemba
Par 36-36 — 72; 7,120 yards

November 12-15
purse, ¥90,000,000

	SCORES				TOTAL	MONEY
Graham Marsh	70	69	71	66	276	¥16,200,000
Tom Watson	71	68	68	70	277	9,000,000
Kikuo Arai	69	70	70	69	278	6,120,000
Bernhard Langer	70	69	69	71	279	4,320,000
Craig Stadler	72	65	70	73	280	3,600,000
Ian Baker-Finch	70	71	70	70	281	3,060,000
Koichi Suzuki	71	66	69	75	281	3,060,000
Haruo Yasuda	71	71	71	69	282	2,095,200
Aki Ohmachi	72	70	67	73	282	2,095,200

	SCORES				TOTAL	MONEY
Masahiro Kuramoto	71	72	67	72	282	2,095,200
Seiichi Kanai	69	68	74	71	282	2,095,200
Tadami Ueno	70	69	70	73	282	2,095,200
Tateo Ozaki	75	69	70	69	283	1,296,000
Naomichi Ozaki	70	70	68	75	283	1,296,000
Tsuneyuki Nakajima	72	74	68	69	283	1,296,000
Tom Kite	69	71	70	73	283	1,296,000
Seiji Ebihara	72	73	67	71	283	1,296,000
Hiroshi Makino	71	68	71	74	284	888,000
Futoshi Irino	70	67	72	75	284	888,000
Masashi Ozaki	69	72	73	70	284	888,000
Curtis Strange	73	72	69	70	284	888,000
Chen Tze Chung	72	67	70	75	284	888,000
Yoshiyuki Isomura	71	66	73	74	284	888,000
Hajime Meshiai	69	68	77	71	285	765,000
Motomasa Aoki	72	69	72	72	285	765,000
Toshimitsu Kai	72	65	75	74	286	738,000
Isao Aoki	71	70	76	70	287	693,000
Teruo Sugihara	71	68	74	74	287	693,000
Chen Tze Ming	75	70	71	71	287	693,000
Hiroshi Ishii	67	72	75	73	287	693,000
Shinjiro Tanaka	74	69	74	71	288	623,700
Nobumitsu Yuhara	69	74	75	70	288	623,700
Anthony Gilligan	72	71	75	70	288	623,700
Curt Byrum	71	77	69	71	288	623,700
Nobuo Serizawa	71	70	72	76	289	565,200
J. C. Snead	75	71	74	69	289	565,200
Ove Sellberg	74	73	71	71	289	565,200
Masanobu Kimura	75	70	73	71	289	565,200
Shinsaku Maeda	74	74	72	70	290	514,800
Taisei Inagaki	70	74	75	71	290	514,800
Tsukasa Watanabe	71	70	73	76	290	514,800
Lu Hsi Chuen	75	73	72	72	292	457,200
Katsuji Hasegawa	76	72	71	73	292	457,200
Yoshitaka Yamamoto	75	68	71	78	292	457,200
Yoshihisa Iwashita	70	74	75	73	292	457,200
Tsutomu Irie	72	76	75	69	292	457,200
Yoshimi Niizeki	71	72	74	76	293	401,760
Tatsuya Shiraishi	75	70	74	74	293	401,760
Toru Nakamura	76	70	72	75	293	401,760
Brian Jones	71	76	74	72	293	401,760
Shigeru Kawamata	73	71	74	75	293	401,760

Dunlop Phoenix

Phoenix Country Club, Miyazaki
Par 36-36 — 72; 6,993 yards

November 19-22
purse, ¥140,000,000

	SCORES				TOTAL	MONEY
Craig Stadler	71	65	69	72	277	¥25,200,000
Scott Hoch	71	71	67	69	278	14,000,000
Hajime Meshiai	73	70	68	69	280	7,280,000
Severiano Ballesteros	69	69	72	70	280	7,280,000
Hiroshi Makino	68	67	72	73	280	7,280,000
Masashi Ozaki	68	69	69	75	281	4,305,000
Tsukasa Watanabe	72	71	68	70	281	4,305,000
Yoshikazu Yokoshima	70	69	72	70	281	4,305,000

	SCORES				TOTAL	MONEY
Kazuo Kaneyama	67	72	70	72	281	4,305,000
Larry Nelson	72	71	68	71	282	3,220,000
Chen Tze Chung	74	67	70	72	283	2,478,000
Teruo Nakamura	73	70	69	71	283	2,478,000
Mike Reid	73	71	65	74	283	2,478,000
Naomichi Ozaki	71	71	71	70	283	2,478,000
David Ishii	67	70	72	76	285	1,661,333
Seiichi Kanai	72	68	72	73	285	1,661,333
Terry Gale	70	71	70	74	285	1,661,333
Norio Mikami	75	71	68	71	285	1,661,333
Motomasa Aoki	71	75	68	71	285	1,661,333
Brian Jones	72	72	70	71	285	1,661,333
Keith Clearwater	71	71	69	75	286	1,232,000
Tateo Ozaki	72	72	68	74	286	1,232,000
Tadami Ueno	66	68	72	80	286	1,232,000
Nobuo Serizawa	72	73	71	70	286	1,232,000
Scott Simpson	69	74	74	69	286	1,232,000
Davis Love III	75	72	68	71	286	1,232,000
Masahiro Kuramoto	71	71	75	70	287	1,078,000
Taiichiro Tanaka	69	76	72	70	287	1,078,000
Ikuo Shirahama	68	72	73	74	287	1,078,000
Lu Hsi Chuen	71	70	72	74	287	1,078,000
Graham Marsh	72	71	72	73	288	1,008,000
Isao Aoki	75	73	70	71	289	946,400
Bob Tway	69	74	71	75	289	946,400
Futoshi Irino	74	71	75	69	289	946,400
Chen Tze Ming	76	71	69	73	289	946,400
Tsutomu Horiuchi	75	72	69	74	290	856,800
Tsuneyuki Nakajima	68	73	71	78	290	856,800
Andy Bean	69	77	71	73	290	856,800
Hubert Green	73	71	73	73	290	856,800
Koiichi Uehara	67	69	75	80	291	756,000
Kenny Knox	68	75	71	77	291	756,000
Katsuji Hasegawa	72	72	70	77	291	756,000
Masanobu Kimura	73	75	72	71	291	756,000
Larry Mize	69	73	73	76	291	756,000
Kazushige Kohno	73	74	70	75	292	631,555
Tadao Nakamura	71	71	72	78	292	631,555
Hsieh Min Nan	73	74	71	74	292	631,555
Kikuo Arai	74	74	72	72	292	631,555
Shoiichi Sato	73	75	73	71	292	631,555
Saburo Fujiki	68	74	72	78	292	631,555
Kinpachi Yoshimura	71	73	75	73	292	631,555
Hideto Shigenobu	69	73	75	75	292	631,555
Yoshimi Niizeki	69	74	70	79	292	631,555

Casio World Open

Ibusuki Golf Club, Kaimon
Par 36-36 — 72; 6,985 yards

November 26-29
purse, ¥90,000,000

	SCORES				TOTAL	MONEY
David Ishii	67	69	73	67	276	¥16,200,000
Sam Torrance	67	69	72	70	278	9,000,000
Donnie Hammond	68	71	70	70	279	4,680,000
Masashi Ozaki	68	75	69	67	279	4,680,000
Mashiro Kuramoto	69	71	71	68	279	4,680,000

	SCORES				TOTAL	MONEY
Graham Marsh	68	69	73	70	280	3,240,000
Severiano Ballesteros	71	71	72	67	281	2,745,000
Naomichi Ozaki	70	66	76	69	281	2,745,000
Tadao Nakamura	70	68	73	71	282	2,340,000
Kenny Knox	74	67	69	73	283	1,759,500
Scott Hoch	72	68	71	72	283	1,759,500
Larry Mize	73	69	74	67	283	1,759,500
Nobuo Serizawa	70	72	68	73	283	1,759,500
Keith Clearwater	70	73	67	74	284	1,056,000
Kikuo Arai	73	69	73	69	824	1,056,000
Kinpachi Yoshimura	71	72	71	70	284	1,056,000
Yamamoto Yoshitaka	70	71	70	73	284	1,056,000
Masanobu Kimura	70	70	72	72	284	1,056,000
Chen Tze Chung	73	67	74	70	284	1,056,000
Doug Tewell	72	69	72	71	284	1,056,000
Brian Jones	71	74	67	72	284	1,056,000
Tsukasa Watanabe	69	72	71	72	284	1,056,000
Aki Ohmachi	71	72	69	73	285	765,000
Shinsaku Maeda	72	70	70	73	285	765,000
George Burns	69	70	71	75	285	765,000
Tadami Ueno	70	73	72	70	285	765,000
Hiroshi Ishii	72	71	73	70	286	695,250
Isao Aoki	71	71	71	73	286	695,250
Bob Tway	73	74	72	67	286	695,250
Saburo Fujiki	73	72	72	69	286	695,250
Chen Tze Ming	70	71	72	74	287	623,700
Lu Liang Huan	74	73	73	67	287	623,700
Hideki Kase	76	69	70	72	287	623,700
Haruo Yasuda	74	70	69	74	287	623,700
Yoshikazu Yokoshima	72	69	72	75	288	572,400
Tsutomu Irie	71	72	73	72	288	572,400
Howard Clark	71	72	73	72	288	572,400
Taisei Inagaki	72	70	75	72	289	543,600
Koiichi Uehara	72	72	73	73	290	471,600
Mike Reid	74	73	74	69	290	471,600
Toru Nakamura	78	69	69	74	290	471,600
Koichi Suzuki	73	73	71	73	290	471,600
Hiroshi Makino	73	72	74	71	290	471,600
Hajime Meshiai	74	72	73	71	290	471,600
Hsieh Min Nan	75	71	71	73	290	471,600
Nobumitsu Yuhara	69	76	73	72	290	471,600
Shigeru Noguchi	70	75	71	74	290	471,600
Hidehito Shigenobu	73	72	73	73	291	396,720
Yoshiyuki Isomura	70	74	72	75	291	396,720
Seiji Ebihara	73	71	71	76	291	396,720
Ikuo Shirahama	75	70	74	72	291	396,720
Katsuji Hasegawa	71	72	73	75	291	396,720

Japan Series

Yomiuri Country Club, Osaka   December 3-6
Par 36-37 — 73; 7,078 yards   purse, ¥30,000,000

Yomiuri Country Club, Tokyo
Par 36-36 — 72; 7,017 yards

(First round at Osaka, final round at Tokyo cancelled, snow.)

	SCORES		TOTAL	MONEY
Isao Aoki	67	71	138	¥3,250,000
David Ishii	69	69	138	3,250,000
(Sunday round cancelled, declared co-winners)				
Brian Jones	68	71	139	1,133,333
Masashi Ozaki	68	71	139	1,133,333
Yoshitaka Yamamoto	70	69	139	1,133,333
Hiroshi Makino	72	71	143	750,000
Masanobu Kimura	72	72	144	600,000
Seiichi Kanai	74	70	144	600,000
Tsuneyuki Nakajima	71	74	145	525,000
Masahiro Kuramoto	76	70	146	400,000
Yoshikazu Yokoshima	71	75	146	400,000
Graham Marsh	79	68	147	350,000
Nobuo Serizawa	73	75	148	325,000
Hajime Meshiai	76	73	149	300,000
Naomichi Ozaki	72	78	150	266,666
Chen Tze Ming	74	76	150	266,666
Katsunari Takahashi	71	79	150	266,666

Daikyo Open

Daikyo Country Club, Onna, Okinawa   December 10-13
Par 36-35 — 71; 6,208 yards   purse, ¥70,000,000

	SCORES				TOTAL	MONEY
Isamu Sugita	65	73	70	69	277	¥12,600,000
Seiji Ebihara	67	68	69	73	277	5,880,000
Hiroshi Makino	68	69	70	70	277	5,880,000
(Sugita defeated Ebihara and Makino on second hole of playoff.)						
Kinpachi Yoshimura	70	70	67	71	278	3,080,000
Masanobu Kimura	64	70	73	71	278	3,080,000
Haruo Yasuda	68	70	73	69	280	2,380,000
Tsukasa Watanabe	67	72	71	70	280	2,380,000
Hsieh Min Nan	70	69	72	70	281	1,554,000
Brian Jones	70	66	76	69	281	1,554,000
Yurio Akitomi	69	74	73	65	281	1,554,000
Taijiro Tanaka	65	73	69	74	281	1,554,000
Hajime Meshiai	67	69	74	71	281	1,554,000
David Ishii	66	71	73	71	281	1,554,000
Yoshitaka Yamamoto	64	71	74	73	282	929,600
Tsuneyuki Nakajima	68	69	77	68	282	929,600
Chen Tze Ming	68	68	75	71	282	929,600
Tateo Ozaki	66	70	70	76	282	929,600
Naomichi Ozaki	69	71	67	75	282	929,600
Yoshimi Niizeki	68	68	70	77	283	728,000
Noriichi Kawakami	69	68	73	74	284	658,000
Ryoiichi Tmomitsu	71	71	73	69	284	658,000

	SCORES				TOTAL	MONEY
Nobuo Serizawa	72	71	72	69	284	658,000
Yoshinori Kaneko	70	71	76	67	284	658,000
Ikuo Shirahama	70	72	76	67	285	581,000
Kikuo Arai	71	73	71	70	285	581,000
Shinsaku Maeda	68	72	72	73	285	581,000
Saburo Fujiki	71	73	69	72	285	581,000
Lu Liang Huan	68	73	74	71	286	546,000
Atsushi Ikehara	68	69	73	77	287	532,000
Yoshinori Mizumaki	70	71	72	75	288	504,000
Isao Isozaki	74	70	73	71	288	504,000
Nobumitsu Yuhara	69	72	72	75	288	504,000

LPGA Tour

Mazda Classic

Stonebridge Golf and Country Club, Boca Raton, Florida
Par 36-36 — 72; 6,342 yards

January 29-February 1
purse, $200,000

	SCORES				TOTAL	MONEY
Kathy Postlewait	73	72	72	69	286	$30,000
Betsy King	70	72	71	73	286	18,500
(Postlewait defeated King on first hole of playoff.)						
Lauri Peterson	70	72	75	70	287	10,834
Pat Bradley	72	72	72	71	287	10,833
Rosie Jones	72	68	75	72	287	10,833
Ayako Okamoto	74	70	76	69	289	6,450
Heather Farr	73	68	73	75	289	6,450
Lori Garbacz	72	76	72	70	290	4,700
Sandra Palmer	73	71	75	71	290	4,700
Becky Pearson	68	72	77	73	290	4,700
Jane Crafter	74	73	69	72	291	3,807
JoAnne Carner	74	74	72	72	292	3,407
Chris Johnson	72	71	76	73	292	3,407
Tammie Green	71	76	75	71	293	2,767
Penny Hammel	74	70	77	72	293	2,767
Jane Geddes	72	70	79	72	293	2,767
Amy Alcott	67	74	78	74	293	2,767
Cathy Morse	72	66	77	78	293	2,767
Jody Rosenthal	76	74	75	69	294	2,166
Janet Coles	72	77	72	73	294	2,166
Dawn Coe	73	76	71	74	294	2,165
Nancy Lopez	77	70	73	74	294	2,165
Lauren Howe	75	72	73	74	294	2,165
Juli Inkster	73	72	75	74	294	2,165
Debbie Massey	75	70	77	73	295	1,797
Sherri Turner	70	77	74	74	295	1,797
Cathy Marino	74	72	75	74	295	1,797
Muffin Spencer-Devlin	72	74	75	74	295	1,797
Julie Cole	72	78	75	71	296	1,560
Lisa Young	75	70	80	71	296	1,560
Marci Bozarth	74	71	76	75	296	1,559
Therese Hession	72	73	74	77	296	1,559

Sarasota Classic

Bent Tree Country Club, Sarasota, Florida
Par 36-36 — 72; 6,170 yards

February 5-8
purse, $200,000

	SCORES				TOTAL	MONEY
Nancy Lopez	73	66	68	74	281	$30,000
Anne-Marie Palli	73	70	72	69	284	16,000
Kathy Baker	72	68	72	72	284	16,000
Heather Farr	72	72	71	70	285	9,500
Chris Johnson	67	72	74	72	285	9,500
Jody Rosenthal	73	72	72	70	287	7,000
Mindy Moore	76	70	73	69	288	5,267
Ok-Hee Ku	73	70	73	72	288	5,267
Juli Inkster	75	70	70	73	288	5,266
Shirley Furlong	74	71	71	73	289	3,595
Julie Cole	72	70	74	73	289	3,595
Terry-Jo Myers	74	67	75	73	289	3,594
Hollis Stacy	72	73	70	74	289	3,594
Muffin Spencer-Devlin	71	73	71	74	289	3,594
Laurie Rinker	75	67	76	72	290	2,693
Missie Berteotti	75	70	72	73	290	2,693
Tammie Green	70	72	73	75	290	2,693
Cathy Morse	68	73	71	78	290	2,693
Cindy Rarick	73	72	73	73	291	2,318
Judy Dickinson	71	73	72	75	291	2,318
Penny Pulz	73	71	72	75	291	2,318
Dot Germain	74	74	74	70	292	1,968
Sherri Turner	72	72	76	72	292	1,968
Missie McGeorge	71	73	74	74	292	1,968
Pat Bradley	72	71	73	76	292	1,968
Kathy Postlewait	72	70	71	79	292	1,968
Lauri Peterson	71	73	78	71	293	1,658
Sherri Steinhauer	75	73	73	72	293	1,658
Shelley Hamlin	75	71	73	74	293	1,658
Colleen Walker	75	71	72	75	293	1,658
Jane Geddes	74	66	77	76	293	1,658

Tsumura Hawaiian Ladies Open

Turtle Bay Country Club, Oahu, Hawaii
Par 36-36 — 72; 6,220 yards

February 19-21
purse, $300,000

	SCORES			TOTAL	MONEY
Cindy Rarick	69	71	67	207	$45,000
Jane Geddes	71	68	70	209	27,750
Alice Ritzman	68	71	71	210	20,250
Lauri Peterson	71	72	69	212	14,250
Hollis Stacy	70	71	71	212	14,250
Pat Bradley	71	71	71	213	9,675
Penny Hammel	72	68	73	213	9,675
Muffin Spencer-Devlin	77	70	67	214	6,718
Patty Sheehan	72	73	69	214	6,718
Janet Coles	75	69	70	214	6,718
Martha Nause	72	70	72	214	6,717
Lori Garbacz	74	71	70	215	4,436
Val Skinner	71	73	71	215	4,436
Bie Shyun Huang	73	70	72	215	4,435

	SCORES			TOTAL	MONEY
Mitzi Edge	72	71	72	215	4,435
Tammie Green	72	71	72	215	4,435
Chris Johnson	68	74	73	215	4,435
Dawn Coe	69	71	75	215	4,435
JoAnne Carner	75	73	68	216	3,090
Colleen Walker	71	77	68	216	3,090
Barb Thomas	77	70	69	216	3,090
Juli Inkster	74	72	70	216	3,089
Marci Bozarth	72	72	72	216	3,089
Barb Bunkowsky	71	73	72	216	3,089
Kathy Postlewait	75	68	73	216	3,089
Missie Berteotti	72	71	73	216	3,089
Heather Farr	70	72	74	216	3,089
Ayako Okamoto	72	73	72	217	2,526
Margaret Ward	71	73	73	217	2,526
Bonnie Lauer	76	72	70	218	2,078
Judy Dickinson	76	71	71	218	2,078
Sherri Turner	75	72	71	218	2,078
Deb Richard	75	72	71	218	2,078
Sandra Palmer	73	74	71	218	2,078
Myra Blackwelder	71	76	71	218	2,078
Debbie Massey	75	71	72	218	2,077
Cindy Hill	73	73	72	218	2,077
Amy Alcott	71	71	76	218	2,077

Women's Kemper Open

Princeville Makai Golf Course, Princeville, Kauai, Hawaii
Par 36-36 — 72; 6,172 yards

February 26-March 1
purse, $300,000

	SCORES				TOTAL	MONEY
Jane Geddes	67	70	69	70	276	$45,000
Cathy Gerring	66	68	71	71	276	27,750
(Geddes defeated Gerring on first hole of playoff.)						
Ayako Okamoto	69	70	70	71	280	20,250
Jan Stephenson	72	70	68	74	284	15,750
Nancy Lopez	75	71	71	69	286	11,625
Muffin Spencer-Devlin	71	70	72	73	286	11,625
Dawn Coe	69	74	73	71	287	7,900
Juli Inkster	71	69	74	73	287	7,900
JoAnne Carner	70	71	70	76	287	7,900
Penny Hammel	69	72	72	75	288	6,300
Cindy Figg-Currier	74	71	71	73	289	5,476
Chris Johnson	74	71	69	75	289	5,475
Missie Berteotti	67	76	74	73	290	4,380
Ok-Hee Ku	74	74	68	74	290	4,380
Beverly Klass	71	73	71	75	290	4,380
Patty Sheehan	75	71	68	76	290	4,380
Alice Ritzman	71	70	72	77	290	4,380
Sally Quinlan	71	77	71	72	291	3,525
Beth Daniel	72	70	77	72	291	3,525
Pat Bradley	77	69	71	74	291	3,525
Lynn Adams	71	74	72	74	291	3,525
Mindy Moore	72	76	72	72	292	2,974
Janet Coles	69	77	72	74	292	2,974
Marta Figueras-Dotti	71	71	74	76	292	2,974
Lauri Peterson	71	70	72	79	292	2,973

	SCORES				TOTAL	MONEY
Hollis Stacy	71	75	72	75	293	2,463
Lisa Young	75	72	70	76	293	2,462
Martha Foyer	72	74	71	76	293	2,462
Deb Richard	75	72	68	78	293	2,462
Val Skinner	74	73	68	78	293	2,462
Heather Farr	73	71	71	78	293	2,462
Colleen Walker	69	73	73	78	293	2,462

GNA/Glendale Federal Classic

Oakmont Country Club, Glendale, California
Par 36-36 — 72; 6,256 yards

March 5-8
purse, $250,000

	SCORES				TOTAL	MONEY
Jane Geddes	74	74	71	67	286	$37,500
Robin Walton	72	70	72	72	286	23,125
(Geddes defeated Walton on first hole of playoff.)						
Colleen Walker	72	70	72	74	288	16,875
Chris Johnson	76	68	74	71	289	13,125
Patti Rizzo	74	71	73	72	290	9,688
Betsy King	67	77	73	73	290	9,687
Cathy Gerring	71	78	69	73	291	6,584
Juli Inkster	77	70	71	73	291	6,583
Janet Coles	72	73	73	73	291	6,583
Jerilyn Britz	74	74	70	74	292	5,001
Cindy Rarick	72	72	74	74	292	5,000
Sandra Palmer	75	74	72	72	293	4,376
Sandra Spuzich	76	74	75	69	294	3,751
Pat Bradley	74	74	75	71	294	3,751
Ok-Hee Ku	74	77	71	72	294	3,751
Laurie Rinker	75	74	72	73	294	3,751
Hollis Stacy	77	74	72	72	295	3,064
Jody Rosenthal	78	69	74	74	295	3,064
Kim Shipman	74	74	72	75	295	3,063
Jane Crafter	72	74	71	78	295	3,063
Jan Stephenson	71	77	75	73	296	2,579
Marta Figueras-Dotti	74	73	76	73	296	2,578
Alice Ritzman	69	78	74	75	296	2,578
Vicki Fergon	73	74	73	76	296	2,578
Allison Finney	77	75	72	73	297	2,238
Ayako Okamoto	75	73	74	75	297	2,238
Heather Farr	75	72	72	78	297	2,237
Sally Little	69	76	73	79	297	2,237
Mitzi Edge	78	75	75	70	298	1,875
Denise Strebig	76	75	73	74	298	1,875
Tammie Green	77	73	73	75	298	1,875
Lynn Connelly	72	76	75	75	298	1,875
Kathy Postlewait	76	73	73	76	298	1,875
Mary Murphy	77	72	73	76	298	1,874

Circle K Tucson Open

Randolph North Golf Course, Tucson, Arizona   March 19-22
Par 35-37 — 72; 6,214 yards   purse, $200,000

	SCORES				TOTAL	MONEY
Betsy King	70	71	72	68	281	$30,000
Jan Stephenson	67	70	71	75	283	18,500
Sandra Palmer	70	72	72	70	284	13,500
Sally Quinlan	71	68	72	74	285	10,500
Amy Alcott	70	73	73	70	286	8,500
Val Skinner	73	73	72	69	287	5,700
Hollis Stacy	73	73	70	71	287	5,700
Debbie Massey	73	76	66	72	287	5,700
Lauri Peterson	69	72	73	73	287	5,700
Chris Johnson	71	72	73	72	288	3,834
Kathy Postlewait	71	73	71	73	288	3,833
Shelley Hamlin	70	71	73	74	288	3,833
Ok-Hee Ku	73	75	70	71	289	3,100
Pat Bradley	75	70	73	71	289	3,100
Laurie Rinker	71	74	69	75	289	3,100
Heather Farr	76	73	69	72	290	2,223
Amy Benz	72	74	72	72	290	2,223
Barb Bunkowsky	74	74	69	73	290	2,223
Cathy Marino	73	74	70	73	290	2,223
Missie Berteotti	73	70	74	73	290	2,223
Laura Hurlbut	72	70	75	73	290	2,223
Patty Sheehan	72	71	73	74	290	2,223
Jill Briles	72	69	74	75	290	2,223
Jody Rosenthal	71	74	69	76	290	2,222
Shirley Furlong	71	72	71	76	290	2,222
Sherri Turner	71	70	72	77	290	2,222
Alice Ritzman	73	74	72	72	291	1,730
Denise Strebig	70	73	73	75	291	1,730
Susie Berning	72	77	71	72	292	1,580
Lisa Young	76	71	70	75	292	1,580
Penny Pulz	72	72	72	76	292	1,580

Standard Register Turquoise Classic

Moon Valley Country Club, Phoenix, Arizona   March 26-29
Par 36-37 — 73; 6,391 yards   purse, $300,000

	SCORES				TOTAL	MONEY
Pat Bradley	75	74	67	70	286	$45,000
Chris Johnson	71	78	72	67	288	27,750
Lori Garbacz	76	73	71	70	290	20,250
Penny Hammel	72	74	72	73	291	15,750
Cathy Gerring	74	74	74	70	292	10,700
Juli Inkster	77	71	74	70	292	10,700
Susan Sanders	72	75	73	72	292	10,700
Allison Finney	80	71	70	72	293	7,425
Jody Rosenthal	75	71	74	73	293	7,425
Val Skinner	77	70	72	75	294	6,017
Dawn Coe	72	72	73	77	294	6,017
Sandra Palmer	75	76	72	72	295	4,984
Sally Quinlan	74	71	77	73	295	4,984
Kathy Postlewait	71	75	75	74	295	4,984

	SCORES				TOTAL	MONEY
Missie McGeorge	78	72	74	72	296	4,134
Betsy King	75	76	70	75	296	4,134
Penny Pulz	69	72	75	80	296	4,134
Rosie Jones	74	77	75	71	297	3,284
Deb Richard	70	78	77	72	297	3,284
Martha Nause	75	77	72	73	297	3,284
Nancy Ledbetter	76	74	74	73	297	3,283
Alice Miller	79	72	72	74	297	3,283
Barb Bunkowsky	73	71	78	75	297	3,283
Jane Geddes	72	77	73	75	297	3,283
Cindy Ferro	74	69	77	77	297	3,283
JoAnne Carner	74	75	77	72	298	2,674
Tammie Green	77	73	71	77	298	2,674
Marta Figueras-Dotti	70	76	74	78	298	2,674
Susie Berning	75	75	78	71	299	2,284
Patty Sheehan	74	78	75	72	299	2,284
Colleen Walker	70	80	75	74	299	2,284
Martha Foyer	69	78	76	76	299	2,284
Sally Little	72	75	76	76	299	2,284
Muffin Spencer-Devlin	75	74	73	77	299	2,284

Nabisco Dinah Shore

Mission Hills Country Club, Rancho Mirage, California
Par 36-36 — 72; 6,292 yards

April 2-5
purse, $500,000

	SCORES				TOTAL	MONEY
Betsy King	68	75	72	68	283	$80,000
Patty Sheehan	77	73	68	65	283	42,000
(King defeated Sheehan on second hole of playoff.)						
Pat Bradley	72	74	69	69	284	26,000
Rosie Jones	72	73	72	68	285	19,890
Colleen Walker	72	74	73	68	287	15,871
Ayako Okamoto	71	76	71	69	287	15,870
Chris Johnson	72	79	66	70	287	15,870
Cathy Gerring	72	75	71	70	288	11,850
Jane Geddes	73	77	67	71	288	11,849
Jody Rosenthal	72	72	75	70	289	10,054
Hollis Stacy	73	72	75	71	291	8,475
Jan Stephenson	71	73	73	74	291	8,475
Amy Alcott	68	75	74	74	291	8,475
Debbie Massey	71	79	73	69	292	6,959
Laurie Rinker	72	77	72	71	292	6,959
Val Skinner	69	75	75	73	292	6,959
Jerilyn Britz	75	76	73	69	293	6,002
Juli Inkster	76	72	73	72	293	6,001
Lisa Young	72	76	70	75	293	6,001
Corinne Dibnah	76	78	72	68	294	5,403
Beth Solomon	74	73	74	73	294	5,403
Beth Daniel	80	74	72	69	295	4,763
Becky Pearson	77	74	75	69	295	4,763
Lori Garbacz	75	73	78	69	295	4,762
Donna Caponi	70	75	74	76	295	4,762
Sally Quinlan	74	73	78	71	296	4,302
Marlene Hagge	73	76	74	73	296	4,301
Patti Rizzo	73	80	74	70	297	3,803
Mary Beth Zimmerman	77	74	75	71	297	3,803

	SCORES			TOTAL	MONEY
Dale Eggeling	72	81	72	72	297	3,803
Martha Nause	72	73	77	75	297	3,803
Lauren Howe	73	72	74	78	297	3,802
Amy Benz	71	83	73	71	298	2,879
Laura Baugh	74	79	74	71	298	2,879
Lauri Peterson	76	77	72	73	298	2,879
Janet Coles	79	73	73	73	298	2,879
Myra Blackwelder	75	77	72	74	298	2,879
Bonnie Lauer	76	74	74	74	298	2,879
Marci Bozarth	71	77	76	74	298	2,879
Alice Ritzman	75	76	72	75	298	2,878
Nancy Lopez	71	78	74	75	298	2,878
Laura Davis	66	83	73	76	298	2,878
Shelley Hamlin	79	75	73	72	299	2,123
Kathy Whitworth	75	78	74	72	299	2,122
Lynn Adams	73	74	79	73	299	2,122
Kathy Postlewait	71	75	76	77	299	2,122
Mindy Moore	73	79	75	73	300	1,740
JoAnne Carner	75	78	73	74	300	1,739
Nancy Scranton Brown	71	78	77	74	300	1,739
Jo Ann Washam	74	78	73	75	300	1,739

Kyocera Inamori Classic

Bernardo Heights Country Club, San Diego, California
Par 36-36 — 72; 6,391 yards

April 9-12
purse, $200,000

	SCORES			TOTAL	MONEY
Ayako Okamoto	65	70	69	70	275	$30,000
Betsy King	70	67	71	68	276	18,500
Patty Sheehan	70	68	71	73	282	13,500
Penny Hammel	68	70	72	73	283	10,500
Laurie Rinker	71	71	75	67	284	6,650
Sally Quinlan	72	71	71	70	284	6,650
Amy Alcott	71	67	74	72	284	6,650
Pat Bradley	69	68	71	76	284	6,650
Tammy Fredrickson	67	72	72	74	285	4,450
Dale Eggeling	71	73	66	75	285	4,450
Kim Shipman	72	71	74	69	286	3,538
Jody Rosenthal	75	70	67	74	286	3,537
Kathy Whitworth	67	73	72	74	286	3,537
Colleen Walker	70	71	72	74	287	3,104
JoAnne Carner	71	75	73	69	288	2,624
Janet Coles	69	76	72	71	288	2,624
Jan Stephenson	72	70	73	73	288	2,624
Denise Strebig	69	73	72	74	288	2,624
Janet Anderson	69	72	72	75	288	2,624
Val Skinner	73	70	70	76	289	2,254
Rosie Jones	71	71	71	76	289	2,254
Marci Bozarth	74	74	73	69	290	1,799
Sherri Turner	71	76	74	69	290	1,799
Mary Murphy	75	72	71	72	290	1,798
Kathy Baker	73	73	72	72	290	1,798
Dawn Coe	71	71	76	72	290	1,798
Sally Little	72	76	69	73	290	1,798
Kathryn Young	70	72	75	73	290	1,798
Elaine Crosby	73	73	69	75	290	1,798

	SCORES				TOTAL	MONEY
Missie McGeorge	68	74	73	75	290	1,798
Allison Finney	73	70	71	76	290	1,798

Santa Barbara Open

Santa Barbara, California

April 17-19
purse, $300,000

Sandpiper Golf Course
Par 36-36 — 72; 6,311 yards

La Purisima Golf Course
Par 36-36 — 72; 6,250 yards

	SCORES			TOTAL	MONEY
Jan Stephenson	74	68	73	215	$45,000
Jane Geddes	69	79	68	216	24,000
Ayako Okamoto	72	69	75	216	24,000
Shelley Hamlin	73	74	70	217	13,000
Laura Hurlbut	72	75	70	217	13,000
Beth Daniel	73	70	74	217	13,000
Allison Finney	75	75	68	218	7,900
Juli Inkster	75	73	70	218	7,900
Val Skinner	72	71	75	218	7,900
Ok-Hee Ku	76	72	71	219	5,371
Marci Bozarth	72	75	72	219	5,370
Amy Benz	72	74	73	219	5,370
Amy Alcott	73	70	76	219	5,370
Alice Ritzman	73	69	77	219	5,370
Marta Figueras-Dotti	71	79	70	220	3,930
Jody Rosenthal	75	73	72	220	3,930
LeAnn Cassaday	76	71	73	220	3,930
Kathy Postlewait	73	72	75	220	3,930
Beverly Klass	73	71	76	220	3,930
Dale Eggeling	68	80	73	221	3,229
Sandra Palmer	76	71	74	221	3,229
Shirley Furlong	73	74	74	221	3,229
Donna Caponi	76	69	76	221	3,228
Gail Lee Hirata	72	79	71	222	2,775
Lauren Howe	77	73	72	222	2,775
Cindy Rarick	71	79	72	222	2,775
Sherri Turner	70	79	73	222	2,775
Sally Little	80	71	72	223	2,415
Missie McGeorge	66	85	72	223	2,415
Cathy Morse	75	73	75	223	2,415
Patty Sheehan	73	69	81	223	2,415

S&H Classic

Pasadena Yacht & Country Club, St. Petersburg, Florida
Par 36-36 — 72; 6,013 yards

April 30-May 3
purse, $225,000

	SCORES				TOTAL	MONEY
Cindy Hill	70	66	69	66	271	$33,750
Jane Crafter	70	74	66	64	274	20,812
Kathy Postlewait	67	71	68	69	275	15,187

	SCORES				TOTAL	MONEY
Lori Garbacz	68	69	71	68	276	11,812
Rosie Jones	71	72	69	65	277	7,043
Penny Hammel	71	70	67	69	277	7,042
Cathy Morse	71	68	69	69	277	7,042
Donna Cusano-Wilkins	68	68	70	71	277	7,042
M. J. Smith	67	69	70	71	277	7,042
Chris Johnson	68	69	71	70	278	4,725
Betsy King	68	75	69	67	279	3,740
Karin Mundinger	71	70	71	67	279	3,739
Mitzi Edge	72	68	72	67	279	3,739
Amy Benz	71	71	69	68	279	3,739
Mindy Moore	68	73	68	70	279	3,739
Pam Allen	67	71	75	67	280	2,873
Jerilyn Britz	72	70	69	69	280	2,873
Elaine Crosby	72	70	69	69	280	2,872
Myra Blackwelder	69	66	71	74	280	2,872
Missie Berteotti	76	66	71	68	281	2,591
Beth Solomon	72	73	70	67	282	2,283
Sally Little	69	73	73	67	282	2,283
Therese Hession	72	71	68	71	282	2,283
Joan Joyce	72	71	68	71	282	2,283
Barb Mucha	71	69	70	72	282	2,283
Kathy Ahern	72	73	70	68	283	1,851
Beverly Klass	67	74	74	68	283	1,851
Pat Bradley	71	73	70	69	283	1,850
Jill Briles	68	73	73	69	283	1,850
Barbara Pendergast	73	70	70	70	283	1,850
Allison Finney	70	70	71	72	283	1,850
Denise Strebig	70	69	71	73	283	1,850

United Virginia Bank Classic

Portsmouth Sleepy Hole Golf Course, Suffolk, Virginia
Par 36-36 — 72; 6,151 yards

May 8-10
purse, $250,000

	SCORES			TOTAL	MONEY
Jody Rosenthal	71	72	66	209	$37,500
Cindy Hill	65	72	73	210	23,125
Sherri Turner	71	67	73	211	15,000
Nancy Lopez	70	68	73	211	15,000
Juli Inkster	73	71	68	212	10,625
Lisa Young	71	75	67	213	7,125
Chris Johnson	73	69	71	213	7,125
Tammie Green	72	70	71	213	7,125
Barb Bunkowsky	74	66	73	213	7,125
Penny Pulz	76	70	68	214	4,793
Betsy King	73	73	68	214	4,792
Sally Quinlan	72	69	73	214	4,792
Marta Figueras-Dotti	77	68	70	215	3,564
Vicki Fergon	75	70	70	215	3,564
Karin Mundinger	74	69	72	215	3,564
Beth Daniel	72	71	72	215	3,563
Amy Benz	72	69	74	215	3,563
Colleen Walker	72	67	76	215	3,563
Jane Geddes	76	72	68	216	2,876
Jackie Bertsch	76	71	69	216	2,876
Kelly Leadbetter	71	72	73	216	2,876

	SCORES			TOTAL	MONEY
Pat Bradley	75	72	70	217	2,521
Patti Rizzo	70	75	72	217	2,521
Bonnie Lauer	73	71	73	217	2,520
Missie McGeorge	75	72	71	218	2,200
LeAnn Cassaday	73	74	71	218	2,200
Missie Berteotti	73	72	73	218	2,200
Allison Finney	74	69	75	218	2,200
M. J. Smith	73	68	77	218	2,200
Amy Read	75	74	70	219	1,777
Beth Solomon	74	74	71	219	1,777
Anne-Marie Palli	76	71	72	219	1,777
Nancy Scranton Brown	74	73	72	219	1,777
Penny Hammel	73	74	72	219	1,776
Hollis Stacy	71	75	73	219	1,776
Lori Garbacz	76	68	75	219	1,776

Chrysler-Plymouth Classic

Navesink Country Club, Middletown, New Jersey May 15-17
Par 36-36 — 72; 6,358 yards purse, $225,000

	SCORES			TOTAL	MONEY
Ayako Okamoto	70	74	71	215	$33,750
Jane Geddes	75	71	71	217	18,000
Colleen Walker	72	70	75	217	17,999
Tammie Green	71	73	74	218	11,812
Mary Beth Zimmerman	75	72	72	219	7,481
Ok-Hee Ku	74	72	73	219	7,481
Sherri Turner	71	75	73	219	7,481
Betsy Barrett	72	73	74	219	7,481
Barb Bunkowsky	74	72	74	220	4,763
Sally Quinlan	75	71	74	220	4,763
Margaret Ward	72	72	76	220	4,762
Amy Alcott	77	74	70	221	3,312
Donna Caponi	77	74	70	221	3,312
Julie Cole	74	75	72	221	3,311
Juli Inkster	74	75	72	221	3,311
Jody Rosenthal	74	75	72	221	3,311
Cindy Figg-Currier	74	74	73	221	3,311
Sandra Palmer	75	73	73	221	3,311
Denise Strebig	75	77	70	222	2,226
Nancy Lopez	78	73	71	222	2,226
Elaine Crosby	76	74	72	222	2,225
Bonnie Lauer	72	78	72	222	2,225
Pam Allen	75	74	73	222	2,225
Shelley Hamlin	75	74	73	222	2,225
Cathy Morse	74	73	75	222	2,225
Alice Ritzman	74	73	75	222	2,225
Lisa Young	72	75	75	222	2,225
Robin Walton	75	71	76	222	2,225
Sally Little	72	72	78	222	2,225
Susan Tonkin	75	75	73	223	1,745
Debbie Massey	71	75	77	223	1,744

Mazda LPGA Championship

Jack Nicklaus Sports Center, Kings Island, Ohio
Par 36-36 — 72; 6,202 yards

May 21-24
purse, $350,000

	SCORES				TOTAL	MONEY
Jane Geddes	72	68	68	67	275	$52,500
Betsy King	72	68	69	67	276	32,375
Rosie Jones	70	68	72	68	278	18,959
Ayako Okamoto	69	69	70	70	278	18,958
Laurie Rinker	69	67	71	71	278	18,958
Cathy Morse	70	69	67	73	279	12,250
Muffin Spencer-Devlin	70	72	71	67	280	9,713
Patty Sheehan	68	70	74	68	280	9,712
Juli Inkster	72	71	72	66	281	6,845
Amy Alcott	73	70	69	69	281	6,844
Jody Rosenthal	72	68	72	69	281	6,844
Kathy Postlewait	72	69	70	70	281	6,844
Lori Garbacz	72	66	70	73	281	6,844
Cindy Rarick	70	70	71	72	283	5,282
Hollis Stacy	71	69	70	73	283	5,282
Chris Johnson	72	72	72	68	284	4,495
Patti Rizzo	66	72	78	68	284	4,495
Sally Quinlan	72	73	70	69	284	4,494
Deb Richard	68	69	72	75	284	4,494
Penny Hammel	71	71	72	71	285	4,057
Pat Bradley	74	71	73	68	286	3,795
Missie Berteotti	71	72	73	70	286	3,794
Deedee Roberts	69	73	75	70	287	3,433
Sally Little	71	68	75	73	287	3,433
Missie McGeorge	70	72	71	74	287	3,432
Marci Bozarth	68	77	71	72	288	3,165
Shirley Furlong	73	72	71	72	288	3,164
Donna White	76	69	75	69	289	2,616
Val Skinner	71	72	76	70	289	2,616
Sherri Turner	71	71	76	71	289	2,616
Ok-Hee Ku	74	71	71	73	289	2,616
JoAnne Carner	70	74	71	74	289	2,616
Nancy Lopez	73	71	71	74	289	2,616
Dale Eggeling	72	69	74	74	289	2,616
Jane Crafter	67	72	74	76	289	2,616
Cathy Gerring	70	69	74	76	289	2,616
Dawn Coe	72	72	76	70	290	2,036
Cindy Hill	74	71	74	71	290	2,036
Lynn Adams	71	73	72	74	290	2,035
Cindy Figg-Currier	73	71	69	77	290	2,035
Donna Caponi	70	75	74	72	291	1,677
Debbie Massey	75	69	74	73	291	1,677
Tammie Green	74	70	73	74	291	1,677
Beth Solomon	74	70	73	74	291	1,677
Bonnie Lauer	74	69	74	74	291	1,677
Amy Benz	74	71	74	73	292	1,362
Cathy Johnston	73	70	74	75	292	1,362
Kelly Leadbetter	72	73	71	76	292	1,362
Judy Dickinson	73	72	70	77	292	1,362
Kim Bauer	75	70	75	73	293	1,002
Julie Cole	73	72	74	74	293	1,002
Kathryn Young	70	74	75	74	293	1,002
Kathy Baker	73	72	73	75	293	1,002
Martha Foyer	74	70	74	75	293	1,002

	SCORES				TOTAL	MONEY
Jerilyn Britz	71	71	76	75	293	1,002
Beverly Klass	71	71	76	75	293	1,002
Sherri Steinhauer	72	73	70	78	293	1,002

Corning Classic

Corning Country Club, Corning, New York
Par 36-36 — 72; 6,062 yards

May 28-31
purse, $275,000

	SCORES				TOTAL	MONEY
Cindy Rarick	70	69	69	67	275	$41,250
Patty Sheehan	71	69	67	69	276	19,479
Betsy King	75	66	65	70	276	19,479
Jane Geddes	69	68	68	71	276	19,478
Pat Bradley	67	68	73	69	277	9,808
Kathryn Young	65	70	69	73	277	9,808
Dawn Coe	68	68	67	74	277	9,808
JoAnne Carner	68	70	72	68	278	6,160
Rosie Jones	73	64	69	72	278	6,160
Robin Walton	68	68	70	72	278	6,159
Laurie Rinker	70	67	68	73	278	6,159
Missie McGeorge	70	70	71	69	280	4,701
Kris Monaghan	70	69	71	70	280	4,700
Colleen Walker	71	68	70	74	283	4,288
Elaine Crosby	71	75	73	65	284	3,629
Kathy Baker	73	70	72	69	284	3,628
Sherri Turner	70	68	77	69	284	3,628
Betsy Barrett	70	71	73	70	284	3,628
Susan Tonkin	74	70	68	72	284	3,628
Jane Crafter	72	75	72	66	285	3,051
Julie Cole	74	68	74	69	285	3,050
Cathy Morse	73	69	72	71	285	3,050
Margaret Ward	73	69	72	72	286	2,613
Patti Rizzo	73	71	69	73	286	2,613
Cindy Hill	71	73	69	73	286	2,612
Kathy Postlewait	70	73	70	73	286	2,612
Joan Delk	69	69	72	76	286	2,612
Lisa Young	70	73	77	67	287	2,127
Beth Daniel	72	70	76	69	287	2,127
Ok-Hee Ku	74	68	75	70	287	2,127
Alice Miller	71	75	69	72	287	2,126
Susan Sanders	71	76	66	74	287	2,126
Jerilyn Britz	68	73	72	74	287	2,126
M. J. Smith	71	70	71	75	287	2,126

McDonald's Championship

Du Pont Country Club, Wilmington, Delaware
Par 35-36 — 71; 6,366 yards

June 4-7
purse, $500,000

	SCORES				TOTAL	MONEY
Betsy King	72	68	71	67	278	$75,000
Ayako Okamoto	70	73	65	72	280	46,250
Allison Finney	70	72	72	67	281	30,000

	SCORES				TOTAL	MONEY
Lisa Young	71	73	69	68	281	30,000
Val Skinner	75	70	67	70	282	19,375
Cathy Morse	66	70	72	74	282	19,375
Cindy Hill	71	72	72	68	283	13,875
Sherri Turner	67	71	72	73	283	13,875
Patty Sheehan	68	76	71	69	284	10,126
Juli Inkster	70	71	72	71	284	10,125
Patti Rizzo	68	73	71	72	284	10,125
Lauri Peterson	68	72	71	73	284	10,125
Cindy Rarick	69	73	71	72	285	7,750
Sherri Steinhauer	68	69	76	72	285	7,750
Shirley Furlong	73	67	72	73	285	7,750
Amy Alcott	68	71	72	75	286	6,750
Kathy Postlewait	70	74	73	70	287	5,875
Amy Benz	71	73	72	71	287	5,875
Jane Geddes	72	73	71	71	287	5,875
Cathy Gerring	73	74	69	71	287	5,875
Beverly Klass	71	74	70	72	287	5,875
Barbra Mizrahie	69	71	73	74	287	5,875
Colleen Walker	74	70	76	68	288	4,479
Mitzi Edge	73	69	76	70	288	4,478
Marta Figueras-Dotti	73	71	73	71	288	4,478
Mary Beth Zimmerman	72	73	72	71	288	4,478
Connie Chillemi	74	69	73	72	288	4,478
Chris Johnson	73	72	70	73	288	4,478
Rosie Jones	71	70	73	74	288	4,478
Penny Pulz	70	72	72	74	288	4,478

Mayflower Classic

Country Club of Indianapolis, Indianapolis, Indiana
Par 36-36 — 72; 6,156 yards

June 11-14
purse, $350,000

	SCORES				TOTAL	MONEY
Colleen Walker	67	70	72	69	278	$52,500
Sally Quinlan	72	68	71	68	279	22,313
Bonnie Lauer	73	69	67	70	279	22,313
Patty Sheehan	72	68	69	70	279	22,312
Patti Rizzo	69	68	70	72	279	22,312
Muffin Spencer-Devlin	71	68	72	69	280	12,250
Cathy Marino	73	70	70	68	281	9,713
Juli Inkster	73	69	68	71	281	9,712
Ayako Okamoto	73	73	70	66	282	7,088
Marta Figueras-Dotti	69	70	76	67	282	7,088
Deedee Roberts	72	69	71	70	282	7,088
Deb Richard	66	72	72	72	282	7,088
Shirley Furlong	74	72	69	68	283	4,989
Kim Bauer	69	73	73	68	283	4,989
Donna Caponi	71	71	71	70	283	4,989
Jane Geddes	71	70	71	71	283	4,988
Kathy Postlewait	73	69	69	72	283	4,988
Betsy King	69	73	66	75	283	4,988
Rosie Jones	69	73	72	70	284	3,854
Nancy Ledbetter	71	72	70	71	284	3,854
Tammie Green	73	67	73	71	284	3,854
Amy Alcott	72	70	70	72	284	3,854
Debbie Massey	74	66	70	74	284	3,854

	SCORES				TOTAL	MONEY
Missie Berteotti	72	73	69	71	285	3,238
M. J. Smith	71	71	72	71	285	3,238
Lisa Young	68	72	74	71	285	3,237
Shelley Hamlin	70	69	73	73	285	3,237
Hollis Stacy	73	71	72	70	286	2,722
Cindy Rarick	69	73	74	70	286	2,721
Kathryn Young	70	77	68	71	286	2,721
Robin Walton	72	72	71	71	286	2,721
Denise Strebig	73	70	71	72	286	2,721
Marlene Floyd	69	73	70	74	286	2,721

Lady Keystone Open

Hershey Country Club, Hershey, Pennsylvania

Par 36-36 — 72; 6,348 yards

June 19-21

purse, $300,000

	SCORES			TOTAL	MONEY
Ayako Okamoto	70	74	64	208	$45,000
Laurie Rinker	71	71	67	209	27,750
Martha Nause	71	68	71	210	20,250
Cindy Hill	72	68	71	211	13,000
Cathy Gerring	69	70	72	211	13,000
Ok-Hee Ku	67	69	75	211	13,000
Val Skinner	72	73	67	212	8,850
Tammie Green	72	70	71	213	7,050
Shirley Furlong	71	70	72	213	7,050
Margaret Ward	72	67	74	213	7,050
Nancy Lopez	74	73	67	214	5,316
Rosie Jones	71	75	68	214	5,316
Muffin Spencer-Devlin	69	75	70	214	5,316
Jill Briles	73	70	72	215	4,066
Cathy Morse	70	73	72	215	4,066
Judy Sams	69	74	72	215	4,066
Sally Little	68	74	73	215	4,066
Cindy Rarick	71	71	73	215	4,066
Missie McGeorge	70	71	74	215	4,066
Anne-Marie Palli	76	70	70	216	3,070
Kris Monaghan	70	75	71	216	3,070
Lenore Muraoka	69	75	72	216	3,070
Colleen Walker	74	70	72	216	3,069
Kim Bauer	74	69	73	216	3,069
Lisa Young	74	69	73	216	3,069
Caroline Gowan	73	69	74	216	3,069
Amy Alcott	77	70	70	217	2,273
Barb Bunkowsky	77	70	70	217	2,273
Dot Germain	75	72	70	217	2,273
Kathy Postlewait	75	72	70	217	2,273
Allison Finney	74	72	71	217	2,273
Juli Inkster	75	71	71	217	2,272
Donna Caponi	71	74	72	217	2,272
Jane Crafter	74	70	73	217	2,272
Marlene Floyd	72	71	74	217	2,272
Marta Figueras-Dotti	69	71	77	217	2,272

Rochester International

Locust Hill Country Club, Pittsford, New York
Par 35-37 — 72; 6,162 yards

June 25-28
purse, $300,000

	SCORES				TOTAL	MONEY
Deb Richard	66	69	73	72	280	$45,000
Amy Alcott	71	71	71	69	282	19,125
Shirley Furlong	73	69	69	71	282	19,125
Laurie Rinker	71	71	68	72	282	19,125
Lori Garbacz	71	67	71	73	282	19,125
Sherri Turner	72	71	71	70	284	10,500
Deedee Roberts	73	71	70	71	285	7,500
Nancy Lopez	72	71	70	72	825	7,500
Marci Bozarth	68	71	73	73	285	7,500
Patty Sheehan	72	69	69	75	285	7,500
Becky Pearson	72	77	68	69	286	5,476
Kathy Postlewait	71	71	71	73	286	5,475
Ok-Hee Ku	70	71	75	71	287	4,800
Marta Figueras-Dotti	72	74	69	72	287	4,800
Kim Williams	75	75	69	69	288	3,930
Cindy Rarick	75	69	74	70	288	3,930
Cathy Morse	70	72	72	74	288	3,930
Susan Tonkin	71	71	69	77	288	3,930
Sally Little	69	72	70	77	288	3,930
Jane Crafter	72	73	72	72	289	3,375
Donna Cusano-Wilkins	68	75	73	73	289	3,375
Betsy Barrett	75	72	72	71	290	2,925
Margaret Ward	73	72	74	71	290	2,925
Penny Hammel	71	74	73	72	290	2,925
Sherrin Smyers	72	72	70	76	290	2,925
Muffin Spencer-Devlin	69	72	73	76	290	2,925
Nancy Ledbetter	67	76	75	73	291	2,595
Judy Dickinson	70	73	72	76	291	2,595
Amy Read	70	74	77	71	292	2,250
Martha Foyer	73	74	72	73	292	2,250
Joan Delk	76	73	69	74	292	2,250
Lisa Young	73	72	72	75	292	2,250
Val Skinner	72	73	72	75	292	2,250
Nancy Scranton Brown	71	74	72	75	292	2,250

Jamie Farr Toledo Classic

Glengarry County Club, Toledo, Ohio
Par 36-36 — 72; 6,221 yards

July 2-5
purse, $225,000

	SCORES				TOTAL	MONEY
Jane Geddes	71	73	69	67	280	$33,750
Jill Briles	73	70	69	70	282	18,000
Nancy Taylor	68	69	73	72	282	17,999
Laurie Rinker	70	71	72	70	283	10,687
Julie Cole	70	74	68	71	283	10,687
Marci Bozarth	72	72	71	69	284	7,875
Ok-Hee Ku	73	71	71	70	285	6,244
Sherri Turner	70	69	73	73	285	6,243
Tammie Green	70	72	77	67	286	4,768
Heather Drew	71	73	72	70	286	4,768
Cindy Hill	69	71	72	74	286	4,768

	SCORES				TOTAL	MONEY
Kathy Postlewait	71	70	73	73	287	3,842
Nancy Scranton Brown	75	70	68	74	287	3,841
Dale Eggeling	71	76	70	71	288	3,195
Shelley Hamlin	73	73	70	72	288	3,195
Becky Pearson	72	73	71	72	288	3,195
Sandra Palmer	71	71	72	74	288	3,194
Cathy Gerring	70	75	75	69	289	2,772
Jan Stephenson	71	73	72	73	289	2,772
Debbie Hall	73	74	70	73	290	2,547
Jerilyn Britz	70	72	75	73	290	2,547
Patty Jordan	74	76	72	69	291	2,104
Mary Beth Zimmerman	73	74	73	71	291	2,104
Robin Walton	75	71	73	72	291	2,104
Lauri Peterson	72	71	75	73	291	2,104
Sarah LeVeque	70	73	75	73	291	2,104
Colleen Walker	72	74	71	74	291	2,104
Cathy Marino	72	74	69	76	291	2,104
Leslie Pearson	72	72	71	76	291	2,104
Cathy Johnston	72	74	74	72	292	1,730
Alice Ritzman	72	73	75	72	292	1,729
LeAnn Cassaday	73	73	71	75	292	1,729

du Maurier Classic

Islesmere Golf Club, Laval, Quebec, Canada
Par 36-36 — 72; 6,371 yards

July 9-12
purse, $400,000

	SCORES				TOTAL	MONEY
Jody Rosenthal	68	70	68	66	272	$60,000
Ayako Okamoto	65	69	66	74	274	37,000
Rosie Jones	71	67	69	69	276	27,000
Barb Bunkowsky	70	72	66	70	278	19,000
Shirley Furlong	66	72	70	70	278	19,000
Kathy Postlewait	69	68	72	70	279	14,000
Betsy King	74	71	67	68	280	11,800
Jane Geddes	71	70	71	70	282	9,400
Dot Germain	70	68	72	72	282	9,400
Penny Hammel	68	70	72	72	282	9,400
Bonnie Lauer	72	72	71	69	284	7,074
Kristi Albers	70	70	72	72	284	7,074
Robin Walton	71	73	64	76	284	7,073
Missie McGeorge	67	78	72	68	285	6,007
Amy Alcott	71	69	73	72	285	6,007
Mindy Moore	73	74	71	68	286	5,207
Colleen Walker	70	74	69	73	286	5,207
Elaine Crosby	73	67	73	73	286	5,207
Alice Ritzman	73	72	73	69	287	4,507
Cathy Gerring	76	66	74	71	287	4,507
Nancy Taylor	71	75	69	72	287	4,507
Betsy Barrett	71	72	70	74	287	4,507
Marci Bozarth	75	70	70	73	288	3,957
Lynn Adams	68	72	74	74	288	3,957
Marta Figueras-Dotti	74	72	74	69	289	3,467
Terry-Jo Myers	72	73	74	70	289	3,467
Sally Little	72	70	75	72	289	3,467
Pat Bradley	69	73	75	72	289	3,467
Marlene Floyd	71	73	71	74	289	3,467

	SCORES				TOTAL	MONEY
Jill Briles	68	68	75	78	289	3,467
Hollis Stacy	72	75	74	69	290	2,697
Ok-Hee Ku	70	76	72	72	290	2,697
Martha Foyer	70	74	74	72	290	2,697
Janet Coles	75	71	71	73	290	2,697
Becky Pearson	73	73	70	74	290	2,697
Kathy Whitworth	73	72	71	74	290	2,697
Sherri Steinhauer	72	71	72	75	290	2,696
Janice Gibson	69	71	73	77	290	2,696
Sandra Palmer	72	73	74	72	291	1,893
Donna White	73	70	75	73	291	1,893
Shelley Hamlin	70	73	75	73	291	1,893
Sally Quinlan	74	73	70	74	291	1,893
Juli Inkster	72	73	70	76	291	1,893
Mary Beth Zimmerman	71	69	75	76	291	1,893
Kathy Baker	69	71	75	76	291	1,892
M. J. Smith	70	71	71	79	291	1,892
Connie Chillemi	73	71	67	80	291	1,892
Amy Benz	73	74	74	71	292	1,338
Sandra Spuzich	75	72	73	72	292	1,338
Cathy Morse	74	72	74	72	292	1,338
Donna Caponi	72	73	72	75	292	1,338
LeAnn Cassaday	71	70	75	76	292	1,338

Boston Five Classic

Sheraton Tara Hotel at Ferncroft Village, Danvers, Massachusetts July 16-19
Par 35-37 — 72; 6,008 yards purse, $300,000

	SCORES				TOTAL	MONEY
Jane Geddes	73	70	67	67	277	$45,000
Donna White	68	73	69	68	278	24,000
Jody Rosenthal	69	66	73	70	278	24,000
Rosie Jones	71	69	72	67	279	14,250
Betsy King	71	66	75	67	279	14,250
Patty Sheehan	69	72	69	70	280	10,500
Becky Pearson	69	68	70	74	281	8,850
Hollis Stacy	70	68	72	72	282	7,800
Deedee Roberts	70	72	71	70	283	6,675
Jan Stephenson	68	71	73	71	283	6,675
Colleen Walker	72	72	70	70	284	5,496
Sally Quinlan	67	70	75	72	284	5,496
Sherri Steinhauer	72	72	71	71	286	4,671
Donna Caponi	73	68	73	72	286	4,671
Dot Germain	71	70	71	74	286	4,671
Kathryn Young	73	72	73	69	287	3,846
Dale Eggeling	72	71	75	69	287	3,846
Marta Figueras-Dotti	72	70	73	72	287	3,846
Cathy Marino	67	74	72	74	287	3,846
Denise Strebig	75	72	73	68	288	3,075
Missie McGeorge	77	69	72	70	288	3,075
Mindy Moore	77	70	70	71	288	3,075
Anne-Marie Palli	73	72	72	71	288	3,075
Joan Delk	73	73	70	72	288	3,074
Cindy Hill	73	73	70	72	288	3,074
Lori West	71	75	69	73	288	3,074
Ayako Okamoto	70	76	74	69	289	2,571

	SCORES				TOTAL	MONEY
Bonnie Lauer	75	70	71	73	289	2,571
Robin Walton	70	74	70	75	289	2,571
Patty Jordan	75	73	74	68	290	2,306
Martha Nause	72	72	73	73	290	2,306
Patti Rizzo	70	73	74	73	290	2,306

U.S. Women's Open

Plainfield Country Club, Plainfield, New Jersey
Par 36-36 — 72; 6,284 yards

July 23-28
purse, $325,000

(Final round postponed to Monday - rain.)

	SCORES				TOTAL	MONEY
Laura Davies	72	70	72	71	285	$55,000
Ayako Okamoto	71	72	70	72	285	23,823.50
JoAnne Carner	74	70	72	69	285	23,823.50
(Davies shot 71, Okamoto 73, Carner 74 in 18-hole playoff.)						
Betsy King	75	73	70	71	289	13,461
Jody Rosenthal	71	72	74	72	289	13,461
Debbie Massey	76	69	74	71	290	9,741
Deedee Roberts	74	73	69	74	290	9,741
Martha Nause	76	69	70	76	291	8,390
Kathy Postlewait	70	79	73	70	292	7,111
Sally Quinlan	75	71	71	75	292	7,111
Rosie Jones	75	71	71	75	292	7,111
Dottie Mochrie	73	72	77	71	293	5,939
Marta Figueras-Dotti	77	70	74	72	293	5,939
Amy Alcott	72	71	76	74	293	5,939
Alice Ritzman	76	74	73	71	294	5,256
Tammie Green	72	74	72	76	294	5,256
Sandra Palmer	71	72	75	77	295	4,790.50
Deb Richard	72	73	75	75	295	4,790.50
Missie Berteotti	73	74	79	70	296	4,394.50
Cindy Rarick	74	71	76	75	296	4,394.50
Patty Sheehan	74	74	77	72	297	3,844.17
Denise Strebig	74	78	73	72	297	3,844.17
Sherri Turner	77	73	74	73	297	3,844.17
Donna White	77	72	74	74	297	3,844.17
*Michiko Hattori	78	73	71	75	297	
Nancy Lopez	73	71	77	76	297	3,844.17
Amy Benz	74	73	74	76	297	3,844.17
Jerilyn Britz	79	71	76	72	298	3,291
Lori Garbacz	77	72	77	72	298	3,291
Anne-Marie Palli	74	73	77	74	298	3,291
Bonnie Lauer	69	76	76	77	298	3,291
*Kathleen McCarthy	74	78	69	77	298	
Hollis Stacy	76	76	75	72	299	2,857.50
Marci Bozarth	72	73	81	73	299	2,857.50
Nancy Ledbetter	79	73	74	73	299	2,857.50
Beth Daniel	73	75	77	74	299	2,857.50
Cathy Morse	74	74	76	75	299	2,857.50
Dot Germain	69	75	79	76	799	2,857.50
Ok-Hee Ku	73	73	77	76	299	2,857.50
Missie McGeorge	78	74	75	73	300	2,477.75
Juli Inkster	78	72	79	71	300	2,477.75
Cathy Marino	78	73	75	74	300	2,477.75

	SCORES				TOTAL	MONEY
Carolyn Hill	75	73	78	74	300	2,477.75
*Cindy Scholefield	75	74	72	79	300	
Dale Eggeling	76	74	77	74	301	2,271.50
Kandi Kessler	74	78	73	74	301	2,271.50
Judy Dickinson	77	71	78	76	302	2,134.50
Dawn Coe	78	69	77	78	302	2,134.50
*Kay Cockerill	73	74	76	79	302	
Janet Coles	76	73	79	75	303	1,962.66
M.J. Smith	75	75	78	75	303	1,962.66
Mary Beth Zimmerman	78	74	77	74	303	1,962.66

Columbia Savings LPGA National Pro-Am

Denver, Colorado

July 30-August 2
purse, $250,000

Meridian Golf Club
Par 36-36 — 72; 6,265 yards

Lone Tree Country Club
Par 36-36 — 72; 6,151 yards

	SCORES				TOTAL	MONEY
Chris Johnson	66	71	70	70	277	$37,500
Shirley Furlong	72	71	69	70	282	23,125
Sara Anne Timms	69	73	72	69	283	16,875
Jan Stephenson	71	73	69	71	284	11,875
Sherri Turner	76	71	65	72	284	11,875
Elaine Crosby	74	72	71	68	285	6,419
Patty Sheehan	71	71	72	71	285	6,419
Laurie Rinker	70	70	73	72	285	6,419
Cindy Rarick	71	70	71	73	285	6,419
Jill Briles	68	71	72	74	285	6,419
Therese Hession	72	69	70	74	285	6,418
Kathy Postlewait	71	71	72	72	286	4,013
Val Skinner	75	69	70	72	286	4,013
Cathy Gerring	70	73	70	73	286	4,013
Rosie Jones	71	71	71	73	286	4,013
Loretta Alderete	74	71	71	71	287	3,263
Dawn Coe	71	71	72	73	287	3,263
Sally Quinlan	70	68	70	79	287	3,263
Kim Shipman	74	72	73	70	289	2,888
Mary Beth Zimmerman	73	69	73	74	289	2,888
Susan Tonkin	69	75	71	74	289	2,888
Marci Bozarth	71	74	75	70	290	2,534
Carolyn Hill	72	72	75	71	290	2,534
Becky Pearson	70	71	77	72	290	2,533
Susie Berning	76	73	71	71	291	2,251
Joan Joyce	72	72	74	73	291	2,251
Jody Rosenthal	71	73	73	74	291	2,250
Barb Mucha	71	73	71	76	291	2,250
Sandra Spuzich	73	75	76	68	292	1,888
Sandra Palmer	72	71	75	74	292	1,888
Kelly Leadbetter	70	74	72	76	292	1,888
Patti Rizzo	70	72	74	76	292	1,888
Shelley Hamlin	70	74	72	76	292	1,888
Nina Foust	75	68	73	76	292	1,887

Henredon Classic

Willow Creek Golf Club, High Point, North Carolina
Par 36-36 — 72; 6,244 yards

August 6-9
purse, $300,000

	SCORES			TOTAL	MONEY
Mary Beth Zimmerman	72	68	66	206	$45,000
Nancy Lopez	73	68	68	209	21,250
Laurie Rinker	68	72	69	209	21,250
Beth Daniel	70	69	70	209	21,250
Heather Drew	70	69	71	210	12,750
Cindy Rarick	74	68	69	211	9,050
Sherri Steinhauer	70	70	71	211	9,050
Colleen Walker	68	71	72	211	9,050
Jan Stephenson	71	72	69	212	6,356
Julie Cole	75	66	71	212	6,355
Jane Geddes	70	71	71	212	6,355
Juli Inkster	73	71	69	213	3,968
Kathy Postlewait	76	68	69	213	3,968
Sally Austin	74	70	69	213	3,968
Kathy Whitworth	68	75	70	213	3,967
Cathy Johnston	73	69	71	213	3,967
Patty Jordan	69	73	71	213	3,967
Susan Tonkin	72	70	71	213	3,967
Dot Germain	68	73	72	213	3,967
Patti Rizzo	74	67	72	213	3,967
Kristi Albers	74	66	73	213	3,967
Beth Solomon	70	70	73	213	3,967
Missie Berteotti	72	67	74	213	3,967
Penny Hammel	72	74	68	214	2,701
Missie McGeorge	74	72	68	214	2,701
Debbie Massey	73	72	69	214	2,700
Sandra Spuzich	72	72	70	214	2,700
Chris Johnson	70	73	71	214	2,700
Martha Foyer	70	70	74	214	2,700
Jill Briles	72	73	70	215	2,110
Penny Pulz	73	71	71	215	2,110
Lynn Adams	74	69	72	215	2,110
Denise Strebig	69	74	72	215	2,109
Donna White	75	68	72	215	2,109
Marlene Floyd	73	69	73	215	2,109
Margaret Ward	70	71	74	215	2,109
Shelley Hamlin	67	73	75	215	2,109

Mastercard International Pro-Am

White Plains, New York

August 14-16
purse, $225,000

Westchester Hills Golf Club,
Par 35-37 — 72; 6,013 yards

Ridgeway Country Club
Par 37-35 — 72; 6,187 yards

	SCORES			TOTAL	MONEY
Val Skinner	67	70	75	212	$33,750
Shelley Hamlin	69	70	74	213	20,812

	SCORES			TOTAL	MONEY
Ayako Okamoto	73	73	69	215	10,215
Sandra Palmer	72	73	70	215	10,215
Dawn Coe	74	69	72	215	10,215
Sherri Turner	71	72	72	215	10,214
Hollis Stacy	72	70	73	215	10,214
Kathy Postlewait	73	74	69	216	4,816
Julie Cole	74	72	70	216	4,815
M. J. Smith	74	71	71	216	4,815
Betsy King	72	71	73	216	4,815
Shirley Furlong	72	70	74	216	4,815
Penny Hammel	74	72	71	217	3,713
LeAnn Cassaday	76	74	69	219	3,179
Cindy Ferro	74	72	73	219	3,179
Bonnie Lauer	72	74	73	219	3,179
Missie Berteotti	72	73	74	219	3,178
Myra Blackwelder	74	76	70	220	2,645
Deedee Roberts	75	73	72	220	2,645
Missie McGeorge	76	71	73	220	2,644
Nancy Scranton Brown	75	72	73	220	2,644
Patty Jordan	78	74	69	221	2,124
Cindy Mackey	74	75	72	221	2,124
Barb Mucha	73	76	72	221	2,124
Cindy Hill	72	76	73	221	2,124
Janet Anderson	72	76	73	221	2,124
Karen Permezel	74	73	74	221	2,123
Amy Benz	76	69	76	221	2,123
Beverly Klass	79	71	72	222	1,631
Carolyn Hill	75	75	72	222	1,631
Tammie Green	72	78	72	222	1,631
Lauri Peterson	76	73	73	222	1,631
Linda Hunt	72	77	73	222	1,630
Lynn Adams	74	73	75	222	1,630
Robin Walton	75	71	76	222	1,630
Mitzi Edge	73	71	78	222	1,630

Atlantic City Classic

Marriott Seaview Country Club and Resort,
Atlantic City, New Jersey
Par 37-34 — 71; 6,008 yards

August 21-23
purse, $225,000

	SCORES			TOTAL	MONEY
Betsy King	70	71	66	207	$33,750
Nancy Lopez	69	69	72	210	20,812
Sherri Turner	77	69	65	211	15,187
Patti Rizzo	70	71	71	212	9,750
Juli Inkster	67	72	73	212	9,750
Beth Daniel	71	67	74	212	9,749
Jane Crafter	77	70	66	213	5,925
Val Skinner	77	70	66	213	5,925
Dot Germain	69	71	73	213	5,924
Rosie Jones	75	70	69	214	4,503
JoAnne Carner	70	73	71	214	4,502
Marta Figueras-Dotti	74	71	70	215	3,830
Laurie Rinker	74	69	72	215	3,829
Amy Alcott	76	73	67	216	3,182
Ayako Okamoto	74	73	69	216	3,182

	SCORES			TOTAL	MONEY
Colleen Walker	74	71	71	216	3,182
Barb Bunkowsky	70	72	74	216	3,181
Missie McGeorge	71	75	71	217	2,592
Pam Allen	73	71	73	217	2,591
Cindy Hill	72	72	73	217	2,591
Patty Jordan	68	76	73	217	2,591
Kathy Whitworth	72	72	73	217	2,591
Cindy Rarick	74	73	71	218	2,087
Cathy Marino	74	72	72	218	2,087
Dawn Coe	69	76	73	218	2,087
Sarah LeVeque	74	71	73	218	2,087
Denise Strebig	73	72	73	218	2,087
Therese Hession	71	71	76	218	2,086
Connie Chillemi	71	77	71	219	1,663
Deedee Roberts	69	79	71	219	1,663
Nina Foust	72	74	73	219	1,662
Kathy Postlewait	72	74	73	219	1,662
Beth Solomon	76	70	73	219	1,662
Sherri Steinhauer	72	73	74	219	1,662
Jan Stephenson	74	70	75	219	1,662

Nestle World Championship

Stouffer PineIsle Resort, Buford, Georgia
Par 36-36 — 72; 6,073 yards

August 27-30
purse, $250,000

	SCORES				TOTAL	MONEY
Ayako Okamoto	70	68	73	71	282	$81,500
Betsy King	71	70	74	68	283	43,400
Jane Geddes	73	71	67	73	284	28,900
Colleen Walker	73	69	70	74	286	20,400
Patty Sheehan	77	70	69	71	287	15,400
Chris Johnson	76	71	68	73	288	10,900
Laura Davies	72	72	75	70	289	8,900
Cindy Rarick	71	74	75	71	291	6,400
Laurie Rinker	71	72	71	77	291	6,400
Pat Bradley	74	70	75	74	293	5,400
*Kay Cockerill	69	74	74	76	293	
Jody Rosenthal	79	76	69	76	300	4,900

Rail Charity Classic

Rail Golf Club, Springfield, Illinois
Par 36-36 — 72; 6,408 yards

September 5-7
purse, $200,000

	SCORES			TOTAL	MONEY
Rosie Jones	69	69	70	208	$30,000
Nancy Lopez	68	71	70	209	18,500
Betsy King	70	74	66	210	12,000
Shirley Furlong	70	73	67	210	12,000
Nancy Ledbetter	71	71	70	212	8,500
Allison Finney	72	74	67	213	4,900
Cathy Gerring	71	73	69	213	4,900
Beth Daniel	74	69	70	213	4,900

	SCORES			TOTAL	MONEY
Marta Figueras-Dotti	74	69	70	213	4,900
Donna Caponi	70	72	71	213	4,900
Myra Blackwelder	70	70	73	213	4,900
Mary Beth Zimmerman	67	72	74	213	4,900
Cindy Figg-Currier	72	73	69	214	2,920
Marlene Floyd	73	71	70	214	2,920
Sandra Palmer	70	72	72	214	2,920
Jane Crafter	70	71	73	214	2,920
Barb Bunkowsky	69	71	74	214	2,920
Cindy Hill	70	76	69	215	2,252
Missie Berteotti	73	72	70	215	2,252
Donna White	73	72	70	215	2,252
Missie McGeorge	68	76	71	215	2,252
Kim Williams	73	70	72	215	2,251
Ayako Okamoto	70	71	74	215	2,251
Dot Germain	71	75	70	216	1,820
Jane Geddes	74	69	73	216	1,820
Sherri Steinhauer	70	72	74	216	1,820
Jill Briles	70	72	74	216	1,820
Kathy Postlewait	68	71	77	216	1,820
Laura Hurlbut	74	73	70	217	1,553
Martha Nause	71	76	70	217	1,553
Kim Bauer	72	72	73	217	1,552
Sandra Spuzich	72	71	74	217	1,552

Cellular One-Ping Championship

Columbia-Edgewater Country Club, Portland, Oregon   September 11-13
Par 36-36 — 72; 6,233 yards   purse, $225,000

	SCORES			TOTAL	MONEY
Nancy Lopez	72	67	71	210	$33,750
Kelly Leadbetter	73	71	67	211	15,937
Muffin Spencer-Devlin	73	69	69	211	15,937
Jan Stephenson	68	71	72	211	15,937
Chris Johnson	67	73	72	212	9,562
Ayako Okamoto	71	77	65	213	6,413
Beth Solomon	70	72	71	213	6,412
Marta Figueras-Dotti	72	68	73	213	6,412
Hollis Stacy	70	69	74	213	6,412
Anne-Marie Palli	73	75	66	214	4,037
Beth Daniel	75	69	70	214	4,037
Dawn Coe	71	71	72	214	4,037
Elaine Crosby	70	69	75	214	4,037
Patti Rizzo	68	69	77	214	4,036
Mindy Moore	72	71	72	215	3,087
Colleen Walker	70	73	72	215	3,087
Kim Shipman	69	73	73	215	3,086
Kris Monaghan	81	67	68	216	2,406
Mary Beth Zimmerman	73	74	69	216	2,406
Shelley Hamlin	76	70	70	216	2,406
Jody Rosenthal	76	68	72	216	2,406
Kathy Baker	72	72	72	216	2,405
Rosie Jones	71	73	72	216	2,405
Robin Walton	72	71	73	216	2,405
Juli Inkster	70	73	73	216	2,405
Patty Sheehan	71	71	74	216	2,405

	SCORES			TOTAL	MONEY
Missie Berteotti	77	71	69	217	1,891
Alice Ritzman	75	71	71	217	1,891
Barb Bunkowsky	72	72	73	217	1,890
Martha Nause	71	71	75	217	1,890

Safeco Classic

Meridian Valley Country Club, Seattle, Washington
Par 36-36 — 72; 6,222 yards

September 17-20
purse, $225,000

	SCORES				TOTAL	MONEY
Jan Stephenson	68	70	71	68	277	$33,750
Nancy Lopez	71	74	66	67	278	20,812
Missie Berteotti	69	69	70	72	280	15,187
Chris Johnson	72	72	69	68	281	11,812
Missie McGeorge	74	67	74	67	282	8,719
Cindy Hill	72	69	67	74	282	8,718
Kathy Postlewait	71	71	69	72	283	6,637
Kathy Baker	74	70	70	70	284	5,850
Patty Sheehan	73	72	71	69	285	5,006
Martha Nause	70	73	72	70	285	5,006
Sue Ertl	72	77	71	66	286	3,521
M. J. Smith	73	74	72	67	286	3,521
Beth Daniel	73	75	69	69	286	3,520
Jerilyn Britz	70	74	72	70	286	3,520
Jill Briles	72	74	68	72	286	3,520
Dot Germain	73	72	68	73	286	3,520
Colleen Walker	72	69	71	74	286	3,520
Dawn Coe	71	75	74	67	287	2,645
Nancy Taylor	75	73	70	69	287	2,645
Marci Bozarth	72	70	73	72	287	2,644
Hollis Stacy	71	71	72	73	287	2,644
Deb Richard	72	73	75	68	288	2,195
Bonnie Lauer	75	71	73	69	288	2,195
Myra Blackwelder	74	73	70	71	288	2,194
Marta Figueras-Dotti	74	70	72	72	288	2,194
Alice Ritzman	72	71	70	75	288	2,194
Vicki Fergon	74	71	74	70	289	1,753
Penny Hammel	75	68	74	72	289	1,753
Deedee Roberts	71	72	74	72	289	1,753
Heather Farr	71	71	75	72	289	1,753
Sandra Spuzich	73	73	70	73	289	1,753
Sarah LeVeque	71	72	73	73	289	1,753
Shelley Hamlin	69	74	73	73	289	1,753
Betsy King	74	69	71	75	289	1,752

Konica San Jose Classic

Almaden Golf and Country Club, San Jese, California
Par 36-36 — 72; 6,303 yards

September 25-27
purse, $300,000

	SCORES			TOTAL	MONEY
Jan Stephenson	69	71	65	205	$45,000
Amy Alcott	70	70	70	210	27,750

	SCORES			TOTAL	MONEY
Shelley Hamlin	70	72	69	211	20,250
Chris Johnson	70	73	69	212	13,000
Ayako Okamoto	69	72	71	212	13,000
Juli Inkster	71	67	74	212	13,000
Sue Ertl	74	71	68	213	6,826
Jody Rosenthal	74	70	69	213	6,825
Patti Rizzo	69	74	70	213	6,825
Jane Geddes	72	69	72	213	6,825
Sherri Steinhauer	71	70	72	213	6,825
Patty Sheehan	69	71	73	213	6,825
Deedee Roberts	71	74	69	214	4,380
Jill Briles	74	69	71	214	4,380
Missie McGeorge	73	70	71	214	4,380
LeAnn Cassaday	69	72	73	214	4,380
Cindy Figg-Currier	69	71	74	214	4,380
Cindy Rarick	73	74	68	214	3,084
Susie Berning	73	74	68	214	3,084
Donna Caponi	75	71	69	215	3,083
Lynn Adams	73	73	69	215	3,083
Alice Miller	75	70	70	215	3,083
Cathy Marino	73	71	71	215	3,083
Betsy Barrett	73	71	71	215	3,083
Debbie Massey	70	74	71	215	3,083
Hollis Stacy	73	70	72	215	3,083
Penny Pulz	72	69	74	215	3,083
Betsy King	71	70	74	215	3,083
Sandra Spuzich	78	68	70	216	2,174
Dawn Coe	74	72	70	216	2,173
Laurie Rinker	76	69	71	216	2,173
Anne-Marie Palli	75	70	71	216	2,173
Cindy Hill	72	73	71	216	2,173
Rebecca Bradley	73	71	72	216	2,173
Dot Germain	73	71	72	216	2,173
Muffin Spencer-Devlin	71	72	73	216	2,173

Nichirei Cup U.S. vs Japan Championship

Tsukuba Country Club, Tokyo, Japan
Par 36-36 — 72; 6,253 yards

October 30-November 1
purse, $260,000

	SCORES		TOTAL	MONEY
Fukumi Tani	72	67	139	$25,000
Tatsuko Ohsako	74	67	141	15,000
Rosie Jones	72	70	142	13,000
Shirley Furlong	71	71	142	13,000
Sherri Turner	70	72	142	13,000
Juli Inkster	72	71	143	11,000
Nayoko Yoshikawa	73	71	144	5,000
Kathy Postlewait	74	71	145	11,000
Atsuko Hikage	72	73	145	5,000
Colleen Walker	70	75	145	11,000
Ayako Okamoto	73	73	146	5,000
Mieko Suzuki	77	70	147	5,000
Val Skinner	76	71	147	11,000
Fusako Nagata	75	72	147	5,000
Jane Geddes	74	74	148	11,000
Laurie Rinker	78	71	149	11,000

	SCORES			TOTAL	MONEY
Chris Johnson	77	72		149	11,000
Patty Sheehan	75	74		149	11,000
Hiromi Takamura	74	75		149	5,000
Yuko Moriguchi	71	78		149	5,000
Jody Rosenthal	74	76		150	11,000
Cindy Rarick	77	74		151	11,000
Megumi Ishikawa	75	76		151	5,000
Ritsu Imahori	77	75		152	5,000
Keiko Matsuda	76	76		152	5,000
Cindy Hill	79	75		154	11,000
Shihomi Suzuki	80	76		156	5,000
Hiromi Kobayashi	81	79		160	5,000

TEAM RESULTS: U.S. LPGA 17.5, Japan LPGA 10.5. Each U.S. player received $11,000; each Japanese player received $5,000.

Mazda Japan Classic

Musashigaoka Golf Club, Tokyo, Japan
Par 36-36 — 72; 6,376 yards

November 6-8
purse, $350,000

	SCORES			TOTAL	MONEY
Yuko Moriguchi	68	66	72	206	$52,500
Ayako Okamoto	68	71	70	209	32,375
Atsuko Hikage	70	69	75	214	23,625
Betsy King	73	71	71	215	18,375
Rosie Jones	76	70	70	216	12,484
Patty Sheehan	73	73	70	216	12,483
Juli Inkster	73	71	72	216	12,483
Patti Rizzo	76	69	72	217	7,840
Debbie Massey	71	73	73	217	7,839
Shirley Furlong	74	69	74	217	7,839
Tatsuko Ohsako	72	70	75	217	7,839
Ikuyo Shiotani	74	71	73	218	6,157
Muffin Spencer-Devlin	77	72	70	219	5,020
Jan Stephenson	74	73	72	219	5,020
Jody Rosenthal	71	75	73	219	5,020
Yuen-Chyn Huang	74	70	75	219	5,019
Colleen Walker	75	68	76	219	5,019
Kathy Postlewait	72	70	77	219	5,019
Dawn Coe	77	72	71	220	3,493
Masayo Fujimura	74	74	72	220	3,493
Kathy Baker	73	75	72	220	3,492
Lisa Young	75	72	73	220	3,492
Cathy Gerring	73	74	73	220	3,492
Sandra Palmer	77	69	74	220	3,492
Marci Bozarth	76	70	74	220	3,492
Hiromi Takamura	74	72	74	220	3,492
Jane Geddes	68	78	74	220	3,492
Martha Nause	74	70	76	220	3,492
Val Skinner	67	75	78	220	3,492
Amy Alcott	78	72	71	221	2,476
Nayoko Yoshikawa	77	72	72	221	2,476
Robin Walton	75	74	72	221	2,475
Gail Lee Hirata	75	74	72	221	2,475
Cathy Morse	73	75	73	221	2,475
Deedee Roberts	73	75	73	221	2,475
Chris Johnson	72	74	75	221	2,475
Fukumi Tani	73	70	78	221	2,475